THE
UNIVERSITAS
PROJECT

THE
UNIVERSITAS
PROJECT

SOLUTIONS FOR A
POST-TECHNOLOGICAL
SOCIETY

Conceived and
Directed by
Emilio Ambasz

The Museum of Modern Art, New York

This publication presents the papers and
proceedings of The Universitas Project, a research
project culminating in a two-day symposium held at
The Museum of Modern Art on January 8–9,
1972. The Project was organized by The Museum
of Modern Art under an initiating grant from
The Graham Foundation for Advanced Studies in
the Fine Arts and prepared jointly by the Museum
and The Institute for Architecture and Urban
Studies. • The Universitas Project was sponsored
by The Graham Foundation for Advanced
Studies in the Fine Arts, Chicago; The Brionvega
Corporation, Milan; The Noble Foundation,
New York; and The International Council
of The Museum of Modern Art • Produced
by the Publications Department of The
Museum of Modern Art, New York • Edited
by Harriet Schoenholz Bee • Designed
by Gina Rossi • Illustrations executed by
Gina Rossi • Production by Marc Sapir •
Printed and bound by Editoriale Bortolazzi-
Stei s.r.l., Verona, Italy • This book is type-
set in Futura and Dante • © 2006 by The
Museum of Modern Art, New York. All
rights reserved • "Vuelta" by Octavio Paz,
translated by Eliot Weinberger, from Collected
Poems 1957–1987, copyright © 1986 by Octavio
Paz and Eliot Weinberger. Reprinted by
permission of New Directions Publishing
Corp. • "Symposium Remarks of The Universitas
Project of 1972" by Hannah Arendt, copyright
© 1972 by Hannah Arendt. Reprinted by
permission of Georges Borchardt, Inc., on
behalf of the Hannah Arendt Estate • Library
of Congress Control Number: 2006922274 •
ISBN: 0-87070-070-7 • Published by The Museum
of Modern Art, 11 West 53 Street, New York, NY 10019.
www.moma.org • Distributed in the United States
and Canada by D.A.P., Distributed Art
Publishers, Inc., New York • Distributed outside
the United States and Canada by Thames &
Hudson, Ltd., London • Printed in Italy

Contents

297 | SYMPOSIUM PROCEEDINGS

Foreword

On January 8 and 9, 1972, more than a score of distinguished architects, planners, scientists, and philosophers from nearly as many countries participated in an international symposium at The Museum of Modern Art, to discuss problems associated with the design of the urban environment. The symposium was part of a study, conceived and directed by the architect and designer Emilio Ambasz, then Curator of Design at the Museum, to explore the possibility of establishing in the United States a new type of institution centered around the task of evaluating and designing the man-made environment. This ambitious inquiry into the relation of man to the natural and sociocultural environment was titled "Institutions for a Post-Technological Society—The Universitas Project" and was sponsored by the Museum and by its associate organization, The Institute for Architecture and Urban Studies, with the aid of an initial grant from The Graham Foundation for Advanced Studies in the Fine Arts and underwriting from the Brionvega Corporation of Italy, The Noble Foundation, New York, and The International Council of The Museum of Modern Art. It questioned the adequacy of prevailing modes of thought and of existing institutions in dealing with the increasingly complex problems of the man-made milieu, and it examined the idea of founding an experimental university in which a broad domain of inquiry might be integrated toward developing modes of thought and action that would be better suited to dealing with those problems.

At the time of the symposium, Mr. Ambasz wrote:

> The Project has been organized into two stages, covering a period of five years. The first stage, concerned with problem definition and the proposal of alternatives to the present situation, culminates with the January symposium. . . . In the second stage the possible ways of bringing such an institution into existence will be explored.
>
> As part of the first stage, a small research team worked for a year, with the consultation and active participation of an interdisciplinary group of research advisors, at preparing a basic Working Paper, which brings into focus several critical issues of this Project. This paper has been submitted to the participants of the January symposium, who are contributing essays, each from his own point of view, commenting on the issues raised by the Working Paper and expanding on them.
>
> These essays will be distributed among the participants before the symposium takes place. The symposium, comprising a two-day series of working sessions, will be open to a small invited audience of specialists to allow for free discussion of the views presented in the essays and a high level of exchange among the contributors. The essays will then be published in book form together with the symposium's proceedings.

While the experimental institution that was the ultimate aim of The Universitas Project (part two of the ambitious study) has not come about, the symposium and its affiliated texts, long housed in the Museum Archives, have finally emerged as a book, and indeed as one of the most extensive and stimulating engagements between architecture and other theoretical and technological disciplines ever conducted. This outstanding element of the Museum's involvement with architectural institutions and pedagogical enquiry constitutes an architectural event of a multidisciplinary nature that was unprecedented at the time. The list of participants formed a truly remarkable array of some of the most noted minds of the latter half of the twentieth century, and the ideas and issues pursued resonate no less today than they did when originally articulated at the Museum's 1972 gathering.

This still-relevant publication, then, includes all of the initial documents prepared by Mr. Ambasz and his team at the Museum, some twenty individual scholarly papers submitted to the Museum, the complete proceedings of the four sessions recorded during the two-day symposium, and a group of postscripts submitted by eleven of the participants after the event. To these basic archived materials, which vividly reflect advanced postwar and Cold War attitudes and immediate concerns of the 1960s and 1970s, have been added a new introduction, written by Emilio Ambasz as he revisits his ambitious Project, brief introductory notes to the various sections, biographical summaries on the authors of the papers and the participants in the symposium, and a postscript to the event written as a fable in 1972 by Emilio Ambasz. On behalf of the Museum's Trustees, I am pleased to see this important work become available to the scholarly community and the public.

Glenn D. Lowry, Director
The Museum of Modern Art

Acknowledgments

The preparation of this volume began more than three decades ago when I served as Curator of Design at The Museum of Modern Art. The development of the ambitious undertaking that resulted in a multidisciplinary conference and a set of scholarly papers by leading thinkers of the day would not have been possible without the support of the late Arthur Drexler, then the Director of the Department of Architecture and Design at the Museum. His willingness to risk the reputation of his department on an intellectual exercise of this nature was most generous and admirable.

The Universitas Project was supported by an initiating grant from The Graham Foundation for Advanced Studies in the Fine Arts provided under the aegis of its remarkable Director John Entenza. Enio Brion, of The Brionvega Corporation, Milan, also provided enlightened and enthusiastic support for the Project, which remained close to his wide-ranging intellectual interests although far from the immediate concerns of his company. The generous support of The Noble Foundation reflected its dedication and commitment to new institutions of learning. The Project also benefited from the support of The International Council of The Museum of Modern Art.

I must express my deep appreciation to all the distinguished participants in this immense undertaking. In addition to the authors and symposium chairmen and participants, whose work is amply presented herein, I am deeply grateful to the Project's Board of Advisors for its generous advice and criticism: Stanford Anderson, Kenneth Arrow, Walter Buckley, Karl Deutsch, Ronald Dworkin, Peter Eisenman, Thomas Farer, Gerald Feinberg, Harry Frankfurt, Suzanne Keller, Arnold Kramish, Rosalind Krauss, Robert Nozick, Carl Schorske, and Alan Trachtenberg, among others, who read and commented upon the drafts of portions of the Project Working Paper. They are to be exonerated from any responsibility in the resulting document; the errors, viewpoints, as well as the sense of hubris this undertaking exudes were entirely my own.

A debt of gratitude is also owed the two individuals who provided essential assistance in the preparation and execution of the written material presented in this volume as well as the staging of the symposium itself. I warmly thank Gilberto Perez-Guillermo for his fundamental support, for having expressed some of my raw thoughts so eloquently and making me appear more clever and knowledgeable than I was, and for having contributed so extensively to making "The Black Book" a presentable intellectual entity. Gratitude is also owed Douglas Penick for his important assistance and support and especially for his questioning everything we did, not out of doubt but on account of his irreducible rigor.

The long-delayed effort to publish the materials that comprise the Project was remedied by the crucial help of Terence Riley, until recently The Philip Johnson Chief Curator of Architecture and Design at the Museum.

His decision to support the publication of the papers and transcripts that had long lain dormant in the Museum Archives led directly to the present volume. We are also grateful to Felicity D. Scott, Assistant Professor of Art History and Visual Studies at the University of California, Irvine, for her great acumen in locating and initially organizing the archival materials and for her scholarly interest and support of the Project from its inception.

At the Museum I wish to thank Glenn D. Lowry, Director, for his whole-hearted support of this publication and for his gracious Foreword. Peter Reed, Deputy Director for Curatorial Affairs, has heartily endorsed the Project and has been instrumental in bringing the book to fruition. Thanks are also owed the Museum's Chief of Library and Museum Archives, Milan Hughston, for his help in unearthing the materials published here; also, much gratitude is owed Michelle Elligott, Museum Archivist, and Jenny Tobias, Librarian, for their critical assistance with the papers and recorded proceedings. In the Department of Publications Christopher Hudson, Publisher, is thanked for his most professional help with a project he inherited but generously made his own. I also thank Kara Kirk, Assistant Publisher; David Frankel, Managing Editor; Marc Sapir, Director of Production; and Christina Grillo, Associate Production Manager, for their expertise in publishing this volume.

In obtaining a renewal of permissions granted thirty-five years ago, we relied on the expert advice of Nancy Adelson, Assistant Museum Counsel. Others, outside the Museum, who provided invaluable assistance are: Elizabeth E. Bailey, The Wharton School; Manuel Castells; Ronald Dworkin; Claire Jacobs Elsen, Princeton University; Rachel Goodman; Professor Miriam Schapiro Grosof; Jerome Kohn, Hannah Arendt Center, New School; Margaret Logue; Jan Murphy, Association of Former Intelligence Officers; Dennis Palmore, New Directions; Marie Jose Paz; Gwen Rapoport; Carl Schorske; Denise Scott Brown; Jivan Tabibian; and Eliot Weinberger.

I particularly wish to express my sincere gratitude to Gina Rossi, formerly Senior Designer in the Department of Publications, for her dedicated commitment to finding a graphic means for embodying the scope of this project and for her handsome design giving visual structure to so many words. I also wish to acknowledge the expert assistance of Cassandra Heliczer for proofreading, Lynn Scrabis for both transcribing and proofreading texts, and Marguerite Shore for translations from the French and Italian. Finally, for the assiduous direction and editing of this volume I am indebted to Harriet Schoenholz Bee, formerly Editorial Director in the Department of Publications. I am most obliged to her for undertaking this project, and extend my personal gratitude for her having maintained immaculate editorial standards during her long and fruitful tenure at the Museum. We who worked there greatly benefited from her discreet and superb help, and I am thankful to her for her committment to the Museum's highest spiritual and artistic values.

Emilio Ambasz

Introduction: Looking Back to See Ahead

Were earth paradise, we would need only to settle on a plot of land so welcoming that, slowly, the land would assume the shape of an abode around us. And within this abode—being a magic space—it would never rain nor would there ever be hardships of any other sort. Alas, we must build houses because we are not welcome on this earth. Every act of construction is a defiance of nature. But in order not to elicit unearthly retribution for such an act (of defiance) we must conceive of our creations as pacts of reconciliation between what we were given and what we are making anew.

The Western notion of man's creations as distinct and separate entities—in contrast with those of nature—has exhausted its intellectual and ethical capital. An emerging man-made garden overtakes the one we were originally given. We must create a notion of production whereby our creations are conceived as an integral component of that emerging man-made nature we are willingly, as well as unwittingly, creating. Our most urgent task is that of integrating man-made nature with the organic one entrusted to us.

In our efforts to master nature-as-found, we have created a second nature, man-made nature, which contrasts endlessly with given nature. We need to redefine all aspects of material production, an overbearing protagonist of man-made nature, but to do so we need first to redefine the philosophical meaning of a contemporary nature.

Can such a philosophical system of thought and creation, aiming not only to evaluate that which exists but, as importantly, that which should come into being, be developed in our present academic institutions? This question is as valid today, if not more so, than it was more than thirty-five years ago when, as The Museum of Modern Art's Curator of Design, I conceived and directed in depth a program of research and postulation seeking to redefine the notion of the *Universitas*, i.e., the whole.

What I envisioned then was that the traditional concept of Universitas be reformulated according to the needs of a post-technological society. The Universitas Project was aimed specifically at defining and establishing a new type of University concerned with the evaluation and the design of our man-made milieu. The issues and the implications involved were, and certainly still are, immense.

It was necessary to define the field of the problem before addressing its specific aspects. The first stage of this project, therefore, was intended as a contribution toward the larger enterprise of inquiring into the nature of our man-made environment. Its purposes were, *first*, to attempt a definition of the objectives to be met in the evaluation, design, and management of the man-made environment; *second*, to question whether our current modes of thought and present institutions, especially universities, satisfy those objectives; and, *third*, to advance a view on the needed modes of thought and the new or restructured types of institutions which will have to be developed to satisfy these objectives.

As the Project Working Paper—or "The Black Book," as it became known among the Project's participants because of its black covers—stated in its section on General Matters:

> The tasks that would have to be assumed by such Universitas may stagger imagination and paralyze hope, but they cannot be relinquished, as they would involve: first, the *retrospective* task of evaluating the consequences that have resulted from having made choices on the bases of values no higher than those derived from an acceptance of consumption as the existential motivator; second, the *critical* task of analyzing the socioeconomic and political institutions of our technological milieu in order to establish the effects they have had on our civilization's systems of ideas and emotions; third, the *prospective* task of envisioning and constantly expanding the framework of private and common values that should guide the physical and socioeconomic design of our society; and fourth, the operational task of developing the physical and socioeconomic methods necessary for implementing these objectives.
>
> The fulfillment of these tasks will, however, require that prior to defining new areas of inquiry and action, and before developing new disciplines, we have the courage of conceiving of this Universitas, both as the model for beholding the meaning of man's condition, and as the way for imagining and implementing the quality of our existence in terms of a humanly made milieu.

It was clearly understood by all participants that the realization of such an institution would not solve all the problems of our emerging man-made environment. At the outset we also deliberately stated our commitment to insuring that this type of institution would not seek to assume the role of a philosopher-king by purposely structuring it devoid of political power. (But what good philosopher cares to be a politician, and what real king wants to inhibit his actions by recurring to intellectual questioning? It is the second-rate ones that should concern us.) At the same time, we did indeed hope that such a Universitas would contribute to finding answers to our need to develop methods for transforming problems into controlled processes and, moreover, propose alternative modes of existence and guide us in the design of those artifacts that might help bring it about.

The Universitas Project resulted from my deeply felt conviction that we must create alternative models of existence proposing a better life to guide our actions if we do not wish to perpetuate present conditions. I still believe passionately that any project not attempting to propose better and more just modes of existence is unethical.

We are all painfully aware that justice, whether social or moral, is a conceit of the mind. Justice does not exist in our given nature, but despite this cruel fact, I felt very strongly then, and do even more today, that it is our ethical imperative to pursue its implementation on earth. Even if we know it to be a delicate structure, held together by such ethereal material as abnegation and altruism but destined to collapse at night, we must rebuild it anew every morning.

My hope, then, and my firm conviction today, is that institutions monitoring, evaluating, and proposing new design models, such as we envisioned the Universitas to become, had to be postulated and fostered to come about. It was a task I felt The Museum of Modern Art, through its Department of Architecture and Design, was in a unique position to sponsor and pursue. The question of why it has taken more than a third of a century for the premises and proposals resulting from The Universitas Project to be published answers to many reasons, all true and honorable. I prefer to suggest that perhaps the wheel was invented many times but only in the last round were its far-reaching meanings understood.

Emilio Ambasz
April 2006

THE
UNIVERSITAS
PROJECT

EDITOR'S NOTE: The Project Working
Paper represents the first phase
of The Universitas Project. It was
prepared and written by Emilio
Ambasz, creator and director of the
Project, and sets forth the ambitious
goals and the procedures for the
Project. It was printed and bound
within black covers and sent to each
member of a selected list of potential
participants, which appears at the
end of the document along with a
proposed timetable. The list and
the timetable proved to be mutable:
not all the listed individuals participated, and others were later invited
to take part in the Project; in addition, the timetable for publication
of the Project turned out to be
off by over three decades, as it
was originally intended for a
date soon after the symposium.
Nevertheless, this document,
familiarly known at the time
of its distribution as "The
Black Book," is reproduced
here essentially as it was
provided to each potential
participant, and forms the
foundation upon which each
invited scholar wrote the
essays that follow.

Institutions for a Post-Technological Society: The Universitas Project

PROJECT WORKING PAPER

A Research Project prepared
jointly by The Museum of
Modern Art, New York, and
The Institute for Architecture
and Urban Studies

Presented by The Museum
of Modern Art, New York, under
an initiating grant of The Graham
Foundation for Advanced Studies
in the Fine Arts

Sponsoring Institutions

The Graham Foundation for Advanced
Studies in the Fine Arts, Chicago

The Brionvega Corporation, Milan

The Noble Foundation, New York

Project Research Group

Emilio Ambasz (Project Director)

Douglas Penick

Gilberto Perez-Guillermo

Contents

✛ Introduction ✛

OBJECTIVES

The Universitas Project is aimed specifically at establishing a new type of University concerned with the evaluation and design of our man-made milieu. The issues involved and the implications are immense. It is necessary, therefore, to define the field of the problem before addressing ourselves to the specific aspects. This present research program is, then, intended as a contribution toward the larger enterprise of inquiring into the nature of our man-made environment. Its purposes are, *first*, to attempt a definition of the objectives to be met in the evaluation, design, and management of the man-made environment; *second*, to question whether our current modes of thought and present institutions, especially universities, satisfy those objectives; and, *third*, to advance a view on the modes of thought and the new or restructured types of institutions which will have to be developed to satisfy these objectives.

PROJECT SCHEDULE

The schedule for accomplishing this Project's objectives has been organized into two distinct, but interrelated, stages:

The first, *postulative*, stage is concerned with problem-definition and the development of alternative solutions. (Material developed at this stage is to be published.)

(September 1, 1970, to December 31, 1971).

The second, *implementative*, stage is concerned with the practical implementation of those solutions that have been postulated in the first phase. The intention of this stage will be to develop the strategies leading to the establishment in New York State of a new type of education-research-development institution concerned with the evaluation and design of our man-made environment.

(January 1, 1972, to December 31, 1973).

(For a detailed description of these two stages and the Project's Working Methods see Appendices.)

PROJECT WORKING PAPER

The present Project Working Paper corresponds to one of the phases of the *postulative* stage and is intended to describe the Project's subject and define the scope of its proposals. It is submitted to a number of leading Contributors to these concerns, who, within their own fields of competence and special interests, will prepare Essays expanding the issues raised by this Project Working Paper. These issues can be seen as roughly falling into two distinct areas:

1. Design as a Mode of Thought

2. The Institutions of Design, and the Design or the Counter-Design of Institutions

These Essays will be distributed in advance of the gathering of the Contributors at the International Symposium to take place in The Museum of Modern Art in January 1972. The Symposium—comprising a two-day series of working sessions—will be closed and kept small, for it is intended to allow for clarification and questioning of the points raised by the Contributors in their Essays, as well as to generate a high level of direct exchange among the Contributors.

(For a list of Contributors and the Symposium Working Procedures see Appendices.)

✛ Preface ✛

This working paper is organized into two parts: the first refers to General Matters, the second to Specific Considerations. The General Matters are further subdivided into two sections, the first of which is intended to describe the scope of the Universitas Project, and the second of which is included to establish a metaphorical parallel relationship between the idea of the Universitas and that of the City.

The Specific Considerations develop certain issues in greater depth, in an attempt to render a more precise context to the previous material.

✛ General Matters ✛

I. The University of Design

1.

As the medieval view of a divine order of things gradually gave way, after the Renaissance, to the view of a world ruled by nature's law, so has this notion of an encompassing natural order come to be replaced by the realization that the milieu we now inhabit is, to a significant extent, artificial—a man-made milieu. More and more, it is this man-made milieu that provides the framework for contemporary man's thought and imagery.

Yet the profile being adopted by this newly emerging milieu is escaping control. To a large extent, man continues to act as though he could trust some external force to put things in order for him. The "happy ending" view of the man-made milieu—the view that technology itself carries the answer to all the problems it raises—is based on the assumption that something like a law of nature is operating behind the technological processes, that, no matter what man does, things will somehow sort themselves out in the end. But there is no functional or historical evidence for this: the structures, functions, and processes of the man-made milieu are best understood as the patterns of interaction of complex adaptive systems and are not analogous to the workings of physical systems.[1] There is no reason, therefore, to expect that the aimless actions of technology will eventually accommodate themselves to some pattern of order. The future will only provide a continuation of the present if facts of technological feasibility, rather than values of human existence, remain the accepted shaping forces.

Opposed to the "happy ending" position, but sharing with it the basic assumption that the processes of technology are beyond our control, are the pessimists who deplore the trend that things have taken but are skeptical of the possibilities for positive action, and warn us that we run the risk of reinforcing the worst of the man-made milieu when we inevitably resort to techniques in order to gain mastery over techniques. Both positions apply to technology attitudes derived from the scientific stance before nature; they refuse to believe in an order that is not in things themselves but which man imposes on his surroundings.[2] They see the future as unfolding from the present, envisioning alternatives they regard as idle speculation. In their refusal to conceive of strategies for action, both neglect to contemplate the possibility that modes of thought may be developed that are better suited than the present ones for giving meaning and order to the man-made milieu, thus enabling man to *design* his future.

2.

The development of a mode of thought appropriate to the task of designing the man-made milieu necessitates a breaking away not merely from old patterns of thought but, to some extent at least, from a whole way of beholding reality, which has been dominant in our culture: the scientific world-view.

Science deals with the given; its aim is to reveal an order that exists already in the world. An endless humility before facts, a total surrender of preconceptions and subjective preferences, is what Thomas H. Huxley recommended as an ideal for the scientist. The aim of design, on the other hand, is to *create* an order in the world; the designer must not yield before facts but, on the contrary, attempt to change them according to some conception of what they ought to be. The natural sciences are fundamentally deterministic, modern science no less so than Newtonian mechanics, whereas in design that which is must not be assumed fully to determine that which can be.

The determinism of natural science, not allowing man the ability to alter, by his choice of actions, the course of things, excludes a concern with ethics. Design, which is based precisely on man's possessing that ability, must, by the same token, give to ethics a central place in its thought, and cannot profitably separate facts from values as science does. The designer, unlike the scientist, should allow his view of things as they are to be affected by what he would like them to be.

Scientific thought cannot properly encompass a mode of thought suitable for design. But science and design are not opposed: they are complementary. The task of science is the analysis of the given, that of design the synthesis of the new. Science performs conceptual syntheses that will aid in its analysis of concrete reality; design performs conceptual analyses that will aid in its synthesis of concrete structures. It is obvious that the two endeavors overlap, and that the methods of science, highly developed as they are, are an invaluable tool in design. But, in view of the ascendancy of science in our culture, and the persistent attempts that have been made to turn the design endeavor into a scientific discipline, we have chosen here to stress our belief that design, understood as the activity by which man creates his own future, cannot prosper within the confines of the scientific worldview.*

Given the dialectical interrelations existing between man-made physical and sociocultural systems, and the fully active, open, and transactional nature of man, it is imperative that the mode of thought capable of structuring and restructuring the man-made milieu would have to comprehend an *empirical,* as well as an *existential,* conception of the Hows and Whys of man's actions and reactions.

In the *empirical* domain, this mode of thought would have to grasp in an operative manner the patterns of interaction existing between man and the natural environment, and, in a more important sense, the constantly changing patterns of interrelations occurring between man and the man-made environment.[3]

The conception of a willed state involves defining goals and norms, relating large amounts of data, developing alternative solutions, and selecting as most satisfactory that solution, which, reflecting acceptable values or values that can in time become accepted, embodies some virtue not presently existent.

Consequently, the explicit analysis of values is to be considered as one of the main features of this mode of thought.

In order to introduce systematic and rigorous theoretical methods, this mode of thought will also have to introduce into its logic as a real factor the notion of an existential operator (man, as the intuitive synthesizer and maker of symbols).[4] Although man is certainly not the only living organism capable

---

*It should be noted, moreover, that the design system of thought—defined as the form generating actions by which man conceives and structures the physical and sociocultural environments as wholes—is not opposed but, on the contrary, complementarily related to what has been defined as technology, i.e., the industrial and cybernetic institutionalization of science. While technology can be understood as the activity by which qualities are organized into quantities in order to turn them operable, the new role foreseen for the design mode of thought should be understood as the act by which man, utilizing technology, synthesizes quantities into qualities.

of altering his environment in order to maintain his essential physiological properties, he is, however, the only entity capable of generating images and undergoing ontological changes.[5]

In the *existential* domain, this mode of thought would, thus, have to conceive of man as he who creates experiential and conceptual structures in order to satisfy needs and conciliate aspirations, which go from the physical to the cosmological, within the boundaries of the natural and the socio-cultural world.

Obviously, the search for such a mode of thought would require a full-fledged body of interdisciplinary imagination and analysis. Two questions, then, present themselves to mind: First, which problem area of the man-made milieu would render the maximum possibilities for research and insight? Second, do our present educational and research institutions have sufficient scope for the establishment of an interdisciplinary exchange, and do they have the power necessary for putting their design proposals into practice?

3.

The *first* question can be answered if we observe the increasingly urban characteristics of our society, and realize that the processes ensuing from such urban phenomena will not become comprehensible nor manageable by solely resorting to the operational and political methods developed for dealing functionally and linguistically with the phenomena of an industrial society and its products. Any attempt at renewing and inventing the language of an urban society can only result from a radical critique and postulation of urban practices and theory. Of all man-made structures, the many levels of meaning that are embodied in the social and physical models of urban existence are the ones that will render the richest source of insight in the development of a system of thought capable of designing the man-made milieu.

As we are reaching a situation in which the only valid approaches will be those comprehending the totality of the world system, the urban models to be considered should behold the natural and the man-made environment—the entire planet—as a complete and totally interrelated problem.

As for the *second* question, of whether the research and teaching resources of our present universities can be tapped to better understand and help develop the new system of thought concerned with the design of our urban environment, a pertinent answer can be extracted from the Ford Foundation's report on Urban Extension.[6] From 1959 to 1966, the Ford Foundation made grants for experiments in applying the nation's university resources directly to the problem of American cities. In the final report, of October 1966, the Ford Foundation stated that the experiments revealed that our present universities have yet to solve a set of critical questions if they are ever to deal effectively with the problems of an urban society. To the question, Are universities presently structured to assume urban commitments? they confirmed everyone's suspicions in stating that "responsiveness to the urban environment calls for an across-the-board commitment. An isolated department or division devoted to urban affairs appears to have limited impact upon the problem as a whole." In addition, the report is explicit in saying that "the difference between the needs of urban extension and those of academic departments are more sharply drawn by university traditions and administrative structure than conditions actually warrant." As a consequence, the present training does not prepare the student of design for the task of assuming responsibilities. He is usually provided neither with the spiritual attitude nor with the intellectual equipment for acting creatively in a world where the posing and solving of problems has become a highly complex task of devising dynamic controls rather than arriving at final solutions.

What conclusions are we to draw from these familiar facts? If we agree with the concept that an education preparatory to designing our urban environment should include all the fields of socioeconomic and physical inquiry and action, which can give sense and structure to the human environment, we would then have to question very seriously whether the present highly rigid and compartmentalized structure of our universities does allow for an effective interdisciplinary approach toward questioning and designing our urban environment.

All these considerations have brought us to the point where we ought to begin considering whether the time has not arrived for formulating the idea of an institution explicitly concerned with the ethical framework of our society, and conceived toward developing the system of thought capable of designing our man-made milieu.

Such an institution will, of course, not immediately solve the problems of our urban environment, but it will come a long way toward transforming these problems into controlled processes. It is hoped that the conceptual scheme of such an institution would benefit from a dissolution of nineteenth-century notions of deterministic systems, which believed that not only did systems have to be simple and general but also that human organizations, in consequence, could be planned rigid and finite. This institution, if it is to be meaningfully new, would require a different notion of "system." We would, then, have to talk of a dynamic concept of "complex system": indeterministic, designed to operate in a constant state of reform and adaptation to other systems, as well as operationally capable of acknowledging private values and emotions as essential factors in the large and difficult process of arriving at forms of commonly shared goals.

This institution should include all the disciplines that can give meaning and order to our social and physical environment. Thus, in addition to its core faculty in physical, biological, and socioeconomic design, it should be flanked by its own faculties in the behavioral and social sciences, in the exact and applied sciences, and in the humanities, which would be articulated according to research topics rather than by disciplines. Furthermore, it would be necessary that this institution take its proposals into the stage of development in order to gain feedback. Such a program for urban development would, therefore, require that both the government and the private sectors of the society be actively involved.

What is here envisioned is that if the traditional concept of *Universitas* is reformulated according to the needs of a post-technological society, such *Universitas* should encompass the constellation of the different Western concepts of the university. The first of such concepts is the humanistic university, as conceived by the Greek Academics, institutionalized by the Italian and Parisian universities of the Middle Ages, and reformulated by John Henry Cardinal Newman[7] in the last century. The second of such concepts of the university is the scientific, specialized idea of a university that deals with the empirical world as envisioned by Francis Bacon[8] and René Descartes,[9] and institutionalized by Wilhelm von Humboldt. The third of such university concepts might be constituted by the idea envisioned here of an institution that would deal with the processes involved in the physical and socioeconomic synthesis of man's aspirations in conciliation with the facts of the natural and the sociocultural environment. This reformulated concept of Universitas, or constellation of universities, would thus represent the philosophic mode of thought in its humanistic university, the scientific mode of thought in its empirical university, and the design mode of thought in its university of design and development.[10] There would thus be, for example, social philosophers in the humanistic university, social scientists in the scientific university, and social designers in the university of design and development.

The tasks that would have to be assumed by such Universitas may stagger imagination and paralyze hope, but they cannot be relinquished, as they would involve: first, the *retrospective* task of evaluating the consequences that have resulted from having made choices on the bases of values no higher than those derived from an acceptance of consumption as the existential motivator; second, the *critical* task of analyzing the socioeconomic and political institutions of our technological milieu in order to establish the effects they have had on our civilization's systems of ideas and emotions; third, the *prospective* task of envisioning and constantly expanding the framework of private and common values that should guide the physical and socioeconomic design of our society; and fourth, the *operational* task of developing the physical and socioeconomic methods necessary for implementing these objectives.

The fulfillment of these tasks will, however, require that prior to defining new areas of inquiry and action, and before developing new disciplines, we have the courage of conceiving of this Universitas, both as the model for beholding the meaning of man's condition, and as the way for imagining and implementing the quality of our existence in terms of a humanly made milieu.

Notes

1. "Adaptive systems possess the ability to react to their environment in a way that is favorable, in some sense, to the continued operations of the system." They are open, i.e., "they exchange materials, energies or information with their environment." A. D. Hall and R. E. Fagen, "Definition of Systems," *General Systems* 1, Yearbook of the Society for the Advancement of General Systems Theory (1956): 18–28.

2. For a critique of technology in ideological terms, see Fragments: Notes on Structure, Paragraph C.

3. In systemic terms, the man-made environment is understood as the interaction between sociocultural systems and physical systems. That is to say, in a man-made environment, man is related to a system of physical elements (objects going from the micro to the macro scale) and to a system of rules (behavior, laws, habits, uses, morals, etc.) that interact with one another.

4. Anatol Rapoport and William T. Horvath, "Thoughts on Organization Theory," *General Systems* 4 (1959): 79–91.

5. Kenneth E. Boulding, *The Image* (Ann Arbor: University of Michigan Press, 1956).

6. *Urban Extension: A Report on Experimental Programs Assisted by the Ford Foundation* (New York: Ford Foundation, October 1966).

7. John Henry Cardinal Newman, *The Idea of a University* (New York: Longmans Green, 1947).

8. Francis Bacon, "The Advancement of Learning," in *Essays, Advancement of Learning, New Atlantis and Other Pieces.* Ed. Richard Foster Jones (New York: Odyssey Press, 1937).

9. For René Descartes's distinction between the faculty of arts (poetry and history) and philosophy, which he divides into the special studies of mathematics, physics, and metaphysics, see his *Discourse on Method.*

10. We first heard the term university of design expressed at a lecture given by Tomas Maldonado at the Graham Foundation of Chicago, in 1967. In his lecture, Maldonado referred to a five-year design education and research program, which, in close alliance with the behavioral, the social, the exact, and the applied sciences would be dedicated to educating environmental designers.

II. Manhattan: Capital of the XXth Century

"Once I have grasped it, then an old, as it were rebellious, half apocalyptic province of my thoughts will have been subdued, colonized, set in order." (Walter Benjamin, in a letter to Gerhard Scholem)

1.

Manhattan, unencumbered by permanent memory, and more interested in becoming than in being, can be seen as the city of that second technological revolution brought about by the development of processes for producing and controlling information rather than just energy. It has, after all, incorporated the worship of communication with the idolatry of the industrial product and, by so doing, provided the ground for supporting any infatuation with the now as the ultimate configuration of reality. However, seen in a different light, Manhattan may reveal an unforeseen potential for conceiving of a quite different notion of city.

Manhattan is, in essence, a network. If beheld as an infrastructure for the processing and exchange of matter, energy, and information, Manhattan may be seen either as the overwrought roof of a subterranean physical grid of subway tunnels and train stations, automobile passages, postal tubes, sewage chambers, water and gas pipes, power wires, and telephone, telegraph, television, and computer lines; or, conversely, as the datum plane of an aerial lattice of walking paths, automobile routes, flight patterns, wireless impulses, institutional liaisons, and ideological webs. In any of these roles, the points of Manhattan's network have been repeatedly charged, on and off, with different meanings. Entire systems and isolated elements have been connected to and processed by these networks, only to be later removed and replaced by new ones.

2.

Were we willing, for the sake of argument, to suspend disbelief, forget coordinates, and imagine that all present structures have been completely removed, Manhattan's infrastructure would emerge—in all the complexity of its physical organization, the capacity of its input-output mechanism, and the versatility of its control devices— as the most representative urban artifact of our culture.

Freed in this manner from its current limitations, we may, to further this transfer operation, remove Manhattan's infrastructure from its present context and place it, for example, in the center of San Francisco Bay, on the plains of Africa, among the chateaux of the Loire Valley, along the Great Wall of China. . . .

Manhattan's infrastructure, thus liberated, belongs to all. But an infrastructure, though necessary, is not sufficient to make a city. The next step is, then, for all to undertake the postulation of its possible structures. The methods may belong either to remembrance or to invention, for, conceived as the idea rather than as the actual configuration, Manhattan's infrastructure provides the framework in which all crystallized fragments rescued from the city of the memory and all figments envisioned for the city of the imagination may dwell in ensemble, if not by reason of their casual relationships (since no reconstruction is hereby intended), then by grace of their affinities. The outcome of such an undertaking may be agitational, and render, if not actual proposals of structures, at least on explicit Inventory of Qualities of urban existence toward a yet to be defined City of Open Presents.

3.

In a first, retrospective, phase, we may, as one of many possible approaches, assemble in a piecemeal manner any surviving fragments of the memory on the infrastructure:

bologna's arcades,
osip mandelstam's st. petersburg,
john nash's regent's park,
gabriel's petit trianon,
katsura's promenades to observe the sunset,
mies's barcelona pavilion,

wallace stevens's wind on a wheatfield,
john soane's house,
frank zappa's los angeles,
baudelaire's fleeting instants,
debussy's submerged cathedral,
michael heizer's land marks,
joan littlewood's fun palace,
ray bradbury's brown clouds,
le notre's gardens of chantilly. . . .

This tearing of the fragment from its former context, this rescuing of the irreducible word from its sentence, involves not only the usual process of design by discriminate selection but suggests, moreover, a process of bringing together where, instead of establishing fixed hierarchies, the fragments rescued from tradition are placed on the same level in ever-changing contiguities, in order to yield new meanings, and thereby render other modes of access to their recondite qualities.

4.

In a second, prospective, *phase, the form of any structure to be assembled on the infrastructure is to come from the domain of invention.*

But envisioned qualities do not come in wholes. They are to be apprehended as they rush by—partial denotators of an inverse tradition, of possible states which may become; and once grasped, they are to be dialectically confronted with the many meanings which can be temporarily assigned to our fragmentary experiences of the Present.

If beheld as icons, the architectural and ceremonial forms, which these constantly changing structures may adopt, represent an instance in the perennial state of transaction between the fears and desires underlying the individual's aspirations and the assembled forces of the natural and the sociocultural milieus. If unfolded, these structures would provide an insight into the goals and the values of their designer: man, the private being and the member of society.

Expanding the Inventory of Qualities of urban existence by this process of interpreting the meaning of the individual values and goals underlying the invention of structures involves bringing the subjective content of these individual values up to a communal objective level so that they may be accepted or rejected by the community.

This process of expanding the community's ethical framework involves observing or projecting the possible effects these values, if implemented, may have on the community, and assessing communally whether these effects are to be enhanced or reduced. As the meaning of these structures can only be interpreted in the context of the patterns of relationships it establishes with other structures, this process generates new meanings, which, in turn, will require further interpretation. By this reiterative process the envisioned structures assume constructive powers. Insofar as they question the context of the Present, they assign it new meanings; insofar as they propose alternative states, they restructure it.

The quality of human existence is the principle that is to guide the communal process of designing and constructing the house of our individual realities. Both methods, rescuing the irreducible fragments from their decayed contexts and interpreting the different possible contexts which may give meaning to imagined figments—in a word, designing structures as a method for inventing and learning about the form that new qualities of human existence may adopt—suggest possible approaches toward interpreting a culture through the structures it creates, as well as aid toward creating the images and developing the models of new sociocultural systems.

But, as we may soon realize once we return to our customary state of disbelief, no mode of coexistence with the city of the memory will be found, nor will the configuration of the city of the imagination become evident until the system of thought and action capable of designing the two according to new ideological and emotional values shall have been developed.

Then, we may see the changing configurations of the emerging city and those of the constantly renewed modes of thought that are developed to design it are always isomorphic. It may also become evident that such structural transformations will only take place after new institutions, concerned with developing such design modes of thought and capable of designing the man-made milieu physically and socioeconomically, have been established. Perhaps, then, after these specific conditions have been satisfied, but not before the unfolded meanings of remembered and invented structures have begun to expand the realm of our valued qualities, will the Universitas become the Univercity, and the City of Open Presents come into being.

✢ Specific Considerations ✢

The following sections are included to provide a context to the previous sections. They regard problems of a general nature, not exclusive to this Project. They are, nevertheless, included not only because they do affect, and are related to, the issues in questions but, also, because we believe that, although some of these problems can certainly not even begin to be solved within the scope of this Project, they ought to form part of the Contributor's largest frame of reference.

As the Contributor will soon observe, these Specific Considerations are not part of a precise logical sequence, but rather a bricolage of related thoughts. Not all of them can, therefore, be consistently reconciled, because satisfying the spirit of one consideration may determine excluding others. Our intention has been not to list a number of precise questions that must be answered but, rather, to render an impression of the attitudes that animate this Project.

I. Design as a Mode of Thought

1.

The task of science is analysis. Science takes systems apart into their basic components; it seeks to discover simplicity behind the apparent complexity of observed phenomena. The man-made synthesis of various elements into a purposefully complex system is not the kind of problem that the methods of science—natural or social science—are intended to deal with. Once such a system exists—or once it is proposed in sufficient detail so that it can be imagined as existing—science can tell us much about the way it works. An airplane is no less subject to the laws of nature than a bird is, and as a given object in the world it can equally be analyzed by the methods of natural science. But an airplane is built for a purpose and adapted to some environment so that this purpose is accomplished; this distinguishes the artificial system from the natural one.*

Of course, the structure of a bird can be thought of, and profitably discussed, as answering to a purpose and being adapted to an environment. But such discussion is really metaphorical: the structure of a bird can be assumed to be necessary, that of an airplane is contingent and can be changed according to its performance. Science is meant to deal with the given; man-made systems are not given but put together so that they function according to certain expectations and satisfy certain desires. They are, in one word, *designed*.

2.

The scientific mode of thought was not intended for the task of design. But some believe that it can be extended, without any essential changes, to apply to the different set of problems that design entails. Two main approaches have been taken toward developing a *scientific discourse of design*: an *empirical* approach and a *normative* one.

To those who take the empirical approach, the problems of design can always be seen as closely akin to the problems of engineering. Now, engineering is not science: it produces artifacts to serve some purpose; it deals not so much with the world as it is as with the world as it can be made to be. Yet those are probably right who believe that the problems of engineering can be brought within the compass of scientific thought. Engineering makes "ought" statements (as science does not) but only about how things ought to be so that some goals are attained, not about what the goals themselves ought to be; and once the goals are taken as set, something like a scientific analysis can be made of the various strategies of action that might be followed. The "ought" statements of engineering can be turned into empirical

---

*See the lucid discussion in Herbert Simon, *The Sciences of the Artificial* (Cambridge, Mass.: M.I.T. Press, 1969): ch. 1.

propositions such as a science makes. This is not true of "ought" statements, which are not about means and strategies but about ends and purposes. When design is looked upon as strictly akin to engineering, "ought" statements about ends and purposes are placed outside its domain; design so conceived can in all probability be systematized into a scientific discipline.

But, if design is understood, more broadly, as the endeavor by which man, consciously or unconsciously, creates structures that give meaning and order to his surroundings, it cannot leave aside matters of purpose and aspiration, and it must be concerned not only with facts but also with values and purport. Natural science deals with an order that can be assumed to exist already in the world, and to be independent of human activity. Its statements are properly declarative and empirical, whereas design statements, being about a man-made order, must also include the normative, and cannot be exclusively empirical and independent of the observer. Even when the design endeavor pretends to operate in strict adherence to the standards of objectivity and externality of a natural science, it will not be able to exclude matters of value; for when such standards are applied not to a natural but to a man-made order, the scientist's commitment to the given, his fidelity to things as they are rather than as one would like them to be, will function, unacknowledged, as the guiding ethical principle. This has the effect, in our present situation, of conferring on the processes of technology the status of a force of nature, and thus discouraging any attempts to control them and change their course. Such "scientific objectivity" is therefore not really objective but plumps for the continuation of ongoing processes, the future as a prolongation of the present.

The future of the man-made milieu does not merely unfold from the present; one cannot predict it from a set of initial conditions as one predicts the future state of a mechanical system. Rather, it depends on what we think it ought to be and what we do to bring this about. The envisioning of alternative futures, which are not contained in the present but which are to be *created*, purposefully worked toward if they are found to be desirable, is fundamental to a design endeavor that is concerned not just with designing strategies and producing artifacts to meet a set of requirements, but with the larger task of synthesis of the man-made milieu, of giving meaning and structure to the productions of man.

• • •

If design takes on that larger task it must not only be an empirical but also a normative pursuit. The future, it has been cogently argued, can differ radically from the present only if it is based on a different set of *values*; to truly create the future and not just extend the present, a change in the overall configuration of values must be brought about. In the view of those who attempt to develop a normative approach to design—in contrast to those who conceive it in empirical terms—it follows that the examination of values should be the main concern of design.** In this view, it is after values are examined that goals are to be set, which, in terms of the new value configuration, are judged to be desirable; and only then is one to worry about how such goals might be reached.

Certainly one should not let questions of feasibility, rather than matters of value, determine the direction that human activity is to take and the choice of ends that should be aimed at. And proponents of the view of design as a normative endeavor are perfectly right when they argue, against the predictive way of approaching the future, that values are the fundamental thing and value changes cannot be predicted. But, by the same token, can value changes be consciously planned? A set of values defines a worldview; it is not something that can first be decided upon and then implemented in the structures that man builds; rather, it emerges dialectically from the interaction between aspirations and conscious intentions, and the actual structures that are meant to carry them out. To argue this is not to give precedence to the actual over the envisaged but to point out that, in the activity of man upon his surroundings, they constantly modify each other.

The view of design as a normative pursuit, like that which sees it as an empirical one, constitutes an attempt at the systematization of the design discourse along the lines of a scientific discipline. It is, in the case of the normative approach, a discipline that validates its statements socially through the agreement of members of the community rather than by empirical observation; but its task is still the analysis of the given and not the synthesis of the new. Conscious, commonly held meanings cannot be new, and normative approaches operate only with these; they cannot create new values any more than engineering can. Where do new values come from? An isolated individual may think of them by himself, and attempt to communicate them to others by means of some structure which embodies them but whose meaning, because it is new, will not be immediately accessible. Or, a structure may be created which embodies new values that no one is aware of, not even its maker, until the meaning of the structure is deciphered and made explicit.

(Gaining access to, or assigning, possible meanings to a structure can be done by decoding according to an established context or by developing a new context to give it meaning.) In any case, it is not before, but after, structures have come into existence that new values embodied in them can suggest themselves to members of the community. The synthesis of structures that have a *symbolic* charge—with levels of meaning that go beyond the commonly agreed and are not directly accessible—is what enables us to invent the future.

** We have in mind those, like Hasan Ozbekhan, who see design primarily as normative planning. See, for example, Ozbekhan's excellent article, "Toward a General Theory of Planning," in *Perspectives of Planning.* Ed. Erich Jantsch (Paris: Organization for Economic Cooperation and Development, 1968): 114.

3.

The scientific procedure is to subsume as many particulars as possible under a suitable generalization. The syntheses of science take place in the head; their upshot is a set of general *principles*, which the scientist then applies to his basic task of analysis. The designer starts not with the particular but with the general, with restrictions that are to be observed and aspirations that he will attempt to fulfill; and the upshot of his work is a particular structure, a synthesis that takes place in actuality. And that structure is a richer design whose meaning is not adequately subsumed under the general considerations that motivated its construction, but suggests new possibilities, a new *beginning*.

The interpretation of symbolically charged structures so that they may enter the semantic domain, their meaning elucidated and their implications understood, is an important aspect of the design endeavor, and one that is akin to a scientific discipline. The designer here, and wherever he deals with semantic elements, does well to avail himself of the methods of science. Where design does not fall within the compass of scientific thought is in the regard that it must give to the uniqueness of particular structures as possibly containing the seed for new beginnings. The scientist, too, must of course be open to phenomena that suggest revisions in his picture of things, even sometimes the need for a fresh start; but properly he clings to his old explanations until they are proven wrong. The designer must, on the contrary, assume that each new structure has the properties of an *icon*,*** in Charles Sanders Peirce's terminology, that it is a new discourse unto itself, totally symbolic until proved, or turned, semantic. The design mode of thought must supplement the scientific with what may be called an *iconic* dimension.

A mode of thought suitable for design must, then, comprehend not only the empirical and the normative but also the iconic. Empirically, the designer deals with the processes of the *infrastructure*, with the allocation and organization of material resources and of resources of information; and, as a normative planner, the designer is concerned with the *superstructure* of ideas and aspirations, values and intentions, our conscious image of what we are and of what we would like to be. In both these capacities, the designer deals with semantic elements, and something like a scientific discourse of design can, in

***The notion of an iconic structure is really a matter of methodological convenience, a way of regarding the productions of man, which can be conceptual or material, or, more often, a combination of both, so that they may point the way to new beginnings. Thus, even a set of scientific principles, such as, for example, Isaac Newton's three laws, can be looked upon, so to speak, as a conceptual icon, which suggests certain aspirations and implies a new set of ideas; from this point of view, Newton's laws can be regarded as symbolic until fully interpreted, not only for their scientific content but for their larger implications, and later integrated into the infrastructure (as technology, for example) and the ideologies of the superstructure (as the hierarchical patterns of mechanical organization adopted by a political system, for example).

all probability, be developed for these two tasks, but not, as we have argued, for the task of synthesis, by which alone a true renewal can take place.

A *synthetic discourse of design* would deal neither with the infrastructure nor with the superstructure, taken in themselves, but with the *structures* that man creates to reconcile the "interface" between these two levels, and with the iconic properties that these structures have. Change comes about through the structures in which man, attempting to satisfy the demands of the superstructure within the bounds set by the infrastructure, gives embodiment to strivings and inner impulses that he may not be quite aware of. The dreams and fears and desires of the structure maker thus find articulation in the symbolically charged uniqueness of a structure. Only the invention of such structures can break the stasis of established patterns.

II. The Designs of Freedom

1.

The Universitas as we have conceived it is not to be a detached observer or passive entity. It must actively participate in the creation of the man-made milieu, be concerned both with the question of what goals are to guide man in this creation and with the problem of how resources are best to be allocated toward attaining these goals. In such pursuits, it should acknowledge what contemporary experience has shown, namely, that authority over resources and means of production (or the opposite position, withdrawal from any such involvement) is not enough to insure the quality of our environment; a desirable environment may only come about if we develop ways for continuously designing and managing it.

2.

Man creates artifacts in order to conciliate his individual aspirations with the constraints imposed by his natural and cultural worlds. In creating his artifacts, he seeks to attain some goals: goals of which he may or may not have a clear grasp and which the actual artifacts may or may not satisfy. Artifacts have to be interpreted after they come into existence so that their true meaning can be learned; and once their meaning is learned and compared with the original goals that motivated their design, man may want to modify them or to design other artifacts, or he may choose to revise his original goals or even his basic values. Man's transactions remain a strictly individual process if his goals can be satisfied by means of his own resources, or if satisfaction can be attained by a mere internal reorganization of his system of goals. But the satisfaction of an individual's goals may require pooling resources with another individual and, in some degree, combining their systems of goals. In this case, a goal proposed by one individual must be formulated objectively, according to agreed convention, to enable the other individual to accept the proposal as an input.

Agreement by at least one other individual to the joint pursuit of at least one such postulated goal establishes a group. A group itself may be regarded as an artifact designed by an individual to satisfy his need to transact with other individuals. A group will, in turn, transact with other groups, and they may all agree to constitute together the larger artifact that is a society. The transactions and conflicts that take place in a complex society often determine that the pattern of this agreement—usually called the *social contract*—undergoes constant transformations.

3.

The measure of a social system, like that of any artifact, is the degree to which it fulfills, and allows to be fulfilled, the purposes of individuals. Informing the following proposal that the Universitas contribute actively to the constant examination and reformulation of the social contract is the desire to insure, as much as possible, the freedom of the individual to will his environment.

One may feel pessimistic about the prospects of such freedom in the present political context. But awareness of a state of crisis and analysis of its symptoms are the privileges of reflection. Designers, even if torn by perplexity, must identify problems, propose alternatives, and develop methods to implement them. The proposed design of the Universitas is meant to help resolve two opposing positions on the present predicament. One position holds that by letting the technological infrastructure proliferate without a harnessing superstructure, we would discover embodied in the products of this technology all goals we may wish to imagine; the other position counters that the individual can best satisfy his aspirations by himself or in small groups at the most, that his superstructures do not require much in the way of support from an infrastructure. The first position subjugates the goals of the individual to the productions of an overpowering technology, the second, to the constrictions of an undeveloped one.

The Universitas must, therefore, be so designed as to help resolve these conflicting positions by acting as a mediator between the processes of the infrastructure and the goals of the superstructure, and by attempting a synthesis of individual goals into proposed states that may be adopted by other individuals. As a guide in our description of the roles that we envision for the Universitas in society, we propose to introduce, first, a working model, outlined below.

4.

Members of a group, as we have seen, are brought together by certain goals, which they have agreed to pursue jointly, and by certain pooled resources—

resources of matter, energy, and information—which they will allocate and structure as they think best with the aim of reaching those goals. But, as it happens with the artifacts that an individual builds, the actual structures that a group creates may not satisfy the goals for which they were created, and may imply other goals, which the members of the group did not have in mind. A structure, after it comes into existence, must be interpreted, and its true meaning learned in the context of its interaction with other existing structures and of the larger configurations these structures establish.

Let us look at this operation in terms of a network model. An individual conceives of some goals that he may want to propose for adoption by others. He reformulates this proposal according to agreed convention and makes a postulational input which, if accepted, establishes a network of group relationships.

The group may then proceed to build a structure, which it believes will satisfy this proposal. A reorganization of some of the points and patterns in the group network takes place. This reorganization is fed back to the network as an internal message, which is then decoded in the light of certain goals. As a result of this decoding, further reorganization may take place; new structures may be built or new goals agreed upon.

Already a simple equilibrial feedback device performs some kind of *decoding* on the messages it gets from its environment, for they are followed by determinate changes in the behavior of the device in accordance with the goal it is designed to pursue: this goal can be said to set up a code by which messages are assigned meanings. A sufficiently complex dynamic feedback network is able to decode messages in a number of different ways—according to different, perhaps contradictory, goals its structure may imply. And the decoding of messages in such a dynamic self-modifying network does not simply trigger a change of behavior but may result in a change of goals—that is, in a process of *code making* or icon invention.[1] A network setting itself new goals is inventing new codes by which it interprets messages—messages that may come not only from the environment but also from within the net itself.[2]

Looked upon as a complex dynamic feedback network, a group of human beings is oriented, by its patterns of organization, toward the attainment of some goals of which the individuals in the group, as a whole or in part, may or may not be conscious. It is by a decoding not only of external messages but also of internal patterns—of the very structures designed to carry out what the group sees as its goals—that the group can become conscious of what its actions and processes are actually likely to lead toward. Discrepancies revealed between the actuality and the aspirations may bring on a change of the existing structures or a revision of the original goals. Like any sufficiently complex network, a human grouping will have various levels of goals; there will be larger, more comprehensive, goals in terms of which the more immediate intermediary goals are to be interpreted. To these larger goals correspond larger configurations of interacting structures; the meaning of any given structure must be decoded from these larger configurations, a proposed revision of immediate goals pondered for its possible consequences in terms of overall purposes.

It is convenient, when considering these code-making and decoding processes, to distinguish two kinds of structures within a network and four functions exercised on these structures. For purposes of discussion, we will consider the case of a group network, although the same concepts would apply to individual and to social networks.

The system of goals shared by the members of the group may be said to constitute a conceptual *superstructure,* which is supported by a physical *infrastructure* into which the available common resources have been organized. In practice, of course, there never is a perfect correspondence between a given superstructure and the underlying infrastructure.[3]

These concepts of infrastructure and superstructure, although necessary for describing *formally* the organization of a group network, nevertheless, are not sufficient for distinguishing *functionally* the different feedback processes that take place with the group network. We ought, therefore, to introduce the notion of four distinct, though interrelated, functions that operate on the group network and govern the interactions among the various infrastructures and superstructures created by the group.

The *information function* performs the task of decoding and of bringing to the consciousness of the group the results of its decoding. It analyzes existing structures for their implied goals and possible consequences; it recognizes and interprets the larger configurations that these structures establish; it projects as possible future states the aspirations and proposals contributed by individual members, and attempts to decode these envisioned structures.

It is through the *postulative function* that new structures are envisioned, alternative goals and the corresponding new patterns proposed, and new codes invented. Whereas the information function decodes, the postulating function makes codes.

In operational terms, the postulative function accomplishes its roles by designing alternative new or modified structures of resources that embody the new or modified goals it postulates for the members of the network to accept or reject.

The postulative function is exercised by the individual members, who, as private individuals, have their own dreams and aspirations, which at first may make sense only to themselves, but which they may be able to recast, in group terms, as suitable inputs for the group network. As a rule, it is through such inputs from private individuals (from such inventors of patterns as artists, social thinkers, poets, and designers) that a group network becomes aware of possible new states it may aspire to, new configurations that would assign alternative meanings to existing structures, and new structures that may be built to replace the existing ones.

It is by the individual members, too, that the *decision-making function* is to be exercised in the group. They must decide, on the basis of the analysis and projections provided by the information function, which among the existing patterns in the group network are to be maintained, which suppressed and which augmented, and which among the alternatives proposed by the postulative function are to be accepted and which rejected.

Finally, we have the *regulatory function*, which is exercised through the infrastructure and is in charge of implementing the choices of the decision-making function by controlling the supply of matter, energy, and information to each of the points in the group network.

5.

The four functions that we have described for a group network also exist for the larger social network. But they may exist in thwarted or inadequate forms. It may happen, for instance, that the information function is effective only within the smaller group networks and not for society as a whole, so that each sector of society makes its own decisions unaware of how these may affect the other sectors or the life of the whole. Or, it may happen that, after a certain stage, the postulative function effectively ceases, goals are set and cannot be renewed, all changes are assumed to be predictable and all points in the social network are assigned fixed meanings; the system is closed.

Closed systems inevitably run down; if a system is to renew itself it must be kept open, and open above all to postulational inputs, which, as we have seen, usually originate with the individual. Since these postulational inputs are for the most part made locally, into the group networks, it is only through an effective information function that these individual postulations can be made to carry into the larger social network.

Other institutions in society may also enact the four functions described in our working model; however, for the purpose of this essay, we shall restrict our argument solely to defining the roles we foresee for the Universitas and for the individual members of society.

We propose that the Universitas, *conceived not as a specific organization but as the prototype for the pre-design structure that would provide the context for the design of new structures,* undertake in formal terms the related functions of information and postulation.[4] Individuals, in addition to exercising the decision-making function in formal terms, would also participate actively, though in a random way, in the performance of information and postulative functions. One of the immediate intentions of this proposal is that the performance of these two functions by the Universitas would strengthen that done by the individuals—the formal exercise of these functions by the Universitas would complement their continued nonformal exercise by the individuals acting on their own. The long-range objective underlying this proposal is to reverse established technocratic hierarchies of decision making by helping the individuals of the community to assume the four aforementioned functions in a decentralized manner.

Such long-range objectives clearly establish the transitional nature assigned to the Universitas. As a transitional institution, it should be regarded as a special type of group network,[5] one analytically attuned to what is occurring in the other group networks, so that it may be able to keep track of local patterns initiated by individuals and groups, of the possible offshoots these local patterns may have, and of the larger configurations they have established or are likely to establish through their interaction—all of which it would be charged with bringing up to a level of social consciousness. And it will be charged with keeping track of, and of bringing to consciousness, not only existing local patterns but also local aspirations, the postulational inputs made by individuals into their group networks. Furthermore, we are proposing that Universitas itself take on a postulative task, that it itself propose, for the individuals of the community to accept or reject, new goals and rearrangements, putting much of the same formal equipment that served for decoding to the complementary task of code making.[6]

As to the decision-making and regulatory functions, it is best that the Universitas not be involved with them except as they are inevitably bound up with the information and the postulative ones.

The right of choice exercised though the decision-making function must remain with the individuals of the community; otherwise, what we get is a dictatorial arrangement—the Universistate. Such active postulating and efficient information function as we propose that the Universitas undertake is meant to buttress the decisions of individuals. The regulatory function should not be exercised by the Universitas either. This, in general, should be as independent as possible from the information and postulative functions, especially since there is the danger that, were the Universitas to become involved with regulating techniques, it might end up accepting the constraints and dynamics of technical feasibility as the main guidelines for its postulations and recommendations.

6.
The laudable ideal that individuals and small groups be able to pursue their own goals by themselves and enact their own local patterns as they see fit usually takes no account of the fact that often the fragmentary and strictly piecemeal enactment of supposedly local goals and conceptions may show them to be bound up in large measure with those of others, and significantly altered by their place in the larger context of society. Because interactions and configurations may extend far beyond an immediate vicinity, it is only through feedback from points everywhere in the network of society that individuals and groups can get to learn if the local patterns they have initiated actually satisfy and continue to reflect what they want.[7] This feedback the Universitas, by its informational action, is intended, within its scope, to supply.

By this feedback process, new goals can be introduced locally, in a decentralized manner (without gravely disrupting the larger fabric of individual and group life), and their circumscribed effects observed empirically. From the pattern of ensuing consequences, it should be possible to establish whether the local goals ought to be extended for acceptance by other individuals and groups.[8] Moreover, the linking of local patterns, which the information function undertaken by the Universitas will attempt to accomplish, may contribute to the expansion and enrichment of these local conceptions through knowledge of how they interact and overlap with those of others.

Beyond this linking action, the more important postulative action, by which the Universitas will attempt to develop methods toward implementing individual and group goals, may contribute to making it possible for individuals and groups to remain independent while marshalling some of the greater technological resources of society's infrastructure for the enactment of their own patterns and the satisfaction of their own private purposes. Moreover, by postulating alternative future states, the Universitas will aid in combating the inducements to accept the outcome of ongoing technological processes as something beyond individual control. By this formal postulative action, and by the bringing of isolated individual postulations to a level of social consciousness, the Universitas may be expected to broaden the scope of envisaged futures and, thus, help bring about the true aspirations and desires of individuals, what their visions tell them ought to be rather than what is presented to them as possible.

The concept of the Universitas, which we have here developed, may serve as a prototype for any artifact designed to support a self-modifying ethical system in which social goals are derived from individual values and come to be agreed upon through the goals that individuals pose and the proposals they enact. If capable of constantly reexamining the scope of existing goals in the new light cast by the individual goals it brings up to a level of social consciousness, such an ethical system would provide a design for individual freedom, where authority is not bestowed on any specialized agent but is defined by the whole of the social network, and remains the sovereignty of each of its individuals.

It is a paradox that any system capable of allowing the greatest possible individual freedom, the fullest possible personal enjoyment of the pleasures of the senses and of the spirit, will not be some sort of unstructured Arcadia but, rather, a highly complex physical and sociocultural artifact. Individual man is not man in isolation (for him, Arcadia would be fine), but man as he willingly transacts with others, joins with them, and chooses to accept the constraints of various patterns of organization. Individual freedom for such a man lies not in the absence of constraints but rather in their *design*: this must reflect his wishes and work toward achieving his aspirations.

7.

We have attempted here the briefest sketch of the roles we contemplate for the Universitas in the design of the man-made environment. The arguments for this discussion were based on a proposed understanding of society as resultant of the interactions between individual networks and their groups. These distinctions were introduced with the intention of providing, on the one hand, a keener insight into the interrelated processes by which man and society invent and modify their goals, and, on the other hand, an approach to designing the social network's functions in such a way that they will contribute to the coherent examination and expansion of society's framework of goals without compromising the independence of the individual and the group networks.

Considerable revision and elaboration will no doubt be required if our abstract outline is to be carried out in actuality. Most of the issues we have raised would certainly benefit from further analysis. We have not touched on such questions as: How do we avoid that the regulating agencies become the protectors of those forces they were created to regulate? What are the political mechanisms by which the individual exercises his evaluative and regulatory functions so as to check on the formal and nonformal exercising of the information and postulative functions? What type of community government system is implied by a network where the sovereignty of the decision-making functions resides in the individual members of the network? What delay will be tolerable in the feedback processes occurring among the four functions?

The truth of any statement regarding the design of our man-made milieu is a sociocultural function dependent on the individuals of the community. We cannot trust, therefore, any answer to be final; a permanent state of questions rather than a conclusive configuration is the ideal.

Notes

1. The internal and external feedback processes by which man, the individual being, expresses his aspirations, and formulates them in terms that are accessible to other individual members of society, have been treated in an article by Emilio Ambasz, "The Formulation of a Design Discourse," *Perspecta* 12, The Yale Architectural Journal (New Haven: 1968). The article proposes a theoretical construct to comprehend the feedback processes by which an individual designs artifacts in order to conciliate the conflicts between his private and his social being. The terminology is different from that utilized here, but the concepts are similar: the artifact resultant from a design process is considered, in Charles Sanders Peirce's terminology, as an icon, whose symbolic content is conceived as an internal system of codes, which must be decoded, i.e., brought up to a semantic level for further information and interpretation of the goals of the individual code maker and those of his sociocultural environment.

2. We can distinguish two types of procedures for goal renewal or modification. By the first one, *internal* to the network, new goals are derived from the meanings which the goal patterns inside the network may generate, consciously or unconsciously, when interacting with each other. By the second procedure, goal renovation assumes the form of *external* inputs originating in other

networks. Both processes allow the network the freedom to break or override established goal patterns, and, thus, introduce the concept of an autonomous, creative function capable of postulating new goals.

3. This network of resources should theoretically be able to shift its position whenever the intersection of the goal patterns determining the point have changed positions. Thus, a given structure can be said to have lost its social meaning when, following the dynamics of sociocultural processes, the goal patterns, which once determined the point, shifted. However, it may happen that due to the inertia of the social network, the infrastructure of resources continues to supply the same position even after the pattern of goals has shifted. On the other hand, a powerful infrastructure may of itself generate "false" superstructural patterns, i.e., not wished by the members of society, but imposed by the demands of the infrastructure's pathology. We have in mind the case where the present production system imposes its own system of demands on the individual and endeavors to establish its own internal needs and goals as those determining the patterning of society's superstructure.

4. The specific tasks that the Universitas is formally prepared to perform in the context of the social network have been described here, in the closing paragraphs of the section "General Matters: I. The University of Design," as *retrospective, critical, prospective*, and *operational*. The first two are tasks of consciousness, which would correspond, to a great extent, to those to be performed by what we have defined as the *information function*. The prospective tasks of envisioning and proposing new goal patterns to be evaluated by the members of the social network, and the operational task of developing the methods necessary for structuring these prospective proposals, fall very closely within the realm of what we have defined as the *postulative function*.

5. As all specialized groups, the Universitas will unavoidably have its own evaluative bias. What should be done is not to reject its actions, but rather to take such bias into account as an explicit factor when pondering the results of its information and postulative functions. Structures run the danger of perpetuating themselves, and the Universitas is not an exception. But it is primarily closed systems that tend to stasis. Designed as an open system, with built-in devices for pattern breaking and for the constant input of outside goals, the Universitas should always remain conscious of changing conditions and capable of rearranging its internal patterns.

6. In a sense, what the Universitas will be doing when it undertakes a formal postulating function is an extension of its information function to postulating inputs that ultimately come from the minds of its own individual members; the Universitas merely provides a formal framework conducive to the postulations of its individuals.

7. This description applies, obviously, to ideal feedback conditions. In practice, we have to allow for and deal with degrees of dysfunctional tolerance.

8. Individuals must always have the freedom to reject postulations they may get, whether from the Universitas or from other individuals. The refusal by an individual to go along with a goal postulated by a group of which he is a member might serve to check the momentum that group patterns often develop of themselves, goals generating structures and structures generating goals without regard for individual values. (We have in mind those participating today in moratorium movements.) Such refusal of a postulational input may well constitute a meaningful counter-input that the individual makes into the group, and, rather than being dismissed as an instance of individual alienation, it merits conscientious examination by the Universitas and by the members of the community.

Appendices

APPENDIX A: RELATION OF THIS RESEARCH PROJECT TO THE MUSEUM OF MODERN ART

Although other institutions are also involved in taking to a level of conscious-ness, as well as evaluating, the system of ideas and emotions embodied in the objects that man makes, The Museum of Modern Art is unique in that it deals with the whole spectrum of man-made objects, from those that gain part of their meaning from a socioeconomic domain, such as industrial design, architecture, and urban planning, to those which gain part of their meaning from an individual domain, such as painting and sculpture. Together, these different man-made objects constitute our culture's system of symbols.

As an institution concerned with problems of values, the Museum is as much interested in the decoding and evaluation of these symbols as it is in all aspects connected with their creation (in this case the establishment of an institution concerned with the creation of the man-made environment). The Museum satisfies its interest in evaluation as well as in synthesis in two different, though complementary, ways: *perspectively*, through its curatorial departments, by dealing with the present understood in the context of the past, and *prospectively*, through such special programs as this project, by attempting to project into the future the possible meanings of a not-yet-understood present.

The fact that all points to be raised in this project will be directly related to the future of our urban communities is in line with the Museum's tradi-tion of pioneering involvement with new urban ideas and its long history of involvement with the community and the quality of its environment. The Museum's auspices for this Project will provide the ground on which to con-duct inquiry unrestricted by parochial interests as well as render the proper international forum from which to present solutions.

APPENDIX B: RELATIONSHIP OF THE INSTITUTE FOR ARCHITECTURE AND URBAN STUDIES TO THIS PROJECT

Through a process of research and design, which tests physical design pro-posals against the actual political, social, and economic constraints of imple-mentation, the Institute is a bridge between the theoretical world of the university and the practical world of planning problems.

The major objectives of the Institute's program are:

A. To propose and develop new methods and new solutions for problems of the urban environment using physical and socioeconomic design as a problem-solving mechanism.

B. To provide a new learning and work experience for students in physical design and related aspects of social planning, so that a new cadre of people can be brought into the research, design, and implementation, and into both the public and private sectors of planning.

C. To investigate and propose, through special programs such as this Project, new types of institutions capable of designing and administering the urban environment. In a certain sense, this involves the Institute in a constant process of transformation and reformulation of itself toward the goal of such institutions.

APPENDIX C: WORKING PROCEDURES

1. Postulative stage
2. Implementative stage

First Stage: *Postulative.* (September 1, 1970, to December 31, 1971)
Annotated Calendar.

1. (September 1970 to July 1, 1971):

Preparation and submission of Project Working Paper to a number of invited Contributors.

Project Working Paper: This Project Working Paper has been prepared with the intention of identifying and defining critical points of concern, and with the hope of advancing several issues of inquiry. It has been prepared by a small Research Team, with the active participation of an interdisciplinary Board of Research Advisors.

2. (July to December 1971):

Period during which Contributors prepare Critical Essays.

Critical Essays: In order to foster the kind of deliberative thought that is essential if we are to comprehend the dimensions of the problems raised by the Project's issues, a number of leading Contributors to these fields have been asked to contribute Critical Essays. Each Essay will be circulated among all other Contributors prior to their gathering in New York.

3. (December 10, 1971):

Critical Essays due: are distributed in advance of the Symposium to all Contributors.

4. (December 20, 1971, to January 5, 1972):

Essay Reading Period.

5. (January 8–9, 1972):

International Symposium to discuss the Critical Essays, at The Museum of Modern Art, New York.

International Symposium: The Symposium will be devoted to critical discussion of points raised by the Contributors' Essays. In order to generate a meaningful level of exchange, each Essay will be distributed to all Contributors well ahead of the Symposium.

Attendance of the sessions will be kept low and will include only invited Contributors and a small number of invited observers. The Symposium will take place over the weekend of January 8 and 9, 1972, at The Museum of Modern Art in New York.

6. (February 1972 to September 1972):

Editorial preparation of the Critical Essays and the Symposium proceedings for publication purposes.

Publication: An immediate result of the Postulative stage will be the edition, in book form (2 volumes) of the Critical Essays, and of the Symposium proceedings.

Diagram of Postulative Stage:

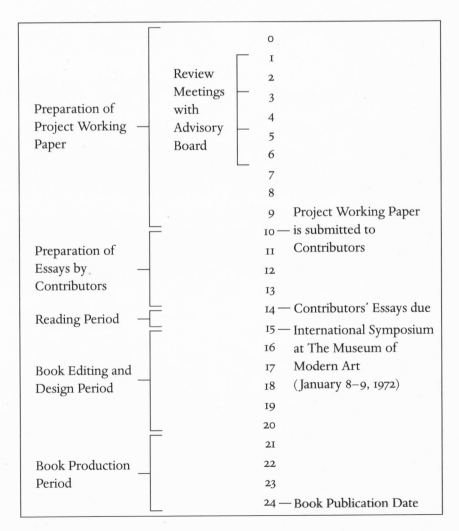

Second Stage: *Implementative*

(Since the second stage can only be planned and executed after the first stage has been completed, the following description is enclosed for informative purposes only.)

Aimed at putting into practice the recommendations to emerge from the individual contributions and the Symposium's proceedings, this stage will be in charge of developing strategies and preparing feasibility studies toward the establishment, in New York State, of a pioneering type of institution, dedicated to the evaluation and design of the man-made milieu.

APPENDIX D: LIST OF MEMBERS

1. Invited Contributors

Louis Althusser
Jean Baudrillard
Kenneth Boulding
Pierre Boulez
J. Burnham
Manual Castells
René Dubos
Umberto Eco
Hans Magnus Enzensberger
Richard Falk
J. Forrester
Michel Foucault
Jermen Gvishiani
Roman Jakobson
Erich Jantsch

G. Kepes
Henri Lefebvre
Tomas Maldonado
Martin Meyerson
Hasan Ozbekhan
Octavio Paz
Anatol Rapoport
Herbert Simon
Susan Sontag
George Steiner
Karlheinz Stockhausen
Alain Touraine
Rexford Guy Tugwell
Sheldon Wolin

2. Board of Research Advisors

*Stanford Anderson
Associate Professor of the History of Architecture, Massachusetts Institute of Technology: *Research Programs for Design Disciplines*

*Kenneth Arrow
Professor of Economics, Harvard University: *Mathematical Economics*

*Walter Buckley
Associate Professor of Sociology, Chairman, Department of Sociology, University of California: *Systems Analysis in the Behavioral Sciences*

*Karl Deutsch
Professor of Political Sciences, Harvard University: *Design of Political Institutions*

*Peter Eisenman
Director of Institute for Architecture and Urban Studies: *Architectural Theory and Urban Planning*

*Thomas Farer
Professor of Law, Columbia University: *Law and Problems, Modernization*

*Gerald Feinberg
Professor of Physics, Columbia University, and Fellow, Institute for Advanced Studies, Princeton University: *Theoretical Physics, Ethics of Technology*

*Harry Frankfurt
Professor of Philosophy, Chairman, Department of Philosophy, The Rockefeller University: *Philosophy*

Suzanne Keller
Professor of Sociology, Princeton University: *Urban Sociology*

Arnold Kramish
Vice President, Institute for the Future: *Technology and Society*

Rosalind Krauss
Associate Professor of Art and Architecture History, Massachusetts Institute of Technology: *Contemporary Art and Architecture*

Teodor Melnechuk
Director of Neuroscience Research Program at the American Academy of Arts and Science, Massachusetts Institute of Technology: *Neuro and Biological Sciences*

Abraham Moles
Professor of Sociology, University of Strasbourg, and Professor of Design Methodology, Ulm, Hochschule für Gestaltung, Germany: *Sociology and Design*

Sheldon Nodelman
Associate Professor of Art History, Yale University: *Theory of Contemporary Art*

---

*The persons listed above following an asterisk have read and commented upon the draft versions of portions of this Project Working Paper. We are immensely grateful to all for their generous advice and criticism. They are, however, to be exonerated from any responsibility; the errors, viewpoints, as well as the overall sense of hubris this undertaking represents are entirely our own.

Joseph Rykwert
Professor of Architecture and City Planning History, University of Essex,
England: *City as a Cultural Artifact*

Carl Schorske
Professor of History, Princeton University: *Cultural History*

Jivan Tabibian
Associate Professor of Sociology, Graduate School of Urban Planning,
University of California, Los Angeles: *Methodology of Social Design*

Alan Trachtenberg
Associate Professor of English Studies, Yale University: *History of American
Ideas and Institutions*

3. Research Project Group

Emilio Ambasz
Curator of Design (Director of the Project)

Douglas Penick
Curatorial Intern (N.Y. State Council for the Arts)

Gilberto Perez-Guillermo
Fellow (Graham Foundation)

E S S A Y S

EDITOR'S NOTE: The following group
of twenty essays represents the second
phase of The Universitas Project.
The papers were submitted by individuals
invited to participate in the Project
in response to the Project Working
Paper. They were read by the director
of the Project and by the panel
of advisors to the Project, and
subsequently sent to all of the other
participants in advance of the
symposium held in January 1972.
In this section, the essays are
arranged alphabetically by the
names of the authors. The
authors represent a wide spectrum
of scholarly disciplines and
nationalities. Their credentials
and backgrounds are given in the
biographical sketches at the back
of the volume. All of the papers
and the poem by Octavio Paz
appear in English, although some
contributions were translated; the
names of the translators are given
where known. The contributions are
given as submitted; they have been
edited only to conform spelling
and usage of philosophical and technical
terminology, and to clarify syntax. Graphic
illustrations for a number of the papers
were executed by Gina Rossi.

Design and Environment: Or, The Inflationary Curve of Political Economy
By Jean Baudrillard

Not every culture produces objects; the concept of the *object* pertains to ours, a culture born of the Industrial Revolution. However, even industrial society, as yet, knows only the *product* and not the *object*. The object truly begins to exist only when it becomes formally liberated as function/sign, and this liberation occurs only when industrialized society, as such, mutates into what we might call our techno-culture,[1] with the change from a *metallurgic* society to a *"semiurgic"* one, i.e., when, beyond the object's status as product and merchandise (beyond the modes of production, circulation, and economic exchange), the problem of the finality of the object's meaning, of its status as message and sign (of its modes of meaning, communication, and of exchange/sign) begins to pose itself. This mutation begins in the nineteenth century, but it is the Bauhaus that enshrines its theory. It is from the Bauhaus, therefore, that we can *logically* date the Revolution of the Object.

This revolution is not simply a matter of extension and differentiation, however prodigious, in the field of products deriving from industrialization. It is a matter of mutation in the status of the object. Before the Bauhaus there are no objects, per se. Beyond that point, and according to an irreversible logic, virtually everything enters the order of objects and will be produced as such. This is why any empirical classification (by Abraham Moles, etc.) is farcical.

To ask whether clothes or a horse are "objects" or not, where the object begins or ends to become, for instance, an edifice—all this descriptive typology is vain, because the object is not a thing, nor even a category, but a status of meaning and form. Before the logical development of that form/object, nothing is an object, not even the daily utensil. After that, everything is an object, from a spoon to an entire city. It was the Bauhaus that established this universal semantization of the environment, with everything judged on the basis of its function and meaning: total functionality, total semiurgy—a "revolution" in regard to the traditional manner, where "objects" (let us give them this name, though it is inappropriate), still fettered, not "liberated," had not as yet achieved a status of their own and did not form among themselves a system based on a rational finality (functionality).

This functionality, which the Bauhaus initiated, is characterized by a double process of rational analysis and synthesis of forms (not only industrial forms, but also environmental and social forms in general): synthesis of form and function, synthesis of the "beautiful" and the "useful," synthesis of art and technology. Beyond "style" and its caricature version, styling, beyond commercial kitsch of the nineteenth century and the modern, the Bauhaus for the first time establishes the bases for a rational and comprehensive conception of the environment. Beyond genres (architecture, painting, furniture), beyond "art" and its academic privilege, aesthetics are broadened to encompass all of everyday life. As a matter of fact, it is from having abolished the separation between beauty and utility that the potential for a "universal semiotics of technological experience" is born (see Jeremy Schapiro on one-dimensionality).[2] Or, from another point of view, the Bauhaus tries to reconcile the technical and social infrastructure established by the Industrial Revolution with a superstructure of forms and meanings. Aiming at the fulfillment of the technical with the finality of meaning, the Bauhaus becomes a second revolution, capping the Industrial Revolution and solving all the contradictions the latter had left in its wake.

Revolution or utopia? Neither one nor the other. As the Industrial Revolution ushered in the birth of a branch of political economy, the systematic and rational theory of material production, so did the Bauhaus usher in the *theoretical extension* of this field of political economy and the practical extension of the system of exchange/value into the realm of signs, forms, and objects. At the level of the process of signification and under the classification of design, there is a mutation analogous to that which took place in the sixteenth century at the level of the mode of material production and under the category of political economy. The Bauhaus marks the point of departure of a true *political economy of the sign.* There is the same general scheme here: on the one hand, nature and human labor are delivered from their archaic constraints, freed as productive forces and the object of a *rational computation of production;* on the other, the environment becomes charged with meaning, objectivized as an element of meaning. "Functionalized" and freed from all traditional implications (religious, magical, symbolical), the environment becomes the object of a *rational computation of meaning.*

THE SIGN OPERATION

There is, in fact, an entire process of dissociation and abstract restructuring that takes place behind the function becoming visible through the object; behind that universal moral law which regulates the object in the name of design; behind that functional equation, that "new economy" of the object, which immediately takes on "aesthetic" value meanings; and behind the general system of synthesis (art/technique, form/function):

1. Dissociation of all complex subject/object relations into simple, rational, analytical elements capable of being reassembled into functional aggregates that will assume, from here on, the quality of environment. It is only at this stage that man becomes separate from that something called "environment" and is confronted with the task of controlling it. After the eighteenth century, the concept of nature as *a productive force to be mastered* came to be developed. The concept of environment takes this, but further and deeper, in the sense of *mastery over signs.*

2. Generalized division of labor at the level of objects: analytical fragmentation into 14 or 97 functions, one technical solution joining several functions of the same object, or the same function several objects; in short, all the analytical moves and counter-moves that permit disassembling and reassembling an aggregate.

3. More fundamental, still, is the semiological (dis)articulation of the object from which the object takes its strength as sign. When we say that the object becomes sign, it is by the strictest definition: the object articulates itself into signifier and signified, becomes the signifier of an objective rational signified, which is its function. This is not at all so in the traditional symbolic relation, where things do not have meaning because of an objective signified to which they correspond insofar as signifying something. Whereas this is the status of the object/sign, which by this token obeys a linguistic schema, "functionalistic" stands for "structuralistic"; that is, a two-part unfolding, with design arising at the same time as the projection of an ideal articulation and the "aesthetic" solution of their equation, because "aesthetics" is nothing else but that which puts an almost redundant seal on that operational semiology.

In fact, aesthetics, in the modern sense of the term, has no longer anything in common with the categories of beauty or ugliness. Critics, public, designers still use the two terms, *beauty* and *aesthetic value*, indifferently, but these are logically incompatible (confusing them is a strategic gambit: it allows one to continue granting to a system dominated by *fashion*, i.e., by values of exchange/sign, the aura of a preindustrial value, of a pre-exchange value, which was that of *style*).

A thousand contradictory definitions of beauty and style are possible. One thing is certain: they are quite unrelated to the operations of signs. The category of beauty comes to an end when the system of functional aesthetics begins, just as previous modes of economic exchange (barter, trade/gift) came to an end with capitalism, with the institution of a rational computation of production and exchange. The category of aesthetics succeeds that of beauty (liquidating it) as the semiological order of the symbolical. Formerly the theory for forms of beauty, aesthetics has now actually become the theory of generalized compatibility among signs, of their internal coherence (signifier/signified), and of their syntax. The "aesthetic" value connotes the internal workings of the whole; it qualifies the ever-shifting equilibrium of a sign system. It very simply denotes the fact that the elements *communicate* among themselves according to the economy of a model, with maximal integration and minimal loss of information (an interior harmonized in blue tonalities, or in a "play" of blues and greens—the crystallized structure of a residential development—the "naturalness" of a green area, etc.). Aesthetics, therefore, is no longer a question of style or content, it now relates only to communication and to exchange/sign. It is idealized semiotics, or semiotics of an idealism.[3]

There is a forever-unresolved ambivalence at play in the symbolical order of style. The "semio-aesthetic" order is that of the operational solution, of a play of counter-moves, of controlled equivalences and dissonances. An "aesthetic" assemblage is a mechanism without errors, without failures, where nothing jeopardizes the interconnection of the elements and the transparency of the process. This is that famous total legibility of signs and messages—the ideal that is common to all manipulators of a code, whether they be cyberneticists or designers. This aesthetic order is cold. Functional perfection exercises a cold seduction, the functional satisfaction of a demonstration and of algebra. It has nothing to do with pleasure, with beauty (or with horror), whose role it is to deliver us from rational dictates and to plunge us once more into total childhood (not in an ideal transparency, but in the illegible ambivalence of desire).

This operation of the sign, this analytical dissociation into a functional couple, signifier/signified, is always a component in ideological schemata of synthesis. That is the operation at the bottom of all actual systems of signification (media, politics, etc.), just as the operational disjunction, use/value–exchange/value, is at the basis of form/merchandise and of all political economy.[4] This is to be found even in the key concepts of design: design reduces all possible valences of an object, all of its ambivalences, irreducible beyond whatever pattern there be, to two rational components, two general qualities, the useful and the aesthetic, which design isolates and artificially opposes one to the other. It is useless to point out the violence done to meaning, arbitrarily constraining it between these two narrow finalities. Actually they are but one: they are the disjointed forms of the same rationality, with the seal of the same value system. But this artificial disjoining permits us to subsequently evoke their reunification as an ideal schema. We separate usefulness from aesthetics, we give them separate names (because they have no other reality, one and the other, than *their being separately named*), then we rejoin them ideally, and all contradictions are resolved by this magic operation! Now, these two classifications, equally arbitrary, are there only as an artifice.

The real problems, the real contradictions, are at the level of form, of the value of the exchange/sign, but they are precisely what is hidden by the operation. Such is the ideological function of design: with the concept of "aesthetic functionality," it proposes a model of reconciling, of formally transcending, specialization (the division of labor at the level of objects) in an all-encompassing universal value. It thus imposes a schema of social integration through obscuring the real structures. Functional aesthetics, which conjugates two abstractions, is therefore itself nothing more than a super-abstraction that enshrines the system of the exchange/sign value by designing the utopia by which the system disguises itself. The operation of the sign, the separation of signs, is as fundamental and also as profoundly *political* as the division of labor. The theories of the Bauhaus and semiotics alike ratify this operation and the resulting division of labor of meanings, just as political economy ratifies the separation of the economic, as such, and the division of the material labor that derives from it.

We must give the term *design* all its etymological breadth. It can deploy itself in three directions: drawing, planning, and "design" (in French: *dessin*, *le dessein*, *le design*). In all three cases, we find a schema of rational abstraction: graphic for drawing, reflexive and psychological for planning (conscious projection of an objective), and a more general one for "design": transition to the status of a sign, operation/sign, reduction and rationalization into elements/signs, and transfer to function/sign.

This process of signification is systematic from the very start: the sign never exists outside a code and a language. Hence, the semiotic revolution (as the Industrial Revolution in its own times) relates to all possible activities: of arts and artisans, of forms and plastic and graphic arts (just to remain within a domain related to design, but once more the term extends far beyond the plastic and architectural domain), which up to now were separate and different and are now synchronized, homogenized according to the same formula. Objects, forms, materials, which heretofore spoke their own group dialect derived only from an idiomatic practice or from an original "style," begin to be thought out and written in the same tongue, in the rational Esperanto of design.[5] They begin, once they are functionally "liberated," to *signal* to one another, in the double sense of the word (and without making a play upon words), that is, they start to *become signs* and at the same time to *communicate* among themselves. Their unity is no longer that of a style, or of a practice, but that of a system. Or, to put it in still another way, as soon as an object becomes part of the structural rationality of signs (as soon as it divides itself into a signifier and a signified), it simultaneously becomes part of a functional syntax (as the morpheme in the syntagm) and is assigned a common general code (as the morpheme in language); all the rationale of the linguistic system takes hold of it. And, besides, if we speak mostly of "structural" linguistics and of "functionalism" of design, it should be clear that:

1. If the structural (signifier/signified, etc.) is evident in linguistics, it is because, and at the moment when, it disengages itself from a purely utilitarian view of language (strictly conceived as a *method of communication*). The two are actually one and the same thing.

2. With design, objects are born at the same time as functionality and the status of sign. This rational and limited finality assigns them in the same breath to structural rationality. Function and structure: the same "revolution." This means that the functional "liberation" of the object never means anything else but its assignment to a code or a system. Here, too, the homology is immediate with the "liberation" of labor (or of leisure, the body, etc.), which is nothing but their being assigned to the system of exchange/value.

Let us resume the essential traits of the homology (sharing the same *logical* process, even if separate chronologically) between the rise of a political economy of the sign and political economy (or material production):

1. Political economy, under the guise of *utility* (needs, use/value, etc., anthropological reference of all economic rationality), is the establishment of a logical, coherent system of a computation of productivity where all production is broken down into simple elements, where all products are equivalent in the abstract: it is the logic of merchandise and the system of exchange/value.

2. The political economy of signs: in the name of *functionality* ("objective" absolute, similar in value to utility), a certain mode of signification is established where all surrounding signs have the role of simple elements in a logical computation and relate to one another within the framework of the system of the exchange/sign value.

In both cases, the use/value (utility) and the functionality, given as final reference sometimes to political economy and sometimes to design, only serve, in effect, as some "concrete" alibi in the same abstract process. Pretending to serve maximal utility, the process of political economy generalizes the exchange/value system. Pretending to maximize the functionality of objects (their legibility as meaning and message, i.e., basically their "value of use/sign"), design and the Bauhaus generalize the system of the exchange/sign value.

And just as a product's utility, beyond grasp when no coherent theory of needs exists capable of establishing it, reveals itself to be simply its utility for the system of exchange/value, so the same functionality of an object, illegible as a concrete value, serves to describe the coherence between that object/sign and all the others, its interchangeability with all the others, and thus its functional adaptation to the system of the exchange/sign value.

The functionality of an object (of a line, of a form) in an oblique architecture, therefore, rests not in its utility or its balance, but in its obliqueness (or, by contrast, its verticality). It is the system's coherence that defines the aesthetic-functional value of elements, and this value is *an exchange/value* in the measure in which it always refers to a pattern as *a general equivalent* (same abstraction as for the economic exchange/value).

It is not by accident that this homology is reflected all the way down to the level of mores. Like the capitalistic revolution, which, from the sixteenth century on, established "the spirit of enterprise" and the bases for political economy, the Bauhaus revolution was *puritanical*. Functionalism is ascetic. This is evident in the stripping, the geometric spareness of its model, its phobia of decor and artifices, in short, in the "economy" of its approach. But this, we might say, is only the "handwriting" (which, after all, has become a rhetoric like any other) of the fundamental doctrine: that of rationality, where the functional liberation of the object brings as its consequence the establishment of an ethic of labor.

One ethic corresponds, three centuries later, to a same logic (and a same psychology).[6] And the terms in which Max Weber (in *The Protestant Ethic and the Spirit of Capitalism*) analyzes the rational economic theory as the interaction between two worlds (the religious and the materialistic—in French: *ascese intra-mondaine*) apply perfectly well, mutatis mutandis, to the rational computation of signs.

THE CRISIS OF FUNCTIONALISM

Before analyzing how this crisis is lived by designers today, we must realize how it was born, that the elements of crisis were there from the start. It derives from functionalism willing its own order (as political economy wills its own order) as the *dominant rationale*, capable of accounting for everything and of controlling all processes. This rationale, necessarily blind to its arbitrary character, provokes at once a fantastic or "irrational" counter-argument shuttling between the two poles of surrealism and kitsch (the first a direct antagonist, the second a subtle accomplice, without their being mutually exclusive—surrealism playing a great deal on the ridicule of kitsch, and kitsch often acquiring a surrealist value).

The surrealist object comes into being simultaneously with the functional object as its mockery, its overstatement. However, these phantom objects, openly dys- or para-functional, also postulate, if antithetically, the advent of functionality as the universal moral law of the object, and the advent of the object itself as a separate autonomous entity, dedicated to allowing its function to be visible through it. Upon reflection, there is something unreal and potentially surrealistic in reducing the object to its function.[7] Moreover, it is sufficient to carry the principle of functionality to its extreme in order to see absurdity arise. This is evident in the case of the toaster/iron, or of the *objets introuvables* of Jacques Carelman, but the overall appraisal of human "aspirations" is just as nonplussing and well-suited to the conjoining, on a dissecting table, of the comte de Lautréamont's sewing machine with an umbrella.

Thus, surrealism also originates in contrast to the advent of the object and the extension of the semantic and functional computation to the whole field of everyday life. In this sense, the Bauhaus and surrealism are inseparable, as the critical, anomalous, monstrous discourse of objects is inseparable from the rational discourse of objects (little by little, the first subversive discourse will make its way gently into customs and will become integrated into the functional universe as an anomalous variant); in its banal version, it is already injected into all our environment today in homeopathic doses.

The shoe-foot of René Magritte, his woman in a skin dress (or, her *naked* dress) hanging on a coatrack, the chest-of-drawers men (or, the anthropomorphic machines): everywhere surrealism plays on the *distance* the functional approach establishes between the object and the subject, or between the object and itself, or between man and his own body; on the distance between no matter which term and the abstract absolute we impose on it; and on the division that causes men and things to find themselves suddenly cast in the role of signs and confronted with a transcending designation: their function. Fusion of the breasts' skin and of the folds of the dress, of the toes with the shoe leather: the surrealist imagery plays on this division while denying it, but on the basis of separate terms and read separately in their *collage* or *superimposition,* which means that it does not return them to any symbolical relationship (which does not allow for the concept of division, since a relationship is tied in with reciprocity and exchange). In surrealism, the symbolical relation only becomes visible as a phantom of the conversion from subject to object and vice versa. Short-circuit between the two orders, that of functionality (overstated and ridiculed) and that of the symbolical order (distorted and fantasized), and the surrealist metaphor assumes the form of a compromise. It seizes the moment when the object is still mired in anthropomorphism and is not yet born, we might say, to its pure functionality, or the moment when the object is about to, but does not yet, absorb man into its functional unreality. Translating into image the extreme of their contamination, surrealism illustrates and denounces the dismembering of the subject and the object. It is a revolt against the new principle of the object's reality. Surrealism opposes the rational calculation that "liberates" the object *into* its function by liberating the object *from* its function and by turning it over to free associations from which no symbolism re-emerges (nor does the respective crystallization of the subject and the object take place), but subjectivity itself, "liberated" into its phantom self.

A subjective poetry where the primary and the associative processes of dreams come to sidetrack functional associations, surrealism, thus, briefly and contradictorily, illumines the growing pains of the object, generalizing the abstraction of life through the functionalization of the object. Merrymaking around the agony of desperate subjectivity, all the poetry of nonsense (Lewis Carroll, precursor to surrealism) illustrates in the negative, through revolt and parody, the irreversible institution of a political economy of meaning, or a form/sign and a form/object structurally bound to form/merchandise. (The Romantics, in their time, were a reaction of the same type to the industrial revolutions and the first phase of political economy.)

But the surrealist overstatement is still a measure of the *relative* extensibility of the political economy of the sign. It plays upon forms, figurative objects, on *representational* contents and meanings. Today, when the concept of functionalism has passed from the isolated object to that of the entire system (a hyperrationality as Kafkaesque as the other)—when the almost artisan functionalism of the Bauhaus has overreached itself in mathematical design and in cybernetics of the environment—surrealism can survive only as folklore. We are, here and now, already beyond the object and its function.

In the actual system of interrelation and information, this "beyond the object" already corresponds to a beyond the subject. The hybrid game of the surrealists, just between the figure of the object and that of man, between function and desire—the two cases, separate in reality, still celebrating in surrealism their impossible conjunction—that subtle mixture of a functional logos and of a logic of symbolism, shattered, dismembered, haunting, resulting in an illogical phantom representation, all this fades away before the cybernetic order where nothing replaces the critical regressive/transgressive discourse of Dada and surrealism.

After surrealism, the explosion of the abstract (dreamlike, geometrical, or expressionist—Paul Klee, Vasily Kandinsky, Piet Mondrian, or Jackson Pollock), last critical blaze of art, responds to the ever-increasing systematization of the rational order. In fact, where are we today? At cinematic manipulation, or "luminodynamics," or the psychedelic mise-en-scène of a debased surrealism; in short, we are now dealing with a reassemblage that is in the very image of real systems, at an aesthetic operationalism (of which Nicolas Schoeffer's *New Spirit of Art* is the biblical specimen) that is indistinguishable from cybernetic programs. The hyperrationality of these systems has absorbed the critical surreality of the phantasmic. Art has become, or is becoming, total design, METADESIGN.

Design's mortal enemy is kitsch. Dispatched by the Bauhaus, kitsch keeps rising from its own ashes. This is because it has behind it the entire "economic system," say the designers who have only virtue to sustain them. Thus, in a 1967 article on industrial aesthetics, Moles analyses the crisis of functionalism as an excess of rationality stripped of design and its rigorous functional ethic by the proliferating irrationality of consumer goods. The "absolute consumer's mentality promoted by the economic machine," buries the functionalist purification deeper and deeper under neo-kitsch. Functionalism suffers and dies from this contradiction.

Actually, this analysis absolves design of all internal contradictions: it is all the fault of "status seeking" and of the "strategic manipulation of desires." But Moles and many others forget that this system, and all the process of consumption that it implies, is also rational and perfectly coherent in itself. The password of functionalism is triumphantly dictated by it every day. It is precisely in the "anarchic production" denounced by our virtuous academicians of functionalism that functionalism reveals itself as adequate to its own ends, which are its survival and its expanded reproduction. Therefore, there is no contradiction: the model of rationality was originally, and remains fundamentally, that of economics; it is but normal if the functionality of the economic system has the upper hand. Design, pure and hard, is impotent in the face of it because this rationality based on computation is *its own inspiration*. Design is based from the start on the same rational abstraction as the economic system. There is no doubt that this rationality is virtually absurd, but it is so, in both cases, for the same reason. Their apparent contradiction is nothing but the logical outcome of their deep complicity. Designers complain that they are misunderstood and that their ideal is disfigured by the system! All puritans are hypocrites.

This crisis, actually, can be analyzed on a totally different level, the semiological level, whose elements we described before. Recapitulating the Bauhaus formula: for every form and every object that exists, we can determine an objective *signified*, its function, that which in linguistics is called the level of *denotation*. The Bauhaus presumes to rigorously isolate this kernel, this level of denotation—all the rest is wastage, the hellhole of *connotation*: the residual, the superfluous, the excrescent, the eccentric, the decorative, the useless. Kitsch. The (functional) denoted is beautiful; the connoted (the parasite) is ugly. Or, better still, the denoted (objective) is *true*; the connoted is false (ideological). Behind the concept of objectivity, all the moral and metaphysical argument on truth is, in fact, at stake.[8]

Now, it is just this postulate of denotation that is crumbling today. We are finally beginning to realize (even in semiology) that this postulate is arbitrary, not just a methodological artifact but a metaphysical fable. *There is no* truth of the object, and its denotation is nothing but the best of connotations. This is not just theoretical: designers, urbanists, and environmental planners are confronted every day (if they ask themselves a few questions) with the decay of objectivity. The function(ality) of forms, of objects, becomes, from day to day, more unattainable, more illegible, more incalculable. Where is the object's centrality, its functional equation today? Or, where is its directive function, and where are its parasitic functions? Who can still say, when the economic, the social, the psycho- and metaphysical are inextricably mixed? I defy anyone to demonstrate that such "superfluous" form, such "irrational" characteristics do not respond, at a longer range, to something in the subconscious—what do we know—to a more subtle equilibrium perhaps, and therefore are not functionally justified somehow?[9] In this systematic logic (because functionality is an *interpretative system*, nothing else), virtually everything is functional and nothing is. This ruling utopia turns against itself. It is not astonishing that, as it fails things by and by, this objective finality is transferred to the system itself, which, in its reproductive process, finalizes everything to its own profit and at the end finds itself the sole owner of extant functionality, which it then redistributes to its own elements. It alone is, indeed, admirably "designed": it is enclosed in its own finality as if in an egg.[10]

If there is no absolute utility of the object left, the superfluous, too, is meaningless, and the whole theoretical structure of functionalism crumbles. This benefits *fashion*, which, not burdening itself with any objective denotation (even though it pretends to it), plays entirely on connotation and, in its shifting "irrational" rhetoric, under the sole license of its *actuality* of signs, takes over the whole system. If functionalism defends itself poorly against fashion, it is because fashion expresses the total potentiality of that system of which functionalism, founded on the metaphysics of denotation, is but one particular expression, arbitrarily privileged according to a universal ethic. From the moment a computation of signs is established, nothing can oppose its generalization, and there is nothing left, rational or irrational. The Bauhaus and design lay claim to controlling, by ownership, the process of the *signified* (the "objective" evaluation of functions), but, in fact, it is the play of signifiers (that of the value of exchange / sign) that has the upper hand, or, is unlimited and escapes all controls (the same happens in political economy for the value of the exchange system: it invades all levels, for and against pious and liberal souls who think they can circumscribe it).

This is what the real crisis of functionalism consists of: nothing can oppose whatever form enters the unlimited combination pattern, its sole function then being its function / sign. Not even the forms "created" by design escape from it. And if the styling which the Bauhaus thought it had disqualified reasserts itself through design, without the latter really being able ever to disenfranchise itself from it and to retrieve its "rigorousness," it is because what it thought was pathological and belonged within the logic of its own "design."

If our era, in spite of the Bauhaus revolution, nostalgically recuperates all the kitsch of the nineteenth century, it is because, in effect, *it was ours already*. The floral motif on the sewing machine or the subway gate is a regressive compromise, but today, by virtue of its rebirth, it takes on the surrealist value of fashion; and this is logical, surrealism in some way being responsible for formalizing as an artistic overstatement the hybrid production of commercial kitsch. Today, although "pure" design condemns the floral motif, it takes the "naturalistic" ideology further still: it is the starlike structures of organisms that will serve as models for an entire city. There is no radical difference between the two. Whether we take nature as decor or as structural model, there still remains, ever since the concept came into existence, its projection as a *social* model. And, any starlike structure is capitalistic.

Even though design is immersed in fashion, we should not lament its fate: it is the proof of its triumph, it is the indication of the hold political economy has over the sign, whose first rationalization came with the Bauhaus. All that which today declares itself marginal, irrational, a revolt, anti-art, anti-design, etc.—from pop to psychedelic art and art-on-the-street— all this obeys, willy-nilly, the same economics of the sign. All this is design. Nothing escapes design: that is its fate.

What we are witnessing, therefore, is much more than a crisis. And it serves no purpose to deplore, as does Abraham Moles, the fatal destiny of consumerism and to call upon a neo-functionalism to bring about "the stimulation of phantasy by systematic effort" (!). This neo-functionalism cannot be but that of a re-semantization (a resurrection of signifiers)[11] and, therefore, a recycling of the same contradictions. Even more likely, neo-function-alism will be in the image of neo-capitalism, i.e., an intensification of the play of signifiers, mathematization and cybernetization by the code. A humanist neo-functionalism does not stand a chance against operational metadesign. The era of the signified and of the function is over: it is the era of the signifier and of the code that begins.

Environment and Cybernetics: The Crowning Stage of Political Economy

This revolution of the sign introduced by the Bauhaus was at least dimly perceived by it and has since been relatively brought to light by the analysts of design. Henri Van Lier (in *Critique*, November 1967) sees quite clearly that "those new forms and their operations throw each other back toward the poles of the system," and that functionality is not utility but, rather, "putting things into reciprocal information, in a position to signal to one another to create significations," adding, as if it followed, "food of all culture and all humanity." The eternal humanistic metaphor: the more signs, the more messages and information we have, the more communication, the better. Having unmasked the advent of the value/sign, and its indefinite extension on the basis of rational productivity, he sees in it, without hesitation, an absolute progress for humanity. This is a reaction analogous to that which sees in the industrial thrust a more or less long-term certainty of happiness and abundance for all. This illusion, which was that of the nineteenth century about material production, starts afresh in the twentieth century about productivity/sign: cybernetic idealism, blind faith in the radiance of information, mystique of information and media.

In both cases the fundamental error is the same: that of remembering only the *value of use* whether of the product or of the sign, and of considering industrial (or semiurgic) mutation only under the aspect of the infinite multiplication of the values of use (signs as messages). Profusion of goods, profusion of signs—maximal consumption, maximal information: this without ever taking into account that what, first and foremost, causes this mutation is a system of the *value of exchange*, an abstract, generalized social form which is not at all the "food of all culture and all humanity." This idealism of the content (of production or of the signification) never reckons with form. This idealism of messages forgets that what settles in behind their accelerated circulation is the hegemony of a code. In fact, both simply forget political economy and its social, strategic, and political dimensions, placing themselves at once in the transparent sphere of value. This optimism may appear to be in good faith; it may take on the benevolent mien of the designer who thinks that, for his feeble part, he is contributing through his creativity to more information and therefore to more "freedom" (hence, the prophetic tone of Marshall McLuhan, exalting the actuality of interplanetary communications). This ideology of communications reigns everywhere—cybernetics passing itself for a neo-humanism, the profusion of messages having in some way replaced the profusion of goods (the myth of plenty) in the imagination of the species.

Everywhere, the ideologists of the value of use are accomplices and ministers of the political extension of the system of the value of exchange. This is how consumption has come to play the role, in the order of material goods, of an automatic starter for the system of production, not at all as apotheosis of the value of use but as a social compulsion blinded by surfeit. Thanks to consumption, the system is successful not only in forcibly exploiting people, but in making them *participate in* its multiplying survival. It is a considerable progress. This participation, however, reaches the entirety of its fantastic dimension only at the level of signs. This is where all the strategy of "neo-capitalism" articulates itself in its originality: in an operational semiurgy and semiology which are but the developed form of directed participation.

In this perspective, where the production of signs, seen as system of the exchange value, takes on an entirely different connotation than it had in the naïve utopia of their use value, design and environmental disciplines can be considered as one of the branches of *mass communications*, a gigantic ramification of human and social engineering. Our real environment now is already the universe of communications.[12] This is where it becomes radically distinct from the concepts of "nature" and of "milieu" of the nineteenth century. Whereas the latter referred to the physical, biological laws (determinism of substance, of heredity, and of the species), or sociocultural laws ("milieu"), the environment is at once a network of messages and of signs, and its laws are those of communications.

The environment is the autonomy of the entire universe of practices and forms—from the day-to-day to the architectural, from the discursive to the gestural and the political—as the operational and calculation branch, as the output/input of messages, as *space/time of communications.* This theoretical concept of "environment" corresponds to the practical concept of "design," which, in the last analysis, is *production of communications* (between men and signs, between one man and another, and between men themselves). Communication, i.e., participation, is a must; in this case, not through the purchase of material goods, but through the informative mode, through the circulation of signs and messages. This is why the environment, just as the *market* (its economic equivalent), is virtually a universal concept. It is a concrete compendium of all the political economy of the sign. Design, which is the practical counterpart of this political economy, generalizes itself in the same dimension and, if it began by applying itself only to industrial products, today it embraces and must logically embrace all areas. Nothing is more false than the limits a "humanistic" design would set for itself. In fact, everything belongs to design, everything springs from it, whether it admits it or not: the body is designed, and so is sexuality; human, social, and political relations are designed, just as are needs and aspirations, etc. It is this "designed" universe that properly constitutes the environment, which, just like the market, is but a *logic* of sorts, that of the value of exchange (sign). Design is the imposition of models and operational practices of this value of exchange/sign. Once more, it is the practical triumph of the political economy of the sign, the theoretical triumph of the Bauhaus.

Just as public relations, human relations, and industrial psychosociology, and just as policy making and participation policies, marketing and merchandizing exert themselves in order to create better relations, in order to reestablish relations where production made them socially problematic; in the same way, design has the task, the strategic function in the actual system, to create communications between man and an environment that exists only as something foreign (once more, like the market). Like many ideological concepts, "environment" stands, by antithesis, for that from which we are separated; it marks the end of a world we were in touch with, where people and things were next to one another. And the mystique of the environment is as large as the chasm the system opens wider every day between man and "nature." It is this schism, this relationship fundamentally broken and dissociated between man and his environment, just as social relations are, which, whether design likes it or not, is the cause and *place* of design. This is where design desperately tries to restore meaning and clarity by means of information, "understanding" by dint of messages. Upon reflection, the philosophy of design, reverberating through all environmental theory, is at heart *a doctrine of participation and public relations extended to all of nature.* We must make nature (which seems to have become hostile and to wish to avenge itself, through pollution, for being exploited) participate. We must re-create with nature, at the same time as with the urban environment, communication through signs (as between employer and employees, between governments and governed), by dint of media and of policy making. It is necessary, in a word, to offer nature an employment contract: to offer it protection and security, to syndicate those natural energies that are becoming dangerous in order to better control them! Because, certainly, all this has no other end in view than keeping this nature in line, making it a contractual recycled participant by intelligent design, under the norms of rational hyperproductivity.

Such is the political *ideology* of design, which today is taking on its planetary dimension in the discourse of the environment. From Gropius to Universitas, the thread is unbroken, leading to what we might call a metadesign, a political meta-economy, which is to neo-capitalism what classic liberal economy was to capitalism.

If we talk of the environment, it is that which has already ceased to exist. To speak of ecology is to acknowledge the death and total abstraction of "nature." Everywhere the "right to" (nature, the environment) witnesses the "decay of." This decay of nature (as vital reference and as ideal reference) is strictly connected with what, in the analysis of the contemporary sign, we have called the decay of the signified (of the real, objective referent of the denoted function, of "truth," of the *world* as the real warranty of the sign— a bit its gold standard—the gold of signified/referent gone, no more Gold Exchange Standard—no more convertibility of the sign into its reference value—there is nothing left, as we see in the actual international trend, but a free interrelation of floating currencies). The Great Signified, the Great Referent Nature is dead, and what takes its place is the environment, which points out both nature's death and its reconstitution as a simulation model (reconstitution, as of a pre-hashed beefsteak). And what we said of "nature" before, that it was always the projection of a social model, is certainly valid for the environment. The transition from the concept of nature, as an objective reference, to the concept of environment where the circulation system of signs (of the value of exchange/sign) abolishes all references and even becomes its own referent, marks the transition of a still-contradictory society, nonhomogenized, nonsaturated by political economy, where there are still models resisting transcendence, the conflict, the becoming outdated—a nature of man torn but present (cf. the affinity of Marxism with a substantive anthropology of needs and of nature)—a history with its revolutionary theory, etc. Such transition is that of an historically conflictive society to a cyberneticized society, to a synthetic social environment, where abstract total communications and an immanent manipulation machinery do not allow for anything to exist outside the system. This is the end of traditional political economy and the beginning of a political meta-economy in a society which has become *its own and sole environment*.[13] "In the same measure in which the manipulation of the environment is successful, will that of man be successful, man himself an object of manipulation, i.e., simple environment" (Alexander Mitscherlich).

The social control of the air, of water, etc., in the name of protecting the environment attests to the fact that evidently men themselves are sinking a little deeper into social control. If nature, air, water, after having been simple productive forces, become rare goods and enter the field of value, it is because men themselves enter a bit more deeply into the field of political economy. At the end of this evolution there may be natural parks, an "International Foundation for Man," as there is in Brazil a National Foundation for the Indian: "The National Foundation for the Indian can insure, under the best of conditions, the preservation of indigenous populations as of the survival of vegetable and animal species (*sic*) which have cohabited with them for thousands of years." (It is ethnocide and massacre, surely, this institution sanctions and disguises: we liquidate and reconstitute—same schema.) Man is no longer even face-to-face with his environment: he is already part of an environment that must be protected.

Notes

1. An echo of the technostructure of John Kenneth Galbraith: neo-capitalist, neo-industrial, postindustrial. Many terms may apply to describe this passage from an industrial political economy to a political trans-economy (or political meta-economics).

2. See Jeremy Schapiro, "One-Dimensionality," in Paul Breines, *Critical Interruptions* (Herder and Herder, 1970).

3. Already in 1902, Benedetto Croce was writing of "Aesthetics as science of the expression and as *general linguistics.*"

4. But this fundamental operation of the form is, in either case, that which is never mentioned.

5. In his own way, and in Marcusian terms, Schapiro ("One-Dimensionality") gives a similar analysis, but in a mechanistic, technological light: "The evolution of design is an essential component of the unidimensional process . . . in the measure in which it derives from the machine's process the matrix form for a total (totalitarian) environment in which the technological experience at once defines and circumscribes the aesthetic and the experiential Universe." Totalizing abstraction, unidimensional homogenization, yes, but by this process the machine or technique are neither *causes* nor original models. The technical mutation and the "semio-linguistic" mutation (the transition from abstraction to code) are two *concurrent* aspects of a same transition to the functional/structural rationality. (The translation into English of the above quotation from Schapiro is from the French text—Schapiro's "One-Dimensionality" not being readily available in the original English at the moment of translation.)

6. These are, in truth, only logical landmarks in what is actually a continuous historical process. However, the moment in which a theory is formally enunciated (which is that of the Bauhaus in the political economy of signs) always marks a crucial point in the historical process itself.

7. Similarly, there is something immediately Kafkaesque in reducing man to his function.

8. Functionalism's Kantian and Platonic heritage, where morals, aesthetics, and truth are fused into a same ideal, is devastatingly clear. The functional is the synthesis of pure reason with practical reason. Or, the functional is the beautiful plus the useful. And the useful is, in turn, that which is moral and what is true. Stir the lot: you have the Platonic Holy Trinity.

9. Something else, anyway, completely eludes all computation of function: ambivalence, by which every positive function is in the same movement negated and undone, annulled by that logic of desire according to which no unilateral finality truly can exist. This level is even beyond the functional complexities. Had we reached a perfect computation of functions, *even of contradictory ones*, there still would remain this insoluble, irreducible ambivalence.

10. We know that the egg, a formal stereotype, as kitsch as any, is an ideal of design. This means that the system's "finality" is simply *tautological*. But the finished result of function is tautology itself—a perfect redundancy of the signifier in the name of the vicious circle of the signified: egg.

11. We shall again have "social" design, with humanistic content, or we shall reintroduce the game, the sport, "free" associations, etc. But let us not be taken in: it will be the *function* of the "game" that counts, the game as a particular function, a liberal-modernistic variant of the same code.

12. Paradoxically (and no doubt symptomatically), the British Ministry of the Environment embraces almost all aspects of it *except* media.

13. It is what Marshall McLuhan refers to as the intensification of modes.

Urban Symbolism and Social Movements: On a New Institution for the Study of the Urban Environment

By Manuel Castells

I. WHAT ENVIRONMENT?

To escape natural determinisms, to shape the world, to fashion the environment—these are elements of the ancient dream at the center of human history. A certain technocratic thought (the dominant ideology of advanced industrial societies) held that this dream could be realized with the aid of science. Many still believe in this possibility, for, despite the apparent progressive deterioration of the framework of life, as the growth rate accelerates, many still expect to find remedies within the vast technical arsenal. Thus, the treatment of *the environment* has become a new frontier for the business world and for a certain sort of politics, and "the defense of nature" has led to the formation of an eco-establishment.

An analysis of the framework of life in terms other than those of technology and cost necessarily assumes a point of view in opposition to this ideology. If one begins with the affirmation that "man constructs his milieu," and if one refuses to reduce this "man" to a technical agent imbued with a universal and ahistorical rationality, then the problem becomes one of a *social relation*. The environment is no longer a physical "given," exterior to human action, but a particular form of matter (human and nonhuman), an *expression*, a relation among elements. But what elements? And the expression of what?

There is a danger here of extending the notion of *environment* to the whole of social life and, thus, of trading a conception of the problem in which everything is "technical" for one in which everything is "social." But any nonideological grasp of a phenomenon begins with the non-separation of nature and culture, or, as it were, with the principle that every "natural" milieu, every "environment," is constructed by social action, which follows its *own* logic but is also linked to a complex of conditions. The knowledge of these conditions, which is never complete, is consciousness.

Thus, if one does not want merely to play with words, the environment, seen as a social relation, must be referred to a specific practical domain. Otherwise, one risks extending one's grasp over the ensemble of social relations and, thereby, referring to the multiple relations of society to productive forces in ambiguous terms. What is connoted by this approach to the problem is the social relation to *cultural forms*, that is, to a certain crystallization of the systems of representation and exchange of the society. But this social morphology is expressed in dress and table manners, just as in architecture and the city. Why, then, this spatial dimension, this direct connotation of the urban and ecological in the problem of the environment? Because, in this domain of forms, social practices seem at once "naturalized," subject to a larger rigid patterning and especially dependent on the necessarily collective organizational process of daily life. That is to say, that "urban forms," i.e., *the most apparent forms of the elements of daily life*, are those that seem to be imposed without the least control and which affect, massively and in an openly collective manner, the ensemble of the society.

From this point of view, an analysis of urban forms is necessarily linked to general social morphology, and thereby to the study of cultural systems. But our analysis must take into account the specificity of the "urban" domain as it reflects a certain sort of social process. This means that research on the "urban environment" must further develop the analysis of ideologies and cultural forms by constructing theoretical elements adequate for the decipherment of *urban symbolism*—that is, the particular social efficacity of the cultural load of these forms and the systems of expressive combination of their formal elements.

That much said, from the moment the environment is seen as a social relation, one is obliged to posit the terms of this relation to the basis of the symbolic load expressed by the forms themselves. Or, more concretely, there can be no cultural expression without social content, without social praxis, and without "actors" seen simultaneously in their allegiances and their conflicts. But the principal difficulty raised by the theme of the environment is that this theme opposes (or reconciles) man and his milieu without establishing the lines of division inside the society, which is then drawn together in a relation to a common problem. And, yet, as soon as one uncouples the technocratic science / nature doublet, as soon as one introduces the social process by which the environment is produced, then there is a differentiation of positions within this productive process and, consequently, a differentiation of interests, which is the expression of social classes. From that point, the transformation of the environment is bound up with social dynamics, and the innovation of forms (most especially urban forms) will depend, in a constant interaction, on contradictory movements at the base of processes of social and political change.

Thus, to the degree that urban symbolism can provide the elements of comprehension of a certain meaning, to the degree that these signs are not merely combinations of other signs, one must, in order to understand a formal innovation, study the production of this meaning, which, at the practical level, entails the observation and analysis of social movements, the principal sources of change in our societies.

In this fashion, reflection on the social relation to the urban environment must include a discussion of some theoretical elements relating to *urban symbolism*, and the problem of urban symbolism must be related to that of *social movements*. Only by following the leads uncovered in a rapid examination of these two themes may one pose the question, *How?* and found a basis for a few remarks on plans for institutional innovation in this domain.

II. URBAN SYMBOLISM

Space has meaning. Its forms and its outlines reflect and articulate one another in a symbolic structure whose effect on social praxis is revealed by any concrete analysis. But this symbolic structure is not the equivalent of an *urban text* organized by the formal crystallization of social action. In fact, following recent linguistic theory, there is a dangerous tendency to develop a semiological analysis of urban space according to which the urban space is the "signifier" (*signifiant*) of the "signified" (*signifié*) *social structure*; it is a question, in that analysis, of a recasting of space as a social fact (which simply sends the analysis back to the ensemble of structural analysis of the urban space) or, more importantly, of a priority accorded to the analysis of forms in the study of the urban phenomenon. In fact, by distinguishing *signifiant* and *signifié*, one posits a certain separation, tension, and autonomy between the two terms, with two important consequences:

1. There is an organization proper to the *signifiants* that is the organization of the urban.

2. The key to this organization is to be found in its relation to the social *signifié*, and the study of the urban phenomenon thus becomes the study of the laws of the compositions of these spatial signs, allowing the discovery, following the wishes of Claude Levi-Strauss, of the history of a society in the remains of its works.

But such an analysis is not possible unless one reduces social action to a *language* and social relations to systems of communication. The ideological shift introduced in this perspective consists of passing from a method for the reconstruction of the remaining traces of social praxis, as seen in its effect on the organization of space, to an organizational principle deduced from inventoried formal expressions, as if social organization were a code and urban structure a body of myths. In this perspective, one meets a symbolism proper to spatial structures *as form*.

But Gaston Bachelard has taught us that images exist within a cooperation of the real and the unreal, "by the concourse of the function of the real and the function of the unreal," and that, "if the house is a living value, it must include an unreality. All values must tremble. An unshaken value is a dead one."[1]

This means that images can exist only when bound up with a social experience, and not only because the image is socially produced but also because it cannot exist ("tremble") outside social relations, just as, finally, there is no language without speech.

Let us define more clearly the terms of the question that has been posed: just as economic and political-institutional factors have their own effects through their spatial modulation and its place in the cities, so also is there a certain specificity of the ideological instance at the level of the urban space. This ideological specificity manifests itself in two major ways:

1. In the ideological constituent, which, at the level of historical reality, is present in each element of urban structure. So, for example, every lodging or means of transport takes a certain *form* that is the product of its own social characteristics, while enjoying a certain margin of autonomy.

2. In the expression, through the forms and rhythms of urban structure, of ideological currents produced by social praxis. *It is on this level, that of the mediation by the urban space of general ideological determinations, that the theme of urban symbolism must be situated.*

If one agrees that spatial forms should be considered cultural forms and, consequently, as expressions of social ideologies, then an analysis of the forms should begin at the conjuncture of a general theory of ideologies and a consideration of the rhythm proper to existing cultural forms. It is in this fashion that architecture has been understood by an entire tradition exemplified by Erwin Panofsky.

So it will be necessary, in order to make progress into this domain, to apply the same principles of analysis as those concerning the ideological instance in general. Notably, and most importantly, *an ideology is not defined by itself but by its social effect; on the other hand, this social effect makes possible an understanding of the contours proper to ideological discourse.*

This social effect, despite its diversity, can be summed up by the double dialectic of the effect of *legitimation* and the effect of *communication*. By the former is meant the role of every ideology in rationalizing certain interests so as to present their domination as an expression of the general interest. But the strength of ideological discourse resides in the fact that it constitutes a code within which communication among subjects becomes possible. Language and the ensemble of expressive systems are always cultural processes, constituted in a dominantly ideological whole. One must also remark that this communication is accomplished through a process of *recognition* among the subjects (recognition of mutual possession of the same code), and that this *recognition* is at the same time *miscognition* to the degree that it is founded on a dominantly ideological code that makes communication possible only through a false apprehension of the experienced situation; thus, the "citizen" can understand "democracy" to the degree in which he considers himself as a juridical individuality above and beyond his class allegiance.

If ideology can be characterized by the social effect so defined, *ideological praxis* is necessarily part of a social process, and any concrete analysis should be able to locate the different *places* in which this process decomposes. If one considers ideological praxis as a message, by analogy to the theory of information, one may distinguish the places of *sender, relay,* and *receiver* in the larger process of the production of an ideological effect.

How do these remarks on the general theory of ideologies help us to understand urban symbolism? One must first stress that it is not a question of pure ideological praxis without relation to spatial forms; nor is it a question of the purely derived effect of the formal structure of a space. *Urban symbolism exists where spatial forms are used as senders, relays, and receivers of general ideological praxis.* This means that no semiological reading of a space is possible within a mere decipherment of forms (the frozen traces of social action), but only within a study of those expressive mediating functions through which ideological processes produced by social relations in a given instance are realized. In this view, the urban space is not a text already written but a cinema screen constantly restructured by a changing symbolism, with the production of an ideological content given by social praxis acting on and within the city. However, the urban space is not simply a blank page on which the ideological praxis is written. It possesses a certain *density*. This density, in order to be something other than a metaphysical entity, must be capable of being socially decomposed. Essentially, this decomposition reveals:

1. Conjunctural effects, that is, the already existing urban forms, an historical product socially accumulated and combined.

2. The symbolic load proper to spatial forms in function, not of their position in the urban structure but of their insertion into the cultural history of forms (e.g., skyscrapers are at once a combination of a symbolism attributed to them by the ideological praxis mediated by space and the symbolism that they receive from their cultural conjuncture—art, design, technology, materials, etc.).

Thus, the larger view of the process of determination of urban symbolism might be expressed schematically as follows:

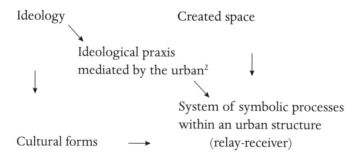

This schema is excessively abstract, and it is quite difficult to attribute concrete forms to the positions and functions indicated by it. One can, nonetheless, if only as a largely inaccurate illustration, propose a few concrete images.

Thus, a semiological analysis of urban renewal projects cannot begin with the general symbolic structure of space, for that would create an infinitely elastic analytical matrix. Instead, the analysis must begin with the ideological content carried by the project, which is itself derived from the effect of the operation of urbanism on both urban structure and social relations. Knowing these effects, one will find a multiplicity of messages that should be logically sent out by the new urban forms: some of these messages will dominate—for example, technical modernity, social prestige, the consumer's wealth, etc. But, while architectural forms can play the role of sender, this situation is complicated considerably at the level of *reception*, because not only are the inhabitants of the project affected, there is also an effect on the surrounding area and, more importantly, a general symbolic effect directed at the entire population. The content of the messages on different levels depends on a series of correspondences or differences among the "sending" forms and the "receiving" forms. But, one might object, the subjects, not the forms, receive the message. Precisely, but this message has a spatial constituent, and that constituent is at issue here. More clearly, the "formal" message is, in this case, the same for the inhabitants of the renewal projects and for those of the surrounding lower-class neighborhoods (*quartiers populaires*). Are the differences in communication entirely explicable by class distinctions? What is the margin of formal specificity of the "urban frameworks" of reception?

Going further, one must certainly introduce the "urban relays," that is, the symbolic mediations, which permit the translation of codes and the combination of several messages into one to facilitate reception. For example, "modernity" transmitted by renovated buildings is relayed differently by being encountered from inside an automobile, on foot, or during a daily passage on public transportation serving the center of the city.

Moreover, although we have spoken only of "forms," one can also think in terms of flux, urban rhythms, empty space, and the relation between time and space, etc.

Finally, these processes are not "willed," nor are they strategies; instead, they are necessary social effects produced in the ideological praxis by a social relation to space. This means that at times the ideological effects produced will contradict the economic effect of an operation because there is no systematic control of the ensemble of these effects. In colloquial terms, it will then be a mistake, a "smudge," which shows the limits of such a situation by the oriented law of the ruling logic that tends, without any success, to eliminate contradictory experiences.

The "concrete" element of such a process must be composed, *situated* by the analysis. Our elementary remarks are intended only to point up a set of problems, to define a theoretical space, which is yet to be thoroughly explored. In the course of research on other questions, we have discovered the existence of these symbolic effects, which were materially identifiable by their reflections in other domains but incomprehensible due to a lack of research tools.

In any case, the essential thing in this domain is to reverse structural semiology and to seek to determine the symbolic load of an urban structure, starting from the social appropriation of space made by the subjects. The strategy, which begins with ideological praxis, must not be allowed to fall into subjectivism, because the praxis can only be understood in its relation to the ideological content it carries and to the place it occupies in the larger process. Beginning with the ideological-spatial praxis to discover the language of the forms, while integrating its relations into the total network of social relations in the city, is the complex but clearly defined perspective that must be developed upon a theme as rich as it is unexplored.

This theme cannot be further developed here, but these few remarks will permit us to reach a tentative conclusion that is decisive for the study of innovation within the framework of life. This conclusion holds that there is no *independent* urban symbolism, as such. Instead, one finds a formal expression in constant change, reflecting the social relations that found it. It is certain that there is a play of interactions between forms and praxis, but the latter is dominant. While the forms can have a relative autonomy in their social effects, they cannot transform themselves by internal movement. The innovation of urban forms is linked to cultural transformations, which, in turn, depend upon social movements. Instead of pursuing this increasingly abstract theoretical enterprise further, we will attempt to adopt a new perspective on the same set of problems, by examining the direct relation between social movements and their spatial expression.

III. Social Movements and the Transformation of Space

What are the paths of innovation in the urban environment?

If the urban environment is understood as a social relation to a certain field of cultural forms, it is clear that any innovation in these forms is linked to the processes of social change. Moreover, since the meaning of these forms is given only by their integration into the society (and not by any ahistorical aesthetic language), innovation can only be described in terms of the transformation of a social meaning.

Does this mean that a transformation of the framework of life requires a prior substantial modification of social organization? In a sense, yes, because it is impossible to produce a redefinition of urban forms and rhythms while the social sources of production of these forms remain unchanged. An analysis of the transformation of the environment should depend entirely on an analysis of social transformations.

But there are no fixed qualitative thresholds that divide the world into totally independent "befores" and "afters." If such discontinuities exist (they are called revolutions), they do not spring from nothingness but, on the contrary, are prepared by a series of faults and contradictions that develop within the old order. So it is with the forms of the urban environment. On the one hand, given the stresses in the processes of transformation among the different levels of social reality, it may be that there are profound modifications of urban forms linked to processes of change other than those directly involving the dialectic of social classes (for example, technical progress taken as a relatively autonomous element). The question then involves determining what are the principal sources of these modifications. There is an answer consistent with our point of departure: to the degree that all technical development implies and calls for a certain social treatment, every modification in the meaning of a cultural form is linked to a process of social innovation.

This innovative process may occur (although rarely in the case of the city) within a rhythm proper to cultural forms: for example, an architectural school. Such a path for innovation seems, however, to depend entirely, in its social effects, on its relation to a more general movement of transformation. This means, without denying the role of exceptional circumstances (genius, etc.), that there is no new cultural content during a *simultaneous* and *interdependent* transformation of the sending and receiving of signs. Or, if you will, there can be no functionalism without a capitalistic intent in the United States, and no surrealism without a definitive crisis in the old sociopolitical European oligarchies.

Thus, we again meet social movement at the foundation of all cultural transformations (and of the transformations of the urban environment) *if* one accepts that specific social movements (e.g., artistic movements) can occur whatever their articulation with other movements (in particular with political movements). *By social movement, we mean a system of practices that tends objectively toward the qualitative transformation of the social order.*

Social movements produce innovation in urban forms in two ways: on the one hand, by the indirect effect that social movements encompassing a major social contradiction have on every domain and, in particular, through the sociocultural movements which they commonly create; and, on the other hand, by establishing a new type of relation that concerns the whole society, for example, the urban space. This second aspect, which is seldom discussed, seems, nonetheless, to us to be an essential source of social innovation of urban forms, while the action of urban planners, as a result of their position within the apparatus of the State, is centered on social and cultural reproduction, rather than innovation.

How is it, then? Do social movements literally reconstruct the city? Is there, in historical situations dominated by a social movement, a new mode of appropriation of the urban space?

Rather than attempt a systematic answer to so vast a question, we can quickly examine the evidence of two recent cases, which we have known both personally and analytically: the social revolutionary movement of May 1968 in Paris and the constitution of squatters' settlements in Santiago, Chile, in 1970–71.

A movement as vast as that of May 1968 in France was destined to have a direct impact on the urban environment, less as the result of durable formal innovations than as the result of new social uses of existing space. In fact, there has been little discussion of this question, although a considerable interest has been manifested in such matters as the environment of Nanterre, which is surrounded by an industrial zone with a sprinkling of shantytowns. What emerges as most significant is the relation to space of each of the major lines of action that were intertwined within the May 1968 movement.

Thus, the occupation of historical buildings (notably the Sorbonne), which seemed at first to be the most important change at the symbolic level, did not, in fact, introduce new patterns of utilization of space. The nonstop assemblies that were held there only mimicked, by reversing and contesting it, the purely ideological and discursive activity for which these spaces were created. The case of the occupation of the Odéon (Théâtre de France) is even clearer. There the "official" theater was replaced by another theater, a continuous one, made up of a parade of artists, intellectuals, etc., who had come to exhibit their share of intimacy. This corresponds perfectly to one of the least significant currents of May 1968, pure ideological revolt by part of the intellectual community, a revolt that threw up to the old institutions their own contested, but ultimately unchanged, ideas.

In contrast, the urban space created by the Movement of March 22 (which was, of course, the kernel of political agitation at the forefront of the movement, but not an avant-garde in the Leninist sense) was entirely different. First, no space was privileged, no form fixed, but, rather, there was a new style, a mode of relation to space, a desire for diffuseness with points of concentration constantly changing as the political lines of force became apparent.

Thus, the "faculty" of Nanterre University, where this movement was born, was not occupied "in the proper form" (red flag, expulsion of the dean, etc.) until ten days later than the Sorbonne, since the March 22 group had forgotten to do it, being too busy elsewhere. At no time was there a symbolic headquarters, and the occupation of offices was carried out on a strictly functional basis, while the group refused from the beginning to join the Sorbonne contingent. Having left its first headquarters at the School of Decorative Arts (Ecole des Arts Décoratifs), which was found too "folkloric," the group moved into the modern offices of an isolated university administration that had been abandoned by its employees. This does not mean that urban space played no role in the activity of the Movement of March 22. On the contrary, it was practically a policy to constitute spaces, which one might call "rupture and reassembly" (*rupture et rassemblement*): a breaking off with the exterior world of repression and regrouping within the community of rebels, in a single movement. The street was the space proper to the Movement of March 22. When the situation was favorable (in relation to the police), the street became a place of assembly, with thousands of people sitting on the pavement around a circulating bullhorn. When the situation was unfavorable, the barricades were very poor military instruments but provided a clear demarcation of allegiances and attitudes, both in terms of frontiers and in terms of activity (building a barricade together was a way of getting to know one another). The fate reserved for the faculty at Nanterre by the March 22 group (which was quite different from that of the other Parisian schools) expresses the same line of conduct. Their first act was to pull down the fences that separated the campus from the neighboring shantytown, after which the inhabitants of the shantytown, especially the children, took possession of the faculty offices. These people then organized surveillance groups that denied entry to administrators, police, etc.

It was, then, a new social content that expressed itself on the campus (a liaison between students and the sub-proletariat) by cutting itself off voluntarily from the rest of the weakly controlled world.

This form of appropriation of space expresses and reinforces the dynamic of the Movement of March 22, a vast breaking away without specific strategic goals. This is a space of divisions whose boundaries are as mobile as the objectives of the revolt.

By contrast, the specific attempt to create an alliance of classes with revolutionary goals inaugurated another relation to space in an episode less well-known than one thinks, but which was the apex of the May 1968 movement—the battle at the Renault factory in Flins (30 kilometers from Paris) engaged in by workers and students in an effort to prevent the police from breaking the strike militarily. During four days of political and military struggle, groups from the May movement (several thousand people) attempted to oppose the government's attempt to regain control of the situation. While it is obvious that the relation to space was not an objective in the minds of the militants, it is just as obvious that a new sort of relation was elaborated and played a considerable role in the relative success of the enterprise (the strike was maintained locally, although the movement was militarily broken by its political isolation). In fact, what characterized Flins spatially was that 14,000 workers were dispersed across a vast expanse of countryside, without the least relation to one another other than that of common work. The struggle was extended throughout the surrounding area, along roads that one traveled in order to stop the police vans or to reach the key points of the moment; through forests and fields, in "combat" with the police, in scheduled but constantly changing assemblies, which re-created each day the density of an activity that then was spread out in time and space. But, especially, the basic element was the fomenting of revolt among the population by the actions of the police. Workers from the factories, inhabitants of the area (who suddenly discovered the sting of tear gas), individual students who had come from Paris, militants from the area who came as reinforcements—all these groups opposed the thousands of policemen who marked the entire space with an expression of the larger society. The automobile became (alas!) a source of solidarity, because constant collective transportation was necessary in the absence of collective means. Great bonfires at night reunited the groups dispersed during the day and structured this space made up of diverse social moments, to say nothing of a host of other elements! It is obvious that the break between industry, countryside, and town was overcome, and that all the participants experienced space in a qualitatively new way. The innovation was less a renewal of forms than of rhythms and personal relations. This "revolutionary space" was an expression of the larger significance of the movement of May 1968. Yet, dependent as it was on the rhythm of the social movement, this was only a spark on a wet plain.

The relation of social movements to innovation appears even more explicitly in the organization and evolution of the "encampments" (*campamentos*) that were created suddenly in Santiago, Chile, in 1970. Taking advantage of a delicate electoral juncture, which limited the possibilities of repression, some 300,000 people illegally assumed possession of unused urban land, where they put up temporary lodgings while waiting for the construction of affordable housing. These *campamentos* were quite different from shantytowns by virtue of their strong social organization, and they will be absorbed, progressively, by the Chilean Popular Unity Party housing program. In direct relation to the social processes underlying the takeover of public lands, these settlements ran the entire gamut of spatial designs and of levels and forms of appurtenances. Lacking the space to do justice to so vast a subject, we may offer two important conclusions from our investigation of these settlements:

1. The urban forms, the types of housing, and the relative degree of innovation that they display, the level of technical achievement, etc., are directly determined by the intensity of the social movement underlining the takeover of these areas. In the Chilean case, the organizing political orientation of the settlement was the determining factor. The more revolutionary the political line of the movement, the more marked the innovation, and vice versa, so that one finds social disorganization in settlements mobilized by pure demagoguery.

2. There is little innovation in the forms themselves. Beyond the general refusal of collective housing, even the most revolutionary settlements present little major innovation either in the type of structure or in their disposition (usually in the "checkerboard" pattern). But perhaps the renovation of forms will follow the transformation of the life of the people, who for the moment are using patterns that they know, that is, the patterns of the past. Furthermore, it is clear that the constraints of scarcity considerably restrict the possible range of formal innovation.

Does this mean that nothing has changed in these settlements or that their urban environment is identical to that of the "emergency settlements" built by the State? Not at all, because the way in which they are (illegally) created conditions their relation to space, in terms of dealing with the problems of daily life, since no preparations are provided for this sort of lodging. But, at the same time, the content of this relation changes as a function of the political line. Given the illegality of these installations, for example, there is no police or judicial apparatus. If there is also no organization of the settlers, the space of the settlement becomes a place of terror, violence, and arbitrary justice. Where there is a revolutionary political organization at the base of the process, however, popular militias and tribunals are formed. Let us compare the effect of these two situations with one of the few formal innovations that are to be found in these settlements—schools held in old buses brought in for this purpose and adapted for it by the inhabitants. The sight of a bus immobilized, fixed by the smiles of the children, or, the transformation of a place of terror into a space where one circulates without fear and learns to identify the constantly changing posters: where is the urban environment? In the forms or in the rhythms? In objects or in social praxis?

The hopes of the Chileans and the Parisians at the barricades invite a brief reflection on the social conditions for the creation of a new urban space.

IV. For a Contestant Institution Concerned with the Urban Order

From this reassembly of the theoretical components of that which we call "the urban environment" and from an examination of the social processes underlying its transformation, we may proceed to an examination of the institutional treatment to be given this problem in a non-bureaucratic sense. Or, if you will, the discussion of institutional means presupposes our prior discussion of objectives in urban studies and a study of their production in society.

Within the University (even the new University) one finds the three fundamental elements of any system of knowledge: *research, teaching,* and *practical application*. The institutional objectives of urban studies, as all will agree, must certainly include studying the meaning and production of urban forms, the support of action designed to adapt the urban forms to the needs of the inhabitants, the training of the personnel needed for these programs of action. But one must be able to state exactly what it is that is to be taught and applied, in terms of the fundamental *problems* that are to be confronted and resolved.

One might think, for example, of an institution built on the thought of a few authorities on the urban environment and dedicated to testing the ideas of these authorities by training the personnel necessary to conduct experiments in practical applications. But this course leads to a paradox: the activity within such an institution would consist of using the urban environment (and the lives of the inhabitants) as an experimental field for these authorities, rather than using the thought of the authorities as a tool in studying the society.

This is problematical, not only from the point of view of value judgments, but also—and especially—from the point of view of our analysis, which it contradicts. *If social movements are at the base of changes in urban symbolism, philosophical ideas cannot replace social praxis as a source of innovation in our environment.* If one believes that change comes from *life*, in all its diversity, rather than from a few privileged experts (which assumes an idealistic theory of the movement of history), the fundamental goal of an innovative institution concerned with urban forms is *to tap the sources of this innovation, that is, the social movements which transform the urban environment.*

The role of researchers is not eliminated, since pure social praxis does not yield its significance unanalyzed. But it is essential to study innovation where one finds it—in praxis that is contradictory to the social order. The false dilemma between the scientism of stasis (reproductive of the social order) and the utopian dream of the ideologist (the indispensable complement of the technocrat) can be obviated by studying the innovation already manifest in advanced social praxis. The role of research is to analyze and project into the future these social practices.

This perspective has repercussions for the other goals of an institution for urban studies. Thus, *practical applications* can no longer be taken as technical recipes but must consist of the furthering of social modification (including the use of pressure groups) to implant certain seeds that have been discovered and analyzed, with a view to generalizing them. Professional training thus becomes extremely dependent on such a goal and begins to resemble the production of men like today's union leaders. Rather than producing technicians, such an institution as we envisage should train "agents of change" (one might say, militants). These subjects must be capable both of analyzing and understanding the production of the urban framework, and they must act to transform it. This requires a recruiting process already engaged in the battle.

The essential problem in this view seems to us to be the problem of the power that would found such an institution. For, if social movements furnish the themes, serve as agents of intervention, and are at the base of recruitment, the institution can only live and grow within a strict allegiance to these movements. *An institution dedicated to changing the environment must necessarily be in the camp of social change in opposition to the established order.*

In fact, the choices are few: it is either a question of a technical applications institute, devoted to technological recipes, although enveloped in a philosophical-social discourse; a matter of a school of thought turned in upon the personal dreams and opinions of a few intellectual leaders; or a matter of linking the institutions up with new forms of life, of monitoring change and attending to its lessons. In short: *neither technocratic scientism, nor ideological utopianism, but study and reinforcement of experiences in the process of transformation of the framework of life.*

For, what we lack is not the impossible but those possibilities that we are obliged to ignore so that mediocrity may continue to be profitable.

Notes

1. Gaston Bachelard, *La Poétique de L'Espace* (Paris: Presses Universitaires de France, 1957): 67.

2. Ideological praxis (*pratiques idéologiques*): the production of legitimation-communication effects.

The Proairetic Factor and the Concept of Asymmetry in Design
By Gillo Dorfles

Rather than give suggestions for a new university of design, I should like, in this brief paper, to make some remarks on the situation of that group of disciplines with which such a university should concern itself.

First of all, the very concept of design, limited to its subspecies of product design, is obsolete today. That which, by now, has been repeatedly defined as the "crisis of the object" is easily apparent in all fields of human productivity, in those of "industrially produced objects" as much as in those of the "artistic object." It is, therefore, preferable today to talk of environmental design and about the confluence of city planning and ecology, thus taking into consideration the two trends dominating the entire environmental situation: the *artificial* and the *natural*, always keeping in mind the interaction of these two components, which should never be separated.

The error of many scholars, of many theoreticians of problems concerning design (and particularly of environmental design and of urbanistics), has been that of not giving sufficient weight to these two components, *nature* and *artifact*. I have already mentioned this in the volume *Artifact and Nature* (Turin: Einaudi Editore, 1968), where I tried to bring into focus the interaction between these two elements in modern civilization. Today, we are implanted in a milieu that is prevalently *man-made*, and we too often forget that at the basis of this milieu, there exists and preexists a natural element. The slogan I suggested in my book was *"naturalize the artificial, and consider even nature as artificial"* (as man-made), which means, consider meadows, woods, lakes, and rivers as having the same requisites—which I would call *semiotic*—as the works of man, having the same need to be included in environmental design; and, on the other hand, consider the various man-made artifacts as part of the natural milieu.

An often quoted example (I believe first underlined by Adolf Loos), which is typical of the subject at hand, is that according to which the great technological structures (high-voltage towers, smokestacks, the tanks and pipes of oil refineries, atomic power plants, etc.) do not wound the landscape but melt with it, without, however, fading into it—since they maintain their autonomy; whereas, any mediocre (or even good) architectural construction often violates the landscape, changes it, or suffocates it. This applies to many analogous situations where the two principles of nature and the artifact—not integrated nor clearly distinct—appear confused. It is as dangerous to try to hide architecture in the landscape (Frank Lloyd Wright) as to wish to overpower it with buildings: their integration must be achieved through reciprocal respect.

One of the first tasks of a Universitas, such as we might envision, would then be to *establish the limitations and the values of the artificial and the natural* (which subsequently find their extension in the study of plastic materials, prefabricated architecture, etc., and also have many points of contact with the actual situation in visual arts generally). In my opinion, a study of environmental design cannot be undertaken without taking into account these preliminary considerations, which have not yet been sufficiently developed and are often completely ignored by the various universities. On the other hand, in the observations proposed by Emilio Ambasz (in the Project Working Paper) there are already some points that are acceptable from the start: I definitely agree with the fact, for instance, that a Universitas must be not only an institute for scientific, sociological, or linguistic research, but also an institution founded on humanistic, historical, philological, etc., research.

The point I wish to analyze in this paper, however, is whether it is possible to isolate at least one aspect of the complex problem of environmental design in order to be able to better define and elucidate it.

I believe it is precisely the *anthropopsychological aspect of the relationship between man and environment* that must be given the precedence. Although, even within this particular aspect (which has had a remarkable development lately) we can very often see distortions due to the excessive emphasis given certain elements to the detriment of others. Thus, it has happened that physiopsychological considerations—as in the case of studies based on proxemics, or technological considerations (by engineers and construction technicians), or linguistic considerations (by semiologists)—have been overemphasized.

If we examine man's situation and function in contemporary society and in his habitat, too often we neglect some factors that perhaps we might consider as being of an ethical nature and without which many observations and analyses are, in the end, unacceptable or useless. I shall quote here but a few of these often neglected areas:

1. The "affective memorization" of territory and milieu by the inhabitant and the importance of the *micro-milieu*.

2. The inter-subjective relationship between inhabitants.

3. The recognizability (i.e., semantization) of territory and of habitat.

4. The excessive or *insufficient present of new environmental and ecological symbologies*.

Among the most urgent tasks that a Universitas should study and fulfill, I would then list the following (quoted as mere examples and impossible to discuss here in greater detail):

1. The need to study and establish some "points of reference" in the habitat for the affective memorization of each individual to hold onto.

2. The creation, *ex novo*, of an iconic symbology, establishing just how much it can be inner-directed or other-directed.

3. The need for a *recuperation of the natural* in order to permit man to maintain his sensitivity to the most important aspects of nature.

4. The need to stimulate perceptiveness in the public in order to enable it either to accept or refuse the discordant elements in the environment (forms, colors, proportions, signs, lettering, etc.).

5. The need to abolish and prevent the concentration of "art containers" (museums, churches, monuments), and to attempt the aesthetization of the entire habitat instead. (The case of Manhattan, in spite of its paradoxical and inimitable quality, is a very clear example of how an artificial environment can offer highly aesthetic sensations through the ensemble of its functional structures—bridges, highways, turnpikes, skyscrapers, etc.—and, on the other hand, altogether antiaesthetic sensations through its "artistic" works— St. Patrick's Cathedral, the Cloisters, the New York Public Library at Forty-second Street, the Fifth Avenue Synagogue. As a matter of fact, even old cities like Florence, Naples, etc., are now reduced to accumulations of territorial monstrosities, where the single historical monuments of the past have lost their magic and, furthermore, any educative function of the "taste" of the inhabitants, just because they are cut off from the new civic functions.)

6. The need to develop—in a semiotic study of environmental design— the *pragmatic* dimension of design and architectural semiotics, above all, besides a *semantic* and *syntactic* dimension: this primarily because as a rule inhabitants (and designers as well) relate to the objects of environment design with a total perceptual disinterest. In other words, today even more than yesterday, there is a lack of any stimulus in the inhabitant to "decode" the structures that make up his milieu, with the result that the milieu remains unread, and its utilization is more and more only practical and economic (and no longer *symbolic* and *aesthetic*).

One of the first tasks of the Universitas should be to develop and reestablish the relationship between man and the environment through a correct semantization of environmental structures, thus inducing that capacity for "affective memorization" (see point 1, above) without which it is impossible even to initiate a discourse on individual and communitarian preferences, which is the subject of this paper.

The core of the problem rests on these premises, i.e., on recognizing that the exercise of a true and proper "preference," whether ethical or aesthetic, is impossible without adequately preparing humanity to exercise this *preferential judgment*.

Further examples, very simple but constant, will clarify still better the meaning of what I propose to state. The above-mentioned impossibility, or near impossibility, of any "affective memorization" (and this seems to me to be the greatest obstacle to any just acceptance or refusal of the environment by its inhabitants) is due, in part, to our consumer society. The continuous substitution of products (product design), as of structures (planning design), not only has the result of preventing man from treasuring the objects of consumption (which might be a good thing), but also leads him to take an indifferent attitude in regard to his "possessions" or those of the community to which he belongs. The detachment felt for one's milieu, the buildings it consists of, those fragments of nature (public parks), which it still contains, is due precisely to the feverish turnover in urban construction, in means of transportation, in human settlements. The same exaggerated mobility of the population brings about an obvious lack of "affective" interest on the part of the individual or individuals as a community. The ethical disinterest is accompanied by an equally profound aesthetic disinterest. (If this is not true with regard to some countries—certain Swiss cantons, certain alpine villages in Italy, certain rural corners of Spain, or the underdeveloped countries—it is certainly true of all highly industrialized countries. And this is what counts, since in a few decades this will be, almost surely, the fate of the whole world.)

Actually, the aesthetic interest cannot be disjoined from an ethical participation, and these two aspects will be shown always to be combined in the preferential element we will be talking about at greater length later.

Other examples can easily be derived from the highlights of today's life in industrialized countries. Think of what has happened to the mountains in winter since mass skiing has come about, with its multiplication of ski lifts, etc. Today, going skiing means being caught in a network of *servicing*, where the most important thing is the functionality of the hotel and the ski lifts, while the very perception of the alpine landscape, of the woods and the mountain air, has been lost.

The same happens at the seaside during the summer, both in Europe and in the United States, on the Adriatic coast as on the Spanish or Yugoslavian ones. Generally speaking, tourism has substituted a peculiar standardized symbology of its own to the previous architectural symbology or ecology. Hence, the advent, every day more unbridled and totalitarian, of the phenomenon of *kitsch*—of standardized bad taste, which now spreads not just to the single object (the curios for tourist consumption), but to the whole environment, the touristy milieu.

It is too easy to attribute all the phenomena of environment or object degradation on the population increase or to mass civilization. They are due, in reality, to a lack of education of the masses and of individuals; to the lack of an enlightened planning and semantization of the milieu by designers. This is why, in the ultimate analysis, it is the responsibility of environmental design first, and also of product design, shelter design, and graphic design, to recognize these errors and to correct them. And this could and ought to be the task of a Universitas dedicated to design.

The fact that an axiological and ethical element, i.e., of "value" and moral meaning, is considered basic to every design activity (as even Ambasz seems to admit in his introduction to the symposium) and the fact that design activity is admittedly inseparable from the consideration of "preferences," both lead to the conclusion that the entire field of design (as of art in general: any distinction in this case is sterile), ipso facto, is recognized as being intimately connected with *proairetic ethics*, i.e., with an ethical condition based on a preferential element (*proairesis* = preference: προαιρεσισ), which should guide design activities and, generally, all environmental planning. This statement—we are well aware of this—is contrary to all those trends of thought on the problem of design that are based on:

1. Exclusively scientific considerations.

2. Mostly economic or technical considerations (as was true during the Bauhaus period of architectural functionalism and was still prevalent in some institutions such as the Hochschule für Gestaltung, etc.).

Moreover, such an orientation brings into play as a major factor precisely the proairetic (preferential) factor, which, as a rule, is not taken into serious consideration mostly because it is considered irrational, nonscientific, romantic, aleatory—like any phenomenon of "taste."

It is my opinion, conversely, that this is just the factor that must be advocated, today and tomorrow, if we wish our environment to respond to all those requisites that, in the ultimate analysis, are the true requirements of the individual, based on the search for his autonomous preferences. This is the concern not only of environmental design but of all the large design family, since each separate branch is strictly bound with all the others.

Naturally, at this point the most difficult problem we will be confronted with will be that of finding a balance between the designer's "preferences" and those of the beneficiaries; to determine to which extent it is possible or necessary to intervene, for or against, the public's preferences; and, finally, to recognize as the most delicate of the designer's tasks not that of *catering* to the public's taste, but of being able to *educate it without forcing it.*

Which, in truth, is the basic element motivating and directing our choices? Those of consumers? It is the *preference* given a certain product, a certain event, a certain process, hence a certain design. Obviously, the consumer society tends to entice, ensnare, and instrumentalize, more and more, the preferential apparatus, so as to manipulate our choice. Thus, the task shall be that of opposing this activity performed by publicity, by mass media, and by all the "hidden persuaders" who are constantly near and around today's man, ready to pounce on him, and, instead, activating that which I would call an *autonomous proairetic and autogenetic factor*, consciously self-determined, not the dupe of a preestablished plan and manipulated by the hierarchy of any establishment.

Perhaps, in this way it would be possible to stimulate a positive action not only on the part of the designer and the planner but also on the part of the public, of the consumer, toward the various proairetic factors whose custodians are the population in general and the individual consumer. I will mention here, very briefly, that some attempts have been made at subjecting the proairetic factor to a logical-mathematical calculation (as done by Georg Henrik von Wright in his book, *The Logic of Preference* (Edinburgh: Edinburgh University Press, 1963), which have proved ineffectual in practice, or at least disappointing. The Finnish scholar (a pupil of Ludwig Wittgenstein) tried to give this problem a solution based on symbolic logic and, although he succeeded in reaching an exact formalization of the problem's essential core, he did so without realizing that its very irrationality made it unsuitable to rationalization pushed beyond certain limits. The proairetic element, although it can be formalized, cannot be constrained into formulae that will be valid once and for all; their validity will change from one time to another, together with the changing of desires, of affective compulsions, of moods, of "taste," etc. The only constant that we must reckon with, from a logical-mathematical point of view, should be the recognition that the proairetic element is always asymmetrical and irreversible, which only confirms those premises empirically noted above.

And here I should like to linger, if briefly, just on this last point, and precisely on *the asymmetry of the proairetic element* and its being intimately connected with *a more general notion of the asymmetry of design*.

The fact that the preferential formula, **p P q**, cannot be inverted to **q P p**, just because this formula implies the inevitable asymmetry of the two components (**p** and **q**), goes to prove how each choice is guided by a preference (as is each preferential choice of a designer, obviously), that, in order to make a choice, it is necessary to slight, or prefer, one of the terms against the other, which immediately results in a decidedly asymmetric condition. The connection between this type of asymmetry and the one I wish to speak of now— the hypothesis of asymmetry in environmental design—is only casual, and in a certain sense the two notions are not even fit for juxtaposition. However, the more detached observer of our times, capable of viewing them from a universal standpoint, in comparing them to previous epochs, will perhaps note, as peculiar to ours, an extraordinary autonomy of taste as well as its unusual asymmetry. In other words, I am of the opinion that in eras preceding ours there was a homogeneity of taste and of artistic currents (and of technical currents as well) that made them less subject to certain deviations and distortions. This might go toward explaining the lack of balance that, today, characterizes not just art, but society and also technology.

I am not saying anything new in mentioning the alternation of symmetry with asymmetry according to the different eras (classic and Baroque; Greece and China; new classicism and Art Nouveau; organic design and functionalism, etc.). Several times it has already been remarked that there is now a pronounced tendency toward asymmetry, even at the level of architectural, urbanistic planning, and at the level of the "distributive characteristics" of a single building. This would be further proof of what I have been saying, and convinces us that the study of asymmetry as an "epochal constant", could be extremely relevant.

These observations, as a matter of fact, remain within the framework of today's quite justified refusal of rationalist and functionalist positions (as asserted in some urbanistic and architectural schemata linked to the "poetics" of the great masters of the modern movement—mainly Le Corbusier and Walter Gropius), and are more closely related to the postulates of Henri Lefebvre, Alexander Mitscherlich, Kevin Lynch, Joseph Rykwert (this, only to offer some points of contact between what we wish to pinpoint here and certain positions taken by contemporary sociologists and urbanists).

The hypothesis of a new formulation of the man-made milieu could, thus, start from an initial consideration of the problem, favoring the asymmetric situations of environmental design (as much as of the "humanized" natural elements belonging to it) against the crystallized situation that gave birth to some of the great environmental planning efforts of the last thirty years, from Brasilia to Chandigarh, from Gropius's plans for Baghdad to British and Swedish New Towns.

We have witnessed, as I mentioned before, the alternation of the symmetrical and the asymmetrical in old civilizations as well as in some recent artistic currents. Though upholding the necessity of asymmetric design today, I certainly do not intend to deny the necessity, for certain structures of our habitat and of product design, of remaining anchored to symmetry, also in view of the symmetry in our organism. However, just as in our organism there exists a functional asymmetry (the predominance of one cerebral hemisphere on the other, cortical differentiations, asymmetry of the internal organs, etc.), so must we acquire a consciousness of the necessity to *subtract the design of our milieu from certain symmetric canons* concerning some functions and some structures, though *not all*.

This is another point that I think ought to be elucidated: we have become too accustomed to considering our universe and our milieu as a projection of our body, and our body as that of a biped, essentially symmetric, whereas many of our body functions and many of our organs are asymmetrical. This results in a contrast artificially imposed by the structures of our milieu and designed objects on our organism, which is, thereby, coerced and enslaved. Quite often today we notice the presence of elements, in product design, architecture, and urbanism, which are offensive for their useless and harmful symmetry.

The hypothesis we formulate here regarding the importance of an asymmetric element in environmental (and product) design obviously should be gone into in greater detail and expanded upon. I can do no more, here, than hypothesize on certain aspects of it. The apparent defeat of architectural rationalism in the 1930s by an International Style more flexible and decorative ("ornamented modern") did not substantially alter the regular and symmetric aspect of environmental and architectural design. The subsequent appearance of Brutalism and of certain informal architectural styles, even of a revival of Art Nouveau, have in their turn evidenced certain formal aspects of design although not going very deep into the authentic structures of the architectural or urbanistic language. (Even the construction of some artifacts, which, to all appearances, seemed etherodox: sinuous and irregular car bodies, urbanistic projects that abandoned the "hyppodamic," concentric, or star-shaped schemata, always ended by maintaining a balance, however arbitrary.)

It is in such ways that the public's aim for an alternative discourse has become increasingly blunted: the absence of an available disorder brought as a consequence the persistence of a preestablished, though unjustified, "order." Now then, I believe that the need is pressing to restore to the consumer the possibility of exercising a choice—by using his preferential capacity, which can only be manifested in rebellion against the framework of preestablished conformism.

Again, as a counterproof of my argument, I should like to bring up—with due caution—the fact that even in the field of "useless" visual arts (those that once were labeled "painting" and "sculpture" and which I prefer to call generally "visual arts") something analogous is happening: the fact that these artistic forms have extended their field of interest to include an environmental dimension, no longer limited to the canvas, or the statue, or the object, is undoubtedly an element worthy of reflection. Recent experiments, such as earthworks, are now well-known. The attempts of Dennis Oppenheim, Jan Dibbets, Richard Serra, Richard Long, etc., to act upon nature and the environment by removing sheets of earth, mowing meadows, opening great pits by means of caterpillars and bulldozers, moving stones removed from the soil, etc.; engraving marks on the iced surfaces of rivers and lakes, in other words, using elements borrowed from nature and "transformed" or set in such a way as to give the environment a humanized character, even though "useless" and imparted from an ephemeral start, denote the acute need in man to accost the *natural element* once more, bypassing technological and mechanical means. And not only this, they denote, almost always, a search that leaves behind any eurythmics and any symmetrical proportionality, turning instead toward the irrational and uneven.

I did not mention this to infer that design (product or environmental design) ought to "imitate" art; we know too well how very dangerous similar comparisons and imitations have been in the past. However, it is well known and evident that a shared *vis formativa* (shaping force) often unites technical and aesthetic works (as shown by the relationships of the Bauhaus period or de Stijl with architectural and urbanistic styles of the same period). Today, we are too often inclined to forget, either willfully or superciliously, the "useless" activities of visual arts and to neglect their intimate connection with those of design. I think this is a fundamental error. The disorder and irrationality of much of contemporary art will not be able to find an issue or a solution except in a new type of order and rationality based on new and different structural and linguistic criteria; on a different, as yet unedited, semiotics of its basic element. It is impossible to hypothesize new directions for environmental design, or new didactic directives, without taking into account the various requisites existing in our society also in the field of "pure" creativity just as in the inherent social order.

To conclude these remarks, which are meant to be no more than a working hypothesis whose elements are still to be clarified and brought to a finished polish, I should like to add that all new didactic methods and also new practical methods in the field of *the man-made milieu* and of *environmental design* should cling to the following premises:

1. Give back to man a *consciousness of the constant interrelation between nature and the artifact* (between natural elements of the environment and man-made environmental elements).

2. Develop in man (and in the designer) the drive toward a proairetic ethical and aesthetic formulation, i.e., toward an emphasis on his artistic and ethical "preferences."

3. Bring about and encourage this proairetic tendency through design of an asymmetrical character (product, shelter, environment, etc.), capable of responding to the present asymmetric tendency in our society.

New Values
By Ronald Dworkin

I.

I would like to gloss a crucial passage in the Project Working Paper, a passage that I found both fascinating and problematical. The passage, which appears in the essay "Design as a Mode of Thought," is this:

> The view of design as a normative pursuit, like that which sees it as an empirical one, constitutes an attempt at the systematization of the design discourse along the lines of a scientific discipline. It is, in the case of the normative approach, a discipline that validates its statements socially through the agreement of members of the community, rather than by empirical observation; but its task is still the analysis of the given and not the synthesis of the new. Conscious, commonly held meanings cannot be new, and normative approaches operate only with these; they cannot create new values any more than engineering can. Where do new values come from? An isolated individual may think of them by himself, and attempt to communicate them to others by means of some structure which embodies them but whose meaning, because it is new, will not be immediately accessible. Or, a structure may be created which embodies new values that no one is aware of, not even its maker, until the meaning of the structure is deciphered and made explicit.
>
> (Gaining access to, or assigning, possible meanings to a structure can be done by decoding according to an established context or by developing a new context to give it meaning.) In any case, it is not before, but after, structures have come into existence that new values embodied in them can suggest themselves to members of the community. The synthesis of structures that have a *symbolic* charge—with levels of meaning that go beyond the commonly agreed and are not directly accessible—is what enables us to invent the future.

I want to explore the concept of *new value*, and I shall begin, I am afraid, rather pedantically, by making some distinctions. The first is the familiar distinction between two readings of the proposition that something—vanilla ice cream, for example, or truth—is a value. The proposition may mean simply that vanilla ice cream is, in fact, valued by someone, that is, simply that he wants to have it. Or, it might mean that vanilla ice cream is of value for someone, that is, that he *ought* to have it. I shall call the first a descriptive, and the second a normative, sense of "value," but I must express a caveat about these terms. A philosopher or a sociologist might say that something is a value within a particular community, and this statement is ambiguous in the way just described. He might mean that members of that community, in fact, value something, like vanilla ice cream. Or, that they treat something as a thing that ought to be valued, like truth, perhaps by maintaining social practices or rules that express that judgment. In both cases, the philosopher's or sociologist's *judgment* is descriptive rather than normative, but in the second case it employs the normative sense of value.

But this distinction leaves room for another that is equally important, namely the distinction between the proposition that something, like penicillin, is of value, and the proposition that something, like truth, is *a* value. Something is of value if it is instrumentally related to some other value, like health or nutrition or comfort, and something is a value if it is a value on its own, that is, something that either is, or ought to be, valued for its own sake, like truth, for example, or liberty.

These two distinctions are independent, and so create four possible categories of value. One may say that members of a community, in fact, simply value something, either instrumentally, like golf clubs, or for its own sake, like entertainment, or that they treat something as a thing they ought to value, again, either instrumentally, like penicillin, or for its own sake, like truth. It seems plain to me on the basis of these distinctions that the passage of the Project Working Paper I quoted means to talk about the fourth of these categories, that is, about what the community treats as a value in the normative sense. But it is just with respect to this category that the idea of new values is most problematical. Let me explain.

Consider the individual, mentioned in the passage, who "thinks of a new value" and attempts to communicate it to others. He has no difficulty if he merely wants to say that he himself wants something not before wanted. The semantic difficulties the passage contemplates would be minimal because his situation calls upon him simply to describe the state of affairs that would satisfy him, and if he has been able to "think of" that state of affairs, the language in which he has thought should be rich enough to allow him to describe it. He has no more difficulty if he simply means to point out that something new should be desired, or should be recognized as something that ought to be desired, because, in fact, it is instrumental in reaching something that already is a value in one of these two senses. He then makes an empirical claim, and one that presents no special semantic or conceptual difficulties. He must have the vocabulary available to make his arguments about cause and effect, because he needed that vocabulary to make the discoveries on which the arguments are based.

But now, suppose he means to make an argument in what I called the fourth category, to the effect that something new ought to be taken to be a value. Now he will have what might be called conceptual problems, but not, as the passage I quoted seems to suggest, because he lacks the vocabulary to describe what he means should be a value. He must have had the vocabulary, even if it was jerry built from other concepts, in order to identify for himself the state of affairs he counts as a value. His problem will lie in finding the means to argue that others should value this state of affairs, however he describes it, for its own sake. When we argue that something is a value, rather than simply of value, we characteristically use backward-looking arguments, that is, we appeal to what we take to be prior commitments of *some* sort. We might appeal to a duty established in social practice, as when we say that the police have a responsibility to act fairly. Or, we might appeal to a standard virtue, as when we say that men must take helping their friends to be a value, because that is what loyalty is. Each of these arguments draws on established social practice not simply to define the conduct in question—treating black prisoners like white prisoners, or helping friends—but to identify a ground for the claim that this conduct is a value, by showing that it falls within a concept, like justice or loyalty, that already occupies a place in the social scheme of values. But how can one supply a reason for a "new" value? There is this apparent paradox: if a reason can be supplied then the value is not really new; if none can be supplied then it is not really a value.

II.

Still, new values *are* created, or at least develop. Consider this example. It is often said that privacy is an important value, but it is a value of modern origin even in liberal Western society. We might pick a date—say 1600—at which very few, if any, men or women recognized even physical privacy as a value of any great importance. But now it is thought by many to be a value of such importance that they speak of a political *right* to privacy, and argue that we ought to sacrifice efficiency even, for example, in crime detection procedures, when this is necessary in order to protect against invasions of that right.

How does such a change come about? We might ask that question from two standpoints. From the external or historian's point of view, the question asks this: What sort of evidence reveals the development of the idea that privacy is a value? Such evidence might consist, for example, of Supreme Court decisions, novels in which a concern for privacy is exhibited, and so forth. From the internal, or participant's, viewpoint, however, the question asks for the kind of argument that can properly be made to a community that does not recognize privacy, that it should, not simply because privacy is of instrumental value but because privacy is a value in itself. Fortunately, we have a model of this sort of argument on record, in the form of one of the most famous law review articles ever written.

In 1890, Louis D. Brandeis and his law partner, Samuel Warren, published an article called "The Right to Privacy." Their argument took this form: they examined a host of judicial decisions in different and apparently unrelated fields of law, decisions involving, for example, property rights in private letters and special problems of copyright. They argued that the grounds stated in these decisions could not, for different reasons, justify the decisions, but that these decisions could all be justified if one supposed that a principle not before recognized, the principle of a right to privacy, was in fact part of the law. They concluded that the principle therefore *was* part of the law.

That conclusion, to anyone unfamiliar with legal reasoning, must seem extraordinary. If we think of the law the way many lawyers do, as simply a collection of rules adopted by legislatures and courts, to be applied according to what these bodies intended when they enacted the rules, the argument seems fallacious. No court, and certainly no legislature, had enacted a principle about the right to privacy. If the judges who had made the decisions Brandeis and Warren examined had intended these decisions to protect a right to privacy, then one might argue for such a right on the basis of that intention. But the argument assumes that these judges had no such principle in mind at all.

Nevertheless, the article is famous as an excellent example of legal argument. Nor is it a solitary example. Indeed, if we look closely at the landmark *judicial* decisions that are often said to have made "new" law, both in America and England, we find much the same form of argument employed. Again, I can offer a famous example. In 1916, Judge Benjamin Cardozo, as he then was, decided the well-known case of *McPherson* v. *Buick*, and in so doing established the modern law of negligence in the United States. He used earlier decisions in the same way that Brandeis and Warren had. He pointed out that the results of a great many such decisions could be explained and justified by supposing that the law contains a principle imposing on each of us a general responsibility not to damage others through our carelessness, and a general liability to make good these damages if we do. This was a "new" principle, in the sense that it had not been recognized before, certainly not in the decisions Cardozo sought to explain by it. Nevertheless Cardozo's opinion was designed to establish the principle as law; and indeed it did so.

I mention these two examples of legal reasoning because they provide concrete instances of arguments in favor of new principles, arguments that are nevertheless drawn from established values. They seem to me to illustrate, in an institutional form, what the Project Working Paper describes as the "decoding of structures." We may take a body of existing rules of law— the results of earlier decisions and statutes—as forming a "structure." Certainly lawyers think of rules of law in this way. We may then take the form of argument used by Brandeis, Warren, and Cardozo in my examples— and, indeed, used by less famous lawyers all the time—as "decoding." We must understand by that somewhat runic phrase, however, the fresh justification of a structure constructed to the tune of other, and older, values.

III.

I, therefore, assume that legal reasoning is an example of what the Project Working Paper means when it speaks of creating new values through decoding structures. I should now like to put this question: Is decoding structures in this way a proper sort of argument for showing that something, like privacy or a new vision of public responsibility, ought to be recognized as a value?

We might start with this piece of armchair sociology. Social institutions, such as business organizations, family structures, unions, and the law, develop their structures in response to a vast variety of often competing normative principles and social and individual goals. The pressure of these different principles and goals takes different forms, ranging from the explicit demands of pressure groups to the subtle forces of an inarticulate sense of justice. The structure of the resulting institutions is, therefore, a social balance sheet, a summing up of the various additions and compromises that have shaped it. If a new principle, like the principle of privacy or negligence, can justify a set of apparently unrelated rules, therefore, it can claim to represent a kind of social decision. I do not mean a decision in the deliberate, formal sense in which, for example, a statute is a social decision; I mean a decision in the sense in which a compromise is a joint decision of those who have compromised. Once the unifying principle is found, however, then the structure is no longer seen as a compromise, but as an achievement, and as an achievement of the society whose common needs and disparate concerns produced it.

But why does it follow, from the fact that an institution can be justified on the basis of a fresh principle, that the community which supports the institution ought to treat that principle as a value? Why does it follow, in the terms of the Project Working Paper, from the fact that a structure can be decoded in the shape of a principle that this principle is a value? I can think of three separate sorts of theory. The first relies on a kind of transcendental psychology; it supposes, for example, that the judges who decided the cases Brandeis and Warren cited were "really" relying on a principle of privacy they did not consciously recognize. If this were right, and if it could be extended generally to cover the case of the slow development of a social institution, then the argument could be made that society had already accepted, albeit without so realizing, the principles discovered in the structure of these institutions. The second sort of theory relies on Hegelian historical metaphysics. It supposes that social institutions, including the law, develop in the form of a dialectic, so that the new principle, which justifies what has been done, although it was not relied upon in the doing, represents a synthesis of the earlier values and has normative force just on that ground.

Each of these theories will have its constituents, but I cannot accept either myself, because they seem to me to run beyond the boundaries of sense and because they seem to ignore what every lawyer knows about his society, which is this: any social structure, and, in particular, the law, contains elements that are irrational in the light of any scheme of justification. When lawyers attempt to justify a set of decisions in the way I described, the justification must be selective; the new principle is not so much drawn *from* as imposed *on* the structure it seeks to justify.

I should want, therefore, to rely on a different sort of assumption. I mean the assumption that in a rational society, institutions, and particularly coercive institutions, must continually be justified and must be administered in accordance with the most plausible justification that can be found. That assumption drives a wedge between the historical explanation of the structure of an institution and the present justification for maintaining and enforcing that institution. It forces those who accept it not only to criticize and reform institutions but to extrapolate from these institutions by taking seriously the principles that justify their present enforcement, and enforcing these principles elsewhere. Decoding, on this assumption, is justified by the combination of two principles of political morality; the principle just mentioned, which requires contemporary justification of social institutions, and the principle of consistency, which requires that the justification of principle from one institution must also be accepted as a standard for criticizing and reforming others.

It is easy to see how this third theory fits legal reasoning. The judge's responsibility includes the responsibility, from time to time, on suitable occasions, to reexamine the existing structure of the law, to see whether the diverse and competing justifications relied upon earlier must now be replaced by a fresh and unifying principle that can stand as a contemporary justification of the law. If so, he must identify that principle, and "expand" the law by enforcing it, in cases to which the previous justifications had not extended, within the limits left open by statute and precedent.

The theory also helps to resolve the paradox about new values described earlier. The paradox took this form: showing that something ought to be taken as a value seems to require a backward-looking argument to the effect that it already is a value; if that is right then new values are impossible. But the analysis I offered, if it is successful, shows that a value can be new, in the sense that it is not formally entailed by any values previously recognized, and yet rooted in the community's institutional practice, in the sense that the community may be committed by virtue of that practice, to recognizing that "new" value.

IV.

I want now to raise, though briefly, two further questions:

1. The argument, thus far, has kept close to the specific examples of legal reasoning I offered as a model for the "decoding" of institutions. Does this model have general application in, for example, political as well as legal contexts? I believe that it does, because I believe that it can serve as a model for understanding the standard arguments in favor of new, or extended, political obligations. Consider the claims, for example, that every child is entitled to a public education that suits his special capacities, or that every man is entitled to a job even in conditions of inflation. These are, or at least very recently

were, claims that appealed to "new" values, in the form of principles of justice not previously accepted in any wide community. Arguments for these new principles may well be found, in the political world, on the same model as I offered for legal reasoning. The present pattern of public education, or of Keynesian economic support, may be regarded as a social institution or structure, and it may be argued that these cannot be justified except by appeal to principles that, if applied consistently, would require reform of these institutions in the way the "new" values would suggest.

2. Does the argument have implications for the structure of an educational institution of the form of Universitas? I think it does, and I shall limit myself to this one suggestion, which many of you will find parochial. The design of Universitas should give a prominent place to the study of law, for law is now the discipline that most dramatically and most self-consciously follows the theory of research and education the Project Working Paper describes as the "design" mode of thought, in contrast to what it calls the "philosophical" and "scientific" modes. For some time, law schools in the United States, at least, have taken themselves to be engaged precisely in creating and studying "experiential and conceptual structures in order to satisfy needs and conciliate aspirations," and have attempted to develop interdisciplinary faculties for this purpose. The Universitas project can benefit by studying the successes and failures of the law schools. In particular, it can benefit by studying the phenomenon of legal reasoning that, as I have tried to show, translates the "design" mode of thought into practice.

Critical Essay
By Umberto Eco

0.1.

It is not clear whether the critical essay should advance proposals on the disciplinary structure of the Universitas, on its organization, on its philosophy, or whether it should comment on some of the points in the Project Working Paper. In the latter case, I tend to think that it must be very difficult to comment on a text scientifically when its pages are *not* numbered, and I hope that the future Universitas will supply more precise elements of code for those who will have to send messages from the center to the periphery and vice versa.

0.2.

Another motive that renders criticism difficult is that the Project Working Paper contains many theoretical hypotheses (which could be discussed indefinitely) and few concrete indications of a possible structure of the Universitas (except in "The Designs of Freedom"). I find it hard to undertake a theoretical discussion because there are too many undefined terms, such as *symbol*, *structure*, or *icon* (concerning this last term, see my final critique).

0.3.

For these and other reasons, I do not want to submit a strictly disciplinary contribution, indicating the types of subjects I would recommend at the Universitas, or other details pertaining to specific pedagogy. I would rather put forward a few considerations, inspired by recent university experience of the last few years (from 1968 to the present day), not to stipulate how the new university should be, but how it should *not* be, and in what terms it would be worthwhile projecting another one.

0.4.

I shall only make a preliminary methodological consideration. In "The University of Design," 2, there is a definite distinction being made between *science* and *design*, which I find too rigid. I do not think it can be said that "the task of science is the analysis of the given" whereas "that of design is the synthesis of the new." Niels Bohr's atomic model is the description of a *datum* that became a *datum* only after Bohr posited it. And, he posited it because it followed a certain operational hypothesis that was, in many ways, antecedent to science. In that sense, I think that both the methodology of Bohr and the project for a university, which would be willing to research in order to produce new ideas, could be synthesized by this sentence of Mao Tse-tung: "To acquire knowledge it is necessary to participate in the process which transforms reality. TO GET TO KNOW THE TASTE OF A PEAR

IT IS NECESSARY TO TRANSFORM IT BY EATING IT." This assertion, naturally, calls for two clarifications:

A. Transformation and reality could be interpreted in many different ways; to understand the structure of a literary text effecting some changes is also a form of science. But it is just as true that a literary text is not merely a written object but also the recipient of the reactions it provokes in its public; consequently, to understand it, it is necessary to see it inserted in its psycholinguistic process.

B. There is one situation in which scientific knowledge can be present in a university without being immediately tied to transformative research, and that is the moment of information on precedent knowledge. But even this information must be selected, in view of the hypothesis of practical work, otherwise the Universitas could easily be substituted by a universal encyclopedia.

1.1.

What is the present situation of the university? Founded in Bologna at the beginning of this millennium, the university as a traditional institution (i.e., as a center of learning of specialized disciplines, of selection of specialists, and of research) historically has ended. Universities will be able to subsist for a few centuries without corresponding to any particular political or cultural reality (as happened in the eastern and western Roman Empire).

1.2.

The traditional university has not ceased to exist due to the student revolts, which were simply the side effect of an ampler process that does not concern the university as such (but concerns the fact that in the university there were the representatives of a new form of proletariat, the students, as a future intellectual labor force).

1.3.

The traditional university has ceased to exist because it is becoming a university for the masses, or Open University. Thus, it is becoming the instrument of an act of justice, allowing all citizens to receive a higher education whose purpose it would be to abolish the inequalities caused by inferior and familial education, determined by class differences. But, as an instrument of higher education, it will no longer be in a position to carry out the selection and the preparation of specialists.

The reasons for this are quite comprehensible:

A. If the university for the masses is to eliminate cultural gaps (which directly correspond to class gaps), it will be able to undertake the teaching of specialized disciplines, but it will have to supply elements of general scientific information, which will place everybody on the same level.

B. If it immediately gives specialized training to the most alert of its components, it will once more become an instrument of social selection.

C. If its purpose will be to give the student mass equal possibilities of learning, it will not be able to form centers of research within its structures.

D. If it does so, it will have created centers of selection and consequently of discriminatory power.

1.4.

The fact that the university would no longer create specializations could be a positive factor inasmuch as it would aim at proposing the figure of a polyvalent technician who should, theoretically, identify himself with the citizen, taking the first step toward the abolition of the division of labor; the students, during their process of education, would also be laborers, and vice versa.

But it is, on the other hand, a negative factor that research should altogether disappear, not as a time of selection of men, but as a time of selection of topics and standards for deeper analysis.

2.1.

The day when a real university of the masses exists (on a universal scale), research could be adequately inserted in other institutions where students with a vocation to research could converge after having completed the university for the masses. But, even so, research should be characterized by some of the components of the new university for the masses: refutation of fetishized specialization, refutation of the difference between the scientific knowledge of data and the practical modification of the environment. Moreover, the researchers should have some characteristics in common with the population for which, and among which, they would carry out their research, and the research itself should continually involve the collectivity, becoming a form of public instruction, a public model of scientific work, which would receive its feedbacks from the collectivity for which the research is being carried out.

2.2.

Let us, then, try and see if between the present university and the mass university of the future we can find a possible intermediary model, which would be transitory and experimental, like the one postulated by the Universitas Project. The model for the traditional university is the following: PEDAGOGY paves the way for RESEARCH, which singles out a NEW PROBLEM for which the SOLUTION must be found.

PEDAGOGY consists of understanding the problems of the past and studying the solutions that have already been given.

2.3.

The model for the Universitas Project seems to be articulated in the following way: around a new problem which has just been singled out: there is a
moment of pedagogy, which aims at making it more widely known, and a
moment of practical solution:

UNDERSTANDING
The Universitas
postulates and gives
context to solutions.

NEW PROBLEM
Which is real and not
abstract: it is a
concrete environment.

SOLUTION
The research collectivity
assumes the responsibility
of decision making and
of regulatory functions.

2.4.

But I wonder how the center of coordination can give context and postulate,
when the problem, as object of the transformation or of the action of design
(Mao's pear), is in contact with the collectivities of research, which are the
only ones inserted in the praxis. How can they receive postulates and information, which are essential to research, from a center that is in no way connected to the research itself (having said that the research identifies itself
with the transformation of the pear)?

   In other words, the moment of information should not be contemporary
to that of the proposition, and the two moments should not be contingent
on the same center, inasmuch as they constitute two different moments of
research, which are neither authoritarian nor theoretically abstract.

2.5.

The Universitas should, therefore, have a center of proposals, indispensable
to the insertion of each process and to the channeling of the choice of situations and environments. But in this "postulative function," the Universitas
should not so much foresee new structures, as propose alternative goals and
new patterns, because these latter ones are the finalities of elaborate research
within the praxis; the Universitas' sole purpose is to discover new problems
and to propose new fields of hypotheses. If "the postulating function makes

codes," as is asserted in "The Designs of Freedom," 4, what remains of research? And how can it be thought that a selected group of artists, social thinkers, poets, and designers, who are, by definition, unfamiliar with decision-making and a direct contact with the collectivity, could postulate valid solutions to those who are researching within the collectivity? If such an obstacle is created, we shall once more have a "gerarchy" of abstraction; the young researchers would be on the lowest level and in direct contact with concrete experiences, and, on the higher level, there would be the center of research in the form of feedback. Thus, the researchers would have "fresh" information, which would be upheld by "canned" theoretical hypotheses ("canned" because they would already have been postulated at the center of research); whereas the postulators would have "fresh" theoretical hypotheses but "canned" information filtered by the "ingenuous" experience of the researchers.

Likewise, it is difficult to determine which information could be supplied by the center to the periphery before the periphery itself uncovered some concrete problems for the solution of which it would need specific disciplinary information.

2.6.

Therefore, I think that it would be useful to reconsider the model of the Universitas (in its four moments: informative, postulative, decisive, and regulative) as a circular, rather than a linear, model.

It would be a self-sustained model with just two external elements: A. Problems Switcher, and an ideal, B. Storage of Cultural Information ("ideal" because this storage actually coincides with the totality of the existing scientific knowledge).

A.
PROBLEMS SWITCHER   ← new proposals to the
↓
1) Suggests the concrete
situation experimented on by
the researchers and by the
local community.
↓
2) From the experimentation   4) The initial situation is
derives the need for possessing   redefined and interventions
new cultural techniques.   in other situations are
                                           proposed.   ↑
↓
3) New hypotheses are tried   B.
by taking new decisions   STORAGE OF CULTURAL
registered in the →   INFORMATION   ↑

Let us try to clarify the various points brought to light in the diagram:

A. The Problems Switcher identifies situations in need of modification. Due to the fact that it is also fed with the results of the preceding cycles, the Problems Switcher is not a scientific authority divorced from the groups of research, but it represents the groups of research in the initial and conclusive moments of new cycles.

1. By the researchers I mean the teachers and the students of the Universitas, as well as the members of the local community. It is at this point that the Universitas carries out a postulative function.

2. During the process of solving a situation, the researchers will realize that they need scientific and disciplinarian information. By "scientific" I mean, in this case, "the record of that which science has achieved in other circumstances and which cannot be directly applied to the situation in question, but which can have a channeling function." The researchers would therefore solicit the Storage of Cultural Information so that it would organize courses, seminars, bibliographies, and various types of documentation.

B. The Storage of Cultural Information could be composed of the researchers themselves, who would act as experts of documentation (by researchers I also mean teachers and members of the local community who could sometimes be more familiar with a previous experience than current teachers or students); and possible experts who would not participate full-time in the life of the Universitas but who would, all the same, be indispensable in the solving of a scientifically oriented problem. Nevertheless, before contributing this information, the experts would, to a certain extent, have to participate in the life of the research community, in the environment pending modification, so as to channel information accordingly. Information that is at the same time scientific, objective, and neutral does not exist.

3. During this phase, the researchers would carry out the function of decision-making and actually begin their intervention in the environment. At every step of the experiment they would naturally be enriching the storage files of information.

4. The researchers would then find themselves in a restructured situation. The problem could either be solved or reset on a different level. The results of a similar process would, on the one hand, enrich the storage of information and, on the other hand, lead to the conception of new proposals (the Problems Switcher would thus be fed).

2.7.

All of these cases clearly indicate that the regulative function does not belong to any of the operative moments; it is the entire self-sustained process that establishes its own auto-control.

3.0

This model brings to light a few problems, such as:

1. The redefinition of certain methodological concepts proposed in the Project Working Paper.

2. The redefinition of the decisive role of the Universitas as center.

3. The redefinition of the relation among teaching, learning, and the students, and between the teachers and the subjects of experiment.

4. The redefinition of the faculty, which should form the Universitas (as defined in "The University of Design," 3).

5. The redefinition of the meditative role of the Universitas between the "processes of the infrastructure and the goals of the superstructure" (as defined in "The Designs of Freedom," 3).

Let us analyze the following points:

3.1. ABOUT CERTAIN METHODOLOGICAL CONCEPTS

A given anthropocultural situation is definable as a series of codes (familiar, proximal, architectonic, linguistic, and others). Who is going to define these codes? If the faculties, as sources of postulation and information are the representatives of science, as analysis of the given, then they possess (and can explain) these codes. But one of the contradictions of class culture (of culture as an expression of the dominating classes) is that it postulates codes which are not the ones the masses relate to; moreover each projectional intervention modifies the initial codes, in the same way as each message partly reformulates the codes on the basis of which it is emitted—if it is not a purely tautological message. Consequently, the Universitas as center of proposals and information cannot be familiar with the situational codes; this could nevertheless be done by the researchers, scholars, and local community who try to understand the situation in which they find themselves concretely in order to effect the modifying praxis within it. One can deal with the semiology of codes only if one also deals with the semiology of the message. "The Universitas as we have conceived it is not to be a detached observer or passive entity" ("The Designs of Freedom," 1). It invents interventions: the dialectical situation that arises between the invention and knowledge of the given is well explained in "Design as a Mode of Thought," 2.

Let us see, then, what happens when a basic concept is attributed the theoretical form it has assumed to this day, instead of it being derived from the modifying process. The various arguments concerning the solutions, which have their own "iconic" or "symbolic" power, do not take into account such items as the criticism that semiology is bringing to bear upon the concept of *icon*. If the iconic sign is (as ingenuous semiology asserts) something that has relations of similarity with the object represented, then the building of new structures which would have iconic value could serve to communicate the wishes of the structure maker to the local community. But the "similarity" of the iconic (or symbolic? Why is "iconic" used in the Peircean sense and "symbolic" used in a non-Peircean sense?) structure derives from an ethnocentric illusion. That which is iconic for a group that has been culturally educated according to certain visual codes, is not so for another group. In other words, would the cruciform plan of churches have the same "symbolical" value it has now if Jesus Christ had been killed by hanging? Why is it that at the time of St. Augustine, the epitome of perfection was the circle and in the twelfth and thirteenth centuries it was the square?

Even admitting that certain structures can be defined as iconic or symbolic, their configuration cannot be established on the basis of the cultural codes of the *directive* elite of the Universitas in its propositional and informative moment, but it must be extrapolated from the system of values of the community where the work is carried out, just as the modifying intervention which acts as scientific instrument in microphysical observation, and as element of indetermination, is configured after it has started to take place. Studying the codes of a microphysical society at the moment of intervention does not necessarily lead to the discovery of the semantic conventions that are supposed to have been given, but it leads to the discovery of certain initial semantic conventions and to the intervention becoming a process of re-semantization, on the basis of new code conventions stipulated by the entire community, which carries out research within itself.

3.2. Decisive Role of the Universitas

Thus, it cannot be said that the Universitas as center of direction and as prototype is not involved in decision making. It is already part of the concrete praxis of modification and it is also politically involved. If this prospective is not accepted, the entire project would be facetious.

3.3. The Teaching-Learning Relationship

It is clear at this point that what distinguishes the teacher from the learner is the former's *wider* experience in terms of information on the preceding science. Teaching derives from the experience conducted concretely and by the local communities, which discover their own problems through the maieutic action of the researchers of the Universitas. But, by means of the maieutic action of the local communities, the university researchers will discover new procedures, new topics and problems, and new criticisms to add to the preceding disciplinary archives.

3.4. The Faculties of the Universitas

Faculties will not exist because the teachers will be with the students and with the local communities in the various environments. At the maximum, for reasons of storage of information, there will be some sections of the Storage of Cultural Information to which the teachers will be able to refer, each according to his own specific area of competence. (But when the research group refers to the Storage of Cultural Information and in the case where elements of social methodology are needed, then also the biology technician should participate in the process of learning.)

3.5. THE ROLE OF THE UNIVERSITAS
It could have a *mediatory* function inasmuch as it would *insert* the processes. As for the rest, it would always be involved in modified reality. If it mediates, it will do so in a dialectical sense rather than in the sense of the mediation of the United Nations between India and Pakistan or between Israel and Egypt.

4.1.
All these observations are based on a concept that I would like to underline. Usually, the gap that exists between teaching and learning is based on the fact that the one who teaches is in command of a skill or technique with which the learner is not familiar, and of which only the results directly concern him. This situation recurs in different forms in the various arts and disciplines, but I shall clarify what I want to say by a few examples.

4.2.
Everybody knows how to walk; then there are a few people who have perfected this ability (Emil Zátopek) and walk better than others. Sport is usually popular because (even in those countries where it is watched rather than practiced) those who watch it enjoy feeling that they are, to a certain extent, experts on the matter. Everybody can sing, even if it amounts to singing in the shower or while shaving. Then there are some who sing better than others (Frank Sinatra or Maria Callas): those who listen to them understand them because those singers are doing something that even they could do to a certain extent. Literature is in an intermediary position: everybody can write, but literary writing is based on techniques that the literate masses do not possess. The visual practices (painting, sculpture) and the environmental practices (architecture, city planning) are in an extreme position: few people know how to draw and nobody knows how to build a house. In this field, people use the product of an unfamiliar skill. Technique is administered by the artist or by the technician, *who acts as a shaman.*

4.3.
Now, if one wants the local community to solve its own environmental problems, it is necessary that it should learn the techniques of intervention, even if crudely. In that sense, the expert (teacher or student) is not in the environment to technically solve the problems of the local community, which cannot know what it wants because it is not aware of other alternatives than the ready-made ones offered by the precedent authoritarian tradition. The

teacher and the student must, therefore, assume the role of stimulators of operative practices. In 1969, in a section of Florence, the students of architecture were trying to single out the urbanistic and structural contradictions, and to do so they filmed the houses, the streets, and the courtyards. Someone suggested that the inhabitants themselves should participate in the filming. One of the greatest ambitions of a public that is present during the shooting of a film for the cinema or for television is to be able to look through the viewfinder of the camera. But this selective prerogative is, by right, only the director's. When the inhabitants of the Florentine quarter were allowed to shoot film, not only did they feel that they were participating in the research, they also singled out and framed some structural contradictions which the students hadn't noticed and with which they had lived for years.

4.4.

Let us take this example from the mapping of the problem to the practical solution. The aim of the Universitas should be to transform the inhabitants of the environment in question, from guinea pigs to advisors and from advisors to collaborators. The technician should be present in order to lead an intervention operated by the collectivity according to recent techniques, and still therefore amateurishly; but the solutions will spring from the personal experience of the inhabitants, who could, nevertheless make use of the Storage of Cultural Information files along with the specialized researchers; thus, they would find out if their proposals are in any way related to solutions which the preceding science has already tried to apply or which it has declared to be useless.

4.5.

This prospective leads us from the university *for* the masses (destined to a limited function of distribution of the predominant culture to vast layers of new subject citizens) to the university *by the masses.*

4.6.

The new Universitas Project must, if not solve this problem, be aware of it and of the fact that a new university cannot be projected before a detailed discussion of this utopia has taken place. *Utopia*, in this context, is not intended in its etymological sense as "something which does not belong anywhere," but in the sense of Possibility: Place Which Must Be Constructed.

Remarks Concerning the New York Universitas Project

By Hans Magnus Enzensberger[1]

THEORETICAL PREMISES

The founding of a university is a political act. This statement can be verified by considering the history of numerous institutions of higher learning founded since World War II (e.g., Nanterre in France; Bochum, Bremen, Constance, and Ulm Academy of Design in Germany; Essex in England; Tromsö in Norway; etc.). This statement is particularly true for a project which, like Universitas, suggests a programmatic basis for analysis and design (*Entwurf*) of socially produced environments ("man-made environments") and which is supposed to be located demonstratively in a metropolitan area—a metropolis whose socially constituted problems have become increasingly obvious over recent years.

Under these circumstances, it has to be expected that, already, the constituting of such a university will bring about vehement conflicts. The initiators of such a project, on the one hand, have to turn to resources that can only be granted by the dominating social groups, be it by means of an administrative decision, a private foundation, or a political patronage: financial and material means of production, real estate, special legal boundary conditions, etc. On the other hand, the initiators intend the project to represent an overall emancipatory social interest, even if this overall interest conflicts with individual (local, regional, national power, and ownership) interests. All of this is clearly shown in the tentative program of the Project Working Paper.

One of the main dangers in the beginning phase of the project is that a theoretical retreat may offer itself as an easy way out of the imminent conflict between necessary means and desirable goals. Hints of such an attitude (whether it is assumed for tactical or fundamental reasons remains unclear) can already be found in some contributions to the Working Paper. The danger of this attitude lies in the fact that it threatens to neutralize the possible benefit of the Universitas Project from the beginning. I would like to describe some indications of such a basic theoretical attitude in the following paragraphs.

1.

Active involvement of "both the government and the private sectors" is expressly requested for the project. Yet it remains unclear under what conditions and in whose interest such an active involvement is desirable. It is certainly not necessary to mention the catastrophic consequences for the American universities that resulted from the system of government contracts, the collusion with war research, and the role a number of faculties played in counterrevolutionary acts of suppression (e.g., Project Camelot). Surely the initiators of the project we are discussing here have thoughts concerning the responsibilities of Universitas, which run contrary to the trends indicated in the examples above. Therefore, it is all the more necessary to separate oneself from such forms of "active involvement of government." The same holds true for the "private sectors," especially when dealing with "design," a field in which the overall social interest is certainly not identical with the interests of individual industries.

2.

To put it in more general terms, some contributions to the Project Working Paper seem to be based on a social theory that shows extremely idealistic, and sometimes naïve, traits. This theory operates with "structures," "models," "interfaces," but neglects and ignores the categories of domination, social power, and material interest. Particularly naïve is the theory of "social contract," as imported from the eighteenth century and barely updated through the jargon of systems theory. In this theory of "social contract," the social group appears in a completely undialectical way as an "artifact, designed by an individual," as though it had not been proved a long time ago that, on the contrary, the "individual" can be defined as the artifact of a group: only if both processes are dialectically mediated can the opposition of the individual to society possibly be understood. Correlative to a theory of society on which such expressions as the above quoted are based, is the fact that at one point in the Project Working Paper the relevance of social classes as such is denied—hardly even worth a subordinate clause regarding class society having lost its meaning. Another correlate is the mythological role ascribed to the "inventors" in the societal process (again, privileged "private individuals" such as "artists, social thinkers, poets, designers," etc.).

3.

The central concept on which the project is based, the concept of design, remains not untouched by such deliberations. This concept is deeply ambiguous, as we can easily learn from its history and its application. On the one hand, this concept belongs to commodity aesthetics,[2] which serve no other purpose than to maximize profits. This could be theoretically deduced from the commodity analysis as performed by Karl Marx. Without as much theoretical effort or philosophical claims, however, a number of popular sociologists, particularly in the United States, have pointed to this aspect of design (streamlining, artificial obsolescence, styling). On the other hand, since the initiatives of the Dutch de Stijl group, progressive architects and planners have always stood for "interests" that reach far beyond the arrogance of an increase of production and profit only—however, they mostly did so without any notion of political economy and without a sufficient theory of the society in which they operate. Until today, the history of design has remained a series of defeats, suffered by the high-flying aspirations of the designers in their battle against utilization by *Das Kapital*. "If an idea collides with an interest, the idea always comes out looking ridiculous."

These remarks grasp and isolate only single strands of the web of argumentation in the Project Working Paper. This is due neither to a polemical intention nor to the "purity" of some ideological position. If these remarks, referring to Marx and his school, warn against idealistic self-deception, then it is not in order to replace it with a neatly prepared Marxism: such a "pure" Marxism only exists in the form of a narrow doctrine. It is important, however, not to regress to pre-Marxist standards. For example, it certainly would be wrong to apply the Marxian class analysis, without modification, to contemporary American society. That would be possible only at the expense of grave distortions. However, one can by no means draw the conclusion, from this observation, that the concept of class society, in general, has become invalid. That would be, as the European saying goes, "to spill out the baby with the bathwater."

A correct working theory of society is indispensable for the Universitas project, not only because, without such a theory, work at the university will attain only poor results, but also because the constitution of the university requires such clarity; otherwise, the initiators will not be able to deal with the conflicts they themselves necessarily create through their initiative: conflicts with the "outside world," as well as internal ones (within the faculty as well as with the students, whom such a project is supposed to, and will, attract). Such conflicts cannot be approached with harmonizing and idealistic concepts.

PRACTICAL PROPOSALS

One basic principle seems decisive to me in order to carry out the project: in its own institutional form, the Universitas has to anticipate the proposals it offers to society as a whole as far as possible. That is, it must be assured that not only the results, which Universitas will publish, but also its very existence, can be used as an effective example.

The first consequence of such a demand would concern the structuring of the university. Obviously, departmental divisions are unsuitable for this university, a point which the Project Working Paper has already made unmistakably clear. However, beyond that, there remains the question of whether, in addition, the project should not do away with other rules by which conventional universities function. The following may serve as possible examples: the faculty hierarchy, the differentiation according to academic rank, the setting up of curricula, the system of examinations, the collecting of credits, the use of quizzes, multiple-choice tests, etc., to check learned material, and the role of sports on campus. The prevailing stress on publishing in the academic world ("publish or perish") also seems to be a highly questionable practice in regard to the Universitas Project. Perhaps these various aspects could be condensed into the one demand that the university reduce the privileges of its members to the absolute functional minimum. This refers to the income of teachers as well as to questions regarding status and prestige. As a criterion for meaningful activity, publishing must be replaced by actual practicing (praxis) inside and outside the university. These problems cannot be solved after the fact; they exist already as the university is being constructed and as the teachers and students are being recruited. During this process, decisions are made that are irreversible afterward. At least two consequences must be drawn from these assumptions. First, it is not possible to evaluate the qualifications of teachers according to conventional academic standards. In this regard, titles and diplomas, and, to a large extent, publications as well, are almost irrelevant. Rather, teachers who are being considered for the staff must have experience, that is, not only professional but also social experience. Second, the contracts reached with members of the faculty must only cover short terms, so as not to create a permanent pensionable teaching staff ("tenure").

The Universitas Project should provide the students with extensive participatory rights in the governing bodies of the university, to a degree as yet uncommon in American institutes of higher learning. This participation must have an institutional basis (the right to vote in all commissions, also in the Board of Trustees, and particularly when such questions are at stake as the hiring of teachers, the curricula, budgets, and disciplinary problems). However, this participation should not be limited to decision-making institutions. Rather, the chief emphasis should be on cooperative interaction at the actual location of the learning process. In any case, student participation in the decision-making institutions has one deficiency: it lies under the constant threat of bureaucratization, since it could be monopolized by ambitious student leaders. To correct this deficiency, it is necessary, in addition, to participation in high-level decision making, that every single course, every seminar, be determined and developed in regard to its content, its goals, and its scope by teachers and students *alike*. The students must be able to elect their teachers themselves and to articulate their learning needs in discussions with the teachers. (There is one institution, which, for many years, has based its extremely successful practice on such premises: the Centro Intercultural de Documentación [CIDOC] in Cuernavaca, Mexico).

Also, in another regard, a university like the one we are discussing here must distinguish itself from all other heretofore existing institutes of higher learning—in its physical constitution and its administration. It is not at all surprising to note that all institutions and needs are overly bureaucratized in our society. The example of Universitas should show that it is possible to control the quasi-natural (*naturwüchsig*) cancer of bureaucracy. The university should not have a central administration building. All administrative functions should be reduced to an absolute minimum and should be performed by people whom they afflict. It is superfluous to make and keep records of every procedure. Correspondence must be fundamentally replaced by telephone conversations. Budget and efficiency control should be exercised by one's own peer group, not by a central administration. Large amounts of office space, which have to be built, heated, and staffed, are superfluous as well.

The teaching and research process is traditionally tied down to specific locations and definite times. Gigantic buildings with lecture halls, etc., are constructed, requiring large expenses and their own personnel (superintendent, campus police, etc.). Besides a very few technical installations, which cannot be decentralized (laboratories), we have to ask whether the separation between working and living locations could not be abolished, along with the separation between working and leisure time. In this respect, the traditional concept of the campus becomes a problem. This concept is based on premises and thoughts of the nineteenth century: technologically, it is on the level of the communication means of that time; ideologically, it is based on the concept of an archaic reservation ("academia").

Such concepts could be replaced by the proposal to build new kinds of apartment houses, to be used by teachers and students alike, and equipped with all service and communication devices possible today. Principally, meetings for instruction purposes should take place in a private, informal atmosphere ("at home") and at times chosen freely, not fixed by a central administration. The overcoming of physical distances and, with it, traffic problems, can so be avoided to a large extent. Each of these buildings has to be equipped with all of the following means of communication: videophone, real-time computer consoles, video recording and cameras, closed circuit TV, and telephone xerography (that is, access to the library via telephone). This allows discussions between groups at very different locations via conference lines, and common use of a central library (books, newspapers, circulars, sound and picture archives). Such a combined living-and-studying building must provide apartments that are the opposite of mere dormitories. Every teacher and every student must have facilities to receive groups *at his place*. In addition, larger rooms are necessary in which larger groups can work together. The apartments should not be distributed according to status but rather according to need: a single professor would receive a smaller apartment than a student with wife and children. Each of these combined living-and-studying buildings must be self-administered. The expenditure for such installations is immense. At the beginning probably higher investments are necessary than for a conventionally organized campus university. However, the maintenance costs would be much lower, due to enormous savings in unproductive (private, institutional, and public) expenditures: the "dead expenses" would be lower, and the productivity of the university, its diversity, and its openness would all be higher.

These practical proposals are related to the preceding theoretical remarks, although not always in a very direct way. A university founded on the basis of these proposals would be quasi-uncontrollable; it is possible to predict neither the results of such a university nor the rules this university would develop for itself. Whoever considers this unpredictability a disadvantage will fight against the founding from the beginning. Whoever considers it an advantage—and that refers particularly to teachers and students—will be willing to fight for such a university. The Universitas Project will be controversial, or else it will not be.

Notes

1. This essay was translated by Wieland Schulz-Keil and Barbara A. Becker.
2. An aesthetic practice, which attempts to disguise the difference between the use value of a product to its consumer and its commodity or exchange value.

Education for Design: Preliminary Notes on a Systems Approach to Total Human Experience and Purposeful Activity
By Erich Jantsch

The notion of design adopted in this paper embraces the design of all human systems—from the "represented context" of human existence (the world as we experience it) through social systems (civilization) to culture, and from human relations through human instrumentalities (organization with human technological capabilities and aims) to human institutions (represented value patterns). These design tasks, focusing on processes rather than on structures, are structured by a multiechelon (multilevel, multigoal) systems representation and based on total human experience, aiming at coordination, not control, from the top. By analogy to inter- and transdisciplinarity in the realm of "rational" knowledge, interexperiential synthesis is discussed as a mode of dynamically organizing elements of human experience into higher-level designs, and transexperiential synthesis as a mode of organizing all human experience and systems in the framework of an encompassing cultural design. The underlying general inquiry process is viewed as based on the dialectic interaction between appreciative and creative phases, which also holds for scientific, as well as artistic, modes of inquiry; the alleged basic difference between the two is doubted. Education for design ought to focus primarily on the dynamic interexperiential steps between the system levels, i.e., on design of human relations, instrumentalities, and institutions. The nature of learning at these three steps is seen to be the cybernetic evolution of measure, norms, and values, respectively. A few key notions for education, structured accordingly, are discussed, and a number of pertinent "rational" topics enumerated.

1. A Basis of Total Human Experience
The idea of an experimental university focusing on "the design and management of the man-made milieu" constitutes a fortunate formulation insofar as the notions of design and management are addressed here simultaneously. They are, indeed, inseparable if we understand them to signify design for manageable systems, i.e., systems susceptible to continuous self-organization and redesign, and management with the aim of bringing the potentials of continuous redesign into play.

But to envisage something for this task, which might be called a university, tends to build possible traps into our thinking. One of these traps has to do with our being used to thinking that management can be taught, and that this can be done by transferring "rational" knowledge and methods for organizing such knowledge to students, based on some alleged "objectivity" of the subject matter and the transfer process. At present, most curricula in management, whether their scope is business or public affairs, reflect this belief. But they all focus on management *qua* control of a system of given design—a narrow view of management, indeed, and one in which management has been neatly isolated from design.

A second and more serious trap is hidden in the idea that design can be taught. It can be learned, maybe, but taught? Even leaving aside for the moment the issue of "objectivity" of the subject matter, we have to ask the penetrating question whether design is not inherently more than just the organization of "rational" knowledge. The arts are certainly an important aspect of design. Can their contents, modes of expression, and "methods" of inquiry be subsumed under "rational knowledge?" This would certainly imply stretching the notion of "rational" knowledge—possibly not of knowledge in a broader connotation—a bit too far.

However, we may try it with the very broad notion of "experience," in which knowledge is included. We may say that, in dealing with design and management, we are addressing ourselves to *total human experience*. In this way we are gaining a holistic notion, as the word "total" emphasizes. However, we may try to identify important aspects of this holistic notion, in order to become a bit clearer about its scope. Such important aspects may, for example, be considered for inclusion as:

— What we *are* (our biological, genetic, anthropological, psychological, social, and cultural nature—composed of basic, as well as conditioned, aspects).
— What we *know* (through sensation and perception, intellectual and intuitive cognition, and conceptualization and learning).
— What we *feel* (through affection generally, e.g., through compassion, love, and hate—in the interpersonal domain; through resonance and dissonance with our natural and social environment; and through aesthetic appreciation of nature as well as of man-made artifacts, etc.).
— What we *can do* (in terms of basic capabilities, skills, modes of expression, and communication—semiotic modes, but also more generally iconographic modes, etc.).
— What we *want* (on the basis of our drives, desires, values, motives, understanding, etc.).

This explication is not supposed to prefigure any sectorialization in dealing with total human experience or design.[1] Rather, it should give a rough idea of a larger system in which knowledge is embedded. Indeed, any idea of sectorialization breaks down when we realize the extent to which all these aspects are interrelated: what we are expresses itself in knowledge through a variety of scientific disciplines, such as biology, psychology, or behavioral science, but it expresses itself also in what we feel, can do, and want. In similar ways, our feelings translate themselves into what we can do or what we want, but also, through intuitive formulation, into what we know.[2] Bringing into play different forms of expression and communication, variations of what we can do, provides new perspectives not only to what we feel, know, and want, but even to what we are as a culturally conditioned being.

So far, in Western society and its forerunners, considerable emphasis has always been placed on expressing all aspects of experience in terms of knowledge—and neglecting, to an increasing extent, those aspects that resisted such reduction to knowledge. Most of the attempts to develop metalanguages concentrated on numbers (the Pythagoreans), the mathematization of notions (Gottfried Wilhelm Leibniz's *calculus ratiocinator*), and the mechanics (Johannes Kepler's *harmonices mundi*, and René Descartes). Ramon Llull's *ars magna*, developed in the thirteenth century, was perhaps the only noteworthy exception; it tried to design a system of figures and bodies in which all branches of knowledge could be represented, thus searching for a somewhat more holistic approach to experience. The representation of continuously enriched experience through knowledge resulted in a "coherent trend toward optimal organization of the cognitive-semiotic modality"[3]— from the axiomatic model of scientific thought (Greek mathematics and philosophy) through the empirical model (early modern physical science) to the "conceptual" model (the contemporary coalition of the formal and experimental sciences).

It is certainly justified to speak, with Milton Marney and Nicholas M. Smith,[4] of a noetic evolution, in analogy to biological and social evolution. This is even a most significant extension of our concept of evolution, which may be expected to have tremendous consequences for the representation and organization of knowledge. The very idea of interdisciplinarity, understood as a mode of organizing "rational" knowledge toward a purpose,[5] is conducive to an evolutionary, as well as normative, view of the noosphere. But, is this all we want to focus our attention on? Are evolution in the animate world, and evolution and normative design in the organization of society and knowledge, the only dynamic categories that set the stage for our discussion of human design? Should we just continue and redouble our efforts to express all our experience in knowledge equivalents and thereby restrict ourselves to a narrow notion of merely "rational" inquiry?

To prepare ourselves better for an answer to this question, we may take a small informative excursion. Noetic evolution often *follows* changes in meaning, human perception, and thinking as well as changes in feeling, forms of expression and communication, and values. The apparent, almost perfect, synchronization of such dramatic changes in scientific and artistic concepts, as occurred, for example, in the beginning of the twentieth century—with quantum theory and the theory of relativity, psychoanalysis, atonality in music, Cubism and surrealism in painting, functionally oriented aesthetics in architectural and environmental design, etc.—may be viewed as originating in preceding changes in the underlying shared experience and appreciation of the world, in "breathing air from other planets" (Stefan George), in other words, as emerging from a broad-spectrum cultural change in Western society. Because of the dominant position of scientific modes of inquiry in Western civilization, there may be little or virtually no visible phase shift between changes in knowledge and changes in other forms of human experience. But this was not always so. To many systematically oriented people, and to many of the great, nonspecialized scientists, the Bible represents a holistic expression of human experience and includes knowledge of a kind that has only been approached, not attained, by modern "rational" scientific concepts. "Cognitive and affective aspects of meaning always go together," states Jean Piaget.[6] It is only due to the more recent impoverishment of our experience outside knowledge and, in particular, of our capability to respond to other than scientific modes of expression, that in Western society we equate progress with noetic evolution and its implications in *forma* of a technicalized world.

2. THE SCOPE OF HUMAN SYSTEMS DESIGN
We may also take another cut at the question of what inputs can "rational" knowledge alone provide for our design task. The purposeful organization of knowledge ties in with our current (and too narrow) notion of *planning*. But underlying planning is a specific cultural basis, by which the modes and directions of planning—or at least of the part of planning that is subsequently implemented—are conditioned. It is, for example, not difficult to see that the present growth-oriented basis of Western and Western-influenced society cannot accommodate planning with the general objective of global ecosystemic stability.[7] In the same way, planning conducive to anticipative action—instead of short-range reaction—seems to run against our present cultural preoccupations.[8] And yet, these two central ideas appear today as absolutely necessary prerequisites to develop planning into anything useful for social-systems design, even to prevent major global misdevelopments. This we can see very clearly in a rational way, too: it is not the knowledge that is lacking, but the cultural basis that would permit this knowledge to be applied effectively.

Thus, *cultural change* is moving into focus. But much more than with what we know, cultural change has to do with what we are and what our human nature is (which, so far, we are capable of grasping much better through holistic notions, such as archetypes, than through any "rational" knowledge dissected into disciplines), with what we feel and what we want. Recently proposed concepts, such as Charles Reich's "Consciousness I, II, and III,"[9] may be regarded as perhaps somewhat naïve attempts to develop holistic measures of cultural change and break out of knowledge-centered and, in any case, futile modes of interpretation.

The answer to the question posed in the preceding section is really not so difficult: of course, there is not only a powerful incentive to develop a non-sectorial, holistic approach to total human experience—such an approach is even a *conditio sine qua non* for any design involving systems of human living. We must bring into play simultaneously not only what we know, but also:

— What we are (the evolutionary aspects of bio- and sociosphere and their feedback, archetypes, and modification, possibly leading to a "quantum theory" of the psychosocial nature of man).

— What we feel (developing our potential to communicate—not just with our fellow human beings, but in a way also with the whole animate and inanimate world, as great artists do).

— What we can do (exploring possibilities to perceive and structure reality, conceptualize, develop new modes of expression and communication, etc.).

— What we want (exploring the potentials and imperatives of value dynamics, accepting and actively playing out the cybernetic responsibility of man in regulating a world, which, in turn, conditions him, etc.).

Thus, what is proposed here is a *systems approach to total human experience and purposeful activity*. But if we really mean it, we have to try to develop a holistic measure of improvement for total human experience and for human activity, respectively. With such an attempt, we get invariably on slippery grounds, because the question of purpose—the ultimate purpose of human life—enters here. There are both evolutionary and avowed purposes, the latter emerging from a particular cultural context. For example, cognition per se (the pursuit of "truth") was, and still is, one of the avowed purposes of Western-type culture. The result is the predominant orientation of scientific inquiry toward the world as it is, not only in the physical, but also in the psychosocial sciences.[10] "Value-free" science has nothing to contribute to our understanding of the world as it ought to become through our conduct of human activity.

If we stipulate in a general way, that improvement is to be measured along the vector of evolutionary development—a plausible, if not compelling, assumption—we have narrowed down, but not yet fully removed, our difficulties. There are different basic images of human and sociocultural evolution, and it may be instructive to quickly enumerate some of them:

— *Linear development*, usually viewed as a deterministic movement toward a mystical, pressure-free end state, a "paradise." Most of these concepts are presented in apodictic fashion as a Messianic promise, which, in evoking naïve hope, acquires a charismatic quality and, thereby, catches the imagination of parts of the young generation. Apart from theoretic-idealistic Marxism with its economic determinism (for which it needs only a revolution to trigger the one and only possible development toward "bringing the good out" in man in an ultimate classless society, and classical anarchism), one may mention as more recent models those by Johan Galtung[11] (the development toward a "post-revolutionary" individualistic-egalitarian—read anarchistic—form of society, with maximum entropy and the impossibility of any leadership), and, somewhat related to it, by Hasan Ozbekhan[12] (a unidirectional process of "ephemeralization" of thought as well as structure, from the "solid" industrial through a hierarchical and flexible technocratic toward a "fluid" fully participative form of society).

— *Pluralistic linear development,* in which mankind is viewed as starting from a common origin and moving along different ways toward a common ultimate purpose of mankind—like moving from the South Pole along a multitude of meridians toward the North Pole. The famous model of this category was developed by Pierre Teilhard de Chardin,[13] who, significantly, labeled the target of the evolutionary movement "noosphere," although giving this term a very broad meaning.

— *Cyclical development,* a central idea to some Asian religions and cultures.

— *"Spiraling upwards"* toward an ultimate purpose, combining linear and cyclical images of development, or *"spiraling upwards and downwards"* in a cyclical development of a higher order.

It may be readily seen that measures of improvement for the development of total human experience and of human activity, if projected against evolutionary trends, will be vastly different for each of the evolutionary images listed. If entropy increase may be recognized as such a measure (Galtung), so may be the contrary (Teilhard de Chardin). Progress toward an end state may be called improvement, or increased dynamic stability, depending on the type of evolutionary metaphor applied. However, one may be reminded here that, quite generally, in a situation marked by growing instability of social, political, and economic systems, a cyclical development "ideal" gains in esteem today due to the rising awareness of the interdependence and the ecosystemic nature of most of the systems of human living, including the "metasystem" of the whole planet Earth.

The purpose emerging now will probably have to do with the conscious creation of a world, carefully designed as anthropomorphic—by which notion we understand here a world made to human measure—and with the ecosystemic stability of its systems: "speciism," as parts of the American youth would call it in contempt, certainly, but there seems to be no choice. We cannot assume God's position, which probably would be that of a "guarantor"[14] of a natural ecosystem from which we have already departed very far due to the specific psychosocial evolution of mankind. But we can be guarantors of human systems. And we are coming to understand that viable human systems cannot be built in the spirit of the cult of the artificial, as expressed in so much science fiction and "futurology" not geared to meaningful planning, but in the spirit of what perhaps Bertrand de Jouvenel expresses most beautifully: man as the gardener of his planet.[15]

In this context, a holistic measure of improvement for total human experience will have to do with the extent to which man grasps his role as cybernetic actor on the planet Earth and is capable of relating his design capacity, i.e., his capabilities of inquiry as well as creation, to this task. This may come to be expressed, and perhaps even partially quantified, in terms of *balance* between the natural and the artificial—implying also balance between "rational" and other aspects of total human experience. What we would really have to develop here, is a measure for *reason* in the meaning C. West Churchman applies to it: "Reason has to do with the way in which human beings understand what human life means." [16] Some of the pertinent indices may be the extent of inter- and transdisciplinary synthesis under the knowledge aspect, the degree to which new modes of expression and communication increase our chances for freedom, the consistency of our values with the ideal of ecosystemic stability of human systems and the world, and the wisdom of love in this context—a love which is no more a set absolute as it is in Christian thought but is seen in a creative perspective. A holistic measure of improvement for human activity is then, perhaps, the effectiveness of design in integrating human systems toward an overall performance "ideal" of ecosystemic stability, i.e., the effectiveness of both inquiry and creation to that end, with specific indices such as flexibility and modifiability of design, propensity for self-organization and engagement of the members of human systems, together with their active motivation, openness to genuine leadership, i.e., proposals for redesign, etc. Obviously, education for design has to be geared to such measures of improvement.

Finally, we may ask ourselves now what precisely we mean by "human systems." Social systems of various size and scope? They are justifiably moving into sharp focus today when we speak of design, normative planning, political processes, and the like. But human systems, approached on the basis of total human experience, mean much more. They embrace also the notion of cultural systems, underlying our social systems. And *culture, too, is a matter of design*. All great cultures were designed, usually around, and in consonance with, a religion. Under "culture," we understand here (as a minimal notion) a shared appreciative system—"carved out by our interests, structured by our expectations, and evaluated by our standards of judgment" [17]—plus a communication system through which sharing becomes possible. Culture includes a view of the world, through the prism of values, plus modes of bringing the latter into play effectively, sharing and distributing them.

In a static world, culture is translated directly into norms, through religious or ideological ethics. But in a dynamic world, we need a set of flexibly applied regulatory principles, in other words a *policy*.[18] Policies must be designed if we take our systems approach to purposeful human activity seriously and if we adopt the general idea of ecosystemic stability.

Thus, when we speak of designing human systems, we mean, at least, designing the structures and initial states of *social systems*, their *policies* (which implies, as will be pointed out later, the designs of *human institutions*), and the *culture* that gives life to them. But we also mean designing human organizations such as governments, industrial corporations, universities, citizen groups, or PTAs that make up social systems and which, by using technology, arts, and other artifacts, act as *human instrumentalities*—and their roles, which they play in the self-organization of social systems, along with them. And we mean, finally, designing a view of the world, built on our total experience, a *"represented context"*[19] *of human existence*, as well as the *human relations* through which we experience our world. The design task is thus at least six-fold, and the constituent parts of it are, in the end, inseparable. This will be elaborated in more detail in part 4, below.

It is obvious that for many purposes of human systems design we have to take a dynamic and very broad, even global, approach, since social-systems policies have to be consistent among themselves and tie in with a global policy, and cultural contexts have to embrace many social systems, even if we aim for cultural pluralism at world level.

3. SCIENTIFIC VERSUS ARTISTIC MODES OF INQUIRY

The notion of design is often juxtaposed with the notion of analysis, the former being considered the essence of artistic creation, and the latter the essence of scientific research. Scientific and artistic inquiry are traditionally taken as neatly separated, at best sequential, activities: "All science . . . is perfect knowledge of a subject—art the perfect application of this knowledge" (Novalis). The thoughtless repetition of such nineteenth-century categorization in our epoch, when scientific inquiry has long proceeded from empirical to conceptual modes and is about to develop an axiological approach, may surprise—if it were not for the recognition that it is traditional Western cultural bias that again acts here as a trap.

Whereas design is readily credited with giving expression to human values, science generally is not. And when some well-meant enterprises cautiously start to explore possible connections between science and value, they often do it in a half-hearted way as if to avoid pulling us out of the trap, which, to so many scientists, has become a comfortable ecological niche. The Nobel Symposium 14, held in Stockholm in September 1969, carried as its title a slogan of more than thirty years ago: "The Place of Value in a World of Facts." But, as Geoffrey Vickers rightly insists, "the challenging study of our day is . . . rather the nature of fact in a world of values."[20] It is not the values, he claims, that are enigmatic, but the facts. And Churchman views "matter-of-facts" as dull birds, sitting on the beautiful deep blue "insight" birds, preventing them from flying around freely, and even sitting on the insights' eggs until they hatch—not another insight, but a sick resentment. [21]

Both scientific and artistic modes of inquiry may be understood as combining approaches of analysis and synthesis—or, to put it perhaps more aptly, they constitute variations of the *same basic process characterized by a feedback interaction of appreciative and creative phases*. But, if we follow Vickers, who has pointed this out perhaps most clearly, both phases of the process—and this is the *crux*—"change the norms to which they consciously or unconsciously appeal. The appreciative phase changes them by the mere fact of using them to analyze and evaluate a concrete situation; for this may affect both their cognitive and their evaluative settings. The creative phase affects them by presenting new hypothetical forms for appreciation." [22] Wilhelm Furtwängler describes the artistic process in music as "an 'improvisation perfecting itself' . . . in the balancing (*Ausschwingen*) of its proper musical form, and yet in every moment, from the beginning to the end, remaining improvisation." Significantly, he sees the norms of artistic design as being "inherent in the specific psychic process, by which a work of art is represented," [23] i.e., in the creative act, not in the created object. For Vickers, this "evolution of norms is a fundamental form of learning; . . . it provides the criteria not only for ethics and aesthetics but for all forms of discrimination." [24] We may retain for discussion below, in part 5, the notion that evolution of norms is central to education for design, or even to education in the most general sense.

Both scientific and artistic modes of inquiry enrich our knowledge and, more generally, our total experience. Some forms of art, in particular dramatic forms, have often been—and are again today—mistaken as mimesis of reality, a reality that is supposed to be understood and mastered "objectively." But great art of all times has neither mimed nor depicted reality, but changed it, *given reality a new structure*. In our time, the best and most self-evident example is probably modern architecture. But the same may also be shown for the contemporary form of dramatic art that is perhaps most alive, the film. [25] The key moments in Bernardo Bertolucci's 1969 film *The Conformist*—in particular, the scene in the dancing establishment in which the two women break through all conventions and, together, start dancing a daringly erotic dance of such grace and beauty that everybody but the conformist feels joy and applauds and joins in the gay polonaise—break up the rigid reality and show it as open, full of chances for freedom, as changing and changeable. And, the tennis game without the ball at the end of Michelangelo Antonioni's film *Blow-Up* is an expression *in extremis* of the creative interaction between a reality that is not ready-made and unambiguous, on the one hand, and seeing, which is the active shaping of reality, not passive sensation, on the other. An artist, says Ingmar Bergman, acts like radar, receiving the "things" of the world and reflecting them back, mixed with memories, dreams, and images. Nothing but this was also the central theme of Oskar Kokoschka's "School of Seeing at the Internationale Sommerakademi für Bildende Kunst" in Salzburg in the early 1960s.

A difference in the essence of scientific and artistic modes of inquiry can only be suggested by a cultural bias such as the one with which we are living in Western society. According to this bias, science is reflective, but art is not; science is "appreciative" and art is "creative" in a unidirectional sense. Also, a holistic approach is much more appropriate for art than for science. "The artist creates a unity out of a variety of elements," says Immanuel Kant; and Johann Wolfgang von Goethe dramatizes, "In the whole lies the demonic."

Under this Western cultural bias, the scientific mode of inquiry has obviously been distorted far more than the artistic mode. The "creative" phase in the process is not officially acknowledged for the scientific mode of inquiry, which is still largely identified with an empirical or experimental approach. Yet Paul Feyerabend, an ardent critic of scientific inquiry, writes: "The inventions and tricks which help a clever man through the jungle of facts, a priori principles, theories, mathematical formulas, methodological rules, pressure from the general public and his 'professional peers' and which enable him to form a coherent picture out of apparent chaos are much more closely related to the spirit of poetry than one would be inclined to think. Indeed, one has the suspicion that the only difference between poets and scientists is that the latter, having lost their sense of style, now try to comfort themselves with the pleasant fiction that they are following rules of a quite different kind which produce a much grander and much more important result, namely, the Truth." [26]

Still, there now remains chiefly the artistic mode as an example that may be used to resuscitate the "creative" phase in all forms of inquiry—this is also the reason why the hopes placed on approaches which are of more artistic than scientific nature, may be intuitively right. As Paul Feyerabend points out, science has, in general, evaded its obligation to criticize ideology; it attempted to reestablish itself quickly and gain back, to the extent possible, the old security after being shaken up in the early twentieth century. Art has remained much more open and critical. "A critical rationalism setting itself the task to inquire into knowledge and behavior, and improve them through critique, cannot leave aside the contributions offered by the artist." [27]

Normative planning, conceived as a nonmechanistic "human action model" and bringing into play the possibilities, as well as obligations, of man as regulator of his systems, may hopefully develop into such an approach reinforcing the creative phase of inquiry. [28] The thrust of current theory building in planning still points in the direction of increasing "scientification," with the ill-defined "policy sciences" often mistaken for meeting a challenge to build quantified mechanistic models of human systems. But planning, in a broad connotation, is inherently design. By its very nature, it is dynamic, systemic in scope, and based on the feedback interaction between appreciative and creative, exploratory and normative approaches. In dealing with knowledge, it is also inter- and transdisciplinary, focusing on the organization of knowledge for the task of building human systems. But a plan also includes other elements of human experience besides knowledge; its immediate aim is not so much to convince, but to motivate. This is the reason why (as some of the foremost philosophers of science and planning agree) a plan can often be grasped best through a story, which may be regarded as a holistic form of relating a plan, drawing on the resources of artistic expression.

If we rely on planning alone, we encounter a major difficulty. In a period of high-pitched dynamics in almost all human systems, the supreme challenge may be seen in a basic change from reactive attitudes to anticipatory action through long-range planning. But, does this not require a maximum degree of reflective consciousness? Not only must we understand the consequences illuminated by our inquiry with long-range scope, we must also *believe* in them to change our modes of behavior and our courses of action. On the other hand, as a general characteristic, reflection often blocks action, as we certainly experience to an increasing and frustrating extent with our medium- and long-range plans. The only way out of this dilemma would be the building of human systems with more space for nonreflective engagement with life, for spontaneity and joy. But this does not yet answer the question of how to build these systems in other than reflective ways. Nor does that type of spontaneity seem to be the right answer, which is cherished so much by parts of the younger generation today, a spontaneity that expresses itself through a naturalist ideal à la Jean Jacques Rousseau, despises structure, and retreats to raw forms and materials close to the chaos from which they originate (e.g., rock music), and neglects altogether the potentials, the challenge, and the current anthropological necessity of design.

Rather, we may think of a form of "super-experience" through some form of *ecstatis* (which, literally, means "standing outside oneself"). Such *ecstatis* may be recognized as the inner core of primitive rites as well as of antique mysteries and the Greek festival. In our time, Jerzy Grotowski's theater is perhaps the foremost example of such a total and "direct" experience. Allen Ginsberg's chanting sessions and, to a lesser degree, the Sunday services at the Glide Memorial Church in San Francisco, and other church experiments, aim in the same direction. What is approached here, more or less closely, is the ultimate in nonreflective knowledge as evoked by the chorus in Sophocles' *Oedipus at Colonus*:

Not to be born surpasses thought and speech.
The second best is to have seen the light
And then to go back quickly whence we came.

Our human systems have become too complex and too interrelated to be rebuilt in the happy artistic spirit that played such a prominent role in the design of temples, cathedrals, palaces, or whole cities in past times. The mutual enhancement of architecture and natural scenery through form and site in the design of Greek or Japanese temples, the classical harmony of the Baroque abbeys in the Austrian Danube valley—which became the spiritual source for the Viennese school of classical music—or the joy, the melodies which seem to flow from the subtle blending of architectural variation in the design of Salzburg or Florence, are perfect physical expressions of such an artistic spirit in building human systems. But these were systems with human dimensions, systems whose parts could be directly related to human life, functionally as well as aesthetically, mythically as well as anthropologically. Most of the systems we are building today will be inhabited by people with technologically extended capabilities, functions, and desires. The modes of design, appropriate for such systems, will have to be more complex, too. Above all, they will have to combine reflective and nonreflective inputs, planning and intuition, intellect and *eros*. No unidimensional criterion will apply to the assessment of such design tasks—the abominable results of the application of crude economic criteria to large parts of urban America are there to be learned from.

With new complex modes of design, where will the necessary creativity flow from? Will we have to set our hopes, as in some sectorialized modes of inquiry, scientific-conceptual as well as artistic, on *individual creativity*—or should we expect the emergence of some form of *social creativity* as it, to some extent, already characterizes more complex and interdisciplinary approaches to technology? Is individual creativity characteristic of nonreflective design, and social creativity of reflective modes? Will we, thus, have to develop new modes of design so as to ensure interplay between both? This would, indeed, become in itself an important design principle for human systems, implying that cultural, political, social, and generally communicative structures will have to be built into human systems accordingly. We have to allow for chances for individual leadership and imagination in participative systems; we have to design policies so as to ensure the inflow of creative imagination as well as dynamic stability of these systems; and we have to design cultural bases that focus on creativity and communication rather than on egalitarian hedonistic ideals.

4. Inter- and Transexperiential Inquiry

In an earlier paper, I attempted to sketch the organization of "rational" knowledge toward a human purpose by applying the structure of a multiechelon (multilevel, multigoal, hierarchical) system (see figure 1).[29] Interdisciplinarity, in this system, constitutes a mode of organization through the coordination of elements at one level from the next higher level (coordination—not goal setting or control!), and transdisciplinarity extends this concept of organization through coordination over the entire multilevel system. It is perhaps significant that Marney and Smith, for their approach to interdisciplinary synthesis, also use representation by a multiechelon system,

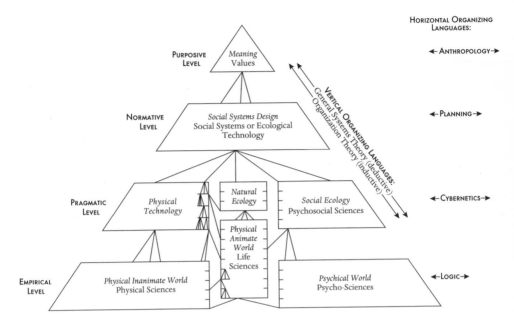

Figure 1: "Rational" knowledge, structured by a multiechelon system. Branching lines between levels and sublevels indicate possible forms of interdisciplinary coordination. [From Erich Jantsch, "Inter- and Transdisciplinary University: A Systems Approach to Education and Innovation," *Policy Sciences* 1, no. 4 (December 1970): 409.]

which seems to be a viable approach to discussing any kind of organization toward a purpose, be it of a physical, social, or noetic nature.[30]

Obviously, structured rationality alone—as much as it can enliven the role of the contemporary university and aid in orienting its basic functions toward a human purpose—has to be considered insufficient for design in a broader connotation. It seems worthwhile trying to extend the multiechelon systems representation to a fuller spectrum of human experience. Figure 2 attempts to sketch such a scheme. In analogy to interdisciplinarity, we may speak here of *interexperiential organization*, characterized by coordination of elements of human experience from the next higher level. Like interdisciplinarity, this type of organization is dynamic in nature, introducing a sense of direction as well as development. Through coordination, the elements of human experience change to some extent in their concepts, substance, direction of development, and modes of expression. We may say, interexperiential organization changes the reality of human existence as we experience it and build it. It ties in with the same dialectic mode of iterative alternation between appreciative and creative phases, which we have identified above with the modes of both artistic and conceptualizing scientific inquiry. We may stipulate now that *design is inherently based on interexperiential organization.* What we also imply, thereby, is nothing less than the recognition that *design changes the reality of human existence in its total context* by changing not only the physical structures of our environment, but also the ways in which

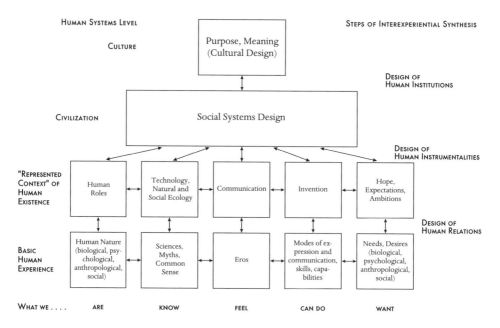

Figure 2: Multiechelon systems representation of total human experience and purposeful activity.

we experience reality, cast it into knowledge concepts as well as into concepts of what we feel, want, and can do, in fact, by changing not only our ways of relating to reality but also ourselves.

Transexperiential organization, in analogy to transdisciplinarity, we would then call the coordination of all systems elements and levels of experience—as is the case within an intact cultural system. We may say, *transexperiential inquiry is a mode of organizing reason*. Cultural design is inherently a transexperiential challenge. The extent to which transexperiential organization may affect systems elements at the lower levels becomes clear if we take a closer look at two notions at the "context of human existence" level in figure 2: as a human role, "man as cybernetic actor in his world" can be coordinated under a cultural heading favoring ecosystemic stability; the Promethean or Faustian notion of *"homo faber,"* which dominates Western culture, cannot. In the same way, it makes a vast difference whether what we want expresses itself as hope or as expectations. As Ivan Illich has pointed out, hope is subject to potential satisfaction, but expectations—at least the familiar "ever rising expectations," which are but "a euphemism for a growing frustration gap, which is, in turn, the motor of a society built on the coproduction of services and increased demand"—engender growth and fixation on "progress" instead.[31] The same interdependence is, of course, even more clearly evident for the interaction between culture and social systems. Daniel Bell speaks of the present "extreme disjunction between the culture and the social structure, the one being devoted to apocalyptic attitudes, the other to technocratic decision making."

Reflecting on the elements at the *level of basic experience* (the empirical level for rationality in figure 1), we realize at once how nebulous most of these forms of basic experience appear in our appreciation, and how ineffectively they are used—if they are used at all—in our rationalized approaches to planning and action. For example, as René Dubos illustrates, we know next to nothing about perhaps the most important aspects of our biological nature, namely the genetic and psychological potentials and limitations of our adaptability to changes in the environment.[32] We know very little, and probably underestimate considerably, the rudimentary instincts still effective in us. In the realm of what we know, we generally exclude myths and common sense, forms of basic experience, which were very important for the earlier phases of mankind's psychosocial evolution. Thanks to Carl G. Jung, we know something about our psychological and anthropological nature and how it expresses itself in "archetypes," but we hardly apply this knowledge to any design purpose except perhaps to advertisements and other forms of "manipulations of the subconscious." In the domain of what we feel, the full meaning of eros in its wealth and all-embracing dynamics has gone out of Western culture—it may still remain with a few artists devoted to a "communion of love," the *Liebesgemeinschaft* between artist and public of which Furtwängler spoke at the end of his life. We have become almost sterile in exploring and developing basic anthropomorphic modes of expression and communication, such as languages, symbols, and icons, forms of artistic expression, sexuality, and even more trivial modes such as fashion, cooking, and celebrating; instead, we have shifted our interest to technomorphic modes of expression and communication, such as computer languages and television. And we are apparently not at all clear about our biological, psychological, anthropological, and social needs and desires. All these basic experiences can be animated, varied, explored, and brought into play—whether consciously or not—through the human purposes implied in a living, dynamically developing culture. "Left alone," many of them are driven to starvation and oblivion.

At the *level of the "represented context" of human existence* (in "rational" connotation the pragmatic level), which stands for the world as we see it through our experience, we find today a pretty uncoordinated conglomerate of human roles, of "wild-growing" technology and social ecology, which fits human systems less and less, of frustrated interpersonal and broken down intracultural communication, of sterile linearity in invention, and of proliferating, cancerous expectations. The picture we gain at this level, may be regarded as typical for a cultural end-phase, for an "end-game" à la Samuel Beckett, not without beauty, but certainly without hope for revival of the same cultural mode. This should not discourage us if we take up the challenge of transexperiential design all the way to the design of a new culture—on the contrary, it may facilitate the task. We are already experiencing a widespread frustration caused by the imposing presence of an almost "autonomously" developing technology. In a transexperiential context, technology will be seen primarily as a way in which man relates to the world, an organization of broad human experience.

The *level of civilization, dealing with social systems design*, and clearly of normative character, reflects what also may be realized in many other ways: that no dissection of the human psyche and human experience is possible at a level where we take a systems approach, bringing together many facets of how we experience reality. The task of designing a civilization, a consistent, if not coherent, ensemble of social systems of all sizes and scopes, has moved into the foreground of interest in planning. This development in our consciousness has been triggered by the decay of the old and the unsatisfactory design of new urban systems, and, in particular, by the devastating consequences that an environmental design, measured against the requirements of the automobile, has had in America. Moreover, it becomes immediately clear that the building of social systems has been increasingly forced into a veritable straightjacket by policies and by a cultural background based on values and criteria focusing on growth and the above-mentioned ever-rising expectations. The example of the automobile, but also of other technologies, which, in the place of human beings, provides the measure for so many of our present "human" systems—television, credit cards, and the deafening beating of the advertisement drum are examples that jump to the mind of the yet "less-developed" European—makes it dramatically clear that social-systems design is a hopeless enterprise without the possibility of simultaneously designing policies (regulating principles) and, indeed, whole new cultures.

The *level of culture*, finally, focuses on the meaning of it all, in other words, on the ultimate purpose of human life. Fuzzy and inaccessible a notion as this may be, man has had remarkable success in pursuing the idea of *creating an anthropomorphic world* to which he could relate meaningfully and which he could develop and shape by bringing his own free will, his humanness, to the task. Art has started in this way as the image forming of a man-related world, and technology goes back to the same origins. Man lives "in a cultural world that is created and maintained by the symbolic transformation of the actual world and the imputation, or projection thereon, of the meaning and values by and for which we live" (D. K. Frank).

To understand better what is anthropomorphic, what is "good" or "appropriate" for man, we need perhaps only to go back to the level of basic experience, to what we are, know, feel, can do, and want. A graphic expression of that would perhaps be a direct feedback link between the lowest and the top levels, bypassing the rest of the system, as it is not shown in figure 2. However, it constitutes the very essence of a multiechelon system, such as the depicted one, that the goals are not imposed from the top (i.e., from "meaning" or from culture), but that the coordination of all goals inherent in the system elements determines the overall goals and direction of the total system. We have only to repeat here Vickers's notion of a shared appreciative system (the backbone of any culture), "carved out by our interests, structured by our expectations, and evaluated by our standards of judgment,"[33] to realize to what extent culture is determined by the "represented context," shaped through the ways in which we experience the world. A new culture will certainly change, to some extent, our basic experience and how we use it to relate to the world; but, at the same time, our basic experience will influence very significantly, too, what we valuate and adopt as a viable cultural design.

Even from a cursory contemplation of the scheme proposed in figure 2, it becomes overwhelmingly clear that social-systems design is not an isolated task in itself, that it finds neither ready-made "building blocks" in the contemporary context of human experience nor a viable cultural basis in Western society—nor perhaps people to design them in a truly interexperiential spirit. Apart from questioning and redesigning both adjacent levels—the context of human existence as well as the cultural basis—design also deals with the steps of interexperiential organization linking the multiechelon levels. It has even to start with them. In order to redesign the "represented context" of human existence, we have to redesign *human relations,* which organize our experience into this context; this constitutes the first interexperiential step from the lowest to the next higher level. And, in order to design social systems, we have to design *human instrumentalities*—organizations with human and technological capabilities, aims, and modes of behavior—along with their corresponding *role patterns.* This constitutes the second interexperiential step, organizing the context of human existence into social systems. And, finally, we have to design *policies* which regulate these social systems over time in such a way that their performance is consistent with the purposes embedded in our design for culture and the meaning it attributes to human life. Such policies are the result of the interplay of *human institutions* in particular *role patterns,* giving life and modifying a tentative first policy design invented perhaps on the drawing board—a theme on which Vickers has written so convincingly.[34] Under human institutions, we understand here the representation of (dynamically changing) sets of values and interests in society, e.g., governing, business (industry), education, health, etc. Designing policies, thus, means inherently nothing else but designing human institutions and their dynamic role patterns. This forms then the final interexperiential step, without which any design for a new culture—which has to be based on the organization of human systems toward the inherent or avowed cultural purposes—will remain a futile exercise.

We may state now that *the overall challenge of human systems design is implicitly the challenge of transexperiential design, involving all levels and all forms of human experience and activity.* And the latter challenge, in turn, is but a reformulation of Churchman's "challenge to reason."[35]

5. EDUCATION FOR DESIGN: A FEW PRELIMINARY GUIDELINES

The challenge formulated at the end of the preceding section constitutes a vast program that needs to be structured. We may ask ourselves, first, what kind of improvement education for design is seeking to achieve in the human "material" exposed to it. For an answer, we may come up with the following two basic notions:

— One principal aim of education is the enrichment of the substance and "effectiveness" of total human experience in the designer. As already stated in part 2, above, this notion may have to do with some balance in the experience of the natural and the artificial, of instinct and culture, as we may also say. Possibly, we ought to add here, but perhaps with a question mark, the designer's awareness of his total experience.

— The second principal aim of education is the enhancement of the designer's capability to organize his total experience toward a purpose through inter- and transexperiential modes of inquiry.

These two aims correspond to different approaches to education for design. One focuses on the substance at the four systems levels in figure 2— an approach which the university has traditionally taken in the realm of "rational" knowledge at the two lowest system levels. The other focuses on the three steps of interexperiential organization between the system levels. There can be no doubt that the latter approach is the more important today, since it enforces a dynamic attitude toward experience and implies an orientation toward a purpose, thus an orientation toward design. Of course, in "bridging" two levels, the substance at these levels may be taken into account as well, but with a view to their "valency" for interexperiential organization toward a higher-level concept. In general, this substance will have to be included to an even much more prominent extent than would be required for "rational" knowledge alone. So much has been done over the centuries to develop science and technology, and so much is constantly present to us, experienced by us, whereas most of the rest of human experience has become "buried beneath the mythology of our culture" (Vickers).

Thus, for the purposes of this paper, we shall consider three basic structures for education geared to the idea of design. These structures focus on:

— The design of human relations as a mode of organizing basic human experience into a "represented context" of human existence.

— The design of human instrumentalities and their role patterns as a mode of organizing the "represented context" of human existence into social systems.

— The design of human institutions and their role patterns as a mode of organizing social systems through policies into culture.

Figure 3 depicts graphically how these three structures are supposed to bridge the system levels of figure 2. In an earlier paper, on a type of univer-

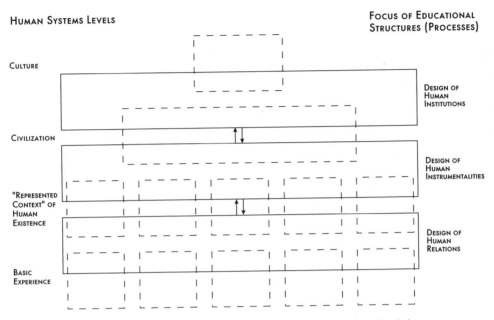

HUMAN SYSTEMS LEVELS

FOCUS OF EDUCATIONAL
STRUCTURES (PROCESSES)

CULTURE

DESIGN OF
HUMAN
INSTITUTIONS

CIVILIZATION

DESIGN OF
HUMAN
INSTRUMENTALITIES

"REPRESENTED
CONTEXT" OF
HUMAN
EXISTENCE

DESIGN OF
HUMAN
RELATIONS

BASIC
EXPERIENCE

Figure 3: Interexperiential educational structures (processes) in relation to the multiechelon system of total human experience and purposeful activity.

sity geared to "rational" knowledge, I proposed a corresponding triplicate structure of discipline-oriented departments, function-oriented departments, and systems laboratories.[36]

In addressing *education for the design of human relations*, we mean not just interpersonal relations, but the general ways in which man relates to his world. This part of education might be viewed as beneficial to *all* people, not just future planners and designers.

Basic to this part of an educational setup for design is Illich's notion that learning has become *measurement*.[37] Whereas primitive man lived in a world without measure and was initiated into reality through rites which made him share mythically in the lives of the gods, learning became a process of measurement in the classical Greek culture. There, man "measured the world with his body and discovered that the world was made to the measure of man." More recently, contemporary man has come to learn "that he is measured by the same scale that can also be applied to things." We may also say, the place of man as a measure for the world has been taken over by technology, whereby not only the familiar scales have been vastly extended, but also quite new scales have been introduced.

But it is not only the scale, it is the overestimation of the very concept of measurement which is put in doubt today in the context of learning. For Illich again, "Men and women who have been schooled down to size let unmeasured experience slip out of their hands. . . . They do not have to be robbed of their creativity. Under instruction, they have unlearned to 'do' their thing or 'be' themselves, and value only what has been made or could be made." [38] The resulting fragmentation of experience has already greatly impoverished human existence and its context. We may even speak of a linearity in the development of experience along a limited number of tracks, the same linearity that has trapped us into patterns of economic and technological growth.

Nevertheless, measure is an important, if not all-encompassing, aspect of design and, depending on what we mean by design, it will be either human measure or the measure of things. In the latter case, consequently, we ought to speak of the design of technological systems *to which man is fitted*, whether the subject of design is a plastic chair, a computer, a moon rocket, or a modern city of a type that may be found in America, but also, more recently, in Germany and in France (the nightmarish La Défense quarter at the edge of Paris, or some satellite towns, which are designed for a quality of life so amiably criticized and ridiculed in Jacques Tati's films). We are virtually drowning in a technicalized environment, which conditions us, but of which, as Marshall McLuhan points out, we are as unaware as the fish is of the water in which it swims.

If we speak of human systems, we mean the use of human measures. This does, of course, not imply throwing technology overboard; rather, it implies fitting technology to human functions and measures. Technology, since its inception, has always been man's instrument to gain leverage (even in the literal sense) in dealing with his environment. But it should not be man giving leverage to some "autonomously" developing technology. At first look, the call for human measures may appear perhaps as retrogression; but we may also understand it as a new phase in a cyclical development, possibly of the "spiraling" type mentioned in part 2, above. The adoption of human measures also implies, quite literally, the acceptance of the *conditio humana*, as it is perhaps expressed most validly in Greek tragedy. There, freedom is gained by *active* acceptance of the laws of the gods, and of the restrictions imposed on man in building his anthropomorphic world. What a great thought for design! Freedom can *only* be gained in this way. Nothing has impoverished our total human experience more than the suppression of this tragic dimension in our lives. Universal boundless love, as proclaimed by Christian thought and more recently by some factions of the "youth culture," cannot do the same—Fyodor Dostoyevsky's parable of the "Legend of the Grand Inquisitor" in *The Brothers Karamazov* states it most dramatically: man cannot be liberated by love alone, he cannot even bear to be free if he is just receiver, not actor. But he can become active only within his boundaries. This is an experience that is central to the idea of design. It ties in with Vickers's notion that "all human liberties are social artifacts, created, preserved and guaranteed by special social and political orders." [39]

As in science, it is also common in human experience more generally to discriminate between "specialists"—the intellectually or the aesthetically gifted, etc.—and to favor a split of education into C. P. Snow's "two cultures," or even into more. This is one of the reasons behind the irrelevance of contemporary education. Any sensitive person living and working with students in Berkeley, for example, will be struck by the intricate interaction of sensuous, emotional, and intellectual experience, which enhances these students' relations to their world so significantly and which is part of what some of us have come to label holistically "the Berkeley experience." But— and this is essential—it is a living experience much more than a formalized learning experience.

Norman Dalkey and Bernice Brown relate an interesting experiment conducted by the RAND Corporation with students from the Los Angeles area. [40] These students were asked to enumerate and rank, by means of a "Delphi" procedure (consecutive rounds of letters with feedback information, to sharpen consensus among the participants who never met physically), first, what they thought were the principal tasks of contemporary university. "Cognitive skills" came out as the winner—no departure from the traditional focus of the university—and "communicative skills" came out at ninth position. Second, the same students were asked to state and rank, in the same way, what they thought should matter most in society in the near future. Of course, "love" came first, "success" only sixth, "dominance" ninth, etc. Asked whether they thought the functions of the university today had anything to do with the society of tomorrow, they answered in the affirmative and requested a rerun of the first "Delphi": now, "communicative skills" came out first, "creativity" came second, and "cognitive skills" slipped down to ninth place, by some irony exchanging its former position with "communicative skills"—a first-rate lesson for design.

It is most significant that these students considered as the two most important foci of the university the principal relations in the domains of what we feel and what we can do, namely, communications and creativity. Yet, these have hardly found a place in higher education. Creativity, under some heading, is taught in management, organizational psychology, architecture, the fine arts—but it is hardly developed in a systematic way, as a means of relating to the whole world. And even less is done for "communicative skills." The interesting experiment of an encounter group for social planners at the University of California at Berkeley was reportedly somewhat disappointing for part of the enrolled students. [41]

Creativity has, inter alia, to do with the development of new modes of expression and communication. In education for the arts, or for architecture, this is sometimes recognized, but hardly in the context of purposeful organization of all forms of basic experience, of a transexperiential approach to design. On the contrary, in a spirit of misunderstood spontaneity, the *l'art-pour-l'art* aspect of inventiveness in expression has come to recent unexpected honors.

In the realm of human relations, we may recognize as a principal approach the conceptual method, in science as well as in art and other forms of experiential synthesis. Richard L. Meier makes the interesting observation that a significant shift has occurred in the background of students who leave conventional tracks and become the brilliant interdisciplinary explorers and innovators: a decade ago, these were still the physical scientists who, in many cases, turned to areas of burning social concern, started to question in a penetrating way both existing human systems and current modes of their design, and attempted to develop some (mostly unsatisfactory and naïvely "scientific") remedy. [42] American think tanks are full of such former physical scientists—the universities had more effective means to curb their interdisciplinary itch. But in more recent years, according to Meier, these innovators who bridge the dissected disciplinary structure and other gaps and "can do everything," turned out to be the students who went through some basic education in architecture. And they are better in dealing with human and social systems, perhaps because they are already provided with a broader spectrum of human experience, and because architecture, after all, deals with human systems design of limited scope.

We are far from a systematic approach to education that would focus on human relations. As an interesting experiment, the undergraduate College of Creative Communication of the University of Wisconsin, Green Bay, may be mentioned here. It blends communication sciences, literature and languages, history, philosophy, and creative and performing arts, but hardly attempts to really integrate them in a purposeful way. Another remarkable approach is taken by the Evergreen State College in Olympia, Washington, which started in the fall of 1971. It permits the largely unstructured exploration of areas of interest by the student himself, aided by the college on the grounds of an individual "contract" set up with the student when he enters. The idea for an international ecosystems university, planned to be located in Marin County north of San Francisco, so far gives particular attention to the "sensibilization" of undergraduate students with the aim of enabling them to relate better to an ecosystemic "represented context" of their world.

Education, geared to the development of human relations, would have to mix formalized and nonformalized learning (living) through novel approaches. The trend among American students to acquire "living experience" in between their formal studies, e.g., by working in the sore spots of the social fabric, and their demands for acknowledgment of such living experiences as part of the formal requirements of higher education, seem to point in the right direction.

Among the "rational" topics, which may, to some extent, be "taught," those are of particular importance which emphasize the dynamic, organizing, and integrating aspects of human relations. They may include, in no particular order:

— Human and environmental biology.
— Psychology and psychoanalysis.
— Behavioral science.
— Critique of empiricism.
— Theory of reflective consciousness.
— Principles of ecosystems.
— Formation of myths.
— Cultural anthropology.
— Semiotics.
— Origin of the arts.
— Forecasting methodology.
— Aesthetics (from the angle of view of natural and anthropomorphic forms and modes of expression).
— Interfaces of human biology, psychology, and aesthetics.
— Communication theory and basic notions of cybernetics.

Education for the design of human instrumentalities addresses perhaps the crucial interexperiential step in our struggle for meaningful design today. Here, Vickers's notion of the essence of education is central: the screen of schemata through which we filter our experience "is itself a product of the process which it mediates and, though tacit, can be developed by consciously exposing it to what we want to influence it." [43] This is just another formulation of the basic idea of an "evolution of norms," which was mentioned as a fundamental form of learning in part 3, above. Christopher Alexander's notion that design is essentially the elimination of "misfit" as the design proceeds by measuring tentative design ideas against tacit criteria, [44] mounts the same horse from the opposite end.

It is not sufficient to set norms and develop approaches to dreaming up social-systems designs that satisfy them. The central theme here is the design of human instrumentalities, of organizations of people, technologies, communication systems, ambitions, expectations, goals, feelings, etc. On the basis of constructive elements available in human beings as well as in the natural and the man-made world—in short, the "represented context" of human existence—these instrumentalities develop their proper roles and, in interaction with each other, *build* and *manage* social systems. The focus of design is thus on the pattern of instrumental (or, in some cases, individual) role playing rather than on the structure of the system in question. Of course, the design of a role pattern will usually imply some idea for an initial structural design of the system and the "positions" of role players as well as the "rules of the game."

Education, focusing on this second experiential step and reaching up to the normative level, will center on the key notion of a *normative method* yet to be fully developed. Such a method would attempt to systematize the inquiry into behavioral and structural norms expressed through instrumental (and individual) role players; it would attempt to translate human and institutional values into behavioral patterns regulated by norms; and it would set a framework for the development of alternative instrumental roles by inquiring into the capabilities, goals, and modes of expression of individuals or human organizations, viewed along with their psychological, technological, anthropological, aesthetic, and social attitudes. The normative method would thus focus on man *together* with his entire world context (including, in particular, also technology)—not in isolation from it. In the realm of "rational" knowledge, we may follow Marney and Smith in their call for innovation in the modification of alternative techniques of systems analysis based on objective-predictive and normative-prescriptive modes of inquiry, a development which has already started forecasting and planning methodology. [45]

Although the involvement with real-life instrumentalities and systems, and their design, appears most essential to the educational tasks in this domain, a few topics may be enumerated, which can be "taught" to some extent, again in no particular order:

— Philosophy of rational creative (nondeterministic) planning and action.
— Innovation processes in the social, political, technological areas.
— Political science (from a normative angle of view).
— Advocacy, persuasion, motivation, self-motivation, coercion, etc.
— Systems approach.
— Organization theory (with special focus on intra- and interorganizational flexibility, and modes of decentralizing initiative).
— Principles of complex dynamic systems (especially social systems).
— Operations research and general approaches to systems analysis.
— Forecasting methodology and theory of strategic planning.
— Social indicators and general experiential indicators.
— Concepts of social-systems effectiveness and cost/benefit.
— Concepts of applied behavioral sciences.
— Decision theory, decision and heuristic models, investment in dynamic systems, etc.
— Decision-making processes, including "nonrational" ones (rites, magic).
— Rational approaches to resource allocation.
— Science, technology, and public policy.
— Policy analysis.

In *education for the design of human institutions and their role patterns*, finally, learning is essentially geared to better understanding or "experiencing" of the evolution of values. As we simulate the dynamic outcomes of bringing into play various value patterns—through human institutions and their role playing—or, in other words the outcomes of various policies for social systems, we try to match them with the purposes embedded in a cultural design. As new patterns of values emerge from this feedback process and are tested against new dynamic designs, we improve our understanding of their effect in role playing.

The key notion for interexperiential synthesis at this step would be an *axiological method*, or value inquiry, which is yet to be built. It should be conceived so as to systematize inquiry about the nature of values represented by various institutional role players, relating them to their behavior, forecasting their implications in an exploratory, as well as normative, sense, and bringing them into play effectively.

The axiological method would focus on the issue of *regulation* of policies for social systems. If we aim at a cultural basis favoring an ecosystemic perspective of regulation, *ecology* in a wide sense becomes the central notion. It embraces physical ecology (including the dynamic interrelationships of both the natural and the man-made milieu), political ecology (which we may base on Vickers's notion of the relations between ourselves as doers and as "done-by"),[46] economic ecology (the relations between production and consumption activities), and the ecology of the appreciative system (again a notion proposed by Vickers, denoting the inner coherence of our systems of values and norms). In short, we are dealing here with the ecology of human institutions for whose regulation man has to assume the responsibility.

The *ethics of whole systems*, Churchman's notion which also may be considered in interaction with the above-mentioned normative method at the second experiential step, may become one of the key elements of an axiological method.[47] It has the potential of accelerating and guiding cultural change as well as providing a driving force for the design of a new cultural image. Ethics of whole systems is a vastly different concept from the traditional ethics of the individual prescribed within intact, static cultures by religions or ideologies. Taking the ethics of whole systems seriously, implies facing moral issues of such dimensions as we normally avoid discussing or even recognizing today. We have only to think of the dilemma into which we get at global level through the population explosion, the simultaneous demands for boosting food production and industrialization on the one hand, and for environmental and resource conservation on the other, and a variety of other imperative demands running counter each other. Any way of dealing with these demands will raise vast moral issues—but so will not dealing with them. We may recognize here a new form of "existential" pressure, comparable perhaps to the former pressures of a hostile environment and of scarcity, which were counterbalanced by man through the design of his cultures, of appreciative systems and means of communication which made it possible to define and secure Man's world against the background of this existential experience—be it through myths, art, or technology. Besides the vast moral issues brought to us by the consequences of social systems dynamics on the basis of Western growth-oriented culture, the pressures mounting within society and mankind due to the increasing gaps and the culturally conditioned phenomenon of ever-rising expectations may also lead to pressures of such an "existential" quality.

The essence of "pedagogy" in this domain is, of course, practical design work in systems laboratories, relating the phenomenology of total dynamic behavior of systems to their spatial and temporal morphology, but also—and above all—to the value patterns in action and expressed through the roles that human institutions assume and play. The aim is a better understanding of, or also better "feeling" for, the interdependence of culture and social systems through policies, and of the possibilities and the feasibility of designing cultures and social systems in a feedback process.

Some of the more "rational" topics that enter here may be considered to include:

— Anthropology of the industrial and postindustrial society.
— Values and value dynamics.
— Ethics (especially ethics of whole systems).
— Philosophy of self-renewal.
— Evolutionary concepts and trends (cosmological, biological, social, noetic, general experiential and value evolution).
— Systems theory (general systems theory, feedback systems, hierarchical systems, etc.).
— Feedback and control theory, cybernetics in general.
— Information theory.
— Dynamic modeling (Systems Dynamics, etc.).
— Theory of normative planning.
— Institutions of industrial and postindustrial society and their changing role patterns.
— Religions and ideologies ("static" policies).
— Holistic interpretation of great art, religious and philosophical systems.

Figure 4 summarizes the aims of education for design at the three inter-experiential steps. The *nature of learning* may be understood now integrally as *triplicate feedback interaction between "loops" built on the same basic principle of iterating appreciative and creative phases.* As we synthesize our basic experience into a "represented context" of our world, measure evolves—human measure in this specific process. As we try to build social systems from this "represented context," norms evolve. And as we aim at synthesizing these social systems and their dynamic behavior into a coherent cultural design, values evolve.

The principal approaches to interexperiential synthesis at these steps provide us also with key notions for education. Again, we find a *triplicate feedback interaction, but here between "loops" built on the common principle of cybernetic self-organization through role playing.* Human relations play such roles in conceptualizing the "represented context" on the basis of human experience; in this process, which we may label *human cybernetics,* the created context acts

Educational Structure	Nature of Learning	Principle Approach to Interexperiential Synthesis
Design of Human Institutions	Evolution of Values	Cultural Cybernetics (Axiological Method)
Design of Human Instrumentalities	Evolution of Norms	Social Cybernetics (Normative Methods)
Design of Human Relations	Evolution of Measure	Human Cybernetics (Conceptual Method)

Figure 4: Focal notions for education at the three steps of interexperiential synthesis.

back on the basic experience and changes it to a certain extent whereby, in turn, the role-playing pattern of human relations changes. In "scientific" terms, this corresponds to the familiar conceptual method. The same basic process goes on at the step of human instrumentalities, where we may call it *social cybernetics*, and where the "represented context" and the tentative design of social systems are interlinked, and change, in a process kept in motion by the role-playing of human instrumentalities. In "scientific" terms, we may hope here for a normative method, which has yet to be perfected. And finally, a process, which may be called *cultural cybernetics*, characterizes the design of cultures in a feedback loop with social systems and their policies, animated by the role playing of human institutions. The corresponding methodological approach may be called axiological method.

The overall task of designing human systems may thus be viewed as focusing mainly on the design of processes rather than structures. The methods to be applied are, therefore, cybernetic rather than heuristic. Of course, the design of such feedback processes in the human, social, and cultural sphere involves the design of structures insofar as an initial system state and an initial role-playing pattern have to be introduced, if they are not given by what exists— but none of these structures is supposed to remain fixed. It has to be kept in mind that the structures of which we are speaking here are primarily structures of total human experience at various levels and may be coupled with physical structures only incidentally. Physical structures, of course, tend to restrict the dynamics and full spectrum of possibilities of the processes.

In the form of a side remark only, it may be mentioned here that the proposed perspective of design entails enormous consequences for methodological development in forecasting—which has already found a formulation, in cybernetic terms, as evolving in a "loop" of exploratory and normative modes[48]—in planning, policy design and analysis, political science, law, economics, sociology, history, etc., but even more so in interdisciplinary approaches to human systems. Some branches of psychology, anthropology, and linguistics are already well advanced in exploring the cybernetic perspective, mainly in the realm of what we have labeled here human cybernetics. Whereas human cybernetics is thus halfway established, and the challenge of social cybernetics has found the response of some of the best interdisciplinary minds today, there is little awareness yet of the potentials and the necessity of cultural cybernetics.

As a backbone of the total and fully transexperiential approach to design one may conceive a *comprehensive normative theory*, which has yet to be developed. Marney and Smith sketch the elements of such a normative theory for the domain of "rational" knowledge only.[49] There, it would include the following five distinct classes of criteria: formal criteria (concerned with syntactical well-formedness and logical consistency); empirical criteria (concerned with conceptual reproducibility and testability); pragmatic criteria (concerned with interpretability and practicability); aesthetic criteria (concerned with cybernetic elegance or simplicity); and evolutionary criteria (concerned with meliorative trends or viability, and stable-optimal organization). From this enumeration, it becomes clear to what extent a general normative approach to total human experience would extend these "rational" concepts. Whereas we may retain the classes of criteria, adding perhaps ethical criteria, the matter of concern for these criteria will change significantly if we extend the scope of inquiry. Certainly, logical consistency, reproducibility, interpretability, elegance, etc., are then no longer essential. Instead, we may tentatively formulate:

— Formal criteria will be concerned with anthropomorphic form and measure.
— Empirical criteria will be concerned with comprehensiveness of human experience involved.
— Pragmatic criteria will be concerned with inter- and transexperiential coordinability.
— Aesthetic criteria will be concerned with systemization (consonance? consistency? harmony? or, generally, composition?) of the organization of total human experience.
— Ethical criteria will be concerned with the improvement of whole human systems.
— Evolutionary criteria will be concerned with meliorative trends and viability.

Most of what I have formulated earlier on the general characteristics and aims of a process of higher education geared to inter- and transdisciplinary inquiry remains valid in the extended framework of education for design—and even more so now.[50] The interexperiential learning processes—through the evolution of measure, norms, and values, respectively—cannot be the subject of teaching in the traditional sense, nor of training in the use of methods. The learning processes in school and in real life have to become identical, they have to be experienced themselves in order to become part of human experience. Whether the instrumental form in which this can be achieved best will be called a university or something else, and whether it will even faintly resemble the contemporary university or not, is of secondary importance. In any case, such an instrumentality will be part of human and social life—it will be political and an instrumental role player itself. And education of this scope, in general, will certainly play an institutional role of considerable importance in our search for viable cultural designs.

As in the transdisciplinary university, students may focus on one of the proposed educational structures only, i.e., on one step of interexperiential synthesis, or may go through two or all three of them. They may "fluctuate" between them, for example experimenting with the design of "soft" institutions and policies, and interspersing this with studies in the design of "hard" instrumentalities or elements of the "represented context," such as technology. Industrial designers of the traditional type may stay within the "human relations" section, whereas architects, city planners, and social planners may focus on the "instrumentalities" step, and some of them on the "institutions" step. For all of them, the proposed approach to education may offer a broader basis of human experience and enhanced capabilities to apply it to design.

What is missing altogether in the present picture is the cultural designer, focusing on human institutions and their roles. Yet without him, even the best-motivated and most sophisticated efforts of interexperiential design will be rendered futile. Only transexperiential synthesis, the coordination of total human experience and all forms of human systems, is capable of providing that sense of purpose and meaning which characterizes a viable culture. As I have stated already, design is inherently a transexperiential challenge: if we fail to develop our responses to this challenge, above all in education, human experience and human systems will become ever more fragmented and further removed from a reality which appears to us as increasingly "inhuman."

Notes

1. Psychological schools have concentrated up to now on such a sectorialization, as C. West Churchman discusses critically in his book, *Challenge to Reason* (New York: McGraw-Hill, 1968): 97; even Carl G. Jung tried, in his book, *Psychological Types* (Bollingen Series XX, Vol. 6, Princeton University Press, 1971), to break the human mind up into four separable functions: thinking, intuition, sensation, and feeling.

2. Some of these interrelations have been discussed in a very stimulating way in Martin Krieger, "Planning and Feeling: Advice Giving in a Sexualized World," Center for Planning and Development Research, University of California, Berkeley, 1971.

3. Milton Marney and Nicholas M. Smith, "Institutional Adaptation, Part II: Interdisciplinary Synthesis," Research Analysis Corporation, McLean, Virginia, 1971; to be published in Richard F. Ericson, ed., *Toward Greater Social Relevance*, Proceedings of The George Washington University Program of Policy Studies in Science and Technology (New York: Gordon and Breach, 1972).

4. Ibid.

5. Erich Jantsch, "Inter- and Trans-disciplinary University: A Systems Approach to Education and Innovation," *Policy Sciences* 1, no. 4 (December 1970): 403–428.

6. Jean Piaget, in Harold A. Abramson, ed., *Problems of Consciousness* (New York: Josiah Macy Jr. Foundation, 1953): 145; quoted in Geoffrey Vickers, "A Theory of Reflective Consciousness," unpublished paper for the Burg Wartenstein Symposium, No. 40, on "The Effects of Conscious Purpose on Human Adaptation," Wenner-Gren Foundation for Anthropological Research, July 16–25, 1968: n. 5.

7. For the most interesting discussion of these aspects, in concrete terms, see Jay W. Forrester, *World Dynamics* (Cambridge, Mass.: Wright-Allen, 1971). Industrial growth and increase in food production—avowed objectives of almost all parts of contemporary mankind—are demonstrated as the principal factors giving rise to future instabilities of catastrophic dimensions in the global system.

8. The most penetrating discussion of this aspect may perhaps be found in Donald N. Michael, *The Unprepared Society: Planning for a Precarious Future* (New York: Basic Books, 1968).

9. Charles Reich, *The Greening of America* (New York: Random House, 1970).

10. This aspect is critically discussed in more detail in Jantsch, "Inter- and Transdisciplinary University."

11. Johan Galtung, "On the Future of Human Society," *Futures* 2, no. 2 (June 1970): 132–142.

12. Hasan Ozbekhan, guest lecture in the framework of the lecture course "Technological and Environmental Forecasting," Department of City and Regional Planning, University of California, Berkeley, April 16, 1971.

13. See, for example, Pierre Teilhard de Chardin, *The Future of Man* (London: Collins, 1964).

14. The notion of a "guarantor" of a system is elaborated in Churchman, *Challenge to Reason*.

15. Bertrand de Jouvenel, *Arcadie: Essai sur le mieux-vivre* (Paris: Futuribles/SEDEIS, 1968).

16. Churchman, *Challenge to Reason*.

17. Geoffrey Vickers, *Freedom in a Rocking Boat: Changing Values in an Unstable Society* (London: Allen Lane/Penguin Press, 1970): 98.

18. The term *policy* is widely misused and underrated. We apply here the same meaning as formulated in Vickers (ibid.: 125): "Policy (consists) in regulating a system over time in such a way as to optimize the realization of many conflicting relations without wrecking the system in the process."

19. The term *represented context* has also been proposed by Vickers (ibid.: 82f.).

20. Geoffrey Vickers, "The Tacit Norm," unpublished paper for the Burg

Wartenstein Symposium, No. 44, on "The Moral and Esthetic Structure of Human Adaptation," Wenner-Gren Foundation for Anthropological Research, July 19–28, 1969: 19.

21. C. West Churchman, "Birds of a Color," mimeographed fairy tale, Berkeley, California, 1971.

22. Vickers, "The Tacit Norm": 15.

23. Wilhelm Furtwängler, *Ton und Wort* (Wiesbaden: Brockhaus, 1954): 79.

24. Vickers, "The Tacit Norm": 2.

25. "Wirklichkeit: Chancen sur Freiheit," *Neue Zürcher Zeitung*, Foreign edition, no. 304 (November 6, 1971): 49.

26. Paul K. Feyerabend, "Problems of Empiricism II," in R. Colodny, ed., *The Nature and Function of Scientific Theories: Essays in Contemporary Science and Philosophy* (Pittsburgh: University of Pittsburgh Press, 1970): 278.

27. Paul K. Feyerabend, "Theater als Ideologiekritik: Bemerkungen zu Ionesco," in E. Oldemeyer, ed., *Die Philosophie und die Wissenschaften, S. Moser zum 65. Geburtstag* (Meisenheim/Glan: Anton Hain, 1967): 408f. See also idem, "On the Improvement of the Sciences and the Arts and the Possible Identity of the Two," in Robert S. Cohen and Marx W. Wartofsky, eds., *Boston Studies in the Philosophy of Science, III* (New York: 1968).

28. For a discussion of various aspects of normative planning, see: Erich Jantsch, ed., *Perspectives of Planning* (Paris: OECD, 1969), especially Hasan Ozbekhan's contribution, "Toward a General Theory of Planning": 47–155.

29. Jantsch, "Inter- and Transdisciplinary University." For the general mathematical theory of multiechelon systems, see M. Mesarovic, D. Macko, and Y. Takahara, *Theory of Hierarchical Multi-level Systems* (New York: Academic Press, 1970).

30. Ibid.

31. Ivan Illich, "The Dawn of Epimethean Man," paper contributed to the conference "Technology: Social Goals and Cultural Options," Aspen, Colorado, August 29– September 3, 1970, mimeographed: 3f.

32. René Dubos, *So Human an Animal* (New York: Scribner's Sons, 1968).

33. Vickers, *Freedom in a Rocking Boat*: 98.

34. See, for example, Geoffrey Vickers, *Value Systems and Social Process* (London and New York: Tavistock Publications and Basic Books, 1968), and ibid.

35. Churchman, *Challenge to Reason.*

36. Jantsch, "Inter- and Transdisciplinary University": 421f.

37. Illich, *Dawn of Epimethean Man:* 6.

38. Ivan Illich, "Schooling: The Ritual of Progress," *The New York Review* 3 (December 1970): 22.

39. Vickers, *Freedom in a Rocking Boat*: 184.

40. Norman Dalkey and Bernice Brown, verbal communication to the author, 1969.

41. Leonard Duhl and Alan Malmanoff, "The Use of Self in Social Change," Seminar, Department of City and Regional Planning, University of California, Berkeley, 1970–71.

42. Richard L. Meier, verbal communication to the author, 1971.

43. Vickers, "The Tacit Norm": 7.

44. Christopher Alexander, *Notes on the Synthesis of Form*, (Cambridge, Mass.: Harvard University Press, 1967); quoted in ibid.

45. Marney and Smith, *Institutional Adaptation, Part II*: 45.

46. Vickers, *Freedom in a Rocking Boat.*

47. Churchman, *Challenge to Reason.*

48. Erich Jantsch, *Technological Forecasting in Perspective* (Paris: OECD, 1967). The terms *exploratory* and *normative forecasting* have been proposed by Dennis Gabor.

49. Marney and Smith, *Institutional Adaptation, Part II*: 45.

50. Jantsch, "Inter- and Transdisciplinary University."

Notes for Discussion on Future Communities
By Suzanne Keller

As I read the Project Working Paper circulated in November, I think it is asking one and the same question in a variety of ways: how to think about and imagine alternative possibilities for the world taking shape.

Such alternatives will be increasingly necessary if we are to solve the massive problems confronting us in every area of life. It is widely agreed that humanity today is caught between two social orders, one on the way out, though not yet past, and the other on the way in, though not yet here. And, while people argue about the meaning of the changes ahead, there is little disagreement as to their pervasiveness and significance.

I go along with the document's skepticism that science will save us. As currently organized, scientists are far more interested in analyzing and unraveling than in imagining and looking ahead. By design or default they, therefore, leave the future to others. The Universitas Project, in its effort to develop new perspectives and new idioms, is thus responding to a significant need.

Since Universitas will not be created nor grow in a vacuum, the larger context within which it will come to life is not without interest. This includes old institutions and vested interests, as well as newer developments in art and life. I will concentrate on some of these. In particular, I am concerned about the kinds of communities now taking shape, because if we "concentrate on making a community structure which is more liveable," as Paul Goodman asserted recently, and if we succeed, "education will take care of itself."[1]

People appear to be hungry for some kind of genuine community, something that will bind them to life and to each other in a less mechanical, less materialistic way. This is true not only of youthful idealists but of the middle-aged as well. As a member of an interdisciplinary team at Princeton, I have recently had occasion to look closely into one of the newly planned communities that are springing up throughout this country. And no matter where one looks and which aspects one examines, the quest for community is plain to see. People buy houses, but the security and shelter they anticipate goes far beyond the confines of gates and gardens. They rush to swimming pool and bridle path, but it is more than recreation that they hope to find there. Such words as purpose, value, meaning, and direction come up spontaneously in their own conversations, in their own, more or less, hesitant attempts to put their intangible longings into words.

The quest for community will be with us for a long time to come. It is a quest that will engage all who plan to live in communities and all who try to plan them. In what follows, I will try to spell out some of the ways in which communities are changing and how the future will impinge on them.

The first point to note is that while most of us are aware of, if not reconciled to, some of the dramatic changes in technology and lifestyles in store for us, we seem to exempt communities from these changes. True, we express interest and concern in the burgeoning population of the planet and how to control it, but we do not give equal time to the habitats that will contain it. One does, of course, hear and engage in debates about whether it is to be extended megalopolis or womblike beehive, metropolis or cluster of small towns, but this still assumes the territorial community as the basic prototype. But, if we are to believe some of the current trends, we may well have to examine this notion of territoriality and of communal self-containment to which it is implicitly linked.

There are those who argue that we must be prepared for some basic changes in these communities of place that we have come to take for granted. When I say we, I mean the world, the planet, even though I am aware that not every country will be directly caught up in these developments. But just as the religion of industrialism swept over the world, irrespective of where one's own small part, grandly called sovereign state, stood with regard to it, so will these new developments enlist the interests, if not the energies, of the entire globe.

Today, most new communities are being designed with the job in mind, especially for the male breadwinner. Access to daily employment is taken for granted, despite some forays into shortened workweeks. But if the nine-to-five job routine will give way to more varied and variable work schedules— which might be grouped by months or seasons—then the linkage between job and residence will be less important. If we are to phase out the unpleasant, routine, and inhuman tasks more and more through automation or reduce the compulsory activity called work to a few days a week or a month, then jobs could be virtually anywhere in relation to one's home base. If, in addition, more and more people will be engaged in nonroutine and individuated work, then time schedules will become even more flexible and less dependent on a fixed location than is the case today.

The flexibility and fluidity required may need a very different domestic organization, and may force us to rethink not only the idea of a dawn-to-dusk work rhythm but the very idea of settledness. As I see it, the mobility of people and ideas will increase enormously in the decades to come and the nomadic impulse already characteristic of sailors, traveling salesmen, and the jet set will be expressed by ever-widening sectors of the public. Instead of returning to a single home base from one's travels one may take one's home—suitably reduced to bare essentials—with one wherever one goes. Hence, we ought not to proceed on the assumption that we will always need a fixed territorial organization in which to contain the round of life. Such containers are bound to be increasingly inadequate as diversity and heterogeneity increase and as permanent residence in a fixed territory becomes only one among several patterns. One need only watch the mass exodus of vacationers each summer and their improvised settlements along seashore and highway to know that the nomadic era is upon us. One need only look at job mobility, employment transfers, residential exchanges, and the like to note that even in the area of work routines, mobility is a pervasive feature of our time.

TELECOMMUNICATIONS IN OUR FUTURE

It seems hard to realize that once upon a time human communication depended largely on person-to-person or face-to-face contact. This had a number of important consequences, not the least being that it reduced the radius of connections within and between settlements and fostered a dependency on the physically contiguous and proximate, which survive in our fantasies as the earmarks of "true" communities.

In contrast to that bygone era, we now have advanced techniques, which extend us in space and time and enable us to transcend these communities of place. Despite our dazzling innovations, however, we are not yet entirely free from our ancient, historic dependencies on the local and the physically near. In fact, one of the unanswered questions is, What is meant by far and near once human yardsticks are displaced by electronic ones?

Another question of interest, and one equally little investigated for all our talk about innovations and discoveries in telecommunications, concerns the interpretation of technical and human communications networks. Note how the telephone, a primitive forerunner of future modes of contact, is, at one and the same time, an impersonal and neutral medium to be used by any- and everyone as well as a personal intimate channel for transmitting powerful messages of love and hate. One wonders just how much of the intended message gets through and with how much of its intended effects. As a dyadic (two-party) channel, the telephone would seem to be subject to all or most of the ills of the dyad, such as misunderstandings, interruptions, and disruptions due to problems at only one end of the line.

In the future, telecommunications will create new patterns of domesticity, friendships, and association. As Martin Luther once said, he was in the world but not of it, so we will be in a given area but not necessarily, and certainly not exclusively, of it. This mobility of mind and spirit will have far-reaching implications for social solidarity, territorial loyalty, and networks of association and service.

The territorial imperative is so entrenched in our way of viewing the world, however, that we tend to interpret everything through its lens, thereby missing the new dimension arising in the midst of older realities. Hence, when newcomers to a community miss their former friends and neighborhoods, this is generally interpreted in physical terms, in the sense of areas left behind, contacts broken, distances intervening. The idiom is physical and spatial. But, already, the telephone is able to dispel this distance in important respects, and, in the future, holography and the like will make it possible to be visually and aurally close to people no matter what the distance.

Of the two basic modes of creating contacts between human beings and their worlds, one brings the person to the experience and the other brings the experience to the person.[2] We have lived by the first, and we are moving toward the second—the electronic encounter with the world. This should enable us to experience the world in a far less fragmented manner than heretofore, and may restore for us the wholeness and richness destroyed by the first industrial revolution. Moreover, once it is possible to transcend physical and geographic boundaries, location will become less relevant to social and economic decision-making. Decentralization, with its dispersion of people and activities and its saving of time, money, and effort, will create new spatial forms.

The communications revolution ahead will also result in a reorganization of such familiar landmarks as the office, the department store, the supermarket, and other central city facilities now located on expensive land not always within easy reach. Instead of people having to seek out these services, they will be brought *to* them, and their location will then become irrelevant. These and other innovations made possible by expanded telecommunications—such as computer medical diagnoses, long-distance socializing—will transform communities, as we know them. It should also transform their basic design.

Despite these possibilities, however, new communities are still being designed with paramount attention being paid to their physical-spatial features, physical accessibility, some effort at comprehensiveness, and the pedestrian ideal. All too many designers still think solely in terms of territories divided into stable zones of activity, with people going to and from work, to and from shopping, and to and from amusements—this at a time of extensive telephone commuting, when the majority of the population does not stay put anywhere for very long, either in body or in spirit. Future communities must, therefore, be designed for mobility as well as for stability. Telecommunications will help forge "telecommunities."

One of these "telecommunities" might be called the spontaneous community, created by the emergence of sudden or unforeseen needs and disbanded when these have been satisfied. In one study by Sam Gaertner and Leonard Bickman, the myth of the callous urbanite was effectively dispelled by charting the willingness of strangers to extend help requested over the telephone to other strangers. Callers would dial a number at random and represent themselves as stranded on a highway with a broken-down car and without another dime, this one having been used to call the present number in the hope of reaching a garage for help. Having told their sad tale, they then asked the listener if he would be kind enough to dial the correct number for them. Quite a number received help in this way.[3] Another study compared the readiness of people to permit strangers to enter their homes to make a telephone call. Comparing cities with small towns, it could be demonstrated that small-town residents are indeed inclined to be more trusting and helpful. Of interest here is the extent to which such spontaneous communities can be created virtually instantaneously by use of telecommunications. Presumably, we should see a rise in such spontaneous and short-lived "telecommunities" in the future.

Another type of community created by telecommunications might be called the altruistic community. In a summary and codification of community responses to disasters, Allen Barton concluded that one of the crucial ingredients for the emergence of a communal helping hand was the existence of central communications nets, without which good intentions, available resources, rescue efforts, and information monitoring were well-nigh impossible. Poorly coordinated communications systems can greatly, perhaps irrevocably, set back the rallying and recovery of a community stricken by a disastrous fire or flood. And here, accessibility to existing equipment, as much as the availability of such equipment, proves crucial. "For most organizations, the loss of telephone service is literally disorganizing."[4] But such loss of accessibility is precisely what follows upon the panic that clogs highways or telephone connections in times of crisis.

Barton goes so far as to make the "ability of modern societies to create an emergency social system" rendered necessary by calamities like fires, earthquakes, or air raids, "uniquely dependent on long range instant communications."[5] And, in outlining a "model of the therapeutic community responses," communications play the expected crucial role in activating "mutual help in situations of collective stress."[6] These include the formal and informal channels of communications as well as the victims' willingness to communicate about their sufferings and the non-victimized members' knowledge of the extent and nature of the catastrophe.

Further proof of the importance of electronic accessibility, rather than of physical proximity, to events comes from studies of collective panic and crisis situations. When calamity strikes on planes, ships, or in nightclubs, access to communications media can become as, or more, crucial as proximity to exits. For one thing, an anxious crowd needs to be supplied with information and reassurance, without which it readily panics. But there is more to it than that. The number of channels is also crucial. When crisis strikes in an enclosed space, it is apparently better to have no exits at all than to have too few exits. One overloaded or inaccessible channel of contact or escape—be it a fire exit or a telephone line—may set off the very panic it was designed to prevent. Where there are no exits at all, so also no hope for survival is generated. Where there are insufficient or inadequate channels, however, hope and desperation, the chance for escape and the terror at being trapped, exist side by side and the single road to life then, paradoxically and tragically, may become the sure path to death.

In view of these findings, it would seem desirable to plan adequate communications systems in new communities so as to prepare them for eventual emergencies. It is not at all certain that we are building such safety factors into the communities now getting under way. We are still not truly convinced that we are about to enter an age of telecommunications, where a clogged telephone channel may be as, or more, serious as a jammed-up highway or a blocked exit in a burning building.

In a famous essay, Melvin M. Webber summarized some of the developments we have discussed as our moving from communities based on territoriality and proximity to "communities without propinquity." These would replace the current place-dependent communities by breaking down the territorial confinement of past communities. Webber does not specifically analyze the role of telecommunications in the formation of such communities, but it is obviously closely bound up with developments in communications.[7] Surely the radius of interconnections is bound to increase the radius of interest and cohesion in the global village of tomorrow and affect human behavior in ways still largely unexplored.

According to many serious observers, the society of tomorrow will be a society of communications, moving information and images as we now move people and goods. "We are," writes Robert Theobald, "moving from an order based on transportation and production to one based on communication, in which decisions and their results become simultaneous."[8]

I do not wish in this brief foray into futurism to ignore or minimize unforeseen problems that the electronic society may usher in. Some feel that we already suffer from communications overload both in terms of what existing channels can carry and what our nervous systems can process. But this reflects, in part, the superimposition, instead of the incorporation, of the new on the old. It attests to our unwillingness or our inability to develop new concepts and designs for living. And yet, it is imperative that we take a fresh look at old truths whose validity we have come to take for granted. Among these are the values of "settling down" in one place and into one life routine; of owning things; of having one occupation, one house, and one spouse for life; in short, of all the idols of domestication: permanence, security, familiarity, and continuity. As John McHale suggests in a recent article, instead of owning, we will be renting things, and we will emphasize the temporary and the transitory. A whole ethos of personal possessiveness—of land, house, car, and kin—will thus disappear and with it a whole chunk of human history.[9]

This will compel a revision of codes bequeathed to us from the agricultural era of history. Our concern with territorial rootedness, with home and homestead, will diminish, as other values take up center stage. This is not to say that each and every individual will adopt the new, but only that the culture will incorporate the tendencies toward speed, diversity, changing scales, and increased self-regulation at every scale, because cultures are connected to life, and that is what life will be like.

McHale also emphasizes the shift to new work patterns in round-the-clock cities, thereby breaking the artificial and, by now, superfluous dawn-to-dusk rhythm of agricultural and early industrial societies. And, he foresees the coexistence of many alternative types of communities and settlements, each presumably with its own characteristic mix of new and old communications media. Among these new communities, he singles out the mobile and flexible instant city; the university city which is inconceivable without advanced telecommunications; the festival city; recreation and museum cities; and experimental cities where new lifestyles may be explored by young and old.

And, as individuals do less routine machinelike labor and are freed from many traditional constraints on their time and talents, many more will be able to participate in the quest for and creation of community.

But along with the new possibilities and opportunities will come new problems. Self-management is one, cohesion and social cooperation are others. As standardization recedes in favor of diversity and individuation, what will create the cohesion necessary for concerted action? Whose values will prevail? How much differentiation can a social aggregate afford?

Current proposals for new communities do not raise such questions. They are still, by and large, standardized in their basic blueprint and in their image of the good life. To give just one example, they give the impression that everyone's family is pretty much like everyone else's. It consists of a father, a mother, and young children, living in a home of their own, with mother keeping the house and father keeping the job as a matter of course. And if there are families where this is not the case, they are automatically considered unfortunate or immoral. This despite the fact that at any given time no more than one half of American families are standard in this sense, and all families vary much more than we seem to realize in their tastes, habits, and ambitions. What will happen to this concept of the family if it becomes simply one among different forms of togetherness in the future? What if people desired to live in a modern version of the Indonesian longhouse or adopt the extended household of medieval times? Where, in the self-contained dwelling nuclei of the planned community, is there room for such innovations?

In this connection, we should not forget that in many, perhaps most, new communities, one common problem concerns the dissatisfied young. Despite the new houses, the new swimming pools, and the excitement of exploring a new setting, they are bored; there is not enough for them to do, and their parents' dream of mobility to suburbia is not their dream. Perhaps they are more aware than their elders of the new forces at work and the new world taking shape. Perhaps, weaned on television and transistors, they are already individually attuned to "communities without propinquity," to the non-place realm. And even if this is not everyone's cup of tea, and some of us would console ourselves that that day is a long way off, we still should not assume that it will never come.

Universitas

Many of the changes touched upon in this brief essay must affect the way we think about design issues—whether these concern the creation of a building, a settlement, or a new institution. New designs for learning need new designs for living, which is why I focused on new kinds of communities ushered in by the electronic revolution.

And, just as community planning is not, to my mind, taking sufficient note of non-territoriality, so I had the impression that the prospectus on Universitas was also not clear on this point. Should the activities it will comprise be in one place, or should it span many places in a far-flung communications network? Perhaps the two should be combined in some way and be territoriality blended with mobility in the manner of a ship, a hotel, or a traveling circus—in which the frame is continuous but the scenery or personnel is ever changing. Or, perhaps the frame will shift and the personnel will stay constant. In either case, the accent will have to be on improvisation, on open-endedness, and on spontaneity. The emphasis should be on learning rather than teaching in a context of active confrontation with life. This is why Universitas cannot be discussed in the abstract, apart from Communitas, which will nourish it. Life and learning, separated for too long, must be joined once again.

Notes

1. Robert W. Glasgow, "An Interview with Paul Goodman," *Psychology Today* 5 (November 1971): 62–65, 90–96.
2. Don Fabun, *The Dynamics of Change* (Englewood Cliffs, N.J.: Prentice Hall, 1967): 1–30.
3. Stanley Milgram, "The Experience of City Living," *Science* (March 13, 1970).
4. Allen H. Barton, *Communities in Disaster* (New York: Doubleday / Anchor Books, 1970): 170.
5. Ibid.: 171.
6. Ibid.: 218.
7. Melvin M. Webber, "Order in Diversity: Community Without Propinquity," in Lowdon Wingo, ed., *Cities and Space* (Baltimore: Johns Hopkins Press, 1963): 23–54.
8. Robert Theobald, *An Alternative Future for America* (Chicago: Swallow Press, 1968): 140.
9. John McHale, "Future Cities: Notes on a Typology," *Ekistics* 28, no. 165 (August 1969): 86–91.

Art and Ecological Consciousness
By Gyorgy Kepes

The forces of nature that man has brought under a measure of his control have again become alien; they now approach us menacingly by avenues opened by science and technology. This does not mean that we have freed ourselves from nature's old scourges: earthquakes, volcanic eruptions, floods, and other "acts of God." The recent tidal wave in the Bay of Bengal left over half a million dead. What we face now are destructive forces of a completely new kind—man generated, cumulative, and of almost cosmic proportion.

A wildly proliferating man-made environment has shrunk living space, dimmed light, bleached color, and relentlessly expanded noise, speed, and complexity. We have contaminated our rivers and lakes through the unrestricted dumping of human and industrial waste, and poisoned our sky, sea, and land with radioactive waste. We have shaved barren our mountains, hills, and fields, and exterminated their birds, fish, and beasts. And, it is not only the destruction of the physical environment that is involved.

Aldous Huxley's comment that by mistreating nature we are eliminating the basis of half of English poetry expresses a deep truth. The world around us—the mobile, luminous richness of the sky, the infinite wealth of colors and shapes of animals and flowers—provides the essential basis for all our languages, verbal and visual, and constitutes the means of attaining a higher, richer sensing of life.

We have had many warnings. Again and again, men in the past have lamented the destruction of their environment and the consequent loss of poetry and beauty. They saw and felt the ruthless impoverishment of life. A hundred years ago, John Ruskin said:

> In that half of the permitted life of man, I have seen strange evil brought upon every scene that I best loved, or tried to make beloved by others. The light which once flushed those pale summits with its rose at dawn, and purple at sunset, is now umbered and faint; the air which once inlaid the clefts of all their golden crags with azure is now defiled with languid coils of smoke, belched from worse than volcanic fires: their very glacier waves are ebbing, and their snows fading, as if Hell had breathed on them; the waters that once sank at their feet into crystalline rest are now dimmed and foul, from deep to deep, and shore to shore. These are no careless words—they are accurately, horribly, true. . . . Ah, masters of modern science . . . you have divided the elements, and united them; enslaved them upon the earth, and discerned them in the stars. Teach us, now, but this of them, which is all that man need know—that the Air is given to him for his life; and the Rain to his thirst, and for his baptism; and the Fire for warmth; and the Sun for sight; and the Earth for his means—and his Rest.

A few years later, William Morris observed:

> And, as yet, it is only a very few men who have begun to think about a remedy
> for it in its widest range: even in its narrower aspect, in the defacements of our
> big towns by all that commerce brings with it, who heeds it? Who tries to
> control their squalor and hideousness? . . . Cut down the pleasant trees among
> the houses; pull down ancient and venerable buildings for the money that a
> few square yards of London dirt will fetch; blacken rivers, hide the sun and
> poison the air with smoke and worse, and it's nobody's business to see to it or
> mend it; that is all that modern commerce, the counting house forgetful of the
> workshop, will do for us herein. . . . Yet there are matters which I should have
> thought easy for her; say, for example, teaching Manchester how to consume
> its own smoke, or Leeds how to get rid of its superfluous black dye without
> turning it into the river, which would be as much worth her attention as the
> production of the heaviest of heavy black silks, or the biggest of useless guns.

Disregard for nature's richness leads to the destruction of living forms and eventually to the degradation and destruction of man himself. And although an increasing number of people realize the urgent need for change, we are all carried along by the uncontrolled dynamics of our situation and continue to develop ever more powerful tools without a code of values to guide us in their use.

Some of our wise predecessors recognized that there are limits to our interference with nature—to the remolding of ourselves and of the world around us. Heraclitus knew that "the sun will not overstep his measure; for if he does, the Erynes, the maids of Justice, will find him out." The fate of Icarus demonstrates the fate of man's overweening ambition to change the world. Some three hundred and fifty years ago, Galileo observed that if we tried to construct mammoth ships and palaces, beams and bolts would cease to hold together. Trees cannot grow beyond certain heights nor animals beyond a certain size and still retain the proportion and materials that give them stability and efficiency.

Such limits also exist in the rate of growth or development. There is an old Chinese fable about a farmer who, impatient with the natural rate of his crop's growth, went to the field every day and gave each sprout a good hard pull to speed its maturation. When the loosened plants all died, he came to understand nature's scale limits—Tao—nature's way.

Every physical form, every living form, every pattern of feeling or thought has its own unique identity, its boundaries, its extension, and its wider context; it contains or is contained by another pattern; it follows or is followed by another pattern. The unique identity, discrete shape, and nature of a space-occupying substance are shaped by the boundary that separates it from, and connects it to, the space outside. An organic form lives and grows only through its intricate transactions with its environment. An optical event becomes a visually perceived figure only when seen against its ground. The quality, feeling, and meaning of a sound is cast in the matrix of the physical processes that generated it; it is not independent of its surrounding silence or the other sounds that frame it. In the same way, the physical, biological, or moral individuality of man is the function of his active relationship with the physical and social environment.

But the world is not made of discrete fixed entities. The boundaries that separate and connect them are fluid. The world's infinitely complex fabric is in a process of never-ending transformation; biological forms, social groups, human feelings and understandings undergo continuous changes. They may merge into larger, more encompassing, and more complex configurations or fall apart into smaller, simpler constituents.

Perception psychologists, investigating the dynamics of visual figure-ground relationships, discerned a dynamic hierarchy of gestalts—perceptual patterns moving toward larger, more inclusive patterns. Our present relationship to our environment is at the threshold of such a process of reorientation. New circumstances have now forced us to see that we can no longer think of ourselves as separate and independent from our environment; rather, together they form a new, higher gestalt.

What are these new circumstances? First, there are the obvious, immediate, and real environmental tragedies. Until the recent past, man had to concentrate his major efforts on safeguarding himself from the inimical forces of the natural world—beasts, cold, sickness, and hunger. At this historical junction, the real beasts are man-created; we face ourselves as the enemy. Nearly two centuries of industrial civilization have defaced and poisoned our environment. Shaped with the blighted spirit of cornered man, our cities are our collective self-portraits, images of our own hollowness and chaos. And, if not properly guided, our immensely potent technology may carry within itself curses of even more awesome proportions. The not yet understood, uncontrolled dynamics of scientific technology could do more than poison our earth; it is capable of wreaking havoc on man's genetic future.

But the man-created circumstances could also bring immense positive potential. In the nineteenth century, inquiry into man's social nature and the study of the Darwinian theory of biological evolution led to the belief that biological and social evolution were closely linked; little attention was paid at this time to the question of how social evolution was involved in the transformation of human consciousness from an early primitive level to its present more advanced one. During the past two decades, this aspect of the evolutionary process has re-engaged the interest of some of the freer and more speculative scientific minds. Simultaneously, there have been momentous developments in genetics, computer and control technology, and economic production. In technically advanced countries, development has reached the point where the traditional purposes of human work—keeping men housed, clothed, and fed—can be transcended, permitting men to take responsibility for the shaping of human consciousness.

Some scientists have read our new situation with confidence, concluding that mankind has entered an important new higher stage of evolutionary development. "We are privileged," wrote Julian Huxley, "to be living at a crucial moment in the cosmic story, the moment when the vast evolutionary process in the small person of the inquiring man is becoming conscious of itself." He has discerned two critical thresholds in this evolutionary process: the first, when, thanks to the development of DNA and genes, material systems became self-varying and self-reproducing, and the biological phase of evolution began to operate; and the second, when, due to the development of conceptual thought, symbolic language, and the cumulative transmission of experience, by tradition mental, or mind-accompanied, organizations became self-varying and self-reproducing, and the human phase of evolution emerged.

Today, we are in the critical stage of the second phase. We are taking the first timid steps toward what could be called "self-conscious evolution." We are beginning to understand that through social communication, it is within our intellectual and emotional power to shape a sounder evolutionary future. The increasing magnitude and complexity of interacting lives must make us realize that our future depends upon an understanding and control of our common system—a self-regulating, interdependent, dynamic pattern that moves from yesterday into today and from today into tomorrow.

But, as the new arrives too fast and too forcefully, and as inherited mores, feelings, and concepts that served both as guides and shelter in our smaller and calmer world are swept away, many of us feel hopeless and helpless. No longer secure in our relationship to the world, we feel our self-confidence is lost. We are unable to respond with imaginative courage to the challenges that face us. Instead of using all our inner resources, sensibilities, intellect, and heart in a common focus, we react with blind one-sided intensity. Our thoughts ignore and discredit our feelings and, thus, lose contact with the energy and richness they can provide. Our feelings, in turn, are repressed and our sensibilities petrified.

Inbuilt into our unguided, imposing technological and material accomplishments is the danger that the life of the majority may be drained of its spirit, belief, and personal meaning. To inject human sense into the external achievements of the man-shaped modern world, it must touch the individual with all the warmth of sensory intensity. The world of the single individual is sense-bound. His contact with the outside world is through sensorial experiences, which, in turn, give the individual his sense of himself. In this context, touch, both physical and symbolic, plays a key role.

A cornered man is compelled to look into himself and gauge his own strengths and weaknesses. He must examine closely the nature of his relationship with his fellow man and with the world. Our unresolved and troubled lives compel us to reassess ourselves, and nowhere is our questioning of goals and means more evident than in the visual arts. Perhaps the responses can indicate what went wrong and where we should look for answers.

In spite of the bewildering stream of conflicting claims and counter-claims in twentieth-century art, there is a common denominator. It relates not so much with what is present as with what is missing: cohesion, com-pleteness, the link between art and life, between man and man, and between man and environment, which provided the vital source of all the great art of the past. Artists have come to recognize that their creative imaginations and sensibilities are neither self-generated nor self-contained: they belong to the larger environmental field of nature and society. After the fervent involve-ment in the revolutions of expressive idioms, in the extensions of morpho-logical dimensions, and in the altering of the rules of the game in form making, the search has assumed new dimensions. Instead of further probing into matters of form, artists today are asking fundamental questions about the role and purpose of art, and beginning to find some answers.

The individual human body has an inbuilt self-defense, a physiological mechanism that protects it from extreme imbalance. Complex, automatic self-regulating devices are constantly either eliminating useless toxic matters from the body or converting what is useful into needed substances. We have begun to see that our extended body, our social and man-transformed envi-ronment must develop its own self-regulating mechanisms to eliminate the poisons injected into it and to recycle useful matter. Environmental home-ostasis on a global scale is now necessary to survival. Creative imagination, artistic sensibility, can be seen as one of the basic, collective, self-regulating devices that help us all to register and reject what is toxic and find what is use-ful and meaningful in our lives.

The underprivileged, the young, and the imaginative artist have expressed their anger eloquently at cowardly inertia and shortsighted selfish-ness. "Look into the mirror. The cause is you Mr. and Mrs. Yesterday," Eldridge Cleaver accuses us all. "They stole my imagination," laments Mick Jagger of the Rolling Stones. For they know in their hearts that without the courage to enter today, we can hardly hope to survive; and without imagina-tive power, we cannot make this move.

Sometimes these voices express the needs and hopes of the richer, expanding world. Jimi Hendrix exclaims, "I want to hear and see everything, I want to hear and see everything," and he adds, "Excuse me while I kiss the sky." In a symposium in 1965, Lucio Fontana, an artist with rare confident imagination, commented, "As a painter, while working on one of my perfo-rated canvases, I do not want to make a painting; I want to open up space, create a new dimension for art, tie in with the cosmos as it endlessly expands beyond the confining plane of the picture. With my innovation of the hole pierced through the canvas in repetitive formations, I have not attempted to decorate a surface, but, on the contrary, I have tried to break its dimensional limitations. Beyond the perforations, a newly gained freedom of interpretation awaits us, but also, and just as inevitably, the end of art."

It must be remembered that what has happened in art is itself a part of a very broad movement in which science has made the major contribution. Through its dynamics of rigorous logic twentieth-century scientific understanding has come to conclusions not unlike those of the artists. Scientists recognize that in the most precise ranges of observation, the observer and the observed interact. When observed and measured with maximum precision, the environment, in both its largest and its smallest realism, cannot be considered an independent objective world anymore.

It is quite understandable that many are sincerely convinced that the application of scientific method to all our problems will provide solutions to the complex equations of contemporary life. Mustering their new energies and their extended tools of the human mind—computer game theory, theories of servomechanism, systems approaches, and the like—men face the overwhelming problems of today with unwavering confidence in their capacity to overcome them. At the same time, such confidence is belied by the fact that the most sophisticated systems applications of technical know-how yet devised are those that have been used to invent means of tearing and burning the flesh from our brother men in areas of the world that, technologically speaking, have never had the chance to live in the twentieth century. But one need not go to distant lands to see that modern man has more cause to fear for his life in the big cities of rich countries than medieval man had in his deepest forests.

Our outdated socioeconomic system would seem to cancel our newly forged tools to build a sounder and richer life. There is an entry in Ralph Waldo Emerson's notebook, written in the mid-nineteenth century, that has an almost symbolic bearing on our plight. Traveling in the outer Cape in Massachusetts, Emerson met some citizens of one of the smaller communities, who complained bitterly about their inability to have a lighthouse built. Their fellow citizens objected to the project on the ground that by warning approaching ships, the townspeople would be deprived of the goods they salvaged from the vessels that were periodically wrecked on the lightless rocks. The lack of moral intelligence that has led to the adulation of objects rather than of lives is a major factor in our failure to realize our potentials. The resistance today of the status quo is not against the scientific technological tools and methods themselves, but against their use in uncompromisingly social applications.

Our potent new tools, both conceptual and physical, contain within themselves an important aspect of new human perspectives. The more powerful the devices we develop through our scientific technology, the more we are interconnected with each other, with our machines, with our environment, and with our own inner capacities. The more sensitive and embracing our means of seeing, hearing, and thinking become through radio, television, and computer technology, the more we are compelled to sense the interaction of man and his environment. Our new tools of transportation, communication, and control have brought a new scale of opportunities to "inter-thinking" and "inter-seeing": the condition of a truly embracing participatory democracy.

The advancement of creative life and, by the same token, of human knowledge is produced by the interaction of the whole community. Through the communication of the knowledge and insights of creative men in many fields, we have the opportunity to make all that is valuable in man a shared possession—a new "common" property of all who seek a higher quality of life.

The notion of the "common" has always been alive for those who kept their human sense unsullied. A party of colonists asked the Indian, Tecumseh, if he would sell them his land. "Sell the country?" he asked in astonishment. "Why not sell the air, the clouds, the great sea?" Emerson once reflected, "The charming landscape which I saw this morning is indubitably made up of some twenty or thirty farms. Miller owns this field, Locke that, and Manning the woodland beyond. But none of them owns the landscape. There is a property in the horizon which no man has but he whose eye can integrate all the parts, that is, the poet."

A new "common"—the potential complex total system now being made possible by our scientific technology—can be explained by comparing it with the growth pattern of an individual human nervous system. It has been observed that the development of the brain increases the range and scope of perception. This increased perceptual range leads, in turn, to a need for greater control within the brain, that is, a greater ability to coordinate the widened range of information. This coordinated, interconnected capital of perceptual knowledge then offers a richer resonance to forthcoming perceptual experiences. In our own extended social and environmental system, we have not yet reached this necessary dynamic symmetry. Either our sensory feelers—our tools of knowledge and power—are growing unchecked exponentially without the coordination and control essential to a deepened and widened sense of life, or our concentrated powers of control and communications network is growing bigger than our individual receptive capacity.

It is difficult to accept as one this world of ghettos, criminal wars, urban violence, and inner erosion that coexists with bioengineering, genetic engineering, the pill, distant sensors, cyborgs, and an ever-increasing communication network. Lost without a frame of reference in the new dynamic scale, modern man responds to his bewildering world either with the unquestioning conviction of a chiliast confidently awaiting the coming of a new technological millennium or with the desperation of a Jeremiah expecting the end of the world with each new step of technological development.

Where can we find a new set of coordinates to guide us through this wildly paced life that destroys so many with its reckless speed? How can we fashion links between the constantly broadening parameter of the experienced world and the diminishing dimensions of its particles? How can we find a living symmetry between increasingly powerful social control and our individual freedom? To achieve redemption for a crime, one must be conscious of the crime committed. Without an ecological conscience, we have very little hope for change. But our imaginative powers and moral intelligence can help us find this consciousness.

Artistic and poetic sensibility and an ethical conscience have served us well in the past. The first massive blows of industrialized civilization were borne by men who still possessed the uncompromising sense of life as an indivisible whole composed of man and nature. In the late eighteenth and early nineteenth centuries in England, where the impact of industrialization left its first ugly scars, Percy Bysshe Shelley and other poets agonized over man's corrupting touch on the richness of the natural world. William Blake raged at the menace degrading labor held for the human spirit, and wrote of "those dark satanic mills." In this country, Henry David Thoreau, for whom trains were symbols of spreading mechanical civilization, observed dryly that, "a few were riding but the rest are run over." The painters, J. M. W. Turner and John Constable, seeing nature defaced by smoke and dirt, projected from their inner resources the missing crescendo of light and color, space and movement. Their intense awareness of the sensorial qualities of life would not permit them to accept either the nineteenth-century mechanical models of scientific analysis or the profit-guided society as an adequate framework for their need for breadth, freedom, and self-variation of life.

In the twentieth-century era of displacement, disillusionment, and social upheavals, the artist has had to face different challenges. He has had to cut through the ego-tangled scene to reach the free horizons that held a promise of the new "common" of man-environment. Clearly, the artist's sensibility has entered a new phase of orientation in which its prime goal is to provide a format for the emerging ecological consciousness. The tasks he assumes differ from previous tasks in kind as well as in scale. The values he uncovers become the values of us all, giving sharpness and definition to the need we sense for union and intimate involvement with our surroundings. Thus, the artist has moved from a marginal role to a more central social position.

First, artists have the opportunity to contribute to the creative shaping of the earth's surface on a grand scale. Major environmental plasticity, for example, has become a fact of great import. Until now, man was tied to the earth's crust: he could move only on the land or swim in or skim across the water. Except for the rare vantage points of high mountains, our globe was given to us only in limited horizons. The new technology has freed us from the ancient bondage of gravitation and opened up vistas of liberating dimension. Today, the artist's creative performance has a new challenge with a new arena and new spectators.

Now, we are all at the threshold of a new scale of consciousness, a complete reorientation; we are shifting frames of reference and thus perspectives. There is no more convincing picture of these expanding boundaries and their consequences than that given by a great troubled poet of the nineteenth century, and confirmed by the concrete real-time experiences of one of our astronauts. "He who one day teacheth men to fly," wrote Friedrich Nietzsche, "will have shifted all landmarks: to him will all the landmarks themselves fly into the air; the earth will he christen anew—as 'the light body.'" Astronaut William Anders, in a newspaper interview, gave this report of his experience:

> The earth looked so tiny in the heavens that there were times during the Apollo 8 mission when I had trouble finding it. If you can imagine yourself in a darkened room with only one clearly visible object, a small blue-green sphere about the size of a Christmas-tree ornament, then you can begin to grasp what the earth looks like from space. I think that all of us subconsciously think that the earth is flat or at least almost infinite. Let me assure you that, rather than a massive giant, it should be thought of as the fragile Christmas-tree ball which we should handle with considerable care.

Man's extended sensors have brought him within arm's reach of patterns and processes both strange and familiar. On the other end of the space spectrum, photomicrographs and electron micrographs have brought micro-dimensions within range of our eyes. Nature has become an artistic challenge again. Artists, instead of representing nature's appearances, have explored ways to present nature's processes in their phenomenological aspects. Wind, rain, snow, nature growth, magnetic and hydraulic processes, and sound events have now reentered the artist's vocabulary.

Some artists, finding it hopeless to formulate their experiences of the expanding new world in sensuous objects or images, attempted to capture the expanding space-time parameters in conceptual nets.

These artistic attempts signify a fundamental reorientation. The dominant matrix of nineteenth-century attitudes was the use of Karl Marx's term *reification*; relationships were interpreted in terms of things, objects, or commodity values. Today, a reversal of this attitude has begun to appear; there is a steadily increasing movement in science and in art toward processes and systems that dematerialize the object world and discredit physical possessions. What scientists considered before as substance shaped into forms, and consequently understood as tangible objects, is now recognized as energies and their dynamic organization. In the visual arts, painters and sculptors have arrived at conclusions not unlike those of the scientists. Artists have liberated their images and forms from the inhibiting world of object. Painting has become the capture and arrangement of visual energies. Through the innovations of a number of contemporary architects and engineers, buildings are also losing their object solidity and opacity to become light and transparent "thingless" events. Buckminster Fuller's airy Dymaxion structures are important milestones on this road. Imaginative younger architects and engineers have moved still further away from weight and have touched upon the possibilities of enclosing space with air currents. Like instant envelopes, these currents could be turned on or off as needed by sophisticated sensing and computing devices regulated by weather conditions. Architecture is making fundamental departures from its traditional position as a discrete, independent, heavy, and solid form catering mainly to the visual sense and is becoming a responding, bodiless, dynamic, interdependent structure answering to man's changing needs and growing controls. The flexible, mobile, transparent lightness can contribute significantly to man's liberation from the fixed space enclosure that separated him from nature's wealth of events. The meanings of architecture and urban configurations have a still more significant revaluation. Buildings and groups of buildings are no longer considered sculptural forms and their space organizations but, rather, as systems of functions, programming life patterns with the participation of the concerned.

These innovations are the physical manifestation of a new sensibility. The scientist-engineer Dennis Gabor once commented that, "The future cannot be predicted, but [it] can be invented. The first step of the technological or social inventor is to visualize by an act of imagination a thing or state of things which does not exist and which appears to him in some way desirable."[1] Imagination is the key to pre-experiencing alternative futures; desirability, in terms of human values, is the decision maker that now selects the right alternatives.

At this stage of evolutionary history, a new attitude toward the environment can be discerned. To the degree that man understands the external environment and, for better or worse, shares its features in his own image, man's inner and outer landscapes will have a new meaning. The uncharted space is in ourselves, in our still unfathomed ethical potentials, in our still untapped imaginative power. Some three hundred years ago, Sir Thomas Browne saw this with his inner eye. "We carry with us the wonders we seek without us," he wrote, "there is all Africa and her prodigies in us; we are that bold and adventurous piece of Nature, which he that studies wisely learns in a compendium what others labor at in a divided piece and endless volume."

Note

1. Dennis Gabor, *Inventing the Future* (New York: Alfred A. Knopf, 1963): 207–208.

What Is Multidisciplinary Man?
By Arnold Kramish

The body of world knowledge is too vast to try to create even the semblance of the Renaissance man, whose knowledge was all-encompassing (if such a man there ever was!). Francis Bacon did not add much to knowledge, but he sensitized man to knowledge. Leonardo da Vinci was a frustrated technologist. He could not translate his inventions into practice because supporting technologies did not exist. The modern requirement, the Multidisciplinary man, is the compromise Renaissance man. He will know proportionately far less of the wisdom generated through ages past and present, but he must admit the existence of other knowledge and be able to communicate that recognition. And now that supporting technology is available, he need no longer be frustrated from lack of information, but must learn the fine art of selection from abundance.

The current concerns on the environment have dramatized, as never before, the views on the relationship of man to nature. Is man disposed, as in the Baconian view, to the constant conquest of nature, and is nature gradually losing its own battle against the ravages of man? Curiously, few of these disputations consider the inescapable fact that man is a product and part of nature. The arrogance of the assumption to the contrary accounts for man's mistakes, not those of nature.

The transgressor in these dramas, whatever turn they take, is almost invariably technology, as if the latter were an even more alien force and a relatively recent intruder at that. Moreover, the assertion has been made that there is a technological man different from the man-animal, characterized as the natural man, and that this technological man is a relatively recent product of a few societies exploiting technology to the disadvantage of the rest of the world.

Claude Levi-Strauss, in his book, *The Savage Mind* (1962), describes the hunting techniques of the Hidatsa Indians of North Dakota. The Indian digs a pit, squats down in it and covers it with twigs, placing pieces of meat at the edge of the pit. When an eagle swoops down to take the meat, the Indian grabs the eagle with his hands. Here, man must become trapped to set a trap, and, in Levi-Strauss's view, he is both the hunter and the hunted. He sits cramped in his pit for long hours, the victim of his own technology. Is this illustration any different from that of modern man experiencing the discomforts and inconveniences of a metropolis so that he may dream of capturing the delights and opportunities of his more "civilized" environment?

In the dawn of time, any animal species that might have developed, whose physical characteristics were such that it required an herbivorous diet, would have died away in periods of long and extended drought or simply by growing healthy and multiplying and dissipating the food supply in an area of finite dimensions. Man is such an animal. Neither dentally nor in the characteristics of his alimentary system is he fundamentally carnivorous. However, in periods of drought or when other means of supply of plant nourishment disappeared, man became meat eating, a transformation that only one or two lower species have demonstrably achieved. To obtain meat, he had to capture or kill at a distance. Undoubtedly, some of the capture techniques (which were true forms of early technology) were similar to those used by the Hidatsa. Other possibilities for survival became evident when man discovered that a chipped stone could cut. Was such discovery the result of an extensive thinking process on how to solve his food problem, or was it instinctive?

Consider another example of primitive technological development coupled with conspicuous consumption. Possibly the earliest complex culture in the New World was the Olmec civilization of the lowlands of the Gulf coast of Mexico. Millennia before the Olmec thrived, men in many areas of the world independently observed that a piece of chipped stone could cut, and cutting gave another dimension to survival. Some men eventually found that chips of certain stones were sharper than those of others. Thus, materials technology was born. Then, man became aware that settlements other than his own had access to better quality stone—all the more reason to trade and to war. And, by accident or by deliberate empirical search (which we would call research), it was found that certain shapes of stones were useful for special purposes in a household and in weapons. Thus, machine-tool technology began to take shape and, as it became evident that the more in number and variety of stones that one had made existence more tolerable, the affluent society was born.

For their flakes and blades the Olmecs preferred obsidian, a volcanic glass, which was not native to their region, but they sought it in ever-increasing quantities disproportionate to their population. Examination of Olmec sites shows that, as time progressed, not only were there more complex blades in a household, but the total number of flakes and blades per household increased. We have no idea of the detrimental side effects, such as the inhalation of obsidian dust in mining and shaping the stone, but surely adverse health effects must have occurred, and it is even conceivable that it was sometimes noticed that the stoneworkers were afflicted with a special disease.

Some of the aspects of the contemporary ecological crisis that appear to puzzle some analysts, such as why a product use and product waste are not linear with population growth, are clearly explicable and have always been present. The factors that underlie problems of complex societies are rarely simple explanations that the entirety of such societies can comprehend, but it is reasonable to expect that a certain proportion of such societies should be educated to understand them.

There is much evidence, speculation, and theory, on the one hand, to suggest that man and nature are fundamentally opposing forces and that technology is the weapon in the battle, but, on the other hand, we also cannot dismiss the suggestion that man is in large measure characterized by technology. If so, he has to live with technology and adjust to and with it, not as an outside force, but adjust as much as he has to adapt to his fears, neuroses, and pleasures.

If this is so, then the adjustment to what appears to be the growing peril of an overabundance of technology must perhaps be found in a manner similar to the way adjustments are achieved when other frailties of the human mind and spirit appear to impair the very existence of the human being himself. It is at this point that one must consider how the mind must be shaped, not solely toward the survival of the single being, but for the survival and well-being of a community of beings. Population growth, communications, and world-girdling technologies have ultimately created a community of beings, which now comprises the planet Earth itself. It is in that context, the context of communities surviving internally and in concert with one another, that we seek and design the educational forms.

In doing so, we should caution ourselves not to repeat the mistakes that we are wont to criticize in others in the past. Under domination of great powers, the health and well-being of people in a number of underdeveloped areas was solicitously improved in order to create larger and more productive labor forces so that greater quantities of palm oil, copper, and other commodities could be obtained. When the natural supply of such commodities ended, these areas were left with greater population, less to feed them with, and, what is even worse, memories of a better quality of life. In modern times, there are similar instances of overproduction of human beings to meet pressing temporal challenges. For example, following World War II the further pursuit of technological visions created during the war demanded the creation of large numbers of "think tanks" or other enclaves in universities, like platonic academies, to nurture the priority technological goals of the moment. Some of these "academies" performed their specific functions for a specific time and then collapsed. Most others have found adjustments to new priorities difficult, to say the least. It is quite conceivable that the overemphasis on environmental and ecological considerations as a primary technological goal could eventually result in drastic overproduction of certain types of talent and mask new critical priorities.

So the new university must be concerned not only with the multidisciplinary or interdisciplinary problems of curricula, but should recognize the possibility of overproduction of specialized individuals. Even in the environmental and ecological sense, the too-narrowly oriented graduate is likely to be developed in substantial numbers.

Key elements in the creation of new institutions oriented toward the solution of the complex problems of modern societies are the faculties and creative thinking that they may be capable of generating. Such institutions, which at this primitive stage of genesis are trying to adapt themselves, tend to be polarized either as an entity in its entirety crusading against technology, pollution, etc., or they are polarized internally. Often the internal polarization is characterized as interdisciplinary research where, in actual fact, the communication between groups is virtually nil.

The past two decades of experience of most so-called interdisciplinary institutions, whether they have been working upon military or social problems, have shown an initial period of amity and cooperation between specialists of various disciplines, who, at first, seem eager to learn from one another. The usual pattern has been that the learning period is brief and that, for example, a physicist soon becomes convinced that he knows all there is to be known about political science, and vice versa. The usual scenario is then that the specialist or groups of specialists tend to carry on independently from others in the organization, under the illusion that they have been converted into multidisciplinary beings and can once again solve problems of a broader nature—but still in the splendid isolation to which they are intellectually disposed and accustomed. Often the individual or group of specialists will then split off from the mother organization as a separate specialized entity.

Thus, there is an inherent factor—a combination not only of individual disposition but of societal factors, characterized by economics and attitudes—which tends to demand both the creation and the destruction of institutions for complex societies.

A new approach is required for yet-to-be-created institutions. The approach must include a very thorough recognition of what is involved in creating a truly multidisciplinary individual. For many of those individuals, specialization in technology is not an essential element. There are many problems to be solved in which technology is only peripheral, but for the large body of individuals where appreciation of the interaction of technology with social problems is an essential requirement, they will have to gain a better appreciation of how technology serves and/or controls man without sweeping condemnation or defense of technology. Is technology the result of some unconscious drive, or is it a perfectly controllable phenomenon of the conscious? Some might put it in other terms. For Sigmund Freud, unconscious phenomena are natural phenomena, and conscious phenomena are cultural. Where does technology fit—in the natural or cultural context?

Man generates his own messages from within, and he receives them from his cultural environment. Most often the internal messages require no external device, but often they do. Levi-Strauss, Freud, and others extensively analyze some of the external devices, such as music and myth. Levi-Strauss calls music and myth "machines for the suppression of time." (Was it his unconscious that motivated him to use the word *machines*?) He points out that, in most instances, the receiver interprets the message of the music, whereas, in the spoken language, the sender decides the message. Now, where is the role of technology in all of this? Marshall McLuhan is happy about increasingly complex communications technology, which provides the music and the spoken word. He sees this technology as a natural and welcome extension of tribal communication to the entire world. Man, having welcomed the Gramophone as a most natural opportunity for private indulgence in whatever music meant to him, has constantly sought in technology a more effective device that would simulate more realistically the natural reception of music, evolving to high-fidelity recording, thence to stereo, and now to quadraphonic sound. There is not the slightest iota of public rebellion against the development of this new and highly complex technology, a technology that not only had its roots in military development, but has military implications in itself.

A multitude of other examples can be given to show how man, in pursuing what apparently is a very natural and fundamental need for "machines for the suppression of time" not only through music, but through play, daydreaming, etc., demands and welcomes any technology that can assist him. Most advanced technologies are incorporated now in toys (dolls as well as scientific kits), in sports equipment (e.g., the same artificial materials developed for certain nuclear and aircraft equipment now prove to be ideal for skis and sports boats), etc.

Technology has its evils, its excesses, its misapplications, but it is also a very *natural* requirement in the evolution of societies. Consequently, we have to approach all attributes of technology not through polarization of attitudes, but through individuals and institutions dedicated to the understanding of the undetachable relationships of technology with man, and man with technology.

Communication
By Henri Lefebvre

I.

The document presented by The Museum of Modern Art interests and concerns the European reader in more than one respect. Not only does it contain the post-industrial and post-technological project for the university of the future, but also an appeal and a demand. It proposes to unify two schools of thought, which are generally distinct and often opposed: Anglo-American empiricism and philosophical rationalism, which we could call "European" to suit the context of this short essay.

Nobody is unaware of these well-known facts. On the one hand, there is a sense of efficiency and operativeness—pragmatism—and, on the other hand, there is a sometimes immoderate use of abstractions and of general theories and concepts, which lack immediate operational capacity.

In spite of concessions and erosions, these well-known facts have not ceased to be valid. Cartesianism, which admits the almost original existence of abstract entities, the Subject and the Object, and which is present in the course of philosophy to this day, still opposes its rationality to a concatenation of facts following logical (formal) schemes; in other words, it opposes its rationality to logical empiricism and positivism. Cartesianism, through European history and laden with history, leads to Georg Wilhelm Friedrich Hegel's (dialectical) thought and, consequently, to Marxist theories. It comes as no novelty that the "grafting" of Marxist thought (to imitate a metaphor used by certain historians) has been successful only when the dominant culture has understood the philosophy, i.e., Hegelianism. It has not had any effect in other circumstances; the grafting has not taken; everything happens as though empiricism were forcefully resisting the domination of the theory, which is upsetting Europe. Why? The question is, in itself, sufficient to indicate the depth of the obvious opposition and its persistence, whether it be overt or hidden.

The proposed topic tries to eliminate all misunderstanding, to bridge the gulf and to achieve a cross-fertilization of these forms, which have heretofore been unduly separated or crystallized in mutual distrust. Is this a step forward? It is to be desired.

II.

Nevertheless, dialogues and conversations are not satisfactory merely for the fact that they take place in an atmosphere of mutual acceptance and recognition. There will still remain some semantic obstacles; from this very moment, some precautions must be taken to indicate the path to be followed and to prevent those who follow it from going astray. For instance, the meaning of the words *ideology*, *structure*, *infrastructure*, and *superstructure* is far from clear in the proposed topic. The context of these terms is not unequivocal. The term *superstructure* denotes both that part of the city which emerges from the surface of the earth and spreads in the light, as well as the unity of ideas and representations. Furthermore, for the American reader, it is possible that there should be some identical or analogous ambiguities in French. The sense and the implication behind the word *ideology*, among other things, have become confused and amplified in the last few years. A clarification would be useful, but it would evade the proposed conceptual frame.

As far as I am concerned ("ego," the signer of these pages) the concept of *iconic structure* used in this text is unfamiliar to me. I am acquainted with the works of Charles Sanders Peirce and the definitions he gives, but I am not in the habit of using them. Can it be said that the *iconic* is defined by the nonpredictable (momentarily or permanently)? This is a methodological problem, which should be dealt with at the outset if the editors of this text desire to be understood and followed throughout a very important point of their development.

There is also another problem. The principal term used in the proposed text, the word *design*, is laden with so much meaning, assumes such importance, and implies so many certainties and problems that the French translator of this text is bewildered. How can it be translated without taking any risks and without audacity? The word *architectonic* could be used to maintain in French the formulas by which the mode of thinking applicable to *design* and to the *designer* takes into account the *empiric*, the *normative,* and the *iconic*. Consequently, the designer can supervise the process of infrastructure while normatively taking into account the superstructure, its ideas and values. As a result, his dissertations could and should be concerned with the space between the infrastructural and superstructural levels, while taking into account their *iconic* qualities and characteristics (materializing the ideal and idealizing that which is material, we should declare these to be "imageable" and "objectifiable").

III.

For the French reader ("ego," signer of these pages, is wrongly or rightly considering himself the representative of this badly defined group!), the Museum"s text uncovers an immense problem, which is none other than that of the United States. By means of hard work and initiative in the field of production, the United States has reached a degree of wealth unknown and even inconceivable until recently. This was said, of course, with the usual reservations concerning the islands of poverty that exist within this wealth, the danger of recession, and the oppressive characteristics that go along with the cumulative process of wealth, knowledge, and technique.

What should be done now? How should the accumulated wealth be employed? This is the new problem that Europeans are considering with astonishment. They do not grasp it fully. An intellectual elite (unfortunately, it is nothing more than an elite), isolated because of its elitism and much more restricted in Europe than in the United States, has brought this question to light. In Europe, it has not yet dawned on the masses, who admit the pursuit of the process of accumulation without considering the break which inevitably follows.

What can be done? Should the accumulation of capital, information and technique, machines and equipment be continued indefinitely? This is the height of absurdity. In spite of the fact that to this day political leaders in all parts of the world have not formulated other projects than that of indefinite growth, their attitude discredits the political element. And this is really how matters stand. In everyday life, the obstacles accumulate, and this circumstance will render unfeasible the project of indefinite growth. These obstacles are occurring much earlier in the United States than in Europe, and the most perceptive minds have recognized them. Will each family in well-off circumstances have two, then three, then four or five cars? How should the roads and the streets be organized in order to allow this onrush to go on and, consequently, to permit the car industry to continue in its role of stimulation and pilotage?

These reasonable questions now contain an element of subversion. It is not surprising that the most lucid American intellectuals now accept "the spirit of 1968" in France.

So what should be done with the acquired wealth, from a social point of view? Gigantic resources could be dedicated to the conquest of space. These same resources could be depreciated by political powers in the waging of war. This policy and strategy could all of a sudden collapse when confronted with the opinion of a democratic country, for want of a rational justification. The problem of finality and meaning remains unsolved.

Is the French reader wrong when he carefully observes the symptoms of a prodigious change, which does not derive from what is *positive* in America, i.e., technology, and from wealth taken for its own sake, but from a *critical point* attained by this process, by a qualitative leap which the quantitative (positive) growth renders unavoidable?

According to this French reader, the United States is questioning its future, which was rendered possible by its past, but which now tends to be banned by a too-certain present. The European thinks that this new America will abandon the strategy of growth, economism, and technologism, the desire for power. He also believes that it will create the post-industrial and post-technological society. How can "elites" and perceptive minds exert sufficient pressure on politicians? That is another matter. "It's their business," thinks the European with a tinge of uneasiness in his admiration. Is it sufficient to reach a high degree of awareness in order to determine events, as Charles Reich asserts in his remarkable book, *The Greening of America*?

Perhaps; in the text of the Museum, this degree of awareness is present and comes across clearly. For the time being, this is essential.

IV.

Europe and France have not yet reached the moment of decision, the hour when "the world will be turned upside down"—this world where the means were becoming the end (production and exchanges). The crucial moment is approaching, but the problem (judging by appearances and excluding unforeseen circumstances) will not be politically posed (that is, by questioning the attitude of politicians) for a few years yet.

The degree of "average" consciousness is infinitely superior to that demanded by Reich. The events of 1968, which have set the problem of a *new society* and which are, more and more, acquiring this connotation, are all the more remarkable. To understand them, it must be remembered that they were the result of an initiative (of a highly cultivated spontaneity) on the part of the students who will fill the vacancy created by the "subject of class" with indisputable practical courage, in the name of deeper theoretical thought.

Today in France, after 1968, there is a new dominating realization, a sad certainty that technology is becoming an ideology. In its name, established forms of authority are becoming legitimate. Production and consumption are being "articulated' more forcefully; circuits are being reinforced. Producing and consuming, commercializing the products of technology, seem to be, for an immense majority, "ends desirable in themselves."

This indicates that in France the "society of classes" has not lost its power, its structure, its restrictive meanings, even though the "subject of class" is fading out. The distance between *infrastructures* and *superstructures* is not diminishing. We are, therefore, still far from the transition toward the post-technological society, while many people are labeling the endless extension of the technological era with such terms as *revolution, socialism,* and *communism!* Under these present circumstances, a society of individuals could intervene, introducing a change; but it would have to be something exceptional and radically new to allow this change to affect society as a whole.

Could it be for this reason that certain articles of the Project and of the text are not in themselves convincing for a "European reader?" And, here, I refer particularly to the accent put on *design*. The project and the text lend this word an eminent and almost demiurgic connotation (so much so that it became necessary to find an almost magical word as equivalent: architectonic). Reshape the milieu? Fine. Transform the environment by tearing it away from its deteriorations and degradations? Fine. Bring the surrounding environment to the level that was once that of the work of art? Once more I agree, enthusiastically. Nevertheless, to carry out this great plan (*dessein*), should one not resort to other concepts, other practices, and other resources than design? Would it not be better to start by a critical analysis of design itself, as a concept and as a reality? And, should not this critical analysis also number among the positions for a *new start*?

V.

The habits of critical analysis of social practice and of ideas and representations go hand in hand with a perpetual distrust. As a matter of fact, this critical analysis reveals *ideologies*, or illusions, when they are least expected. It drags them out of their hiding place, so to speak, even in the most *apparently* innocent and objective ideas.

The concept of *design*, used in the text as the key concept, is laden with such heavy meanings (*sens*) that it cannot bear them. The text recedes, therefore, toward a situation, which is ours, and which the text qualifies as one of "pre-design." This situation seems, at the same time, full of conflict, less structured, easier to bear, and lighter on the whole than that of the *designer*. But it is necessary to get out of it. How? By means of an invention or "epistemological production?" By the discovery of an "ethical system?" By the clarification and adequate insertion of a structure that would generate the matrix of a new system?

The fusion of scientific and moral considerations obviates the need for ideology. At first, the designer was entrusted with an historical mission, which was consequently withdrawn from him. By our endeavoring to condense the concept, it has been given an ambiguous context, which is both scientific and moral. Is it possible to plan the construction of the post-technological university on an ambiguous foundation? What values and what ethical system could we, in such a way, transport into the future? What faded visions would we not risk encountering (for example, that of the malignant city as the destroyer of nature, the divine creation, and the primary environment)? The apparently new system of values, which is the generating nucleus ("matrix") of new forms of knowledge and practice, thus risks dragging behind it a hidden metaphysic, the image of nature at its origin; the same nature, which had been society's field of action for centuries and which was then replaced by "artifacts"; it should now be reconstituted within urban artifice.

This image is merely used here as an example, and nothing in the text could lead one to attribute it to the promoter of the project. Its diffusion and influence authorize some form of allusion.

VI.

I want to go back once more to the mission attributed to the *designer*. As the demiurge of modern times, it reunites the ethical and the aesthetical, knowledge (founded epistemologically) and art, surpassing them. It *molds* space (using superlatively elaborated "molds"), as had once been done by the artist, but this time with more powerful means.

This platonic demiurge benefits from the knowledge contributed by *design*: the adaptation to circumstances, efficient intervention, and operational thought. The creation of qualities is placed without rupture in the motivated line of action.

What infinite power, thinks the critical reader, is indirectly given to this Superman for the projected university! Would not this be entering the post-technological era by concentrating on a single individual or group of individuals all the virtualities of technology, or acquired wealth, thus creating super-technocrats?

The ideology, here, would consist in denying the problem, both by asserting that it has already been solved and by declaring that it has no solution.

Is it solved because the thaumaturge of the future receives a statute from a group or network, or "collective subject?" Is it solved because all that is expected from him is that he perfects the antecedent "artifacts?" No. The state of crisis referred to in the text has not been transcended by images—all the more so since the *postulative* (propositional) function will become essential, with all the dangers involved in strategic proposals. On the other hand, the text simply places it along with the other functions and under an informational, epistemological umbrella (metaphorically speaking).

VII.

The hypothesis of a *generating nucleus* of possibilities does not eliminate the need of pointing out some obvious objections. Such a nucleus as we have in mind would generate a reality. The hypothesis implies that these results would have a cumulative character.

But why should a universitary mission be attributed to this generating nucleus? It could create a real space, the space of the future just as well as, if not better than, a course of action. Thus, the Spanish architect Ricardo Bofill, in a project rendered unfeasible by his country's present situation, wanted to form a group and a network whose mission would literally be to secrete a space that would become its own living space. And this plan transcends communities such as we know them because it gives more consistence and meaning to communal life. Modern communities usually occupy existing space, which they transform; they create neither their own space nor their own morphology. The setback that frequently follows probably occurs as a result of this critical error.

This project does not have a more accentuated utopian character than the Universitas. The generating group of its experimental space should take decisions and make definite choices. Could these practical responsibilities make it degenerate into a dictatorial organization? That is not certain. As for the feedbacks foreseen in the text, could they really take place in terms of a group or network, which would only promulgate abstract models?

VIII.

The Museum text proposes the following functions for the university of the future, consequently for the network that would be established with and around it: informative, postulative, decisional, and regulative.

It seems to me that the *critical function* is, at the very least, underestimated. I know that one could reply that European and French criticism tend toward hypercriticism, toward a systematically negative attitude. Could be, but the danger in substituting a certain "positiveness" to radical criticism is an even more preoccupying threat. The ethical system, or system of values, could in itself be modified, but how? If the nature of radical criticism does not destroy this system, it will reestablish itself without modifications. The feedbacks would absorb all the disturbances, divergences, and variations.

Constructive thought will have evaded global problems—those tied to existence as a whole—and this could be the snag. Conceptual thought that assumes critical negativity, derives from globality or from the concept of a totality. And, it also brings to the surface questions such as, How should it be approached? How can it be defined? How can it be reached? How can it be modified?

IX.

The idea of *criticism of space* could be surprising. Space? It cannot be dealt with as a "someone" or as a "subject." How can one criticize something from which critical thought can detract nothing, either in the way of representation (since space is in itself a representation of sorts, tied to material factors) or in the way of action (since the empirically perceived space supplies us with a framework of action).

What is to be done in the meantime? Has not space changed in the course of what we must still call "history?" And, has it not changed under two basic aspects: in the mind, and in practice (socially)? For example, it is possible that the space of an oriental society (the Asiatic system of production) does not coincide with that of a European society unless one excludes certain subsets, certain subspaces, from the latter, that of industrial enterprise and production, among others. To assemble the constituted subspaces after this process of exclusion, by doing away with the other specific elements in every society through a process of production, is both a logical and a questionable operation.

As paradoxical as it may seem, I shall criticize the space in our society, that in which we live, by setting up a dissertation, which will not be a dissertation *of* this space, taken in itself, but a dissertation *about* this space; will define this space with relation to other mental and social spaces, whether they are of the past (historical) or of the future (possible and conceivable); and will give an internal criticism of it, a criticism that would be inherent in its definition.

The determination of space bears, to my mind, two essential traits:

1. The space we live in gives unprecedented priority to the *visual*. It sees itself and lets itself be seen as a sight for the pure gaze—"pure" in the sense of "fixed." A mirror space? We live in it and lose our body in it. Like Alice, having been led to the other side of the magical surface and reduced to our own reflection, we face the creatures of our good and bad dreams.

2. This space, which is homogenous inasmuch as it is visual, remains nevertheless disarticulated. United before our eyes and dominated by the authority of the onlookers, the elements and aspects of space, its formative factors and constituents disperse into specialized spaces, places of social segregation, fragments sold retail, places polluted by useless signs and meanings, separate microworlds (of painting, literature, of an individual writer or painter), etc.

This is where the relationship between infrastructures and superstructures in society is to be found, and this leads directly to the next question: Will the *designer* continue working in this space, as he is still doing at the moment? Or, will he conceive and carry into effect *another space*, the space of another society and of another life?

X.

Following this direction, it is impossible to avoid a complex re-elaboration of "classical" concepts, which have become commonplaces. Let us consider the concepts of *domination* and *appropriation*: they are generally confused. A *dominated* space is often mistaken for an *appropriated* space, whereas the domination of space derives from technology. A highway exemplifies a perfectly dominated space. It is not, therefore, appropriated. This clearly indicates a city broken up by highways and parkways, which fracture it for no other purpose than the circulation of vehicles. *Appropriation* does not exclude the necessity for technology, exchange, circulation of goods and people, but it does exclude the *usage*, and the relationship between space and everyday life. Around us, domination has eliminated appropriation. In order to find spaces that are well appropriated, although still only slightly dominated, we must go back in time to historical cities and villages—whence their charm, their attraction, and their example, which we should not receive passively by naïvely transposing the past into the future.

Should it be the designer's task to differentiate the appropriated from the dominated by carrying out the appropriation? If the answer is yes, I agree, but without any illusions on the difficulties involved.

XI.

The university of the future must break away from the usual and generally accepted concepts of knowledge and its diffusion. It is accepted that the university should teach, that is, transmit knowledge that has been acquired and consolidated epistemologically. This fetishism of the established cannot help but concern the establishment. An analysis of knowledge reveals in it the following three elements: the *categorical* element (elaborated and codified concepts); the *thematic* element (topics in the process of being elaborated); and the *problematical* element. Should not the university of the future center on the *problematical* rather than the *categorical* element? It would, in such a way, avoid the conservative character that has been present in official programs (which have been, more or less, disputed by the opposition) in all the countries around the world. Within the problematical element will be found the experimental and utopian elements, certainty and doubt, attainment and risk.

XII.

It is, nevertheless, out of the question that the categorical element should be left intact and stagnant. It is inconceivable that the problematical element should not affect the accepted and the acquired concepts by a criticism taken to the extremes of its established and stabilized concepts as "categories."

It would be particularly appropriate to introduce new categories. I propose the following, which are as yet only slightly elaborated, and which are tied to the problematical element: the day-to-day element, the urban element, space, and the criticism of space.

This proposal can only be brought to bear in the course of a development that would transcend the present proposal.

The Education of an Urban Administrator
By Edward J. Logue

Once again it is becoming fashionable to say that our cities are hopeless, they can't be saved, and they will be abandoned to those who are not welcome in the suburbs and probably couldn't afford to live there anyway.

Some take the view that this is too bad but that nothing can be done about it. Others think it is a good thing, that a congested urban lifestyle isn't really any good for the human race anyway.

The continuing spread of blight after more than twenty years of federally aided urban renewal is proclaimed as proof positive that urban renewal is a bad thing. The economic and social errors incorporated into too many public housing projects are taken as documentation that public housing is bad housing. The slow pace of rehabilitation except in a handful of rather special urban neighborhoods is presented as still further evidence that even putting away the bulldozer does not make any difference.

Finally, the just plain ordinariness, often drabness of publicly assisted housing, other public construction, and even private construction in urban-renewal areas is offered as proof that government is incapable of promoting, or even creating, high standards of urban design.

I would like to express very strong disagreement with these views and discuss, particularly, the opportunities and difficulties one confronts trying to get good design, and cite some specific examples out of my own experience.

I am disturbed by the trend so popular in Washington over these last several years of creating gimmicky new programs, my favorite example being Model Cities, which promised more than it could possibly achieve and quickly became mired in local controversy, fueled, among other things, by an uncertain, erratic, and inadequate supply of federal money. Each program was announced with great fanfare as the new solution. These new solutions seemed to serve two purposes: to hold out new hope and to justify cutting back on already existing programs, which could have been refined, improved, and, if necessary, redirected.

It is perfectly true that the design of most low-income public housing projects is banal. Their lack of aesthetic appeal and their tendency to have more than their share of social problems has led them to be largely unwelcome to most neighborhoods, and particularly resisted in all but the most blighted areas where the desperate need for any kind of housing is all too clear.

I would like to put forward the proposition that the failure to have good urban design standards for public housing in this country is responsible for most of the inadequacy of public housing today, and, more important, responsible for its often well-deserved unpopularity.

Let me make clear that urban design, in this sense, and as I use it generally in this essay, is much more than architecture, although it includes architecture. If we examine the history of decision making on any public housing project, we find, nine times out of ten, that urban design decisions were taken under other headings, which all but guaranteed failure.

Good urban design connotes to me, above all, a sense of appropriateness and a sense of humanity. There can be architecture as "far out" as the new Boston City Hall, which is a strikingly human building once you get to know it, or, as ordinary as the average Beacon Hill townhouse. If you examine the latter, one by one, with a handful of exceptions they really are quite ordinary. But set down on those streets, some with long, some with rather short vistas, with a sense of scale, a very human scale, Beacon Hill adds up to an urban space and place as nice as any I know in the United States.

But, back to public housing. Bureaucrats decided, from their point of view, which is that of managers and operators of public housing, to stack as many units as possible in one place because that, they thought, would make their job easier. They did not anticipate the consequences. Think of what a different place that infamous Boston public housing project, Columbia Point, would be if instead of stacking them up, they had used the ample land available and followed the scale of the nearby South End townhouses. In fact, it would have saved a lot of money because the South End townhouses were built on filled land, the same as Columbia Point, and they were put on spread footings, and did not bear the high piling costs of the Columbia Point project. But even projects as bleak as this are not beyond salvation, as M. Paul Friedberg has demonstrated in the marvelous playground at the Jacob Riis Houses on New York City's Lower East Side.

Take another public housing problem: personal safety. The public housing bureaucrats decided that for reasons of cost they, of course, would not have resident superintendents. Despite the fact that in many projects there is a fairly substantial number of elderly people or welfare people who could use the rather modest income. It would have been a relatively simple thing to require that at least one apartment on the ground floor of each elevator bank have either a mom-and-pop candy store with the door open, a concierge, or some other kind of human presence which would improve the prospects of safety at relatively modest cost. This would certainly be a lot cheaper than extra security forces.

On another policy level, if you are a resident of public housing and begin to make more money so that you go above the income limit, you get thrown out instead of being asked to pay more rent. Success equals eviction. That translates into the most motivated families being the ones who have to get out first.

And, last, let's come to the matter of architecture itself. The public housing bureaucrats make specifications so detailed and so rigid that it is no wonder that you can spot a public housing project almost anywhere in the United States without the need for a sign or any other identification. No wonder the talented members of the architectural profession refuse to have anything to do with them.

Typically, public housing projects are built without the kind of supporting facilities in the form of schools, day-care centers, churches, recreation centers, or shopping facilities that would transform them into living communities. And, to use one of my favorite examples, it is unheard of that a public housing development have anywhere in it a tavern.

Even the briefest of visits to a British Council Housing development, such as Roehampton in London, demonstrates how unnecessary this approach is. This is a very large project, larger than most of our American projects, yet it has a combination of high-rise and low-rise buildings, it has a town center with not only a greengrocer, a chemist, a library, a public school, but indeed a pub. We could build attractive human public housing in the United States if we decided that we care enough. It need not cost any more. We just need to get a different set of rules.

Let's go on to the area of urban renewal. Each of us can list a rather large number of unsuccessful urban renewal projects, which are unattractive and which may very well be inferior to what they replaced in terms of urban design. That is because there was not anybody around to insist that the new developments must not yield to the purely commercial constraints or the ordinary real-estate speculator.

But there is ample evidence that it does not have to be that way. I would offer as an example the Government Center in Boston. If there is a sufficient commitment to urban design in the right place, extraordinary standards can be achieved.

Or, in a residential area, the Wooster Square neighborhood in New Haven is still my favorite example of the fact that neighborhoods can indeed be rehabilitated, that new housing can be built to fit in with the gracious old housing that has been fixed up, and that new community facilities can make an old-fashioned neighborhood attractive once again to a variety of ethnic groups.

New Haven and Boston, I believe, are examples of places where high standards of urban design have been achieved. (See Vincent Scully for a dissenting view on New Haven.) But the process was far from automatic. It required education, and I was among those who went through a learning experience on that score.

The average well-educated American decision maker, whether in public or private life, usually has had no exposure whatever to urban design in his academic training, and he comes to these decisions with not only a minimum of preparation but with little awareness of how design decisions are made. Most university presidents, most elected chief executives, and most public and private administrators have no awareness or concern about the importance of urban design. They usually don't even know what they like.

I can give you an example, if I may, of three ignorant men who held positions of responsibility in New Haven at the same time. The late A. Whitney Griswold was President of Yale University, Richard C. Lee was the Mayor of New Haven, and I was the city's Development Administrator. Each of us enjoyed the process of building. We had, you might say, edifice complexes. If one knows where to look in New Haven, one can see examples of the first buildings built under the administration of these three men: they are terrible. We just didn't know any better. But, we all learned, in different ways: there are today probably more well-designed buildings in New Haven—done by Yale, by the City, and by the urban-renewal program—than there are in all but a handful of cities in the United States.

I won't identify the others' failures, only my own. The Southern New England Telephone Company building in the Oak Street urban-renewal project, for example, is a squat ten-story, 500,000-square-foot building, with no appeal. I cringe every time I see it. But the memory of it has led me, over the years since its completion, to be appropriately demanding of good design when it hurts. That is the real test. Everybody one asks is for good design—until it hurts. It counts only when you insist on it all the way.

★ ★ ★

The essential question of our time, as I see it, is whether it is true that the American city can no longer afford to concern itself with good design. Is it possible anymore, for example, to build a city that is livable with motorcars? Do the work practices and bargaining agreements of the construction trades permit buildings that are both innovative and economically feasible? In the day-to-day struggle in the marketplace between beauty and cost, who can effectively arbitrate that unequal struggle on behalf of the public interest?

If I were not a believer in the possibility that good design can indeed be achieved in the tough arena of practical affairs, I would not for a minute be interested in my present job as President of the New York State Urban Development Corporation. That is one of the challenges that make my work satisfying. It might be argued that in a career going back to the earliest days of the Urban Renewal Program in the 1950s, I was a tardy convert to the essentiality of design control. All of us have experienced, I am sure, the phenomenon of the convert becoming even more zealous than those simply born into the faith. The truth, however, is that I always knew I cared. Perhaps it had something to do with being born and brought up in Philadelphia, a city not without style and grace. I went to school on Rittenhouse Square and learned at a formative age what a delightful place a modest public square can be.

My main problem was that when I got into this business, I didn't know anything about the subtleties of the relationships between architects and clients, and, more specifically, the fundamental truth that the architect doesn't exist who doesn't need a demanding client.

The City of New Haven is where I learned that essential lesson. I was in good company during those formative years of my urban experience, because Yale's President Griswold went through a similar process of education in bringing good design to the postwar Yale campus.

Some of you whom I have met from time to time on the ecologically brilliant parking lots outside the Yale Bowl are aware that I am a graduate of that venerable institution. When I married my wife, Margaret, her father William G. De Vane was not only a distinguished professor in the humanities, but also Dean of Yale College. So when I came back to New Haven at a time when the university and the city were both renewing themselves, it was a fortunate coincidence for me to hear from the inside, as it were, the agonizing reappraisals from the president of the university concerning the architectural evolution of the collegiate monuments to God, Country, and Yale. The key circumstance in the aesthetic education of President Griswold was when someone brought him together with Eero Saarinen, who made a master plan for the development of the campus. The Ingalls Hockey Rink, the Kline Biology Tower, and the Saarinen colleges, themselves, took Yale out of the rut and into the forefront of campus design.

My own baptism in design control in New Haven was the Southern New England Telephone Company headquarters building, smack in the heart of our ambitious plans to arrest the flight of business from downtown New Haven. When SNET expressed a willingness to shift from another site, to build 500,000 square feet of office space, which would pay a lot of taxes and, to cap it all, had already engaged a distinguished firm of architects, you can perhaps understand our excitement. What we failed to appreciate was the impact of a bureaucratic client, such as a public utility, on architectural expression, and what we lacked was an adequate review procedure to protect us from the deadening influences of a businessman's committee searching for the most inexpensive common denominator in the short haul.

When we were renewing Wooster Square, a transitional area of New Orleans–style iron railings mixed with decaying brownstones, the good Italian-American residents of the neighborhood dug in their heels against the high-rise design suggested by the architect and too easily accepted by us. And the neighborhood was right. The proposed plans were out of scale with the neighborhood and out of scale with family living styles brought to New Haven from an older, nobler culture. When the time came to build a school there, we let the neighborhood decide what they wanted and where. (They opted for a dual-purpose school-community center, with bocce courts, card rooms, a branch library, and double-sized swimming pool—made possible by applying renewal funds to the normal education building budget.)

My friends like to rib me from time to time over my "architectural monument" in New Haven—the magnificent Paul Rudolph parking garage dominating the Church Street project, now occupied by Macy's and a new downtown hotel. The Rudolph garage is clear, strong, simple, and works superbly well for a not uncomplicated requirement of modern urban development. It has strong texture and it is in scale with its setting. In short, it fits, as the Pan American Building fails to fit the townscape of Park Avenue.

When I moved on to Boston in 1960, I was determined to carry out what I had learned in the school of experience, and I had a marvelous set of instruments with which to work. We were able to accomplish what we accomplished in Boston because the concept of federally sponsored urban renewal had not yet been fragmented and dissipated in favor of Model Cities and the War on Poverty, nor had it been undermined by the false hope that we could simultaneously carry on war in Vietnam and have butter on the table at home.

The Boston experience was predicated on the assumption that in order to achieve good design we needed a plan, a comprehensive approach, integrating the essential elements of a viable and rewarding urban experience.

Why do we go to Europe to visit those ancient cities, and what do we do when we get there? Why is a little piazza in Capri, a tiny little thing, something that you never forget once you see it? Why is it such a pleasure to walk along the Seine in Paris or down the Spanish steps in Rome? Why is it that young Swedes, when they have their choice, opt for the Old Town in Stockholm? And why is it that the Park Slope district of Brooklyn is suddenly undergoing rejuvenation at the hands of young couples searching for a more satisfying lifestyle?

Good design encompasses a good deal more than the gracious elements of attractive architecture. The enrichment of urban living means the right combination of building and space, a sense of scale in which the human dimension is not engulfed, the presence of a vitality that does not disappear at sundown. It includes a decent regard for the small details, such as windows, resting places, lampposts, surfaces, and colors—the amenities that mean the difference between something ugly and dreary and something beautiful and alive.

The cheap and banal results of uncontrolled urban expansion are visible all about us. A couple of blocks from my own apartment is a forty-story atrocity, the product of undirected search for profit that is much worse in design than anything the Public Housing Authority has ever done. I happen to think that, in spite of all the limitations imposed by high construction costs and a seeming disregard for the special qualities of particular building sites, it is still possible to rebuild our cities so that they will be pleasant places in which to walk and work and live.

In Boston, we at the Boston Redevelopment Authority attempted to draw both people and investment back to Boston's historic core through the imaginative use of good design. In the Government Center, the layout was as irregular as the old city blocks, which formerly occupied the site. It contained places to sit and to walk, treating the open spaces as gathering places, not unlike the piazzas I mentioned before. Plazas and walkways at ground level are one of the antidotes to the higher densities required to make some urban developments feasible. We went to some trouble and expense to provide a fountain there, with a bosk of trees. Whenever I go by that spot, particularly in the pleasanter months of the year, people are sitting there just enjoying it. How do you measure that in an urban budget?

We took a downtown area in which there had been only one new commercial building built in twenty-five years and tried to make good design fashionable. After the first new office building was in place, it served as a challenge for others to equal. We were only interested in a city of quality, and somehow the word got around.

We created an architectural advisory committee and imposed the process of a design review on our developers. We couldn't name the architects, but we reserved the right of approval. Serving on that committee were the Dean of the Harvard Graduate School of Design, the Dean of the School of Architecture and Planning at M.I.T., and the Dean Emeritus of M.I.T. When the developers saw the names on that committee, they knew we were serious about having topflight architects. I don't believe that any public official is taken seriously as an advocate of good design until he demonstrates his willingness to pursue good design before and after it begins to hurt. And, sooner or later, it inevitably comes to that. Basically, architecture is an irresponsible profession when it comes to costs. When we ran a competition for the design of Boston City Hall, the essential rule was that the winner had to provide cost estimates showing that the job could actually be done within the budget using his design. So the goal of protecting good design until it hurts has to work two ways: both the client and the architect have to be tough about it.

It is also important not to do too much tinkering. One should start with a well worked out plan—read carefully by someone who cares about design details—and stay with it when the hard decisions need to be made. It is absolutely indispensable to look the developer straight in the eye and say you're going first class or you're not going at all. He won't believe you the first time or even the second time. But after a while he will get the point.

At the New York State Urban Development Corporation, the process has been extended to its logical conclusion. We pick all our architects directly. Those of you with any experience in politics know that this is not always as easy as it sounds. We not only look for the very best of the established architects, but also for the most promising among the younger generation of newcomers to the profession. And that includes professionals of promise from the ranks of ethnic minorities. The relationship between a public official and architects is not always the easiest. In dealing with architects many public officials, since price competition is not permitted, look to them as a source for campaign contributions. That process is not calculated to enhance considerations of design. By the same token, talented architects discover that public officials usually don't have control of their own bureaucracies. Bureaucrats can wear down good design by nibbling it to death. But there has been a general failure in our society to understand the enrichment of urban and suburban living that could come from better design in the comprehensive sense of the term.

The cities, in my opinion, ought to be made competitive with the suburbs, so that the choice between them could be made for real reasons rather than on the basis of the basic essentials of living—the quality of schools, the state of public safety, or the quality of housing. I am a city man, myself, but I recognize the attraction of the suburbs apart from the conditions that have triggered the flight from our urban centers in recent years.

I remain convinced that moderate-priced housing can be built on budget, meeting federal cost limitations, and very attractively, once you decide that is what you are going to do. One of the keys is to take every advantage of the economics and amenities made possible by technological advances in the building industry. At the Urban Development Corporation we have established a Technological Department with the responsibility to design into our projects those tested improvements that are already available. Our authority to build by the code of the State of New York rather than local building codes has enabled us to introduce cost-saving innovations into our designs not otherwise possible. Furthermore, our position as a large-volume producer of housing means that we are a significant market for the products of industrialized housing manufacturers.

We have concluded agreements to utilize a guaranteed number of wood modules for low-rise construction and precast concrete panels for high-rise construction during the coming year. Speed of construction is, of course, the essence of the battle to produce new housing within feasible budgets. We learned in Rome, New York, where the city was faced with a loss of an economically important military facility because of a shortage of housing, that it was possible to use modular construction to build, in a very short period of time, homes that have turned out to be very well-received by their grateful new tenants.

There is a good deal more to design than the physical components of a new housing development. We decided, as a matter of principle, at the Urban Development Corporation that the social environment of projects occupied exclusively by low-income tenants had proven to be a human disaster. Our developments are planned to include, on the average, seventy percent moderate-income tenants, twenty percent low-income families, and ten percent low-income elderly. It is our goal in our new-town-in-town on Welfare Island to create a comprehensive community of diverse ethnic background, varying income and age groups, a demonstration, if you will, that a truly cosmopolitan neighborhood is still possible in the urban environment. The key to the accomplishment of all this is the opportunity to start from scratch in the creation of an innovative public-school system on the island. The presence of quality schools will be as important to the style of life in the designed community as will the absence of automobiles. (Welfare Island is so small and New Yorkers so undisciplined that I can't imagine what we could have done in our plans to accommodate the automobile.)

The idea of New Towns is to tackle the environment at the broadest scale—land-use, neighborhood size, commercial and employment opportunity—in order to provide attractive living on a human scale and with all the necessary services. In the United States there is no tradition and little public acceptance of centralized planning controls, such as those that have enabled European countries to redirect some of the forces of deterioration.

Scenic and historic areas have been sacrificed to sprawling development, biologically important wetlands filled in with garbage, landmark buildings obliterated by ribbons of concrete. Our interest in the potentiality of New Towns at the Urban Development Corporation (we have two in upstate New York in different stages of planning in addition to Welfare Island in New York City) is to test the hypothesis that man can indeed control his environment by intelligent design to the greater benefit of human values.

I would like to make a few final comments on the elements that I think must be in place if we are going to achieve high standards of design in our cities and, therefore, both keep the people we have and attract others back. After all, the competition is only a suburban shopping center, and that is not the toughest competition in the world.

First, there must be commitment. The commitment must spring from either the chief elected official or the public administrator who has primary responsibility for public development decisions, preferably both. If there can be that commitment at the top, it becomes a relatively simple matter of diverse procedures for the selection of architects, the review of plans, or the establishment of controls, which can make good design the accepted, expected thing. It may be a private group, or an influential individual, such as J. Irwin Miller, the patron saint of good design in Columbus, Indiana. But without the commitment from the public leadership, it is a pretty uphill fight.

Second, there must be a power base or a system. There can't be just recommendations. Representatives of the public interest must have, through one means or another, the right of approval or disapproval, and they must be willing to make their decisions quickly, competently, and honestly.

And, finally, unless they are terribly well-educated, the chief executives must restrain the impulse to make all the design decisions themselves, but obtain the services of qualified professionals. Then back them up.

What Is the Most Challenging Role for the Capital of the World in the Continuous Happening that Makes Up the Future of Design?

By Richard L. Meier

Capitals are places that lead a society. They can sometimes command change; they always insist upon authorizing it. Capitals are also the foci for forces hoping to legitimate change, thus making it acceptable to members of the society; they undertake initiatives that open up long-range possibilities. New York was formally designated the diplomatic capital of the world when the victorious and neutral nations got together in 1945 to decide what place had leadership, élan, accessibility, communications, and a stock of knowledge that would nurture the infant United Nations. Within New York, the chosen site became mid-Manhattan. Then, despite a dimming of the hopeful future for international organizations, which had been earlier sketched out in journalistic terms, the physical infrastructure for managing the great enterprises of the world was installed within a short distance of the United Nations.

Manhattan, as a community, has neither power nor influence. It is merely the hugest feedback mixer and modulator that has ever been put together. The most astonishing balancing acts one could ever imagine are undertaken daily in its towers and slabs. Out of this action, which occurs at a more rapid pace and manipulates greater magnitudes, by far, than any other locale in all of human history, comes experience, insight, judgment, learning—as well as irritation, exhaustion, criticism, despair, rebellion, and anarchic reaction.

That, briefly, is the urban setting for The Museum of Modern Art. Surrounded by static machines dedicated to incremental decision-making, the Museum has launched a proposal that appears to ignore its neighbors and competitors. It ambles about stylishly in a metasystem populated with abstractions and ephemera. The Universitas Project proposal, as presented for our discussion, is an unfinished symphony that presents a number of resonant themes—it is, moreover, the handiwork of some great phrasemakers. From this vantage point, it appears that the first question is whether it can be finished, the second is whether it can be performed in that environment, and the third is whether it can achieve recognition as a masterpiece and live in the repertoires of the companies of players (designers) of the future.

Undoubtedly, the first two questions will be answered by others, so what follows will be a response to the third. It will explore what kinds of opportunities exist in the vicinity of the Museum for building a viable first-rank institution for design based upon the theory and practice of organization.

A Recent Parallel

The potentials of the future are best analyzed with the aid of recent history. Where has this kind of thing been promoted before? Are the successes and failures experienced in that effort associated with forces that survive in Manhattan? The biggest effort by far is that of the College of Environmental Design on the Berkeley campus of the University of California. It went through gestation, birth, and a brief period of nurture during the decade of the 1960s before it faced the vicissitudes of budget cuts and open competition.

The preliminaries were based upon the rhetoric of the 1950s. This is not the occasion to dredge up those archaisms for quotation. Suffice it to say that they were eloquent enough to bring William and Catherine Bauer Wurster to Berkeley from M.I.T. Then came the delicate parlaying between separate faculties that finally led to what is now known in the business world as a conglomerate. It contained a small school of architecture under great pressure to grow, a free-floating department of city and regional planning of recent vintage, a department of landscape architecture that had evolved from ornamental horticulture in the College of Agriculture, and a group of designers in textiles, pottery, glass, and other materials who had been orphaned by the dissolution of home economics and were in search of a new academic mission.

As campus planner, Dean Wurster laid out a complex for the fine arts and applied arts, so that the new building to be provided would be neighbored by structures dedicated to music, art, and anthropology. Reinforcement, it was hoped, would result from proximity. Faculty members undertook the design of the building so the face exposed to the world was under close internal control, subject only to the prejudices of a Board of Regents and a legislative subcommittee. The name of the conglomerate was another matter, since many were proposed, but none could be readily agreed upon. Dean Wurster obtained vigorous and unanimous dissent on only one—Environmental Design. In order to force agreement he threatened to submit it to the President and Regents. Lacking concurrence, the Environmental Design label was attached to the new College, and it has since been widely adopted by new and reorganized design schools.

Another important decision was that of scale of operations. There it seemed necessary to defer to local precedents. Just as San Francisco was built in the wilderness and became an "instant city," recognized by its peers less than a decade after its founding, so Berkeley similarly set out to become "instant ivy." It built up a library and embraced the classics with all the vigor of the tycoons and empire builders who won the West. Its engineers left Paul Bunyan behind when rerouting rivers. As science began to move into the limelight, its organizers' references to *gigantism* in research instrumentation were called heroism in the Soviet Union, and "Berkeleyitis" in America.

Again, over the virtually unanimous objections of the faculty on hand, the scale of operations was set to push the College of Environmental Design to become far larger than any predecessor very quickly, supposedly without compromising quality.

Educators elsewhere in the university had qualms, primarily because undergraduate students brought into the College by the respective units tended to come from the bottom quartile in academic achievement of students enrolling at Berkeley. Their competences were not picked up by tests. Would the new College of Environmental Design scrape bottom and become a haven for athletes worried about eligibility?

Fortunately none of the worst fears were realized. An all-university change in calendar from the semester to the quarter system forced a complete restructuring of the curriculum: obsolete courses were revitalized or abandoned. Many modern views crept in, and general student unrest stimulated the relaxation of many unnecessary rules. The planners de-emphasized design after joining the College, taking up with the nearby development economists and the systems engineers first and then linking up with public health, law, social work, and a number of minor social programs. The architects opted for technical competence, many set at the expense of design and subdivided into specialties to get some leverage. The landscape architects left their gardens to plan open spaces at the regional scale, even New Towns, and suburbs. The smaller scale designers failed to get into the industrial arts, and have not yet found a clear direction. Simultaneously, the academic quality of the entering students has risen to the top quartile, with the College of Environmental Design reaching its quota before any other category of undergraduate education. This phenomenon is perhaps more attributable to the decline in the images of engineering, science, and business among students leaving high school and junior college than any reform in the curriculum. Superior students now read avidly and widely, so the library is woefully overtaxed, and the studios are underpopulated.

The device used for promoting academic quality is the offering of a Ph.D. The presence of doctoral students raises the level of discussion of the average master's candidate seminar. Faculty are kept up-to-date, interacting with new researchers equipped with advanced methodologies. Frontiersmanship gets into the atmosphere. Slowly the standards of criticism can be raised; inconsistencies seem likely to remain, but criticism is less likely to be erroneous, judged by the existing stock of knowledge elsewhere in the university or in the books.

The impact of this new institution upon the post-technological society is yet to be experienced. Many students have taken up careers in business and government with other than design responsibilities, a development noted in other schools as well, but it seems to be more significant in Berkeley. A few years after they start, the immediate environment begins to change. An important feature of the scale of operations is that the most advanced students are systematically rerouted into the teaching of design; they design experiments to discover semiquantitatively how well various new techniques of transmitting concepts work in situations where their elders slide by intuitively with a lick here and a promise there. Therefore, many of the graduates will be teaching, although not necessarily in academic surroundings. The content of the teaching is as much psychology, systems synthesis, economics, public health, and politics as it is the elements of environmental design. By producing innovators and ingenious teachers, as well as a few designers, Berkeley will have a large multiplier and, therefore, a significant impact upon society, perhaps also the design professions, but in a way that could not have been envisaged in designers' prose at the time of conception.

This background serves not only as parallel, but also as introduction. The context within which the students react to the Universitas is explained. However, they obviously speak for themselves; they rise above their institutional connections.

Voices from the Future

When students from Berkeley's College of Environmental Design were asked to respond to the Universitas proposal, their reactions turned out to be remarkably similar, whether at the masters, doctorate, or post-doctorate level. For the faculty, this is worrisome. Have we managed to generate that much consensus? Certainly the level of agreement was not anticipated. What follows is a typical example.

Thoughts on the Universitas Proposal

With the first reading, I really didn't understand what the Universitas proposal was about. With the second reading, I began to copy quotes. I am enthused and troubled by the proposal. The philosophy and approach laid out, in my opinion, is close to ideal—but then so is the philosophy and approach of graduate environmental study at Berkeley. How might Universitas function and produce in ways that Berkeley doesn't?

After all, we have this fantastic faculty with high-level expertise in many departments, a lot of very bright people, and a lot of freedom. Most of us are committed to positive, humanistic reordering of our world, and some of us share some of the guiding principles expressed, such as:

1. The belief that there is overreliance on examination of what exists to explain what might or should be.
2. Skepticism of the promise of tackling today's and tomorrow's problems with only technological scientisms.

What promise does Universitas hold that doesn't already exist? One strong point in your favor—for me, the most significant aspect of this proposal—is the commitment to application. It is central and critical to your success and will become crucial when problem definition becomes displaced by the actual design process. One must have people sincerely directed toward implementation and application or the institution almost certainly will lose momentum. Universitas will begin to circle on itself and become ordinary University.

It's my belief that the design/implementation/construction/testing orientation set forth in the proposal will partially, at least, eliminate some of the problems I have observed and felt in the social and behavioral factors segment of Ph.D. and masters programs at Berkeley:

1. Complete separation of analysis and actual design and, as a consequence, somehow a lack of commitment.

2. Little practice with three-dimensional synthesis and testing of ideas.

3. Absence of production pressures, lack of direction seen or felt.

4. Lack of interchange of ideas at the formulation level—all ideas are properly shielded with academic armor before presentation.

I'm not satisfied, on the other hand, that other problems experienced at universities are solved or on the way to solution in this proposal. It does not:

1. Insure against inadequate communication and perpetual ambiguities, misunderstandings.

2. Give thought to the group dynamics that are set up as a result of intergroup rivalries, jealousies, and leadership struggles.

3. Explain how Universitas connects with existing institutions: existing design professions, existing university systems, and economic and political structures.

Will it change them? How? Use them as resources? Become a resource for them? Ignore them? Rival them?

There appear to be several conflicts within the proposal itself:

1. Early mention of "changing values" as a primary task, then later in the operational description "implementation of societal goals is a primary task"—but perhaps this is not seen as a potential conflict?

2. The relationship to science is unclear. What can be adopted from science? Rejected?

I would like to have seen more attention given to the actual mechanics envisioned for all phases of the design process, i.e., 1), the production of construction documents; 2), who takes care of building technology? 3), who might the "clients" really be?

Perhaps this comes later. I guess what I am saying is that I want to be convinced that the concepts Universitas promises will, in fact, be applicable and realizable in a very real sense and, at this point, I'm not.

George Holman, Ph.D. student, Architecture

The following fragment is presented for its outlook. The question raised in discussion was the following: Some things will be excluded from consideration in the study of architecture that the lay population will assume is included. What are they? Where might a reformulation begin?

On the Classification of Architectural Objects

I:

Within the total set of architectural objects that have been and are now produced in our culture in the last decades, it is possible to isolate some that are the output of 1), a system of principles, 2), specific codes in close dependence with those principles, 3), a system of rules governing the relationship "selection of the code/function of the object." Function of the object should be understood in the following sense: being the object of an ideological product it is considered functional when it serves and is coherent with the strategy that determined its insertion in that context. These objects have in common a certain array of traits that constitute its "architectureness," or the status of being produced by architects following principles that started developing during the Renaissance and whose diachronic formation can be traced without break, up to the present.

The remaining architectural objects that have been produced can be distributed according to the following taxonomy:

1. Mass-consumption system (by which I mean those objects in which the "selling function" is so strong that it is the dominant element determining the design of the object at all its levels).

2. Vernacular system (a kind of *"langue"* underlying the production of most of the "unremarkable" objects).

3. Revival systems (objects that are travesties or parodies that, in some cases may be classified as pertaining to the mass-consumption system).

The mass, vernacular, and revival systems have their own specificity of principles, codes, and rules governing their production. Within the system that produces "architectureness" and among the remaining systems there are some well-established relationships (i.e., the architecture yielding system is believed to be superior in relation to the others). On the other hand, there are also well-defined relationships among the set of systems that generate architectural objects in our culture and in the architectural systems outside Western culture (i.e., some of the alien systems mentioned earlier constitute the source of signs from which our system of architecture takes raw matter, material, upon which it builds myths). The point is that in order to satisfy the expanding demand for architectural objects, the relationships among the systems I have so briefly described will have to be changed; possibly this taxonomy will become obsolete and other rules will govern architectural objects and their production.

II:

We can safely say that until now the different practices that are responsible for the production of artifacts in our culture have been determined by following what we can call a "horizontal layers division principle," i.e., the level of houses, the level of art, the level of clothes, the level of furniture, etc.

In order to satisfy the future demand for different qualities of objects, design practices will have to be restructured following the "vertical set division principle." The main parameter that will determine the unity of the sets is the homogeneity of the reading code in the user-consumer; as a direct result of this partition of the fields of design practice, more specific strategies could be adopted more rapidly. The existence of the same rhetorical structures comprehending the production of a full vertical set is a basic point to be explored. The sociological unit to be designed for, which underlies a vertical set, would be that of a subculture, a large group, or even a multinational firm.

Rodolfo Machado, Ph.D. candidate, Architecture

The following study endeavored to show the objective differences in perception between art and architecture, testing propositions underlying current styles by using quantitative methods developed recently by psychologists.

On Aesthetic Preferences for Visual Complexity

The object (of this study) was to find out whether a direct relationship existed between the complexity of an architectural subject and the amount of "pleasingness" found in it by a cross-section of respondents. As a measure of complexity, two components of information load—the quantity of information and the diversity of information—are used; as a measure of aesthetic preference, a seven-point scale of "pleasingness" to "unpleasingness" is employed. To measure, the quantity of information in each of the (sample) squares was counted. By the use of boundary lines, the whole picture is reduced to a large number of small, distinct areas. To obtain the diversity factor, a second group of random squares was selected; these were counted for the number of different kinds of bits (areas).

Michael J. Harlock, M. Arch. 1972

What follows is a general approach now under investigation for discovering the attributes of designed environments, and the subpublics that respond to the respective attributes; it is economical, fast, and convenient. It represents one of the most fruitful outcomes from marrying psychophysics to design.

Multidimensional Scaling for Architectural Environments

In the evaluation of environmental quality, the relevant variables cannot be specified arbitrarily; rather, it is necessary to use those attributes which are subjectively used to judge the environment if human responses are to be modeled. Once these attributes are identified, the second problem is to assess how typical environments rate with respect to the attributes, so that the physical features of the environment, which influence the subjective evaluations, can be quantified and utilized in partly specifying an appropriate environment.

The concept of the attribute is fundamental to this approach. An attribute is a perceived characteristic of environments, a way in which one environment is seen to differ from another. One person may call a room warm and another term it hot, while both agree that it is warmer inside than out. Individuals may differ on their evaluations, yet still utilize the same perceptual structure. The physical features that relate uniquely to an attribute are not obvious. Temperature is related to "warmth" as a possible attribute, but is air speed? The problem of identifying attributes independent of the limitations of psychophysical methods and the verbal interface is a complex problem, and there have been several approaches. The simplest approach is to ask individuals to rate their environment on several scales, and to then compute the average for each space on each scale. There is no assurance that in such an approach the subjects are using the same interpretation of the rating scales, or that in rating only one environment they are perceiving the range of possible conditions. Words are limited. Since our environment is relatively tame, our vocabulary does not have a score of words to describe fine environmental differences, as, for example, polar tribes have for snow conditions. The term *glare* generally means excessive light, but there are a variety of distinct perceptions or attributes inherent in the term. Thus, a single rating may contain any one or a combination of several responses, which should be separated in describing the environment for control through design.

An approach is used in experimental psychology where the environment is varied according to well-described physical variables, and the human response recorded. Any controllable environmental variables can be subject to any of several variants of this research approach. Unfortunately, there is nothing in the approach that assesses the relevance of the variables to architectural environments. Even though repeatable responses are obtained to correspond to some physical measure, it is not assured that an attribute has been found. The response may be based on a mixture of several attributes, or a variety of physical variables may lead to the same variations in response. These, too, may be explored in the laboratory, but the process is a lengthy and, perhaps, unrewarding one.

A less innocent form of psychophysics is used in the methods of developing engineering criteria for architectural environments. Variables are explored on the basis of complaints of glare, noise, and drafts only to the extent of controlling the excesses of past technology, and rarely extending the work to avoid future problems through more understanding of human response. Under a philosophy of benign surplus, it is necessary to supply "enough" light for the most detailed task while "controlling" glare. Aside from broader environmental issues of power generation, just how much light is worth how much glare? The problem is one of trade-offs on the perceptual level, which have not been adequately explored. To answer the question, the first step is to assess the perception of light quantity and the perception of glare, since without relevant attributes trade-offs are not meaningful. Would you trade two quard for a maglevark, or are these terms possibly as irrelevant to your perceptions as illuminance and intensity?

The adequacy of engineering criteria cannot be assessed without an external criterion based entirely on human perceptions, a way of finding what are the human perceptions, a way of finding what are the humanly relevant attributes of the environment, and how particular environments rate relative to those attributes. Despite the previous lack of suitable assessment methods, my own observations of "well-engineered" environments, and the increasing prevalence of such environments through industrialized building, have led to a sense of urgency in developing alternative criteria based on human responses.

Like factor analysis, the method is based on rating scales, as shown in the figure below:

Rate: (1   2   3   4   5   6   7)   Your name _____

        very   average   very   Library _____
        poor   good

__ general impressions

__ type of light fixture

__ arrangement of fixtures

__ color scheme

__ color of light

__ glare from lights

__ glare from surfaces

__ gross light distribution

__ modeling

__ quantity of light (1 = too little...4 = just right...7 = too much)

Since the method assumes that any one scale may share meaning with the other scales, or may have several interpretations related to different attributes, the choice of terms is not critical, although they do roughly delimit the scope of the study. The process involves each subject rating each environment on each scale.

The analysis is based on the differences in each individual's ratings between different environments. On each scale, the differences in ratings between all pairs of environments (a matrix) is accumulated across individuals in a way that preserves the individually perceived attributes of the environments relative to that rating scale. The method was devised by Horan and essentially makes the difference between two environments for any one scale equal to the root-mean square of the differences in ratings by each individual.

The quantitative results are matched by qualitative results; the scaling methods make no distinction between aesthetics and psychophysics. The color scheme was evaluated according to two attributes, one relating to the presence of bright colors favorably, and the other relating more to rich but muted natural wood colors. The first attribute may be interpreted as "colorful/colorless" and the second as "organic/plastic."

The attributes, once understood, are relatively easy to consider in design. Perhaps the best way to grasp them is to visit the spaces with a scorecard, or to view the spaces through slides, but many aspects are not as easily seen through the distortions of photography. Since many of the environments had serious faults, they form the basis for a large number of the attributes, and the faults may, in turn, be identified and avoided in design. It is important that examples exist that illustrate the faults, and that they have occurred in modern architectural designs. Such problems do not just happen to other architects, but are likely to occur in anyone's practice. Some of the faults are due to misapplication of new technology, such as mercury vapor lights, and excessive illumination levels, which could be eliminated given sufficient experience.

Technology is changing quickly so that the slow process of gaining such experience means that many poor environments will be produced before the problem becomes common knowledge. A professionally oriented evaluation system could avoid these problems through adequate assessment before installation, or at least its coordination with the initial use of new technology. Properly armed, the profession need only make the same mistake once.

Hugo G. Blasdel, Ph.D. candidate, Architecture

This selection seems to be overweighted on psychology. There are studies started among students that have been inspired by 1), the theories of culture and language, 2), accumulating knowledge about human development, 3), living systems theory (ecology), 4), political economy in its resuscitated form, 5), morphological technique in the solution of poorly formed problems, and 6), regional science. Needless to say, they are moving far beyond the competences of the design school faculty, but fortunately other members of the university faculty are quite happy to work with such students because they are asking intellectually interesting questions. Henceforth, the development of design theory and criticism must be carried out in a locale with access to documented knowledge and a broad-based company of investigators.

Entrepreneurial Thinking for the Museum

What a ripe opportunity! A non-profit organization with just about the best location in the world, with assets upward of a hundred million in the right market, and control over the property in its immediate surroundings, but unable to meet the next round of pay raises from its current income. Image-conscious executives managing more than $200 billions of capital are within calling and lunching distance. Image-mongers on Madison Avenue and image-preservers on Park Avenue are just as close. And here is a highly significant undertaking putting out unique and sometimes novel images just waiting to be turned around.

It seems that no one on the scene has been seeing the Museum as the silent marketplace. The galleries have long known that option values are built up as Museum visitors twist their necks. Gentlemen and their ladies put cash behind their preferences. Greedy, tax-evading types among the newly rich have been bidding up the prices of the old and not-so-old masters. The brokers in this trade know how sensitive prices are to what is seen and talked about; many are not above a little kiting on the side for a favored artist or the right owner. However, the antiquarian market is limited; the future of design is much more promising. Moreover, the huge exhibits of the latest forms in ultramodern technology, now held in the Armory and the recently constructed convention centers, have gotten as big as they can get. Very soon the action must move into new territory. How shall the new images be presented? A museum is better than a stadium.

Artists and designers, like athletes, need competition to bring out their mettle. Artists are still highly disorganized; their mode of operation resembles that of the nineteenth-century inventor, the would-be Edisons of yesterday in search of the patron who would support the development of their brainchild. The greatest need that artists have is obtaining the attention of the public. Bizarre behavior is usually one way of getting attention; it is a fair substitute for a good agent. Most designers, however, go to school to pick up their trade, and then join an organized group, very much as athletes develop their skills in interscholastic performances and then join a bush-league team with the hope of working their way up through the minor leagues to the majors, where the acknowledged stars are awarded the top trophies. The competitions for designers are still very haphazard in comparison to the sports playoffs or the Olympics. Nor are any Nobel Prizes handed out for outstanding contributions to knowledge as an alternative means for distinguishing between a mere high-level competence and a top-rank performance. Indeed, the degree of organization of competition in design appears to be arriving at a stage where professional athletics was before World War II.

One of the principal reasons for introducing hierarchical stages of competition is that it focuses attention upon the scouting and judging process, which, for design, is still grossly inadequate—the best man or the most interesting idea have a good chance of escaping notice altogether. After a few years of trying, the innovating designer is forced to find some other way of making a living, by which time his concept will have been buried under a barrage of new proposals, bad and good. It may be lost altogether, or, more likely it will be reinvented over and over until some lucky designer achieves the recognition that the concept deserves.

A large part of what is backward about design is its elitist clique of critics. The situation is not unlike what existed in the days when there were gentlemen and players, but only gentlemen could define what was "good form." Rather quickly, however, as soon as leisure time was created by a reduction in working hours, each social stratum created its own game, a medium of communication regarding performances and anticipations, and a quasimarket in wagers so that fans could back their tastes with cash. A rich language of commentary evolved that was so stuffed with neologisms that the newcomer needed an interpreter. Behind this facade of banter and criticism was an inner circle of entrepreneurs, managers, trainers, and inside dopesters whose whole life revolved around the competitive process presented by the game to which they were dedicated. Thus, a public that kicked, bounced, or batted a ball sometime in its life participated vicariously, but intensely, in the series of tourneys by which the winners were selected. So much for the analog.

The process of user criticism of design is just now undergoing scrutiny. Students and designers are shaken, for example, to discover that children from among black, yellow, brown, and white immigrants prefer relatively traditional park equipment and disapprove of the contemporary design approaches. Similarly, residents of New Towns most severely criticize their communities regarding just those features that urban designers use to discriminate good design from the ordinary product. Famous designers have advanced their careers independently of the powerless elements in the society, and have escaped to undertake new commissions before there was a chance for the clients forced to live in their environments to organize and make proposals for reform and redesign. Artists and designers who are producers for the contemporary scene have successfully managed to insulate themselves from the majority of the users, so the gap between the producer and consumer remains as great as it ever was.

A constructive suggestion is heard in some of the salons from sociologists, economists, statisticians, and planners who have been reading Alvin Toffler's more technical contributions on the social function of the arts, and the art of measuring the quantity and quality of the arts.[1] He made such clear proposals that it is possible for social entrepreneurs and institution builders to top his proposals by setting up even more efficient means for collecting the data and using it while it is still fresh.

Consider, for example, the following project:

Let us find and develop the connection between the designer-artist and his public. This can be done in a manner similar to that developed to keep the design and research engineer in contact with the flow of knowledge, the so-called Selective Dissemination of Information (SDI) system. In this case, a person who is willing to allocate some of his attention to the analysis and criticism of imagery, whether natural or man-designed, would be able to tune in on his television set to preliminary presentations equivalent to those of a museum catalogue. They can be made available on the new channels provided in the "wired-up city" (cable-distributed television of high standard) that is coming into existence almost everywhere in North America this decade. He chooses those which fit his mood and style, and the computer submits his choices to factor analysis. He may be assigned to several different specialized publics, whereupon the system is able to present much more specialized collections addressed to his tastes. Moreover, it is able to identify publications and showings of designs and artistic materials, and bring them to his attention. Through contacts with high-grade reproductions, the real thing, and the criticism of the new work, it should be possible to build up a much broader culture explosion than the phenomena of the 1950s and 1960s. Many people would undertake such explorations as they played an amateur's role in the arts-and-crafts classes, others when they were in the market for a house or cottage and needed to decide about the environment and the interior.

Now look at this development from the point of view of the artist-designer. He or his agent could identify the local market for his style. While competing in the bush leagues, he may well aspire for more recognition. Then he would submit his creative work to the minor league competition to which the more sophisticated publics direct their attention. If he is able to hold their attention, his work is displayed in metropolitan museums and galleries (major leagues). If it is deemed meritorious it can be nominated to the world competition, which is held, naturally enough, in The Museum of Modern Art. This is not much different from what happens now, when the present system works at all, but recognition of talented output should be quicker and sooner.

Under such circumstances, "man as image generator" can set about "renewing and inventing the language of an urban society." Certainly it fits into the assertion that "the only valid approaches will be those comprehending the totality of the world system" to choose still another resonant statement from the prolegomena.

Students in New York should be those who showed promise in discovering publics in the world's metropolises or those philosopher-critics who find persuasive arguments for explaining the source of value attached to the imagery by the respective publics. Thus, criticism becomes an exercise in logic, sociology, anthropology, history, politics and poetry; as such, it has content and is vulnerable to tests that enable people to agree about quality in creative output, as well as quality that is determinable in the biological and behavioral sciences.

Economic Underpinnings

The bane of the urban arts has been economics. How does one make a market in aesthetic excitement and charge a price that will maintain a vigorous creative enterprise? How can that enterprise be managed so that the output will follow closely the changes in taste in the public, and not be caught with all of its assets tied up in obsolete inventory? What technical expertise is likely to benefit if these problems are solved?

These questions have been purposely framed in terms that could be applied equally well to Manhattan's "rag trade," where styles change with the season, the year, and the business cycle. In high style it is the large merchandiser who creates the relatively dependable market; in advanced design it is the large private organization. This is where the head offices of the multinational corporations come into the scheme. Knowledge—reasonably firm, verifiable, and true for at least a few years—about transcultural imagery is becoming essential to their operations.

Any firm that finds a formula for reducing the frequency of error or misunderstanding in the communication of nonverbal patterns and images by half would have a strong edge in world competition. Product design and advertising require a linkup with publics that are very likely little different from those that would express their tastes by choosing what they like from thousands of creative contributions. Therefore, market shares should go up for the competent firm. Such connections are already elementary in the strategic thinking of Madison Avenue (by which I mean that comments indicating comprehension of the principles have percolated all the way out to Berkeley). However, the really remarkable organizations are those that build up self-selected participants—employees, consultants, collaborators, agents— who play together, like an orchestra or a football team, and are able to capture some synergy for their enterprise through nonverbal communication. To a small extent, this level of communication has been achieved in the last decade by firms like Xerox and IBM, and in the previous decade by General Motors. Each of them moved into a dominant position in their chosen field of competition. Many of the leading firms, therefore, are alert to the rewards from transcultural and intraorganizational communication and will hire consultants to teach them to communicate with greater range and precision if they are convinced that the consultants have demonstrable competence. Public enterprises need advanced design skills also, but they are likely to buy them only after the lead sector of private enterprise has shown the way.

The design professions, it appears, have unusually good prospects. Actually, they have not been at all bad in the past, since, in terms of earnings, they were ahead of civil engineers and biochemists, but behind electronic engineers, physicists, and mathematicians at the end of the last decade. Once man reached the moon, however, the supply of hardware scientists overshot demand; meanwhile the soft sciences dealing with the environment have been getting headlines, although not yet many new jobs. Thus, a large share of the university output is facing a depressed market and must lower its expectations. Since there should be no oversupply of new design graduates in the 1970s, the salaries and commissions of the design professions should rise relative to the others. It would not be surprising to see them firmly in the second quartile of the professions, with incomes behind those registered in medicine and law, but ahead of almost all others.

Costs for producing a new design professional need not be high. At Berkeley they are less than for a physicist or an engineer. An analysis of university costs for 1968–69 revealed that on a fully allocated basis the average student-year came to:

Architecture	$1,500
City and Regional Planning	2,000
Landscape Architecture	2,300
Design	1,500

Due to faculty salary freezes, including no adjustment for inflation, these costs have not changed significantly between then and the 1972 projections. The above figures indicate what full tuition should be if all state subsidy were to be eliminated.

Most of the cost is less visible; it is borne by the student and his family. The student foregoes earnings at the level of semiskilled labor and junior technical employment. These private costs were estimated for the same period, but wages have increased by twenty percent since then. Therefore the total cost for the production of design professionals in 1972 prices is estimated to be:

B.Arch. (last degrees now being granted)	$ 36,000
M.Arch.	45,000
M. City Planning	44,000
M. Landscape Architecture	49,000
M.A. Design	39,000
Ph.D. City and Regional Planning	67,000
Ph.D. Architecture	65,000

(These figures do not allow for the extra social costs of dropouts, but such students usually finish later in some other specialty, such as business, where design training can be a major asset, so the correction should not be very significant.)[2]

If returns are higher than average, and costs about average, one comes to the conclusion that a social profit can be obtained by producing design professionals. Moreover, a school at a mid-Manhattan location, which would bolster the world-capital function of New York City, should generate many secondary and tertiary benefits.

These arguments were undertaken because they constitute one of the budgetary tests of worthwhileness. What they say to the slide-rule men in Albany is that, independent of politics, there should be substantial net benefits to society from a design school. This conclusion must battle many preconceptions about designers acquired when the budget makers and efficiency experts were themselves in school and are reinforced by their (i.e., the designers') tendency toward irreverence. The impulse is to stop all proposals of this sort unless they had been incorporated in a larger balanced plan for the State. However, economic arguments suggesting improvements upon the master plan may prevail if the new projects appear significantly superior, when calculated according to procedures acceptable to economists specializing in investment in human capital. Full calculations have not been presented here because they tend to get immersed in technical detail, but I have gone deeply enough into the issue to discover that the design professions should, for the next decade at least, have a preferred position. Design education should yield a social profit even if the designers are funneled into the purely American positions open to professionals; an abnormal profit should result if the product goes to work in international organizations, but the extra benefits would be distributed around the world.

For any city that functions as a world capital in one or another activity, a global distribution of benefits must be expected, because it could not function very long as a center for exploitation of others for its own selfish benefit; colonialism, as an accepted way of life, died in the early 1940s.

New kinds of organizations will arise as vehicles for the services of designers. In them a mix can be made with the skills of systems analysts, engineers, psychologists, lawyers, and others before the complete service is transmitted to the customer organization. SUNY-Buffalo illustrates how closely these organizations can be allied to the educational process with its Buffalo Organization for Social and Technical Innovation. Experience shows that there will need to be an assortment of unusual kinds of organizations that work at the interface between the faculty and students of a top-rank school and the pioneering users. What the designers will actually do for their salaries is expressed most clearly by Gerald McCue, in *Creating the Human Environment* (1970), as a series of eighteen roles, each of which is expected to generate several kinds of future actions.

RECAPITULATION

Ambitious, philosophically founded objectives cannot guide an institution launched in Manhattan, which is the nearest approximation we have to the capital of the planet. If a design-based school is to live and prosper it must interact with its milieu—the environment of the big, complex, or unique decision. Scientific, technical, financial, political, and documentary supports exist very close at hand; only a bit of bargaining is required to mobilize them for teaching and research. To fit this niche, the new institution must be large to be influential, it must reach maturity in very little time, and it must have a mechanism for maintaining top rank in its field.

That mechanism could be provided by The Museum of Modern Art if that institution is willing to make itself the impresario of a refined competition for attention in design and the allied arts that is user-oriented rather than elite-directed. The new telecommunications media provide a basis for producing and distributing catalogues of imagery and designs for everyone willing to pay attention. Since almost everyone at some time in his life must make choices regarding personal or organizational style in order to fit comfortably into the physical and cultural environment, we must expect to find many different public tastes, with the pluralism reaching a peak in the affluent, postindustrial societies. The wired-up city coming into existence this decade has sufficient capacity for presentation and feedback response for such a catalogue, and computer programs already exist for categorizing and developing individual tastes. Therefore it is technically possible to set up local, regional, societal, and world-level competitions. The equivalent of the Olympics of design would be held continuously in mid-Manhattan, with one or more public at a time interacting with groups of designers.

Design skills are very much like the jam on the toast—desirable and tasty, but, as compared to the original bread, not essential. Nevertheless, Talcott Parsons, when analyzing the social functions of the professions for the new *International Encyclopedia of the Social Sciences* (1968), came to the conclusion that the social conditions were becoming ripe for the designer to arrive as a cultural hero. Respect for the product of the present schools is registered by the level of lifetime earnings, which, in prospect, exceeds the averages posted by engineering, sciences, and education. Estimates of costs and returns suggest that these kinds of investments are not misplaced when aimed at large-scale production of design skills. The social costs of starting out big appear to be small.

The special returns achievable from the unique location should be much greater than the average design school. To realize them, however, and to stay top-rank, will require a multiplicity of organizations, a whole new philosophy of design criticism aimed at avoiding the faults of elitism, the evolution of one or more international language of design equivalent to the specialized languages of science and technology, and careful scientific-technological study of the processes of nonverbal communication by members of the faculty and its assorted organizations. In these agenda, there appears to be both room and opportunity for the appearance of cultural heroes, particularly if their wits are sharpened by more rational competition for attention than exists today.

Notes

1. Alvin Toffler, "The Politics of the Impossible," in Bertram M. Gross, ed., *A Great Society?* (New York: Basic Books, 1968); and Alvin Toffler, "The Art of Measuring the Arts," in Bertram M. Gross, ed., *Social Intelligence for America's Future* (Boston: Allyn and Bacon, 1969).

2. Belle L. Cole, "An Economic Analysis of Tuition and Finance for Professional Education: Application of Cost-Benefit Analysis to Education in Design and Planning Fields," Report No. 7, Institute of Urban and Regional Development, University of California, Berkeley (February 1970), 170 pp. reprod.

Notes on the Demilitarization of the University
By Martin Pawley

> Seldom in the history of modern civilization has there been a greater
> need felt by everyone for a new key to our mythologies, a key we
> nervously feel is about to be found. For if we are at a moment of terror
> we are also at a moment of great expectation and wonder, for which the
> young have a special appetite. To meet this challenge, the universities
> need to dismantle their entire academic structure, their systems of
> courses and requirements, their notion of what constitutes the proper
> fields and subjects of academic enquiry.
>
> —Richard Poirier, "The War Against the Young,"
> *Atlantic Monthly* (October 1968)

Most people concerned in further education feel some sense of the terror
and the anticipation described above by Poirier; unfortunately, in my experience, it is generally blurred and diffused by what can only be called realism.
A "new key to our mythologies" *is* desperately necessary, but the problem is
to sort it out from the great bunch of keys lying on everyone's desk, and
within a very short time at that. Abortive research projects, a high wastage
rate among students, a distrusted staff, a career anticipated without relish,
problems whose solution requires the self-sacrifice of whoever should first
begin the attempt; the difficulties are enormous. And, if we accept H. G.
Wells's dictum that the survival of humanity depends upon the outcome of
a race between education and catastrophe, those difficulties may well be the
final and most vital of all. In writing this critique of The Museum of
Modern Art's Universitas Project, I am sensible that in many ways I have
strayed beyond the brief into analogies and parallels of an apocalyptic and
perhaps inappropriate nature. My excuse (like that of the student of architecture who converts a small housing project into the redesign of a whole
city) is that the problem under discussion is contingent upon so many other
factors that to consider it in isolation is to forfeit all reality in dealing with it.
Thus, when I stray from the consideration of a proposed new institute of
urban design into a consideration of the critical state of the university system as a whole, and from there into parallels between the university and the
army, and beyond into the equation of success and failure with victory and
defeat, I hope the reader will bear in mind that the matters Universitas proposes to investigate are of overwhelming importance, not merely to the academic world, or even the world of the design professions, but to the lives
and aspirations of millions of ordinary people, the occupants of the great
cities of our planet.

THE UNIVERSITY: ORIGINS AND MODELS

In management courses, it is taught that there are only two historical models for the administration of our institutions, the church or the army. The derivation of the university from the first of these is beyond dispute, although, from the twelfth century, their chief purpose has been as lay corporations charged with the education of the learned professions throughout Europe and the former colonies founded by European states. In the Middle Ages, the word *universitas* was not confined to scientific bodies, since these did not then exist in the modern sense; it was used, instead, as an equivalent to our word *corporation*, and this is the Roman sense of the word. In fact, the university was not so called because of its embracing the whole world of knowledge, but simply because of its being a comprehensive collection of one class of the community—students. We read in black letter books of a University of Tailors and suchlike, although all such institutions, whatever their vocational purpose, grew from the schools at one time attached to almost every cathedral and monastery in Europe.

The University of Paris, to which the term *universitas* was applied as early as 1206, grew out of its ecclesiastical framework when disputes between teachers of theology and teachers of other subjects led to the secession of the doctors of theology from the university and their incorporation into a separate college, or faculty. Their example was followed by doctors of canon law and medicine, who also formed separate faculties. These faculties consisted exclusively of the actual teaching doctors (*doctores regentes*) of these three branches of knowledge. The masters and bachelors (*baccalaureus*) remained members of the university proper, which, from the secession of the theologians, canonists, and doctors of medicine, came to be called the Faculty of Arts. From this period, private families or religious orders established colleges within the University of Paris. Originally, they were intended for poor scholars, who were to live in them subject to certain discipline. By degrees, as more numerous and able teachers were employed in these colleges, they assumed the character of boarding houses for all classes of students. The word *collegium* was, at first, applied only to the students; only much later did it come to signify their hostel, or accommodation.

By 1224, when the University of Naples was established, the scientific study of medicine was making rapid strides, and law, philosophical pursuits, and literature had come to be regarded as the profession of a class whose members might or might not be priests. The universities founded after the Reformation adopted, in general, the organization of their predecessors—the political incorporation, the privileged jurisdiction and power of making bylaws, and the faculties and modes of conferring degrees, which custom had established. But the altered circumstances of society had changed the nature of their external relations. The same political power was not conceded to the new universities, as had grown up with their predecessors, which also saw their influence whittled away; and although other sciences had their practical utility recognized in the same way as law and medicine during the earlier period, the application of mathematical learning to the purposes of war and navigation did not lead to the foundation of new faculties but only to an extension of the miscellaneous category known as the Faculty of Arts. Throughout Europe, a decline in the status of the university preceded the French Revolution and the rise of Napoleon. The extension of elementary and secondary schools had raised the standard of education among the classes that did not receive a university education; the invention of printing operated in the same direction. Eventually, the diminished privileges and restricted jurisdiction of universities led to their being regarded merely as schools of a higher order.

The reestablishment of the university in France, following its closure by the National Convention in 1793, took an entirely different form, and one that served as an international model for the incorporation of applied science into separate university faculties. Throughout the nineteenth century and beyond, the structure of the university increasingly absorbed the study of technical matters deriving from the progress of the Industrial Revolution until, by the twentieth century, the greatest number of students and teachers were involved in what came to be called science subjects. The later expansion of the university and para-university system, which followed World War II, centered on scientific and technical learning, and it was into this context that design education, itself derived from the ancient Faculty of Arts, made its way. In a sense, the University of Tailors re-emerged in technological guise, and precisely that quality of academic indignation, which is aroused by such a term, emerged also in the realization that vocational training had again become the basis of most university education.

It is my contention that the new University of Tailors, of which the classic and also notorious example is in Berkeley, California, where 20,000 students occupy a single campus, represents such a change in administrative and theoretical structure that the ancient derivation from ecclesiastical models has been rendered meaningless—only the terms *university*, *faculty*, and *student* remain. The effect of the continued use of these terms has been to confuse discussion about the aims and purposes of the university (particularly in the field of design education) to the point where the importance of the imagined continuation of ancient traditions prevents rational consideration of reasonable changes.

I suggest, in fact, that the presently unsatisfactory nature of university courses proceeds, to a great extent, from a failure to apply a more appropriate critique based on the second great administrative model—the army. Since Napoleon, the structure of the university has become militarized to such a degree that only the continued use of such terms as *college*, *faculty*, and *professor* successfully obscures it. A case could probably be made for the existence of the same confusion in our understanding of other institutions, the technical implications of modern warfare having penetrated deeply into industrial production, advertising, government, and, indeed, into the control of the economy itself—Keynesian economics, for example, being in part the adoption of measures previously thought appropriate to a war economy in time of peace. There is also the matter of the involvement of the military in university research, heavily criticized in recent years, as well as the presence of officer training units on campus, but these, though significant, are remote from the central psychological fact of paramilitary organizations and its effects upon the self-image of teacher, student, and administrator, which are the areas with which I wish to concern myself for the remainder of this paper.

The University: Crisis of Morale

Before proceeding to a detailed examination of the usefulness of the military analogy, it is perhaps a good thing to consider more general factors, the question of morale, for example. Historically, the concept of the morale of students seems not to have been considered as a basis for university reform. An embarrassingly large number of famous figures in the fields of music, literature, science, and the arts have left on record their contempt for the universities at which they studied and, more often than not, failed to take degrees. Edward Gibbon, Lord Byron, Arnold Schoenberg—the list, with time and patience, is endless. Yet, it was only with the rapid expansion of the university system in all countries that followed population expansion, free education, and the arrival of social services of all kinds that the disaffection of the student began to assume an importance directly related to the future of the university itself. This disaffection can generally be shown to derive from the funneling down of ambition and energy, which, in the vast majority of cases, follows graduation.[1] The free-ranging inquiry and, more importantly, the lifestyle that university education confers upon those lucky enough to receive it, comes to an abrupt halt when the time arrives to look for a job. The present absence of jobs or roles even remotely comparable to the promise of university life is probably the dominant factor in the disabusal of the university student today—and to say this is to ignore a number of high-flown causes cited by students themselves. The collapse of the career is the very basis of student demoralization, just as doubts about the goals, means, and real necessity of a war constitute the basis of demoralization in an army—as witnessed by the French Army mutiny of 1917 or the heroin addiction and "fragging," which afflict the American Army in Vietnam today. In military terms, once meaning and purpose come to be discussed or debated among the troops—let alone acted upon—the battle is lost, the army doomed. The great triumph of the old French Malthusian system of university graduation was that for those who *did* graduate, a high-status occupation was assured. At the present time, not only is the supply of high-status jobs inadequate to the number of amply qualified graduates, but the whole question of what constitutes high status has been cast into doubt. The concept of university education as "a vacation between your mother and your wife" may have been adequate to middle-class undergraduates of a particularly docile and hedonistic type, such as those who emerged (as Poirier has said)[2] from World War II; but it is scarcely adequate for those who read daily in the newspapers or see nightly on television *evidence* of how incompetently and unjustly life is arranged nowadays. It is more than ever inadequate for generations reared on knowledge of the Oedipus complex, flagellated with doubt about marriage, deeply dubious about the value of the nuclear family, entirely skeptical about the political system that governs their country. To be brutally realistic, it has been precisely the failure of old-fashioned commerce and industry and old-fashioned politics to provide seductive roles for even that small percentage of the population who receive a university education, that has ensured that student protest and disabusal have grown from being a nuisance to being a disease to being a cancer that seems to threaten the very form of the society within which it exists. It is the manifest *incompetence* of our existing institutions that commands change and mobilizes the forces that will bring it about; not because the goals and aspirations of our great societies are shabby or mediocre—which they may well be—but because they are patently impossible to achieve with the present disposition of wealth and resources. From full employment to adequate housing, all the principal goals that form the substance of political debate today are mirages. Hence, the army grows restless; when told to attack again across open ground in the face of artillery and machine guns protected only by the shabbiest of illusions (a khaki uniform), the troops react as they did in France in 1917, in Russia in 1917, in Vietnam in 1970.

THE UNIVERSITY BODY COUNT

The concept of "casualties" among students is interesting. In Britain it has been amusing, in a sardonic way, to observe the status change that "graduates from the new universities" have undergone since the arrival of serious unemployment in 1968. Today they are referred to as "the disappointed, disoriented intellectual proletariat,"[3] who "foolishly imagined" that a degree was a passport to a well-paid job and a life of ease. Just who abetted them in these foolish imaginings, apart from their parents and teachers, community leaders, religious leaders, newspaper soothsayers, and politicians, it is difficult to say; but they are almost certainly the same persons who today urge graduates to employ their skills in molecular biology driving lorries, or to emigrate—although, just five years ago, the last was thought to be a kind of treacherous ingratitude. But, of course, the real student "casualties" never graduate—in a very real, sense they never reach university at all. Of those who do, a relatively high proportion flunk at some stage, and it is a truism among university teachers that the ones who do flunk are very often the best. In my own subject, architecture, the dropout rate in British universities is higher than for any other discipline,[4] in fact, double the average for all subjects (23.7 percent against 11.3 percent). This figure is especially interesting in view of the number of university departments of architecture that have been formed since 1958, when the Royal Institute of British Architects decided that training for their profession should be a university course rather than an apprenticeship. To compare such figures with battlefield casualties is, of course, to some extent to relate incomparable magnitudes, but I will quote Walter Millis on the American army in World War II: "It is probably correct to say that a casualty rate of ten percent in any single action, or over any comparatively limited period of operations, would have been considered unacceptably high. When the capture of Tarawa atoll in April 1944 cost seventeen percent in casualties it was considered something of a scandal."[5]

Now, whether a high drop-out rate can be considered "something of a scandal" depends upon an acceptance of not only the analogy between the university and the army, but also between a university course and a military campaign. In simple terms, I might propose that the students represent fighting soldiers, the tutors their officers, and the professors their generals. The modern university is, after all, a career open to talents in the manner of Napoleon's Grand Army, the purchase of commissions an anachronism scarcely to be found anywhere in the world today. Let me go further. Is there a general staff? Yes, the professional institutions where applicable, the learned society where not. Are these politicians who can make or break generals? Yes again, the very same representatives of government who do indeed control the armed forces. Is there a military-industrial complex? Certainly in the field of design education there is, in the form of the interlocks between the university faculties, their "research" satellites, and the construction industry. But, is there a war? That is more difficult to answer partly because, in the modern world, a whole range of partial wars has sprung into existence; cold wars, guerilla wars, states of armed conflict, preventive wars—the line between war and peace is no longer clearly drawn, even when it is self-evident it is not always admitted. In the present condition of the university, it might be said that there is undoubtedly a "war of nerves" in progress. This would explain the "cracking up" of the troops, the desertions, and the increasing emphasis upon discipline and "tough measures." Today's professor does not walk on foot among his soldiers after a battle suggesting that they name their children after him.[6] Instead, he makes contact rarely and formally, trading upon his remoteness and exalted station. There are notable exceptions, but not to my knowledge in design education. There, a Western Front mentality obtains, with frozen-faced martinets urging yet more frontal attacks on targets palpably absurd in the light of the ecological plight of mankind.

THE UNIVERSITY AND THE REAL WORLD

The architectural profession in most Western European countries and the United States consists for the most part of salaried workers for whom professional status is an illusion fostered only by their own institution—which is, in turn, dominated by a minority of principals in private practice on their own account. Eighty-two percent of graduates from the Architectural Association School of Architecture in London go directly into salaried employment in public or private sector offices, and by national standards that is a low figure. Their education, insofar as it prepares them for any career at all, prepares them for a *prima donna* role as "form givers" to a society eager for their help and advice. The career of "form giver" does not exist, neither does the society eager for their help and advice. What, then, is the role of the professor who instructs them? He is a general! He says to each successive year of freshmen: "This is our plan of attack. It has not succeeded yet, but my only advice is that you should try harder. Good luck." As with the most insanely hopeless attacks on the Somme in 1916, a statistically predictable few do survive. They are the raison d'être of the system. Next year they will teach. For the others there are the myriad distractions of private life. How far this abortive pattern is repeated in other areas of university education others will know better than I; suffice it to say, that to my knowledge such a dislocation is common in Western Europe.[7]

The war of nerves is, thus, the pitting of obsolete training against an obstinate reality. The generals fear to explain the nature of that reality to their troops because to do so would be to acknowledge the deception they have practiced hitherto; in any case, they probably retain illusions about it themselves, illusions fostered by the terms *professor, faculty*, and *university*.

The ultimate foundation of the apparently profound irrelevance of even "vocational" courses (which, admittedly, I am assuming to apply to other fields of study apart from those with which I am familiar) becomes clearer if an extension of the military analogy is applied, the idea of university education as a form of military service. Here the concept of open warfare does not necessarily arise; we are, instead, concerned with different processes more directly relevant to the skilled manpower requirements of the modern state, with its economy constantly running at the equivalent of wartime production. We are talking about projected increases in gross national product, which would be inconceivable if separated from notions of re-armament and a permanent military establishment. We are talking about the world as it has been since the Great Depression. To quote Millis, writing of the introduction of conscription in the United States during World War I: "Then, as later, there were many to embrace universal military training for reasons other than strictly military. It would be a means of 'disciplining' the young and improving their physique. It would teach them 'patriotism.' To draft a man to risk death on the battlefield is to give him (if he survives) rights and claims against the state which the ruling groups of 1915 (like those of 1783) might be unwilling to meet; but to draft him for 'healthy' peacetime military training would only regiment him into a military structure that would teach him to be cooperative, obedient, and docile to those who profit most from the operations of the state and have the largest voice in forming its policies."[8]

In view of the presently obvious polarization of university education and military service, I am well aware that any suggestion that the two are equivalent in their overall effect requires some elucidation. This must begin with a brief description of the changes that have overtaken the nature of warfare in the last century.

It is common in military history to describe the American Civil War of 1861–65 as the first "total war." This means, in effect, that for the first time in history the decisive effect of single battles was reduced if not obliterated by the capacity of industrial production, railway networks, conscripted armies, and high-speed telegraphic communications to repair the consequences of any individual action so that gaps forced by the enemy could be plugged before he had time to capitalize on them. The process begun in that struggle developed rapidly so that by 1914 it had transformed the purely military struggle into a struggle of economic power. The gradual collapse of the South during the American Civil War, resulting from the destruction of its railway network, the exhaustion of its manpower and industry, and the strangulation of its supply system was echoed with greater force by the exhaustion of Germany in 1918 and again in 1945. Napoleon could seal the fate of a whole country by defeating its army in one battle—as at Jena—the generals of 1864, 1917, and 1943 could only hope to wear down their opponents by greater or lesser depletions of their resources as a result of whole campaigns. The German army, for example, lost as many men as Napoleon had taken into Russia in one single campaign, at Stalingrad; but Hitler was able to fight for two more years on three fronts (four, if the air war is included) after that debacle. However, in all countries the price of this total mobilization of resources was the intervention of strategic planning into all aspects of social and economic life. The tendency of the victorious combatants to introduce enlightened social legislation in the aftermath of the two world wars (evidence of the "rights and claims" of the conscripted soldier who had risked his life, as Millis observed), is only one side of this coin. The other is the now almost total dependence of industry and commerce, finance and education on nationally ordered priorities, themselves derived from imperatives based on the needs of a war economy.[9] In Britain, Germany, and America, the restoration of full employment after the Depression was achieved only by rearmament. The foundations of post–World War II prosperity have been identically based on military or quasi-military production, state intervention in industry, and perhaps more importantly, on a "defensive" political motivation. To put it simply, the total mobilization of society, which took place during the world wars, has left an indelible imprint on both the mechanisms and the management of the modern world; the University of Tailors—microbiologists, computer scientists, technologists, managers, designers, and philosophers that we know today—is overwhelmingly a function of that total mobilization. Its "cost benefit" is calculated on precisely this basis; comparisons of the "scientific power" of different nations are made entirely on this quantitative ground.

It is hardly surprising, therefore, that the mutinous state of the troops in the graduate cadres of the university should excite the concern of their managerial masters. If the "territorial reserve" of graduates has become next to useless for the instrumental role assigned to it, if the professors (or generals) have lost control of standards of functional achievement, it is hardly surprising that they should seriously consider reducing both the numbers and the power of this rambling, dissident, and thoroughly unreliable army. In Britain, C. Selby Smith notes, in the Graduate Appointments Register, that, "from a cost benefit point of view a Higher National Certificate is more valuable than a degree: it offers a significantly higher return on money invested."[10] From such warnings to remarks about "the disappointed, disoriented intellectual proletariat," is but a step. Clearly, the evils of a standing army, which were so well understood by our forbears, are now reflected in the "evils" of a university system sustained on an enormous scale by state finance. In Britain, the university population greatly outnumbers the army; if—as our managerial authorities seem to think—the "standing university" has become nothing but a breeding ground for social deviancy (if not revolution) then the case for its *demilitarization* would seem to be far more pressing than the more usually advanced arguments for "tighter control" or "tougher measures." To restate an earlier point: it is the failure of the managerial state to provide *roles* for its graduate reserve that has precipitated student revolt, in much the same way as the failure of earlier European kings to pay their soldiers endangered their thrones. The three-year degree course, like the two-year period of military service, does, indeed, create a massive reserve of trained manpower, in theory ready for almost any demand the technocratic state may wish to make upon it. Our present crisis proceeds from the fact that economic and organizational failure has broken down the demand structure toward which the supply of graduates is being directed. Our soldiers have no world war, our graduates no roles fit to receive them. The conscript soldier of two world wars was fed on promises of a better life after victory had been secured; only an uncertainty about victory or a lack of enthusiasm for the cause of battle itself caused him to mutiny or desert. Present university discontent exactly parallels mutiny and desertion: the victory is in doubt and the cause itself is mocked.

Mutiny: Its Causes and Effects

Before leaving this necessarily brief exploration of the university as part of a military process, it is well to describe at greater length one of the examples mentioned earlier, the mutiny in the French Army that succeeded the disastrous Nivelle Offensive of April 1917. I propose to make one or two generalized extrapolations upon it in order to demonstrate that the basic analogy, if effective, indicates that dissatisfaction within the university (whether expressed through militancy or declining morale) is, indeed, a profoundly ominous portent for the future of Western societies and a most serious indictment of their presently erroneous course of development.

The Nivelle Offensive, in inception and execution, represented a European military equivalent to the Ghost Dance movement, which, for a time, linked several depleted tribes of North American plains Indians in a futile last-ditch opposition to the hordes of white settlers who had dispossessed them of their vast lands and livelihoods in the twenty-five years that followed the end of the Civil War. Its strategy was based on a system of incantations designed to make Indian warriors immune to rifle bullets. The incantations were wholly ineffective, and the movement itself dissolved after the massacre of Wounded Knee (December 29, 1890) at which 120 men and 250 women and children were killed, mostly by artillery fire. Twenty-seven years later, faced with the incomprehensible deadlock of the Western Front, the French General Staff—like so many Indian chiefs—agreed to a massive offensive against almost impregnable German positions. The plan, devised and propagandized by General Robert Nivelle, fell into German hands almost immediately. Undeterred, the general confidently predicted a "massive rupture" of the enemy line, an advance of six miles in the first twenty-four hours and thereafter a "general pursuit," which would end only in Berlin. Despite grave misgivings, the attack was launched and within three days had led to the loss of 120,000 men with a maximum advance of six hundred yards. One week later, mutiny had spread to sixteen army corps; other regiments obeyed orders to move to the front but persisted in baaing like sheep to indicate that they were lambs being driven to slaughter.[11] Twenty-one thousand French troops deserted outright; a total of fifty-four divisions, three quarters of a million soldiers, ceased to be operational.

Official reaction to this disaster took two forms: five hundred mutineers were executed, a further hundred exiled to colonial prisons; at the same time, a number of heads (including Nivelle's) rolled at command level, and the conditions of the troops were eased by the announcement of liberal leave and the abandonment of all such offensives in the future. A direct consequence of this policy was the Maginot concept of fortress warfare for future national defense as well as the "configurational" pattern of military administration with which the French army met the Germans again in 1940.

To argue that neither savage repression nor marginal reforms represented a practical solution to the problems of armies locked in a technical impasse is to state a truism. The real answer at the time was no answer, and, in consequence, the matter was decided by economic and industrial attrition. In exactly the same way, ruthless repression and/or marginal reforms do not represent an answer to the presently deadlocked relations between the university and the economic system in most of the advanced countries of the world. They represent no answer, and, consequently, the same process of exhausting attrition is at work, a process that can only end with the mutual estrangement of both parties through an alienating process of privatization. It seems to me indisputable that this process can only lead, at some time in the future, to a kind of technological equivalent of the French collapse of 1940. When any nation (or all nations) finally attempts to confront the massive problems of a disintegrating social structure, urban breakdown, a polluted environment, and a growing shortage of basic resources with a new kind of technological offensive, it will find the university—the inevitable center of any such effort—to be imbued with an incompetence, defeatism, and plain lack of creative resources equivalent to that of the French Army at that unhappy time.[12]

The arguments for major changes not merely in the strategy and orientation of the university but in its relation to the totally mobilized state are unanswerable. The real tragedy will be if that very unanswerableness is interpreted as an excuse for doing nothing. It is in this context that all projects for new forms of university structure should be considered, particularly in relation to design teaching with its *direct* relevance to the implementation of technological programs.

University and Universitas

Viewed in the light of the foregoing, whose apocalyptic tone was intentionally adopted as a counterbalance to the excessively urbane tone of the Universitas Project Working Paper itself, the Universitas Project seems to me to possess structural weaknesses. Aside from the introductory remarks about the uneasy relationship between design and the scientific method (with which I concur, although I apparently differ over the interpretation of their meaning), the authors of the report seem principally concerned that multidisciplinary working on complex urban problems should become *structural* rather than stochastic, as it is at present. Quoting a Ford Foundation report on the present impossibility of integrated study in existing universities is not equivalent to proving the possibility of such work at Universitas; even less is it any guarantee that the production of politically unpopular programs *for* action by such teams (assuming that they produce them, and there are strong reasons, as I shall explain, for concern that they might not) would be any more likely to lead to action than are maverick studies produced in our university schools of design, architecture, and planning at present. It is the relationship between the army and the people that is important in terms of its efficiency; so also is it the relationship between the university and the State, which determines not merely the quantity of influence it can have, but also the quality of that influence. Based, as it is intended to be, upon the existential possibilities of the individual in an ethical situation, Universitas does not address itself to the political possibilities of that individual, nor his economic status, nor his influence within the society of which he is a part. If it is assumed that, like a Bauhaus graduate, the student or teacher emerging from Universitas will have seen a vision which he will afterwards propagandize unceasingly, then it should be noted that graduates of the contemporary military university tend, by and large, to have seen visions too, and the results are not encouraging as far as the fate of any academic body of thought is concerned. The instrumentality of any new university structure *must* extend beyond its doors deep into the political consciousness of the people; if it does not, there can be no hope of effective action resulting from the propagation of what it teaches. And, if there is no effective action—merely further intellectual bolstering for such action or inaction as exists already—then the central problem of academic morale is not even addressed, let alone resolved.

It is a truism that we must attack the problems created by our technology with yet more technologies—we have no other recourse. But it is also true that such technologies are merely instrumental; the motivation and power to *use* such instruments is political in origin, and it proceeds from the acceptance of an analysis of a situation, from an explanation of the world. Such explanations conceived in the isolation of the university strive hard to achieve popular currency and, hence, political effect, but this process is constantly thwarted by the political reality of that very isolation in which they were conceived—isolation, moreover, which tends to devalue the analysis itself. The terrible existential truth of service on the Western Front in World War I is a paradigm here: numerous authors, as well as newspaper accounts, attest to the supreme ignorance of contemporary civilian populations as to its real nature. Chauvinism, an atavistic faith in military victory, an insane hatred for the enemy—whose social structure was identically stressed, whose conscript soldiers were identically dying—marks the home front utterances of 1914–18 just as it marks the irrational confidence of our own politicians in ancient methods and unworkable strategies today. If the purpose of the Universitas Project is to devise a new answer to urban collapse and environmental crisis, then it must *connect* with that crisis through action and a social integration beyond the university itself. In its isolation from political and economic forces capable of implementing revolutionary new programs—as opposed to merely documenting them—the university already contains the seeds of its ultimate downfall. The urban confusion and ineffectiveness to which it proposes to address itself is real enough, but is Universitas real?

The failure of the project will not be significant by itself, but its place in a long chain of failure involving intellectual solutions to concrete problems, the real keys to which are held in other hands, will contribute mightily to the collapse of public faith in all such institutions and the individuals who promote them. The real questions to be asked of Universitas now are the famous Roman questions: Who will pay and who will benefit?

Notes

1. David Martin, "Trouble in the University," *The Listener* (November 23, 1967).
2. Richard Poirier, *The Performing Self* (New York: Oxford University Press, 1971).
3. Angus Maude, in *The Sunday Express* (London), May 2, 1971.
4. The University Grants Committee: "Enquiry into Students Progress."
5. Walter Millis, *Arms and Men: A Study of American Military History* (New York: Putnam, 1956).
6. Which Napoleon did after the battle of Austerlitz. See Count Phillippe Paul De Segur, *Napoleon's Russian Campaign* (London: Michael Joseph, 1959).
7. This is certainly the case by my own observation in most British university schools, such as Manchester, Edinburgh, Leeds, or Sheffield. It is also tragically true at the reformed Beaux-Arts in Paris, at the Academia in Copenhagen, at Otaniemi in Finland, and at the two Dutch university schools, Delft and Eindhoven.

8. Millis, *Arms and Men.*
9. This whole question is analyzed at length by Jules Henry in "Psychological Preparations for Modern War," a paper delivered to the Congress of the Dialectics of Liberation, London, 1967. It is also discussed in his book *Culture Against Man* (New York: Random House, 1963).
10. C. Selby Smith, "Training Qualified Manpower: Costs and Benefits," *The Graduate Appointments Register* (July 1968).
11. John Davidson, *Haig: Master of the Field* (London: Nevill, 1953).
12. This conclusion is, to some extent, substantiated by the 1966 Ford Foundation results quoted in the Universitas Project Working Paper.

Return (Vuelta)
By Octavio Paz

> Better not to go back to the village, to the subverted paradise . . .
> —*Ramón López Velarde*

Voices at the corner's turn

        voices

through the sun's spread hand

        almost liquid

shadow and light

        The carpenter whistles

the iceman whistles

        three ash trees

whistling in the plaza

        The invisible

foliage of sounds

        growing

rising up

    Time

stretched to dry on the rooftops

        I am

in Mixcoac

      The letters rot

in the mailboxes

        The bougainvillea

flattened by the sun

        against the wall's white lime

a stain

    a purple

passionate calligraphy

        I am walking back

back to what I left

      or left me

Memory

  the imminence of the precipice

       balcony

over the vacuum

   I walk

and do not move forward

    I am surrounded

by city

  I lack air

My body deserts me

    Noon

    fist of light

that pounds and pounds

      To collapse in an office

or onto the pavement

     to end up in a hospital

the pain of dying

   like that

    isn't worth the pain

I look back

  that passerby

is nothing now but mist

     Nightmares sprout

in the bellies of movie houses

      Catacombs of gas

electricity sewers

    dreams

desires

  The vegetation of disasters

ripens beneath the ground

     They are burning

millions and millions of old notes

in the Bank of Mexico

                          Paralytic

architectures

                stranded districts

rotting municipal gardens

                       deserted lots

mounds of saltpeter

                  camps of urban nomads

cans   shingles   plastics   sanitary napkins

thoroughfares of scars

                   alleys of living flesh

Funeral Parlors

             whores

               pillars of vain night

wait by the coffins' show-window

                         In the drifting bar

at dawn

          the enormous mirror thaws

the solitary drinkers

                contemplate

the dissolution of their faces

                   The wind

on the dusty corners

              turns the papers

yesterday's news

             more remote

than a cuneiform tablet

               smashed to bits

Cracked scriptures

             languages in pieces

The signs were broken

             atl tlachinolli

                was split

burnt water

There is no center

plaza of congregation and consecration

there is no axis

the years dispersed

the horizons disbanded

They have branded the city

on every door

on every forehead

the $ sign

We are surrounded

I have gone back

to where I began

Did I win or lose?

(*You ask*

what laws rule "success" and "failure"

The songs

of the fishermen

float up

from the unmoving riverbank

Wang Wei to the Prefect Chang

from his cabin on the lake

But I

don't want an intellectual hermitage

in San Angel or Coyoacán)

All

is gain

if all is lost

I walk toward myself

toward the plaza

the space is within

it is not a *subverted paradise*

it is a pulsebeat of time

places are confluences

flutters of beings in an instantaneous space

The wind whistles in the ash trees

fountains

almost liquid   light and shadow

voices of water

shine   flow   are lost

a bundle of reflections

left in my hands

I walk without moving forward

We never arrive

Never reach where we are

Not the past

The present is untouchable

(*Translation by Eliot Weinberger*)

Comments on the Proposed University of Design
By Anatol Rapoport

1. PURPOSE

Design implies intent, and intent implies foreknowledge.

We humans like to view ourselves as the only creatures with a genuine ability to foresee future events and to guide our actions accordingly. There was a time when we did not claim this exclusiveness. The foraging activities of ants and squirrels were once held up as examples of industry and foresight. The skill of beavers and spiders was compared to that of architects and engineers, who first envisage the finished product and only then put materials together according to the preconceived design.

The theory of natural selection, coupled with the stimulus-response theories of behaviorist psychology, "debunked" these anthropomorphic interpretations, making it appear that concepts of rationality and foresight are not applicable to animal behavior. In the light of these theories, the work of the spider spinning its web and of the beaver building its dam is governed not by an image of the future finished product (design) but by sequential behavioral responses to stimuli initiated by the state of affairs at a given stage of construction. Each stimulus evokes an appropriate response; each response determines the next stage of activity, which evokes the next stimulus. As for the mechanisms underlying the proper responses, they are supposed to have been "selected for" in the process of evolution. The organisms possessing the "right sort" of mechanisms, in consequence of favorable mutations and recombination of genes, are assumed to enjoy a survival advantage over others not possessing them and, thus, to replace the latter in the course of the history of the species.

This tendency to "explain away" apparent purposefulness or foresight in nature (excluding man) has characterized the development of natural science since the scientific revolution of the sixteenth century. It began with the birth of modern mechanics, where what Aristotle called "effective causes" (acting on the state of affairs here and now) replaced so-called "final causes," which admitted the influence of the future on the present (teleology).

The expulsion of teleology from physical science has, in fact, initiated a reorganization of the scientific picture of the universe, so that events appeared to be governed by deterministic laws. At times, probabilistic laws had to be added to make possible consistent and unified explanation, namely, where the grossly observable events were composites of vast numbers of minute events, which, because of their minuteness, could not be observed, described, and related to each other. Examples are events treated in the kinetic theory of gases and the genetics of populations. Later, it turned out that events on the subatomic level also had to be described probabilistically, for other reasons having to do with the paradoxes arising in the concept of causality on that level. However, the extension of the deterministic view to include probabilistic models was not an abandonment of the fundamental *nonteleological* orientation of natural science. According to this orientation, a scientific explanation of events is still defined as one in which what happens at a moment is to be explained by reference to what has happened *up to* that moment, not by reference to some future state of affairs toward which a system is assumed to "strive," as a goal to be attained. Thus, design, in the sense of a principle that guides actions (events) in accordance with a preconceived plan, was virtually eliminated from the conceptual repertoire of physical science as it was applied to the description and explanation of events.

Life processes, especially the behavior of sensate things, are much more difficult to explain in the framework of nonteleological orientation. However, the discovery of homeostatic mechanisms and of the role of "feedback" in the behavior of systems interacting with their environment—a fundamental concept of cybernetics (mathematical theories of regulation and control)—have greatly aided the extension of the nonteleological conception of explanations to areas of inquiry where life processes, including behavior, are at the center of interest.

2. "Freedom"

The notion of purposefulness and goal-directedness persists most strongly in our conception of our *own* behavior. We have introspective, that is, *direct*, knowledge of our own state of consciousness, and this awareness makes it practically impossible to give up the notion that, at least as individuals, we have "free will"; that is to say, that our actions are, at least in part, governed by deliberate pursuit of preset goals. These goals appear to be images of objects, conditions, or events not yet realized, sometimes not *ever* having existed except in our imagination. This direct introspective perception of these nonexistent objects, conditions, etc., imparts the vividness of reality to the idea that our actions are guided by goals and purposes. And this direct perception of our own freedom, coupled with the conviction, imparted by science, that the rest of nature is passive (governed by impersonal laws), gave birth to the comparatively new idea that man can mold his environment to serve his goals and so can become master of his own destiny. In short, design, being a concretization of imagined objects or events into plans of action, is an affirmation of freedom.

It is important to note that there are other conceptions of freedom, almost opposite in that they are based on the *absence* of preset goals, maximum "spontaneity" being the central feature. From the standpoint of each of these conceptions of freedom, it is possible to argue that its opposite conception is based on an illusion. Those who identify freedom with spontaneity point out that, once goals have been set, the actor is under compulsion to work for their realization. Moreover, goals are not chosen independently of each other; the realization of some goal strongly influences the choice of the next. Hence, a commitment to specified goals, by channeling man's activities, seems to be the very antithesis of freedom. Those who identify freedom with "control of one's own destiny" point out that the absence of restraints on impulses subjugates man to impulses and ephemeral appetites, and so makes him a creature of momentary environmental forces.

Because of the introspective origin of the notion of freedom, any conception of freedom must, of necessity, be subjective. Hence, the difference between the two notions cannot be resolved on the basis of evidence; they represent a cleavage of fundamental values. To those who identify freedom with the pursuit of preset goals, collectivist ideals are congenial, for organized collective action is indispensable for the realization of distant, commonly held goals. Those who identify freedom with spontaneity are more apt to distrust large-scale organization of human life.

The goal-setters often hold up the ideal of humanity freed from dependence on environment; the libertarians tend to associate this ideal with a disastrous alienation from nature. The former see in science and technology the means of man's emancipation. To the latter, burgeoning technology is destructive of freedom, and science seems to dull man's capacity for other (to them, more important) forms of cognition.

Both views are right, and both are wrong. Each selects an aspect of the human condition and defines freedom in terms of it, neglecting the other aspect. That man's survival potential depends on his ability to foresee imagined objects and events, and so to design tools with which to wrest his subsistence, is not subject to doubt. That, at times, man becomes a slave to his artifacts is also painfully apparent. That man is a social animal cannot be disputed. That certain forms of social structure reduce man to "manpower" is a recurrent theme of history.

The dialectic opposition between social organization and "individual freedom" can be seen clearly only in historical perspective. Man was almost certainly a social animal even before he became man. Therefore, certain models of the origins of social life inherent in libertarian social philosophies must be ascribed to myths. In the American Declaration of Independence, for example, it is stated that man is "endowed . . . with certain inalienable rights," and that *to secure* these rights governments are instituted among men. In the theory of government presumably based on that declaration, "freedom of the individual" is assumed to be something given by nature. In adopting a social mode of life, the "naturally free" individual supposedly trades some of that freedom for certain benefits conferred by organized society, including the protection of his freedom. There is a strong resemblance between this model and an earlier one offered by Thomas Hobbes, according to which men banding together in societies gave up *all* their freedom to the sovereign in exchange for protection of their lives, supposedly in jeopardy because of the "war of everyone against everyone" that men in the state of nature wage against each other. The difference between the social-contract model and the Leviathan model is partly a quantitative one. In the former, especially in its American version, the individual gives up only a minimum of individual free- dom in order to secure that very freedom. In the latter, the individual gives up all of his freedom, because, in the state of nature, his very existence is endangered. The two models differ also in their conception of human nature. According to the libertarian conception, man is "naturally good" and estab- lishes relations to others for the purpose of cooperation. According to the authoritarian conception, man has no natural propensity to cooperate and must be forced to do so.

In both conceptions, however, the individual is the first "given": a society is organized one way or another by putting *individuals* in relation to each other or in relation to an authority.

3. Individual and Social Awareness

Examination of man's biological position gives little support to the concep- tion of society as a coming together of individuals, originally "free" in the state of nature. Most primates are social, living in groups of some scores of individuals, held together by mammalian patterns of family life and by advantages of mutual protection, not against each other but against external enemies. We cannot, of course, imagine what it feels like to be a monkey or a baboon, but it is quite likely that these animals have a much more diffuse awareness of their individual existence than we have. In the case of social insects, it is highly unlikely that the individual ant or bee has any such aware- ness, possibly no more than does a cell in the body of an animal. In fact, some biologists would treat the anthill or the beehive as the "organism" that main- tains itself by the specialized activities of its "differentiated" cells (queens, drones, and workers) and even "reproduces" (swarming).

Libertarians emphasize the awareness of the individuality as a supreme human value, and it probably is true that awareness of individual existence is unique to man. Even so, it is not necessarily the case that this awareness has been central in all human societies. In some, it is secondary to identification with a group, bound together by kinship or tradition; nor is such identification confined to "primitive" societies. Under certain conditions, men of "highly civ- ilized" societies find themselves in situations where awareness of individual exis- tence dissolves in identification with a collective. War is the most conspicuous situation of this sort. In war, even the so-called "instinct of self-preservation" is often extinguished by strong passions of collective identification.

In short, it is reasonable to assume that both kinds of awareness are pres- ent in man—an individual awareness, probably much stronger than in any other animal, possibly unique, and a collective awareness. However (and this is a crucial point), the extent of collective awareness that may arise in man is not "given by nature," as it is in the case of social animals. It is a product of history. Moreover, human collectives incorporate a consciousness of purpose or goal-directedness similar to that of which an individual is introspectively aware. Hence, collectives as well as individuals can be aware of their autonomy. Characteristically, the autonomy of collectives manifests itself in pursuit of preset goals rather than in spontaneity.

Whether the goal-directedness of collectives enhances or frustrates its members' goals or aspirations (which may exist side by side with collective goals) is a central issue in any philosophy of society. The American aphorism, "that government is best which governs least," is an expression of the view that the hegemony of collective goals is oppressive. The opposite view holds that man realizes his "freedom" only in cooperation with others. Moreover, since the latter view of man's freedom is frequently bound up with "independence from nature" or with maximum control of the natural environment, and since the realization of this goal requires highly organized effort by large numbers of people, highly disciplined social organization seems indispensable for the realization of "genuine freedom." Communist social philosophy expresses this ideal most clearly.

4. Coercive Organization and Reaction Against It

Since a "natural" human collective is not given, if we suppose that the earliest human collectives were continuations of their biological prototypes, we may suppose that they comprised primarily kinship groups and owed their existence not to some coercive organizing effort but to a natural identification of its members with the group.

Coercive organization came, probably, with the necessity of undertaking activities that required the coordinated work of larger groups than those comprising primitive collectives. Possibly this necessity arose with the beginning of agriculture in the Neolithic age. On the one hand, agriculture in some areas, such as Mesopotamia, required artificial irrigation and, therefore, "public works" with large labor forces directed by engineers. On the other hand, permanent agricultural settlements introduced the concept of land *possession* and with it competition for possession. This happened as soon as the increase in population, resulting from increased reliable food supply, made good land a scarce resource. Organized, planned warfare, as distinguished from clashes between accidentally colliding groups, was probably born in this way.

Warfare is in itself a large-scale, organized, collective activity. Even more important are the products of warfare—the subjugation of some groups to others (to be exploited as labor, which now began to yield more than its keep) and the resulting centralization of power (indispensable for *institutionalized* warfare). Thus, the patterns of large-scale social organization of early "civilizations" become predominantly despotic.

The great "ethical" religions arose about the time of empire building. They may have been a reaction against the devastation and suffering brought on by continual warfare associated with the enlargement of realms under centralized control. If so, then we must suppose that the idea of the "free individual" or, at least, of the essential "intrinsic worth" of the individual, as well as the idea of universal brotherhood of man, arose in "dialectic opposition" to the historical process that bound ever larger numbers of people into disciplined collectives, typically subjugated to the goals and aspirations of ruling cliques.

The evolution of war-waging states and empires was a self-enhancing process. The development of military technology made possible the development of large military machines, which, in turn, made possible the conquest of large territories, thus the recruitment of ever larger armies and the development of ever more effective techniques to insure their coordination. It was organized warfare that gave rise to the State and, with it, to world politics.

At the same time, the enlargement of the body politic to include huge, culturally diverse populations gave rise to the idea of man, as distinct from kinsman. The concepts of world politics and of the brotherhood of man have become ethically incompatible, but they may have had the same origin in the steady expansion of the scale of human cooperation, whether coerced or voluntary.

Contemporary conceptions of man in society are heirs to the legacies of both traditions: one derived from the ethical religions with their emphasis on the worth, and occasionally the freedom, of the individual and their preoccupation with conscience; the other derived from the concept of society as an organized entity with its own goals and purposes, claiming the loyalty of its members to these goals. Both conceptions have, of course, undergone transformations. In its secular version, the freedom of the individual was separated from transcendental justifications with which it had been bound up in religions. It became "axiomatic," something that needed no further justification. Also, the purposes of states are not publicly identified with those of potentates or ruling cliques. They are only questioned by those who challenge existing social systems. This very challenge, however, is an embodiment of the idea that the State (or some other form of social organization) *could* have goals and purposes not attributable to any ruling clique but rather (ideally) identified with the realization of autonomy of all its members. In other words, there is a rather widespread view today (which, however, is not unchallenged) that the dialectic opposition between the freedom of the individual and the realization of large-scale social goals can be transcended in a synthesis. According to this view (humanism), man's emancipation can be brought about by some specific form of social organization that makes large-scale cooperation and coordinated effort possible but at the same time safeguards the autonomy of the individual to an extent consistent with the common goals of society.

If such a social organization can be achieved, "design" on a broad scale seems possible: "man" can design both his physical environment and his forms of social organization. He can state goals to which "society" can strive and, by means of science, discover and put into effect means to achieve these goals.

5. Is Mankind an Actor?

The humanist view, then, is an iteration of faith that "teleological" causation, according to which events are pulled toward a goal ahead instead of pushed by history from behind, does have a place in human affairs, even though science has largely expelled it from the nonhuman sphere. The humanist view asserts the meaningfulness of the term "actor" applied to both human individuals and human collectives. The question is how comprehensive can a human collective be and still retain the characteristics of an "actor?"

Note that the notion of the State as an actor antecedes the humanist view, in fact, is in some ways antithetical to it, as, for example, in Georg Wilhelm Friedrich Hegel's concept of the State as the embodiment of the Absolute Idea and in modern authoritarian concepts of the State. The State also appears as an actor in so-called "realist" conceptions of international relations. There, personifications of states are not expressed in humanist terms, for, in the "realist" conception of international politics, the autonomy of individuals is either outside the conceptual repertoire or is simply assumed to be realizable only by an identification with the State and its goals. In the humanist conception, not the State but "society" appears as the assumed actor.

It is precisely here that ambiguity arises. What sort of an actor is "society"? Who acts on its behalf? Is one to take as final the contemporary organizations of societies into nation states and the boundaries of society to be those of a nation state? If so, how is one to deal with the stubborn fact that many, perhaps most, perhaps even all, societies coextensive with states pursue goals that cannot be demonstrated as coinciding with the goals or aspirations of its members? How is one to deal with the fact that goals of different states clash, and that, when they do, states often resort to violence destructive of the most essential needs of their members?

People who subscribe to the humanist view sometimes answer these questions by pointing out that "society" can become an actor enhancing the goals and aspirations of its members only if it is organized on the global scale, say, under a world government. For the most part, however, discussions of the "goals of society," including proposals for designing social organization on rational, human principles, employing means suggested by science, still go on predominantly at the level of the State (with which "society" is tacitly identified). In a way, keeping the discussion on that level is dictated by the obvious circumstances that the State is the largest unit of social organization presently existing, which is at all in a position to implement decisions regarding coordination and direction of effort in pursuit of "the goals of a society." The implicit identification of "society" as an actor, even within the confines of presently constituted states, requires careful reexamination.

It is worth reiterating, at this point, the fundamental assumptions underlying the very notion of design. When stated explicitly, they seem obvious, but, for that reason, they are often not stated explicitly. Then, the important question, whether the assumptions are satisfied in each concrete instance, is lost sight of. Design, as has been emphasized, implies a preconceived goal and a well-defined actor. If a house is to be designed, presumably the goal is a house with specified characteristics to be built at a cost within a specified range. The actor is an architect under whose direction the house is to be built. The architect, in turn, may be guided by the goals of the future dweller of the house.

However, the house may be just one unit in a larger complex, say, a neighborhood or an entire city. In that case, the goal may be not just the conception of the dweller as to how he wants to live and how much he wants to pay; the goal may be that of a community of people whose lives are interdependent. The designer is then a community planner or a city planner, guided by the presumed collective goal of the future dwellers. The design of such a complex must include not only the dwellings but also the facilities related to the interdependent lives of the inhabitants—transportation systems, supply centers, facilities for educational and cultural activities, etc.

In a still larger context, the city is only a unit in a more comprehensive "system," say, a nation. The "design" of a nation implies an even stronger assumption—the existence of a common goal among people who will not even live in physical proximity to each other, whose interdependence derives from the economic, social, and political institutions of the nation. The relative weight of these factors compared to those of the physical environment becomes quite great, and so the job of the designer becomes exceedingly complex.

Finally, one can talk of "designing" the patterns of human life on our planet, but hardly more than talk. Design on this scale presupposes the discovery of "human goals," and, while it is always possible to find groups of people in agreement on what "human goals" should be, or even "are" (derived, say, from some transcendental principles or an extrapolation of biological needs), these groups are hardly in a position to do more than suggest utopias.

6. Design as Actually Practiced

In actual practice, design is undertaken on much smaller scales. The smaller the scale of design, the easier it is to define or to ascertain the goal to be served by the finished product. The architect designing a house for a single dweller can consult directly with him, explain the implications of several variants, taking into account the client's preferences for the various features compared to their costs. The engineer designing a machine is in an even more fortunate position from the point of view of facing a well-defined problem, for the performance of the machine is evaluated in terms of easily quantifiable variables: efficiency, life expectancy, costs, etc. The same applies to the designer of a weapon, taking into account the appropriate "desiderata," e.g., destructive potential, accuracy, mobility, etc.

The practice of design guided by scientific knowledge in strictly circumscribed situations (with well-defined, especially quantifiable, goals) has been an unqualified success in the sense of a record of achieving *specified* goals. There is, thus, a strong pressure in the minds of people impressed by these successes to extend the practice of design to more generalized situations in which the goals to be achieved are not so precisely defined: where, in fact, the identity of the actors whose goals are to be served is not easy to establish.

In projected "planned societies," the fictitious actor, "society," and its goals are simply assumed to have been defined. As a rule, such projects remain no more than projects. On occasion, however, designs encompassing the activities of large populations (implicitly identified with "society") and seriously affecting their lives are actually put into effect. However, the actors whose goals are served thereby can, by no means, be identified with the people who follow the prescripts of the design and the people whose lives are affected. This happens when a small number of people have power to direct the activities of a large number of people, whose goals are either of no concern to the people in power or are simply assumed to be coincident with theirs.

The organization and the conduct of war is an obvious example. The goal of a war maker is victory. At his disposal are material and human resources. The "design" of a war is the job of specialists guided by long historical experience (which conscientious and committed specialists diligently study) and a considerable store of scientific knowledge relevant to the design of weapons systems, etc. In traditional military thinking, no distinction is made between the material and the human resources. The destruction of both in the course of military operations is subsumed under costs, to be weighed against the benefits of victory. The benefits accrue to the victorious war makers, who, throughout most of recorded history, have been potentates of kingdoms, princedoms, and empires. The benefits were perceived as accretions to the potentate's domains and to his power vis-à-vis other potentates. The needs and aspirations of the subjects were, for the most part, ignored; those of the soldiers were at times manufactured in the course of training by indoctrinating an appetite for "glory" or identification with the traditions of fighting units or with the personality of the commander.

After the French Revolution, a new factor appeared in European wars: nationalism, which prescribed an identification of the population with the "nation," its language, its history, its autonomy. Similar techniques were used, on the whole successfully, in the design of a "socialist society," as in the Soviet Union, following the Revolution of 1917. The success of the revolution itself was a consequence of the dissolution of power of the Tsarist autocracy and its network of enforcing agencies. In the process of crushing whatever resistance remained (manifested in the civil war), power was consolidated in another network of enforcing agencies—the Communist Party, and eventually (because of the strict military-like discipline internalized by the self-selected membership of that group and of its central organs) culminating in despotic autocracy. The latter dissolved, but the principle of totally centralized authority has remained. The planning of economic and cultural development continues to depend on the decisions of a body analogous to a general staff and transmitted in the form of orders down the organizational channels.

In a way, planning of this sort can be called successful if by "success" we mean the achievement of the planners' goals. In the case of the "first socialist society," two goals were clearly realized: first, a rapid increase of productive capacity essential for industrialization; second, the preservation of discipline, which makes continued centralized planning possible. The realization of both goals depended on a strong commitment by the bulk of the population to the program, or at least of enough people to bring pressure on the rest.

It seems that commitment to "social goals" as defined by power wielders is easiest to achieve when two conditions are fulfilled. First, the criteria of goal attainment are clear, and progress toward the goal is plainly discernible. Second, there is confidence in the designers of strategy in the pursuit of the goal. These conditions were fulfilled in the heyday of nationalism, when national morale was highest in wartime, especially in the victorious phases. The commitment to the task of "constructing a socialist society" was probably most pervasive in the Soviet Union during the periods of heavy sacrifices marking the early five-year plans, because the results of the efforts were made highly visible, and the creation of plenty was imminently expected, which was assumed without reservation to be both a necessary and a sufficient condition for a "socialist society."

It is difficult to ascertain to what extent the same commitment to increasing material wealth and to preserving a monolithic ideology has remained in force after a sustained half-century of effort, after contacts with the outside world became more frequent, and after faith in the infallibility of the leadership has been shaken. There are no facilities for undertaking objective investigations in search of answers to these questions. We have evidence, however, that in countries where complete militarization of effort in pursuit of explicitly set "national goals" is not or cannot be sustained (except possibly in wartime) such commitments are rare. At times, attempts are made to evoke them (e.g., in de Gaullist France). Typically, however, as in Western "liberal democracies," national planning is of limited extent, confined to the implementation of policies (largely economic) of political parties that happen to be in power.

In countries like the United States, where centralized planning on the national scale is itself suspect, being contrary to the dominant ideology, even the modest programs of some European welfare states are rarely undertaken or, if they are, they remain under constant attack by opponents of any aspect of a planned economy.

Nevertheless, design constantly goes on. Only, it goes on at levels pertaining to the goals of special groups. A large enterprise, in choosing its policies, looks to the future and considers how this or that policy will affect its competitive standing vis-à-vis other enterprises. A real-estate firm "designs" a subdivision, but typically only with the view of insuring proper returns on investments. Military establishments support research that produces knowledge useful for the design of future weapons systems, in which they have full support of their government in implementing plans for their growth. This is "planning on the national level" but the goals derive from a special assumption (unassailable in the present political climate) that national security depends on military strength.

7. The Proper Concern of a Science of Design

Clearly, a science concerned with design of these kinds (the subject matter of cost-benefit analysis, operations research, etc.) cannot be identified with the stated goals of a university of design concerned with the creation of a livable environment for man rather than with specific goals pursued by specific power-wielding groups. If man is the actor with whose goals the designer is to be concerned, then the goals of man must be envisaged. One is tempted to say "must be discovered," but that would be a fatuous statement, since no one can seriously indicate a method that would allow us to discover "the goals of man," at least in the present stage of human history. It may even be a serious error to suggest that "the goals of man" have an objective existence and that, at least in principle, it is possible to discover them by properly conducted inquiry. More likely, "the goals of man" may emerge *in the process* of inquiry and may be determined by the direction of the inquiry itself. At any rate, since the "goals of man" cannot be claimed to be known by anyone, the dedicated designer stands in danger of succumbing to his own conception of these goals. Or, his acquaintance with mankind may be confined to people of particular social strata, and he may mistake these people's aspirations (and their ability to realize them) for those of humanity.

A case in point is the design of attractive urban communities, with which many architects and city planners of North America and Western Europe are concerned. The style of life of the prospective dwellers in such communities may be well-known to the designers, and so also may be the ways this style can be brought into better accord with the aspirations of the people concerned. It is a far cry, however, from designing and building such communities with the lofty ideals of modifying man's environment in accordance with man's needs. Those who can live in pleasant urban communities designed for personal comfort and according to their own ideas of "healthy community relations" constitute only a minuscule fraction of humanity. Moreover, it is not at all certain that making life for these people even more comfortable than it is and imbuing them with a community spirit, of which their present life patterns may have deprived them, will have any beneficent effect on humanity as a whole. The question raised here is not whether it is justifiable to make the comfortable more comfortable, but whether there is not a danger of mistaking activity of this sort for a significant contribution to "modifying man's environment," and thereby trivializing the very concept of "creating an environment fit for man."

Mistaking a particular community, or even a relatively well-governed nation (such as the small democracies of northern Europe, where rational environment planning is gaining ground), for "man" is not as dangerous in itself as the consequence of leaving out of account the long-range effects of modifying some selected aspects of the environment. These dangers are now the increasing concern of conservationists and ecologists and, of course, should be central in the orientation of a university of design. The theme of this paper, however, is focused elsewhere, namely, on the creation of a semantic environment that *permits* the implementation of designs for a living physical and biological environment.

8. Obstacles to the Creation of a Livable Environment

The recognition that life on this planet is a system of interdependent processes suggests that any meaningful design of a livable environment must be on a global scale. Since, however, the largest social organization that can implement action programs is still the State (except in very few areas where "international cooperation" can be undertaken), the designer stands in danger of succumbing to an unwarranted assumption that underlies so-called liberal ideology, namely, that in "democracies," among which at least one super- power is usually included, a primary commitment of people in positions of authority is the promotion of "general welfare." If general welfare is not being promoted, the failure is ascribed to insufficient knowledge about how it can be done.

The view (that inadequate social action is a consequence of lack of knowledge) is particularly pervasive in the so-called peace research community. Peace research is usually defined as the totality of investigations on conditions that facilitate or inhibit the incidence of wars or the preservation of peace. In this way, peace research is conceived as something analogous to medical research, which is the totality of investigations on conditions that facilitate or inhibit the incidence of disease or the preservation of health. The implication of the analogy is that, just as disease can be attributed to lack of knowledge of how to prevent or cure it, so wars can be attributed to the lack of knowledge of how to prevent or to stop them. The analogy is a false one. It may well be that not enough is known about how to prevent or stop wars, but the incidence of wars is due not only to lack of knowledge of this sort, perhaps not even primarily, but rather to the circumstance that, at present, no institutions exist that can translate into effective action whatever knowledge is available or can be obtained. In contrast, institutions do exist which can implement the findings of medical research.

The designer of human environment on the global scale is in a position similar to that of the designer of "peace strategies." Even if he were guided by reliable scientific knowledge about the effect on man of this or that designed environment, and even if the projected environment were enthusiastically approved by all those to whom the idea could be communicated (how many, incidentally?), the implementation of the design would have to depend on the existence of appropriate institutions, which, in fact, do not exist.

If one accepts the hypothesis that man's inability to design his environment in accordance with his needs is only partially attributable to lack of knowledge and, perhaps, primarily to the lack of appropriate institutions, then the very least that a program of the university of design must include is a program aimed at investigating *and publicizing* the obstacles to the creation of such institutions. The same sort of program should, in my opinion, be included in every serious effort in peace research. In fact, peace research ought certainly be included in the program of the university of design, since war is unquestionably a prime factor in making man's environment unlivable.

An investigation of the obstacles to the creation of institutions committed to the design of livable environment necessitates the abandonment of the "liberal" assumption that only lack of knowledge (or some inadequacy of individuals in decision-making positions) stands in the way of man's ability to improve or redesign his environment. A serious investigation necessitates a thorough analysis of the ways special groups (defined in terms of social roles, not individuals), in pursuing their own perceived interests, *stand in the way* of creating institutions dedicated to the aspirations of humanity as a whole. It necessitates the abandonment of the "voluntaristic" models of collective action, according to which the goals of a collective reflect the intentions or the aspirations of the individuals in it. It is this assumption that keeps alive the delusion that men in power, being human and, on the whole, reasonable and seldom malevolent, have aspirations not unlike those of most people; that, if they act in ways that brings misery to millions, it is through error or through ignorance.

The assumptions about the psyches of individuals in power may well be correct. But the assumption that the "psyche" of the power complex, which these individuals compose, is some sort of composite of the individual psyches is unwarranted. Carrying out a death sentence demands the coordinated action of scores of individuals, not one of whom may want to deprive the victim of his life. Nevertheless, executions are carried out. The sum total of the actions of the participants is not a sort of "average" of what each one of them wants to do. Similarly, the protestations of rulers that they do not want war, or that they hate war, may be entirely sincere, but they are nevertheless irrelevant to the mechanisms that trigger wars and keep them going. Again, practically no one wants slums, urban sprawl, pollution, or overpopulation. That we continue to be victimized by these plagues is neither a consequence of someone's malice nor even a consequence of ignorance. Not men, but social roles, determine social action. Social action, therefore, depends mainly not on men's good will, nor even on their wisdom, but on the ways social roles interlock in the social structure.

So much for the minimum program of the university of design: in addition to investigations on the desiderata of human environments and the technical aspects of realizing them (in any case, central to the aims of that institution), it should also undertake investigations of the institutional obstacles standing in the way of realizing these desiderata or of creating institutions capable of realizing them. Most important, the educational aims of the university of design should include *publicizing* the obstacles, in the interest of general dissemination of relevant knowledge.

9. The Semantic Environment

A more comprehensive program of a university of design must be based on the recognition that man lives in two environments. One, the physical, is only partially man-made, although its man-made aspect is steadily becoming more important in shaping modes of human existence. The other environment is the semantic, which is entirely man-made.

Here we must make a digression for a brief survey of the origin of this latter environment, unique to man.

Anatomically and physiologically, man differs from other members of his order (primates) no more than they differ from each other. The size and complexity of man's brain is generally supposed to be the crucial factor that has determined the vast difference between man's way of life and that of other primates, indeed, that of all other animals. Yet it is impossible to specify precisely in anatomical and physiological terms how the structure or functioning of the brain has made man's life what it is. The usual way of explaining man's way of life is by pointing out the special role played by language and other symbolic systems as man's unique survival mechanisms. This explanation, however, involves concepts beyond the range of biology. If we stay, for the moment, within the scope of biological concepts, all we can say is that man modifies his environment on a much vaster scale than any other organism.

Actually, all organisms modify their environments by their very life processes. They also adapt to existing environments. On the basis of the relative importance of adaptation and modification, a rough scale can be constructed, on which the most "primitive" organisms will be found on the bottom and man, the most "complex," at the top.

Imagine an idealized "primitive" organism as a single cell immersed in a life-sustaining medium. "Life" on that level can be defined as a process that keeps the organism in a steady state that is *not* a thermodynamic equilibrium. A thermodynamic equilibrium implies maximization of entropy, roughly a state of affairs where there are no gradients in the system, temperature, pressure, concentration of substances, etc. being uniform throughout the system. A system completely isolated from its environment, that is, with boundaries impenetrable to either matter or energy, must approach such a state. Biologically, a state of thermodynamic equilibrium would mean death. A "minimal" definition of life implies the existence and the sustenance of gradients, that is, the maintenance of a system in a more or less steady state of nonequilibrium. Such maintenance is possible only if the system is open, for example, if its boundaries are penetrable to substances flowing in from the environment (nutrients) and substances flowing out (wastes). Moreover, for the steady state to be maintained, the nutrients in the environment must be replenished, while the waste products must be carried away; otherwise, the exhaustion of the former and the accumulation of the latter in the immediate vicinity of the cell will preclude the maintenance of the steady state. If the cell is immersed in a flowing medium with just the right concentrations, this "problem" is automatically solved. In general, however, the medium itself will be characterized by gradients. In some regions the concentrations will be more nearly "right" than in others. Thus, mobility is of survival value. In the simplest case, mobility is a consequence of simple tropisms: differences of concentrations induce forces that propel the cell toward the more favorable regions. Tropisms can be viewed as the simplest mechanisms of adaptation to the immediate environment.

Biological evolution is a history of cumulative adaptations. The immense variety of directions followed by these adaptations accounts for the vast variety of life forms. Some organisms, immersed in environments where certain potential nutrients are plentiful in the immediate vicinity, have not developed mobility (most plants and some sessile animals) but, instead, have developed complex mechanisms for utilizing these plentiful nutrients (e.g., carbon dioxide through photosynthesis). Others (most animals) came to depend on mobility and ultimately on patterns of *behavior* much more complex than simple tropisms, enabling them to search for food and to escape from other organisms for whom they serve as food.

The ability to maintain a steady state by means of physiological homeostatic mechanisms and by means of behavior patterns is only one crucial characteristic of living organisms. The other is reproduction, making copies of oneself. Minute variations in the copies, transmitted to succeeding generations, are at the basis of biological evolution. Natural selection, conferring greater survival potential on "favorable" variations and eliminating the carriers of "unfavorable" ones, is said to account for the adaptation of existing life forms to their environments. In animals with nervous systems, adaptiveness is, to a large extent, reflected in behavior patterns, essentially coordinated motions directed toward finding and ingesting food, finding and coupling with mates, escaping enemies, etc.

Some animals with sufficiently complex nervous systems need not depend on genetic variations in successive generations for adaptive modifications of their behavior patterns. They may be able to modify their patterns during their lifetimes. Such modification is called learning. The physiological mechanisms of learning are assumed to depend on the plasticity of neural processes, as exemplified in conditioning experiments.

If learning depends, as is supposed, on selective modification of neural pathways leading from receptors to effectors, facilitating some and inhibiting others, then learning may be viewed as an analog of the evolutionary process within the nervous system of the individual organism, where something analogous to natural selection acts upon the neural paths. The time scale of this process is shorter by several orders of magnitude than that of biological evolution. In the latter, it is the evolving species that "learns" through the elimination of the maladjusted and the greater survival potential of the better adapted. In the learning individual, the process depends on the acts of the individual, perhaps thousands of acts during its lifetime, spaced over periods of time by many orders of magnitude smaller than a generation.

There is a fundamental difference between the "learning process" embodied in evolution and its analog in the individual organism. The first is cumulative (over generations); the second is not. The genetic modifications of organisms are transmitted from one generation to the next so that subsequent modifications incorporated by natural selection can be added to those already incorporated. In fact, which modifications will have survival value, and will be incorporated, depends vitally on what is *already in* the genetic complex. For instance, greater visual acuity is likely to be a favorable modification if an animal already depends to a great extent on efficient vision, but not otherwise. Modifications of behavior through learning result from the experiences of an animal and, being somatic, not genetic modifications, are not, as biologists generally recognize, transmitted to succeeding generations. Thus, an experienced old animal may be able to cope with its environment more effectively than a young inexperienced one. But the extent to which the old animal can transmit its "knowledge" to progeny is quite limited, confined, say, to the propensity of the young to imitate the adults.

The unique role of language in our species is that it combines the *speed* of individual learning with the *cumulative potential* of evolution. What human beings have learned in the course of their lifetimes can be transmitted to succeeding generations because the transmission of this knowledge does not depend on a genetic mechanism. It is accomplished through language. Moreover, with the appearance of writing and other permanent records, the retention of what has been learned over generations does not depend on the memory capacity of individuals. The records constitute a collective memory store, larger by many orders of magnitude than the memory capacity of any individual. Nor is learning confined to what goes on between the learner and a physically present teacher. The entire store of accumulated knowledge is, in principle, available to a learner. Furthermore, language enables man to extend his experiences far beyond the events of which he is a witness or a participant, and also to extend the range of experience to events that never actually occurred and events that might occur—a range limited only by the vast combinatorial imagination inherent in symbolic, theoretical, and metaphorical language forms. Thus, a human being is not only a product of biological evolution, which modifies him only very slowly; not only the product of his personal experiences, relatively limited in space and time, but also a product of cultural evolution, a process that shares some of the characteristics of biological evolution but differs from it in the crucially important respect that, in contrast to the latter, it does not depend on genetic mechanisms.

The man-made environment is a result of this cultural evolution. Man is not the only animal that depends on specific modifications of environment for survival. Birds' nests, termite hills, and beaver dams are, like our dwellings, roads, and factories, specific modifications of the physical environment. Like our own artifacts, those constructed by animals also undergo evolution, but not *cultural* evolution. The manner of construction and the uses to which the artifacts of animals are put depend almost exclusively on the genetic makeup of the builders, not on modifications resulting from learning, culturally transmitted through generations. Nor are the artifacts cumulative. Each generation either uses existing ones or starts from scratch. In short, the crucial difference between man and other animals is that the man-made environment evolves quite independently of the biological modifications that man may have undergone since becoming man.

Until recently, this *time-binding* aspect of cultural evolution has been represented as man's principal survival mechanism. Man's anatomical adaptation to his physical environment is not impressive. Living in cold climates, he is nevertheless practically furless. Although he is a meat eater, he lacks a biological endowment for catching swift prey or killing animals stronger than he is. He is a mediocre runner and an even poorer swimmer. All of these "natural" adaptive skills have been "neglected," as it were, in man's evolution, because he does not depend on them for survival. From the beginning, man set out to modify his environment, and it was widely assumed until recently—primarily in societies where the modification of the environment by artifacts has been most advanced—that this reversed strategy has conferred on man a survival potential far greater than could be achieved by a specialized adaptation to a particular environment with the consequent dependence upon it.

The "reversed strategy" of evolution, molding nature to suit man's perceived needs rather than depending on biological adaptation to the environment, is made possible by the semantic environment—the accumulated store of knowledge, attitudes, and beliefs coded in words, as carriers of meanings, and transmitted by words and other symbols from generation to generation. This environment defines the limits of the extent to which man can design future environments. Some ideas will naturally crystallize in some semantic environments; others will not. Some may occur but will not germinate. Some will lie dormant until the semantic environment becomes favorable then will sprout. The frequent incidence of simultaneously and independently conceived inventions and scientific discoveries attests to the latter phenomenon.

Changes in the semantic environment instigate social changes and, eventually, different forms of social organization and, in turn, are instigated by them. It follows that any program of research or education centering on the problem of designing an environment fit for man must include the task of making the semantic environment hospitable to radical institutional changes that may be necessary in order to realize the design. For, in fact, the semantic environment is subject to pollution, quite as much as the physical environment. Every generalization of experience coded onto a verbally stated belief, dictum, law, theory, or doctrine is a "secretion" into the semantic environment. At times, these secretions act as catalysts or fertilizers; at times, as toxins or pollutants, inhibiting actions indispensable for overcoming obstacles in the way of designing a livable environment. Examples of the latter are the well-known shibboleths that serve to preserve the existing power structures of societies by providing a rationale for their legitimacy or benevolence.

10. POSITIVIST SEMANTIC ANALYSIS

Critiques of the semantic environment were undertaken in the United States during the 1930s. Their principal aim was to expose the vacuousness of abstract terms used both by demagogues and by the defenders of the status quo. An influential figure inspiring these critiques was Alfred Korzybski. The central theme of Korzybski's first book, *Manhood of Humanity* (1921), had been that the "time-binding process" (cumulative cultural evolution driven by transmission of accumulated experience through language and other symbols) was man's unique survival mechanism.

In his second book, *Science and Sanity* (1933), Korzybski examined the "obverse" side of language in human life. He maintained that people mistake verbal maps for the territory that these maps are supposed to represent. Pre-scientific language, under which Korzybski subsumed everyday language, the language of philosophy, theology, politics, etc., perpetuates the internalization of false maps of reality; for instance, by picturing the world in terms of fixed classes and categories instead of dynamic structural relations; by inducing "either-or" orientations, which Korzybski thought were reflections of internalized Aristotelian two-valued logic, and so on. Korzybski insisted that in reacting to words as signals, which evoke conditioned responses, people "imitate animals" and, therefore, fail to make use of language as the instrument of time binding.

Only the language of exact sciences, Korzybski maintained, being structurally similar to the reality it represents (to the extent of available scientific knowledge) and equipped with self-corrective devices, puts man into contact with objective ("nonverbal") reality. For example, the language of mathematical physics is that of mathematical relations among operationally defined variables. Thus, it avoids notions of "agencies," which pervade pre-scientific anthropomorphic conceptions of causality. The language of probability theory introduces "infinite-valued logic" in place of Aristotelian either-or-oriented, two-valued logic, and so on.

Korzybski believed that the language of science is a reflection of sanity, which he defined as the awareness of and distinction among the levels of abstraction. Pre-scientific language, on the other hand, he pictured as inducing "un-sanity," confusion of orders of abstraction, above all, mistaking the structure of language for the structure of reality. "Insanity," in Korzybski's estimation, was the extreme manifestation of semantic pathology.

Korzybski's ideas had a strong affinity to those of the logical positivists (the Vienna Circle). He insisted, however, that his concern was not with the logical aspects of language, central in logical positivism, but with the psychological. A common ground, nevertheless, can be clearly seen in the insistence by both the logical positivists and by Korzybski on a critical examination of the *meaningfulness* of words and propositions, and on a categorical demand for what P. G. Bridgman later called operational definitions. An operational definition is supposed to indicate what one must *do* in order to exhibit the referent of what is defined as a set of *observations*. Also, the truth of assertions is declared to be embodied in the predictions embodied in the assertions, not in the correspondence between the assertion itself and one's preconceived notions, influenced by the structure of everyday language, of what is true or what sounds true. In short, Korzybski advocated the application of scientific modes of thought and cognition to all human affairs, a sort of language hygiene.

Korzybski's writing stimulated a crop of popularizations, among them a best-seller by Stuart Chase, titled *The Tyranny of Words*. In that book, Chase took literally the injunction that a word, which cannot be demonstrated to have a directly perceivable referent, is only an empty sound, to be expunged from serious discourse. In this way, he disposed of all abstract terms abounding in the language of philosophy, politics, economics, etc., and with them of all philosophical, ethical, and political discourse. For example, whether fascism presented a threat to democracy (the year was 1938) he declared to be a meaningless question, because both *fascism* and *democracy*, having no immediately perceivable referents, were no more than noises like "blah-blah."

It may be difficult to understand how such a blanket dismissal of the most intense human concerns could have been seriously offered and seriously received, except for two circumstances. First, the time was just right for "debunking" florid oratory, demagogy, and hard-sell advertising that had reached the proportions of a deluge, as radio entered its golden age. Second, the pragmatic no-nonsense attitude has always been congenial to Americans. It can be found in a wide variety of contexts; for instance, in the positivist philosophy of law as expressed in Oliver Wendell Holmes's famous dictum: "The prophecies of what the courts will do and nothing more pretentious are what is meant by law." It is found in the attitudes of American culture heroes; Thomas Alva Edison is said to have preferred as protégés young men who knew "facts" (e.g., could remember the speed of sound) over those who bothered about "theories." It is reflected in Henry Ford's vulgar remark: "History is bunk." The juxtaposition of practicality and intellectuality to the disadvantage of the latter is in the American tradition.

Korzybski used the phrase "social engineering" to refer to a rational design of social relations, an obvious extension of a technocratic orientation to social problems. The phrase has since acquired a pejorative connotation, being associated with the manipulation of mass behavior for exploitative purposes. Korzybski, however, used it to denote a problem-solving orientation to human affairs. The idea is appealing. The engineer, designing a bridge, orients himself entirely toward specified characteristics of the bridge, each expressible in terms of measurable physical parameters. He *knows* before the bridge is built that it will serve the purpose for which it was designed, because he knows the laws of physics governing the behavior of materials. To people enthusiastically embracing technology, the engineer's success naturally suggests promising procedures in the approach to "social problems." To be sure, the "laws of human behavior" are not known to the extent that the laws of physics are, but this is seen as an indication that, in future, effort expended on a "science of man" (Korzybski's phrase) will yield comparable knowledge to be used in improving social and even interpersonal relations.

The plea for extending the technocratic orientation to social problems has met with a wide positive response in the United States for reasons already mentioned. In the 1950s, the years of political quiescence, it was fashionable to proclaim the "end of ideology." The implication was that political strife based on polarized ideological loyalties was a thing of the past and, at any rate, had no place in the United States. Such strife was made obsolete by the "open society," presumably achieved in the United States. The political arena of such a society was a fluid one with constantly shifting ad hoc alliances. The issues were all concrete and specific, reflected not in ideologies but in "interests," sponsored by numerous interest groups, whose multiple, many-directional and many-dimensional pressures added up in a resultant representing, by definition, as it were, the optimal resolution of conflicts of interest.

For instance, S. I. Hayakawa, perhaps the best-known popularizer of positivist semantic analysis, wrote as follows about the situation in Watts (scene of violent race riots in Los Angeles in 1965):

> Power in America is always limited and shared power, exerted by alliances and coalitions of political parties, business groups, churches, unions, minority blocs, and the like. New Left leaders adroitly escape power (and therefore responsibility) by refusing to enter into alliances or coalitions, which they term "making deals" and "selling out." Standing on their ideological purity, they prefer blazing rhetoric of moral denunciation to the give-and-take and the hemming-and-hawing of practical negotiation— for jobs, for better schools, for housing, for political support.
>
> From the New Left, therefore, Negroes can expect nothing: not money, nor power, nor jobs, nor better schools, nor housing, nor political leverage.
>
> The only hope for minorities, including the Negroes of Watts, lies in the broad center of both major parties—in those whose minds are neither in an imaginary past nor a visionary future, but in the realities of the present— in those, who in the pragmatic commonsense tradition of American life, will continue to hammer out the agreements and accommodations that we all must make to live together in peace and progress.[1]

In 1950, I myself wholeheartedly embraced the anti-ideological, pragmatic orientation. Assuming that an internalization of the scientific method of cognition would produce a culture able to examine *itself*, I wrote:

> A culture-studying culture! What a relief that would give us from the clamor of economic ideologies, for example! Here is one group shouting that taking a profit on the exchange of goods and services is utterly immoral. Another group shouts equally loudly that everything people hold dear—human character, scientific advancement, the sanctity of religion and the home—depend on the preservation of the profit system! Freed from moralistic shackles, a culture-studying society can study possible ways of organizing economy and *try* them. While the champions of "ideologies" engage in lofty and ever self-righteous arguments about the superiority of capitalism to socialism, or vice versa, the self-studying society would examine under what conditions what degree of control over what industries is required for optimum efficiency and adequate

insurance both against scarcity of commodities and against the excessive concentration of economic might in irresponsible hands.[2]

Implicit in this view is the assumption that "everyone's interest" could be referred to experts, who would take account of the realities of the situation and design rational solutions according to specified conditions of optimality, unencumbered by constraints imposed by traditional prejudices, taboos, or ideological compulsions.

In the light of the events of the last decade, the positivist-pragmatic orientation seems to me to be grossly inadequate. Operationalization and concretization of meanings create the impression that a situation has been formulated in a way that allows us to deal with it as a technical problem. Accordingly, the relevance of specific kinds of expertise seems apparent, whereas the essential aspects of the situation may call for an entirely different approach. Moreover, the "we" who use the solutions of technical problems to advantage are easily identified. The identification of the "we" who would make use of the solutions to social problems, if such were available, *may itself be an essential aspect of the situation to be dealt with.* In fact, to identify the "we" is already to prejudge the situation. There are, thus, severe limitations on the extent to which social impasses or dilemmas can be formulated as well-defined problems yielding to technical solutions.

The attractions of this approach are nevertheless considerable. It seems to remove social conflicts from a sphere where they are unresolvable to the problem-solving sphere, where scientific knowledge can be brought to bear on them. Nor can it be denied that in many instances it *is* possible to do so. It is also true, however, that in many instances the insistence on concretization of issues shifts our attention away from the *structure of* the social relations that produce the conflict, and which often is the root of the trouble.

Another circumstance to be taken into account is that the rationales with which entrenched power elites resist institutional change now depend far less than formerly on obscurantism, shibboleths, and appeals to the ideological purity (against which positivist semantic analysis has been usually directed). The language of establishments is now replete with technical terms, and the pragmatic orientation has been largely accepted as a guide to rational action. Not appeals to the sanctity of private property, but projections of the gross national product and of trade balances are now exhibited as guidelines of economic policies. In designing foreign policies, more recourse is taken to the so-called "realist" conceptions of international relations than to moralistic or ideological rhetoric. Experts and advisers from academe are invited in droves to the decision-making centers, at times even as participants in the decision-making process. The paraphernalia of rapid information processing have become standard fixtures in the arsenal of aids to decision making. It can, therefore, be maintained that the pragmatists, in their appeal for a "scientific orientation" in human affairs, are beating a dead horse. Science enjoys more prestige than ever in the citadels of power, and even "social science" is given a voice, to the extent that "social scientists" can answer or can promise to answer questions that policy makers want answered (in return for research grants).

11. CHANGING THE SEMANTIC ENVIRONMENT

The co-optation of science and of the pragmatic orientation into the service of entrenched power has created a peculiar complex of attitudes among those who see existing institutional power structures as obstacles in the way of improving the human condition. The old dichotomy between entrenched power and its challengers used to coincide with opposite attitudes toward science. When science was young, the established church combated the philosophical implication of its findings—the materialist conception of the world, nurtured by celestial mechanics and the theory of evolution. Progressives hailed these findings and saw in science the means of man's emancipation from misery, superstition, and dogma. Contemporary power elites, on the contrary, enlist science in the pursuit of their goals. It was, therefore, inevitable that revulsion against the ruthlessness and inhumanity of the power elites (as exemplified, for instance, in the recent conduct of a genocidal colonial war) would be linked, mistakenly but understandably, with the rejection of science as a world outlook. To Ivan Turgenev's rebel Bazarov, living in the 1840s, science was the only authority, and any belief or commitment that could not be formulated in the language of the materialistic science of the day was sentimental nonsense, a symptom of weak-mindedness. Revolutionary Marxists had science inscribed on their banners. To many, perhaps most of, rebellious youths today, science is, at best, irrelevant to genuine human concerns, at worst, an instrument of oppression and a fountainhead of death technology.

Therefore, the task of changing the semantic environment with the view of removing obstacles to the design of a livable environment presents problems quite different from those that were central a generation or two ago. The obstacles, as pointed out, are now, as then, institutional. The institutions, however, are now defended not by appeals to tradition nor to supernatural authority but by appeals to a potential of making the institutions more "rational." Witness the sentence introducing Robert E. Osgood's *Limited War* (1957): "How can the United States utilize its military power as a rational and effective instrument of national policy?" Policies are defended by appeals to expertise and to information allegedly available to decision makers but not to the public, on the basis of which decisions appear rational or at least appeared rational at the time they were made. In this way, the charge that "science" is not being enlisted in the design of policies can be parried, at times successfully.

Thus, there is a pitfall associated with the admonition addressed to establishments to make "more rational" decisions. Consider the sharp attacks currently made on the United States military establishment. These are of two kinds. One line of attack emphasizes the destructiveness of the military machine, which for almost a decade has been devastating countries where people live on the edge of subsistence. The same line of attack exposes the threat, which the mammoth war machine, coupled with its opposite number, presents to man and his works, accumulated through centuries of creative effort and toil. The other line of attack charges the military establishment with scandalous extravagance and inefficiency. It exposes the waste of resources on weapons that become obsolete by the time they are produced, projects undertaken under political pressures, duplication of effort by different services competing with each other, irresponsibility and incompetence of information-gathering agencies, and so on.

The latter sort of attack can be, and has been, interpreted as "constructive criticism." Indeed, it often originates within the establishment itself. It can be forestalled and disarmed by appropriate "rationalizing" measures, such as stricter control over procurement agencies, more efficient coordination among the services, more sophisticated cost accounting, and so on. These measures, however, are irrelevant to the "destructive criticism" leveled against the military establishments by the enemies of the institution itself. From the point of view of these critics, the failure of a weapons system, the waste of billions of dollars on pork-barrel projects, etc., appalling as they are, must appear, if anything, as *alleviating* rather than aggravating the threats inherent in the very existence of military machines. For, if the "constructive criticisms" were met, the machine would become more effective and, therefore, even more menacing than it is.

In general, destructive and constructive criticisms of institutions have incompatible aims. The aim of the latter is to "improve" the institutions, whose legitimacy and raison d'être are acknowledged. The aim of the latter is to destroy the institutions. Institutions are more difficult to destroy if they are made to "work better," thus justifying their existence more convincingly. Therefore, from the point of view of the enemies of the institutions, "constructive criticism" is self-defeating.

The question of whether the very existence of an institution (not the way it functions) is an insuperable obstacle to the design of a livable environment should be asked with reference to every specific institution. In retrospect, we know that certain institutions were such obstacles and so had to be destroyed, because "improving" them would be a contradiction in terms. Chattel slavery was one of them. War, in the opinion of many, together with its supporting institutions, is another.[3]

In my opinion, a critique of this sort ought to be incorporated in the program of any educational institution purporting to be emancipated from obsolete conceptions and independent of "mainstream" or official ideologies.

Another purpose that can, perhaps, be served by critiques aimed at the foundations of what passes for scientific objectivity is that of re-winning rebellious youth to a commitment to intellectual values. As has been pointed out, the rejection of these values is probably rooted in the co-optation of science by entrenched power as a "value-free" mode of thinking: the rebellious young associate "science" with "megatechnology," with the hegemony of the technocratic outlook, with the reduction of people to statistics, with computer-dictated decisions, etc. A critique aimed at the fundamental rationales underlying these perversions of science may help to reverse the anti-intellectual bias of the rebellious young. It turns out that a critical examination of these rationales leads to the conclusion that science applied to human affairs *cannot* be value-free. This conclusion is not at all the same as an a priori insistence that science must be value-*oriented* in order to serve human needs. This insistence can be easily refuted by the formal definition of science as a method of arriving at "objective truths" by deliberately excluding questions of what ought to be from inquiries into what is, which is the proper sphere of science. As we shall see, however, values enter perforce into abstract structural analysis of certain concepts, in the sense that without introducing values (as genuine ethical categories, not merely as "utilities") the analysis of these concepts leads to unresolvable paradoxes. The critique can thus serve as a means of building a bridge between "rationality" and "morality" and so of removing the apparent contradiction between them, which incites those oriented toward human needs to reject "rationality" and those oriented toward power to reject "morality."

In short, the aim of the critique of fundamental rationales is to weaken the ideological hegemony of power elites by changing the semantic environment from which they derive ideological support.

I shall exemplify what I call a structural analysis of concepts by three examples: a critique of the concept of "rational decision," a critique of formal definitions of "democratic decision," and a critique of the so-called utilitarian calculus, vaguely defined by Jeremy Bentham and revived in modern garb as cost-benefit analysis.

The analysis presented here will be purely formal without reference to the content of the pertinent situations, except by illustrative examples. The task of applying it to specific situations requires, of course, a coupling with empirical evidence—a task properly left to specialists in various content fields.

12. A Structural Analysis of "Rational Decision"

In every definition of rationality there is an implicit concordance between goals to be achieved and means used in achieving them. However, even in the simplest case of a single goal and a choice of means, the definition of concordance alone is not sufficient for deciding whether a given choice of means is or is not rational. The decision is clear-cut if only one of the available choices of action achieves the goal and if the actor knows which it is. Then we can say with some justification that the actor is rational if and only if he chooses that course of action. If, however, there are several courses of action that achieve the goal, or if the actor has false knowledge about which action or actions achieve the goal and which do not, the matter of evaluating his rationality becomes more complex.

In the first instance, we may want to know whether he has chosen the "best" among the several effective actions, and the answer to this question involves more detailed knowledge about the goal preferences of the actor, for instance, his evaluation of the costs and benefits of the various courses of action. In the latter instance, we shall probably wish to avoid a definition of rationality based entirely on ex post facto evidence, such as that the actor is rational if his choice actually *did* have the desired consequence. We would, in that case, be denied the possibility of calling an actor rational if he chose the action that he *thought* would lead to his goal. We would deny rationality to the ignorant, whereas, rationality and knowledge or irrationality and ignorance should be distinguished.

On the other hand, if we call an actor rational if he chooses actions that he thinks or believes will achieve the goal, we are denied the possibility of defining rationality of beliefs. Some would evade the issue, assuming that beliefs ought not be classified as rational or irrational, that rationality should be defined only in terms of the concordance between actions chosen and beliefs that they will achieve the desired goals. In this view, the superstitious person acts as rationally as one whose beliefs are founded on objective evidence. If, however, we pursue this assumption to its logical conclusion, we must decide that everyone is rational. For what a person "truly" believes can be ascertained only by how he acts on his beliefs (reports of beliefs are also actions). Thus, if an actor chooses a course of action in preference to other courses, this is prima facie evidence that he "truly" believes it to be the most effective in achieving his goals. (If he says it is not, we can assume that he did not declare his "true" goals.) If everyone is "rational," then the very term "rational" is redundant. If we believe that the term is useful in characterizing acts and actors, we must find some criterion that separates rational from irrational acts.

One way of admitting actions based on false-to-fact beliefs as "rational" without making the definition of rationality altogether tautological is by absolving from "irrationality" beliefs held in common by a predominant majority in a community, or in a culture, to which the actor belongs. This definition sometimes serves the purpose of evaluating rationality. However, it puts beyond the scope of any theory of rationality the problem of evaluating the rationality of a community or of a culture. This does not disturb the proponents of the definition, because they usually maintain that the concept of rationality can be meaningful only relative to a particular worldview and is, therefore, inapplicable to the evaluation of rationality of a culture or a common worldview. This viewpoint, too, can be pushed to extremes that make it hardly tenable. Granted that the rationality of a "culture" cannot be evaluated, does this mean that the rationality of any collective is not subject to evaluation, be it a culture, an organization, a cult, or a gang?

Perhaps, in refusing to judge the rationality of whole cultures, the cultural relativists are confusing rationality with other, at times, equally justifiable, bases for action. Consider a magical ritual. On ex post facto grounds, the means chosen to achieve stated ends are usually ineffective (excepting, of course, the effects induced by belief in the magic, such as psychosomatic illnesses). On the basis of beliefs accepted in the culture, the ritual is a rational act. When it comes to the rationality of beliefs, a defense of this rationality is often made on grounds other than effectiveness of achieving *stated* ends. Instead, the cultural value of the ritual itself is pointed out. It provides a sense of community; it allays anxiety, gives the participants a feeling of control over the natural environment, etc. Beneficial effects of this sort may be quite real, but taking them into consideration removes the acts from the sphere of either rational or irrational acts. Acts that are valued in themselves, or for the inner satisfaction they provide, are not, thereby, "rational" if the *instrumentality* of the act is essential in judging its rationality. Instrumentality means that the specific goals to be achieved by the act must be explicitly stated on demand. I shall confine the discussion to this conception of rationality.

In what follows, we shall avoid troublesome ambiguities and simply assume that the actor knows at least the range of possible consequences of each of his available actions. If, now, each action has one and only one consequence, and if the actor's preference order for the consequences is known to him, the decision problem is simple: the actor can choose the action that leads to the most desirable consequence. Further, if he has reason to believe that some supposedly available actions may become unavailable, he can choose a *strategy* of the following sort: choose the action that leads to the most preferred consequence; if that action turns out to be unavailable, choose the action that leads to the next most preferred consequence, etc. Finally, we can say that the actor is rational if and only if he chooses that strategy. Thereby, the problem of defining a rational act and of deciding whether an actor has acted rationally is solved in this simplest of cases.

The situation is more involved if the actor knows the *set* of possible consequences associated with a given act but does not know which one of that set of consequences will actually obtain. Here, it is useful to imagine another fictitious "actor," called nature, or something of this sort, on whom the choice of consequences among those associated with the act depends. As the name implies, nature in making her "choices" is indifferent to the goals of the actor. We can, therefore, assume that nature makes her choice by chance. Accordingly, we specify a set of "states of the world," among which nature makes her choices without regard to the action chosen by the actor. This situation is illustrated through the matrix in figure 1.

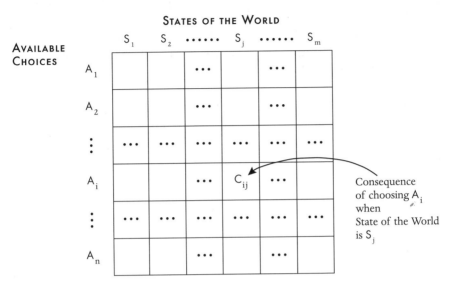

Figure 1

The horizontal rows of the matrix represent the choices available to the actor; the vertical column, the "states of the world," i.e., the choices available to nature. Once both choices are made, a consequence is determined and is entered in the corresponding cell of the matrix.

If the actor can assign numerical "worths" (utilities) to each of the possible outcomes and also probabilities (relative degrees of belief) to each of the possible states of nature, the concept of rational decision can be extended to apply to this sort of situation, called "decision under risk." Namely, the actor chooses the action that maximizes the statistically expected utility. Decisions guided by this principle are called "calculated risks."

So far, we have assumed that the "other actor," who partially controls the outcomes of his choices, is neutral, with regard to the first actor's goals and preferences. The situation is different if the other actor is a "real one" with goals and interests of his own. In the simplest case, these are diametrically opposed to those of the first actor. This opposition can be expressed by assuming that the second actor's utilities for each outcome are numerically equal to those of the first but with opposite sign. The decision problem then becomes a "zero-sum game."

In this case, too, a rational choice can be prescribed to each actor. It has the property of assuring for the actor in question the largest utility (now called "payoff") that he can assure for himself under the assumption that the other actor will also act rationally, that is, in a way that assures *him* the largest possible payoff.

The game-theoretic definition of rational choice is complicated by the fact that, except in special cases, the "best choice" is not one of the available choices but a "mixture" of them. That is to say, the actor must make his choice depend on the outcome of a chance device. What he controls is the probabilities of the chance device that correspond to the various acts available to him. Resort to such "mixed strategies" is necessitated by the fact that, in general, the opponent's knowledge of one's specific choice confers an advantage on the opponent. A "mixed" strategy denies this knowledge to the opponent. (In some kinds of games, however, this is not the case; notably, so-called games of perfect information, like chess.)

It would seem, one could go on in this manner, generalizing the concept of "rational act" to more and more complex situations; for instance, involving more than two independent actors or actors whose goals and interests are only partially, instead of diametrically, opposed. It turns out, however, that there are obstacles in this path having to do with the circumstance that *the concept of rationality becomes ambivalent as soon as the decision situation passes beyond that envisaged in the two-person zero-sum game.*

As an example, consider the following sequential choice situation:

1. Actor **A** must choose between A_1 and A_2.
2. Actor **B**, knowing how actor **A** has chosen, must choose between B_1 and B_2.
3. Actor **C**, knowing both **A**'s and **B**'s choices, must choose between C_1 and C_2.

Thereupon, the payoffs are accorded to the players according to the following rules:

If all three (actors) chose X_1 (where **X** stands for either **A**, **B**, or **C**), each loses one unit, i.e., gets a "utility" of –1.

If all three chose X_2, each gets a utility of +1.

If two chose X_1 and one chose X_2, then the two get +2, while the one gets –2.

If two chose X_2 and one chose X_1, then each of the two get 0, and the one gets +3.

This game can be illustrated by a decision-tree shown in figure 2.

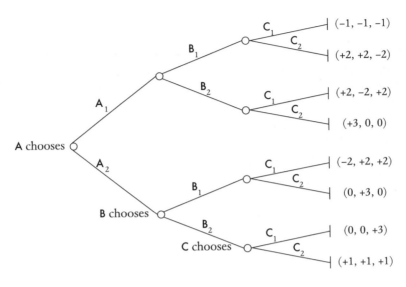

Figure 2

Let us analyze this game from the standpoint of each player, to see what his "rational choice" might be. **A** is the first to choose. Suppose he contemplates choosing A_1. He wants to know what the final outcome will be, so he puts himself into **B**'s position and asks what **B** would do if he (**A**) chose A_1. If **B** should choose B_1, then **C** would choose C_1 rather than C_2, since the first choice leads to a payoff of –1 for **C** while C_2 leads to –2. So the payoff to **B** would be –1. On the other hand, if **B** chooses B_2, **C**'s best choice will be C_1, and consequently the payoff to **B** will be –2. Therefore, **A** can suppose that, following his choice of A_1, **B** will choose B_1 and **C** will choose C_1, resulting in a payoff of –1 to **A**. Pursuing the same analysis of **B**'s and **C**'s choices following A_2, **A** finds that this choice will give him a payoff of –2. Comparing the payoffs resulting from his two choices (assuming "rational" choices by the others), **A** decides that A_1 is the rational choice.

Similar reasoning leads **B** to the conclusion that B_1 is his "rational" choice and **C** to the conclusion that C_1 is his rational choice. It turns out that, while each of the players chose "rationally," each got a payoff of –1. Had they chosen otherwise, each of them might have received +1. We have a paradox, which cannot be resolved without a redefinition of *rationality*.

Upon reflection, one sees that a binding agreement among the three to choose A_2, B_2, and C_2, respectively would give each a payoff of +1 and so would be to the advantage of each. This, however, brings other questions to the forefront; for example, whether it "pays" for **C** to keep the agreement when it is his turn to choose. If he breaks the agreement after the first two have chosen A_2 and B_2, respectively, **C** gets +3 instead of +1 by keeping the agreement. Invocation of sanctions for breaking the agreement introduces features extraneous to the game originally defined. Of course, these can be examined separately. The point to be made is that, within the rules *as defined*, the concept of rationality remains ambivalent, since *individual* rationality prescribes one choice to each of the players, while *collective* rationality prescribes the other.

The next point to be made is that the formation of a "coalition" among the players for the purpose of effecting an agreement (so as to be guided by collective rationality) presents its own problems. Suppose that, in order for the coalition of three to form, first a coalition of two must form, which will then invite the third player to join. Suppose, then, that **A** and **B** have formed a coalition in order to coordinate their strategies to mutual advantage, and suppose that, for the time being, **C** has not joined it. By coordinating their strategies, **A** and **B** can bring the game to any of the four branch points (in figure 2) where it becomes **C**'s turn to choose. Let us see which of the four points will give **A** and **B** the largest return. If they bring the game to the lowest of the four points (by **A** choosing A_2, then **B** choosing B_2), clearly their return will be 0 to **A** and 0 to **B**. This is so because, at that branch point, **C** will certainly choose C_1 to get +3 rather than C_2 to get +1. Similarly, we see that if they bring the game to the point just above the preceding one (**A** choosing A_2, **B** choosing B_1), the returns will be −2 to **A** and +2 to **B** (since **C** will again choose C_1). Again the *joint* gain will be 0. At the next above, the same situation will obtain. If they bring the game to the uppermost of the four points, their joint gain will be −2. It follows that, if **A** and **B** form a coalition, the most they can get jointly is 0. **C**'s situation is more fortunate. If **A** and **B** act so as to get the most they can, that is, if they bring the game to any of the branch points except the uppermost (which they must avoid, since in that case they will jointly get −2), **C** can get either +2 or +3, that is, at least +2. It follows that the player who *does not* join the coalition has an advantage in this game. Consequently, we can expect that no player will be in a hurry to join a coalition with another. Each will hope that the other two form a coalition so that he, as the odd man, will get +2, while the members of the coalition will get jointly only 0. But if every player declines the invitations to join a coalition, no coalition will form. We have seen, however, that if each plays "for himself," the most he can hope to get is −1, even less than he can hope to get as a member of a two-player coalition. On the other hand, if all three join in a coalition, they can coordinate their strategies so as to bring the game to the outcome whereby each gets +1, namely, choosing strategies A_2, B_2, and C_2 respectively. Question: is it or is it not rational for a player to join a coalition?

The question cannot be answered as it stands. It is *individually* not rational for a player to join a two-player coalition already formed; but it is *collectively* rational for all three players to join in a coalition. It is also noteworthy that players acting in accordance with the prescripts of individual rationality lose (if all three do so), while players acting in accordance with collective rationality win (again, if all three do so). The whole problem, then, hinges on the definition of "the actor." Not only does the "collective actor" win, while three individual actors lose, but also the three *components* of the "collective actor" (the erstwhile individual actors) win as members of the collective.

"In unity there is strength" is a piece of age-old wisdom. However, there are almost insuperable obstacles in the way of creating a global collective actor, and by no means the least stubborn of these is the inability of decision makers (especially of powerful states), obsessed with the problem of the "rational use of available power," to transcend the concept of the "national interest." Therefore, the homely lessons taught by the structural analysis of elementary games are likely to be lost on them. The impact of such analysis on the semantic environment is to be sought elsewhere—in the ammunition it provides for demolishing the claims made by champions of "national interest" to the effect that they seek the most "rational" courses of action under constraints imposed by a "realistic appraisal of the situation." The point is that "individual rationality" is inadequate in many situations, while the achievement of collective rationality involves the internalization of values like mutual trust, commitment to *unenforceable* agreements, and so on, that are beyond the scope of the "thinkable" for self-styled "realists."

13. Formal Criteria of Democratic Collective Decisions

Assume the pragmatists' model of a society as a conglomerate of many actors, each of whom may have different preference orders for available choices. If different choices by different members are compatible, "freedom" in this society can be defined simply as the composite freedom of its members. Each chooses according to his own preferences. Problems arise when the choices are not compatible, when the society as a whole must make a choice, obligatory on everyone. (Laws are "choices" of this sort.)

Democracy is often defined as "people's sovereignty," implying collective decisions on matters of public concern. To make the definition meaningful, the actual rules governing the making of such decisions must be specified. They are, in fact, specified in constitutions of states called "democratic." Thus, the definitions of "democracy" and "democratic" tend to become circular: "democratic societies are those with 'democratic' rules of collective decision." To avoid circularity, we must start from the beginning and examine possible decision processes that deserve to be called "democratic."

Assume a collection of individuals, each of whom prefers a set of possible actions in some given order. We seek some rule according to which, when the preferences of all individuals have been examined, the society, as a whole, chooses a preference order on the actions. What shall we require of such a rule if we can reasonably call it "democratic?"

First, it is reasonable to demand that the preference order chosen by society should reflect, *to some extent,* the preference orders of its members. That is to say, if the rule of choosing the social preference order is such that, no matter what the preference orders of the members may be, the social-preference order for a given set of actions remains unchanged, we cannot call the rule democratic. The notion of "people's sovereignty" must reflect *some* responsiveness in the preference order chosen by society to the preference orders of its members.

Second, we can reasonably demand that the preference order chosen by society reflect more than the preference order of some one individual, for if that were so the individual would be a dictator. If "democracy" is to have a meaning compatible with our intuitive notions about it, then it certainly should be incompatible with dictatorship. Note that, if there exists a group of individuals in the society who always have exactly the same preference order with respect to any set of actions, then, for all practical purposes, this group acts like an individual and should be considered to be an individual. To impose the preference order of this (fixed) group as the social preference order is tantamount to admitting dictatorship.

Third, the rule determining the social preference order should not be "malevolent." That is to say, should all members in a society except one be indifferent between action **A** and action **B**, but the one individual exception prefers **A** to **B**, then the rule should be such that the social preference is for **A** over **B**. (If a choice benefits just one individual and hurts no one else, it should be made. Of course, the same applies to the case where a number of members benefit from a choice, while no one else is hurt by it.)

Finally, we can expect that if, besides previously available choices, others are added which *do not include* the choice to be made by society, then the added choices should not affect the choice that *is* made. That is to say, suppose, according to the preference orders stated by individuals and our rule of making a social choice, choice **A** is made. Suppose now the same situation where, in addition to the previous alternatives, another alternative, **Z**, is added. It is conceivable that with the addition of **Z**, and taking into account its standing in the preference orders of members, the social choice switches to **Z**. If it does *not* switch to **Z**, however, then it should still be **A**.

Now, in any situation where there are only two alternatives to choose from, each time a choice must be made, any number of rules satisfy the above conditions. For example, a simple majority rule satisfies the first three, whereas in the last it is irrelevant because the addition of another alternative makes the issue no longer an either-or choice. Nor is the simple majority rule the only possible one. More complex rules may specify conditions where larger majorities may be required to "pass a measure." The rights of certain minorities may be protected, by requiring *them* to give their consent (determined by a process within their ranks), etc. In short, when we are dealing with only either-or choices, the usual decision rules, derived from conventionally established parliamentary procedures, satisfy our minimal requirements for a "democratic" decision rule.

The matter looks very different as soon as there are more than two alternatives. The problem is illustrated by a famous paradox discovered by the eighteenth-century French mathematician-philosopher the Marquis de Condorcet. Imagine a society with just three members, A, B, and C, who are to choose one of three available alternatives, X, Y, and Z. Assume that A prefers X to Y and Y to Z (therefore, X to Z); that B prefers Y to Z and Z to X (therefore, Y to X); and that C prefers Z to X and X to Y (therefore, Z to X). Suppose the social decision rule is by "majority vote." Then, since X is preferred to Y by both A and C, who are a majority, the society should prefer X over Y. Next, since Y is preferred to Z by both A and B, again a majority, the society should prefer Y to Z. But Z is preferred to X by both B and C, who are also a majority. Therefore, the society should prefer Z to X. But then we find that the society prefers X to Y, Y to Z, and Z to X. These preferences are incompatible, and so no choice is possible.

This special case illustrates only the failure of the majority to rule in a situation involving three members of a society and three alternatives. It has been shown, however, that whenever more than two alternatives are available, if there are no restrictions on how the members may order their preferences, no social decision rule can exist that will satisfy the above, apparently minimal, requirements of "democratic" social choice.

It is not necessary to conclude on the basis of this analysis that "democratic decisions are impossible." The requirements may be "minimal" in the sense that they seem eminently reasonable. However, the demand for an appropriate rule of social decision is also "maximal" in that it is a demand for a rule that will apply to *every conceivable* set of preference orderings, each freely chosen by every member of the society. As a matter of fact, "every conceivable" preference ordering of every possible set of alternatives is not likely to occur in human society. Usually, the alternatives considered are perceived as ordered on some "ideological basis." For instance, a set of alternative economic policies usually will be perceived as ranging from "most laissez-faire" to "most socialistic"; a set of alternative foreign policies will tend to be perceived as ranging from "most dovish" to "most hawkish," etc. In the light of these perceptions, a member of society will tend to take a "position" on the "private enterprise-socialism" axis or on a "militaristic-pacifistic" axis. If every set of alternative policies could be ordered along some axis of this sort, social decision rules could be easily devised to satisfy the "minimal requirements" listed above.

We know that such orderings of issues along "ideological axes" actually occur. At any rate, individual preference orders for alternatives are not independent. Rather, issues are *linked* by reference to the general orientations, which they suggest, by reference to the coalitions that sponsor them, etc.

In this way, the collective decision process *can* operate, but only at the cost of giving up the concept of completely independent issues and completely independent actors. The ideal "non-ideological" democratic process with independent issues and independent voters not only does not exist, but *cannot* exist because the minimal defining assumptions are inconsistent with each other.

This finding does not tell us anything that we did not already know through experience with things political. It does, however, expose the fallacious nature of the model that pictures a democratic society as an atomistic one, a notion borrowed from classical economies where the individual producer-consumer in "free interactions" with others of his kind is put at the foundation of the economic process.

Elementary structural analysis of the possible formal bases of social decisions turns our attention perforce to ideological factors and to the coalescence of members of a society into power blocs—features that are de-emphasized or suppressed in idealized conceptions of individualistic democracy.

14. Utilitarian Calculus and Cost-Benefit Analysis

In the preceding example, it was assumed that, given a set of alternatives, each member of society simply orders them on a preference scale. Nothing was assumed about the "*degree* of preference" one may have for the alternatives. In principle, these degrees of preference can be determined. Suppose, to begin with, the alternatives are different amounts of money that an individual is to receive under identical conditions. It can be reasonably assumed that any larger amount will be preferred to a smaller amount, since even if the individual "actually" prefers the smaller amount he can always get it if he receives the larger amount by the simple expedient of throwing away the difference. At a first approximation, we could assume also that the "degree" of his preference for the larger amount is proportional to the difference. Actually, there is evidence that this is usually not the case, the equal increments of money are not of equal "worth" to the individual. For instance, a raise in salary from $10,000 to $20,000 will be typically felt to be "worth more" than the next (equal) raise from $20,000 to $30,000. These observations gave rise to the notion of the "utility" of money.

In principle, an individual's "utility function" for money can be measured by offering him certain hypothetical choices (provided he makes these choices with sufficient consistency). The zero point and the unit of this scale can be chosen arbitrarily. The scale establishes only the relative worth of the increments. To fix ideas, suppose that the zero point of the utility scale is fixed at $0 and the unit at $10,000. Suppose, next, that the individual is offered a choice between two alternatives: receive $5,000, or a lottery ticket that entitles him to $10,000 or to nothing, depending on the outcome of some random event, the probability of a favorable outcome being 0.5. (The outcome of a toss of a fair coin is an illustration of such a random event.) The man will choose the one alternative or the other. If he prefers $5,000 above the lottery ticket, he is offered another lottery ticket, with larger probability of a favorable outcome, say 0.6. If he still rejects the lottery, increase the chances still further. If the individual prefers $10,000 to $5,000, as we have assumed, then as we keep increasing the probability of winning $10,000 he must at some point change his choice, for he will certainly change it when the lottery gives him a one-hundred percent chance of winning $10,000. Usually, the preference will switch at some point before this extreme is reached. Say the individual becomes indifferent between $5,000 and a lottery ticket with eighty percent chance of winning. Then, by definition, $5,000 is worth 0.8 utility units to him, and we can say that his preference for $5,000 over $0 is four times as large as his preference for $10,000 over $5,000.

Similarly, a utility scale can be established for any set of alternatives. Given any three alternatives, A_1, A_2, and A_3, preferred in that order, an individual is offered a choice between A_2 for sure and a lottery ticket, which gives A_1 with a certain probability or A_2 with the complementary probability. The probabilities are calibrated until the individual is indifferent between the two choices. Thereupon, the ratio of the two utility differences is determined.

The introduction of utility scales permits the attachment of a "worth" to every alternative. The idea of achieving the "greatest good for the greatest number," another basis for defining democracy, stems from this apparent possibility of defining the "social worth" of each choice. It would seem that, by adding the utilities assigned by each member of a society to each of the alternatives that present themselves, one can determine the utility of each alternative to the society. All one needs to do, then, is choose the alternative with the largest social utility.

Upon closer examination, however, this model, too, turns out to be unrealizable, for it is based on the assumption that the utilities of different individuals can be added. In consequence of the above *operational* definition of utility, they cannot. Since the zero point and the unit of that scale can be chosen arbitrarily, it follows that choosing different zero points and different units for the utility scale of an individual leaves his utility determinations invariant, but does change the contribution of his utility for an alternative to the total (society) utility. One way the addition of utilities can be justified is by fixing, once and for all, the zero point and the unit of utility for each individual. So far, no procedure has been suggested for doing this, nor even imagined. The other way of justifying the addition of utilities is by choosing a single utility scale for the entire society. This is what is done when planning is undertaken on a national scale. In this way, a meaning can be attached to "the greatest good for the greatest number" (more precisely, finding a course of action that maximizes this assumes "social utility" or its statistical expectation).

In some situations, the procedure can be reasonably justified. In designing public health policies, safety procedures in mass transportation, etc., it is relatively easy to agree on a "social utility" within those contexts (reduction of incidences of disease, of traffic incidents, etc.). In each case, however, there is a "trade-off," which may be ignored for a time until it becomes conspicuous. For instance, traffic volume can be increased and fatalities per passenger mile reduced by covering a country with a network of fast, safe roads. *Now* we know the social price of this "solution," which had not been entered in the initial calculations.

Cost-benefit analysis becomes a menace when the "trade-off" continues to be ignored because some interpretation of "social utility" is ideologically unassailable. Such is the case with cost-benefit accounting applied to "national defense." Monstrous growth of war machines is justifiable by identifying their destructiveness with "national security." Bizarre "civil defense" schemes, projecting a subterranean existence for a population, are seriously entertained on the basis of calculations of how many lives can be "saved" in case of a nuclear attack. At the same time, diplo-military "postures" are evaluated on the basis of "acceptable" losses in "nuclear exchanges," etc. United States war operations in Southeast Asia are said to have been guided by cost-accounting practices introduced by Robert MacNamara, carried over directly from automobile manufacturing.

Moral indignation against these caricatures of "rationality" is entirely understandable. Here, too, however, waves of moral indignation break against the rocks of self-styled "realism." Structural analysis of the underlying concepts (like "utility"), by exposing their meaninglessness beyond certain highly specific contexts, may help to undermine the alleged "rationality" and "objectivity" on which modern power elites and their technical experts claim to base their policy decisions.

Thus, the aim of structural analysis is similar to what the aim of positivist semantic analysis had been: to strip away the impregnable armor surrounding certain key concepts that have polluted the semantic environment, clogging the flow of new ideas. However, structural analysis goes deeper, beyond pragmatism and beyond the conventional acceptance of the purely instrumental, "value-free" role of science.

To be sure, the pragmatic approach also considers "values"—namely, utilities assigned to possible outcomes of decisions—and it perceives the task of applied science to be that of finding courses of action expected to maximize the stated utilities. In this way, applied science serves the actor whose utilities have been given or assumed. But utilities can be assigned in any manner whatsoever and different assignments change only the parameters of the problem, not its *structure*. It is in this sense that values and "rationality" *are separated* in the pragmatic approach; and it is in this sense that pragmatists, for the most part, insist that science is "value-free," or, at any rate, emancipated from ideological bias.

In structural analysis, questions of value enter not as utilities but *as questions about the identity of the actor*; for instance, whether the actor of a party with a set of interests, acting in pursuit of these interests, or a collective, an amalgam of parties with originally divergent interests, now merged to take advantage of collective rationality. As was shown, the notion of rational decision cannot even be unambiguously defined unless questions of this sort are answered. And questions of identity and of identification with collective interests are at the very basis of ethical concern.

It is in this sense that values and rationality *cannot be separated* in structural analysis: values enter perforce in the very definition of the actor.

Consider, for example, the implications of defining the actor in the design of policies where social goals are identified with "national interest," and national interest, in turn, is identified with power. There is no reason to suppose that "national interest," conceived in terms of notions passed on directly from the era of absolute monarchies, cabinet wars, and colonial conquests, has any relevance to what humanists would like to define as "social goals." But the tacit identification of the actor with the nation state freezes this identification, even in the minds of men of good will.

SUMMARY

Nothing of what has been said should be interpreted as, in any way, minimizing the importance of what is usually understood by design. It goes without saying that a university of design should include programs of research, education, and dissemination of information in matters directly relevant to improving man's physical environment by intelligent use of space, and wise utilization and prudent husbanding of resources. It goes without saying, also, that the program should pay special attention to long-range consequences of modifying the environment. Hence, the architect and the engineer, the city planner and the conservationist all have central roles to play in the enterprise. Little or nothing has been said in this paper of these roles; they will, undoubtedly, be defined by the corresponding specialists.

What has been said was meant to emphasize aspects of the problem that are often bypassed: the obstacles in the way of putting ideas to work. If these obstacles are not recognized and faced, the enterprise may find itself in a position where its really important and creative products remain utopian schemes, while its "salable" projects serve only the especially fortunate portions of humanity, or, worse, nurture the very social forces that produce the obstacles in the way of improving the condition of mankind.

For this reason, the revolutionary, in a way, "subversive," function of the enterprise should be given most careful attention. A principal aim should be radical change in the semantic environment, which, in turn, will mean that loyalty to established social orders will be eroded. In particular, if the university of design performs its task successfully, a persistent illusion of our age will be shattered, namely, that the impasse in which mankind presently finds itself is a "problem" to be solved by finding proper techniques—more technology, or more conservation, or application of advanced cost-benefit analysis to make policies more "rational," or invention of methods of conflict management and conflict resolution, or psychotherapy. All of these uses of applied science have their proper functions. However, the principal obstacles to the creation of a livable environment are not the inadequate functioning of established institutions but the very existence of some of them—institutionalized war making; institutionalized distribution of de facto power, not mentioned in constitutions; institutionalized education aimed at perpetuating the existing institutions, not necessarily through explicit indoctrination (which is ineffective in the long run) but by making access to the means of livelihood and social acceptance (which only a few can dispense with) conditional upon internalizing conventional values and adhering to conventional life patterns.

The question remains as to what extent a university of design can contribute to the breakdown of institutional obstacles blocking the design of a livable environment. The answer hinges not only on creating centers of learning as countervailing institutions, where the young are immunized against a polluted semantic environment and are inculcated with loyalty to mankind instead of to entrenched power. This can be done, because the young are all too ready to reject ossified ideologies and shabby conventional wisdom. The difficult problem is that of making a place for emancipated men and women in the workaday world. They can't all take refuge in Academe, where, by resisting certain pressures and temptations, they may still be able to make a living without serving power. Even if all were so accommodated, the enterprise would be self-defeating, for the goal of the university of design will be served if emancipated men and women enter the world of production and service. Presently, this world is organized into corporate and government institutions, and, as a rule, acceptance of existing institutional structures and commitment, or at least service, to their goals is virtually a precondition for entering that world. How to create opportunities for combining adult responsibilities in the world of work with a genuine commitment to what I presume to be the goals of the university of design is a problem with which the enterprise ought to be most seriously concerned.

Notes

1. S. I. Hayakawa and Barry A. Goldfield, "Reflections on a Visit to Watts," *ETC.: A Review of General Semantics* 23 (1966): 305.
2. Anatol Rapoport, *Science and the Goals of Man* (New York: Harper & Row, 1950).
3. *Editor's note: At this point in the narrative, one page of Professor Rapoport's essay was inadvertently omitted from the Museum's archival copy of his manuscript; attempts to recover the page have been unsuccessful.*

Notes on the Universitas Project Working Paper
By Jivan Tabibian

The Project Working Paper variously defines or characterizes design as the creation of an order in the world, changing the facts of this world in the process, according to some conception of what they ought to be: as the synthesis of new and concrete structures and, finally, as the activity by which man creates his own future.

This means, of course, that the Universitas Project wants to succeed, ultimately, in educating men who are designers in the above meanings of the word. We are, therefore, concerned with the design of design education. There will be ample opportunity elsewhere to discuss the organizational/practical issues related to institution building in the context of education and professionalism. Here, we must first discuss some philosophical problems related to the premises upon which this undertaking is based, since a series of implicit models about man and his society underline the Project Working Paper.

In the advanced technological society, the significant problems confronting man are due to the social/institutional consequences of the process of structuring and restructuring his man-made environment. While man is the maker of this environment, now the social/institutional component seems to have become a strong determinant of man's condition itself. Without exploring the specific historical relationship in which man finds himself today vis-à-vis his social milieu, there is always a danger of considering the man-made world as an object and man as, unavoidably, the subject. It is the concrete possibility of man experiencing himself as object that must be considered as an important design problem and significant variable.

The superstructures discussed in the Project Working Paper have to be translated into affective, cultural, and experiential terms; without such translations, we tend to reify the autonomous idea of our man-made milieu and divorce it from the consciousness of those who experience it as the fragmented and fragmenting manifestations of our fractured society and disjointed identities. It is the destruction of our holistic relationship to a community that may account for our tendency to confuse the means with the effect. Post-technological man is a post-community man, where his roles, determined by the dialectic of *techne* and society, substitute in a disconnected way the immediacy of his continuous experience of self in the fold of the polis. The synthesis of new structures presupposes the resynthesis of the self as subject and the mending of the rupture between the "I" and the "me." In this context, it becomes apparent that the optimistic and pessimistic attitudes toward technology share the same mechanism of resignation. In both instances, we relate to technology as objects. To be motivated by the facts of technological feasibility, the mechanism and consequences of which are so well discussed under the rubric "megamachine" by Lewis Mumford in *The Myth of the Machine* (1970), can be explained only if we understand the emasculation of the "I" in favor of the "me." The values of human existence to which the paper alludes cannot emerge simply out of man's intellectual confrontation of his own existence, but must be experienced, unselfconsciously in a manner wherein the conditions of his existence are inextricably linked to the existence of others. The values of human existence in the post-technological society often tend to be reparative in nature. They attempt to mend, structurally or subjectively, the fracture of reality and meaning. The humanism of rebellion and the humanism of mysticism, the humanism of heroic stoicism and the humanism of self-assertive absurdity, all attempt to impose meaning after the fact, a bit like prayers to bring back the loss of innocence.

We have burdened man's intellectual confrontation of his existence too much with therapeutic functions related to the affective significance of his experience of living. We, thus, confuse—to paraphrase Anton C. Zijderveld—the problems of freedom with freedom itself. The impact of the scientific/analytic mode has been more extensive then even recognized in the Project Working Paper. To subject freedom to analysis is to translate experience into cognitive consciousness. This transformation, incidentally, is possible for two rather unrelated reasons—first, that it may be all that is left to us and that, therefore, we had better reconstruct the image as best we can, and, second, the rationalist tradition cannot allow for any kind of legitimacy other than the one that stems from systematic inquiry and analysis. If this is the case, design as synthesis will require the designer to transcend his rationality and participate through his experience in the irrational, at least at the level of exploring goals and establishing priorities. The commitment to survival neither is, nor needs to be, rational, and this applies to the survival of an individual as well as that of the species. The a priori acceptance of survival as necessary and desirable preempts all further decisions of their urgency or seemingly ethical significance. It is true that action, ethics, and the quality of life are complementary to the concept of survival. But, what is suggested here is that truly qualitative and normative judgments must recognize the empirical and metaphysical contingency of life. With this logico-ethical certainty eliminated, the synthesis of structures is less bound by the necessities of function and can afford to position superstructures ahead of infrastructures, thanks to the ambiguity of purpose. Life or death propositions reflect and substantiate the dichotomous nature of our normative schemes. It is the ambiguity of life *and* death that permits a construction of meaning and reality that is not bound by linear structures.

At this point, an illustrative digression may be worthwhile. The case in point is the prevailing orientation toward the future, demonstrating a convenient and telling depersonalization. It is seldom my future, or our future, except for rhetorical emphasis. The epistemology of my future cannot deny my consciousness of my own death qua consciousness and not experience. It is this that is a constant dimension of my future; it contains its own finality, at least in a specified form. This is also true for our collective future. Our true future is in our extinction. It is only by abstraction and separation that we can extricate our future from the imminence of our mortality. In this sense, our future is all the relevant future that there can be, and that is why it is intensely normative and cannot be, in any fashion, value-free. Thus, as construction rather than projection, the future is an order that remains to be created by design, and resolved. Otherwise, we would deny ourselves the right to hold a future state of consciousness into the future with the same feelings of awkwardness that one might sense upon discovering the inevitability of one's happiness sometime hence. The personalization of the future also publicizes it because, while within the future we may passively accommodate our unique experience, the construction of our multiple futures may not necessarily resolve in harmony. Whose future is the designer to create? If it is only his own, the design task we have is drastically extended and expanded because that would be the task of redesigning society through such strategic new structures as to permit all individuals to fulfill their existences through a decentralized design process. But if, on the other hand, we were to create designers whose synthesis is, in the largest sense, public, then the questions of political economy and political ethics remain all unanswered. Of course, these anxieties could be dissipated if we were to reinvent the demiurgic role of the designer and wed it to that of the philosopher-king.

We must now examine by what methodology Universitas proposes to realize the idea of an institution, "explicitly . . . conceived toward developing the system of thought capable of designing our man-made milieu." The task of those designing Universitas is quite similar to the task to be assumed by those who will later hopefully emerge out of the ongoing universities. They both have the task of creating structure, out of which might emerge new meaning. The Working Paper's position on this issue is justifiably tentative and vague. Though, on the one hand, convinced that this may be the only way to break the cycle and induce material and epistemological change, it ultimately bases its faith on the innovative qualities of structures and their iconic characteristics. It is a combination of imagination and randomness that guarantees the openness of meaning. This, the paper suggests is the (if not the only) way that new values, embodied in structures, can emerge and suggest themselves to members of the community. This view of the spontaneous emergence of values out of new structures, I am sure, holds great appeal to many of us, because it implicitly reassures us in one swoop both of the élan vital and of the potency of mind augmented by freedom and choice. More seriously, it can promise a system whereby not only can we account for discontinuities in history but also can link man's image making to the inexorable curve of his spiritual progress.

The desperate need for true renewals and fresh starts may have led us to believe in the promise of their fulfillment, as well as to search for the means of their realization. Skepticism about the quasi–sui generis nature of innovation and renewal through structures, I hope, is not interpreted as fatalism. What these questions suggest is that, although structures may have iconic qualities and although man as image-maker and symbol decoder expands through the interpretation of unique structures, both their meaning and values in general, it is imperative to take another, closer look at the process. More simply put, the following questions come to mind:

— What is the empirical, epistemological, and normative linkage between old structures and new yet-to-be-designed ones?

— What are the dangers of the articulation of symbolically charged unique structures, or the deciphering of the iconic properties of new structures generating values that contradict present or future desirable norms? What assures us that open-endedness moves toward the future humanization and existential actualization of man? Do we have a way, in short, to know that the meaning of icons unfolding will, in fact, cumulatively synthesize into a new coherent and desirable superstructure, which, in turn, will permit the continuation of the process?

— And, finally, how can we justify the assertion that breaking "the stasis of established patterns" can be accomplished through the invention of structures whose iconic properties may dialectically combine and transcend existing infrastructures and superstructures?

It is presumed, I believe, that the Universitas Project and team are considered the beginnings of such a unique structure, with as yet undeciphered, but eventually articulated and actualizable, new meanings and new values. This new structure, it is further presumed, will not only, in turn, affect old epistemologies but strive to redefine old infrastructures. We know, however, that although substantially unpredetermined, specifically unknown and unknowable, the direction that the unfolding of the Universitas' iconic quality will take is not to be left to chance. At least, we would know which values emerging from this new structure would be considered as objectionable. The directionality of iconic interpretations is less independent of the superstructural context of the designer than one might want to believe. True discontinuities in the direction are more likely to occur, if we were to let those people design who, because of their position in the social infrastructure, would depart from superstructures that have so far been alien or asymmetrical to ours. It is essential, therefore, to understand that the infrastructural and superstructural position of the would-be designer is of paramount importance. In some ways, if the designer's symbolically charged new structures are to break the stasis of established patterns, his existence must have, in some ways, broken the existing harmony between his societal infrastructure and normative/ideological superstructures.

A new role for the designer, and a new role for us, as designers of Universitas, is necessary. This role may be the first new structure with iconic meaning that will have to come out of this enterprise. The designing of this role will also test our methodology, because we will have to carve this new role out of old ones. The synthesis of a new role out of the constraints of our existing infrastructures and superstructures will show to what extent we can control the inflow of old empirical and epistemological dimensions.

It may be a truism to say that the roles we structure will, in some ways, influence, if not determine, the range of iconic qualities of the structures we ultimately design. This, of course, is neither unexpected nor necessarily counterproductive, except that there is another level of dependence that compounds the incest. And, this is the issue of the choice of method and problem ultimately reinforcing the existing ideology, rather than permitting such designs to liberate new meanings out of symbolic charges. The case in point is, of course, New York as the object and environment of the design exercise. The linkages between the retrospective, the critical, and the prospective tasks are very intimate, and they often bathe in the secure glow of the same ideology. The informational function that is meant to govern the retrospective and critical tasks will generate as much new structure as will the postulational and, in some ways, smuggle in the old social superstructures. New York will dictate not only its own analysis, but also a method of analysis that legitimizes the conception of the city as an artifactual icon of significant epistemological and normative, as well as empirical, value. The choice of ideal typical cases quite often leads to the reinforcement of old epistemologies rather than the invention of new ones, because the perceptions of interface between the infrastructure and the superstructure are both dictated by and governed by that interface itself.

Ideal-typical constructs are ways to mend the fractured pluralism of our daily experiences, and they reflect dialectically the consciousness (in epistemological or normative terms) of the empirical world. On another level, and with more than methodological consequences, is the ideal-typical construct of the social contract as the determinant of the pattern of agreement in social transactions. This model, while capable of accounting for the idea of *freedom*, seems to be less appropriate for dealing with the question of *power*. In fact, one must surmise that power here is a residual category. As such, power would vanish once an ongoing transactional open system, accommodating individual choices and harmonizing them with others through a complex dynamic feedback network, actualizes freedom. The proposed mediation between the processes of the infrastructure and the goals of the superstructure is not as might be suggested: inherently conflict free in the political sense.

The discrepancy between infrastructural processes and superstructural norms happens to constitute the elements of power upon which rest the real and perceived status of political elite. Therefore, that mediation, or synthesis of some individual goals into structures to be adopted by others is ultimately a political act, and needs to succeed on a level that is more than symbolic or ideational.

It becomes unavoidable, at this point, to raise some basic social-philosophical and social-theoretical questions and wonder whether, in cultural and political terms, the infrastructures are not the repository of power, with the superstructures being, in the Marxist sense, no more than the legitimizing and reinforcing manifestations. Or, should we revert to a stricter idealism and assume that consciousness and ideology determine the distribution of power and regulate the flow of the network. Of course, we can expand our analysis and move away from a monolithic integrated model of society to a pluralistic one and say that the real issue is the reconciliation of various superstructures in society, each of which is linked (a neutral term) to some corresponding infrastructure. The synthesis is, thus, a new step in the confrontation between ideology and utopia, and the choice cannot be avoided. Universitas must recognize the fundamentally political nature of its own epistemology or relegate itself to the pure role of reflection. The meaning to emerge from new structures is not disconnected from the meaning that one *hopes* the new structures will generate. This a priori direction, this parti pris is the extension of our own political ideology. In this sense, design is a political process because the intentionality of the act does not simply imply a judgment about the world, but also proposes a redefinition of the agreement in the social contract.

It is one thing to permit the refusal of a postulational input; it is another to transform it into a meaningful counter-input. Both, in some form, depend on the criteria by which the anticipated pattern of ensuing feedback consequences are judged. This judgment, as well as the judgment of empirical events, follows a code. Thus, the new synthesis must not only create new consequences but also generate a new code by which to evaluate these consequences. If the new code is desirable simply because it is new, we have missed the boat, even if, in the process, we have toyed both with anarchistic and revolutionary fantasies. On the other hand, if this new code is yet inconceivable, but we are sure it will correspond to the needs of its own actualized social contract, then we are optimist-progressivists. Or, it may be that we choose what the new code should be, specify its range, and let it happen. In that case, we are the dialectic counterculture whose reformism chooses the sign as the weapon, signification as the strategy, and consciousness as the battleground.

Finally, as in most instances of innovative social design, we find ourselves in a situation where we think we are damned if we do and damned if we don't. There is a close relationship between the fact that we want to break a vicious cycle, and yet the tools and values with which we want to break away are nurtured and sustained by the system that we are breaking away from. This dilemma, rather, this paradox, of course, varies with intensity whether one perceives culture as an all-encompassing and pervasive system, outside of which little if any human activity can exist, or whether man's inner creativity can transcend culture and ultimately transform it from outside through psychodynamically determined perturbations.

Along these lines, the Universitas Project team is either incapable of true innovation because it is already caught, infrastructurally and superstructurally, in the existing social system, or it has to rely on the genius of its revolutionary creativity in terms of synthesizing meaning free of existing values. If these, in fact, were the alternatives, one might hesitate where to bet. But, it may be possible to postulate a third alternative. Thus, one can conceive of the Universitas team as having to be characterized not so much in terms of existing social roles and institutions but, rather, as the outcome of a pattern of interstitial spaces between the well-defined roles and social infrastructures and superstructures. The pluralism of our social system, and its fragmentation due to the pressures of technological organization, have the singular salutary effect of creating cracks in the wall, so to speak. These cracks are the zones of indeterminacy and amorphous tension that exist between the rigid boundaries of our bureaucratized roles. Often, they provide a haven for an escapist privatism, supported by mutually neutralizing magnetic fields. But these cracks can also become the springboards from which new roles can emerge, which are less dependent on their coherence with the old ones. We can, in fact, plant a tree, or hang a painting in that crack. The interstitial space has its own iconic qualities, which can be decoded, often independently of the space surrounding it. The Universitas must examine its opportunities for innovation in terms of the potential of its team to emerge from, and exploit, interstitial social spaces, where what we are not, rather than what we are, can better define what we can become.

The University Between Theory and Ideology
By Alain Touraine

1. VALUES AND STAKES

Social activity and organization have always been directed by the image a society has of its capacity to act on itself. The weaker this capacity was, the more limited was the part of the available product taken from consumption and put into accumulation and, especially, investment. Consequently, social changes grew slower, and this creative and transforming capacity became, more and more, understood and defined as a principle exterior to the social practice, as a meta-social order, a logos, and not a praxis. Giving birth to the order of disorder, a different world was taking shape above the social activity and its empiricism. Whatever the name of its principle may be, God, the sovereign, or the laws of marketing, it always designated a world of essences different from, and giving its meaning to, the social experience.

But, we have gradually entered a type of society where these meta-social warrants of social organization have been progressively destroyed by our increasing ability to act on our life conditions. By its ability to create languages and systems of signs, by its ability to realize rapid technological and economic changes, and seize the fire of the sky to build bombs more destructive than Jupiter's thunder, our society uses its capacity to act on itself in a direct and practical way.

Disenchantment—what Max Weber called *Entzauberung*—seems to me to mark the end of the "values" and of the recourse to an image of man, therefore, the destruction of essences.

The societies with smaller capacity to act on themselves—I will say, with a smaller historicity—were caught between the world of essences and the rules of maintenance and reproduction of the social organization. On one side, the gods and the kings armed with the hand, symbol, or order—the royal hand of justice, the invisible hand of marketing—on the other, the rules of exchange that anthropologists have started to formulate. Between the two, between the order above social action and order under it, only events occurred, and the myths too, when human unity and experience were to be comprehended.

Industrialized societies have overthrown the rules of social-order reproduction and, at the same time, secularized the principles inherent in the production of this order.

And, like André Malraux, referring to his conversation with Jawaharlal Nehru, one can say that when gods are dead and, consequently, when man is dead, action is what is left.

But whose action?

Can we say that society is forced to plan its operations and its transformations? Yes, without any doubt, if we intend to show that our life conditions are, more and more, dictated by decisions and action programs. No, if such an assertion forces us to reintroduce a meta-social warrant of the social order, to put the society at the place vacated by the departure of the gods and call values what was once called the order of the world.

The stronger the historicity of a society and the more instrumental its representation of creativity becomes, the more, then, does the unity of society disappear, and the power structure extend its influence and increase it constraints.

One must not say that force replaces idea, that power replaces religion. But one must recognize that the historicity of a society, its capacity to act on itself, is becoming, more and more, the direct stake of social conflicts, and that, consequently, the unity of the values tends, more and more, to be only the name given by the ruling-class ideology to its domination. If an ancient society found its unity in the essences it referred to for its existence, the present societies can only find it in the unity of a totalitarian power. Clearly enough, decisions are not necessarily taken in a totalitarian way; they are very often the result of negotiations and transactions, limited and temporary agreements. But, when such is the case, it becomes even more obvious that we have to replace, in our analysis, the unity of values by the network of conflicts woven around the control for social development, around a capacity for transformation, deprived of intrinsic orientation, which defines a cultural field, and not some social choices, social action modes, or social and political organization patterns.

One always tries to avoid this conclusion by saying that planning only organizes, in a coherent but empirical way, the adaptation to changes. But, then, planning becomes just the prerequisite condition to having proper political discussions, just a set of information-reducing uncertainties, as a French planner once said, and thus decreasing the part of the irrationality inherent in marketing; it informs every decision maker on the implications of any of his decisions, reminding him that no act is isolated and showing him in advance the effects of the move of one element on the rest of the system.

But such an answer is not satisfactory and only avoids the main problem. Information is not a decision. The coherence of initiatives does not define a "one best way."[1] And, if I just used the expression of Frederick Winslow Taylor, so rightly criticized by generations of psychologists and sociologists, it is because the confusion between coherence of means and definition of goals is as threatening today as it was when rationalization only occurred at the level of the working process.

Those involved with planning and design rightly remind us that the action of society on itself cannot be reduced to the adaptation to changes that would bring us back to the liberal illusions of the nineteenth century. Decision making is a choice, and this choice supposes goals, preferences, and the intervention of an actor. What I dispute is only that society can be called an actor.

If I object to an analysis in terms of values, it is because it seems impossible to me to confuse two very distinct ideas in one single affirmation.

On the one hand, a society is defined by one type of historicity: it organizes its cultural and social field according to certain modalities of its action on itself. It is defined by what Michel Foucault called an *episteme* and Serge Moscovici called a cultural model that is an image of the creativity which in our society is "practical," i.e., based on science and technology.

On the other hand, the social organization is not the simple shaping of these cultural orientations. The nature of social relations is dependent on class affinities, that is to say, on the nature of social control exercised on cultural orientation. The ruling class is the fraction of society that identifies itself and also uses social relations by identifying them with its private interests.

The society is not a system in movement. Society curls back on itself, acts on itself, and this "consciousness" is not necessarily linked to a dichotomy of the society, which allows this reunion between operation and transformation.

The ruling class naturally tends to self-identity with the action of society on itself and, thus, tends to speak in the name of society as a whole, to identify its interests and its ideology with the totality, and mask its very nature as particular agent.

In a society defined by its movement and its ability to change, this ideology of the ruling class can no longer rely on the essences and meta-social warrants of the social order. It, therefore, relies on the idea of a society-actor and a society-leader of changes. The systemic ideology is the new form of the functionalistic ideology, only liberated from the too openly idealistic appeal for values or the more archaic call for functional requirements of the equilibrium and reproduction of the social order.

This criticism is not directed against an analysis of society as a system. On the contrary, the *episteme* of the past industrial society is systemic. It replaces the one of the industrial society based on evolution and history. But a society acting as a system is to be conceived as a system of social and political relations, defined by the opposition between an elite class, ruling historicity and identifying it with itself, and a popular class, which defends itself against the grasp of the ruling class and, at the same time, appeals to the historicity of society against the private appropriation that the ruling class imposes. At any given moment, this dialectic of social relations is experienced and denied by the social actors.

Experienced, because even when the domination of the ruling class is the strongest and can rely completely on the political institutions, the opposition it meets lives on and manifests itself in the necessity for the dominant class to use repression and, therefore, to doubt its own discourse.

Denied, because of the permanent conflict between opposite utopias, which identify one of the actors of the social conflict with the historical field in which he acts and propose a unified and integrated image of society.

Opposite utopias differ in the fact that the one of the dominated class shows an aim toward social transformation, an image of a future, whereas the dominating ideology, more directly embodied in a social practice it tightly controls, is more "practical" and claims to be the ideal directly corresponding to the "tendencies" of the social reality. The dominant utopia is, at the same time, more constantly present and less systematically formulated.

In any given concrete field of the social organization, the more one tries to bring out "the idea" of a social practice, the more one gets into the flow of the dominant utopia. It is not possible to avoid it by opposing a contrary utopia, which could only be the expression of nostalgia for a removed past. The only way is to acknowledge the contradictions and the conflicts hidden, not only by the dominant discourse but by the social practice. It would be in vain, for example, to imagine an urban utopia opposed to the present urban reality. One has to accept looking, first, for the signs of urban crisis, and recompose the complaints and claims whose spontaneous expression is not clearly structured. It is a critical approach, which can be partly sustained and guided by the knowledge of counter-utopias, but goes much further and harks back, not to the unity of the discourse but to the social relations system and to the conflicts through which the cultural field socially takes shape.

2. Rhetorical and Ideological Knowledge

These remarks, as brief as they may be, are, nonetheless, sufficient to set up in general terms the problems of the university in our type of society and distinguish the two complementary aspects of its role.

On the one hand, the university is what may be called an agency of historicity. It has an essential role in the creation of a knowledge pattern and in the shaping of a cultural model. In that sense, its role is "theoretical" and contributes to defining the social and cultural level of society.

On the other hand, the university has a set of functions, later to be distinguished one from the other, which places it inside social relations and social organization. Here, the university cannot any longer stay "neutral." Either it is an ideological instrument for the ruling class with a meritocratic and technocratic role, making the social choices and interests under the appearance of professionalism and technicity, or, it is an instrument of social criticism dissociating the historicity of a society from its controlling power, bringing into light what the ruling forces keep hidden, and making obvious the existence of choices and interests in which the dominant discourse only speaks of rationality, modernity, and adaptation to change.

A more radical position could be taken by defining a type of university as a direct political instrument for the dominated popular classes. I set aside this case not because it doesn't exist but because no one then can really speak of the university as such, any more than one can in the case of *"les écoles de cadres"* for the ruling class. Indeed, in either case, the autonomous relation to historicity and especially to scientific knowledge disappears, and that takes us out of the university field. Nobody can pretend to call a university an organization that does not acknowledge the existence and the constraints of scientific knowledge.

Let us admit, at least, conventionally, that the university only exists with the two functions, theoretical and ideological, inherent in the institutions of creation and transmission of knowledge. One can accept the necessity of political schools; it does not eliminate the need for universities unless one places itself in such a dependent society, unable to control its own progress, that the only way out is to break through and explode.

The university system in Western countries, and especially in the United States, was based for the past decades on the conjunction of professionalism and technocracy.

The university is technocratic in the way that it presents, as something evident and natural, the identification of science and progress with national power and the reinforcement of the great production devices—links that are as firmly defined, if not more, in Soviet-type societies.

It is not necessary to proclaim that professionalism is the mask of technocracy. It seems to me that both orientations are simply complementary, and that the teacher's professionalism often even comes into conflict with the technocratic orientation of the university system, without questioning it. When this professionalism triggers an opposition, it is from the inside. The university serves science, as witnessed by the rapid progress of scientific knowledge, but it does not question the relationship between science and power, nor the disequilibrium in the use of resources for different domains of knowledge; even less does it question its own role and the subordination of the entire university system not to science but to the reinforcement of the great production systems. It is too ready to forget that it is an instrument of selection and social hierarchization. In the United States, as well as in France, one can see being formed or reinforced a hierarchy of establishments in which the level of "scientificity" is, above all, an instrument for recruiting different and hierarchized social categories. At the top, general scientific knowledge is the mark for the selection of the ruling elite. Applied sciences are instrumental in the formation of executives, and a simply professional formation is sufficient for recruiting what Ralf Dahrendorf called the "service class." The educational demands of the popular classes are largely diverted either by the mechanisms of school neglect or by the creation of subordinate schools, which guarantee that children will not surpass their parents' educational level, thus accomplishing "the cooling out function" that Burton Clark mentioned regarding the American junior colleges. The more general the college educational process becomes, the higher the general instructional level of the masses and the stronger this hierarchization, so that school education is less a means for reproduction of social inequalities than a means for creating new inequalities and a new class hierarchy.

Inside this technocratic system, professionalism combines two different orientations. The first is aggressive—it claims for the knowledge producers the right to administer universities. Scientists readily challenge the power of the administrators and the influence of prominent local citizens, especially when these two are apart from centers of decision. They prefer to get the necessary funds directly from private or public agencies. But they resist, simultaneously, the new constraint that can be put upon them. For the sake of fundamental research and academic freedom, they try to build a scientific power, or at least to increase their autonomy inside the power system. The second orientation is defensive, more corporate, and even bureaucratic; this is even stronger because teaching is more a means of limited social climbing. Then there appears a university culture that can be strongly out of focus compared with the requirements of the ruling classes. This case occurs more frequently in Western Europe than in the United States or, above all, in the Soviet Union, where the association of science and power predominates even more clearly.

The university, therefore, finds itself divided, beyond its teaching activity, between ideology and rhetoric.

Ideology—the discourse that reproduces the social order and, more precisely, reproduces the exclusions proclaimed by the ruling forces and their institutional means of action—always functions on the opposition *in-out*. It masks the social relations and opposes those who subscribe to values and norms against those who are deviant, marginal, outsiders. It presupposes the "objective" existence of a social frame and hierarchy, and sits as a judge, who ascertains need, insolvency, or insubordination, and condemns them. The entire school system is an ideological machine because it is an instrument of social selection and defines a "normal" type and a hierarchy of activities and forms of expression.

What I call university rhetoric is quite different. The school norms do not coincide generally with the norms outside the school world. The university rhetoric is the operation by which a professional milieu becomes isolated by identifying its role in the production of theory and scientific knowledge with its interest and its own social and cultural characteristics.

The relationships between ideology and rhetoric are complex. The more important the scientific activity, the stronger is the university rhetoric. Ideology, on the contrary, triumphs when the university has more of a role of reproduction than production of the social order.

The crisis that just upset the universities in most of the capitalist-industrialized countries—the situation in communist countries being institutionally quite different—challenged, simultaneously, these two aspects: the technocratic orientation of the university as well as the liberalism and professionalism of the teachers.

The university is criticized for being unadapted to, and submitted to, technocratic rule.

My intention here is not to analyze this crisis, but only to consider the notions of reform of the university that have been brought about or given force by this crisis, and which have greater breadth and depth than has been the case before.[2]

3. REACTIONS TO THE CRISIS

A.

The first reaction is defensive. It defends the elite institutions, which, sustained by their own power, are able to escape the traditionalism and the direct pressures of the modernizing power. This reaction is not necessarily conservative, but it is in favor of the elite. In the United States, it revives the traditions of the best liberal arts colleges, renewed between the two world wars under the influence of Robert Maynard Hutchins and his reform of the University of Chicago. During recent years, these colleges have not been much affected by the crisis and were an arena for student activism comparable, in a way, to the French preparatory institutions for the *Grandes Ecoles*. Professionalism, then, affirms itself both in its scientific aspect and its university liberalism. The goal is to form social elites with enough of an open mind so that their new members will be agents of change, which requires the acceptance of a certain amount of rebellion. The report on university goals and governance, published at Harvard under the direction of Martin Meyerson and Stephen R. Graubard, is the most characteristic document of this liberal elitism in the United States. Evidently, such propositions do not furnish a total solution and can only renew a certain capacity of initiative and innovation at the top. And, most of the forming systems allow a certain freedom of action to those already selected through a long series of social and cultural tests. The novelty of these propositions is that they take action at the time of the decline of the liberal arts colleges and try to transfer their active spirit to the best university colleges.

B.

In a completely different and even opposite direction, attempts are made to go back to the main orientations of the nineteenth-century American "universystem": the concerns of community "service." Two themes are present in the reform projects.

On the one hand, the university has to be replaced in its urban milieu in order to break the isolation of the campuses planned and created to allow the formation of a social elite away from the ghettos, the "minorities" of the multiethnic society, which is viewed as a menace to the Yankee establishment. The most striking example is that of New York University, which, by suppressing any kind of selection for admission to its many campuses, has opened college education to social categories that otherwise could only apply to subordinate schools. Adult education is becoming essential. In France, the universities at Vincennes and Grenoble adopted a policy that tends to give as much chance to the students who already have worked as to those who have always remained inside the school system.

On the other hand, preliminary inequalities have to be acknowledged, and the university has to be forced into diminishing them, instead of maintaining, or even aggravating, them.

But this requires a transformation of the recruitment and the pedagogy, special programs for the "risk students,"[3] and an absolutely new critical effort to detach knowledge from the discourse proper to social class.

C.
Finally, the financial crisis that affects the university system is to be considered as a force toward change, although the causes of this are not related to any reform movement.

The United States is emerging from a long period dominated by the expansion of its power and by the central importance given to its confrontation with the Soviet empire.

During this period, science and power have been tightly interrelated, and their union has been one of the main bases for the development of the technocratic domination. The Black rebellion, the opposition to the Vietnam war, the student upheavals—especially in the best universities—and the urgency of the urban crisis have deeply wounded the native pride of the ruling class and brought to light the inner problems and contradictions of the richest society in the world.

This led to the assertion, many times denied and apparently in no need of demonstration, that national power was based on the accumulation of knowledge and on the reinforcement of the great management apparatus of information. Carl Kaysen noted appropriately that the relationship between science and technical progress was not as direct and simple as one might think. The university system is, therefore, asked to fulfill other functions than the mere production of knowledge, and these may prove to be still more important for the dynamism and solidity of the society.

4. KNOWLEDGE AND CRITICISM

In observing these trends, it is possible to define more accurately the choices offered to the university system. But this presupposes, first, a critical analysis of each of the above-mentioned themes. Each of them applies to one of the three main functions of the university. The university has a production function, an adaptation function, and a reproduction function.

The reproduction function corresponds rather directly to what is called education, and especially general culture, or general education, which is a composite whole from the point of view of its content, but whose unity is given by society's definition and especially by society's dominant ideology—by what society wishes to keep as heritage from the past. The insistence on the content of teaching, on the values to be transmitted, and on the formation of the personality generally reinforces the transmission of a cultural heritage and the keeping up of a hierarchized social order. Even when the appeal to general education is associated with a criticism of specialization, of instrumentalism, even when it appears to be a criticism of an education too much bound up with professional recruiting, it just gives a refined ideological cover to the defense of property.

The adaptation function is not limited to supplying the labor market with the specialists it needs. It is placed in the perspective of change, and, therefore, it entails constant attention to the demands outside the institution, whether it is the educational requirements for admission or the demand for college graduates in the society outside. Those who advocate opening out the university to the demands of society, pulling down its walls, developing its role in community service—those who insist on the necessity of its concerning itself, above all, with the great social problems, and especially with those posed by the urban environment—give predominance to this adaptation function, conceived in its most dynamic and open aspect. But, I do not think it possible to dissociate this "opening out" from a basic conformism, more or less mixed with honest sentiments and the search for limited reforms. To put the university at the service of society is to put it at the service of power and influence. The unions, the reform movements, and even the subjugated groups can, of course, have a certain influence. But it can only be very inferior to that wielded by the ruling forces.

At the end of the nineteenth century, during the most inventive period in the history of the American university system, while campuses opened to applied studies and strived to develop their service role, it is the formation of a national ruling class beyond local community elites that was the main result of the university development, rather than the support which was given to new social demands; and those who could not accept this state of affairs often had to pay with their jobs for their opposing attitudes. One may also ask what will become of a university system that defines itself as a response to demands and, therefore, diminishes the autonomy of the development of knowledge. Most institutions often enhance this adaptation function. More rarely do they question the role of elite colleges and universities. When isolated, the university's role is mostly to adapt the entire society to the orientations imposed by the ruling class.

Finally, we come to *the function of production of knowledge*, which has been mentioned previously in this essay. In a society where technical and scientific knowledge has such an important role, it is impossible for this function not to have a central role. Still, do we have to mention again that this production function is also the one that associates the university most directly with the ruling class, the big word, *research,* serving as a cover for the elimination of all critical roles for the university, and scientific professionalism easily identifying itself with submission to a power that provides research funds.

The university revolution has tried until now to overthrow the old hierarchy of these functions. From a conservatory-university we passed to a laboratory-university. The reproduction role is not disappearing, but it is transforming itself. From the transmission of a body of knowledge, of behaviors and expressions reserved for an elite, this role tends, more and more, to become the keeper of an academic and social hierarchy. This function, therefore, is exercised as a complement to the production function, just as the performance of social domination accompanies the initiatives of the ruling class.

Of the two, the adaptation function, which was predominant at the time of progessivism, becomes more than anything the response to social changes determined from inside the power of a ruling class.

The novelty and the importance of the university crisis come from the fact that it challenged this conjunction and this hierarchy of functions, which can only be taken as a repressive move, because no university system in our type of society can give a subordinate role to the production of knowledge. The intention is, on the contrary, to break up the apparent unity of this production function and to understand that the current hierarchy of functions is only the expression of the link between the university and the ruling class. Obviously, this link does not prevent the university from accomplishing a scientific task, but it connects this task intimately with the reinforcement of the social domination.

One may conceive, in reverse, of a university system, which would give up defining itself as a unity, as an institution, and which would tend to be the place where the creation of knowledge is cut from the organization of the social order. This is only possible if the forces, not of change, but of demands, receive a privileged welcome in the university.

This breakup and change of the social role of the university presupposes two conditions, which are, therefore, the two main problems set before the university today.

First, scientific activity has to be dissociated from the university organization. It would not be the dissociation on the Soviet or French model between research centers and universities. I mean to say that scientists must have a work organization of their own, which guarantees them security, independence, and efficiency, but that the demand for education must be separated from the supply of transmission of knowledge.

The students, themselves, must establish the status of the demand for education, and an independent management will relate this demand to the supply from the scientists, and negotiate their mutual adaptation. Professional and scientific independence is essential, but there is no reason why it should be related to a function of authority. This notion is directly opposed to the concept of *academic freedom*, i.e., the government of the university by the teachers. Professionals, experts, do not have to be executives or supervisors. It is fundamentally important to bring into question such practices as required courses, the curriculum, and even degrees.

Scientists do not have to monopolize the teaching body. And, I find this proposition rather close to the reactions of the teachers themselves. It is impossible to consider teaching their main task, when the research requirements are more and more constraining. At the same time, very few wish a complete dissociation of teaching and research, and the French example demonstrates in fact that, when this happens, it has more unhappy effects than favorable ones.

How can we combine these two equally strong trends without admitting that teaching should belong in a significant way to people other than the scientists? Let us only state precisely that the task of choosing teachers from outside the university should be done by a university government composed of scientists, students, and outside members chosen by the first groups and represented equally. Let us add, also, that modern techniques should allow self-teaching by groups to a degree difficult to conceive until now.

Second, the concept of *student* has to be questioned equally fundamentally. Nothing proves that university studies have to be undertaken during youth and without interruptions. In the United States, the cohesion in the studies of a group of the same age is already less strong than in Western European countries. The idea of permanent education should become absolutely central and, in consequence, suppress the privileges of upper- and middle-class youth. One has to take into consideration Ivan Illich's directive: away with a school society. The conjunction of these two sets of transformations seems to me required for the needed separation of scientific knowledge and social order. The adaptation function to changes does not disappear, for that matter. On the contrary, it will act at an intermediary level between the supply and the demand of knowledge.

The university government cannot be reduced to its administration. In the United States, university presidents, at the time of Charles William Eliot, Andrew Dickson White, Daniel Coit Gilman, William Rainey Harper, James B. Angell, and many others, played an eminent role and managed to relate the society demands and the demands inside the university. Their action was taken according to the sources of revenue for education—tuitions and donations. Similarly today, support has to be given to a university government capable of combining the production of knowledge and student demands, which go beyond the simple acquisition of knowledge. This role can be fulfilled in an innovative way only if the majority of funds comes from public institutions, which is mostly the case today.

With such a process, decisions will, of course, be in agreement with the ruling interests, but the more directly they are linked with representative institutions, the more likely they are to escape the exactions of the technocracy.

This is why scientists must have an autonomy and independence as strong as possible and must not depend on the local personalities for their careers and work. The student demands must also be expressed with an equal independence. The demand for education is, nowadays, an opposition force against the technocratic power, and even the decisions, of the representative institutions. Youth is not yet involved with the system of production and is as sensitive to the needs of personality as to the constraints of the professional roles. Youth is open to change. However, its lack of practical experience makes it more susceptible to ideological systems and to propaganda, and less capable of recognizing the importance of exploratory intellectual research, detached from application. I will not say that students are, by nature, the "critical" actors in the university. But, the critical role of the university will be best assured if scientists and students are able to act more directly in their own fields, and, at the same time, led to combine their efforts in order to resist external constraints, which, in their turn, must be strong enough to stem the risk of the university becoming a generalized corporation.

These considerations, worthy of further development, bring us back to our point of departure. They are the concrete expression of the criticism I made at the beginning—of planning and design as being oriented by a coherent and conscious system of values, therefore, of preferences and choices. I am convinced that such a strong determination, whatever its intention may be, can only serve the ruling class, and that its most positive role is probably to be an instrument of modernization for this class.

Despite all the criticisms that this conception has provoked, and which often were legitimate, I think the concept of the *multiversity* marks an important progress over the search for "the Idea of a University," to recall John Henry Cardinal Newman's phrase, and his archaizing theory of the nineteenth-century British university.

The university is not above the ruling power. It is never simply a Citadel of Learning.[4] The more it affirms its unity of conception and operation, the more it plays an ideological role of integration of the social order agreeable to the interests and the actions of the ruling power. What it needs the most is to be aware that its unity is its independence, and its opening out the necessary condition of an independent growth. The university cannot be an instrument of the social forces and a mere arena for their struggles, since it does not exist as autonomous entity if it loses its role of production of knowledge. But the university has to choose—it cannot but choose—between established order and the opposition. And the more it will help the opposition, the more it will allow the hidden to come into light, the silent to speak, the forbidden to occur, and the more also it will serve the development of society and the progress of knowledge, which is its fundamental and permanent mission.

Notes

1. Original in English.
2. I have already done this in several volumes: *The May Movement: Revolt and Reform* (New York, Random House, 1971); *The Post-Industrial Society* (New York, Random House 1971); and "The Academic System in American Society: A Report for the Carnegie Commission" (1972).
3. Original in English.
4. Original in English.

On Making Things Safe for Designers
By Rexford Guy Tugwell

1.

Any discussion of planning and designing has to begin with semantic distinctions. Both words, unfortunately, have accumulated ambiguous meanings. Even in dictionary definitions, each tends to become a synonym for the other, and this makes it impossible to use either one apart from the other or to make a distinction between them. A plan is described as a "design"; and a design is "deliberate purposeful planning."

There is more: it is said that a "plan" is a "drawing or diagram drawn on a plane," or "an orderly arrangement of parts of an overall design or objective"; and this could as well be called a design. Again, it is said that to plan is "to arrange the parts of a design." On the other hand, to design is "to conceive and plan out in the mind," "to have a purpose," or to "devise for a specific function or end."

This, obviously, becomes hopeless. It is necessary to find some clearer distinctions if each is to be identified and discussed with any hope of finding how each is really related to the other.

For the purpose here, then, a plan will be understood to be an assessment made of resources available to a social organism together with an arrangement for their disposal. It is assumed that they will be brought into a comprehensive expression of intentions. Planners, then, will be understood to be engaged in such diverse activities as analytical research, the weighing of alternatives, and the putting together of a resulting proposal (or perhaps alternative proposals) for activities during a future period.

Designers, in contrast, will be thought of as engaged in making visible the creations made possible by a proposed disposal of resources. A planning agency will produce a synthesis whose products materialize in designers' minds. Planners will depend on designers to make explicit what they propose.

Even the dictionary, when mentioning synonyms, recognizes the difficulty. It says about "plan" that it is "a design, plot, scheme or project devised for making or doing something or achieving an end." It goes on to say that a plan always implies mental formulation and, sometimes, graphic representation. A design often suggests a particular pattern and some degree of achieved order or harmony.

This is somewhat more helpful but it would be difficult to infer from the definition the sort of work planners actually do when acting for a social organism or how designers are related to planning.[1]

Professionals of both sorts have suffered from these ambiguities. Designers have been supposed to be engaged in planning when they were merely laying out spaces for particular uses or were fitting their objects to the spaces allowed. Planners have been thought to exceed their terms of reference if they did more than "physical planning," and, obviously, this is not planning but designing. On this misconception, most so-called "city planning" departments have been erected. It would be more accurate to call them designing departments. The duty defined for them is merely the indication of uses for space. They have no duty to consider the resources needed or their division among many claimants. This was convenient, since it served as an excuse for not estimating the probability of achievement. Since "city planners" are actually designers working without essential terms of reference, little attention may be paid to their conclusions. And, in many instances, they are engaged in regulatory duties guided by a "master plan," more properly called a "master design."

Designers suffer equally with planners. They are excluded, in most of their activities, from knowledge of the resources available for their conceptions, and, as well, from considering the effects of environment on their models or of their models on the environment.

It is necessary to speak of another ambiguity. For decades, there has been active opposition to planning for the nation, a hostility arising from an incredible misconception. A planned society was commonly supposed to be one rigidly marked out by a central authority and brought under the discipline of rigid ideologues. This, of course, was anathema to those who believed in free initiative. So the process was considered to be undemocratic and was identified either with the communism of the Soviets, with the national socialism of the Nazis, or with the fascist corporate state. That a planning agency could and should become the coordinative mechanism of a pluralistic society was only slowly recognized.

That budget-making regulatory agencies and subterranean bureaucratic devices for looking further ahead than the customary annual appropriating sessions of legislatures or, for that matter, of corporate directors, were actually piecemeal approaches to planning, was deliberately not recognized for fear of rebuke from those who pictured it as an alien philosophy.

Times change, however, and a new generation has lost most of its old fears. Planning seems clearly about to be recognized as an indispensable activity if pluralism is to be prevented from degenerating into chaos.

Curiously, city planning grew in favor during the decades when national planning was unmentionable. That it was mostly confined to its physical phases did immensely reduce its usefulness; but it was so obvious that fiscal resources were a condition of materialization that budget making was slowly recognized to be a planning responsibility. Public planning agencies are gradually taking on the comprehensiveness essential to practical guidance. The transition stage has been long and tortuous; it is not yet over; but that it is coming to an end seems certain.

2.

Design is a word still likely to arouse suspicion among professional planners. To them, it has a narrowing and static connotation. This is because those in official positions have been confined so long to physical arrangements, to marking out locations on paper, explaining their utility, and then seeing them put aside by politicians with other ends in view than the general good. The change they have waited for would allow them to study the available resources, indicate their most effective uses, and have a part in making final decisions. This implies, for the whole agency, a central position in social organisms.

It begins to be assumed that this is what is meant by "planning" and that a planner is one who participates in directive activities. With some caution, because analogies are never quite exact, theorists compare individual and social organisms. These last, they point out, have a physiology too. They also have a comparable need for informed direction. An individual who makes a decision does it because he visualizes consequences he desires. He has a conception, a model, of what will, in the end, appear. He may, indeed, if he is at all rational, create several of these and make a choice among them. While doing this he will consider whether what he desires will be within his means. This propensity of individuals defines the role in social planning of designers. They do for the social body what is done for the individual body by its thinking apparatus. The designer has an obvious and indispensable part in the planning process. By making manifest and comprehensible what may emerge from the whole process, he makes a decision, when it comes, more likely to satisfy otherwise hazily formulated desires.

Illustration may be helpful. For a manufacturing concern, the designing of its products is so important that it may, indeed, determine their acceptability; but its planners, as distinct from its designers, have a wider responsibility. They must assess available materials, markets, locations, and the relations of the organization with others operating in the same sphere. Each of these words implies careful foresight and weighing, and requires that trained specialists of various sorts shall work together. Rational administration depends on this finely organized cooperation.

The same is true of a public service organization, whether it provides facilities or serves some other purpose. In a city, for instance, there must be an assessment of future revenues and careful distribution among claimants. The conflicting demands for schools, hospitals, and other facilities have to be assessed in such a process. At this stage, designers who know what a school or hospital should be, are depended on to offer preliminary models. Later, when these have helped in determining the resources necessary to the accomplishment, they make a final contribution by actually creating the drawings for the facility. Even then, of course, they work within strict limitations. The amount allocated is the condition they must consider as they go to their drawing boards; then they do what they can with the support allocated for their project. This may be less than seems sufficient for the purpose—it almost always is—but the condition it imposes has always to be taken into account by creators.

Consider the postal service; it has to estimate future demands, locate centers of distribution, engage and manage its employees, and determine its probable revenues. Similarly, the Social Security complex must forecast the numbers it will serve and deploy its facilities within an allowable grant. So must the diplomatic service, the park and forest services, the regulatory agencies, and even the executive office of the president. All must accept conditions set for them by allocations from a general fund.

Going concerns regard the design of facilities as preliminary to all their other activities. They must consider these while they are conceiving and creating their operating organisms. By then, they will have fought many battles to establish their positions, and taken such measures as they can to safeguard the integrity of their agencies. The planners would like to make such battles less necessary by a factual showing of comparative needs; and for this last, they must depend on imaginative designs.

If the definition of design is a comprehensive one, as it should be, showing the shape of the whole, the relation of parts to one another and the potential amenities of what may emerge, the planner will be the first to say that this is the foundation of his creation; but if it is only a commodity, a facility, or a building here, an interspace there, features—localized features—he will say: "First I must estimate the need, then find the resources to meet it. Going on from there, I must determine and delimit quantities and locations; and, finally, I can hope the designers will give it the utility and grace necessary to its acceptability."

If planners have a fault, however, it is that their effort to achieve practicality will defeat their own purposes. They have a certain reluctance to consider designs as definitions of purpose. They are so accustomed to associating designers with commodities or with such specifics as buildings, or, at the widest, local environs, that they may not recognize the materialization of the end in view as indispensable. An individual could not make intelligent choices without this visualization and neither can a social organism. The qualities and skills of both planners and designers are needed, and needed from first to last; but they must work in harmony, not in competition.

For this to happen, however, the planning organization must have a proper position in the organic whole. It has been defined as a "collective mind," referring to the similarity of its contribution to that of the directing apparatus in an individual's organism. In this conception, it will be seen, a complex social organism without such a referral and coordinating mechanism is comparable to an individual who has never developed an adequate mind. There are retarded social organisms as well as human ones. Much more could be said about this, but the reference to the mind as the deciding mechanism of living individuals will perhaps convey what is intended without further elaboration. The analogy is much more exact than might be thought at first. Cities and nations do have anatomies, their activities have recognizable rhythms, they proceed out of the past into the future as they labor to make what is coming better than what has been. For decisions about what needs to be done, for coordination of activities, the mind makes the body whole. This is a fair description, also, of social organisms. That they must have such a central organ to survive is a logical following conclusion.

3.

If what has been said is recognizably true, it is only logical to say that the designer, who for some reason must ignore the organism he works in, is lost. If he cannot consider environment before he undertakes his special work, he will be embarrassed, possibly even overwhelmed, by the incongruity if not the downright worthlessness imposed on his product by its surroundings. A whole will not emerge; it will be fractionalized by even the most successful partial improvements.

This handicap is true of any designing effort but is most visible, because so publicly exposed, in urban groupings as they are so often constructed. They may have a defensible internal purpose; but it will be defeated by association. They may have admirable qualities of many kinds and may even be very beautiful indeed. Contemporary efforts at renewal often do result in the erection of admirable buildings, sometimes clusters of them, perfectly suited to specific uses, but too often they are surrounded by shabby, decaying neighborhoods. However self-contained, they cannot be insulated from the prevailing condition.

Many cities have encouraged the positioning of such islands at their decaying centers. Los Angeles, Baltimore, Cleveland, Kansas City, and Cincinnati are examples. St. Louis and San Francisco had better fortune because of their waterfronts, but on their other sides, not far away, there are the familiar obsolete residential areas, and grimy warehouses or factory lofts. These clearing and renewal convulsions run their course, and all too often end with a few squares transformed but with what was there before still close by to characterize the area. Moreover, those who worked in the office buildings or lived in the apartments, having been dispersed for the transition period, have found that they could not come back. Some light has come into the darkness. It lifts the spirit to see what can be done; but reflection is depressing. What about all the rest?

The fact is that all the rest is held in the grip of owners who were not participators in the syndical effort of renewal. A certain amount of capital was made available, furnished by such investors as insurance companies, pension funds, and savings institutions; properties were assembled with complex maneuvers and arrangements participated in by city officials; but these usually became so costly as to defeat the renewal purpose. It is almost always necessary to substitute for it another—better paying—use. The old owners will have taken their profits and departed or, perhaps will have successfully bargained for so much that the new facilities are beyond the means of any but those who can afford deluxe quarters. Something wounding has been done to the whole organism.

At most, the island may have given some opportunity for the display of new possibilities; and there may have been experiments in the use of new materials and new ideas for living and working. Such coming to terms with urban necessities is good, and it was thought and said a few decades ago, when such projects began to take shape, that they would demonstrate what could be done and that their example would generate wider renewals. That hope has been disappointed. The projects had only a limited viability in the real-estate market. A few people or organizations could afford the expense, but customers were few. Other persons and enterprises had to find cheaper places to live and work; and those places were what they had always been, cheaply built, badly maintained, and ugly with the neglect inherent in private landlordism. They were more crowded because of expulsions from the old places cleared for renewal. These, just beyond the plazas and fountains at the foot of the high-rises, are slums quite like the ones that for centuries surrounded the places cleared for the cathedrals. The historical similarity is depressingly exact.

Would it have been as well if these efforts had not been made at all? It is true that they are an indication of what could be done if designers worked in ideal situations with appropriate scope for their conceptions; but if they had not been built, and there had not been the mistaken belief that example would prove infectious, the problem might have become embarrassing enough to have caused a more general renewal, not islands but environments, not buildings or blocks but neighborhoods, cities, metropolitan areas, or even regions and nations. There might have been planning, not merely localized designing.

4.

Nothing, perhaps, gnaws the soul of the artist so much as confinement imposed from outside, when he knows it will defeat his purpose—and, besides, is not necessary. There is something wrong here. It has been shown often enough what the aspiring grace of contemporary design can do; but not what it might do if allowed—if it had freedom of space and terms of reference comprehending the whole, rather than just restricted parts. Thinking of capital or of land in this way is, unfortunately, not usual. That these should be made available for public uses seems somehow to be beyond comprehension. It is because of this that the designer is cramped. He can think only of the physical changes determined by private owners with no interest in the whole.

Such institutional innovations are needed as will free spaces from the grip of such obstructionists and open the entire organism to renewal.

What innovations would be needed? First, the pooling of land, thus making it available for appropriate public purposes. If every piece of land in a city were equal in value to every other piece, the city could be transformed. Vast blocks cover the entire space between streets because, only in this way, can developers get the return they want from the huge investments in the plot where the building is located. The same is true of residential development, both urban and suburban. The conditions of life for tenants are determined by the speculative values of the land and returns to developers, not by its best uses.

One way to escape this restriction would be to institute public ownership. As things are, the city encourages speculators. Taxes are a percentage of assessments, and the more costly the land and the more crowded its use, the more the city extracts from its owners. If the land belonged to the city it would not tax itself. Its revenues would be got by charging the costs of government to those who benefit from it. Real-estate taxes would disappear and be replaced by more broadly based sources of revenue. This condition would give designers a chance to think of wholes instead of parts, to ask themselves what the city should be like instead of what it must be like to maintain income from property.

A less drastic way of equalizing would be the pooling of private lands. It should not be too difficult to establish compulsory associations and require all property owners to surrender their titles in exchange for shares in a corporation. This would have much the same freeing effect as public ownership.

After land, capital must be available, and in the vast quantities only to be found in the channeling of savings to public uses rather than private ones. Capital is now gathered and used for speculative purposes. This may well require the public ownership of savings and loaning institutions. This would be a radical innovation but it might make much more radical ones avoidable in future.

Another way of finding the necessary capital would be the taking of governments out of partnership with developers and their financial backers. Because real-estate taxes are depended on for revenue, the most profitable uses for property are encouraged; and these are the very ones most likely to defeat any comprehensive planning for public uses.[2]

5.

The suggested institutional changes would do more than open the way for freer comprehensive designing. They would make possible a change in the effect of time, the worst enemy of the creator. It might be recalled that the Book of Common Prayer speaks of death for individuals beginning at birth. This is even truer of objects created by designers. Their obsolescence begins at the instant they are finished and progresses to decay and uselessness. Adaptation, rehabilitation, and replacement may prolong their usefulness, but time will have its way in the end.

One difference between the planner and the designer is precisely that the planner deals in time; he breasts the river of objects, forces, and arrangements coming out of the past and going on into the future and, making use of its elements, tries to shape it for improved uses. The designer, however, is tempted—and often succumbs—to ignore time, to reach for the glories of permanence. By trying to defeat time, he fastens on society objects inevitably growing obsolete. He reaches for the monumental, not the adaptable.

Yielding to this temptation is made more likely by the propensity of designers to think of themselves as artists. There are, actually, many likenesses between the two. Both are creators, seekers of something beyond mere utility, imperishable beauty, perhaps, or a coming to terms with nature. It is a law of nature, however, that there is only relative longevity for any object. Some will last longer than others, but none will last forever. Even the magnificent churches of the Renaissance were subject to the perishability of the rites they were created to express. Buildings may last a thousand years, as museum pieces do; but their obsolescence, however gradual, is certain. Most other creations have far shorter existences.

What actually happens in the real world of technological change and enlarged demands is that facilities lose their attractions very rapidly. A school building more than half a century old is regarded as an incubus; but there are many of them in our cities. Education has escaped them; but they still exist. They were designed as monuments.

Objects of art are not affected by this obsolescence; indeed, they may grow more valuable with age. They may crumble or fade or become esoteric; but, as creations they are unique and permanent. Still, it is unsettling to consider how many sculptured figures are relegated each year to lesser and lesser prominence, how many paintings are stored in museum basements, and, on a larger scale, how many buildings, once much admired, become, like Grant's Tomb, objects expensively maintained only for obscure reasons, not even historical or sentimental.

Projects designed for use, rather than to be enjoyed by viewing or listening, are frankly intended for the present, and always have an uncertain future. Objects of art are for a forever defined by the destructive penetration of decay. This is regretted, as the prolonged existence of useful works is not.

There is another thing. The designer uses an accumulation of knowledge and techniques. He has for foundation the materials and methods of his predecessors. No one expects to paint better than Rembrandt, to sculpt better than Praxiteles, or to write better than Shakespeare—differently, perhaps, but not better; but it is expected that better houses, schools, and hospitals will be built than ever have been built in the past, that better utensils, packages, and wearing apparel will replace the old. Supplanting objects of utility is encouraged.

It is, of course, quite right that admired creations—even buildings—should be designated as public treasures and preserved for future generations; but it is quite another thing to expect that they may continue to serve their original purposes. There is a rule here, a guide. It is that use shall be the criterion, present use, not the one once considered acceptable.

It is true that some uses change more rapidly than others. The technology of transportation, for instance, has been revolutionized in a generation. Old streets and roads are choked with automobiles. Gradually, the congestion has been reduced by widenings, by new freeways, by bridges, and by traffic controls. In another generation, this costly network may, in turn, have outlasted its usefulness. There will be another convulsion of change. Already its forms begin to appear. Streets, it seems, will be several storied, and access to buildings, even those of merchants, redesigned. Motive power will be different and vehicles unrecognizable in the imaginations of the present generation.

What has been said about the creations of artists and designers is true of living and working places, not only of monuments and buildings. Far back in history, the city was a stylistic whole, designed for unchanging uses and for stable numbers. The centers of life—sacred structure, marketplaces, universities, forums, theaters, public centers—were accepted as necessary and had proportions so well understood that designers no more thought of departure from tradition than did the poet who undertook to create a sonnet, and they had positions considered appropriate in civic life.

Unruly change disturbed all this, and a characteristic of change is that it accelerates. So slums crowded the cathedrals, universities crumbled, commerce was interrupted or expanded, forums were not needed when discussion was no longer allowed. When industrialism and nationalism developed, the cities rapidly became so large that recasting them for contemporary convenience became costly, and besides, property owners resisted. Their streets and buildings simply proliferated like some primitive forms of animal life. The original designs were blurred, their housing and merchants' places, their factories, and their social facilities were located where speculators and landowners preferred to have them. There were occasional convulsions of reconstruction such as occurred in Rome, in London, and in Paris in the nineteenth century; but rebuilding was never comprehensive; a future of constant change was not prepared for.

Washington is an example of one grandiose attempt to design an urban complex for the future. Pierre Charles L'Enfant's vision of elegant avenues with a concentric pattern proved to be worse for the succeeding motor age than the simple grid of the engineers who laid out Manhattan—worse in the sense of resisting adaptation as technology changed; but the automobile made both conceptions obsolete. There was never a deliberate choice made between the city and the motorcar. They simply collided and injured each other—two incompatible designs, both conceived for one time and its circumstances, both lasting into another age. This is what designing without planning can result in—something approaching paralysis.

Perhaps the city is beyond the capability of man to keep compatible with his changing needs. It is possible to think of schools built for no longer than current educational techniques are likely to persist; but it would be a colossal enterprise to build a whole city, say, for the decades until the technologies of transport and communication have been revolutionized. Such a thing can only be visualized as an ongoing process, accomplished by changes undertaken year after year, according to estimates of what is to come. It can only be done by abandoning permanence as an objective and undertaking, on a serious scale, what is here defined as planning.

6.

How differently from one another the cooperators in a planning complex work! The researcher and analyst assemble facts and assess their meanings; they then establish trends and point out probabilities. Their results are shown in statistics, charts, and reports. They use such abstract terms as education, health, conservation, and welfare. The designer, by translating these terms into something visible, understandable, shows where a trend ends, how the abstract emerges into the specific. The statistic becomes a model.

The researcher or analyst deals with developing probabilities; the designer is essentially a creator, using the stuff emerging from the minds of scientists and inventors. The organism's deciders, catching the designer's vision, may make use of it to propose its use for the benefit of the whole. The momentum of the tide coming up out of the past, to be mastered by the planners, is not quite irresistible or unchangeable; it may be slowed down, diverted, or enlarged; and elements may be selected for development or suggestion. It may not be changed by much at any one time, but still such efforts may have significant results. Invention and innovation are always appearing, and conflicting managerial efforts are endless. Some, serving private ends, have to be disciplined for public purposes. It is a never-ending effort. Its results may possibly be called progress.

In this river of efforts, facts, demands, and arrangements, certain ones most likely to be significant for a future period can be detected; and there will be others whose viability is likely to pass more rapidly. It is the first duty of the planning complex to discover these probabilities and to assist in making decisions concerning their development.

It should be understood that although research and analysis are necessary to planning, they are only part of the whole activity. Comprehensive planning can only be carried out by an agency established to monitor all the impacts of the past and share decisions concerning the future.

It must be said again that, in this process, the designer is the objectifier, showing what can be done with what there is to do with. His values and techniques are related to the past and to the future, just as others' are; but his relationship is unique. Are there new materials and new ways of shaping them? Are there new needs because of new discoveries about individuals or their organizations? Are there wider environments to be brought under the control of the organism? It is the designer who must be looked to for materializing larger visions, enabling deciders to visualize what they are deciding and helping them to find the true utility of proportion and elegance. It is he who must show the way to harmony and seemliness.

7.

It is certainly possible to avoid obsolescence in the things necessary to the organism. Whether what is possible will be understood and will be undertaken is another matter; but the possibility must be examined unless we are simply to accept a permanent state of unacceptable degeneration in all the facilities of civilization. The resolution must be fairly complete; otherwise existence for everyone will become more and more unsatisfactory. It will be like confinement in a crumbling and patched museum full of objects once well-fitted to understood purposes but long since outmoded—the purposes changed, the facilities became worn and neglected.

If the way of escape is the adoption of the collective mind already spoken of, the anatomy and functioning of this central organ are of intense interest. It will have connecting tissues running to it from every part of the whole organism. These tissues will carry messages of need, claims on the general body; also others describing its potential productivity, therefore, the available resources. In the center, these will be brought together—watched and measured against claims. The result will be a statement of intentions and possibilities. It will be a comprehensive statement, made up of designs together with estimates of income, preferential expenditures, and essential justifications. It will be for a measured time and subject to quick revision.

This statement will be passed on to the organs of acceptance, made up of the elected officials who, in a democracy, establish policies according to the preference of those they represent. They will not be free of responsibility for the general good as they have been in the past, but will have to consider the statement passed to them by the agency for planning. They may accept or they may reject; but if they reject, they will have a responsibility to say why, and to say it openly. When there is accord, the organism can proceed into its next phase. This, of course, is action in response to demands and judgment concerning those demands.

The agency itself will have done more than accept, weigh, balance, and judge. It will have digested what is useful for the future and will have suggested the allotment of resources for the necessary activities.

Designers will have had an important part in this. The planner cannot tell from his abstractions, his statistics, what ought to be done, only what there will be resources enough to do. The designers will be aware of the possibilities in the materials and techniques just appearing and will show how they translate into arrangements of facilities and acceptable goods.

It was not a designer who thought there should be bridges across the waterways of New York; it was planners. But it was designers who told the planners what the bridges would be like if they were built. The contrast between the oldest and newest of these, the Brooklyn, so massive and unwieldy, and the Whitestone or the Verrazano, so spare and graceful, is an illustration of technical progress taken full advantage of by designers.

A similar illustration is furnished by the contrast of the Louis Sullivan Stock Exchange Building on Michigan Avenue in Chicago, just now being demolished, and, say, the new John Hancock structure less than a mile away. The one, remarkable for its time, was heavy with stone and iron, the other towers—more aspiring. It can, because of modern materials and new construction methods. In the same neighborhood are the in-between buildings of Ludwig Mies van der Rohe.

In the same city, near the University of Chicago, is one of Frank Lloyd Wright's prairie houses, the Robie House, conceived before air conditioning was invented, with wide overhangs for protection from the prairie sun. It has been kept as a museum piece; but it is a kind of prison for its users, so dark that on the brightest days its lights must be kept burning.

The lesson from these instances is that unless the facility to be created is to become a nuisance when some time has passed, it ought to be replaceable, and provision for its replacement ought to be made. This is certainly not an easy condition for the designer; but that does not make the generalization less true. Bridges will continue to be needed; so will buildings. But both can decline in usefulness and will decline more rapidly if they are not adaptable to new conditions and new methodologies.

8.

Planning as a process, with the planning agency as a directive center for social organisms, is by now a recognized necessity for public enterprises of all sorts. This is true of the governments of cities most obviously, but also of the federal government.

Reorganized procedures for federal activities already go far beyond the old limits set by the custom of annual appropriations. Budgets now recognize the lead-time for development projects requiring capital expenditure. Congress is gradually surrendering to necessity and giving up the allocating prerogatives it clung to so long. There are fewer demands for favors in placing facilities, fewer attempts to protect supporters, and less blackmailing of the executive departments. Reform in such matters is reluctant; legislators give way only to outraged pressures. The changes will not be sufficient until legislators are no longer all representatives of districts or states but are elected at large. Local demands are insistent and nearly always inconsistent with national needs. A change of this kind will require a constitutional amendment and may be long in coming; but the nation clearly requires responsibility to a national constituency, and this is a logic that sooner or later must prevail.

These changes are occurring. It will be helpful to adopt more appropriate terms for this discussion in the years ahead. So it seems sensible to accept the definition of design that is closest to the etymology of the word: a pattern for the making of a product. This develops easily into the expanded meaning of making an integrated whole by disposition of its components. This suggests that such an effort will have to consider the materials to be employed, the uses of the product, the fitting of parts to the whole, and the effect on those who may use or see it. It is more than style or decoration; it is the organism in operation, described in specific and visual terms.

A plan, then, may appropriately be defined as a projection for the future of needs to be met, of the resources available for meeting them, and of a schedule for accomplishment. The usefulness of such a statement is conditioned on its making explicit a view of just what is proposed. The consequences of proposals are impossible to judge unless they are made explicit; and unless the consequences are foreseen, the journey into the future will be a blind one.

9.

It will be understood, perhaps, from what has been said why it was that the Center for the Study of Democratic Institutions concluded, as it did, after years of study, not only that the nation needed a revised constitution but that it should include provision for a planning branch. This branch, coequal with the others, as is the American scheme of separated but interdependent powers, would, if adopted, act in the way suggested here, as a collective mind, a coordinating and integrating center at the heart of government. Its responsibility would include the surveying of likely resources for the future and would suggest their disposal in the best interests of the whole organization.[3]

The branch would develop its plans over sufficient time to allow for protracted study and deliberately encourage public discussion. It would look ahead for at least a decade and make its estimates by projecting the trends passing through the present from the past, modified by the constantly appearing new influences: invention, discovery, ingenuity—the emergent forces whose impacts are difficult to foresee but when assiduously looked for can be taken account of much earlier than if they are simply allowed to intrude on organisms with no warning and no preparation for accommodation.

Some emergencies of this sort appear unexpectedly, but many more simply develop from known or discoverable sources. Illustrations are not difficult to find even without the apparatus of prediction. There will be new sources of power, food will be manufactured from chemicals, new materials for building will replace those now in use. These are simple and basic changes to be looked for immediately. Others are more dimly perceived: the genetic management already talked of by scientists, the conquest of old diseases and the appearance of new ones, the abolition of useless armaments now absorbing so much of the world's irreplaceable materials and so much of its energy.

These are the early-warning duties of the imagined planning agency. Its more specific rationalizing ones, looking to the comprehensive disposal of resources, will be represented by the making of budgets for submission to the other branches—the legislative and the executive.

The procedure is simply conceived. The planning branch itself would have a paralegislative body, called, perhaps, a commission or board, not made up of professional planners but of appointees with special capability for assessing what the planners propose. The actual proposals would originate in a department variously made up of researchers, analysts, engineers—and designers, working under the commission. These, it will be understood, would have, among them, the necessary skills and capabilities.

For the nation, this department would serve as a net to catch the proposals originating in many subordinate governments and needing to be reconciled with the general resources estimated to be available. Reduced to a statement, appearing at last as a budget with illustrative attachments, this, after scrutiny from the commission or board, would be forwarded to the executive branch for examination and then sent on to the final deciding body, the legislature, with such comments as may be required.

The legislature, according to the model, may approve; if it does, the government for the budgeted period will proceed as indicated. It may not approve; if it does not, the planners, acknowledging the objections of the legislators, will go back to their analyses and make another proposal. This procedure puts final decisions where they should be in a democracy: in the people's elected representatives. At the same time, however, the carefully articulated scheme will have a certain advantage; those who oppose it must accept responsibility for disagreement with something long studied and put together with care.

This is a very brief description of the proposal included in the Center's model. Its proponents argue that its acceptance would substitute rationality for the present method of trading for advantage. It would put the general interest above that of private and local ones.

It is argued here that such an agency would produce the situation so long desired by designers: a favorable environment for their creative talents. They need not fear environmental encroachments; they would not be imprisoned by irrelevant limits; they would be part of a general coordinated operation in the public interest.

It is true that the Center's model is for a national constitution and that creative work is done under many other auspices, very often not even governments, but sometimes, of course, the governments of cities; but if it had been a city charter rather than a national constitution, the principle would have been the same: planning as a central coordinative agency for rationalization of resources and demands.

It is generally supposed that creative people resent discipline. It may be that the discipline they resent is a forced subjection to conditions they know to be unsocial; but talented workers have always had to work with the materials at hand for results defined by the art they have chosen. A potter must work with clay to make useful or pleasing objects; an architect must work with the materials at hand to produce a building for certain uses; a writer must speak to an audience in language it understands. These are not the confining conditions that are resented. They are, in fact, the disciplines he has mastered and pursues with satisfaction.

To have rationalized social organisms is to have the kind of ambient desired by all creators. It is not total freedom; but no such condition is conceivable. What it does provide is the tolerable discipline of understood and accepted purposes.

Notes

1. The dictionary quoted here is Webster's Collegiate, Seventh Edition. The ambiguity is not the fault of the dictionary's compilers. It merely reflects common usage.

2. The suggestion of pooling is not new; it was explored by this author in "The Real Estate Dilemma," *Public Administration Review* (Winter 1942).

3. This constitutional model was published in 1970 by James A. Freel and Associates. It was the thirty-seventh version of a project repeatedly revised and discussed at the Center.

Whose Utopia?
By Sheldon S. Wolin

My comments upon the Project Working Paper of the Universitas Project will be divided into two parts. The first attempts a characterization and criticism of the utopian idea set out in the paper; the second sketches an alternative account of our present condition and the implications that it has for a new form of politics and a new focus for a university.

I.

The assumptions and proposals in the Project Working Paper serve as a reminder that utopian thinking need not be the expression of exploited classes or oppressed groups. It may reflect, instead, the aspirations of established groups and interests that feel that they have been denied the full power and recognition that is their due. Such thinking need not be callously indifferent to the plight of powerless and deprived classes and may even seek to alleviate their distress. Yet, the essential nature of this form of utopianism does not derive from either a passionate protest against injustice, inequality, and misery, or from calmly reflecting upon the possibility that the existing order may be fundamentally deranged. Rather, it is inspired to remove obstacles to a fuller, more "rational" exploitation of the potentialities of existing society. It proposes forms of social organization designed to facilitate the power and influence of individuals and groups whose skills and resources are most directly related to what it considers the emergent possibilities of society. Social projects of this sort may be characterized as "the utopias of the shadow establishment" to emphasize that their opposition is "loyal" and their disagreements limited.

A few examples, drawn from the Project Working Paper, will illustrate the modes of thought and analysis characteristic of utopias of the shadow establishment. First, there is a strategy that disarms potential critics by adopting language that was once truly radical but is now formulary. It recites the litany of *alienation, existentialism, Vietnam,* and the like, as though its utopia intended to incorporate the protest implied by these symbolic words. But, by a kind of transformative grammar, it divests these words of their radical connotations.

This is accomplished by homogenizing these words, as well as others, like *freedom* and *creativity,* so that they can be accommodated to a common, abstract status, that of the "normative." Once this is achieved, they can be peacefully absorbed into a theoretical formulation, in this case "systems theory," which, as we shall see, is diametrically opposed to the spirit and substance of the original words. Once the linguistic transformation has been accomplished, *freedom,* for example, becomes merely another "input" with no trace of the historic tension between "freedom" and any "system." Second, it is characteristic of this form of utopianism to present itself as a via media between two extremes, each of which is caricatured. The Project Working Paper locates its position between those who blindly accept technology and those who blindly reject it. It is unperturbed by the fact that the extremes are espoused by practically no one, except Wernher von Braun at one end and Jerry Rubin at the other; its purpose is to present a reasonable utopia. No matter how "open" or sensible such utopias may be, they, like the extremists, have their share of dogmas: dogmas of the irreversibility of history; of the fundamentally benevolent nature of modern science; of the generally desirable, because progressive, direction of Western society; of the reliability and value of modern social science; of the essential neutrality of all forms of power and invention; and of a material solution to the problems of the poor and the oppressed.

Dogmatic thinking is troublesome, not because it is necessarily wrong but because it is reluctant to consider some of its basic assumptions as problematic. Thus the Project Working Paper ignores the possibility, which is being voiced increasingly by responsible critics, that modern science is itself a problem. The paper assumes, instead, that science is neutral. At this date, it is surely apparent that science is more than a method of inquiry, which can easily be conscripted for "values" other than those it is presently serving. Science presupposes a sustaining culture that will reinforce and inculcate certain values intimately associated with scientific activity, e.g., quantification, precision, predictability, manipulativeness, efficiency, and a particular form of rationality. By not grappling with the problematic nature of modern science, one runs the risk of ratifying its present form, which not only includes a particular structure of values, but a web of interdependence with corporate capitalism and governmental bureaucracies. Under such circumstances, a utopian proposal, which declines to come to grips with these affiliated structures of power, becomes little more than a plea for a "piece of the action," the very definition of a utopia of the shadow establishment.

As the foregoing suggests, the Project Working Paper projects a conception of the future blended from the ameliorative elements of liberalism and the power-potential of science and technology. This is perfectly expressed in the particular theory chosen to describe the way society works and how it might be changed. "Systems theory" is a metaphorical way of thinking, which likens society to an interrelated and interdependent whole. Its conception of a whole is drawn from cybernetics and communications theory. The typical formulation defines society as a "perpetual conversion process [which] takes in demands and support as they are shaped in the environment and produces something out of them called outputs."

For our purposes, it is not the refinements or claims of the theory that matter, but the characteristic ways of thinking that inform it and their consequences. We may note, first, that it represents a thoroughly technological way of thinking, not only in its choice of metaphors but in reflecting a crucial quality of that thinking and, indeed, of the history of technological progress itself. Western technological development has been noteworthy for a view of progress that treats the past as something disposable, something to be overcome and superseded. Similarly, the concept of a social system is abstract in the special sense of being ahistorical. Cybernetic or communications systems do not have histories, only "states" (e.g., of equilibrium or homeostasis). One consequence of this is the way that such systems reduce "memory" to a problem of information storage and retrieval, rather than, say, an attempt at the recovery of significance. More important, to abstract a society from history has the effect of denying the existence of inherited claims, such as those descended from historical injustices or oppressions.

A second consequence of systems theory is that it dismisses the age-old problems of social and political domination while failing to furnish an alternative vocabulary for talking about them. In adopting the vocabulary of "infrastructure" and "superstructure," it performs a kind of lobotomy that dulls our sensibilities to the coercion inherent in present-day social, political, and economic forms and relations. Then it is possible for the authors of the paper to discuss the "design" of cities and universities without realizing that *design* is a professional euphemism for control over people and things, a euphemism, that is, for power.

Finally, systems theory is, in some striking respects, a bureaucratic ideal. Several of its major concepts, such as input, output, coding, decoding, feedback, noise, and the like, contain specifications for what can be admitted into or omitted from the system; they have, in other words, specific criteria for what shall "count," and these criteria embody an implicit notion of legitimacy. In these respects, a system forms a parallel to a bureaucracy: it must depersonalize and dehumanize and, in so doing, exert pressure toward homogeneity, equalize the incoming units, encourage uniformities, and discourage diversity and deviance.

As the Project Working Paper reveals, the utopians of the shadow establishment do not confront the possibility that the existing order may be deranged in its fundamental structures and principles. Instead of perceiving inherently wrong modes of material distribution and reward, of class structure, justice, and political power, they are apt to describe the existing political or economic system as temporarily victimized by inept decision makers, who have committed "mistakes" or made irrational "choices." It is no accident that the Universitas Project makes little or no fuss over questions like racism, colonialism, war, the inanity of most forms of work, or the triviality of much of what passes for culture. Nor does the document make an effort to explain how and why existing society has evolved to a state in which it is regarded without affection and with a mixture of rage and frustration. The silence about basic issues and the ahistorical outlook underlying it are inherent in a form of utopianism that seeks to redeem the present rather than to explore the future in the hope of redeeming or expiating the past.

II.

Before sketching an alternative, I must first state the theoretical viewpoint that informs it. The viewpoint issues from a particular understanding of our historical situation and it runs as follows: the contemporary world is a created world, remarkable for being the product of organized, systematic thought. Wherever we look or wherever we are, we are surrounded by mind-created objects, the artifacts of science, engineering, technology, modern methods of production, communication, and transportation. We dwell in a world of premeditated processes and structures, the vast majority of which are the end result of systematic knowledge, that is, bodies of knowledge, which, to an extraordinary degree, are derivations from some explicit theory.

During the past several years, there has been a growing awareness that our forms of knowledge have given us power to introduce rapid changes, but only in certain directions and in accordance with certain values: mass production for mass consumption, for example. The same holds true for the large-scale structures that are designed to produce, say, students or welfare benefits in large amounts and according to certain specifications. Our ability to do these things and many others is possible because of the unprecedented magnitudes of power made available by science, technology, and the arts of administrative organization and business management. Our power is uniquely dependent on the economies of large scale, on the efficient organization of hierarchical structures of domination and control, and on the widespread dissemination of bureaucratic attitudes and values. Above all, these forms of power seem to require continual expansion or growth, as is demonstrated by the failure of recent efforts to reduce expenditures, to cut back education or welfare, to reduce our military commitments abroad, and to control industrial pollution.

In routinizing the dynamics of growth, an extraordinary "heaviness" has accumulated, which weighs upon and inhibits innovative action. We frequently acknowledge this when we complain of the difficulty of changing directions in foreign policy, urban growth, and the utilization of natural resources, or when we seek to reform existing structures of education, taxation, welfare, or business.

Given these circumstances it is obvious that much of contemporary utopian thinking is merely a variation on the theme of dynamic growth, another way of projecting the forces immanent in recent history, another form of the futurism that has obsessed Western society since the seventeenth century.

To be genuine, a contemporary alternative must be radical. Its radicalism consists in breaking with the dynamics of future-oriented growth. The goal is not to re-create a preindustrial arcadia, or, more crucially, not to settle for a no-growth society. Rather, the goal is a society in which growth is measured by intensity and by the proliferation of smaller forms. This conception of growth may be described by saying that it presupposes that growth consists in the enhancement of human experience through activity; that it exists in inverse proportion to the scale of the structures in which it occurs; and that, for the immediate future, it will be experienced mainly in the form of divesting human life of its dependency on large and impersonal structures. At this time in history, social and political blueprints are doomed to failure. The weight and immobility of existing structures render blueprints futile. Fortunately, these structures have their vulnerabilities. Accordingly, I should like to offer not a blueprint but a strategy: the general strategy can be described as the strategy of de-structuring. Its overall purpose is to encourage individuals and groups to undertake a new form of experience, the experience of extricating themselves from dependence upon large-scale, rule-bound, bureaucratized structures and from the tempo of life that these future-oriented, exploitive organizations impose upon us. This strategy is intended as an alternative form of utopianism, but its emphasis falls upon experience rather than upon a premeditated theory, the experience of exploring and inventing new social, political, and economic forms of common endeavor while divesting oneself of the old ones. It requires a vow of hostility toward the major forms of concentrated power—political, economic, educational, and cultural—and a commitment to seeking new forms of decentralized, localized autonomy. What is at stake is a post-bureaucratic future.

The politics appropriate to this form of utopianism would be a politics never before cultivated in modern times, a politics of reversal dedicated to changing directions, reducing the tempo of growth, dismantling bureaucratic complexes, and making power available to smaller groups whose vitality is expressed in intensive development rather than extensive growth, excellence rather than quantity, publicness rather than privacy.

Although the strategy of destructuring and the politics of reversal seem novel, they are not unprecedented. The Protestant Reformation, particularly in the phases represented by Martin Luther in the sixteenth century and the English Dissenters in the seventeenth century, was a vast assault on ecclesiastical bureaucracy, as well as a search for alternative forms of religious association. No single structure endured as a monument to their efforts, but the experience itself left a deep and persistent mark on most Western societies.

If a university were to assist in the de-structuring of society and in promoting the politics of reversal, it would have to be established upon the experience of the last decade. Specifically, it would capitalize upon the unrest in many of the major vocations and professions, such as law, medicine, teaching, social welfare, penology, and ecology. That unrest had a remarkable focus, which combined professional skill with public concern and directed the combination toward local communities. It embodied an alternative both to the revolutionary nihilist who took no account of the need for skill and knowledge and to the liberal reformer who could only offer administrative solutions to social problems while denying the experience of responsibility to the groups affected.

The faculty and students of this new university would have as their task the broadening and deepening of the action-oriented vocations; the devising of new strategies of de-structuring and reversal; and the critical discussion of the values embodied in "public concern." Hopefully, such a university would assist in developing a new political outlook, dedicated to a politics of nurture rather than to a politics of exploitive growth.

SYMPOSIUM PROCEEDINGS

EDITOR'S NOTE: The symposium, the third
phase of The Universitas Project, took place
over the course of two days on the weekend
of January 8–9, 1972, and consisted of four
sessions organized thematically. These were
recorded on tape, and the transcripts are
presented here as accurately as possible,
given the difficulties of clarity with
regard to the technology of the time,
of several gaps in the tapes and the
original transcriptions, of comprehension owing to the various
accents and rapid exchanges that
occurred, and of identifying several
of the speakers. Each session was
conducted by a chairman, and
comprised a panel of participants
as well as other speakers and comments from members of the invited
audience; the event was not open to
the public. The symposium began
with Octavio Paz reading his poem in
Spanish, followed by a reading in English
by the translator Eliot Weinberger. Some
of the presentations were conducted in
French and translated on the spot for the
convenience of all of those present. Only the
English translations appear here, and they
are indicated as such at the beginning of each
speech. At the head of each session, the names of
the chairmen, panelists, and other participants are
given; most of the speakers are the authors of papers
given in the previous section of essays.

Universitas Symposium: First Working Session, Saturday, January 8, 1972

Editor's note: The symposium was opened by Emilio Ambasz and by a poem read by Octavio Paz. The first session was chaired by Stuart Hampshire, and included panelists Ronald Dworkin, Hasan Ozbekhan, Octavio Paz, Anatol Rapoport, and Jivan Tabibian. Other speakers were Christopher Alexander, Hannah Arendt, Umberto Eco, Henri Lefebvre, Meyer Schapiro, Carl Schorske, and Alain Touraine.

EMILIO AMBASZ: Good morning. In the name of The Museum of Modern Art and the Institute for Architecture and Urban Studies, I want to welcome the guests of the symposium and, especially, the contributors who have written very insightful essays and come, many of them, from far away, to participate today in this meeting.

I want, also, to express our gratitude to the Graham Foundation for Advanced Studies in the Visual Arts and the Noble Foundation, who have underwritten this research project, and also to thank the members of The International Council of The Museum of Modern Art and the Brionvega Corporation, as well as Mrs. Douglas Auchincloss, who have very kindly sponsored this symposium today.

It is not a commonplace to say that many institutions are looking, today, for a redefinition of their roles. In our case, the Museum's traditional function has been that of aesthetic evaluation. I believe the Museum should so continue in this evaluative function, of bringing to a level of consciousness the meanings of the ideas and the emotions which are embodied in the objects which man makes. In such an endeavor, of course, the aesthetic cannot be separated from the ethical, and this is especially evident today when what we are undergoing is, perhaps, what could be seen as a shift in evaluative attitudes. The once all-pervasive attitude of formal certainty is beginning to give room, perhaps, to an attitude of lucid perplexity. We are beginning to complement the concern that we have for universal constants with a more dynamic approach that requires that we constantly reformulate our doubts. And the complement between aesthetic and ethical evaluation is the more evident in the case of the Architecture and Design department, where we have to deal constantly with the objects that man makes, his architecture, and his cities—and we have to deal explicitly with the socioeconomical context to which they pertain.

Now, the department attempts to implement its concern in evaluation, as well as in synthesis by means of two different, though complementary, ways. One, through its collections, its temporary exhibitions, we attempt to understand the present in the context of the past. Then, second, prospectively, by means of such programs as this endeavor, we attempt to project into the future the not yet well-understood meanings of the present. This research project and this symposium represent one phase of one of such projects.

The Universitas Project is a critical and prospective inquiry into the relation of man to the natural and to his sociocultural environment. It is specifically planned to explore the possibility of establishing, in the United States, an experimental type of institution centered around the task of evaluating and designing the man-made milieu. Now, by *design* here, I do not mean the narrow, professional specialty but, rather, the large enterprise whereby man creates structures and processes in order to give meaning and order to his surroundings. The projects that are involved in this design endeavor are especially significant today when there is no hope, no conviction that the aimless actions of present technology and society will somehow accommodate themselves to some providential pattern of order. The Universitas Project starts from the recognition that although human activity, more and more, shapes its milieu, the shape which is being taken by this man-made milieu has so far escaped our control; and what the Project, therefore, questions is whether the prevailing modes of thought and the existing institutions that we have are capable of dealing with the problems of the man-made milieu. The project examines the conception of the Universitas as an institution in which a broad domain of inquiry would be integrated toward developing systems of thought and of action, which could be better suited to dealing with the problems of the environment.

Now, this Universitas—which may, perhaps, find embodiment in an experimental type of university—we have presented as a metaphor for a society, for the institutions of a society, which understands the creation of its milieu not only in terms of hierarchical material production but, eminently, in terms of full participation in the acts of cultural invention. We organized the Project into two stages: one, of a postulative nature, in which we attempted to define the objectives that would have to be made into the design and evaluation of the man-made milieu; second, we attempted to question, as I said, the systems of thought that we have and institutions which exist; and, third, we attempted to advance certain views as to possible types of modes of thought and institutions that may have to be created. The second stage, which would follow this first stage, would be one of implementation, where we will attempt to develop strategies to, perhaps, implement some of the proposals that have been put forward by the first stage. This symposium is, in a certain way, the culmination of the first, postulative, stage. In order to prepare the postulative stage, we have worked for a year with a small group of people and with the advice of a research group, of advisers, into preparing a Working Paper, and this Working Paper was submitted to a number of contributors who have written very thoughtful essays, which we are gathered here to discuss. The essays, as well as the proceedings of this symposium, as well as certain other writings that may follow the symposium, will later be published in book form.

The point, as far as the proceedings for today, is that, as you know, the symposium will consist of four successive working sessions, and each session will be centered around a panel which is made up of some of the contributors, and we have thought that the four sessions could be centered around the following topics. The first session would be concerned with problems of value in design, with the broader and more philosophical issues; the second session would be concerned with problems of semiotics of urban structures; the third session would be concerned with problems of planning and forecasting; and the fourth session with the social and political matters, the role of the university in society.

Now, I will introduce the chairmen of the sessions, and then each of the chairmen will introduce, in his turn, the members of his panel. After introducing the chairmen, I will ask Mr. [Octavio] Paz to come to the rostrum to read a poem that he has prepared. The chairman of the first session is Mr. [Stuart] Hampshire; the chairman of the second session is Mr. [Thomas A.] Sebeok; Mr. [Arthur] Drexler is the chairman of the third; and Mr. [Carl] Schorske is the chairman of the fourth.

What I want now, before we enter into the first session, is to ask Mr. Paz to read his poem. Mr. Paz is one of the leading poets writing today; he is also a brilliant essayist on many subjects, political as well as of a philosophical nature, and his essay on [Claude] Levi-Strauss is the one that really called our attention to bringing him to this symposium. At present, Mr. Paz holds the Charles Elliot Norton professorship of poetry at Harvard University.

OCTAVIO PAZ: When I accepted the invitation of Emilio Ambasz to participate today in this symposium, I did not know what I had done. I accepted because, being very much distressed by the sight of modern cities, especially my own city, Mexico [City], I wanted to know if there was a way out. But when the Project Working Paper arrived, and later some of the essays, I trembled, trembled in doubt. What kind of contribution could I give to the symposium, and in which language? I say "language" not only in the linguistic, but in the intellectual, sense.

Henri Lefebvre has described this symposium very aptly as an attempt to overcome an old *malentendu* between [René] Descartes and [David] Hume, the empiricist tradition of the Anglo-Americans and the Hegelian Marxists of the Europeans: philosophy, as crossing of the English channel or, if you like, *le canal de la manche*. All right. But I am not British, and neither am I European. Some of the contributors speak, following the general title of the symposium, about the post-industrial society. Again, I belong to a country still trying to become an industrial society. Nevertheless, it was too late to desist; and, also, because I am interested, very much interested, in the problems and ideas that appear in the Working Paper and in many of the essays, I decided to participate, to participate as an outsider, but from a point of view of language, and from a point of view of political and cultural geography: I mean, as a Mexican and as a poet—or better, as a Mexican who happens to write poetry.

I said "another language" because one thing is the language of concepts, and the other the language of images. Are poets relevant to the symposium? Reading in the Working Paper the paragraph about the City of Open Presents, which I would prefer to call the City of Open Presence, I say "yes." But I think we should not forget certain names in our symposium: [William] Blake, who saw London and dreamed of an open Jerusalem in an anticipation of [Charles] Fourier. [Charles] Baudelaire, who wanted to banish le végétal irrégulier from his geometrical city; [Walt] Whitman, the poet of Manhattan, the poet of open spaces; [Arthur] Rimbaud, who saw, before they were built, our megalopolises; the surrealist poets (but they are already folklore for M. [Jean] Baudrillard) who had rather marvelous ideas pour aménager Paris; and [T. S.] Eliot and his (our) wastelands.

I don't know if the spirits and the gods speak through poetry, but I know that through poetry speaks the body. Mr. [Anatol] Rapoport has remarked that we live in two environments: one physical and the other semantic. The second is not only superimposed on the physical, it is fused with it; semantic and physical spaces are united in the cities, and you cannot separate one from the other. In this sense, cities are as poems, you cannot reduce the poem to its meaning or to its material properties—for instance, sound—the poem is more than a text, more than a texture; it is a body. The semantic space of the city is not only a system of meanings—plaza, church, palace, brothel, university, jail, gardens. They are configurations of signs, but whether they are made of stone walls, and wood, or brick, they are bodies. And bodies will radiate meanings and images, or, to use the modern parlance, they emit not only denotations but connotations; they cannot be reduced to concepts only. A city is a metaphor, and it is built on a metaphor. The poem I am going to read is about how metaphors are now being destroyed. I wrote it in June of this year. It has an epigraph of the Mexican poet [Ramón] López Velarde. During the Mexican Revolution, he went back to his village, saw the destructions of the civil strife, and wrote a poem in which he calls his village a "subverted paradise." He was very much influenced by [Jules] Laforgue, as you can see.

Well, I, too, went to my city after many years of absence, and I did not find a town razed by civil war, but debased by modern progress: the known blend of American businessmen and Mexican oligarchs and politicians. I will explain some of the words and passages: Mixcoac was a village, and now it is an anonymous district of Mexico City. The whores standing near the funeral parlors, the police have expelled them; and now the funeral parlors don't show the coffins in the windows, as in my youth. But, of course, they have suppressed neither prostitution nor death.

Atl tlachinolli: a Nahuatl expression, meaning burning water, really, burnt water, water in flames—Novalis said wet flame, la flamme mouillée. It was the hieroglyphic of Mexico, Tenochtitlán. The Aztecs, in their wanderings near the lake of Mexico, the Aztecs saw a bundle floating in the waters. They fished it out and found two good sticks to make fire. The meaning was *atl tlachinolli*: the marriage of water and fire. This metaphor was the founding stone of Mexico City. Now, they have sealed with concrete and plastic the old prophetic mouth where water and fire spoke.

[The poem, *Vuelta*, is read in Spanish by Mr. Paz, and, then, in English, by its translator.]

ELIOT WEINBERGER: "Return"

> Better not to go back to the village, to the subverted paradise . . .
> —*Ramón López Velarde*

Voices at the corner's turn
                voices
through the sun's spread hand
                  almost liquid
shadow and light
           The carpenter whistles
the iceman whistles
            three ash trees
whistling in the plaza
            The invisible
foliage of sounds
         growing
rising up
     Time
stretched to dry on the rooftops
                I am
in Mixcoac
       The letters rot
in the mailboxes
       The bougainvillea
flattened by the sun
          against the wall's white lime
a stain
    a purple
passionate calligraphy
          I am walking back
back to what I left
         or left me
Memory

the imminence of the precipice
balcony
over the vacuum
I walk
and do not move forward
I am surrounded
by city
I lack air
My body deserts me
Noon
fist of light
that pounds and pounds
To collapse in an office
or onto the pavement
to end up in a hospital
the pain of dying
like that
isn't worth the pain
I look back
that passerby
is nothing now but mist
Nightmares sprout
in the bellies of movie houses
Catacombs of gas
electricity   sewers
dreams
desires
The vegetation of disasters
ripens beneath the ground
They are burning
millions and millions of old notes
in the bank of Mexico
Paralytic
architectures
stranded districts
rotting municipal gardens
deserted lots
mounds of saltpeter
camps of urban nomads
cans   shingles   plastics   sanitary napkins
thoroughfares of scars
alleys of living flesh
Funeral Parlors

whores
            pillars of vain night
wait by the coffins' show-window
                        In the drifting bar
at dawn
        the enormous mirror thaws
the solitary drinkers
                contemplate
the dissolution of their faces
                        The wind
on the dusty corners
                turns the papers
yesterday's news
                more remote
than a cuneiform tablet
                        smashed to bits
Cracked scriptures
                languages in pieces
The signs were broken
                atl tlachinolli
                                was split
                        burnt water
There is no center
                plaza of congregation and consecration
there is no axis
            the years dispersed
the horizons disbanded
                        They have branded the city
on every door
                on every forehead
                                the $ sign.
We are surrounded
                I have gone back
to where I began
                Did I win or lose?
                                (*You ask*
what laws rule "success" and "failure"
                                The songs
of the fisherman
                float up
from the unmoving riverbank
                        Wang Wei to the Prefect Chang
from his cabin on the lake

But I
don't want an intellectual hermitage
in San Angel or Coyoacán)
All
is gain
if all is lost
I walk toward myself
toward the plaza
the space is within
it is not a *subverted paradise*,
it is a pulsebeat of time
places are confluences
flutters of beings in an instantaneous space
The wind whistles in the ash trees
fountains
almost liquid   light and shadow
voices of water
shine   flow   are lost
a bundle of reflections
left in my hands
I walk without moving forward
We never arrive
Never reach where we are
Not the past
The present is untouchable

STUART HAMPSHIRE: Well now, the panel will proceed to discuss the papers that have been circulated to the participants in the conference. Let me just, briefly, introduce the members of the panel: Professor [Ronald] Dworkin, who comes from Oxford, and Professor [Anatol] Rapoport, who comes from the University of Michigan, Dr. [Jivan] Tabibian, on my left, who comes from Los Angeles, and Dr. [Hasan] Ozbekhan. I think I ought to explain the procedure, clearly, that I hope to follow. And that is this: that I, as chairman, will pick out, as best I can and as briefly as I can, the main points from the three papers which have been submitted and are comments on the original Working Paper. Thereafter, I will ask the members of the panel to speak, each for about four minutes, adding anything they would like to add in view of the attempt that I've made to focus the discussion, or, if they choose not so to speak, not so to speak.

And then there will be a discussion, including the panel as a whole and the other participants. And I hope that, by this means, the discussion can remain fairly focused on one or two points which are common to the papers that have been submitted. So I begin, first, with Professor Dworkin's paper, which addresses itself to a question which is by no means confined to this single panel, but which you will find running through the papers that have been suggested—namely, the question, Where do new values in a society come from? And, evidently, if one is considering the projection of new institutions, which are to serve new purposes, both moral and aesthetic, one has to address oneself to this first philosophical question.

And, he raises what he regards as a paradox, and certainly it is a paradox. Namely this: that if a reason can be given for introducing a new value, whether it be moral or aesthetic, then it seems that the value isn't really new, since the reason-giving process is, in part, an assimilation of a new value to values already recognized. And, if no reason can be given in support of the new value that is proposed or projected within a society, then it can't, strictly speaking, be said to be a value in any sense which carries with it the suggestion that a value has rational backing. For, in general, giving a reason for an ideal that is put forward, or a state of affairs which is willed, is showing that this ideal or this state of affairs is, in some way or other, in accord with what the audience, or the person to whom you are speaking, would recognize as a virtue or principle already stated. For example, and this is an example which he takes, so I'll slightly alter his sense in giving it, take the value of privacy, highly relevant to questions of design. This has become an aspect of liberty of the individual because of certain concrete conditions, which exist in the modern world; it has become something to which people attach value and regard as an aspect of the individual's tolerable or good life, that a certain degree of privacy should be possessed. Now this value has arisen out of concrete conditions, that is, out of the technologies, which have threatened the privacy of the individual. Now, if we start to project it as a value, as indeed we do, then we look for the principle that would justify representing the right to privacy as an extension of human rights already recognized, or if not general human rights, rights of a particular society. Now, Professor Dworkin makes a suggestion of a very general character, which seems to me to be a very important one, though he derives his suggestion primarily from the example of law. That is, he suggests that we have a twofold process of justifying values, by a complicated interaction between the looking for a general principle and the considering of particular cases.

For example, in the example just given of privacy, then, the law will look back retrospectively, and look at past cases which have been decided as cases of liberty, and find that there's a gap in the justification given for these cases, which would be closed if privacy was recognized as a value, a distinct value, which should be built into the legal system, and recognized, or into the general social consciousness, and recognized as such. And some such processes, I understand, did in fact happen (or so he will correct me), where Justice [Louis D.] Brandeis was concerned—that he did, in fact, disinter from old cases a justification of the decision in virtue of a new principle, or new before he formulated it, of privacy. So what we have here, as a characteristic, at least of the law and perhaps of other value systems (I'm going to suggest it is a characteristic of value systems in general), is that you make explicit general principles which lie behind particular cases and which have formed the decisions you've made in those particular cases, or which society has made, even though you or society didn't know that this was a principle which was guiding you.

Not only is *this* so, but it works the other way, that once you've formulated or made explicit a principle—say the principle of privacy as an aspect of liberty—then this affects how you in the future decide particular cases. (It isn't at all the case that you simply decide from the specific; you go from the specific to the general, but you also go from the general back to the specific.) And, thus, there is an interaction between your intuitions as to how particular cases should be decided and the general principle, which you extract from your intuitions. Now, this, I think, we are familiar with as something one would expect in a legal system because, in the legal system, you expect the values to be governed by precedent and to have a historical sanction—that is, you expect the law, for reasons that are plain, to be something which is continuous in its development, and continuous in the principles it acknowledges. Because, the law must be something that is known and, thus, the law is governed by precedent; there are other reasons, but that's one reason. But let us forget the example of law, because what we are concerned with are more general moral and aesthetic issues.

And, take what Professor Dworkin suggests, and try the hypothesis that this is entirely general for value systems as a whole, both moral and aesthetic: that is, that in all cases where we think of our values, moral or aesthetic, as being expanded across time, they are done in this way of extracting from the past, gaps in the explanation which one would have given for decisions that one made, or values one recognized, and then filling the gap by a new value. This has the implication, of course, of what you might call a "massive conservatism" in the development of values, by analogy with law, that is, that in all cases we seek across time to preserve a certain continuity in the values that we respect—that it crosses time, and the giving of reasons is always, in part, an assimilation of a new value to a past value. There is this double interaction.

Now let me give you an example which seems to me to make the point clear and bring it somewhat nearer to our subject of design: supposing one is speaking of language, grammar, or correct use of language—or, correct use of a specific language, perhaps, better, say what is "good English." Now, in the case of what is good English, obviously what is good English evolves over time, involves a value, and it's a value which you certify by reference to classical cases. That is, users of the language (but obviously there is a circle here) who use the language very well, what makes them classical is just that they do use it very well—but you allow that they expand the language as they go along; they are themselves governed by certain inertial principles, in a way, where values are concerned, that is, language, which is highly rule-governed. It's impossible for a poem to be read without there being some mention of the past of poetry. So that there is always this assimilation to the past, but, nonetheless, good English is something that changes over time, and new principles of construction, or principles of poetic syntax, or principles of grammar, or principles of poetic structure of a more general kind, pass into the language. Now, it would seem to me, therefore, that what he's speaking of, under the heading of this particular phrase that he uses, which is "decoding structures," is something quite general to values as a whole, and the importance of it is this: that, in our discussions, many of the papers, you will find, by the participants, return again and again to this question, If you have a project for a new university, and a new way of teaching design, and a new grouping of the teaching of visual arts in universities, to have such a project, where does it come from? Is it something you just invent out of your head, like an eighteenth-century projector, as it were, or does it emerge out of some concrete social situation, out of some social conflict, out of some real social change that is going on? And, if you don't answer *this* question, in what sense are you different from those who used to be called utopians? What is, as is sometimes expressed here, the "infrastructure"; how will it come about, what will sustain it?

Now, if we take Professor Dworkin's account, then it's plain, I think, it's easy to see that new obligations, such as the obligation to respect privacy, like new requirements put on education, have to be recognized as emerging from some actual experience which people have had. Just as, a new extension of the art of writing English verse emerges from some actual verse written—it has to emerge in some way from actual experience, that is, the experience of students and teachers. This is easy for the law because the social conflicts are there all the time, and are visible, and the law is itself an adversary system. But the suggestion in Professor Dworkin's paper, to me, is that there is this interaction which is both across time, that is, assimilation of the new to the old, showing a continuous development, which is characteristic of course of political projects, that they do do this—and also of legal ones—and secondly, the complicated relation between the general principle and the specific case, which is misrepresented in so many positivist and empiricist accounts of value judgments. Now, that is what I extract (and really I must apologize, I am just abstracting) from Professor Dworkin's paper, which leads directly on to other papers both in this panel and other panels.

I turn now to Professor Rapoport, who, equally, is concerned with the question of values and, in fact, gives a very interesting account, really in the manner and the form of an intellectual autobiography, at a certain point, of the phase through which social thought passed under the influence of contemporary philosophy, which you might call the positivist phase; and the writers to whom he refers are Stuart Chase and [Alfred] Korzybski, and others, whose theories of meaning now appear to us all, I think, of extraordinary naïveté. And, the theory of language, that the language of science somehow corresponds to reality in some privileged sense, and that we should dismiss from our vocabulary all words that don't refer to actual observables, which Bishop Berkeley would have thought a naïve way of going about things and certainly must be thought so in the twentieth century. Professor Rapoport's point is that this theory of meaning was linked with what he calls positivism and pragmatism, and he says, very interestingly, in the light of the events of the last decade, he has come to be suspicious of this mode of thought to a certain degree, at any rate, of its generalization (I think I don't misrepresent him; if I do, he will correct me), and what he means by the "light of the events of the last decade" is further spelled out when he speaks of the cooptation of social science by the power elite, in, so to speak, an adoption of the spirit of [Yevgeny] Bazarov by advisers to the United States and other governments. That is, a spirit of extreme dismissal of issues of value and any appeal to intuitions of value that people might have from discussions of public policy or social planning. And, thus, from our point of view, when considering the social sciences, which is part of a projection of any university of design, there is what he calls a sentimentality about scientific objectivity. This seems to me a point of the utmost importance, and linked to the point just made by Professor Dworkin, namely, that we have passed through a period where it was thought somehow a betrayal of rationalism or of clear thinking and a retreat into subjectivity if we looked for a distinctive rational structure to a discussion of new values in relation to old values, in the middle of any intellectual inquiry. Somehow, it lay outside the proper sphere of intellectual inquiry in its purest sense. Now, with this went a very naïve idea of social science, as somehow something which should be strictly modeled—and included in the social sciences, after all, jurisprudence, sociology, and, I would say, moral philosophy—that all these things should be somehow modeled on the language of physics. We've passed, I think (when I say "we," certainly the academic philosophers of the Anglo-Saxon or Humean tradition), passed away from thinking of this, for the most part.

In the latter part of his paper, Professor Rapoport discusses the theory of rational choice in complex situations, where more than one person or social group are involved, which is a long, continuous subject, which he refers back to [the Marquis de] Condorcet, and this is a sphere of rationality, which really is related to action but, nonetheless, is strictly a disciplined subject amenable to very strict intellectual techniques. It still leaves aside, so it seems to me, the really important issue—raised by Professor Dworkin and raised by other speakers—of how you weave into a continuous projection of a future institution moral requirements, which are still things you can argue about no less continuously and exactly than you can argue about means toward ends.

Now, Dr. Tabibian makes the suggestion, in his paper, that maybe (it's the same suggestion which I've been dwelling on all the time), and I quote, "a logical rationalist bias seems to infuse the Universitas Project," the project of the Working Paper. It seems that there is a logical rationalist bias in it, which means a bias which takes science (let's say the physical sciences) as a model of clear reasoning, and he wonders whether the project doesn't presuppose that social conflict between groups, or maybe between classes, depending what view you take, is somehow dispensable. In fact, he does wonder (I think I don't misrepresent him; if so, he will rapidly correct me) whether the project isn't really a return to the idea of the wise man advising the enlightened despot, as it were, an eighteenth-century conception that one might invent an institution which broke down the barriers, which, themselves, were due to historical development, political development over time, and reflected power balances within society. And, somehow, one might make, as it were, a leap altogether and project something which really was in accordance with the blueprint of entire intellectual rationality and detachment, and wasn't this imagining that we might have, as it were, Joseph II, or a modern equivalent, which might be a foundation or something which would bring into existence an intellectual design without it being at all plain what power relationships would be involved. Or, who would have an interest in bringing it? And, I want to ask this: he puts this in terms of a familiar metaphor of infrastructure and superstructure, which, personally, though this is of course a deep theoretical matter, I prefer not to think of it in that way, but to think of it in a less causal way, that is, not that the infrastructure determines it in any exact sense but, rather, in the way I was thinking about it in terms of Professor Dworkin, that one has to think of who now living is carrying on (what groups of people) a form of life which encounters frustrations, which they would feel would be solved by this kind of project, and then, of course, the answer suggests itself: well, maybe the students.

Now, I will say no more about that, because other papers in later panels, which deal explicitly with the events of 1968 in France, or, at any rate, mention them, and the whole question of student utopianism, and the lack of institutional embodiments of student ideas and ideology, that this is a question which will come up later. But it's plain, I think, that it's out of actual necessities of education, particularly mass education, as in America, higher education, that you have to think of what interests would there be in projecting the particular ideals of education in design, that is, breaking down the established barriers which are suggested in the Working Paper, and there are various things that are said later about this by other speakers. But, Dr. Tabibian's point is that we mustn't take the demiurgic role of the designer, we mustn't think of the designer as somebody who can design institutions—one would think, I presume, of the Bauhaus or whatever else has been historically important along these lines—as arising out of specific historical conditions, and ask ourselves, what would be, now, the rule for persons who have an interest in going a step beyond this.

In other words, he says we've got to break out of, in our thinking, that is, the vicious circle that the design of an institution is limited by a social structure which itself projects past designs; how do we get out? (That's the relevance of what Professor Dworkin says.) Dr. Tabibian's own suggestion is that there are what he calls interstitial spaces in society (that's because he is generally taking a determinist picture of society where there is an infrastructure and a superstructure); maybe there are certain areas of indeterminacy, and out of those could develop a demand for a radical realignment of education. For example, a breaking down of the notion that higher education is primarily intended for the young: it might very well turn out that the demands for continuing and adult education, which would themselves break down, have a tendency to break down existing divisions, existing ways of conducting universities.

But, that's the sort of thing you would have to work out, you would have to show, roughly, a breakdown, I think this is his suggestion (at least it's what I am taking, what seems to me to be extremely relevant out of his remarks), that you would have to show a breakdown in our present institutions (for urban planning, for training architects, for conducting architectural schools, for running universities); you would have to show the point of breakdown which would lead, produce cadres, groups of persons interested in developing along these lines. So, all the way through, we have this philosophical problem: What is the relation between new values and the ways of life, or forms of life, out of which they're generated? And, how do we avoid simply projecting a dream, or alternatively, imposing a particular form of social analysis, say the Marxist social analysis, and arbitrarily prolonging that into the future, and saying that *that*—some unspecified form of social revolution—will produce these sorts of institutions?

Well, those are the philosophical, or quasiphilosophical, points that I extract from these three papers, and certainly very central ones. I would now ask Professor Dworkin whether there's anything he'd like to add, or what, and then there will be a discussion among all of us.

RONALD DWORKIN: Thank you. I never like what I've said so much until I hear it summarized by Stuart Hampshire. It sounds much more lucid than I thought it was. I would only want to add this: I was struck by Stuart Hampshire's suggestion that the analysis that I had offered—which I did take to be a general analysis of arguments about new values and not simply confined to the law—his suggestion that this was, on the whole, conservative. In one sense it *is* conservative, but I think only in the sense that any argument that something is a value must be conservative. That is, it must connect with some predicate, something that has gone before that serves as a platform for argument. But, the sense in which it's conservative, and the degree to which this kind of conservatism allows for genuine change, seems to me to be a subject open for considerable expansion. Perhaps it will be in this discussion.

It is true that this assumes a notion of precedent that is, in a sense, common to and employed by the law—but of course it's a great debate within legal theory, a debate which has been made part of politics by Richard Nixon's jurisprudence, for example, the extent to which this notion of precedent requires a kind of slavish adherence to the verbal formulae that have been used before and the extent to which it allows creativity. Now, the suggestion that I wanted to make, I think, can be expanded in this way: that if you take the commitment, which I think serves as the platform from which to argue that something must be a value, if you take that commitment to be represented by society's—that is, the legal system's, or society's in a more informal sense—determination to continue to enforce certain laws or to continue to employ certain social institutions, then what is required is a justification of those laws or that institution which must be applied consistently. It is, therefore, open to people, at any time, to say, as Brandeis did in the case of privacy, "We cannot justify what we are doing and what we propose to continue to do, consistently; we have to abandon part of what we have been doing in order to have a consistent principle on which to base the rest of what we are doing."

In the paper that I contributed, I gave this example of a more general application of this kind of argument, social rather than distinctly legal problems, and I think it's an example that indicates the degree to which this form of conservatism is, in fact, open to radical argument: one might say that the economic system that the United States now employs, with its heavy use of support, Keynesian and other forms of support, for the environment, is simply no longer consistent with free-enterprise models but assumes certain economic rights, for example, rights to security, which must be recognized to be implicit in what we now do, in the way in which Brandeis said that the principle of privacy is implicit in various separate items in the legal system. If that is true, then we have, to that degree, in that way, recognized a much more radical principle than we acknowledge that we've recognized, but we enforce that principle unfairly, that is, we depart from the free-enterprise model in favor of those who are politically powerful; in fact, a consistent application of this principle would lead to a dramatic revision of social-welfare schemes, for example, a dramatic revision of our notions of the relative importance of unemployment and inflation as competing goals, and consistent adherence to this principle would, for example, require minimum levels of support for individuals, far in excess of anything now contemplated, and a tax structure very different from anything we now contemplate. Now that is a conservative argument in this sense: that it appeals to principles which, it is said, must be accepted if we are to continue to enforce the kind of economic system that we have, broadly; but it's radical because it says that to do this consistently would require tearing apart a section of these institutions to make them compatible with this larger principle.

ANATOL RAPOPORT: I was most favorably impressed with Professor Dworkin's concept of a new value as arising as a sort of a synthesizing principle. I was impressed with the idea because it is applicable to other fields as well, most of all, of course, to science. A very important new theoretical construct usually arises as a synthesizing principle, whereby many observations, experimental results, and so on, that had been explained ad hoc, more or less, that had not been connected to each other, become, in virtue of the new principle, connected and lucidly understood.

About this "paradox" concerning new values—a value is not new if it's recognized, and if it is not justified it is not a value—I have two things to say. First, in my lexicon, a value need not be justified. An instrumentality for the achievement of the value needs to be justified, either on pragmatic or theoretical grounds, but a value is something which is valued intrinsically, by definition (I choose to define it that way, and this is the way I understand values); therefore, a value need not be justified, it is only existentially perceived, and not rationalized in terms of being an instrument to achieve certain other goals. So I do not see any paradox on that score, but, nevertheless, the question arises, How do new values arise, how do we become aware of them? And, I think, a rather easy answer suggests itself: we become aware of values to the extent that we are deprived of them. When there are developments, for example, and there are social developments, which result in deprivations that previously had not been so sharply felt, then it is precisely those deprivations that become sharply felt that are then formalized in terms of "values." I would say that privacy, at the present time, is a good example of that, since there are so many encroachments of privacy, sharp and dramatic encroachments; for that reason, privacy becomes an important value.

To take other examples, the values of communal arrangements which characterize so much of the thinking and feeling of the young, I think that they come to the forefront simply because industrial society, particularly industrial society based on an ideological individualism, has deprived people of what may be a very fundamental human need, that is, the feeling for community and affect, and so forth, and when deprivation becomes especially sharp those values come to the forefront. During the Industrial Revolution, or perhaps even before the Industrial Revolution, as the new class of entrepreneurs, adventurers, organizers, professionals, and so forth, became numerically large and socially important, the old institutional arrangements of the feudal system made them feel very sharply the deprivations, because they could not practice their professions, could not undertake their business ventures, and so forth, without certain changes in the social system—so the value of individual liberty, and so on, came to the forefront. So, it seems to me, that we become aware of new values, first, if there is something to begin with in the human makeup that made it possible for this value to be considered as a value, and, second, when the social arrangements are such that we especially feel deprivation of this value; this is when the new value comes to the forefront.

The reservations I have with respect to Professor Dworkin's approach have already been voiced, that is, I, too, consider it to be a conservative approach. I am very much interested in what he said about the dialectical opposition between conservatism and radicalism. One may be conservative in the sense that one asserts that an old value has to be preserved, but radical in the sense that one must point to new instrumentalities in order to preserve that old value. Well, this is fine, but this is not what I had in mind when I had the impression of this conservative approach. It seems to me that Professor Dworkin does tacitly assume that society is an actor, that society has values, and society, then, has at its disposal instrumentalities for achieving these values, legal systems being one of them, and so forth. I challenge that idea. I do not think that any society is an actor. In society there are conflicting interests, and usually it is the elite of the society that has the freedom of action. Now, the division between the elite and the others may be very sharp, or it may be not so sharp; in this sense, we have societies with large concentrations of power, where a great majority of the population, or perhaps even only a minority of the population, is, nevertheless, very much deprived of fundamental satisfactions of values. There you have a sharp division between the ruling elite and the exploited, and we have also societies where these are not quite so sharp. So we do have a gradation, in this respect: I would not, by any means, subscribe to the dogma that all societies are necessarily despotic, and necessarily have a sharply differentiated exploiting and exploited class, but, nevertheless, this differentiation exists in all societies now existing, and it particularly exists in those societies which have glossed over the division between the exploiter and the exploited. I have two societies particularly in mind, both of which claim to be classless societies in a very fundamental sense, and both of them, in my opinion, rest very heavily upon the ruthless exploitation—of another sort, not necessarily of the sort that was envisioned by Marx—but of another sort, which I hope will come out in discussion. And those are the two superpowers.

Now, I believe that the dialectic opposition should be recognized between various dichotomies, and that the Universitas should be devoted to dealing with them in a frank and honest manner. First, there is a dialectic opposition between intuitive perceptions, the existential mode of thinking, and rational analysis. Mr. Hampshire emphasized that part of my paper where I criticized so-called rational analysis, positivism, scientism, and so forth. Perhaps I have overemphasized it in this paper, simply because at any time one bends over backwards *against* the tide. I do, nevertheless, recognize that it is impossible to omit or to disregard rational analysis in favor of intuitive perceptions, such as mystic philosophers and, perhaps, artists and poets would have the major mode of thinking. There is definitely a dialectic opposition between the two, it cannot be glossed over, it cannot be compromised, and one of the tasks of philosophy, education, science, and so forth, today, is to deal honestly and openly with that dialectic opposition.

Another one, which is even more important, I think, is between the needs of the hungry and the needs of the affluent. And, I do not mean to say that the needs of the affluent should be entirely ignored—after all, it is the hope that, one day, the hungry will become the affluent, and then they will have the same needs as the affluent have—but, nevertheless, this opposition exists, and it has very practical consequences. Take, for example, the whole field of thought that concentrates on ecological problems, conservation, and so forth. This is a luxury of the affluent. When the affluent do not need to industrialize further, they can pay attention to such things as pollution, the supergrowth of industrial plants, and so forth. When you look at the hungry, they need to industrialize; if they're going to survive at the present numbers that populate the earth, they have to, somehow, expand their means of production, whether it's of food or other products, and the problems are entirely of a different nature. I remember that Mr. Paz mentioned the fact that his country is not a post-industrial country: it strives to become an industrial country, and most countries try to become industrial countries, not post-industrial countries, and, perhaps, those needs have to be taken care of before, even, the needs of post-industrial society are taken into consideration.

And, finally, the third dichotomy that I think is relevant to the idea of the Universitas is this: Is education to be a help or a hindrance to the educated person in getting along in this world? Someone once remarked that education is the process which conceals from the stupid and reveals to the intelligent the extent of their ignorance. Now, as I say, the education may be a help, and it may be a hindrance, and the paradox at the present time, I think, that is behind a great deal of the unrest and discontent among the youth in universities is that educational assistance has been designed to be of help to them in getting along in a certain type of society, but if they reject that type of society, then the educational process that helps them get along in that type of society becomes "irrelevant." And that's what all this talk about irrelevance is.

On the other hand, if education is going to be such that they are helped in their present emotional needs, then, by that very means, it may be a hindrance to them in living a simple, ordinary, normal kind of a life that education was supposed to prepare them for. So this is a very, very important paradox and dichotomy, or dialectical opposition, and it has great relevance, in my opinion, to the plans of the Universitas. Who are going to be the students in that institution, and what are they going to learn? Are they going to learn a type of design that is saleable? And, let's face it, the design of cities, the design of great buildings, and so forth, is made by people who are in the power elites, wherever they are; they are not made by the hungry. So if they are going to learn the type of design that can be sold, even though it is superior, aesthetically, ethically, morally, in every sense, but if it is saleable through the power elites, then, by that very fact, they are going to serve the power elites. And, suppose they didn't want to serve the power elites, how are they going to be educated? If they're going to be educated in the techniques of making a revolution, then perhaps an entirely different kind of institution is needed, and then the question arises, who is going to support that institution? Where are the funds coming from? Who is going to build the buildings? Where are the professors coming from? Who are going to be the professors, and so forth? Now, we need, of course, both types of education, but how to combine them in one institution, this is beyond my modest capacity of answering.

JIVAN TABIBIAN: I should first try to bring up some of the points that I was trying to make in my paper and complement what you just said, and then refer to the comments that were just made by professors Dworkin and Rapoport. I find that we must, in some ways, examine both some methodological questions that are raised in the [Project Working] Paper, as well as some general theoretical problems, in terms of values and implementation, and, particularly, the question, in general, of how do we go about it, and are we really sure that we will reach where we want to go. I find sort of as central to my opinion about this paper the question of roles. I believe that as long as we do not design new roles through which to carry out our performance in a new institution we will, in some ways, maintain continuity with past values; that the transmission of values in our context is somehow through the performance of certain roles that we would assume as individuals. And, to go directly to the ray of hope I see, is that maybe, however, there is a possibility of conceiving of individuals in a highly fractured and pluralistic society, participating in so many roles that they are able to find themselves, once in a while, in those interstitial spaces, namely, spaces within clearly defined boundaries of roles, where, because they participate in so many multiple roles, their multiple allegiances, and their multiple loyalties, and their multiple obligations, so to speak, also permit them to evade all those obligations, and not go all the way into any one of them. In the absence, so to speak, of all-encompassing and monolithic role structures, this complexity permits us to squeeze through in between alternative responsibilities that we have; and I even thought, in some ways, about the composition of the Project team and discovered, for instance, that if one thing characterized it, it was that there was a tendency in the group not to be, role-wise, purist. They had not, for the longest time, stuck with the most clear and explicit roles, intellectual or otherwise. They were trying to combine, to mix, to synthesize from the multiple and competing intellectual and social obligations they had, new conceptions of their own responsibility—as well as new methods and methodologies of their ways of analyzing the world. Namely, both in theoretical and in social terms, the Project team reflects the tendency to synthesize from the old, new possibilities, simply because none of us is fixed and solidly entrenched into any particular position. Maybe this, therefore, gives some promise.

The second thing is that, now, if we move from the Project team and the designer to the society at large, I think that the Project Paper does not, in some ways, emphasize enough the basic motivation behind our dissatisfactions. The reference to the man-made milieu and man's relationship to the man-made milieu, in terms of the presence or the absence of meaning, I do not think is explicit and clear enough in terms of what seems to bother everybody, and I do not mean by everybody, us, but the population at large, society at large. I think there isn't enough emphasis on the *experience* of alienation rather than the *notion* of alienation. There isn't enough emphasis on the *connection* between the fact that people, in general, feel disconnected with their social environments and their *inability* or their *unwillingness* to try to mold that social environment to satisfy their needs. Maybe the word *despair* is too strong, but I would say that we are in such a situation where the more frustrating our relationships are with others and with society at large, the less potent we feel in terms of structuring that environment. I think that the inability to make our environment fit our expectations is not due to either technical failure or, in some ways, to an ethical failure—it is neither lack of responsibility alone, nor the lack of technical knowledge that is the failure of design; it is, in some ways, the defection of will that stems from the concrete experience of the disconnectedness, the concrete experience of not experiencing the direct feedback of one's own actions. The remoteness of feedback, in terms of one's direct action, is what, in some ways, extends the gap between the self and the results of one's choices. It is one thing to speak of choices; it is another to experience the consequences of your choices directly. We are, by the multiplicity of our social and bureaucratic roles and organizations, removed from direct experiences of the consequences of our own acts. I think that any attempt to create new values by the selective design of new institutions should address itself to the question of how do we, so to speak, bring back and collapse the distance between man and his own experience of his own acts?

Another thing that, in some ways, was interesting is that not only is there a logical rational bias through the whole thing, but there is a sort of taking for grantedness that men as individuals and men as a species ought to survive. This is not difficult to detect, but it is surprising to look for it, in some ways. And, this has come to my attention almost since the very recent concern with ecological problems. I still am very anxious to see a justification of why men believe that men should survive, in the sense that, I'm not saying men should not, but as long as we take that as a point of departure, it becomes such an absolute from which flow both normative and methodological implications. If that is to be taken for granted, in fact, in some ways, the definition of rationality ultimately becomes that principle which does not contradict that original, so-called, taken-for-granted notion. In that sense, rationality is the pursuit of those methods with which one maintains that primitive commitment to survival. I think that even for purposes of an exercise, one should momentarily deny the necessity of the principle of survival and explore what alternatives are available, for instance, rather than thinking in survival terms, to think about, for a short period of time, reorganizing society for the pure pursuit of quality rather than continuity. I think the notion of continuity is, in some ways, one of the corollary notions of the question of survival. I am not proposing that we do not, but I am, at least, proposing that we consider the possibility that we *should* not. And this, incidentally, brings up the question of planning (and I have tried in my notes to make references to the question of futures in planning), and say, for instance, that it is the avoidance of the notion of extinction, and, therefore, in simpler terms, of death, which, in some ways, makes us think about the future in impersonal and depersonalized terms. I would suggest at times that by sort of accepting the notion of death and, rather than putting in such opposite terms "life" *or* "death," rather reintegrating in terms of life *and* death, which is experientially more relevant: life *and* death would lead us to talk not about *the* future, but would lead us to talk about *our* future, and would lead us to talk about, personally speaking, about *my* future. Because: my avoiding speaking about my future is basically a way of avoiding my speaking about the necessity of my death and the contingency of my life. I think, therefore, I suggest that there is a psychological way, sometimes, of coming to epistemological problems, if we understand the question of our ability to tolerate the experience of our own contingency.

And, as to the methodological problems I was raising (though I have not explicitly said so), many of the constructs of the paper use ideal typical categories. I find the use of the urban form, and the particular case of New York, as well as the theory of social contract, as ideal typical constructs, and I propose that the choice of ideal typical constructs leads to the choice of certain more specific techniques of inquiry that one later cannot deny. Let me, particularly, explain this in the case of the social contract. The social contract as proposed is not simply a social-theoretical position, but it leads necessarily both to methods of determining the presence and ultimately of methods of inducing what one might call social consensus. And, the question that is raised is how, while raising the question of social consensus as a critical issue, how do we reconcile this to the form of almost anarchical individualism that is further suggested in the paper, where, by some open feedback process in a complex network of social interactions, the choices and decisions of a large number of individuals are all naturally harmonized?

This is where I see the question you raised in terms of the dispensability of social conflict. I ask, therefore, the question, Is social conflict dispensable because it is not inherent to nature, in which case, it is a philosophical position that needs to be defended? Is it to be dispensable technologically? And, if it is not, is it to be designed, in which case, the solution of conflict is not the denial of conflict but is its resolution in a certain direction. The resolution of social conflict is not value-free; the resolution of conflict implies the success of one point of view over the other. We are either in the Universitas, direction-free, or we are not. I suggest that if we are direction-free, that denies us the right, at this moment, to be critical of the previous direction. To the extent that we have taken a moral or aesthetic position toward the past or present, we have implicitly taken a position toward the direction of the future, even if, at the very least, in negative terms. We may not know what future we want, but it is implicit in the paper as to what future we do *not* want, and the future that we do not want constrains the direction of our choices. It is in this case that it becomes almost inevitable to conceive of the designer as a demiurgic character.

And, if I have one more minute, I would like to refer to some of the points raised, first to the question of values supplementing or coming as solutions to existing needs. If we accept (I am just going to point to some of my feelings about it) that kind of definition, we are thinking of deprivation, and if we think of values supplementing what is deprived of now, we are thinking of values and of human nature as a closed and finite space, and within this finite space we are trying to give values a negative definition—a definition by negative space. It is, assuming there is a finite quantity, within this finite quantity that space is taken as necessity, X happens to be actualized, X is *less* than the finite necessity, and the difference is to be made up by that which we will actualize in the future. What I am saying is a definition by negative space, therefore, necessitates the conception of space as finite, and if it is metaphorical of values, therefore assumes that no really new value can be invented. This is neither objectionable or not, it is just a position we must be explicit about, and is a conception of culture that really assumes the absolute fixity of human nature. And, finally, the question of the making of values: I believe that my understanding of what was proposed in terms of the invention of values in Professor Dworkin's paper is more the process of making explicit values rather than creating new values. The question of making things explicit, or recognized, or accepted, or making it part of social consciousness, bringing it to a level of awareness, is a process different than the *invention* of the value. We must, I propose (through our discussions at times), make the distinction between whether we are inventing a value, or whether, by some process, we are bringing to the fore and to the level of awareness a value that is already there but that has not yet, in some ways, been defined.

HASAN OZBEKHAN: I shall be very brief. I, as you might have noticed, did not prepare a paper. There was method in my folly. I'm very glad I didn't, because now I am able to talk a little bit about the very interesting things that we have heard, instead of trying to repeat and clarify what I would have written. I was very interested in the dynamics, this morning, of our discussions. We started with a very beautiful poem that Dr. Octavio Paz read us, and which made us all extremely nostalgic for those pillars of the night, namely the prostitutes who are still remaining among the disappearing metaphors of our world. And, after that, we went almost immediately to Professor Dworkin's idea of justification and Dr. Rapoport's criticism of it, with Mr. Tabibian suddenly synthesizing and criticizing, I think, both viewpoints. I believe the conference has gotten off to a good start, and what I would like to contribute to this is that I believe that, in some sense, there is really not that much argument among the viewpoints expressed at this table this morning. I personally am very sympathetic both to Professor Dworkin's and to Professor Rapoport's views; I think justification, however—unlike Professor Rapoport—I think justification, the very idea of justification is a very important one in value-formation theory, which is, more or less, what we have been talking about. It is absolutely true, as Professor Rapoport said, that values do not get justified, but their instrumentalities do; but, the fact is, in my opinion, that values become manifest through their instrumentalities and, therefore, if the instrumentalities are justified, then values must be, in some sense, either verified or justified continuously.

Now, this brings forward not a dichotomy, but an interesting relationship between that which is instrumental and that which is intrinsic, and that particular relationship, in my opinion, is a stylistic one and has to be looked at in that particular form. However, this we cannot perceive, nor can we cognize, except in the sense of what Dr. Tabibian talked about as the ideal typical constructs, which, in some sense, is the past projective mode of thinking and leads us to reasoning and dealing with reality in terms of experience. If this is admitted, then obviously value formation is not a fundamentally creative act, as we would like it to be—even when we take into consideration the requirements of the "ought" that normative thought imposes upon us. But the important thing here (and I am not going to go into the interstices that Mr. Tabibian talked about) is that I believe a distinction could be established fruitfully between experience and what the Universitas, as described in the brochure we have gotten, tries to put forward, which appears to me to be a mode of continuous experimentation. The difference ought to be elaborated. You see, experience arises from the past projective mode, namely from the imposition of the ideal typical constructs on our thoughts, but experimentation could be reduced to that which I believe, almost subconsciously, we are all aiming toward, and it is the ephemeralization of structures. What we are suffering from are structures that are too heavy and too well set, which cannot be dealt with and which have become unmanageable, and all the metaphors, there-fore, are beginning to disintegrate under our inability to manage the great structures that we have created and that surround us. Justification in terms of experimentation, and experimentation in terms of the ephemeral structure is perhaps the major idea that the Universitas is proposing. The only trouble, of course, there, is that the methods for justification remain old and the loop closes back into the ideal typical constructs, which impose both a particular vision and a particular solution to the problems proposed. Now, if the Universitas has a mission, it is precisely that of inventing not necessarily the values but the *methods* in which an ephemerally structured reality—both phys-ical, aesthetic, maybe ethical—can be conceived of in relation to totally new methods of thought. This is all I wanted to say for this morning.

PAZ: I will make a very brief commentary. I was very much interested in this idea, if I understood you well, that new values are not invented but discov-ered. You discover in your practice new values, or as Professor Rapoport says, we see them. Now, how can we see them? We can see them because if they are hidden in the social practice, in one moment there is a break of society, and they appear; and I will make an example, for instance, in poetry, when we talk about a good poem, or about a good poet we say that he has a unique language, or that in this poem appears something that doesn't appear in the style of this period. Shakespeare is unique, or [John] Donne is unique. Well, [Noam] Chomsky thinks that poetry, in some way, is a linguistic deviation, which could say that every time there appears a new poem we are seeing a transgression of language: a creative transgression of language. If we apply this idea of transgression, linked with values to social practice, we will find the same thing. New values appear when there is a new force in society that is breaking society and bringing new values. Then, new values are first criti-cal, and in our society creativity is linked with criticism. New values mean not only, of course, they are hidden in society, but in order to appear there must be a criticism of society and a transgression, as in poetry. What I think the new university must, in some way, embody is this critical spirit, which is also a creative spirit—this spirit of transgression.

HAMPSHIRE: Could I just dwell on that example for a moment, because I think it's very relevant to this question of inventing and discovering. Supposing one speaks of the poet as a deviant and unique, then it may still be that the critic decodes, to use Professor Dworkin's language, the structure which gives the poem its power, even though this was by no means present to the poet. But not only is that true, but that he then goes back and reads the poetry of the past, in terms of this structure which he's discovered in something quite new—I mean, he looks for it in the poetry of the past—now this seems to be an extremely common process of argument about values. If we take the concept of good design, for example, or good manners, or good any-other-very-general-thing, then, on the point of conservatism, I think Professor Dworkin is absolutely right in saying that, of course, new forms develop, and then you decode the structure which lies behind, then you go back and you see some element of this already existing in the past, though we didn't recognize it: it wasn't made explicit.

PAZ: What I should say, for instance, about good manners, that *extreme* good manners mean, also, a break in good manners. Then this is an exaggeration of good manners. Then, in the case of the critic, when the critic decodes the structure of the poem, yes, but in this moment he is making a creative criticism. That is the only thing that I wanted to say, that criticism and creativity are linked.

TABIBIAN: The notion of transgression and criticism is an essential one. I think what is the difference here is that existing social norms reward the transgressive nature of the poet's behavior, and in the area of institutions related to the pursuit of, so to speak, intellectual matters, the present university, a transgression is not rewarded. The question is that our intellectual institutions are organized for the purpose of confirmation and for the purpose of reinforcement rather than for criticism in the sense of transgression. Methodological appropriateness, historical accuracy, procedural purity, these are the ones that, in some ways, establish the criteria among which a hierarchy is formed. But this is only a partial, and, in some ways, distorted emulation of the, so to speak, process of scientific growth. [Thomas] Kuhn, in his discussion of scientific revolutions, shows that scientific thought itself has progressed on the basis of transgressions, mostly accidental, sometimes by choice. Now, what we, even the social scientists, are doing is emulating a distorted and degenerate notion of science, where confirmation and reinforcement of existing paradigms maintain the mode of thinking, while, in fact what is necessary, the proper word here might be *criticism*: criticism as revolution, criticism as the denial of existing paradigms. Not so much in stylistic terms, but we must necessarily destroy some of the existing paradigms. Now, to do so, what is required, from a sociological point of view, is to get outside those institutions whose viability depends on that kind of reward system. So there will be no Universitas unless it can structure itself socially in such a way that what is rewarded is transgression rather than confirmation. So it is a case of social design, in that sense, by rearranging who gets what chips for what kind of bad behavior rather than for what kind of good behavior. Most of us from universities know very well that, in that sense, at least at the University of California, good behavior and bad behavior are defined in the state capitol, and not along the lines of paradigmatic revolutions in social thought.

RAPOPORT: I wonder if one can seriously defend the point of view that transgression should be rewarded as such, simply because it's transgression. With regard to the scientific revolutions I would also like to point out that they came about when there was a certain build-up of pressure, a certain build-up of tension. The old paradigms simply did not serve in the light of experimental findings that could not be explained in terms of old paradigms. That is where, to use the Marxist cliché, quantity changed into quality and you had a discontinuous jump so that the paradigm was discarded in favor of a new one. I would also like to go back to an earlier point raised by Mr. Tabibian, and I would like to ask him whether he would not consent to this amended value concerning human survival, that is, would he not think that it is worthwhile for the human race to survive, at least so long as to seriously consider the question whether it should survive or not?

TABIBIAN: In the context which I meant, it is a choice that takes no time. It is a choice that takes the courage of inquiry rather than the pondering of meditation.

RAPOPORT: Well, if no time is set upon the business of survival, then I do not think we have a choice, I think that the question is answered for us.

TABIBIAN: Well, I am not sure.

RAPOPORT: You're worried about immortality?

TABIBIAN: Immortality?

HAMPSHIRE: Surely, your point was that there is one way of defining rationality, which is in terms of usefulness for survival, and I don't think it's at all the case that we're all agreed on this panel. It seems to me that Professor Rapoport really does believe that we can't argue about that, but then, it seems to be false: we do every day argue about that. We argue very clearly about whether something is well written or whether something is well constructed, or not [well] constructed, or whether somebody plays the piano well or ill. These are things that we are always arguing about. And I would say that we argue about whether something is just or unjust. We always have, it's just that philosophers, from time to time, in very unfortunate phases in the history of thought (and such names as Korzybski, I'm bound to say, are associated with them), don't recognize this simple fact, that we are, all the time, arguing about values. And I don't mean about means toward ends. And, I take Dr. Tabibian's point to be that there is a way, if you hold this positivist belief, that you can't argue about values, and that somehow it's irrational to argue about whether a law is just or unjust. If you take a legal positivist view or a positivist view of aesthetics, then you're apt to say that whatever serves the survival of the human race, take a kind of pseudo-evolutionary view, is rational. So that there is a genuine difference here, which is a fundamentally philosophical one, and I'm bound to say there is a difference across the table. But I don't want to confine the discussion—incidentally, I'm sure it is not the intention of the organizers: other participants, at some stage or other, will perhaps speak. I think there are some speakers here. Perhaps, at the very end we could have half an hour for our guests to speak—certainly, of course, Professor Dworkin, break in.

DWORKIN: Of course, there are some things that I want to say, but I agree. A lot of people, presumably, have things they want to say, who haven't been heard from yet. Then, to continue.

UMBERTO ECO: I have an objection to a proposal of Mr. Paz, which is good in principle, but it allows us to distinguish better the question. The parallel, the comparison with poetry is to be revised, in a sense: poetry, or art in general, is an already shaped transgression, and the critic has to immobilize, isolate the rule. The kind of values that social designers are looking for are still unshaped for transgression, and here is the difference. In your comparison, the social designer is not a critic who has to find an already-shaped transgression, but it's someone like a poet who has to decide what is the value to put forth. In this sense, I agree with both the declaration that values are not new but are to be recognized, and that any value can't be justified. But *which* values, we can, we won't, or we must recognize as valid? Because: not any value is valid, from my point of view. I think there is a way to justify the value: the value can be justified structurally in demonstrating that it is systematically connected to the older values we do accept. And we can demonstrate that such or such a value is too easy or it is not consistent with older values we consider. Faced with new values, we have a parameter. It is our value system, it is not a closed parameter but anyway it is a parameter, a theory. Without the theory no empirical research is possible because we can't recognize data as significant data. So, any discourse about new values is very amateurish, in this sense. If we don't start with a system of assumption, and I think Mr. Tabibian said something of this kind, if we don't decide we have some hypothesis about new society, new Universitas in this case, we can't recognize values. In other cases, we are in a very aesthetic—in the sense of aestheticism—position, the discovery of new values. Eating people is a good value for a cannibalistic society, but it is not this kind of research we are faced with.

DWORKIN: Well, I think what I want to say connects with this point, but it's principally addressed to Professor Rapoport's point about values and their justification. I noticed that you were quite careful to say that you defined the concept of value in such a way so that value can't be justified, so that, in a formal way, you're not disagreeing with Professor Hampshire, at all, are you? You're simply saying that when you use the word *value,* you mean that which can't be justified. But then, I would want to ask you whether you think that when people do argue about values, as they do, whether you would want to say, well that's not a value argument in my sense, or whether you would want to say that it is a value argument in your sense but that the argument is an illusion, that there is no genuine disagreement or that there is no rational argument possible, and people have fooled themselves for centuries.

RAPOPORT: No, certainly not the latter. This is the point of view that I have rejected, and Professor Hampshire very correctly pointed out that I had rejected it. People do argue about values, and those are very fundamental arguments. Let's examine the nature of these arguments. There are some things where values clash, and these clashes are not of any consequence or importance, such as, for example, whether oysters are good to eat or not. There's no sense arguing about such a thing if it is only a matter of personal taste. So, in this case, agreeing to disagree is a perfectly natural resolution of this conflict if it is a conflict to begin with—it can become a pseudoconflict, in the sense that a person who faces another whose tastes are different from his ascribes to him either wickedness or foolishness, or whatnot, and it is these kinds of socially trivial arguments about values which I would dismiss as being of no consequence. However, people do argue about fundamental values, for example, there are people who maintain that the preservation of power of a great state is a value, and it is a value in my sense of the word, in the sense that it is intrinsic; it is sometimes rationalized but it need not be— it can also be taken as fundamental. Rationalizations can, of course, be attacked, logically speaking, because one can question whether the preservation of the power of this or that particular state will indeed achieve, let's say, a better world.

Those are questions that have to do with either theory or empirical evidence, but that's not what the value argument is about. The value argument is about whether it is a value. Now these are socially important values, and I would not say that these arguments can simply be dismissed as being unresolvable on empirical evidence, or logically, and, therefore, one can simply agree to disagree. An example was just given: What do you do with people who think it is a value to eat other people? Well, you restrict them so they will not be able to do it—very simple. So that there are arguments about values that cannot be resolved on logical grounds, and they cannot be dismissed because they are socially important or not trivial, and, therefore, they lead to conflicts, and these conflicts must be recognized as such. In one sense, it may be possible on a certain level for the conflict to be resolved, in the sense that some people bring other people to their point of view; they convert them, so to say. I usually take a dim view of these prospects. But on occasions, partially, they sometimes come about (well, those are every complex conditions under which they do come about); they usually come about under those conditions where people simply cannot implement their particular values so that, therefore, in the long run, they have to give them up. So the conversion does sometimes happen. But some conflicts about values are unresolvable, and those are situations with which one must simply deal.

DWORKIN: When you say *unresolvable* do you mean that no justification can be given, that nothing can count as justification, or do you mean that, in fact, neither side will convince the other, no matter how long it goes on?

RAPOPORT: Both.

DWORKIN: Well, yes—there's a very big difference. You said that you define value as something for which no justification can be given, I think you said, and then later you said you think that when people do attempt to justify values they are doing something that makes sense. You wouldn't want to say that, in any sense, they're fooling themselves about what they're doing.

RAPOPORT: Excuse me: I did mention rationalization. I mentioned this: that people sometimes do try to justify values, but in doing so they are simply rationalizing.

DWORKIN: Oh, well then they're fooling themselves. Because they think they're giving reasons for their values, and you do think that that's massive self-deception.

RAPOPORT: It can be, certainly, yes.

DWORKIN: Well, I'm sorry to press you, but you think that if it is a value they're talking about, it is self-deception, not simply that it may be.

RAPOPORT: No, the value is generally held. Let me give you an example. Let's suppose some value is justified by reference to some supernatural being, a god, who has commanded this type of value or this type of behavior. If one has no reason to suppose that any such being exists, then this is not a justification of a value but only its rationalization. But that does not mean they are deluding themselves: they actually hold that value.

DWORKIN: Well, yes, I wasn't thinking of them deluding themselves in holding the value, but they're deluding themselves that they can have a reason. Of course, it's possible that their reason is not, in fact, a good reason; it may be based on something that is factually false, the case of rain dancing, for example, or rituals, things you mentioned. But what I'm still unclear about is, Do you think that although, on some occasions, people offer rationalizations instead of true justifications, there are other occasions in which people do hold something as a fundamental value and do have genuine reasons, not rationalizations?

RAPOPORT: In that case the values refer to the reason. Unless we face infinite regress we must somehow come to principles beyond which one cannot go.

DWORKIN: That's what I thought was coming.

RAPOPORT: You've got me trapped.

DWORKIN: No, on the contrary, I think that anybody who thinks he has *you* trapped on any strategic thing, that is the definition of hubris, I think. No, I don't think I have at all, but I do think that you suggest that you hold the view that the only kind of argument is a chain that goes back to a starting point.

RAPOPORT: A logical argument necessarily must be of this sort. There are other arguments.

DWORKIN: Well, are other arguments good arguments?

RAPOPORT: They are certainly made and, in some instances, they are unavoidable; in other instances they are justifiable. For example, arguments that have to do with affect: supposing I held a value which you did not hold, and it was important to me that you also share it—well, I would make arguments which are, in no sense, logical arguments; I'd try to convey my feeling about this thing and perhaps evoke some kind empathy in you toward the things that I feel. This kind of communication is extremely important in human affairs.

HAMPSHIRE: Is that the kind of communication in the Supreme Court?

RAPOPORT: Well, I wouldn't know.

PAZ: One thing I should ask. It is really very interesting, this problem—I remember now—about values; and you were talking about cannibalism. Well, in a very high civilization, the Aztecs had the practice of opening the breast of the prisoners and eating, as a ritual thing, one part of the heart. When the Spaniards arrived they were horrified with this practice: they found that the Aztecs were barbarians. At this moment, some Spanish soldiers raped some Indian women, and Moctezuma went to see [Hernan]

Cortés and said, your soldiers are doing horrible things to my people, and then Cortés put these Spaniards in jail and, following the practice of the time, first, they put iron bars in their hands, and then they tortured them. And the Aztecs were horrified about this judicial practice of the Spaniards. We have two systems of values. How can we justify? That is very important. How can we decide, not inside one civilization, but facing two civilizations?

OZBEKHAN: But, I believe this whole discussion is getting to what, ultimately Professor Rapoport had said, that one cannot talk about values but one talks about their interpretations, and the instrumentalities, which is the same thing, basically. The point is that in any argument of values the ultimate fundamental value, if you want to take the chain argument, is the good. Now, the good is interpreted very differently in very many civilizations in contradictory and conflicting ways. Now, the problem arises, therefore, in the discussion of these instrumentalities, these institutions that apply those different aspects of the good and in the interpretations of the human beings, the individuals. So, therefore, I do not believe that it is a resolvable, or a very fruitful, kind of discussion to wonder whether the Aztecs were ethically more pertinent or whether the Spaniards were ethically more pertinent. Because, they were probably within their own ambience; they might have been pertinent to themselves—as long as it is to themselves.

RAPOPORT: But to stop the argument at this point is simply to accept the position of cultural relativism. I happen to reject that position.

PAZ: Yes, that is a contradiction.

OZBEKHAN: What I don't understand, Professor Rapoport, is how can you argue the way you do and yet reject that position?

DWORKIN: It is interesting.

RAPOPORT: Where is the inconsistency? I don't see it.

OZBEKHAN: Because you said that fundamental values cannot be argued and only that instrumentalities can.

RAPOPORT: No, I did not say that they cannot be argued, in fact, I must accept the fact that they are argued. I'm trying to analyze the nature of these arguments and their possible consequences. Of course they are argued. I say that they cannot be argued on logical grounds, simply because any logical argument demands a regression to certain fundamental principles which are assumed.

HAMPSHIRE: Well, perhaps, Professor [Meyer] Shapiro?

MEYER SCHAPIRO: I would like to continue with the important points made by Professor Rapoport about relations between values and their realization. Our chairman gave, as examples of real arguments on values, the question: Is that just or unjust? That presupposes we have a value called justice. Which is not in question. There is a difference between asking, is this poem good, or is poetry a value worth pursuing? Now, I believe that we are never, or very rarely, in the situation, except perhaps in the example of truth in oysters or some other food, we are rarely in the situation of dealing with one value, the pursuit of any value of consequence, which brings us at once into the relationship to consequences or to ideas, which are not altogether clear or altogether consistent.

One of the things that struck me in Professor Dworkin's exposition is that the imagined existence of a law, which as a law was accepted, was clear, was generalized, but what grabs our historical sense is that at any point, laws have some elements of obscurity, or their full extension is not known, and even their meaning is not fully known. That is why all new situations bring about some question as to the interpretation of the law. But, also, there are people for whom the effect of the law is not the same as for others. That, at once, implies some discontinuities or some difficulties in the law, and if one tries then to relate it to institutional life, one also comes upon the same fact, the institution is not a perfectly clear, definite thing; it's connected with very particular people. Not all people who are affected by the institution have quite the same relation to it. And it is out of that unstable, complex, unclear situation that there may be—though there aren't always so—there may be seeds of change, of criticism, or of revolt. Now, if you want to make a revolt with regard to one law, you may find that it requires revolt against many other laws which are connected with it.

Now, to make a revolt which involves so much change requires an act of faith, because the cost and the risk of making large-scale changes multiplies the difficulties and complexities and instabilities, since people have become accustomed to what exists, even though they suffer from it. Now, in any case where you want to make a radical change, and a large-scale change—and we have not discussed the question of scale of values, scale of laws, or scale of projects and change here, and nothing could be more important for evaluating any of these interpretations of the concept—if we enter into the problem of scale, and then foresee changes in many relationships and values, we have to ask, What are the risks and the costs? We then try to be rational; we try to find guarantees in precedents, or in our idea of human nature, or the system, or types of control we have, as to the consequences of commitment to new values, or commitment to new instrumentalities for realizing the old values. War is an example of a commitment to instrumentalities for realizing old values. But that involves tremendous cost and risks. We cannot be sure at all; we are in a theological situation where we ask whether faith is self-justified, or whether actions are justified by faith.

Now, our answer to that depends upon what will happen to us as a result, and the "us" is not homogeneous, the "us" is not the same set of people. I think that is clear in several of the discussions this morning. How then do we resolve it? There arises the question of rhetoric and of persuasion and of influence. We are in a domain of persuasive politics, and that's where the questions about semantics and ideals and beliefs all come into play. But, then, that itself becomes an instrumentality, which has its costs and risks—what we said about the superpowers depends, precisely, upon the power to determine, or see, to influence people's acceptance or rejection of things. Hence, the question of rationality comes back again within those fields where we speak of nonrational affective values and faith. Where those affective values are to be realized, and on a large scale, and thereby involve dozens of other values or situations. And the act of faith has to pay attention to the costs, to the risks, and that is a problem of a highly practical, technical, and difficult kind. And yet, we do not have an adequate technique for foreseeing far beyond the present moment. Hence, we are always involved in this affective moment of faith. We are in a theological situation, again, as it were. We make our faith the value to serve us the way religious values served at one time, but with command of tremendous resources of analysis and rationalization and pre-diction, which, nevertheless, we know very well in our hearts cannot go beyond a very limited distance and depend upon so-called probability or sta-tistics, which ignore individuals, which are statements about what the global consequence or result will be, or what a mean value, what a mode, is, and yet it is in the name of the individual that all this is done.

We are involved in real paradoxes and difficulties, whether we regard value as ineffable, as beyond rational criticism, or whether we regard reason as the means of realizing the values. I believe that values can be argued and talked about, that genuinely new values do arise in the course of experience, that the reference to the past is important but not sufficient, that the institu-tion is not something that acts as a block, and I believe that Mr. Tabibian is entirely right in his criticism of the views which isolate, in an abstract way, cer-tain terms in that manner. But I would call attention to our actual experience, in the last fifty years, of attempts to realize values in a supposedly rational way, and I say "supposedly" not because I deny that they are rational, but because the limits or boundaries of that rationality are not understood, are not foreseen, nor are most of the consequences foreseen. But the commit-ment to the value then commits one to the consequences, not by some mys-terious necessity but because a power has been created to maintain them. All these considerations are known to every newspaperman in the world, and to everyone who follows events, but the theoretical discussion tends to move just outside the sphere of the experience of the costs and the risks.

Hampshire: Thank you. Professor [Alain] Touraine is going to speak and then Mr. [Christopher] Alexander, then Professor Dworkin, and then Mr. [Martin] Pawley. Perhaps there might be time at the end for a general discussion as well.

Alain Touraine: I want to address some very brief remarks to the concept of values such as it has been in broad use by Mr. Dworkin. I have the impression that we are confusing two things here. It seems to me that we were thinking about values, and now we are thinking actually about norms—ways of differentiating good and bad behavior, ways of defining the rules of the social game. So, if we follow that line, a main question I would like to make to Mr. Dworkin is: How can we speak about some specific values without referring to a certain principle of unity? He himself mentioned several times that values should be thought of in a coherent system of values, and if we refer to a coherent system of values, we have a series of excluded, forbidden, illegal, deviant, marginal behavior. Now, on the whole, I think, if I can go back the example given by Mr. Dworkin, which is that, if we take the case of privacy, it's a cultural orientation in our society, let's take it as given, which cannot be defined by the opposition with an opposite orientation. We have the struggle for more privacy and for more expropriation rights. We accept more infringements on private situations or traditional situations and, at the same time, we defend more freedom.

Now the problem seems to be to understand the values not as principles, as elements of a discourse, but as conflicting elements in a social practice—not to locate values at the level of ideology, at the level of the organization of a social order, but as elements of social transformation. I want to be more clear on that point. I would say that values, or cultural orientations, appear because society has a certain capacity to transform itself, and there is always a conflict between the mode of transformation of society by itself, and the resistance of certain natural structures in human existence and in social organization. When society had a relatively limited capacity to transform itself, on one side we had some abstract principles—natural order, the will of God, and so on—and, on the other side, we had the resistance of communities, system of kinship, all kinds of systems of exchange in local communities. Now, in our society we have a much more practical capacity to transform ourselves, and, in opposition to that, we have the development of values, like privacy, that mean the maintenance of the individual human being, the maintenance of the structure of language, of expression, of the unconscious, of the dreams, of the imagination, and so on.

So, if we refer to the problem of design, in the broad sense, we see that cultural orientations in a specific society are not coherent, are not an integrated system of norms without some general orientation, but are always opposed to each other, and so design cannot be the action of a certain central actor, planning the relationship of a social unit with its environment, but it is a management of puzzling, conflicting tendencies. And it's always obvious that each society tries to suppress these oppositions, which are not social conflict, which are cultural oppositions. Every society tries, by rhetoric, by law, by food, by the teaching system, through all kinds of ideological systems, to come back to a certain unity, and, instead of accepting that, instead of replacing the problem of social and cultural orientation of a certain society by the fake unity of its discourse, I think the main problem is to come back to the conflicts which are structurally linked, where the historical nature of society, where the capacity to transform itself and to have a constant but always moving opposition between its achievement and its destruction, in all societies we have that, and so I think the word *values* can be very dangerous because instead of starting with a practice of society, and the very movement or transformation of society, or action of society itself, we risk to be prisoner of the image and the discourse that a society or the ruling elements of a society give about themselves.

CHRISTOPHER ALEXANDER: I'd like to go back to the question that Professor Dworkin started with. It does seem to me to be the most important one, faced by this meaning, since the Universitas project is supposed to be concerned with the creation of new values. The question, what kind of arguments would you have about the formation of these new values is pretty fundamental, and I've been getting only kind of a shadowy feeling so far from the discussion on this point. First of all, there seems to be some doubt that these new values really do emerge out of nowhere. I want to quote two examples, very beautiful examples given by Robert Redfield, of the emergence of pacifism in two individuals. One of them was Ikhnaton, the Egyptian priest king, and another was an obscure American Indian. Both these men suddenly, and apparently out of context, decided to do what they could to prohibit violence in their societies. Ikhnaton refused to wage war on the surrounding peoples; he didn't last very long; but it was a very, very long time ago. [The American Indian]—he was the chieftain's son of a small tribe in New York State, I think, where it was the practice to kill certain prisoners of war—one day said simply, This must stop; if you want to kill these prisoners that you've taken today you'll have to kill me too. And Redfield talks about the fact that it is clear that new values are being forged, more or less, out of context. I take it as very, very fundamental to ask, Where do these things come from and how can one argue about them? And, for the sake of concreteness, I wanted to talk about two examples of emerging values that are going on right now—very small points, the smaller the better, I think, because they make the discussion easier. One of them is the value that there must be a limit on noise level. And the other is the value that we should not go on shooting tigers. I give these examples because I don't think either of them can be handled in the way that Professor Dworkin proposes or in the way that Professor Rapoport proposes.

Situations have come to being in industrial society in our world, where one moves toward these values because it is clear that if we don't there is some sort of threat. I don't think it's a threat to survival, exactly, I think it's quite wrong to argue that these values are really, in some sense, extensions of past values and principles—in fact, I think that's only public relations, I think that when Brandeis explained that the value of privacy was actually an extension of past values, this was really only public relations. You can't persuade people to take it seriously unless you do this, because what seems to me essential in the argument is that, in each case, there is a dim awareness, in fact, that our capacity to become whole, to realize ourselves in the world, as it is growing and changing, is threatened, and in order to preserve our capacity to become whole as individuals and groups, and to realize ourselves, we invent these values to maintain that very, very fundamental matter. And, I believe these are the kinds of arguments that are really given, if you say, well my God, the decibel level is going up every year, we'll soon be in the loony bin if we don't do something about this. The matter of the tigers, I think, is much more obscure; there's a sensibility that if we go on shooting and killing species, that we are going to be the losers. Again, in some sense, our capacity to become whole, the wholeness of our fabric, is being undermined, and that is why we invent this value. And, it seems to me that this appeal to the wholeness of the situation and to our own capacities to become whole as individual persons in society, that, actually, is the basis for the invention of these new values.

DWORKIN: I won't try and reply to everything that was said by the last several speakers. I do want to make one general point, which I think was touched on by each of them. And, I'm going to describe a theory, perhaps it's something of a straw man, this theory about discussions of values, but I think there's something of this view in what lots of people say generally, and have said this morning, about arguments over values, and I want to try to expose that if I can. And that is this: you have a conception of an argument about values that runs something like this—when someone says that's an unjust thing to do and another person says no, you're wrong, that's perfectly just; what's going on here, according to this theory, is that each of these people has some place, some back pocket, a rule book about what is just, a theory of justice spelled out into various rules. And, what ought to happen, if these people are rational, at this point, is they ought to take out their rule books and compare them to see whether they're both using the same concept of justice defined in terms of a list of principles which help you to define, in particular circumstances, what's just. If they are proceeding from the same set of rules, in the back pocket, then what remains are issues of fact, which we can then specify and argue about intelligently. If, on the other hand, it turns out these rule books are very different, then we have to change our view of what this argument is, and suddenly it doesn't become a kind of ordinary argument; we think of it in terms of a conflict of value systems, and then we have to talk, perhaps, about power, or we have to talk about persuasion as being the only thing that goes on, we have to talk about forms of argument that are not, on the whole, logical arguments, or something of this sort; and I think perhaps what Mr. Schapiro meant when he spoke about the difference between argument about what is justice and argument about whether a particular thing is just is, perhaps, brought about by this shift in the form of argument when you discover that these people are using two very different rule books about what justice is.

Now, it seems to me, there is something fundamentally wrong with this picture, and I think what's wrong is this: that when people say that something is just or unjust they're not relying upon a rule book in their back pocket, because they don't have one. That, in fact, the joinder of argument that takes place when people use concepts like this has to be explicated in a much more complicated way, and I think it probably comes down to something like this: that the supposition and the background of this discussion then becomes expressible in terms of two propositions. First, that there are cases, more or less—what might be called paradigm cases—in which people, these two participants, would agree that an act is unjust, though they may be very simple cases and very far removed from the case at hand. That's the first idea, and the second idea that each one has is that some principle or other, or some group of reasons, makes these various unjust acts unjust, though neither party may be committed to any particular theory about what this is. If that's right, that fundamental argument about values becomes, we might say, a distinct form of argument, but still a form of argument, namely, a competition made necessary by the fact of a particular disagreement about what principles can be found, and defended, though it may be that neither of these will be principles that existed beforehand and that people will vouch for.

Now, I think that is what happens when a term like *privacy* or *justice* enters an argument. I think people are not backing any particular theory but, rather, just backing the supposition that there are reasons of a certain sort, framed very broadly by this notion of justice or privacy or something else. Now, if that's right, then the task of analysis, of trying to understand and help an argument of this sort, whether we're talking about noise levels or tigers or art, for that matter, is to try and understand this distinctive form of argument arising from the fact that people might agree on certain paradigm cases, agree that principles can be found, or reasons can be found, but disagree about what these are. And it's in that spirit that I suggested what I called the *decoding*. I did not mean that, indeed, I think I denied in the full version of my paper, that anybody recognized these before. What I'm suggesting is that this is a competition to try and justify what we are otherwise committed to doing. It seems to me that the analysis might very well fit a case like shooting tigers, for example, when you sense that there are values at play here—taboos, restrictions, concerns, competition. Then (this, it seems to me, is what philosophy of a certain sort is about) it becomes trying to identify why and to see where a partial justification that might be deployed would lead you. The process of justification seems to me the process of fitting something to cases both real and hypothetical in which our intuitions tell us that we're committed to a particular kind of behavior.

The noise level, I must say, seems to me rather a different one. I think it important to distinguish out cases in which we are all subject to a similar kind of harm, and we begin to recognize that harm by seeing that we're deprived of something, we're beginning to be deprived of something that's terribly important to us. And, as the noise level of a community increases, so we increase our sensibility to this fact that we're all in the same boat. When we're all in the same boat, I think, the metaphor of society as actor doesn't become a dangerous one; I think that Professor Rapoport's point is absolutely right, dead-on right, when what is in dispute is not the idea of a common goal, but a conflict in principles. A conflict between competing notions of how you flesh out what privacy is or what justice is. At that point, the supposition that there is a common goal, which is a utilitarian supposition, I think, which infected liberal political theory in America for a very long time, has to be washed out with cynical acid. We must see that there is an enormous difference between the kind of investigation appropriate to the concern when we jointly throw up our hands and holler and say we're being deprived of something mutually important, from the case in which somebody says: even though most of us want something that's important, we can't have it because this offends principles of justice. At that point, the notion of society as one actor becomes dangerous; I think that we then have to talk about principles rather than policies.

RAPOPORT: Thank you, Professor Dworkin, I would have said exactly the same thing if I had your eloquence.

HAMPSHIRE: Mr. Pawley isn't going to speak at this time; he is going to make his statement on another occasion. So, Mr. Tabibian.

TABIBIAN: I think that the discussion about values seems to imply several things—to point in several different directions. One is that we are, at times, confusing our need to account for the origin of values with our attitudes toward the consequences of values. If one were to account for the, so to speak, genesis of values and where they come from, the reference to principle and general principles can be accounted for in a very different way. One must, therefore, decide whether principles are sort of absolute necessities that are coexistent with mind and intellect and, therefore, have an inherent and intrinsic and ultimately transcendental quality to them. Whether principles are essences that occur or whether they occur in an accidental and independent way from human experience or whether principles are convenient generalizations and abstractions that, through cultural change and evolution, have become shortcuts and labels and condensations to basically refer to and describe, again, notions of consequence and social conflict.

Let me take it this way—the question of value is this, quite often: let's look at conflicts of value as being conflicts about anticipated consequences of that conflict, and we expand "consequence" from the physical and the material to the perceptual, to the cognitive, to the normative. Then, there is as much anticipated, so to speak, fear, dissatisfaction, and avoidance of conflict, of a value due to its perceived consequences. It's not that it's intrinsic to the value. If we were able to think of values without consequence, then we would be in a pure case of having determined whether there is an inherent quality to it over which we are disagreeing. If we translate, therefore, these abstract principles to either social or psychological experience and deny to it a sort of autonomy, that there is an autonomous spiritual realm, but, rather, believe that that which eventually manifests itself as spiritual and intellectual is a level of abstraction that grows out of social and psychological experience, then value becomes a completely different subject to discuss.

Now, as to the question of the origination of new values, such as in the case of tigers or the lack of stopping of the commitment of violence, the question is that they indicate, if not substantively new things, they indicate a certain direction. I would like, always, to distinguish between the substance of a value, its unique quality, and the direction in which that value is going. I believe that both not shooting tigers and the revolt against noise are very consistent in the direction that we are already in. They are directionally continuous rather than substantively old. Their direction is presumed in terms of a trend that is culturally very, very obvious. That is, by the way, the kind of directionality that I was trying to detect in our paper, in the Working Paper, which is the almost taken for granted directionality of greater humanization of our civilization. In that case, not shooting tigers is almost extending to animals the status of humanity and encompassing them, including, by the way, historical relics and monuments and buildings. It's an old form, an extension of animism in some ways to believe that historical monuments should be preserved.

We must, in some ways, therefore, distinguish between the motivation for a value and the expected consequences, the consequentiality. It is essential, because when designing new values we might, in fact, create them by changing the perception of the consequences of old values. In fact, a new value may be no more than a changing perception of the consequences of old values. It would, in fact, eventually be thought of as a new value.

Hampshire: Are there any other observations?

Paz: Just one thing. I was thinking, perhaps we could say something, first, that values come from society, not from nowhere. And they are symptoms of the direction society is going to take. Then, we think in modern society we will find that in the old times values tended to be one value—absolute values—but now we are thinking that values must be critical and plural. Before, the important thing was society as one actor: the state, the king, the god. But now it seems that we attach value to plurality, criticism, confrontation, dissidence, transgression, and perhaps that is the sense of the new university.

Hampshire: Yes, I think it is a fundamental case, the not shooting tigers, but I wouldn't agree that it's a small one. On the contrary, it seems to me to be a very large one because, supposing we do distinguish, as is suggested, the genesis, how we come to have this moral feeling, and in the case of some of us, disgust about shooting tigers, a very strong moral feeling, then one can, say, ascribe to historical or genetic questions, that this feeling could not have been felt by certain societies at certain times, or by such persons as us, insofar as you carry us back into the past. So, for a certain time, and because a particular view of human beings' relation to the natural species would be the prevailing view and should exclude this, which was, indeed, reflected by suggesting that this was somehow assimilating tigers to human beings, when, actually, I think it's the other way around, that human beings are by some of us assimilated to tigers, in other words, that you'll regard human beings as not placed in nature, like owners of a garden which belongs to them and they can do anything they choose with it. Now, why is this thought, that the destruction of natural species is an unforgivable act, developed now? You might give as a reason that just because there's been industrial progress, which looks like it could go on forever and it then it meets a stop and there's a threat to the survival of the human species, that that's why we have the thought, and therefore we're giving a genetic explanation—but not of the validity of the thought. It wouldn't have occurred, I suppose, if we had been successful in this attitude that we could indefinitely dominate nature and do whatever we wished with it; then, I suppose, that perhaps you might argue on historical grounds that the thought couldn't have occurred.

But this still leaves open your question of how do you show the validity of the thought. Well, that I would imagine is really never direct, nor always indirect, that is, if you held a certain view of the human soul, and that it had a special destiny in the whole of the observable universe, and was somehow ancillary to what happened to human beings, then you wouldn't regard the shooting of tigers as shocking or, rather, the destruction of the species, for the same reason that those who do not have that view—that the human beings are by no means the center of the universe—have a completely different argument why. Therefore, it would become an indirect, or philosophical, argument, I would suppose, even though it's true that this wouldn't have happened if our technology hadn't gotten to a certain point. So, if you take this infrastructure-superstructure view, you can easily say that this ideology develops out of something that's happened to technology. Because we would have been optimistic had our technology not received this rebuff that it has received in the last thirty years. On the other hand, there's a playback the other way, that's why I myself don't like the infrastructure-superstructure, because, in fact, people do come to take a different attitude toward technology in consequence of what's happened. And this plays back into the actual infrastructure and out of that comes such themes as we're now considering. Now, Professor Schorske.

CARL SCHORSKE: I would like to address myself to Professor Dworkin's position, in relation to our general concerns because, while I was enormously persuaded by your arguments in the paper and here, with respect to the history of the law, I find it, in some way, inappropriate to the pursuit of the intellectual aims that we have before us. If I could begin just with the word *decoding*, I have the feeling that what you were really discussing was a problem of encoding, and decoding was the beginning of that process. That is, you had the specific case, the specific case was in need of a principled explanation, the principle was discovered by a kind of penetration of a complex set of phenomena, values, practices, etc., so that a gestalt was found, and then when this gestalt was found it became respectable by being given sanction by the social authority. Now the law, in particular, involves the social authority, and I feel, precisely for that reason, the innovative side of the process is seriously neglected by the model you put before us: what is stressed, rather, is that point at which what has been innovated has indeed been recognized by the social authority, which is now prepared to endow it with the respectability of law which only the social authority already constituted has in its hands. From this point of view, I feel not that I'd like to argue with your description of the way law works but whether it is really relevant to the kind of thing we're trying to get at here.

HENRI LEFEBVRE [in translation]: I apologize for speaking in French; my excuse is that there is one place in the world where my English was understood and that was in Hong Kong. I have considerable admiration for the discussion that has been going on for the past hours, I am full of respect and admiration for all those who have spoken. I find myself in a country where, obviously, people still believe in values, and I have the feeling we are in a slightly puritanical atmosphere, where one discusses the merits of values but doesn't dare go so far as discussing values themselves.

I come from France, a country that had three, four, five revolutions whose purpose it was to destroy values, and we've been doing all right. In

France, we do not believe in law, we do not believe in information, we no longer believe in justice. We know, for instance, that law equals power equals money, although law, information, justice, and other such values have been spelled out very well by the French in the past. We, therefore, find ourselves in rather disagreeable circumstances, as though we were in a boat that still had a motor, and that is still capable of being steered: the motor is the economy, the steering is politics, and other than that there's nothing on this barren ship that makes it livable.

So, we find ourselves now in a quite interesting situation. We are forced to create new values, since we cannot live long without values, but between the disappearance of the old values and the creation of new values there is a gap, an interstice, as it was said this morning, but this interstitial time, as it not only involves space but also time, sees a lot of things happening, and some of them are quite unpleasant, some are pleasant and interesting, and this is what I wish everybody.

HANNAH ARENDT: Since I am not an American either, I somehow share M. Lefebvre's attitude: I don't believe in values either. But he still believes in something, which at least one of your discussants here doesn't believe in, that one cannot really live a resolved attitude very long. Our hearts are really stabilized in the value of life, and I'm afraid that, besides, if we have the time for justification of life itself, where are we going to get it from? And M. Lefebvre, like everybody else, believes still in the so-called value of life, so, if you question this, then you are really in trouble, because how can you hide the justification of life from living beings? You would have, in order to justify life, for instance, to justify the life of an individual regarded as absolutely useless; but if you want to justify the life of an individual, you have to invoke mankind, as a nation, as a class, or some kind of collective. But if you also question the life of the species, then you would have to step outside life. Perhaps somebody on Mars or somebody absolutely transcendent could decide whether the life of the species is worthwhile, but we wouldn't know, according to what criteria, how we should measure that.

SCHAPIRO: As an addition, Samuel Butler, in his notebooks, wrote: "The question of whether life is worth living is a question for an embryo and not for a human being."

HAMPSHIRE: Well, I think, probably, our discussion for this morning has reached an end. In any case, it only remains for me to thank those who have contributed the papers.

Universitas Symposium: Second Working Session, Saturday, January 8, 1972

Editor's note: The second session was chaired by Thomas A. Sebeok, and included panelists Jean Baudrillard, Manuel Castells, Gillo Dorfles, Umberto Eco, Gyorgy Kepes, and Meyer Schapiro. Other speakers were Henri Lefebvre, Octavio Paz, Anatol Rapoport, Carl Schorske, Denise Scott Brown, Jivan Tabibian, Alain Touraine, and Rexford Guy Tugwell.

THOMAS A. SEBEOK: We are still waiting for one of our panelists, but I think, perhaps, we can begin now. The very able organizers of this conference were in the position of an innkeeper who has two bedrooms to rent with twin beds each, and about twenty-five guests, and they have to put these twenty-five people into a total of four beds. This morning's bed, I suppose, could be labeled *axiology*, roughly speaking; and in this afternoon's bed we put everybody who was judged to be interested in what has come to be known as a *doctrine of signs*. Now, the doctrine of signs has become one of the obsessive preoccupations of the last decade, and of our age, and I think we have not seen the climax of this yet. And, perhaps, to put this material into some setting, I ought to say something about the doctrine of signs in a very, very capsuled form. As most of you know, the doctrine of signs is originally a medical concept which is associated with the name of Galen and other Greek physicians; it then underwent philosophical development in the works of the Stoics, particularly Chrysippus, and the Epicureans; and reached some sort of a climax, perhaps a first great milestone, in the work of St. Augustine.

Skipping practically everything that happened in between, I would say at the end of the nineteenth century it underwent a curious bifurcation. One development which took its cue from the work of John Locke, his *Essay Concerning Human Understanding*, through the enormous contribution of Charles Sanders Peirce, who I think is a giant of the field, and then it was developed rapidly in the mid-twentieth century by Charles Morris, [Rudolf] Carnap, and others; and, on the other hand, it underwent a somewhat different development from the impetus of the Geneva linguist Ferdinand de Saussure. And these two tendencies developed in a different way in the Germanic-speaking countries and the Anglo-Saxon world, on the one hand, and also the Slavic world and East European countries, and, on the other hand, in the Romance-speaking countries, particularly France and Italy, and the Spanish-speaking countries, particularly Argentina, and also Brazil. Now, in very recent times, the two tendencies have somehow coalesced, and people like Umberto Eco, who is sitting here at the table, and his book, *La Strutura Assente* [1968], one of the most interesting books in the field, is a kind of a synthesis of these two points of view. It's very easy to identify which tradition people work in simply by looking at the label. If you see the label *semiotic* or *semiotics*, and various variations thereof, you are roughly in the Locke–Peirce–Morris tradition. If you see the words *semiology, semiologie,* and variants thereof, in various Romance languages, then you are in the tradition of Ferdinand de Saussure. The word has criss-crossed in a most extraordinary way; in English of England we now say sometimes *semiology,* whereas in Parisian French we sometimes now say *semiotique.* Compare, for example, the work in another field—cinematography—of an Englishman called Peter Wollen, who published an essay called "The Semiology of the Cinema," and precisely, simultaneously in America there appeared an essay by Sol Worth of Pennsylvania called "The Semiotics of Film." They're very similar, but these two labels, as they occur, brand one as being in one tradition and the other in the other tradition. The papers, which are going to be presented around this panel, are, I sense, practically all in the Romance tradition, in a tradition of *semiologie,* rather than in the Peircean tradition of *semiotic.* The panelists might take issue with me, but I sense that this is where the papers belong.

Now, I am not going to follow the procedure of Mr. [Stuart] Hampshire: I am not going to try to summarize what the panelists have said. Rather, I've gone through the papers and have sort of extracted from them some kind of polar terms, opposites, or, to use a term that was used this morning, the terms in the dialectic that are used, and it is interesting to observe that a number of them repeat. I would say, however, one thing that is curious is that the one panelist who is perhaps the most semiotically oriented—namely Umberto Eco (he is, after all, author of one of the books in the field, and he is Secretary General of the International Semiotics Association)—is the one that least belongs in the field of semiotics. I would say, that it could be perhaps, by an operation, be transformed into a semiotic work; and I use here the word *transformed* as a nontechnical term because the word *transformation* is used in several of the papers in a very nontechnical way. The word *transformation* is another shibboleth of our time: in linguistics it is used, of course, in a very technical and particular way, but it has spread beyond linguistics and is now used in a very loose way in many fields.

So, let me now turn to the various papers and try to state what the terms in the dialectic are, as they appear to me. First of all, I turn to M. Baudrillard, who is sitting over there, and behind him his interpreters, and the terms that he has used are *object* versus *product* or *object* versus *sign,* and he has bifurcated the word *sign* in the classical way into *signifier* and *signified,* or, in the medieval terminology, *signance* and *signatum.* He talks about technical-social infrastructure, on the one hand, and he opposes this to superstructure, of forms and meanings, on the other. He then talks, in the Bauhaus context, about function and structure, and I'm not quite sure about the word *structure,* what the word *structure* means in our context here. I was thinking this morning, when M. Lefebvre made his witty remarks about French society of the present day having no sense of values; I would say, on the contrary, they worship *structuralisme*—you can't do any work in France without being either structuralist or anti-structuralist, although I think the term is being replaced by *semiotic* rapidly. Another opposition that M. Baudrillard used was *beauty* versus *aesthetics*, which he equated with the opposition *symbolical* versus *semiological*—not *semiotic*, note, but *semiological*. Then, of course, this fundamental opposition is between design, on the one hand, and environment, on the other; and the word *design* is also opposed, in a different way, to *kitsch*. He says kitsch is the enemy of design.

I now turn to Mr. Castells, sitting on my right, and he used at least the following four oppositions: *physical* versus *cultural*, which I take was also an opposition that permeated the discussion this morning, and which, in [Claude] Levi-Strauss's terminology, would be called the *raw* versus the *cooked*, or nature/culture, whatever you want. He used the opposition between urban space, on the one hand, and social structure, on the other, and then a very intriguing opposition, which I thought about quite a bit last night, the opposition of text, on the one hand, and the cinema screen, on the other, and a great deal could be made of that, but by Mr. Castells rather than me. And, finally, he used the opposition *code* and *message*, which is also one of the fundamental oppositions used in semiotics as well as linguistics.

Mr. Dorfles, who is sitting on my left, used as his key opposition *artificial* versus *natural*, which is again the nature/culture opposition, and he introduced another one, which is also echoed in some other papers, namely, *symmetrical* and *asymmetrical*, which also has interesting implications.

I don't know quite what to make of Umberto Eco because, as I say, his paper is not semiotic, although, as I remarked earlier, it could be transformed into a semiotic discourse. He opposes, on the one hand, the traditional university, which is a kind of metaphor for the present, versus the mass university, which is another way of labeling the future. He also opposed the array of special disciplines and universities, more generally, versus the transfer or the circulation of general information.

And Mr. Kepes, whose paper unfortunately did not reach all of us, but it did reach me late last night, uses a series of oppositions, which echo some of the previous ones and introduce some new ones. He uses the opposition *dynamic* versus *static*, he uses *conceptual* versus *physical*, and then he echoes Castells's opposition between *symmetry* and *asymmetry*; and he also introduces a very interesting opposition, which in linguistics has played a great role, namely, the opposition of goals and means. We now talk about goal-directed linguistics, which is also a concept important in biology; and, finally, he uses the opposition, which his work in general is known for, *science* versus *art*.

Now, I have gone around, except for Mr. Schapiro, who has not written a paper, who did not have an opportunity to write a paper, but who will comment, the second time around, on the papers that are in front of you. I will now ask each of the panelists to make a brief statement and, as I say, we will end up with Mr. Schapiro, who will comment at the end on these matters.

JEAN BAUDRILLARD [in translation]: I shall speak French during my interventions. I will, in spite of the presentation which has been made, I will use the non-semiological or anti-semiological approach. When I referred to the shift from the product to the sign, I was referring to the traditional political economy of goods, as the political economy of sign. When I talk about economics of signs, I expect to make a critique of the sign in the same way as in Marxist economics—goods were being criticized or reviewed or examined. When I talk about value, I talk about value in the terms of economics. But, instead of applying that idea to things, such as in traditional Marxist theory, I would apply it to signs. I was, indeed, myself, also surprised this morning that we spent so much time about values, the disappearance of values, and the necessity to recreate values. Values would then be cultural, but it seems to me at the present time there are absolutely no values to be reckoned with except values that lend themselves to exchange. Values are economical, and economical only, and the only values we deal with, whether they're sign, design, or anything, are placed under the sign of economics.

It is true that after we reviewed, studied, or argued over a number of things and then about a number of signs, we found that it is only actually some sort of bourgeois entertainment. The question that is really at stake is the one of the foundations of values, and the foundations of values, whichever way we look at them, are also bourgeois. If we want to redesign something, it is very important that we turn our back to those bourgeois values, and that we question them in the same way as we questioned the economics on which they rest. We have to reexamine and restate the question of the ends we're pursuing. I do agree with what Mr. Tabibian said this morning, that people do not need values, that they need destruction, that we are oversaturated with values, and those values only perpetuate an order which is distasteful to us and that we want to destroy before we set about the task of starting on another one.

I will go further than Mr. Tabibian, even, when he questioned the necessity to fight for the survival of man, namely, the survival of the species "man." I do wonder whether values envisaged in the context of survival or, in other words, of accomplishment within the perspective of economics as we know them are not a unilateral pursuit. He seemed to question happiness, and some of us ask ourselves questions on happiness, but happiness takes place within a certain system, and that certain system is what we are questioning; and I would suggest the radical alternative that we can find in the works of psychoanalysis. Psychoanalysis told us a long time ago that man was moved by at least two impulses, the impulse toward death as well as the impulse toward life, and that man's inner workings are very ambivalent, and that there is a lot more to what he is pursuing than values themselves and the satisfaction of those values. I refer to some of the works of anthropologists: we know that archaic societies, or primitive societies, have found a way to give collective reality to life and death as well, in a ritualistic manner, and therefore achieved a social equilibrium which we have lost; and it may be that there would be values to be found in rediscovering such an equilibrium for ourselves.

MANUEL CASTELLS: Just an introductory remark: I think that for a discussion to be fruitful it has always to be referred to some concrete decision, to some concrete situation. And that decision and that situation are here, the Universitas Project. So, the final aim of my contribution is to examine the project of a new institution for the innovation of urban environments, and not to engage in some discussion on urban semiology that would require, in my opinion, to be grounded on a specific research matter. However, any criticism of the Universitas Project must be supported by a careful examination of a large number of problems, quite complex problems, whose treatment needs a very long theoretical roundabout way. Otherwise, our arguments would be just opinions, and the opinions are perfectly subjective. And, since I don't believe in elites, my final criticism will be the logical implications of the sociological analysis of some issues concerning, directly, the environmental question.

So, the first of these problems is the meaning of the term *environment* itself. If we refuse the metaphysical idea of a natural environment, as everything we treat is involved in human action and it is for that reason that we are thinking of it, we start our discussion considering the environment as a social relation. But, which kind of social relation? We have, I think, to define the field or the level of social structure that we are indicating when we speak on environment. My answer is: we are speaking of cultural forms; that is, we are speaking of the expression of the cultural values and representations in the forms of human life. But we have to be more specific yet. The environment concerns a more specific vision of general social morphology: the forms it concerns, the forms whose process of production and whose process of consumption are necessarily collective and indivisible. So, the urban environment, that is, the system of collective forms which addresses the everyday life in modern society is, in my opinion, the most achieved expression of the particular relationship between people and cultural forms in mass society, as the American tradition, often called the monopolistic estate of the capitalists.

Now, if the environmental question is related to urban forms and if these are cultural forms, we have to examine, first, the process of urban symbolism at the same time as a general symbolic process, and as a specific process because it is urban; and second, the process of innovation of such a system of cultural forms both in the relationship of that system to cultural change and in the particular ways of change in the case of spatial forms.

So, regarding the first question—I mean the process of urban symbolism—our proposition is to consider the urban forms not as a text but as a happening (that's the cinema screen I was talking about before). I mean, of course, the urban forms, as any forms, have a symbolic meaning, and that meaning is organized in a system where the relationships define the sense of the elements. They are signs, of course, but the structural semiology makes, in my opinion, two fundamental mistakes in the interpretation of that system.

The first big mistake: it considers the urban as a signifier and the social structure as a signified, so the city is nothing else but a symbol. However, we know that the city, as any concrete reality, is all at the same time—I mean economical, political, ideological, and so on—as the distinction between levels of socialist structure is a theoretical one, and any empirical analysis must consider the specific combination of its level in the social processes. So, there is no urban text but urban symbolism; there is no text, structurally, but the process. The symbolic system of urban forms is linked to economical and political urban processes and to the social general action.

The second big mistake: structural semiology specifies the meaning of the symbolic system by the combination of the different messages. In that case, no structural transformation is made possible, but only the production of new messages by the increasing complexity of the combinations. A sign does not make sense except for another sign. But the production of the new messages, and, of course, of the new codes, is impossible inside the system. So, to change the symbolic you have to introduce new elements by the intervention of a new kind of social relation. Even more, to make sense of each particular code you have to refer to its social effects, I mean, to the role of that particular message on the social structure. This implies, in my opinion, that if the urban forms are ideological expression you cannot understand it by *any* semiological analysis but by the social effect of these forms, that is, finally, by their impact on the economics or on the politics.

So, to understand urban symbolism, you have to apply the general theory for the analysis of ideological culture. That is, first, ideology has, at the same time, a function of legitimation of dominant social interests and the function of communication between the subjects, and this communication legitimates, in that way the social interests. Second, the work of this communication is composed, essentially, of three kinds of elements—senders, receivers, relayers—and each of these elements has very particular characteristics. Third, ideological expressions are dependent on social practices and are characterized by their effect on these social practices. Now, with these general elements of the theory of the knowledge of ideologies, the urban forms can be understood since they are elements of one of the channels of communication. They are specifics because they're collective characteristics, and, of course, we have to study carefully this kind of specificity. But the messages change all the time, because of their depending on the changing situation of social practices.

So, urban symbolism is not to establish the whole permanent myth of a city, but to discover, at each moment, and for a specific social process, the way these forms work regarding their effect on the social structure.

SEBEOK: I think we must assume that most papers were read by most people, and so I'm trying to cut these introductory statements short and we'll come back to discuss the ideas.

GILLO DORFLES: I'm sorry, but I must assume that most of the papers have not been read by most of the people; and, of course, I was told that everybody would have read the papers and that there would have been a discussion about our papers, but I think that's quite impossible because, for instance, it's impossible for me to make a resume of my paper in a few words. It's quite impossible; there are several difficult and complicated questions that ought to be discussed with a lot of time. And so I think the only thing I can do is just to read two or three sentences, and, perhaps, that can give a slight idea of what I wanted to say, but not of all that I wanted to say.

If we examine man's situation in contemporary society and in his habitat, we see that there are some factors which, perhaps, we might consider as important, which are neglected. I will make just a few; I will tell only a few of them. First is the affective memorization of territory and milieu by the inhabitants, and the importance of the micro-milieu. I hope you understand what I mean by affective memorization: everybody has to be able to memorize the milieu where he belongs. If this memorization of one's own milieu is impossible, then we have a great danger for the interrelationship between man and society. I think this is one of the most important things, and I think it could be discussed for a long time to make sure that it is really important.

A second point is the recognizability of the territory and of the habitat; that stems from what I said before, of course. Nowadays, we are no more able to recognize the true meaning not only of the buildings but also of the natural ground where we live. And so, this affective memorization of the milieu is made impossible

Then, a third thing is the need to study and establish some points of reference in the habitat to make the affective memorization of each individual to hold onto.

And now, I think one of the first tasks of the Universitas, as we think it should be developed, is to reestablish the relationship between man and the environment through a correct semantization of environmental structures. I will read one more sentence, and then I will end. Further example, very simple but constant, will clarify still better the meaning of what I propose to illustrate. The above-mentioned impossibility, or near impossibility, of any affective memorization is due, in part, to our consumer society. The continuous substitutions of products, as of structures, not only has the result of preventing man from treasuring the objects of consumption, which might be a good thing, but also prevents him from being able to take an indifferent attitude with regard to his possessions, or those of the community to which he belongs. The detachment felt for one's milieu, for the buildings, for the fragments of nature which it still contains, is due precisely to the feverish turnover in urban construction, in means of transportation, in human settlements. The same increasingly more exaggerated mobility of the population brings about an obvious lack of affective interest on the part of the individual. The ethical disinterest is accompanied by an equally profound aesthetic disinterest.

That is what I wanted to say, just to make clear that at the basis of all the crises, which we now have in our design and in our society, there is this lack of possibility of affective memorization and also a lack of the right semantization of architecture and of the milieu.

UMBERTO ECO: I agree with Gillo Dorfles because I believe that when a scholar writes fifteen pages he cannot synthesize a problem, he can't synthesize it reasonably, his fifteen pages, in ten minutes. So, I will only remember the titles of my items in order to allow further reading of my text. Unlike M. Lefebvre, I would speak in English because, in my life, I have found only one place in the world where my English is understood, and this place is New York, so I beg your pardon. In my paper, maybe I committed the mistake to think of the Universitas as a real initiative to be realized concretely, so I tried to discuss concrete points, and my paper is divided into two parts, apparently without connection to each other. The first one is about the structure of a future Universitas, and the other one is about the kinds of signs the designer has to manage and the types of codes he must foresee, and/or provide, in order to make these signs understandable to the people for whom we are working.

But the two topics are interrelated because only by knowing what an urban and architectonic design sign is can we conceive a way of organizing an institution supposed to be able to teach and to transform, at the same time, the man-made milieu.

The starting point of my paper was the present state of the university, not Universitas, in the world, maybe since May 1968, but in principle since 1088, the year the University of Bologna was founded, the first in the Western world. Well, at this time, it is finished: the university as an institution is finished. It can prolong its life like the Roman Empire for several centuries, but it doesn't matter.

The traditional university finished with the arrival of an open or mass university, which, in order to eliminate the selection provided by class difference, and so on, is destined to transform itself into a big lyceum, into a big high school, supposed to transmit traditional science. I mean by traditional science the corpus, the treasury of what science has built until now, which is not research, because research is exactly the transformation of this treasury into something new. I think that a mass university can't perform this task; it will be no more a place of research. This is not a tragic perspective; it will be an important means of reestablishing a level of equality between people arriving from different classes. But, obviously, we have to discover and to invent new places for research, which remains always important. In this interstitial space and time, a project such as the Universitas Project, like the bridge between an open and mass university, which doesn't exist anymore, and the future place for research, a project like this has many chances. But we have to consider exactly how to organize it. The traditional university, in a way, was split into three pedagogical moments for the transmission of the treasury of science. After, for a little elite there was the moment of research as the postulative moment, postulation of new trends and new problems at the moment of solution, science research, and science of the right things.

Reading the book provided for these meetings by the organizers of the Project, I had the impression that the model of the Universitas is organized like this: one moment, a centered moment, the faculty moment, the center of Universitas, which has two functions, postulative and informative—if you want—understanding of some situation and proposal of new problems. And after, around this center, you have the periphery, the peripherical centers where students are working with communities, which are supposed to be centers of decision making and of regulation.

The main criticism of my paper deals, in the first part, with this point, because I don't believe that if students and teachers are really working in peripherical centers, in direct contact with communities, with people, in order to understand, to individualize, and to solve problems, I don't believe that one abstract center could give either postulation or information about—what? Science is not a new tool, and information has to be individualized, isolated, and discovered functionally in order to solve some problems. So I tried to design a model of work, which is circular in this way. The center could exist only as a phantasmic center; the center would be the moment in which the periphery converges in order to discuss and to revise the problem. The center initially is only a problems switcher that indicates the possible existence not of problems but of places and of situations in which, maybe, new problems can be foreseen.

The first real moment is a concrete situation experimented on by the researchers, students and teachers, and local community. In the second moment, from experimentation derives the need for possessing new cultural techniques. At this point, the center could function again as a storage of cultural information, but it always could be a phantasmic center in the sense that the owners of this information storage are the same researchers and students working in the peripherical nodes, who converge in the center in the moment in which such or such information is needed, is isolated, following the needs existing in the situation. After, in the third moment, always in the peripherical nodes, new hypotheses are tried by making new decisions, and, obviously, these discoveries are registered in the storage of cultural information. And, at a fourth moment, always in the peripherical nodes, the initial situation is redefined, and interventions in other situations are proposed. The treasury of this discovery constitutes new proposals for the central problems switcher. In this sense, the regulative function is not the private ownership of the center of one of the nodes, but it is the entire process, self-sustained.

Proposal making, information making, and decision making are the common activities of the peripherical nodes, and the center, as a summary of this initiative, is profoundly and deeply committed to decision making. Maybe, in this perspective, such a Universitas is more difficult to realize: it will encounter too much difficulty. But, in my opinion, it is the *only* way in which we can also conceive the problem treated this morning about new values. No panel can discover new values, obviously, but only a group of people working with other people.

Such is the first part. I do not know if I have five minutes more in order to summarize the second part, which deals with the need of a redefinition of an amount of theoretical and methodological concepts. One of them, and I agree strictly with the views of Mr. Castells, is that we can't conceive of forms, urban forms, objects, as something that is already filled with meaning in itself. Forms are containers empty of meaning. The meaning, to be filled in forms, is proposed by what I call the local codes, and maybe you call social structures, and so on, but the history of architecture is full of failure when architects imagine transforming the world in proposing new forms without knowing the meaning of these forms in such or such situations. In this sense, I disagree with a lot of friends of mine, who believe in a sort of inner significance, an inner symbolic power of form. I note here: would the cruciform plan of churches have the same symbolic value it has now if Jesus Christ had been hanged? The meaning of a form is given in the field. So, I don't believe that a center of a new Universitas could propose new form in order to redefine the man-made milieu, and for this reason I believe in the work of peripherical nodes, which are supposed not only to inquire about the existing codes and the way in which people give things to form, but also to subvert the existing codes, to help people to transform the reading of given form, and, maybe, to propose new forms.

Well, this is not, obviously, the paper. A third part concerned the situation of the designer until now as a shaman, a medicine man. It's impossible to transform a community by giving to people the result of a technique the people do not possess. Why do we appreciate singing so much? When we hear Frank Sinatra or Maria Callas, we feel something that we, too, are able to perform when shaving ourselves, unless they are performing it in a better way. Anyone is able to walk, but a [Emil] Zátopek is more able. And this is the possibility to understand and to emphatically reproduce extraneous techniques. In the field of literature, but particularly of visual arts and architecture, the people are always obliged to accept the final product of a process of which they do not know anything. The problem of participation is the transformation of desire—not in a maker of forms but in an activator of a communal activity of proposing forms. Participation, in this sense, is to offer to working people, working in peripherical nodes, continuous suggestions about new techniques, new endeavors, maybe in amateurish ways, but in order to resuscitate energy that exists but is not exploited. Because the architect, the designer, is a shaman, entitled with charisma, entitled to propose results, the problem of a Universitas working only by peripherical nodes is a problem of the transformation of local communities in operators, makers, and collaborators, where obviously the medicine men are more entitled to check the process, to transform the amateurish proposals into technical proposals. This is a general perspective of the paper. Thank you.

GYORGY KEPES: I am really in a rather embarrassed situation. I feel like somebody who arrived at the wrong date at the wrong party. I don't know anybody, at least not as I should, and also I somehow feel, and increasingly feel, that I'm in a party where people wear sort of intellectual tuxedos, if not long tails, and we are speaking almost different languages. I am a painter, and I was also surprised to see my name in the program as a researcher in visual structure. I was puzzled by the meaning of it and am still puzzled.

UNIDENTIFIED SPEAKER: It means painter.

KEPES: I don't want to go into detail—you know what it means—because today nobody knows what a painter means. But, the fact is that I submitted a paper where I tried to somehow indicate what I feel in a rather vague way the artist's role could be today in this very critical situation where we really, all of us, know that we are experiencing this crisis of scale. The artist, like everybody else, tries to find his way of living to fit in a constructive way in this moment of time. And I suggested, in a rather metaphoric way, that the artist has to be a very important role to give some images or hints or directions or metaphors of a new relatedness to the environment and to the other human beings. I used the title, "The Artist and the Ecological Consciousness": what I implied by it is that, today, in disguises of scale, there are new responsibilities of insights. The artist has some very important inner challenges—to give some type of honest image from within—but he believes one could get a new kind of scaffolding for life. To give some hint of what I mean by "crisis of scale," it's just, I'm sure most of you know this beautiful paragraph in Galileo's dialogue about the nature of scales, that if you have a bridge which is perfectly sound structurally in a fifty- or hundred-foot span, and if you try to enlarge it or magnify it two or three or five times its original size, the bridge will collapse. Every situation, everything has its own rules of the game, and if one goes beyond it one is facing chaos, as we are facing it today. Galileo implies that in this situation there are two possible directions one can take, as an engineer or designer: either to find a new structural solution or to find a stronger material which would survive under the new scale situation—or, one has to find both.

And, it seems to me today we all face the whole issue: that in this type of exploded, completely insane scale of event which happens by the dynamics of a certain stage of history, individualism, whatever is affiliated with it, we created this new situation, and we have to face it. And in this new situation we have very concrete tasks for all of us. And, to have this Universitas that we are speaking about, we have to read our own individual self and our individual direction as to how to fit in and give something which makes sense. And, it seems to me, rightly or wrongly, that what we call artists, which is getting, more and more, to be an evasive notion, have some ability to be almost like genetic coding, like the DNA, to envision in images, forms, in events, whatever, forms that the artists may have used to give an image of a possible completeness within the condition, the context of the time.

Just to give one more metaphor: if one could compare art to any other thing in life it is love, love in the really most intense and most deep and most complete sense. If one can have a real love, what we very rarely have today, then the sensors, the emotions, the affective, and the ideation, or whatever you like to call it, the horizon of the life coincides. In our present corroded world we separate the sensors from the emotional, or the ideational, and we are not living. And, on very rare occasions there are artists still today who have this chance to converge and synchronize all these labels of human response to the world. And, as a new Universitas, I think this type of quality of insight in very concrete terms has great significance; and I thought, later, if it is not too vague for your terms, it would be interesting to explore its concrete potential, how the artist could fit into these new systems, not just in terms of semiotics, not just in terms hard to define, the terms in more and more refined levels, but go to the core of the matter and to sense—and I mean the deepest sense of "sense"—these roles that the artists could give.

MEYER SCHAPIRO: I was invited too late to this meeting to be able to prepare an adequate paper. But I've read the papers that were submitted to me, and I shall speak, first, of some general impressions of the character of the papers. From the original conception of the meeting, namely, a collective discussion by people from various fields, various interests, of the possibilities and requirements of a new university of design, I was led to think that the problems would be focused upon real difficulties today in conceiving such a university and realizing it. I shall not speak of the obvious economic difficulties of starting a new university under the financial economic conditions of the moment. It is often valuable, at a time when one cannot realize a goal, and one is, therefore, not involved in responsible tactical considerations about every detail and its realization, to imagine what such an institution would be, how it might function. And, in the course of such a pre-discussion, one might learn things that one could not easily learn under the pressure of a deadline for setting up a university. So, my criticism is not of the fact that one undertakes such an enterprise at a moment as unfavorable as the present one, but, rather, that the papers that I have read give to the problem of the university, or introduce to the problem of a university, considerations, questions, challenges, which are, to my mind, far beyond the scope of any university in the world; however, I am not surprised by that. The very existence of institutions being in question today, one is bound to look into the reasons for that, and the consequences, but there is an additional reason why it should happen particularly in reflection on a university of design.

It is architecture, more than any other art, which has been the great stimulus to utopian thinking. An architect is a man who works on paper, who is free to draw, to outline, who uses concepts of structure, of fitness, of function, of form, who creates objects, which last for centuries, perhaps, if they are successful; who is, at the same time, a master of feeling, insofar as we use the word *feeling* for the intuited and not easily definable qualities of things, and things which have an immediate appeal, which affect our tastes or distastes. There is that aspect.

And second, the architect, unlike the painter, has to count, he has to measure data, he has to estimate costs, he has to consider the uses of the object, the individuals who will relate themselves to it. Architecture, therefore, is in a very peculiar situation among all the arts with respect to awareness of the effects of the building upon the totality of life. We tend to forget, for example, that when, in the Middle Ages, Nôtre Dame de Paris had to be built, it required an expenditure according to a nineteenth-century economist, of a 120-million-dollar investment. Now, multiply that by ten and imagine an economic enterprise today of over a billion dollars. Now, there was no economic enterprise in the whole Middle Ages which required such an expenditure of resources, and a collection and direction of the energies of human beings. Obviously, the construction of such a building transformed the economy of the place where it was realized, and it changed the whole appearance of the community with such an experience—that of architecture as having a special position within the appearance of the community and its actual deployment of its resources, not in one generation but for many. And, when it was finally completed, it became part of the life of the community in ways quite unlike that of any single building in our own time, unless perhaps, the Pentagon building.

Now, this conception of architecture also appears in the notion of the architectural form as being a model of rationality and beauty and utility, altogether, at a time when no other competitive objects of that kind existed. That led to the view that the planning of buildings could serve as a model of the highest forms of reasoning, logic, and completeness. It is in terms of such an experience that [René] Descartes, in order to illustrate the superiority of reason over accidental movements and action, in his *Discourse on Method*, contrasts the unplanned grown city with the city which is laid out by the will of one man, and, therefore, shows the properties of rationality as exhibited in a complete way. And, later philosophers constantly use the example of a building. Descartes, himself, in a debate with someone who objected to his views, gave the model of a house which is to be built through a reparation of foundations, and upon that are built stories, and so on. The very idea of foundations, and of habitation, and of form in connection with it is so embedded in architectural experience, we are not surprised that a writer like [Immanuel] Kant would speak of an architectonic of pure reason. It is the architectural metaphor, or terminology, that has provided the models for the basic forms.

But the same thing has been said, in another sense, by socially minded thinkers who, when they wish to give an account of the form of a society, and wish to compare a society which is stable and unified with one which is disintegrating or which is not homogeneous, point to the cathedral as a model of medieval society, and a modern street or building in multiple styles, without a style, which is beautiful, which is thoroughly coherent or consistent, as an example of the loss of community, and integration, and consistent thinking within our own. Given this deeply embedded set of ideas about the relation between architecture and society, we are not at all surprised that architects, in the eighteenth and nineteenth centuries, and we see it already during the period of the French Revolution in [Claude Nicholas] Ledoux's plans for an ideal city, in which the center of the city is a *bourse*, by the way, and his designs for the houses of individuals which are given forms that symbolize their occupations for everyone to see, and in that way there is a reconciliation of the collective and the individual, as if they together can adequately represent the whole of society.

Given that attitude, we can see how writers like [John] Ruskin and Frank Lloyd Wright, and others constantly point to the building and to the building use as a substitute for the society as a whole, or as a model. And, architects who feel constrained in their work by the circumstances of their work conceive of easy transfer of the ideas of good architecture to the whole society. Architecture then becomes a model building, a construction; the very word *structure* is already present in the very nature of architecture—and, various considerations as to harmony, proportions, stratification of parts, the whole symbolism of the building as representing the society—so that a medieval writer can say that the stones are the plain people and the columns are the bishops, and so on. And the differences in class stratification are translated into differences in the function of the part of a building in the whole. Recognizing that, I read the various papers as examples, in a way, of a more advanced situation, and with a deeper consciousness of the problems in which an architect or designer or urban planner finds himself, I was not surprised that there should be so many considerations of architecture itself as a means of revolution—or the criticism of architecture as a revolutionary criticism of society. We are doing, as Mr. Dworkin would truly say, we are doing what is being done when new values are introduced as new, but with some tacit or open reference to an ongoing practice or tradition with regard to these very objects.

Now, when I read an account of modern architecture as ideological and, in some sense, therefore, alien to the real needs of the society as a whole or of a large group in the society, and read a call for the destruction of such conceptions of architecture, which are bound to be ideological, I see also a deviation from the responsibility of the problems set by this conference, namely, how to develop an adequate organ for the laying and practice and advance of architecture as an art, as a technology. Of course, everyone today is aware that you cannot build on a large scale, or replan a city, without becoming at once involved in considerations of property, of authority, of power, of needs, of different living standards, of effects upon numerous features of the environment, both the outer environment and inner environment of human beings. And too little has been said about this concept of the inner environment, which biologists take for granted as fundamental in studying the behavior of the organism and its conditions for survival.

The example of the Bauhaus, which M. Baudrillard analyzes—and I think he is right in pointing to an ideological factor in their attitude toward technology, toward technique as an important, if not sufficient, ground for developing a new style—that whole criticism of the Bauhaus, it seems to me, takes us away from the important lesson that the Bauhaus has for the creation of a new university. It is briefly this: we know that, at any moment, there are competing notions of the right style of building. Some of these are inherited notions. They are part of a tendency to uphold what one has learned, especially if one cannot take risks toward the new. Other notions, of great strength and idiosyncrasy, are projected by exceptional individuals who want to impose their own new ideas. But they must have a chance to realize that idea.

How can they do it as single isolated individuals? Some, like Frank Lloyd Wright, not only manage to find those that will commission them to build, but they also preach and write and talk. Another example is Louis Sullivan in this country. These architects, because they have a conviction and a faith about the value of their architecture, which we can then criticize ideologically, thereby, have the will to act architecturally and to influence the opinions of other architects and also to create, as it were, a taste for their architecture in their world. This experience of the Bauhaus is, to my mind, therefore, beyond any judgment of the ideological character of their taste for a particular functionalist approach. Actually, [Walter] Gropius and those with him changed their views within a two-year period, between 1918 and 1920, their program underwent tremendous change, a response to a widespread change of sentiment in Germany, particularly with reference to expressionism. The first plans or statements of the Bauhaus have a highly romantic, expressionist character. The statements after 1920 are of a more sober kind; they are a response to a demand for rationality, for a rehabilitation of Germany after the war, for new possibilities of construction, and perhaps are parallel to the decline of expressionism itself. The great sociologist Max Weber, in a letter written just before his death, said that what Germany needs after this curse of expressionism is a new *Sachlichkeit*; he used the word three years before it entered the literature of art. He felt that demand as a sort of therapeutic demand, that, given the present conditions, given the failure of revolution, or the untenability, in his mind, of revolution, the only viable answer, the only viable solution to the problems of a Germany that had undergone war and defeat, was to apply the logic of reason, sober criticism, cooperation, and all the rest. And yet, if we study the course of the Bauhaus over those years, we find a very interesting change taking place, granted the attempt to systematize a style, and that is not at all easy, not simply a matter of dogma. It is an effort of imagination and experiment: to create a new curriculum adequate to all the problems that will arise in the course of commissions that they may get, and to train pupils so that they will have a sense that what they are doing is coherent, purposeful, oriented, and is guided also by master architects, people who have proven themselves as creative men. What was the consequence of that? We see that for a period of about ten years they had an enormous influence throughout the world because nowhere else in the world is there such a school. They became a model because they tried to solve seriously the problem of a viable school which is influential through its strength, through its rationality, and through its capacity to solve certain problems. Fortunately, because of the men who did it, and it was not an accident, since only men of real talent and intellectual vigor can achieve it, what developed was a powerful school far in advance of any other school in Europe.

I do not mean to say that only under such conditions can such a result be realized. We see a parallel to it in France, with Le Corbusier, in Holland with [J. J. P.] Oud and his associates: we see a parallel type of architecture emerging. But that itself was a sort of confirmation of what had been done by the Bauhaus people. They were, as was said earlier this morning, in the right direction with respect to certain optimal solutions or possibilities that were given them.

But they are not, therefore, exempt from criticism. They were aware, to some degree, of the limitations of their point of view. They invited Paul Klee, who brought the temperament of a completely different time to their school; they invited [Vasily] Kandinsky, likewise. Both of them, under the influences of the ruling ideas, tended to become more like the architects. And, we notice, also, that as these ideas and as this practice came into greater and greater conflict with existing social and economic situations in Germany, that the directors and the type of student and attitudes changed. So that toward the end of their existence, the director was Hannes Meyer, a communist architect who went to Russia to carry on his work, but his work had no effect there, and he was unable to produce anything viable there.

Now, I'm sorry that I have to interrupt at this point, because I wanted to make a further point about the aesthetics, the aesthetic problem. Anyone designing a new university of design today must ask himself, what shall we teach and how shall we teach, if there are deep conflicts of aesthetic attitude? If we take the painters as the model, or if we give painting an important place in it, then we are confronted by a spectrum of aesthetic ideas ranging from what is called *anti-art*, but is not really anti-art—that is simply a slogan to advance a particular aesthetic. The most fanatical anti-artists wanted anti-art to be as good as possible, and what makes it as good as possible has to be understood.

But, given the great range of styles of art and the constantly shifting vogues of one or another style, how can one prepare a curriculum, or develop a method of teaching which will endure for a sufficiently long period in which one can test the validity of these ideas, or in which one can create general grounds of practice. That is an extremely challenging and difficult question. The discussions of the necessity of making the school serve the community as a whole, as if such a whole existed in an unproblematic way, the conception of the love of beauty and the love of the environment as being a sufficient guide to it, or the need for the destruction of all the previous aesthetics or even the university as it was in the past, although they may be discussed in certain tactical terms, these do not permit one to prepare foundations for a really practicable school of design, a university of design. But, they all bring up considerations which are important, but they are brought up in such a way that the concept of the social function of the school leaves it completely in the air or, in some sense, confuses the question of the values or requirements which a new school of design must meet.

The people who started the Bauhaus and enabled it to live for ten or twelve years have the immense merit of having really shaped an institution which, in that period, was able to give to artists and designers, painters as well as architects, a notion of an ongoing, consistent, advancing practice. Naturally, it produced also, as has been said, types of kitsch in imitation of it. It produced every sort of variable mixture with other styles, which seemed impure, but the great merit of that achievement should not be lost sight of, nor should the significance of that achievement as a model for our own thinking as to what is involved in creating the university of design. Some of it is psychological, political; some of it is practical and some aesthetic. One cannot create a new environmental design without taking a risk of some bold hypothesis about the very actions on the drawing board and about the conception of buildings and environment, which are not simply political. I must conclude by saying that when a revolution takes place, it is made in the same language, using the same semiotic systems as existed in the preceding society. One is still bound to the best available instruments for one's communication—rhetoric, activity, influence—as before. And, one builds upon it; but one cannot lose sight of either that continuity or of the eternal problem of planning the university or a school, for which, as I said, the Bauhaus offers us a number of guidelines, not for imitating that style, but for the process, the risks, the ethical values, the intellectual values which, I believe, made possible the success of the school.

SEBEOK: Thank you very much. We have approximately one hour for discussion now. I suggest that we start as we did this morning around the table, and then, if we have time, expand it to the larger circle of the group sitting out there. Have any of you any comments around the table?

CASTELLS: I promised you before to speak on the Universitas Project by a long roundabout way but it was . . . in the corner, so I had to reassert the essential argument regarding the remarks just made by Professor Schapiro. If we agree that the urban problems are cultural problems and if we agree that the definition of that kind of cultural problem is made by social effects, it is, of course, logical to conclude that the social innovation that forms depends on cultural innovation and it depends on social change. So we can demonstrate, I think, that any important social change is made by a social movement, I mean, by systems of social practices organized in a way that is contradictory with the structure of dominant law. So, if that is true, you cannot have formal innovation, cultural innovation, without at least one of these two sources: first, general social transformation made, too, by social movements; second, some kind of anticipation of this general transformation by the innovative social practices you can observe in the relationship of this social movement to this space and to the urban forms.

If that's true, the institution that wishes to innovate an urban environment has to be closely tied to these sources of social change—I mean, social movements—and closely tied at the three levels of its university institution. I mean, at the level of production, you have to get the material of your research and the observation of these practices everywhere in the world. Secondly, at the level of training, you have to teach people, you have to work to train people, who are engaged in the practice of social, urban transformation. Third, at the level of application, you have to push the new experiences which are transforming our urban life. So, if that's true, the essential problem we must treat is, of course, the problem of power. By which power could this kind of institution be supported? I mean, which power is able to, at the same time, allow the institution an existence of such a university and to link this institution to the needed social sources for its objectives. In my opinion, there is no solution for this contradiction. There are some possibilities, but they are tactical possibilities, no possibility, in my opinion, in the long run. And, I tell that regarding the remarks recently made because, of course, you can have an innovative institution; it doesn't make sense to adjust the institution to the expression of a new kind of symbolism, which is required by a new stage of dominant ideology but inside the same structure laws of this ideology. I mean, you have ideological, not innovative, rearrangement, adjustment; you don't have cultural transformation because you don't have political transformation.

DORFLES: I wanted to say only a few words about Castells's and Eco's speeches—or against, if you want. Namely, I quite agree with the importance of social forces and influence of social forces on architecture and on milieu. And, also, I quite agree on the different readability, on the different ways of reading architectural monuments in the different ages. But, I think, in our epoch we are witnessing a very special danger, namely, the lack of the right way of decoding architectural features. There is what [Jacques] Lacan calls the *glissement du signifié sous le signifiant* (the gliding of the signifier under the signified). We see, for instance, a church that looks like an air terminal; we see an air terminal that looks like a cathedral. We see a skyscraper that looks like a monument, and so on. We don't have the right way, the right semantization of the different architectural buildings. And this is something that was not so in the past, in the old times, where every building had for that period, of course, the right meaning, the right way of being decoded by the population. That's why I say it was so important for us to re-acquire this possibility and to make sure that the designers knew how to do it, how to really have the right way of semantizing their work.

SEBEOK: Any other panel members who would like to comment?

ECO: Only a little problem for Dorfles. I think that an air terminal looks like a cathedral because it *is* a cathedral. We are not living in a period with a great order. My problem is: for whom is the air terminal a cathedral—for you, for me, for the executive, the average man using airplanes? Maybe there are strata of the population for whom the air terminal has the appearance, the exterior form of a cathedral without an inside fire. When I spoke about the peripherical nodes' work in discovering a new exigency of interpreting and using buildings and urban forms, I thought exactly of that problem. The new Universitas is concerned with the kind of people for whom the cathedral has no mass inside. And maybe they want to celebrate another kind of mass inside. This is a good field of research.

KEPES: I would just like, if there is any chance, to suggest a direction because I was a little worried that we go in as many directions as we are here, and a little convergence would not be very harmful. And, what Dr. Schapiro was doing, I think, was very important, focusing on a concrete issue, how in a certain stage of history a certain group of men, or minds, created at least a temporary solution for their own moment. And what we have to face (and that was the reason, I think, to come together, to feel out at this moment a direction which has, in a certain way—I don't mean in technical terms—a corresponding meaning, but which gives at least for us a certain crystallization point, how to proceed) is how can we involve our own competence to all these new ways of formulating an education process? And I think it may give us, if we take it as a concrete issue, some chance to find some correspondences and maybe some, I don't dare to use *value*, but value in it.

What we face today, I think, is quite obvious, that we have a chaotic urban environment, a polluted natural environment, and a completely polluted inner life. We are confronted with a completely different image of the world, through the scientific discoveries, new vistas of nature, and we didn't learn yet how to digest and channel this knowledge into an education process. And what I would like just to submit, as a beginning, is that one of the great tasks today is to find an image correspondence, and I don't mean a flat projection on whatever pictorial surface, but somehow a projection of these new invisible relationships, what twentieth-century man has to face in comparison to the visible relationship, what you were speaking about. The new vistas of nature revealed by science, if one can oversimplify this, have, as their key characteristic, the significant aspect of it, invisible significance, invisible in the sense that you hardly can see this tangible, manipulable, physical reality. This new vista of nature creates a completely different frame of reference of seeing. And, this different way of seeing will guide man to structure the visible relationships of his world. But, if he escapes in making the artistic or imaginative consequences from this new reality, we can talk about the social background and the condition factor of the social background; it doesn't mean that we can and should evade, because we cannot evade, the social relationship in the background. But, I think this new reality is a very important issue to understand on every level of human responses, including what we call artistic, aesthetic (all these terms are wrong or dated, but we don't have anything better). And, what I would suggest, if you feel it makes sense to have a response, is to see what would be a certain aspect of this new education process where the new reality could be translated into a didactic process.

Because what the Bauhaus did, and one can discuss it ad infinitum, but still, what they did was they accepted mass production as key for object making, and it was not really the object that was important, but the process producing the object. And, now, our own basic issue is not creating objects but services, or the whole terminology; what you see rampant in every direction of contemporary cultural life is the participatory process, the process and not really the tangible object. Now, how to find a translation of this new invisible relationship into an educational process, I think, would be worth exploring.

SCHAPIRO: In Mr. Kepes's text, he attempts to present in an eloquent and poetic way the great affinities of modern science and modern art as a guide to the future of an architectural or design school which will be inspired by or find a model in the revelations of microphysics, let's say. Now, I'm rather doubtful of that as a description of contemporary art. I cannot forget hearing Fernand Léger speak with tremendous enthusiasm in my presence about an automobile graveyard. Never had he seen such a delightful accumulation of intricate, overlaid forms—all mechanical. And never had he received an assurance of the ephemeral nature of such products and, therefore, the necessity of perpetual creation. He was able to derive, therefore, from the evidence, the example of rubbish and the discarded, an inspiration for an art, which was itself very severe, architectural, and the rest of it. And, I know today, among painters, similar impulses toward the violent and destructive, the broken, and we cannot, therefore, take it for granted that the response of a painter to the charm of an electron-microscope photograph is itself a sufficient ground for either aesthetic or human relationships. I remember always, stated by a doctor whom I revered, this: We do not eat electrons; we eat bread. The scale, or the level, on which we understand these micro-objects is not the one in which we actually live. We deploy them as instrumentalities.

This use of science as a model for art is, to my mind, also, though it may serve particular artists as a great stimulus and there may be beautiful works arising in that way, when it is generalized in the way in which you speak of it, it seems to me, again, to have an ideological component of shifting from the human frame in which things are done to some other field where the problem has less conflict, where the successes and where the difficulties of experience do not exist in the same way. The life of a scientist and the life of an artist—the testing of the results of a scientist, the testing of the results of an artist—are so far apart that we can imagine an artist who finds a great security in the sureness, at least the public assumption of the sureness and exactitude and the truth value of the scientific work. I believe that very often, in the discussions about the architect's role with regard to the environment, there is a tendency to place in the work of a particular profession, or an architect, the salvation of a society. Some will find it in improved psychology: if psychologists did their work properly, all social problems would be solved. It was once proposed that every cabinet in the United States should have an anthropologist as a member to explain how foreign peoples behave—not ourselves, but the other peoples. And it is also often proposed that the problems of society are all engineering problems—we need social engineers. These are, to my mind, parallel transpositions of the central focus of problems, which are fundamentally economic and political, to neighboring fields where a certain beauty or truth may be achieved but where they will not have the leverage for transforming a much larger, more complex whole of an entirely different scale than the operations within the special field—this canvas, six by nine feet.

SEBEOK: If you don't mind, let's let Mr. Kepes respond, and then we will open up to a wider discussion.

KEPES: I think your response to what I said is based upon a misunderstanding because I nowhere imply, in fact, I try to emphasize that we are representing certain fragmentary scientific images. Science means much more. And, if I may just report a conversation I had with Niels Bohr some years ago when he was at MIT, which was for me a really major experience, and it has, I think, a very important illuminative aspect to suggest what really we are speaking about. He explained to me, we had dinner together, and he had yin-and-yang cufflinks on his shirt, and he told me his students gave him this present, and he started to monologize, saying that actually this whole notion of complementarity was in his mind much before he became a physicist. As a young boy, he heard about a story where a man was stealing bread and he was arrested, and he heard from his parents (Niels Bohr) that the man had a sick wife and children at home and he had to steal because that was the only way they could survive, and he could not resolve in himself for long, long years this conflict between one frame of reference and the other frame of reference. The reason I mention it is because science is not this image making or projecting, but science is a complementary principle and a great number of other things. And, basically, the most important thing is the rediscovery of the continuity in the world from the human to the physical, so that we don't have anymore this sudden wedge between the human level and nature, which the oriental, this Taoist philosophy, always knew. And science gives a new key to see nature differently, where we are not separate, above the existing entity, but where we have a very definite structural continuity with everything.

And that is what I meant by science and not really the prettiness of a few electro-micrographs, or whatever may be. In this book I did some fifteen years ago, what I tried to show was the *continuity* between man and nature and not the prettiness of the pictures.

SEBEOK: I have the hand, first of Mr. Rapoport, and then Mr. Paz.

ANATOL RAPOPORT: I would like to amplify these remarks a bit. There is a very good counter-example, where science and art did merge in a very meaningful sense, and that was in the Renaissance. The beginning of naturalistic painting coincided with the experimental method, in direct contact with observation. But what I wanted to say really was something different, coming back to the initial remarks of Professor Schapiro with regard to the permanence of the architect's products, which makes his position rather unique, he being essentially an artist who must also deal with social forces, with business, with projects, and so on, and the things that he produces have a permanence that lasts sometimes for several centuries.

Well, coming back to this planned city during the French Revolution, where each house, each dwelling, reflects the occupation of its owner. Houses, as I understand, are supposed to be designed for several generations: does that mean that several generations have the same occupation? That is, of course, the logical consequence of this sort of design. From that we can draw a very important lesson. What is the average viability today of a social order, and of its ethos, and of its aesthetics? Look out the window and what do you see? You see monuments to the power of business. To what extent will they be valued as monuments after the power of business is gone? To the extent that the pyramids are valued today, or perhaps Nôtre Dame in Paris? Admittedly, they are valued, and unless one took a rather eccentric view, one would be rather dismayed to see them destroyed because the social order on which they were based was destroyed. But, nevertheless, this is a very, very serious problem. Can we conceive of an architecture that does not depend on this permanence of an ethos, and aesthetics and ideology, and, nevertheless, be designed in a sense that the architect is supposed to design? Planned cities and buildings, and so on, that are supposed to last for centuries are somehow supposed to straddle several, possibly now, more and more, rapidly changing ideas of what the social order should be.

PAZ: If there is time, perhaps I will make a very brief remark—three minor points. What I have to say is not in the center of the discussion, and it's about, again, some remarks on the paper of M. Baudrillard. It's a lateral question, but for me it is very important. When he defines the object, he thinks that, in a very intelligent way, surrealism was a negation of the object, infusing subjectivity in the object, and making the object re-associated with another re-association. Of course, he is right, and I should add that that is the old romantic irony. Humor in the surrealist sense was an inheritance of romantic irony. Where I disagree with him is when he thinks that now it belongs to folklore. This kind of passionate negativity can be humor or it can be poetry, and then he thinks that kitsch is not folklore; well, I think kitsch and surrealism, not only kitsch and surrealism but kitsch, humor, poetry, all these have some relationship. As, also, M. Baudrillard said in a right way: they are not denotations, they are connotations. Now, we must distinguish between connotations. For that, I think the best thing to remember is one anecdote of the Japanese poet Basho that André Breton, who also perhaps belongs to folklore now, loves. This anecdote was: a disciple of Basho went to say, I have made a haiku, and it was rather a very amusing haiku. He said, I have a dragonfly, I take off the wings, and it is a stick. That is humor, that can be kitsch. Then Basho says: That is nice, but real poetry is different: there is one stick, I pull the wings, and it flies. That is the connotation, but this is not cultural, this is rebellion, this is revolt, and this is still alive, in political terms. These 1968 students, they were not marked so much by political thinking, by Marxism; they were much more marked by, much more responsive to, poetical thinking. The quotations were [William] Blake, Breton, all the romantic and surrealist traditions in Western civilization.

M. Baudrillard has said something very intelligent, that our society expresses life and ignores death. Well, I don't know if it's really true, because this society is a murderous society, we use war, use imperialism, use bombs. Of course there is one dissociation: we have dissociated life and death, and that is why we can kill with better conscience, because we have dissociated, we have hidden death, but death is still a reality in industrial society, in the capitalist version, and in the so-called socialist version of the East.

But, we don't need to go to primitive societies to see how we can reintegrate death. Not in this murderous way. We can reintegrate death in our society: art is a way to reintegrate death—humor, again, poetry. And, I am thinking, for instance, of a poet such as [Rainer Maria] Rilke; we don't need to see primitive society to see how we can face death. We can read Rilke. We find how we can reintegrate death in our societies. And that is the thing I wanted to say, that art, in the sense of critical art, of our society, is not folklore and is not kitsch: it is still a reality, and it is still something that is alive, still alive as rebellion in the Soviet Union, still alive as rebellion in France, or here.

BAUDRILLARD [in translation]: I should like to go back to the problem of death. I do agree that death is a very important problem, and that it is a reality we can hardly dismiss. Our societies, indeed, are societies of death, but what I mean to say is that we have eliminated the connection between life and death. In the society that I would call a society of achievement, on the values of achievement that we have, the values of economics, of equivalence, of abstraction, of rationalization, we only stress the life impulse. Of course, the death impulse remains, but it is subterranean, it comes up every once in a while but in a sort of shamefaced manner, through the death that we spread or the breaks in the social contract that we tolerate. I think that we do not offer any solution to that aspect of death as is common; death only comes as a destructive or disturbing element in the life that we have learned to accept. We live, I think, in a superrational mode, and the economical realities and the values that we live by are superrational, are abstract, and death only emerges every once in a while as an element of instability, of catastrophe, I agree, but it isn't assumed and it isn't absorbed.

I wanted to add one thing about the university of design. It seems to me that it is a rather problematic endeavor, because that basic ambivalence between life and death can hardly, it seems to me, be solved or resolved by design. It seems to me that design or a university of design are highly rational, collective undertakings. They can become, in one way or another, dialectic, but they will not solve that basic ambivalence that I mention—even where it is placed beyond the value system on which that university would rest. I do agree that art, poetry, and, in some ways, May 1968 in Paris are of a slightly different order. They are a radical alternative, not because they go beyond the value system that we labor under but only because they are means of destruction, because they destroy the values that we live by. In that sense, they are an alternative because they are not dominated by the value system, and because they are destructive of it and of the social order that those value systems have created. The problem, however, that we are debating, is the problem of the creation of an institution, and of an institution that would solve that ambivalence—not an institution that would satisfy needs as others have in the past, and that is something I cannot see in the context. I know that they are pragmatic problems to be solved, the problems of needs, of functions, of values; I see them, but those needs, those functions, those values have been established, or grounded, on the economic system that we live in. And we can reexamine them, we can change them, but we are still subservient to the economics of the world we live in. And I think that we are searching, trying to solve the question—we're not going to do it, we are only going to change or metamorphize the problems as we know them, but we are not going to create anew or solve anew.

SEBEOK: At this point, there are six names on my list here and only twenty minutes, so I will call on these in this order and ask them to be very brief: Mr. Touraine, Mr. Tugwell, Mr. Schorske, Mr. Tabibian, a lady whose name I don't know over there [Denise Scott Brown], and, finally, M. Lefebvre.

ALAIN TOURAINE: I will be very short. I'm struck by the parallelism between this morning and this afternoon's discussion. In the morning, the question was raised of the existence of values and the system of values, and some doubts were raised, too, and rightly enough I think. And this afternoon, one of the main questions is, Is a city an urban system, integrated as a system of forms and symbols? And, we could say the same about the school system, for example—any aspect of social practice—is it a symbolic system? And we can defend this idea in two different ways. First, in the policy way maybe in the past, some cities could be considered as symbolic systems. I don't think it was so. I think in some societies where we have the systems of order, what we have is architectural systems organizing the isolated world of values. I don't think we ever had a Mayan or a Zapotek city that was planned, where there are ceremonial centers and the people could live scattered around; and in a Greek or Roman city it was the same; Versailles was a civic center. Ledoux's city was not a city, it was a convention and civic center, and people could be around, like foreigners or the slaves of antiquity. And, more and more, this isolated world of value disappeared: it dissolved into social practice the more we see the decline of the positive concept of order, and we have a certain decline of architecture, too. So what we see is, to a certain extent, apart from the fact of some utopians trying to maintain the old idea of a city that some people like to refer to as a model for new cities, referring to the Middle Ages, to the barbarian type of city.

Apart from that, what we have is what we would call a negative conception of the symbolic urban system—the idea that, after all, the city is an ideological system: it is a system of signs, which denote social power. And I would just say, very rapidly, that I certainly would agree with what Mr. Castells said, that this vision is a very dangerous and superficial one. We don't have, either in the urban system or in the school system, an integrated system. If class domination is expressed to a certain extent by an ideological system of integration, it is expressed, at least, to the same extent by a system of exclusion and prohibition. So, in a city today, in a school system, we never have an integrated system but a divided system. There is a center and the periphery: the people who have the noble education, and the people who have an inferior education, and so on.

And it's more and more so; I would say that, more and more, our cities can be read at different levels. At the first level, systems of communication are transforming themselves for practical, economic reasons. Secondly, there are the expressions of an opposition between social classes, noble and inferior neighborhoods. Third, is the expression of political bargaining and transactions. And, fourth, to a certain extent, we have the influence of an integrating ideology.

Now, if it is so, what is the role of design? I think the role of design—probably I would agree with M. Baudrillard—is not to imagine an integrating model of a city, but to have a *dis*integrating role and to show how, behind the false unity of social phenomena, we have actually not just social forces, but different levels of social relations, which are working, sanctioning, and interacting. And so I think, for example, one of the remarks made by Mr. Dorfles was very interesting. More and more we have polysemic buildings, and we have an urban structure which should be flexible and polysemic, and I think that maybe one of the main purposes of design should be to be able to create ambiguous buildings, ambiguous neighborhoods, ambiguous cities, and to try to find, behind the false unity of a map, of an open terrain,

of a certain social organization, the social forces at work, and their changing interaction.

REXFORD GUY TUGWELL: I think your twenty minutes are almost used up, and
I shall only make one comment about architecture. It seems to me that the
architecture problem is something more than was indicated. I read in the paper
the other day that the last important Louis Sullivan building in Chicago is
under the wreckers right now. Everybody was surprised to hear that it had
been built as a stock market. Actually, it has been used as a university for the
last twenty-five years, so perhaps Louis Sullivan would have been glad to have
had it torn down maybe fifty years ago.

   Also, there's a Frank Lloyd Wright house out on campus at the University
of Chicago. It's called a prairie house because it has long extensions from
the roofs. Frank Lloyd Wright had the idea that this was a protection from the
prairie sun. But after air conditioning was invented these things made the house
dark. The lights burn all day, and the people who function in it are very annoyed
with their circumstances. I have more to say tomorrow morning, so [I will
end here].

CARL SCHORSKE: I would just briefly like to say that I thought the example
Professor Schapiro raised about the Bauhaus was introducing a note of high
realism into the proceedings, and, in the sense that I feel (I don't know whether
others do) something like the shadow of the Bauhaus as an institution hover-
ing around the Universitas Project. I'm not sure this was in the minds of the
framers of that Project, but one has the sense that the aspirations do seem to
share something with the Bauhaus. I would like to subject that to a kind of
scrutiny, however, that would produce quite different results, I think, from
what is either in the Universitas Project or in the interpretation that Professor
Schapiro gives to its history, while fully agreeing with Professor Schapiro about
the admirable professional ethos that informed that group of men.

   I think the social experience of the Bauhaus in defining their function in
relation to a series of clients is a really horrendous example of what can happen to a Universitas, or any other institution of the same sort, including the
universities in our own strife-ridden social context. I think it worth observing
that the Bauhaus had, from the beginning, to be extremely conscious not
only of possible economic clients but of political support. Thanks to the
recent collection of documents that [Hans M.] Wingler put out, we're in a
much better position to see how that tragedy ran its course. In the center of
it is the suppression of the socialist republics of Thuringia and Saxony, which
Wingler, for some reason, makes no point of. This suppression was done by
the so-called parties of the democratic center and under the leadership of
Prime Minister [Gustav] Stresemann. So that it was the liberals who knocked
the political top out from under the Bauhaus, at which point they had to

move from state patronage to an attempt to construct a combination of city patronage along with a whole lot of economic interest groups, not the least of which were the older guilds. The whole definition of design labor, of furniture production, and so on, became a social issue as to how the Bauhaus should turn.

Now, it was at this point that Gropius and the chief people in the Bauhaus decided political neutrality was the right road, in the professional interests, and the great days of *Neue Sachlichkeit* came from an acceptance of the political facts of life, which was that the economic marketplace was ruled in the determination of the customers, the patronage of the Bauhaus. I can't recite the whole story, I don't know the whole story accurately, indeed, the whole story has not been told, and I may already have made one or two factual errors in reciting it. Though, about the fundamental character of the change in the patronage structure, I'm sure that I am right.

I would also like to say that there were two tendencies in the Bauhaus, one of which was mentioned by Professor Schapiro, about Hannes Meyer, who went in the direction of working with urban government, trying to get contracts to build workers' settlements, low-cost housing, and this kind of thing. Thus, the attempted political neutrality ended, first with the exclusion of communist students, then with the exclusion of the painters, who were viewed by the new conservative governments in the 1930s as a particular source of radicalism and of danger. So that the relationship between the painters, who expressed the artists' criticism of the society, and the architects—or designers, industrial designers—who were trying to produce products for the society, who accepted the existing modes of production, became enshrined in that decision that the painters should be shut out. And finally, of course, the people who defended the political neutrality themselves, in principle, Gropius, [Marcel] Breuer, and so on, had to withdraw from the game, and left it to [Ludwig] Mies van der Rohe, who was content to go forward with, in effect, the anti-political stance. I do believe that, in the end, they got swallowed by the Nazis, but there is something instructive in the problem of trying to build a school which is truly on admirable principles of modern design, professionalism, recasting the definition of how one relates to society, and then being swallowed by the political forces, unable to suppress their breaking out inside as well as outside the society.

I don't try to argue that, had they gone another route, they would have survived, because the institutional matrix indicated a dependence on some social element, and whichever one they had associated themselves with would have been doomed by the rise of Nazism—whether they were communists, social democrats, whatever, if they weren't Nazis they would have been doomed. But I think it is instructive that the attempt to go in for pure objectivity, and pure professionalism, in the last analysis, really did fail, and was shattered by the rock of politics and social tension.

JIVAN TABIBIAN: On the connection between the success of the Bauhaus: I was thinking that for Mr. Schapiro to explain why they succeeded, that there was a notion that they succeeded, but I did not understand why. Their success, and I think there was some success—not on the level of institutional survival but on the level of influence and the generation of a new way of looking at the world—their very success can be explained along the lines of what Baudrillard was saying, namely, a complicity with the broader scale of social forces. For having moved from the product to the legitimization of the process, it was destined to be successful simply because it legitimized an economic and political process that preceded the Bauhaus and got legitimization through it.

Therefore, we are, similarly, if we want to, capable of designing a Universitas that will, in some ways, succeed if it only manifests and makes explicit and articulates inherent forces in the existing social system which are not yet translated but are potentially there. In some ways, it is the actualization of reformist and liberal utopia, which many people believe are not connected to existing social and economic forces. Intellectual elitism, in many instances, is nothing but complicity with existing relationships, except cast in different terms.

And, the final point about ambiguity and ambivalence: for a very long time, I did believe that maybe we can change things by institutionalizing ambiguity and ambivalence, and then I became, more and more, somewhat skeptical about this possibility, because ambiguity should not so much be design, as, what we're talking about, the ability of individuals to tolerate ambiguity, and to live with ambiguity. Rationalization performs a function; it performs a function that in some ways replaces the security of the community that existed in history—entire communities, the entire society. The security of the monolithic community is being replaced today by a rationalist frame—a frame of mind by rationalist ideology. Now, we can only supersede rationalization if we are able to construct a personal situation for individuals where they do not need that rationalization, and where, having acquired their sense of security by some form of identity, they can tolerate that ambiguity. Ambiguity would be experientially intolerable in a society that provides no other order but the order of reason. Therefore, there is a connection between the rationality of values and the lack of an integrating communal principle that underlines the experiences of all of us in society. I think we must understand that unless the individual's well-being can be substantiated by the integrity of his identity, rationalization performs a necessary, but ultimately destructive, function.

DENISE SCOTT BROWN: Let's discuss, first of all, the notion of the Universitas. A university for design has a very exciting potential, but I believe it's defined here too narrowly. Why should one not consider economic and social design as well as physical design? Today we talked as if it were a new school of architecture, yet in every academic discipline students are in revolt against the action-averse stance of their masters: against academics who measure trends and write histories, or who produce internally consistent theories but don't get their feet muddy in action—in the intangibles and irrationality that action involves or in interdisciplinary work that is messy.

Because the Universitas would give training in action-oriented decision making and design, many fields that should be oriented toward action might orbit its programs. Urban physical design and architecture would be subsets within this broader and, to me, more exciting possibility. If this is what Universitas is (or even if it is only a new kind of architecture school, suited to our times) then what we've been considering here today is too much university and not enough Universitas—our orientation toward problems has been academic rather than professional.

This morning's discussion of values, for example, was a kind of a metaphysical *pilpul*, suitable for a Saturday. But a truly action-oriented analysis would be somewhat different—would view the same subject matter in a different light. I think we should be discussing the design of instruments that would elicit new values, or asking ourselves what types of instruments could help to mediate value conflicts. How would these fit into a new Universitas? Professor Schapiro dealt with this problem when he asked: How do you teach action—or design, as he called it—when there are differences in values? And he and others have analyzed the Bauhaus as a case history and a cautionary tale for future designers. This seems to me the right approach.

As for the semiotic analyses: no one told me why this subject related more closely than any others to architecture and design. Why was this the most important starting point for a Universitas? We had some good discourses on semiotics and interesting consideration on what aspects of semiotic thinking would go into a Universitas education. But why is it the first topic? Educators who are planning a professional school should start with questions of priority.

HENRI LEFEBVRE [in translation]: Regarding the problems that created some sort of confrontation between Jean Baudrillard and Octavio Paz, they exist, but it seems to me that they are irrelevant to science. If we have the introduction of rationality in a society, it creates its mode of expression that upsets it. Rationality, or rationalism, does not satisfy the death impulse, but it does create a catharsis to it. I shall take an historical example: when the Greek city was created or, rather, was developed and organized, at the same time Greek tragedy developed and satisfied the death impulse. One could say, also, that at a time where the merchant impulse made itself felt in the British Isles, Shakespearean tragedies offered a catharsis for the death impulse. What our society will produce or offer along those lines I do not know; I don't think anyone does; and don't think we are competent to decide upon it. That was the point I wanted to make.

One other thing I wanted to say is that I have witnessed, listened to a great many monologues, some of themes very interesting, as well as modest attempts at dialogue, but few and abortive. I would like to suggest that we have accepted as a hypothesis, that maybe there was a hypothesis that ran under the whole discussion this morning and this afternoon, that possibly economics or psychoanalysis or semiotics could confront the problems of the new life we would like to solve or the future city we would like to build. But why would any one of those disciplines be the tool we're seeking? We're confronted with an entirely new problem—an absolutely and completely new problem—and why do we not create an absolutely and completely new science. Actually, "absolutely and completely" are overstatements: we can take some inspiration from the Bauhaus, from previous rebellions, from communities, and other forms of knowledge, but what I would like to offer as a conclusion is that the problems are new, and the science we are after is unknown.

SEBEOK: Thank you very much, all, for your participation and patience, and continue your monologues and dialogues over the cocktails.

Universitas Symposium: Third Working Session, Sunday, January 9, 1972

Editor's note: The third session was chaired by Arthur Drexler, and included panelists Christopher Alexander, Hannah Arendt, Erich Jantsch, Arnold Kramish, Edward J. Logue, and Rexford Guy Tugwell. Other speakers were Emilio Ambasz, Manuel Castells, Percival Goodman, Gyorgy Kepes, and Denise Scott Brown.

ARTHUR DREXLER: Good morning. I'd like to begin by introducing the panelists this morning and by making a few, I hope, brief remarks, intended to locate the subject of the symposium. This morning, we have with us Mr. Erich Jantsch from Austria, who is consultant to the organization . . . .

ERICH JANTSCH: All wrong; not any more.

DREXLER: Well, we're off to a good beginning. Mr. Jantsch, will you identify yourself.

JANTSCH: Yes, I am actually without a job now, but in ten days I will be Visiting Professor of Systems Science at Portland State University, and, after that, Visiting Scholar of Public Health at the University of California at Berkeley. That is all now.

DREXLER: Good. Mr. Kramish.

ARNOLD KRAMISH: I represent the United States science community at UNESCO and the National Science Foundation and other United States science organizations; previously, the founder of the Institute for the Future, and previous to that, with the Rand Corporation and the University of California.

CHRISTOPHER ALEXANDER: I'm Chris Alexander. I'm an architect. I work in Berkeley, California.

EDWARD J. LOGUE: I'm Ed Logue and I'm president of something called the New York State Urban Development Corporation, which is a new little thing the governor created a couple of years ago.

DREXLER: Mr. Tugwell.

REXFORD GUY TUGWELL: Well, I'm afraid that you'll get the impression that this is an entirely California morning, and I'm a Californian, too, so we're in a majority, you know. I'm from the Center for the Study for Democratic Institutions in Santa Barbara, at the moment.

HANNAH ARENDT: Well, I'm not from California. I teach: my name is Hannah Arendt. I teach at the Graduate Faculty of the New School for Social Research, and my field is rather something like political philosophy.

DREXLER: This will save me the problem of eulogies, and is probably the neatest way to do it.

Yesterday, I think we had some extremely interesting discussions on a fairly abstract level, and I found myself paraphrasing their content more or less like this: that it seemed to me that by the time I left yesterday, I had, on the one hand, the picture or, rather, perhaps, the proofs that action is indeed impossible; life itself is called into question; and the possible first subject for a curriculum of the new Universitas is removing the sting from death. We invented, my colleagues and I, the title of this program, and we thought perhaps "Thanatology," and then "Prospectus in Thanatology" became a better title.

On the other hand, at the other end of this, was the admiration of the Bauhaus. And, I found this, personally, very problematic because, of course, anyone who has had experience of trying to teach architecture, much less practice it, understands that the deficiencies in the formulations of the Bauhaus and, on a larger scale, of the modern movement as a whole, are, of course, what have contributed so much to the present impasse in the practice of architecture and, for that matter, design. The problem, it seems to me, the subject that I think we are trying to find, is how to reconcile the formal problems of the discipline of architecture, planning, and design or, using design as the broadest term, how to reconcile the formal problems of that discipline with the ethical implications.

The Bauhaus, as we all know, attempted to avoid the ethical implications. That is, I think, however, that that is only a very partial statement of what the Bauhaus assumed it was doing; and certainly some of the people from whom the Bauhaus drew its ideas conceived of their work as having very substantial ethical implications. The outcome of all that, however, is something very tangible and very much in evidence; it was cited yesterday, I think, by Professor Schapiro.

Now, behind me—you can all see it—is the new Avon Corporation's skyscraper going up on Fifty-eighth Street. It is a new and ingenious effort to shape a product, namely, a package of space that has commercial value, to give shape to that product according to a legal configuration, a legally defined physical configuration. Further downtown, in almost exactly the same position on an east-west axis, is another version of the identical building, by the same architect. It is not without significance that the architect,

Gordon Bunshaft, whom I happen to admire very much, refers to this package of space as a three-dimensional security. If the architect, who is most clearly associated with this kind of work and most admired for his enormous professional competence, himself, thinks of it as nothing more significant than a three-dimensional security, it tells us something about the condition of architecture, and we can also draw conclusions about the problems of training people to continue this work. Not only is it almost impossible now to try to persuade youngsters to take up this mission, it's rather difficult to persuade Gordon Bunshaft to continue doing it.

The talk this morning, I hope, will be, at least to some extent, on what the mode of operation might be for a Universitas concerned to reconcile problems of performance and ethics that baffled Plato and Aristotle but should not hinder us. And, I thought we might best begin by asking one member of our panel, who is very directly engaged in trying to cope with this, and I mean, of course, Chris Alexander, who has a very interesting project in the works; and I'm going to ask Mr. Alexander to speak on that first, and then, after that, I hope other members of the panel will pitch in.

ALEXANDER: I've been a bit baffled by some of the discussion yesterday, so I'm going to start by just restating what I understood to be the problem of this conference. The way it was explained to me was that there was an intent to create a community which would address itself to the problem, How should we live? And, it would function as a university in the sense that all the intellectual resources of this community would be constantly concerned with that question and would be making experiments, and trying to implement the conclusions that were drawn so that this whole community would be an evolving experiment dealing with that question. I did not understand it to be a traditional university, in any sense, and my remarks have to do with this problem as I've now defined it.

I have, possibly, two things to offer. One of them I could offer to any community, and an extension of it, which I'll explain, is particularly appropriate to a community that is going to bring this much intellectual pressure to bear on its own nature. Now, first of all, I'd just like to talk about the architecture of communities: as I understand it, what I believe would be necessary in any community, not particularly the Universitas Project. And, I start with the assumption that it is absolutely essential for all the people in society to be shaping the environment for themselves. That is, I reject completely the idea that a few professionals called architects or planners are going to take over this function; I regard it as an intolerable abrogation of liberty. I think that the making of one's own environment is as important as a practical and as a symbolic act as the act of speech is; and for just about all of human history, up until the Industrial Revolution, this was commonplace. Until the Industrial Revolution, all towns and buildings were in effect made by their users. Of course, there were specialized craftsmen involved in many cases, but the organic and living character of preindustrial human settlements, is largely due to that one fact: that the fabric of variety created there—literally, if there are ten thousand people in a community—is the variety created by ten thousand people, and it lives for that reason: it is not created by ten people or a hundred people.

Now, this is a pretty difficult problem: to try and re-create this in the modern world. Most of us have been taught that these matters are so difficult that only architects can tackle them, and the publications, first of all of the architects themselves, and more recently of the popular press, *Time*, *Life*, and so on, have impressed upon everyone the fact that this is a matter for specialists, that you can't hope do it for yourself, and so on. And, it is also true, I mean, that is, that the practice of this kind of thing is so remote from most people now that if a person were asked to take part seriously in designing his own house or to take part in designing an office building where he was going to work, he would hardly know what to do. He would throw in a few casual suggestions, feel extremely insecure, be willing to bow to the better judgment of the architect at all turns, and not really be able to take charge of this process.

Now, as I say, it's a very, very difficult question: How can one create this situation? My colleagues and I have been working for almost ten years on this and have recently, in the last year or two, I think, finally managed to solve it, at least in a rudimentary way. The solution hinges on a device called a "pattern language," which is a combinatorial system of images. I simply don't have time to explain what it's really like, but it takes the form of a loose-leaf book, if you like, which one can leaf through, write in, and do many things like this. Anyway, this language, which is based in its nature on the similar devices used in traditional cultures by people to design their own environments, allows a person directly to create a building, a part of a building, a part of a neighborhood, according to the principles present in the language and according to that person's own judgment and feeling for the immediate context he's dealing with.

I must be brief, but just to give you examples of what we've been doing: we've reached the point now where, for instance, a housewife can come into our office, knowing that she wants to build a house. She can sit down with this material, assuming that she has a site in mind; within about two days of hard work, she has produced what one would have to call a beautiful, organic, subtle, buildable design—somebody who didn't know anything about architecture before. We have recently been working with a psychiatrist, some miles east of Berkeley. He and his staff, using this process, have designed a mental clinic for themselves. There was also some small involvement of the patients in this. And that is going ahead to construction now.

We have, in the last few months, been working for the University of Oregon at Eugene, and have initiated a campus-wide process there, where it is now understood that all future construction on this campus will be in the hands of the students and faculty acting as designers. And, only last week, we were helping the people in the music school design about a three-quarter-million-dollar extension to their present facilities: they were perfectly able to do this. Just, again, to give you a feeling for what it was like: it was a matter of representation, of course, there were the dean of the school, two faculty members, and two students. The five of them and two of us spent a week on the site designing the building right there, and by the end of the week they had produced a wonderful extension of their building.

I'm on my way to Sweden tonight, where we have the opportunity, I believe, to try and initiate this process in a New Town outside Stockholm, where, again, if we succeed, the understanding will be that—in this case, we're talking about forty thousand people building a growing community, between now and 1985—if it works out, we will put the same tools into the hands of this community as it grows, so that this town will be a living town in the same sense that the towns of the past have been living towns, not a dead thing made at the drawing board: now, so much for the practical side of the matter. I believe it is essential that this community represented by the Universitas would handle itself in the same way.

To try and make the connection between the practical problems and the ethical problems, I want to talk a bit now about the nature of these pattern languages. The content of this language, or these languages, consists of concepts dealing with the organization of space, of human groups, which are highly concrete and which embody value. I'll just give an example, a very small example: if you ask yourself how a group of this size, all of us sitting in this room together, could best have the kind of meeting we're trying to have, you would see that there is, at the moment, quite a bit of difficulty created by the fact that there is almost no eye-to-eye contact between the people in this room. There is a little bit, of course, between the panel sitting here and you, but between you and you there is none. And, it is rather difficult to hold a communal meeting under these circumstances, and, to make that kind of thing work, what is needed is a room not much different in size from this one, perhaps slightly different in shape, essentially a bowl-shaped room with, essentially, tiers of seats so that each person is looking at most of the other people. If there are people who start the discussion off as we are doing, then we could be sitting somewhere near the middle.

Now, I just want to talk about this example for a moment, because the fact that this works, what I just described, of course, is partly based on common sense, partly based on what you could, if you wanted to pretend to be sophisticated, call psychology and anthropology and things like that. And, you can draw evidence from various fields to substantiate concepts of this sort. Apart from being a practical solution to a problem, it is actually a value, in the sense that it embodies a new institution in a very physical way; very simple, but if the room were like that we'd all feel differently about what we were doing and it would, to that very, very tiny extent, change the culture that we were a part of.

Now, these languages that I speak of, that allow people to design their own buildings, contain hundreds of concepts of this kind at all scales, ranging from details of windows and doors up to rather large-scale questions dealing with transportation, distribution of work, and families relative to each other—all kinds of questions of that order. Now, under normal circumstances, in the projects we've been doing, we have not been able to get the people concerned with their environment to play a great role in the development of these patterns. In other words, it is quite hard work, it takes a good deal of experiment, empirical investigation to establish even one of these patterns. As I say, there are hundreds of them at stake, and in the normal kind of time pressure that people have, they just don't have that much time to devote themselves to elucidating these things, to challenging them, modifying them, doing critical experiments that will find out whether they really work, or whether they're not working so well, and all this.

I believe that the Universitas, in this sense, has a unique opportunity because not only could it take charge of its own environment in the way I've described, but its function could be the continuous evolution through experiment, discussion, and observation, of the language which they themselves are using to build their own environment. And that fascinates me very much, simply because (this is extremely important at the moment) we've been in the position that a relatively small number of people, drawing, of course, on whatever we can, in many, many fields, are providing this material to a very large number of people. Now, I don't object to this, but, at the same time, it leaves it rather impoverished. We don't know that much, we don't have that much opportunity to find out things, and so on. So that, by opening it up in this way, and allowing the evolution of the languages to be themselves part and parcel of the communal process, then this thing is going to become enormously enriched and very much better.

ARENDT: I don't know; it seems that Mr. Drexler knows I came here entirely unprepared. And, now, listening to Mr. Alexander was very interesting. I just want to make a few remarks on what you were saying.

Number one, you compared, quite rightly, the way we live in our environment, and expect experts to deliver us, so to speak, prefabricated [buildings], as against a traditional way in which communities shape their environments, and how this, of course, came about because these communities had something in common and, therefore, shaped it. They didn't do it consciously. You seem to me to reverse the whole process, namely, by somehow persuading communities to engage in something in which they were not engaged before but which was natural before: whether this will succeed—I by no means think it's impossible—whether or not this will succeed or not seems to me quite open to question.

The second thing that I would like to remark on is connected with this. You very nicely pointed out the shape of the room as something about the way we feel in space; our spatial feeling, if I may say so, has something to do with how we relate to each other, and there's no doubt about it. And, you gave us an example that we have a certain relation here to each other, whereas this community has none. Now, if we talk simply, objectively, spatially, not psychologically, then I would say that what gathers us together is, first of all, spatially, the table. Take the table away and, so to speak, that will also separate us from each other and we will lose that which binds us together, and this seems to me quite important. And, if we take this now one level higher, then I would say: your chance to build up this community would be this table, that is, metaphorically speaking, it is the same concern. You would have to have people, and what really brings them together would be their common concern with this kind of environment, that is, that they want to live in such a kind of self-shaped environment. The extent to which people do not want to do that any longer seems to me to lie less with the architect than with the interior decorator. What has always surprised me so much is that people would hire an interior decorator to design the way they are going to move between their furniture. It never occurred to me before I heard about it, and saw everybody doing it.

Now, one of the reasons why this can be done is, of course, or it seems so to me, that they do not think of their environment as something really stable. You know, I have great sympathy for this three-dimensional security because I think that this whole question of shaping the environment has something to do with the simple fact that man is a temporal being and lives only a certain time on earth, and during this time changes a great deal. And, therefore, because he is such a futile, temporally limited being, he needs something that is more permanent than he himself. And, only under these conditions, it seems to me—that is, if you can arouse in people the old feeling that, because they are unstable, they need some stability in the objective world—that this is the real difference between objective and subjective, because our subjective feelings are by no means permanent; on the contrary, they are the most unstable thing there is. And, the only thing by which we can, so to speak, recognize ourselves and acquire a certain amount of stability is that we have the same chair, for so many years, and will not throw it out simply because one of the legs is no longer so good, but we will ask somebody to fix it because that is our chair, and that is the way we orient ourselves. That is, what is really involved in this whole business is a world of feeling, feeling for objectivity, and a change in these exclusively subjectively directed ways in which we think or act about these things. If we think about objects—and I've heard much said here about their functional use, and so on—even those who are most outspoken against the consumer society are not even aware that they talk about all objects as though they were consumer objects, that is, as though they have only a very short life expectancy in the world. For instance, if I make an omelet, the life expectancy of this omelet, as every woman knows, is very short; either it's being eaten right away, or it goes into the garbage can. Whereas, even the most flimsy pair of shoes has a much longer life—if I leave it alone it will survive. That is, it is a use object and not a consumer object, and this permanence goes in a direct line up to the art objects whose permanence, as we know, is almost unlimited. I mean, we all can still appreciate the Parthenon, no matter what our philosophy may be.

So it seems to me that all of this is involved here, and it would be nice if one could start it, so to speak, from the architecture, or the designers, and get people again to have this community feeling. But, they will only have this community feeling if they are really interested in having this kind of environment, which you cannot throw out of the window and don't want to throw out of the window every five years or so.

TUGWELL: I have great sympathy with what Mr. Alexander has to say; I'm old enough to have grown up in a village myself. On the other hand, I don't know of any surviving villages at the present time which are like the one I grew up in, and probably happily so. And, I'm afraid that he's ignoring some institutional problems, which I wanted later to call attention to, and particularly economic ones.

I can't imagine, for instance, what he has to say to the eight million people of New York City or the ten or twelve million people of Tokyo. It seems to me that most of them are doomed by the institutional situation that we've inherited, to live in apartments; and apartments are not something, which, from their technical quality, can be very much interfered with by the people who are going to live with them. They'd fall down, or something. And I think that the economic problem we've inherited in this country is especially serious, that is to say, the speculative ownership of land, and the difficulty of finding space in which to do planning, and so on, but this is something I wanted to get to later. I'm afraid, Mr. Alexander, that what you're talking about is a wonderful thing for a few people.

DREXLER: Well, I'd like to ask you a question about this, precisely. Ms. Arendt used the metaphor of the table as the thing that defines this group, by at one and the same moment uniting us and separating us. Throughout history the table, so to speak, has normally been provided by architects, as the public place in any community. The nature of that public place (I think, and everyone will correct me if I'm wrong) has historically been indicated by—I hesitate to use these phrases—a ruling caste; but the nature of that place has been provided, or indicated, or proposed, either, it seems to me, by a priesthood or by those who lead the society, or who are at least capable of articulating its aspirations. How, in the effort that you're describing, is the table prepared? Is it prepared? Are you getting at a society that is "tableless," or is there the hope of eventually producing it as a collective effort?

Secondly, on another level, not the level of metaphor but on a purely practical level, who provides the infrastructure of services? To what extent is there self-determination, even on the village level where Mr. Tugwell is assuming it can still operate, perhaps, if not in the urban?

TUGWELL: Well, that's the way Mr. Alexander described it.

ALEXANDER: May I? What I would much prefer to do is perhaps to answer some questions after everybody has had a chance to speak. I'd like to hear what all the other kinds of things are and then try and make more of a mélange.

KRAMISH: I think I'm in the happy position of agreeing with both of you. I don't see how we possibly can enlarge the decision and implementation processes to include all of the people, each individually taking a hand and shaping the community. You made a reference to this in your first point. Whether you like the terminology or not, I think this still has to remain the responsibility of a responsible, hopefully, small group of elite people, in a sense.

So the question resolves as to how this elite shall responsibly carry out their tasks. Unfortunately, there are lots of elites, who are still fractionated into humanists, technologists, scientists, etc., and I don't see much progress in maintaining that fractionation. Each group is now gaining an awareness of the other group; they're either sympathetic to them or they're antagonistic to them, but at least the awareness is growing. Now what do we do with the awareness? So far, after awareness, this subjective feeling Ms. Arendt talks about takes over, and the technologists attempt to rationalize what they are doing, by throwing in a few humanistic parameters, and the humanists want to get back to nature, reject technology, etc., and it's essentially an anti-technology stance because they experience pollution, noise, etc. They're afraid of it.

When we worry about all of the people, when we try to balance these parameters, obviously a balance has to take place eventually. (There's no thing that says technology is the answer.) Let me put it in a different manner, let me put it in the context of being a physicist, of the Heisenberg uncertainty principle. At a technical level, the Heisenberg uncertainty principle says, essentially, that if you attempt to measure energy with extreme preciseness then you can't know anything about time; or, if you attempt to measure momentum with extreme preciseness then you can't know anything about position, and vice versa.

It seems to me there's an uncertainty principle involved in what we're attempting to get at. If we follow technology with extreme preciseness, then we have to give up all humanistic considerations. If humanistic considerations, which are extremely subjective, are dominant, without taking into account what benefits technology can bring, then you might as well stop doing technology. So, what we have, then, is some equation which is a product of these two parameters, which are inverse to one another, and we have to find the means for carrying out this process. The science people lately have become intoxicated by a new science called "technology assessment." This implies not only the assessment of one technology versus another, to see whether one technology can do a job without polluting, or with less pollution, or one technology can do a job cheaper than another. It also involves the interjection, presumably, of the humanistic values.

Now, what I'm pleading for is not an exercise in technology assessment on the part of the technologists or the part of the humanists alone, but that same sort of exercise, which I would prefer to call "value assessment," because there are many things besides technology and humanism in the values, which would incorporate the kinds of techniques you've hinted at: the table techniques and the special design configurations, so we can go about this technology assessment more reasonably.

And, I also urge that this so-called elite, which is working on these problems, continuously changes; even though we can't include the entire population of a city, or whatever we're trying to include, we have to be sure that it is continuously sampled. These types of groups, think tanks, or whatever we call it—if we call it "technology assessment institute" in the future—tend to become inbred and incestuous, and this is one thing we would certainly have to avoid. I'll have some other comments at a later time.

JANTSCH: I think, perhaps, I'd better speak now, because I feel some aggressions mounting in myself; I felt it throughout the symposium, actually. And this has to do with the fact that I feel that the issue of design is either not at all addressed or addressed at a very low level and with very small scope. It was practically only during the discussion yesterday when Ms. [Denise] Scott Brown brought up, also in a slightly aggressive way, the same problems which bother me. I think we have here a split into, perhaps, two or three types of discussions, with no, or very little, link between each other. One is an old-style disciplinary discussion in sociologists' language, city planners' language, architects' language with a very nice French Cartesian framework and the terminology which is cast in disciplinary terms and which—without going into details here—I would brush aside as irrelevant, readily, for problems of design, because we are not dealing with science here in an old perspective.

My feeling, by the way, is that science is design, but we have to get the new culture to get this through, because scientists today try to stipulate their activity in science as being the opposite of design. Now, this old disciplinary type of discussion I felt also present in the presentation of my friend Arnold Kramish, and I would say that his way of putting C. P. Snow's two cultures together in an uncertainty principle alienates me very much because it is integration between the two, which we ought to look for, and I do not think that we should perpetuate this type of separation between technology and humanistic attitudes, as it would imply. Also, I would say (and this is just as a side remark), that the mentioning of one of the more recent fads which are on in America, technology assessment, is I think regrettable here, because technology assessment is nothing but a very small sector of a planning process which has been elucidated and developed in theory much further than the National Academy of Science and engineering have been able to grasp. There are some very prominent committees which have cast the name of "technology assessment." So I think we ought to speak of planning, of the full-scale normative planning process, in which technology assessment is a part of technological forecasting at a strategic level, to put it precisely, and we have to deal with design. And I think there is a framework developing which makes it unnecessary to go back to C. P. Snowish types of terminology, and this is what some of us call a "systems approach."

The systems approach, like the word *systems*, and like other words which are in some circles considered good, is at last getting into the terminology of very narrow-minded disciplinary people, such as economists and sociologists. But I would say that the systems approach, to me, is, first of all, an approach to designing *human* systems, and, in a moment, I'm going to say what I mean by that; and it is about the self-organization of human systems, self-organization in two ways: Self-organization internally: how does a community, for example, organize itself internally, which is one of Chris Alexander's themes. But also, how does it organize itself externally, that is, how does it want to interact with the environment, with the world of which it is part. Both aspects are very important. I have commented on some of these things in my paper, which almost nobody has received and almost nobody has read, and the copies are, anyway, so pale that I wouldn't be tempted to read such a copy.

But, let me say, at least, that we should recognize three levels of human systems. The lowest level is human relations, and I do not mean here the interpersonal relations which are normally addressed with this term, but our general way of relating to the world, our way of forming what Geoffrey Vickers calls a "represented context." At the higher level, we would have social systems, in general, social systems which in their totalities can form civilization, and with which we are dealing at the level of cities, countries, and so on. But at the highest level, this would all be futile if we did not address at the same time our cultural systems, which are also subject to design. I have the feeling that the culture is being taken for granted here, and we have to conform to it, that values are taken for granted. We cannot put them into play—whether invented or not; this is another question. But, we cannot bring them into play willfully, and this means that we do not function, that human systems, viewed in this narrow perspective, would not function as purposeful systems; they would function as anything lower which could be mechanized, in a way. If a human system is really operating as a self-organizing, purposeful system, it sets its own dynamic principles, its own rules of conduct. It forms its own ethics, not out of a blue sky, but out of a cultural system, which is also subject to a learning process.

I have gone, in my paper, into some detail, describing what I see as important learning processes at these three levels—and, by the way, also using notions from Chris Alexander's book and from Geoffrey Vickers's book—but using them at all levels.

At the human relations level, I would say that this learning process, which I will not describe in more detail here, is such that measure evolves. That is all that we are talking here about: architecture. I'm interested in architecture, but I'm not interested in discussing design, and the design of human systems in the terms of architecture. This would be a sectorial approach, again. But to me, also, I think it is a theme Ms. Arendt brought up, namely, the theme of human measure, is one of the crucial themes here at this level of human relations, at this human systems level.

At the social systems level, is where, in a learning process, norms evolve. Norms: this means our own ethics of how to conduct and how to regulate our own systems. And that is the subject, by the way, of the normative planning theory of which Hasan Ozbekhan is one of the foremost exponents and which will, hopefully, become the core of a normative theory, of which only a few elements are gradually taking shape. One of the most important problems here is one of the unsolvable problems, but really not a problem, but a human condition; here, at this level, is a dichotomy between individual ethics and what [C. West] Churchman called ethics of whole systems. And right up to now in intact cultures, cast in formal religions or ideologies, we have been given a set of norms as a more or less rigid set, to apply in such a way that we can apply to our individual lives, so that we did not need to question what is good for the whole social system and what is not.

If we take our role as shaping our own system, the self-organizing systems, with man as a cybernetic actor in it, really, if we take this seriously, then we must question also the subject of the ethics of whole systems, and this, if you just start thinking—nobody has developed this in detail—if you just start thinking along these lines, it probably makes you aware that there are vast differences between the individual ethics by which we live and the ethics of whole systems. You can't, for example, make the thought experiments to say: people whom we regard as great people, great politicians, great artists, people who have done something which is recorded in history books, were their ethics personal ethics or were they an ethics of the whole system? I would think that many of the great politicians would probably not be recognized as so great from this point of view. I do not say that we resolve this to one side. It is one of these tensions, bipolar ways of making our life more dynamic, that we will constantly be moved either to the individual or to the system's side, and we have to live in between, we do not have to resolve it, we should not resolve it, but we should live in between and gain a source of energy by it.

And, at the highest level, the cultural systems, which is really the thing we ought to address most clearly in design, is where values evolve. And there we have to ask ourselves, in what ways can we guide, can we design this evolution of values? And I have heard here in this symposium several times that institutions, by which some people meant, obviously, organizations, which is a lower level of institutions, find values, or institutions as expressions of, or crystallizations of, value patterns, find a place in a static society; we have to develop the theme in a quite different way. We have to see how institutions, and by this I mean the institution of business, of government, of higher education, and so on, how they develop their roles, their role playing, just as in the way in which Geoffrey Vickers describes it, and thereby build these cultural systems, build these values, bring in the values, become the motor of it, you know. This is a nonphysical type of human system and institution, which is actually the active element in building the culture. I think this would be the most important, the core theme of any full approach to design. Well, I think I'd better stop here (I could go on).

Logue: Well, Arthur [Drexler], I think you've got a problem. You've got six people here and they all want to talk about what they want to talk about, not what Mr. Alexander wants to talk about. I'd like to say just briefly, however, I feel that not having read any of the material on [Mr. Alexander's] work, I feel teased. To somebody who's been involved with working with communities and urban renewal projects and giving them, I like to think, a real partnership, I've seen community involvement make plans a hell of a lot better, and a hell of a lot more acceptable, than they otherwise would have been. To carry that one step further, and say that, for example, in built-up communities, that you're going to allow them to design, that's where I feel teased. I'd like to know: Is the product very much different? I'd like to know why, if a housewife can design a house in a week, why it takes an architect three months? There's something not quite fully stated there, and I don't suppose there's time to state it this morning. So I think what I'd like to do is to ask Mr. Alexander's permission to send a couple of people, one an architect and one very definitely not an architect, out to Berkeley to see what he's up to. It's a new twist to me on the community participation we hear so much about, but I'd like to be sure that it is better and that the rather broad claims made for it this morning are, in fact, borne out.

ALEXANDER: Let's arrange that. I would prefer not, at the moment, to answer all the detailed things that were raised about my remarks, because one has come up, which is so fundamental that, unless we address it, I don't think we'll be able to get much further. And that is the question of whether there should be an elite doing this, or whether there should not.

Now, I oppose absolutely, the notions expressed by my friend here (or I shouldn't say my friend). It is, of course, central to the whole process of society today, and if we could go into this matter as to whether planning is to be done by an elite or whether it can, in fact, be done by everybody, we might get it straighter.

I was frankly astonished by what you said. It seems to me that in order to take the position that an elite is to do this, you have to assume that you have the right to certain pleasures and liberties, which you specifically want to withhold from others, and that is a rather far out state of affairs.

LOGUE: May I suggest that it's an argument without meaning, a discussion without meaning, because it's impossible in the United States today to proceed in that matter; it just can't be done. Maybe it could have been or should have been done, but it can't be done any longer.

ALEXANDER: But, that's a different question. The question of whether it's feasible is something else. He actually said that he didn't like the idea and that he thought it had to be done by an elite.

LOGUE: No, I didn't say I didn't like it. I'm saying the planning process of an elite doing it is not a relevant thing; it's impossible. It is not longer possible in the United States to have an elite do the planning, whatever kind of planning, your kind of planning, my kind of planning, anybody's kind of planning. It's no longer possible.

TUGWELL: Can I offer a possible illustration? My wife recently redesigned the kitchen in our house, and I tell you, I'm almost afraid to go into it, because it's so complicated, and I'm sure that if I touch anything it'll go to pieces. She did the arranging, but practically nothing in it was invented by her, it was all brought in from outside. It was the product of factory technology, and back of that, of course, a great deal of science and research, and so on. Now, you must be counting on a great background of technological material, which is not known to the people you're talking about, who are doing the designing. And this is the structure of our society today. These are the things we have to do with. Isn't that so?

ALEXANDER: One can make all of this available to people in a very, very simple way; this is the whole point.

TUGWELL: Yes, but all of these things are available now; more will be available in the future, and who will invent them? Who will produce them? Not the people you're talking about.

DREXLER: May I interpose something? It seems to me that underlying Mr. Alexander's effort is the assumption that, if people who have no special training and no demonstrated special ability are somehow enabled to manipulate the givens of technology, that new configurations will emerge that somehow bear a closer relationship to what those people would, indeed, prefer to have as their how-to-live arrangements. Is that reasonably accurate?

ALEXANDER: Yes.

DREXLER: All right. One could add to this the observation that among the existing elites, each one believes in the efficacy of the others. It is only within a given elite that its own efficacy is questioned. And I'm using the word *elite* as a very unsatisfactory term: what I mean by it is simply people who have been trained to do something.

LOGUE: I wouldn't say that is true.

DREXLER: Well, I think it is true, to the extent of a trained group that I'm familiar with, that is, architects.

LOGUE: I don't feel that way about architects.

DREXLER: You don't, but architects feel that way about architects.

LOGUE: I question the efficacy of the practice of architects—and lawyers.

DREXLER: Oh, you do question the efficacy of architects, then you know enough about the discipline to be able to question its efficacy. Well, the question—since the elites lose confidence in their own efficacy, then it is not too difficult to follow Mr. Alexander's impulse that one has to turn to something else in order to let something emerge—the question is, Is it really possible? Does it, in fact, yield anything in any way different?

ALEXANDER: May I give an example of the question that has to do with this elite/not-elite matter? I'm really addressing it to Mr. Logue. I'll just tell a story about one thing that happened up in Oregon. It had to do with something that is still happening. When we arrived on the scene, there was a proposal to build an extension to the student union building, at somewhere between two and three million dollars, a large hunk of a building which was going to be added onto the existing student union. Now, one of the patterns that came out of our work and that was then reviewed by the campus student-faculty committees that were working with us, essentially made the statement that centralized student unions were extremely bad for the campus community on the grounds that they established a particular piece of territory as being student territory, and, by implication, created at least the feeling that the rest of the university was not student territory, and that in order to bring these matters to rights it would be advisable to distribute the same facilities for coffee and snacks, recreation, and things like this, all over the campus, so that there's ready access from different departments and that there was some of it everywhere.

Now, we got into a fairly drawn-out political battle, because this three-million-dollar building was in the works (it was not under construction). And, then, the following kind of thing happened: it so happened that this building had been designed actually by a group of, well, the administrators of the union, of course, and a couple of architects, and quite a heavy representation of students. So that we were told that this was outrageous for us to be questioning this particular project, since this, of all projects, was the one which had had tremendous community involvement, represented the wishes of the people, etc. We doubted this, went into the matter, and found that the students who had been involved in this project were a particular, minute, special interest group attached by bonds of common intercourse with the people who were most anxious to push for this three-million-dollar building. They were representing themselves as spokesmen of the fifteen thousand students, but when we presented these notions to a small sample of students at large, we found that students by no means wanted this centralized student facility, and, in fact, thought that the plan that we had proposed was a much more sensible idea, which they wanted to do.

Now, at that point, tremendously hairy meetings were held, we were accused of trying to take three million dollars away from the university by threatening the project, etc., and what is now happening in order to settle the matter is that a very, very large random sample of students is being consulted, with the idea of ultimately having a student referendum on this matter. This is going on right now, and I'm quite confident that the results of this thing will be entirely different from the so-called student involvement in the earlier project.

Now, I think Mr. Logue is right, that there is a temper of the times which, in effect, insists that there be some form of representation of users, and this is quite true. But, my story illustrates the fact that unless this matter is taken seriously, wholeheartedly, and pushed all the way, you don't get the same results.

TUGWELL: Could you tell us how the referendum is worded; what's the question that's asked?

ALEXANDER: It's been a very, very delicate matter. Roughly, what's happening is that the two opposing views are each being given about three pages to explain themselves, and there is an exchange of views being held by the opposing parties, if you want to call them that. We're looking at one another's material, until we feel confident that they're adequate representations of what we believe. And then, it's being done first as a random sample.

TUGWELL: Well, I'm just interested in the parameters; this raises some very interesting questions, I think. What students are there for is an education, I suppose, and I think there's grave doubt being cast on the question of whether a campus is the right kind of thing to get an education from. And I suppose those are the questions that don't get asked at all. The institutional questions seem never to get asked; everybody assumes that the institution is there and it can't be questioned.

ALEXANDER: I think that one can easily make the mistake of taking every little question back to apple pie, god, and country, but the fact is, that there is a day-to-day reality in the matter.

TUGWELL: In other words, you do accept the conditions that are set.

ALEXANDER: No, I think it's perfectly proper to question the existence of the university, I think it is perfectly proper to question everything about the way it functions, but it is also sensible to question the construction of centralized student facilities, which are plainly going to do nothing but elaborate the previous order.

TUGWELL: Well, I don't think you've answered my question, but I know what the answer is, I think.

DREXLER: What would you do if the result of the referendum was the demand, or a demand, for a procedure that you thought, that you were convinced, was inimical to precisely the thing you were trying to accomplish?

ALEXANDER: What sort of procedure?

DREXLER: Well, you have a concept of what the physical configuration of this should be. You have some guiding idea about it.

ALEXANDER: Well, we've already made it clear that we're not even interested in pushing it unless somewhere of the order of seventy-five percent of the student body feels that it's right, because we don't want to be finicking around whether it's fifty-five or anything. If a massive body of support shows that this concept is actually more sensible than the one that is being proposed, then I think it should go ahead.

DREXLER: In other words, you're ready to sacrifice twenty-five percent of the student community? Well, I'm trying to get at something, that, at some point along the way, you are declaring prior rights, and you're doing it on a quantitative basis, not presumably on quality.

TUGWELL: The real question is that they may not be able to have what they want.

DREXLER: Well, evidently. But what I'm questioning is the mode in which the decision is arrived at. It apparently is being arrived at democratically, which means that it is a quantitative decision.

KRAMISH: No, I think this is a very, very crude technique. In this particular situation, I'm wondering whether the decision taken in this manner, for this body of students, this year, corresponds to the will of the body of students four years from now, and their thinking, the temper of the times, etc. After all, this is a more or less permanent institution, or at least something for twenty or thirty years, which you're setting up.

PERCIVAL GOODMAN: Mr. Chairman, you know, I don't think we're here to debate whether Mr. Alexander's pattern language is a correct method of handling the particular subject that we are here for. And I think that we're wasting a lot of peoples' time in quibbles about what Mr. Alexander's idea is about. His theory, whether correct or incorrect, will be demonstrated by the kind of proposals he makes, notably, to try them out in practice; and I think we ought to discuss what this conference is about, and we have very little time, we have just a little over an hour left to get down to some brass tacks. And I see great guys, like Tugwell and Logue, and my dear friend Hannah Arendt, here, and I think that they have a lot to say, and I think I'd like to hear what they have to say. And I'd like to say something.

DREXLER: I am sorry if we've seemed to focus too heavily on Christopher Alexander's work, but it seemed to me that he is involved in the ethical confrontation that we're trying to identify, as, indeed, is Mr. Logue, and everyone else here. Percy, do you want to ask a specific question of members of the panel?

GOODMAN: I didn't want to ask a specific question, I wanted to give a specific recommendation.

DREXLER: All right. You want us not to talk about Mr. Alexander's work.

GOODMAN: Well, yes. It seems to me that we are gathered here for the purpose of discussing what kind of new teaching methods would be usable in
our time, because apparently the present teaching methods for teaching
about the environment, and how to solve the problems of the physical environment, are unsatisfactory. Otherwise, none of us would be here. We all
agree with that. Both teachers and practitioners agree with that. I think that's
what we ought to talk about, and not talk about a whole set of rather vague
principles, when we are, in fact, in a rather desperate situation. And I think
it's a desperate situation—unless we're all just twiddling our thumbs—that
has led many people to give up a weekend when we don't have too many
weekends to give up.

DREXLER: Does anybody on the panel want to address himself immediately to
that formulation of what this discussion is?

LOGUE: I'm sure Mr. Tugwell does, and I know I do.

DREXLER: Fine.

TUGWELL: Well, I guess so, but you and I are the voice of experience, perhaps,
or something like that.

JANTSCH: I've certainly come here to discuss the Universitas Project, which is
supposed to be something different from existing architecture and city-
planning departments.

DREXLER: Well, gentlemen, Mr. Tugwell, will you lead off on it?

TUGWELL: I don't know that what I would volunteer would be of the nature of
what you're talking about, but it does seem to me that this Universitas proposal, from its very name, carries a very large connotation. Now, what I have
to say is, perhaps, irrelevant to what you have in mind as a school of design,
or a university of design, but it is my conviction that unless the environment
is freed, far more than it is at the present time, from man-made strictures (not
those imposed by nature because designers have always had to accept what
nature imposes and to work with them); but we ourselves, as a community,
as a civilization, have imposed unnecessary restrictions on ourselves, it seems
to me, so that we're not free as we should be to make a civilization, and, shall
I say, educational institutions, which are necessary and acceptable under the
circumstances. And the circumstances, of course, are the increase of technology and the great difficulty there is for any student now to arrive at a point
where he can work on the frontiers of technology. This is a very difficult discipline at the present time. I often say I'm very glad that I was educated fifty

years ago and don't have to go through it now, because I don't think I'd make it, and maybe some of the rest of us wouldn't. But some will, and they'll work with this great structure of technology which has come down to us, and which we now have to work with.

And it's a very bad thing, I think, a very dangerous thing, to have stupid people working with this, because they can be very dangerous. They can be very dangerous if we give them the technological results of what's been done over the past, and allow them to arrange it the way they want to and to do the things they want to do with it. And I think this is, perhaps, our chief problem at the present time. Our elite that you talk about is working for people they ought not to be working for. And it's very dangerous, very dangerous indeed; it's so dangerous that it involves cataclysm. And we all know that now, and yet we don't change the institutions that have allowed it to come about. So I would plead for more freedom to arrange resources, to plan resources, the developing resources, the new technologies together with what nature gives us and is giving us, in ways that will contribute to, shall I say, social utility, or the kind of life that we would like to have. And I think that we can gain that freedom, but we can only gain it by changing some institutions to which we have very great attachments, and sometimes don't realize how they constrain what it is that we ought to be doing at the present time. Well, I do not want to develop this too far, Mr. Chairman, but this is my thought.

DREXLER: Could you identify some of the institutions you're referring to that ought to be changed?

TUGWELL: Well, they go to government, of course; they go to economics. We have, for instance, if we talk about the city and architecture, the architect works within constraints, which he ought not have to work within. Suppose, for instance, in your imagination, that land was not controlled by people who make a speculative profit out of it, but was controlled by the public. I don't necessarily think that the public ought to own it, but the public ought to have the say about what it's to be used for. And if it did have that say, and if we had equalized values, we could then look forward to the planners using resources, or allocating the resources, to use that land in ways which would contribute to the kind of civilization we want. And the designer could then make the kinds of things that we would like to live with and in. That's only one illustration, but you can think of many others, of course.

But, think of what this implies for government, for instance. It implies that government shall do a great deal more and, perhaps, a great deal less in some ways, than it's doing at the present time. The cities would have to be freed from the constraints that they have now from overhead. This runs, I think, to no less than the abolition of the states, as we know them now. The only source of funds for the purposes that we have in mind comes from the nation as a whole. They come from what we call the federal government. That's where the tax powers lie; that's where the representative government has its center. And we decide that those people who go to Washington shall be able to lay our taxes and to distribute them. And they ought not to go through several layers of bureaucracy in order to get to where they're supposed to be used. And when they do get to where they can be used, there ought to be freedom for the designers to use them in ways which we've decided we'd like to have them used.

LOGUE: First, I would like to agree with Mr. Tugwell on the really extraordinary importance of institutional and organizational change. I don't happen to agree with him that planning should be separated out in the way he has proposed so eloquently and for so long. But I think we have adequate examples of the kind of institutional changes that can be made in the United Kingdom, where they've just, in this past year, created a Ministry of Environment, which I would suppose everybody in this room would think would be the finest thing that could happen in the United States if we could do it tomorrow, and I don't think we'll get to that.

JANTSCH: No, I don't.

LOGUE: Well, we can get to that. Now, what they've done in the way of reorganizing London into a two-tier system, a lot of people feel would be a great thing for the City of New York. And the way they have public control of land without public ownership would do an awful lot—they have a lot to teach us.

But I'd like to speak from another perspective, if I may, as, if you will, a potential customer or employer of the graduates of this institution. I sometimes feel that if we ever create this institution it will only have a faculty and students who will become part of the faculty and not go out and work.

But, over the last fifteen years or more I guess I've hired some, at least, five hundred professionals, and for most of that time I've been conscious of the fact that they're inadequately educated, and they've got to learn on the job, whether they come from architecture or, particularly, city-planning schools, or law schools. Now, I think we have a need for an institution of this kind, and I'd like to make some very pragmatic comments about it.

I can't resist the comment that after, I guess it's seventeen years in this business, the idea that design and construction are ready for the post-technological society seems to me stretching the facts by a rather wide margin. And, I know that after three and a half years of dealing with architects and contractors in New York, we're nowhere near the industrial society.

TUGWELL: Not to mention the unions.

LOGUE: Well, we right now pay a thousand dollars per dwelling unit more than we should because Local 3 of the Electrical Workers Union will not allow us to use BX cable. It's a very pragmatic problem, and they tell you what they'll do to the BX cable if you try to put it in anyway.

But, I said in my paper, where I obviously had a difficult time making the transition to the somewhat rarefied atmosphere here, that we had to be wary of discarding established concepts like urban renewal and public housing just because they've made so many mistakes, particularly in the area of design. I tried to suggest that most of those mistakes were made because design was rather low on the priority list. And then I used, as I've done before, the example of three people: the late A. Whitney Griswold, the President of Yale, Richard C. Lee, the long-time Mayor of New Haven, and myself, as three ignorant people coming to power, you might say, in New Haven at more or less the same time. And, I can show you in New Haven the three different buildings that each of us was first responsible for, and they're awful. Mine is the Southern New England Telephone Company, a gross building. But yet if you look, somehow or other, Griswold, clearly an educated man, Dick Lee, clearly not an educated man, and me, a lawyer, we somehow, I like to think, learned. But, there was no formal process for that learning. It's quite obvious that whatever process there is, there's nobody in the telephone company anywhere in the United States who's ever been exposed to it. I can tell a telephone building in any state in the union without having it identified to me.

Now, this does suggest, not that we somehow try to identify decision makers and the power elite in their graduate and undergraduate years, but it does suggest that we ought to be able to find a way to train people in an interdisciplinary way so that they'll be available for these decision makers in a significant way. And I, therefore, am inclined to think that this university shouldn't focus only on design, it should focus on what *Time* called "urbanology." I get a little bit frightened at the tendency here to reach out into all of the disciplines so that this educational process would never end. I get concerned about the notion that somehow we can begin somewhere other than now and somewhere other than here. We have to begin here and now.

I get concerned that there's a discussion about whether we begin with a power elite, because, in fact, only the power elite has the resources to provide the salaries that will make the faculty come here instead of somewhere else. But we also have to consider, in a way that we haven't, so far as I am aware, the powerless. This is the first meeting I've been to in a very, very long time where there hasn't been a single Black face. And I think their involvement and the involvement of other minorities in other parts of the country, is something that needs to be part of this institution.

Finally, it seems to me that if I were to take [as an example]—because I don't deal as easily in abstractions as examples—we have a very extraordinary institution in Berkeley, and this symposium, somehow or other, reflects that because more people come from Berkeley, from the College of Environmental Design, than from any three other institutions represented here. If we can get the superb preparation that is being given to students at that college, in all of its disciplines, and we can somehow or other marry it with the discipline that's provided at the Harvard Business School, because, finally, these things do get settled on the way you raise and spend money, and if we can somehow or other add to that, if I may pick my own favorite school of public affairs, the Yale Law School, the people who make things happen in government, we could turn to people like that: we who are in this business in the public sector, could turn to people who had that kind of training, without it taking them ten years so that they're useless for productive work, they would find ready employment very quickly.

I would hope that it would be a problem-solving institution, and I take the trouble to say that because I tried for many years to work with the Joint Center for Urban Studies at Harvard and MIT, and I found that they were a problem-creating institution not a problem-solving institution. I think they've now tried to turn that around.

Finally, I suggest, and I might as well say it bluntly, that I hope it will be the hallmark of this institution that it has the ability to communicate, not one faculty member with another in esoteric language that is not used in decision-making chambers, but the ability to communicate with decision makers who can make these things happen.

It's interesting, again, Mr. Tugwell, that as we think about all of this, that there is an institution like this, somewhat like this, at least, as I understand it, in the process of formation in the United Kingdom; it's the Staff College being created for the Ministry of Environment. So maybe we should be in London and not here.

JANTSCH: I would like to attack Mr. Logue on at least three of the notions that I found so wrong in his speech. And the first one is that the Universitas Project should be problem solving. I think this technological mode of thinking is about the most dangerous you can find in dealing today with society, and, as far as I'm concerned, it has broken down. There are no problems to be solved, once and forever, as there are in planning by networks, and so on, for technological products: where you have a problem with the material, you develop the material, then this problem is solved, and you go on to the next problem. In society it's quite different than that.

And, as Hasan Ozbekhan once said—he isn't here—there is a *problematique,* which is something quite different, which is a dynamic situation evolving that has such characteristics that, from time to time, on the surface, something you might identify as a temporal problem comes up, and you can do something about it but you can never solve it.

The second notion I would like to rectify here, and this same notion has been brought up by our chairman before, is that you should train people. Training people means to me you duplicate existing skills or you stuff them with accumulated knowledge. And, Mr. Logue said that you should train people for interdisciplinary work. You cannot train people for interdisciplinary work; you can stuff them with various disciplines, but not for interdisciplinary work, because interdisciplinary work is organization toward a purpose, and that means you have to make these people creative, you have to make them designers. You have, also, to make the scientists into interdisciplinary designers, and that cannot be done by training; that can be done by work and stimulation.

And, the third thing is that Berkeley would have such a fine College of Environmental Design. I am in a position to comment on that because I was a faculty member there last year. And I can tell you Berkeley is a very fine university in one thing: because there, as in no other university I have seen in the world, the thinking of the students has split from the thinking of the faculty. The students are the ones who are motivated and purposefully oriented in an interdisciplinary way. They know what they want, they go around and use those faculty members who are willing to play with them, in this way. They use them as resource persons. And, I must say, I've learned more from them than they have from me. And, they were all very happy in this. But you have in the faculty this rigidification, this establishment of rules, the compulsory establishment of methods, even. If you don't use, in several departments, Berkeley's method of statistics you are not considered qualified to teach at Berkeley. If you do not express your papers in applied behavioral science terms, which is one of the most dangerous fads around in Anglo-American countries, I think, then you are asked to leave, whether you have tenure or not. So I think the same, by the way, also holds—these old stereotypes of decades ago, you cannot use them anymore. You cannot use the Harvard Business School anymore, the Harvard Business School is gone, you know; there are a few intelligent students there, who know what to look for and how to apply it, but for all those who study the case method—what has been done and the idea of applying the same cases in the future—it's utter rubbish.

We have to improve, and we have a new challenge before us, and we have to live up to that challenge, and I thought the Universitas Project was about that challenge and not using the "fine examples" of this or that existing school.

LOGUE: May I comment? I think it's interesting (I, of course, don't agree with any of that), it has been true for at least forty years, I guess, that the cream of the applicants for law schools in the United States, deeper than any other institution, have gone to Yale and Harvard. And there are many people, and when I was a student at Yale I felt it; we thought we were the reason, as students, for the greatness of the institution. Somehow or other, the students remained great, and the faculty, maybe they're just a convenient reason for the students to gather. I think there's more to it than that: the same thing is true at the Harvard Business School. They get the pick of the students interested in that, and maybe the faculty are all old fools, but somehow or other they must perform some function and teach some classes. It may also be true that, and as far as I know it is true, that the students are what give distinctive quality to the College of Environmental Design, but the fact that the faculty are there must bring a few of them. I think that is nonsense.

Second, the notion that you can't train people interdisciplinarily, and that they have to come to work situations half-prepared, I think is nonsense. I know it's nonsense, as someone who has to take untrained people and make planners understand something about law, and make lawyers understand something about finance—that they would be more useful public servants if they had a more full education. And, I think this urban problem in this country is in such a mess that we need as many fully trained possible people as quickly as we can get them.

And, I realize that one can make a distinction between research of various kinds, but I do think that there is merit in a problem-solving approach. I do think, for example, that if the systems approach, if you like, were applied to the problem of abandonment in New York City, a serious and growing problem, with the same level of resources and commitment that some of the NASA problems were dealt with, that that would be useful, and I would hope that we would not try to do that with in-house government staff but that this Universitas would do that. If it was to be just another place for scholars to get together and talk to one another, I, at least, don't think it would be useful, and since I happen to know that there is a limited amount of resources which can be employed in this area, I would hope that if this ever got to be a decision that I could persuade people that you were wrong, and that we expect useful work out of this outfit.

JANTSCH: Don't tell me that, because I never said "no useful work."

LOGUE: *Immediately* useful work.

JANTSCH: More useful work, then.

LOGUE: There are problems that government is not solving that perhaps this institution could solve, or suggest a solution to.

TUGWELL: May I put in a word of caution? I had some experience as a teacher, and some experience even as an undergraduate teacher, and the worst thing that happened to us in undergraduate colleges of my experience was that the people who wanted students after we got through with them were determined to dominate our curriculum. It seems to me that you're asking that you be allowed to determine the kind of education that people have that you happen to want.

LOGUE: Excuse me, that's true of everybody on the panel here.

TUGWELL: Would you deny that for me, please?

LOGUE: No, I won't deny it; furthermore, I think it's true of everybody who's spoken. But, that, perhaps, is why what I really want is something like the Ministry of Environment Staff College. Because, after all, the Yale Law School is not going to shut down when this thing opens up.

TUGWELL: I just don't think that's good enough. I don't think any of you people who are operating ought to determine what kind of education the next generation has.

LOGUE: Who should?

TUGWELL: If you want to train them, you train them after you get them.

ALEXANDER: This is just getting extremely confusing. I'd like to ask Emilio Ambasz to clarify the following point, please. Are we talking about a university whose function is to define a new way of living, or are we talking about a university which is going to provide professionals for UDC? Now, these are totally different ideas. I'm getting absolutely confused, one moment I think I'm talking about one, then the other. Please clarify this point.

EMILIO AMBASZ: America has given a great contribution to surrealism, and I don't see why this project should not be seen in that light. The intention of the Universitas Project was certainly not to produce a situation where there would be a production— understanding the Universitas in terms of participants in a production system as established. So, therefore, it was never intended to be producing people that would be serving the present needs. If one were to define the specifications as to what institutions need, I think they wouldn't be asking for that because then they would have to assume the responsibility of those they trained for their own performances. After their functions or their needs become obsolete in five years, are you going to become a patrician, and sponsor all your peasants, while they walk around? You have the responsibility of having asked for them, so you have to assume it.

   As for the Universitas, it was first seen, of course, when it would go into the implementative the stage, there are three or four different ways of going about that. One simple way would be to say, fine, the sun is rising in Peking, we can all go there, and this is one proper context for total participation, indeed, there is one system there. The other one is to say that, indeed, we want a university that has no place. It is everywhere, and perhaps one can use the example of the UNESCO or a center for information, which is constantly exchanging communication, and that there would be another type of model. A third model that one can have is to say, indeed, if we have to wait for a total set of social structures to be changed before the Universitas comes about, it will not come about; the intention of the Universitas was that it should, perhaps, participate in the changes through its actions.

As to how you would define the context, how it could operate, I can only give a private opinion, and it's not the institution's opinion, of how we would go about it. After all, the Museum can only initiate a thing like that, present an idea, in terms of its responsibility in the forefront of institutions concerned with the creation of the man-made environment. It cannot assume the responsibility for implementing them.

But, if one were to assume the responsibility for implementing it here in the United States, one could say that, perhaps, the only place where it could be done, and, again, I say this as a guess, would be in New York State, perhaps because it is the only state so far that has the Napoleonic system, in the sense that it has an Urban Development Corporation that has the power to implement some of its decisions. It has a state university system, which is in the process of growth. It has a Metropolitan Transportation Authority perhaps in the beginnings of some coordination of its transportation system. So the problem of where the Universitas could start is everybody's guess.

My proposal would be that I would start the Universitas in the context of a new city, and have a real new city, and a situation where we create a city with, let's say, just a guess, seventy, eighty thousand people, where the Universitas is, in a certain way, the laboratory. Or, let's say the city is the laboratory for the Universitas—but the Universitas is, in its turn, to perform two types of functions: one is to be a reflective function, or a reflective role, for the inhabitants of the city, the other is to fulfill some active roles in how the inhabitants can change their city. That would mean, of course, public authority that owns the land and doesn't sell it. Whether they want that piece of property without the Universitas, whether it would be a Ledoux scheme, where we have now, in the middle of the city, the Universitas and we no longer have the boroughs, as it was said yesterday, it may be seen in that utopian category. If it is so designed that infrastructures capable of admitting certain changes in elements, which can later be subtracted, the fact that the Universitas is in the middle of it, and it can later be removed or changed, or through its action become the Universitas of the whole city, as a metaphor, it's another thing.

You were just saying that new cities are to be created. You can then have a sort of tactical device: go around the other way, say, well the experience of the British, as you know, Mr. Logue, has been quite clear. New cities created, which have not the investment of tertiary industry, in terms of research and services, have usually become dormitories to the existing cities to which they were neighbors. In this case, if you were to say, well, a new city has to be started not as a decision from an educational or social viewpoint but, eminently, as an economical decision, you would have to say that one of the, perhaps, industries to eradicate would be a university. If you were to say what type of university you would have, at this moment, to say as an experimental situation, then perhaps the university should be one concerned with the city itself, which means physical design, social and economical design. Were you to say what type of participation the individuals would have in that situation, well, you could perhaps go and be relatively strategic and say that should you be a permanent university, you have tax benefits, as you know, in a certain way, from a federal source.

So, if I were to strategically take a decision on how you can operate in the present system and establish it, you can say: fine, seventy thousand people can populate such a city, or such an institution. But the fact that they are students of a university and they have a number of federal benefits, they would react in talking about a model which exists in an interstice. But the actions of the members of the city, the production of theirs, is their own life; that's the cultural production. They are constantly changing—constantly changing, of course, assuming that they are students of that Universitas, and by students I mean participants, I do not mean a situation of the receiving end. But it was never particularly intended that we should be proposing a university to train people to perform certain tasks for already-existing institutions. That was very clearly the point.

ALEXANDER: I'm not talking about training *anybody*, as far as I'm concerned.

AMBASZ: Indeed, I am not talking about training. That's the last thing we're talking about.

DREXLER: Are you assuming that the product of the model that you've just described has some bearing on the rest of the society in which it occurs?

AMBASZ: Well, yes, indeed. Number one, you should perfectly well make clear one simple point, that on my head there are several hats. One of them is the one that has formulated, perhaps in a relatively abstract way, this problem of the Universitas postulated as a set of needs, and then brought a number of people to help us elucidate what this Universitas should be, and this was the purpose of having asked for the papers and also the purpose of having gathered people to discuss each other's contributions, so we can perhaps arrive at a certain set of ideas; whether they're contradictory or not is not the point.

If we're talking about the Universitas as having a bearing upon society, perhaps I don't get your point: what I meant, in this case, when I was talking about a product of that city, would be for having in the case of a master example—getting instructions, being trained, and responding accordingly—perhaps the idea of creating a seventy- or eighty-thousand-member city in the State of New York, as an example, as a pilot project—that has a long history in America. After all, America has been the place where most of the European utopias have been created, so it's about time that a certain type of American utopia be enacted in the United States. Whether, by its type of actions or by its operations, it would have a bearing on society, I, personally, would limit it, in the sense that it's seventy to eighty thousand people, where the Universitas produces two types of informational roles: it is aware of the effects of the processes which occur in its city, and, therefore, it evaluates them, it reflects upon them, and perhaps—with the participation of the citizens—proposes certain changes. And for that I insist the Universitas may have a skeleton staff of people who are educators and physical designers, social and economical designers, but they are not the ones that postulate all things: it has to be done in participation with the members of the city. They have a second role, which is that of bringing information in from the outside from other cities, of introducing it, and in that way it has, of course, the complementary role of exporting information and, in that way, the bearing [on society], if that was your question?

DREXLER: Yes, it was the question, and I think you have answered it, except for one thing that I'm a little, myself, unclear about. It seems to me clear enough that nothing in the [Working] Paper, in the formulation, suggests that the purpose of the Universitas is to simply staff the existing organizational procedures in order to confirm and reinforce the present methods. At the same time, if the model of the Universitas, wherever it might be located, if indeed it has a physical location, it seems to me that in order to perpetuate itself it must, in some sense, be involved in problem-solving. All right.

Then, on this basis, presumably it does at least connect up with existing and available technologies.

AMBASZ: We're only talking about the facts of the resources which exist to make it possible, to only happen in one circumstance, perhaps, and it may be perhaps a totally erroneous evaluation.

DREXLER: All I'm trying to do is see if I can effect some bridgehead between what seemed to me not really as opposed positions, as they might otherwise be made to seem.

LOGUE: I want to comment on that a bit. I'm sure you're not serious in thinking that I have the notion that this whole institution should be created to serve the institution that I am responsible for; it just happens that there are quite a few such institutions. If the Universitas is going to come into being, unless you're going to propose that a whole new set of institutions be created, unless you're going to propose that these people go out and do work unrelated to their educational experience, I suggest, respectfully, that they're going to have to work for existing institutions. But, more important, if they were better trained than the product we get now, I think they would do much better work and they'd correct some of the mistakes that we're making before we make them. And, then I'd like to make you an offer: it so happens that the State University of New York at Buffalo is building a new campus north of Buffalo in a town called Amherst, and it just so happens that we're going to build a New Town around it. I don't know whether we can wait till you get created, but, in fact, the situation exists. It's not eighty thousand, it's about thirty thousand, and we may have a lot of time to wait because we're being sued.

We're being sued for a reason which is interesting, and maybe the Universitas would help ameliorate; it's a national problem, which is that suburban people in this suburb don't like the idea of having as neighbors some of the Black poor people that we're going to bring in because they're going to work at the university we expect. But when you try to take that specific piece of land, some three thousand acres in all, and that very large educational institution, and this New Town planned around it, I respectfully suggest that if the Universitas were in being it would be up to its eyeballs in problem solving immediately. And I wouldn't care what you called it, I'd be satisfied with your nomenclature.

DREXLER: Yes, that's what I meant about how it would perpetuate itself. Ms. Arendt, would you like to comment on some of this?

ARENDT: Well, I was struck by a few things, which I will just throw out. Number one was the business of the elite, which really occurred in everything—in every single one of the discussions. Now, Mr. Alexander had the question of the elite: it's of course always the same, namely, who selects the elite? And Mr. Alexander had a certain proposition of a self-selected elite. Of course, it would be, as Mr. Tugwell said, a wonderful thing for very few people, and the question then always is, as in all these plans, whether this will become an elite. I will, for a moment, disregard that this word has such a bad connotation, and just take it for what it actually says, because we can very badly do without it. So either this becomes actually an elite, that is, something which will put certain standards of living, of having an environment, of having communication, etc., on others, or it will become one of the many, many little communes and communities which we know from history, which never had a very long life to live until it was being absorbed again into the society at large. We can, of course, say that the whole crisis today is the crisis of the elites. That is, that those who are in power and who are the elites and partly empowered by ourselves are no longer recognized by us as an elite, and the whole antiestablishment mood, which I share, is still very typical.

Now, the question is, What can one do? And, I also don't quite know what one means by training for interdisciplinary work, except that I know that everybody talks about it today, and it has become a fad. Mr. Logue has limited this, and then I would agree that if he says somebody who's trained in law ought to know a little bit about finances, and somebody who's trained in economics had better know about the law, too. But that is not what is usually meant by that. What is meant is to educate people in such a way that they can take part in the whole spectrum of modern life; whether this can be done, the word *interdisciplinary* is very bad for that. Actually, every normal education should enable the citizen qua citizen to take part to the extent of his ability in as many spectra of public life as there are. So, there's actually only an education for citizenship. How can one make this education for citizenship, which must be done at the undergraduate level, because on the graduate level specialization is absolutely essential, how can that be done with universities of eighty to one hundred thousand people? I don't know, and I don't believe that's possible, and I think all these institutions are in a crisis today, and it's very, very questionable whether the world will survive this century—including the university.

When this gentleman (whose name I don't know) proposes a model city, with a very interesting limited number—you know Plato said 5,400—so you say eighty thousand, but the notion is pretty much the same, isn't it? And, if you would do that, it would be only, as I see it, a variation of what Mr. Alexander actually proposes, that is, to put models according to which living standards [would be formed], by which we would eliminate this obnoxious business of abstract standards, and the so-called values where nobody knows where these values are actually derived from, etc. That is, you want to put forward examples: to put examples is, or can of course be, very fruitful; it is politics, whether you call yourself architects, or whatever, this means to go into politics.

I'm pretty sure that something or other will arise in the next twenty or thirty years, simply because it is a question not even of life or death. I was struck by the word *urbanology*, that is, the science of the city, and I thought should that be like the science of philosophy, where the owl of Minerva flies only when the day is over? Doesn't urbanology, that is, really the science of the cities and that we want to discuss, and to study it now—what has been there simply up to now—doesn't that spell the death of the cities? I think that the great cities actually may be saved by problem solving here and there, but, by and large, I think the great age of the great cities is really over. And the notion that came up here, of the eighty thousand or Plato's 5,400, seems to me very typical, because many people actually think along these lines though they don't know to put it as articulately as you do.

DREXLER: Mr. Castells.

MANUEL CASTELLS: I was very interested by the discussion of this morning on Mr. Alexander's thesis, which is, in my opinion, directly related to the Universitas Project if he assumes that it is not to project on a new professional situation. And I think this is good preparation for some kind of dialectic between utopia and politics: I mean, the propositions of Mr. Alexander are pointing to the problem of technocracy and to the call of freedom for the people to have their own environment. But the answer, the logical answer, is how can you manage when you have institutions, when you have economical determination of the world, and, finally, if it is true, that it is just in utopia where you have it. But, of course, that kind of discussion will continue always. The point is that social practice in history now is asking this kind of question in a practical way. For instance, I had a group of students who are making a study of China, on urban practices of the Chinese revolution. They were in China this year, and they found that in the Chinese urban communities, the people are building up their communities in the way in which Mr. Alexander was speaking about. I mean, they're using, of course, technicians, but the division of labor is a technical division, not a social division. And, I mean that the possibility to change, to adapt their forms and their wills and their dispositions of the special forms is being done by a continual discussion between the people and the technicians, who are also teaching the people. But that's possible not only because of social and political revolutions, and so on, but because of continual revolution. That has been possible now, and was not possible before the cultural revolution of Chiang.

So, I want to say, of course, you have to build, to realize also important goals; you have to build institutional problems. But, in the meantime, have we nothing to do? I don't know, but I think we always have something to do because we are always in change. But, the things to do are not the same in the different stages of the process of change. That means that to go directly to the final goal could be a bit dangerous for the same goals you are trying to defend.

I mean, more completely, the work done by Mr. Alexander or the work that could be made by an institution, such as the Universitas Project, has to be done as an alternative solution. It can be a utopian project, and that must probably be quite dangerous because it's going to be thought of as a prototype. I mean it is going to be sold in the same way that the Bauhaus objects are now being sold everywhere in the world. But the other possibility, of course, is to try to do something in the way of disrupting society, and, I think that the real alternative is not between utopian and ideological projects but between a professional institution on one side and a disruptive institution on the other side, which means that kind of disruptive institution, that is a theoretical problem we don't have solved.

DREXLER: Mr. Kepes.

GYORGY KEPES: I was listening with a certain type of irritated interest yesterday to many of us, and myself included, and I was very happy when Percy Goodman reminded us that we came here for a purpose. And I assume it is a very good idea to remind us again that we try to find some way, a frame of reference, to place this very complex problem that we are speaking about. And, as I was listening to the last few speakers, including Ms. Arendt, I felt that we forget a very essential, embracing variable, which is really our crisis of scale.

When you are speaking about an environmental reduction, when you have a small city, whether it is an image or model of Plato, or is a new model, we forget that we are living in a fabric of a total situation. Just to dramatize it, I was reading recently of pollution in Holland, which is rather devastating, which has not originated in Holland but which has originated in Western Germany, and there is a certain unit of the total field where they are completely undefended against events, processes which are beyond their particular political system.

Now, when we are projecting a small city with this absolutely beautiful, crystal clear Universitas, and, just again to dramatize a point, for some rather known reasons, we will have some pollution, really on a fatal level, and invade this beautiful little crystal universe, then we are really confronted with our essential problem. And our major issue, what we all have to face individually, institutionally, and at every level, is this new scale. And, if we try to invert the direction of this and assume that we have a beautiful prototype, this whole resolution in a small scale, as a model for the future, I think we have a very dangerous kind of misguided notion about the total.

I think what [Castells] said, I very much agree that we have two kinds of tasks to face. One is really a university of subversion, an institution that faces reality and can be angry, passionately angry about issues that we have to be angry about. And this anger has to find its focus.

And, yesterday, when I was angry myself, I was not very articulate. But what I tried to say is that there are very important spokesmen, in every stage of history, with the anger of men with the image of a better world. During the beginning of the Industrial Revolution, when England was first polluted, and the light, the color, and the space disappeared from the life of the individual, there was the artist's imaginative power, the angry artist's imaginative power—sometimes the anger was not explicit—that projected the images of light, color, really the most invaluable orchestration of a [J. M. W.] Turner, [John] Ruskin, or [John] Constable. And when the immense creative power began to be degraded, it was a [William] Blake image for the creative imagination that gave the direction of how to look at it. And, if you read carefully nineteenth-century history, it has just everything that we are talking about. If you look at the connection, for example, between Turner and [Joseph] Paxton: you may know Paxton's proposal to the British government to fight against pollution and create beautiful arcades through the whole of London, where one can still live a human life. I feel, if we speak about what we are speaking about, without neglecting this tremendously significant ingredient—the imaginative power of the man who still has within himself the ability to feel coherently and feel with an intensity, or the glow of this intensity—then we neglect something, very much so.

If you look at what happens among the young people, the underprivileged, and the artists, there are three issues which come to the fore. One is the kind of technological fetishism or utopia—Bucky Fuller is a hero with a big halo, and everybody is dreaming about finding a new system when everything will be resolved. And, again, I have to confess I was listening with great irritation to the new type of technological fetishism, which is semiology— which is in our new education industry. And, I fear there are great dangers: again, an assumption that by having this tool and polishing this tool you can resolve the essential.

The other major issue, where the young people are involved, and justly involved, is the social revolution. I do not speak on any political platform or anything like that, but there is a system, which evidently didn't live up to the new demands of the scale. And the system has to be changed. And this change has to find its tools. Now, until the last maybe hundred years, there were different proposals to find the technology of change. We have different conditions now, and we have to find a different technology of revolution.

And the last, which seems to me the most important—it was quite neglected here—is if you look around, almost the most significant part of the present scene is the young search for a lifestyle. The inner emptiness, the ego prison: man cannot bear anymore his own prison, and he tries to find a new community, and his new community has many ramifications, many aspects. And this one we just neglected, because assuming that if we resolve adequately the environmental transformation, we have still a tremendous major task to face, the man who is suddenly facing a new cosmos, first with a new knowledge of science, and second, the new cosmos of this new scale of complete interdependence, but where we have to respect the fact of life. And, I think, if one could start this conference again, I think we should first outline the coordinates, survey the variables, and try to work within this clearly defined territory the issues that we should explore. Forgive me, sir, for taking too much time.

DREXLER: Thank you. Mr. Goodman. We have about five minutes left and one other person has raised a hand.

GOODMAN: It seems to me that everything that Mr. Kepes just said I really support one hundred percent, and what I'm saying, in certain ways, is an extension, on a different level, of what he said, I think, very eloquently indeed.

I don't think there's any point in trying to teach something new unless you have something new to teach. One of the things I think that we have to teach is this question of what Mr. Kepes calls a new scale. Now I call it a change, in the good old Marxian way, of quantity to quality. You know, you put straws on a camel's back, at some point that last straw breaks the back. And, it seems to me that the quality of our life today has become of that sort, and that the last straw is about to be put on the back. This morning's *Times*, for example, gave a beautiful example of it. The Tokyo metropolitan government is considering establishing radio links with most of the city's schools, to provide an early warning system against the so-called photochemical, or "white smog." Schoolchildren have been among those most severely affected by this smog, which is produced by the action of strong sunlight and oxygen in the exhaust gas from vehicles. Many thousands of Tokyo residents were reported to have suffered from sore throats and sore eyes last year as the result of this smog.

Now this is a sort of building up of what we all can look forward to. Now, it seems to me that our job here, at least from my point of view, is the problem of the physical environment. The problem of the physical environment in our time consists of vast population increases. It consists of the possible exhaustion of resources if they are used as they are presently being used. And it consists of a pollution that Kepes just mentioned. And, it consists, also, of the fact that when the developing countries, as they are called, develop to the level of the United States or Holland or Germany, what happens to resources, what happens to the pollution, and the rest of it?

Now, we all think we are bored to death with what the ecologists have been saying about population, and the rest of it. We all know what the principle of doubling is: and the principle of doubling is, simply, that there are three and a half billion people in the world today, and by the year 2000, twenty-eight years from now, there will be roughly twice that number of people, and some thirty years later, there'll be twice *that* number of people. So, instead of having three and a half billion people, there will be seven billion, and then fourteen billion people. Now, if the amount of pollution that exists at the present time is intolerable to the Tokyo schoolchildren, I think it will be pretty fantastic by that time.

Now, I wanted to take up another problem, and I'm giving this because I think it is the background for a curriculum. It has been estimated that if the developing countries developed, that we would need about ten times the amount of energy used when they were developed than if they had not been developed. And, in view of the fact that the United States now uses thirty-five percent of the world's energy produced annually, how are you going to provide for this increase in energy, especially when it has been proven, I think, rather dramatically, that our resources are exhaustible, and they will be exhausted not too far hence. Recently, it was said that by the year 1980 we will have used up all but ten percent of our oil resources in this country, and we will have to go to oil resources that are very difficult to get out of the ground, and the rest of it.

And so we go on. How are we going to provide for the kind of population growths that are talked about in the world today, when in order to provide for a decent standard of living, according to these technological standards that everyone seems so blithely to take for granted here, if we find that, for example, in the Netherlands (as Kepes has mentioned the Netherlands), in 1968, the people in the Netherlands used twice as much tin, I give that as one example because it struck me as being outstanding, as all the people of Africa—thirteen million people using more tin than 280 million people, the population of Africa in 1968? What do you do about a situation, Mr. Logue, when during the last ten years the State Power Commission has pointed out that the use of power in New York State increased by ten percent and the population increased only by .6 percent? Now, this is a fantastic kind of increase in power usage. What do we do when we have a city like New York—and it is pretty typical of the rest of the country—trying to dispose of five pounds of solid waste each day and a good piece of it is not biodegradable because it happens to be plastics, what do we do with all this stuff? And, we could go on and on with these kinds of figures.

Now, it strikes me that our problem of a Universitas, is to provide a decent environment for people. And if we think, in the United States, that we can, for example, use something like forty to sixty percent of the world's annual production to maintain our standard of living, we are living in a dream world, because there are six-hundred million people in India and eight-hundred million people in China who are not going to be favorably inclined toward our misuse, to my mind, of the world's resources.

So what actually should happen? Two months ago, about, or three months ago, the Civil Engineers Society of New York came out with the recommendation that all new buildings in New York—skyscrapers, office buildings—should have operable windows. Now, they came out with that suggestion for two reasons. One is that we had a bad fire in New York, and a lot of people were damaged by this fire. And, second, the amount of energy being used by these buildings for air conditioning and mechanical ventilation, and the rest of it, was simply horrendous. Do you people know that the World Trade Center, for example, is going to use as much energy every day as the City of Schenectady, which has a ninety thousand population? Does

Mr. Logue know that thirty thousand tons of air-conditioning waste, thirty thousand tons of air conditioning is required at the State University up at Buffalo, and that this is all going to be dumped into the lake to thoroughly pollute the lake? That's what I was told by the engineer of the project, and I suppose he knows.

These are the kinds of problems, I think, that we should address ourselves to. How, in fact, should we frame simple laws, like a law, say, for the preservation of natural resources? Now, the architects, the planners design a house. And what is looked at by the building department or the Department for Environmental Protection—or whatever one pleases to call it—is not only whether the beams and the posts are strong enough to support the building but also how much energy is being used. Why do you want an interior bathroom, which requires mechanical energy, the fan, and the rest of it? Do you need air conditioning? Is the architect's real problem now not to turn the difficulties of architecture over to some mechanical engineers with some gadgetry that has to be replaced every twenty years? Or, in fact, is the architect's problem to so orient his buildings, so gather in solar energy of those buildings that he can dispense with a great many of the things that are being done today?

This is what I call the humanization of technology, and the humanization of architecture, and I think that is what we should devote ourselves to. Now, I would like to recommend to everyone, to have everyone read the *New York Times* amusement section today: this article by Walter Kerr, who asks the question, "How live is the live theater?" When you get home, read that little bit. This has an absolutely immediate application to what the curriculum of the Universitas should be about.

DREXLER: You might have mentioned that the *New York Times* uses several thousand acres of trees each week.

GOODMAN: Well, look, I want to tell you something, that in a month or two months, the United Nations is having a conference in Stockholm, which is called "On the Human Environment." And what that conference is about are the very kinds of things that I just mentioned in passing here. And it would seem to me that if the Universitas were being founded on the basis of trying to design a better human environment, not simply for the stinking people in New York City or in the United States, but for the stinking people of the whole world, I think that the United Nations might possibly, out of its budget, find enough money to finance such an organization.

DREXLER: Denise Scott Brown?

DENISE SCOTT BROWN: If we're undertaking an exercise here in participatory institutional planning—an exciting endeavor, that's why there's excitement in this room now— maybe we need clarification on three types of questions: to do with location, content, and process.

Location: Where in this society does the Universitas fit? I think we've been mainly discussing this topic today. Should it, together with the legislative, executive, and judiciary, be one of the powers of government—what Rex Tugwell called "the directive arm of government," or the "fourth arm of government?" Or an arm of the executive? Or a department within an executive agency, for example, HUD? Is it a university—a great university like Berkeley or Harvard, with complex ties to power, action, and organization? Or is it an institutional gadfly like the Center for Democratic Studies? We tend to accept that it's a university, but there is a broad range of alternatives, including a separate small college. Maybe it is all these things, but there are more opportunities than we talked about.

Content: Curriculum planning is also very exciting, as many people here know. What could be the curriculum of this type of institution? We haven't really looked at this question, although we've brought up various subjects— values, semiotics, citizen participation. The latter has many models: a philosophy of planning action and citizen participation would be fascinating to develop as part of the curriculum. Also systems thinking, problem solving, technology evaluation could be taught in this kind of institution.

Process: What processes will we be learning about, allying ourselves with, acting within, undertaking? The processes will depend a lot on the location. Obviously, a fourth arm of government would operate under entirely different procedural mandates from those to be followed by an adviser to UDC. So again, where is this institution?

The issues of location, content, and process can give a sturdy framework for our considerations. But what more is needed?

As an educator in a professional school, I'm particularly interested in educating for action. How do you train people for action? Academe trains people for criticism, which is part of action; for analysis, which is part of action; but seldom for synthesis, which is the real focus of action. And, particularly, how do we train people for creativity? That's an important topic for a Universitas.

DREXLER: Good. I want to thank the members of the panel and the audience, and we adjourn for lunch.

Universitas Symposium: Fourth Working Session, Sunday, January 9, 1972

Editor's note: The fourth session was chaired by Carl Schorske, and included panelists Suzanne Keller, Henri Lefebvre, Richard L. Meier, Martin Pawley, Alain Touraine, and Sheldon S. Wolin. Other speakers were Emilio Ambasz, Hannah Arendt, Manuel Castells, Arthur Drexler, Kenneth Frampton, Percival Goodman, Gyorgy Kepes, Edward J. Logue, Octavio Paz, and Anatol Rapoport. Jivan Tabibian summarized and concluded the proceedings.

CARL SCHORSKE: Ladies and gentlemen, may we open the last session of the conference. We are to deal this afternoon, as you are doubtless aware, with the social context in a more explicit and direct way, supposedly, than has been the case up to now, and with the relationship of educational planning, in the area of environmental design, to that social context.

I should like to begin with some questions, which I have derived from the substance of the papers. I should, perhaps, say that this block of papers, if you've had an occasion to read them—although they are obviously very different in points of view—have a certain homogeneity in their coordinates, and this homogeneity is reflected in the questions that I have derived, which I hope will serve at least initially as a framework for this afternoon's discussion.

I should also say that at the end of the morning session, with the positions taken by the last few speakers, happily provided a transition, not often encountered in conferences such as this, from one portion of the proceedings to the next. It seems to me that the political and social questions were coming alive as the morning's proceedings reached their close, and that was appropriate for what there remains for us to do now.

Now, the questions fall into two parts, it seems to me, social and educational. With respect to the social questions, one: What kind of society have we now, and what limitations does it impose on the potentiality for environmental design and education in it? This first question (What kind of society have we now?) is essentially analytic, and leads to a second question: What kind of society are we to expect, or, depending on your temperament, what kind of society are we to work for? This is either a prognosticatory question, or a question of the investment of the will in the social process, let us say. Both these types of questions—analysis and prognosis—are reflected in the documents in your hands.

Then, the second class of question is educational. How can a vocation in environmental design be defined and shaped under the conditions we now have, or under the conditions that we anticipate? In short, this raises the question of the aims of education, in a larger sense. And, under that, what is the matter with traditional university structure for filling the needs in this area?

Why can't we use those instruments; why do we sit here wondering about creating a new type of university?

A second sub-question, under the aims of education is this (and this clearly emerges from some of the papers): Must we school for revolution before we can school for design? I put these questions very sharply and very bluntly to point the discussion. Is there a place for something like Richard Wagner's *Kunstwerk der Zukunft,* a model which is offered us in the midst of contemporary social reality pointing forward toward one yet to be realized? And, if there is a place for this, can schooling or education provide it, or must we, rather, put in suspension the educational task in the area of spatial reorganization in favor of, in effect, political or social activity?

Now, having set forth these two kinds of questions, one, the social and, two, the education and design problems, let me very briefly, and with some distortion, try to set up a spectrum, a scale, on which the panelists here lie, in relation to these two questions. It struck me, as I read the papers, that there were social optimists who were quite prepared to work within the perspective of the society as it now is, or may well be—that is, maybe without a serious intervention by themselves or by design planners—and another group that were social or political pessimists with respect to the existing state of affairs and with the degree to which the educational process, as such, could contribute in the present social conditions that confront the environmental plan.

Very loosely speaking, Doctors [Richard L.] Meier and [Suzanne] Keller belong to the optimistic school. Dr. Meier's plan, as I read it (I'm not trying to give a full summary of his work now, please understand me, and every speaker will correct my distortions as they go, but I'm trying to keep within these coordinates), starts with a kind of social optimism; Dr. Meier does, with respect to the real possibilities in a market-organized society for the social designer, the well-educated, a kind of team of social designers to move in and find creative activity. He believes, I think, that we are shifting, in the United States, from aerospace to urban problems; we're going to transfer resources. He has enormous, I would almost say, eighteenth-century confidence in the bounty that would necessarily ensue from continued stress on productivity and technological progress in the society. And, he feels that with a proper application of promotional techniques, market-analytic techniques, to design skills, that the market can be much more fully exploited for the kind of creative, cultural revolution which a designer is likely to be able to produce. The designer is for him, in fact, on the threshold (I may exaggerate a bit, but I do it to provoke some response from him) of really becoming a cultural hero; and the market is, how should I call it, the pedestal upon which this historical new role can safely be placed.

Now, as for Ms. Keller, she sees technology, again, in eighteenth-century fashion, as liberative. She is the cheerful Haussmannisée, if I may put it that way. . .

SUZANNE KELLER: You may not.

SCHORSKE: ... who is responding to the dissolution of domesticity, which she sees as happening, the evaporation of the territorial unit with work access as a major problem. She is responding to that in a way of social and cultural optimism, arguing that the increase of leisure, which our productivity is creating for us, will also liquidate our being bound to place, to territorial locus, and open entirely new vistas in design and planning that have not yet been thought of. There is, here, a perspective, which is, again, if I may say so, on the [Georges Eugène] Haussmann line, something like [Charles] Baudelaire's *Invitation au Voyage*, where you can go on a trip, so to speak, with the unexpectedly emergent beneficence that is resulting from our technological bounty.

Now, as I turn from these to the other group of commentators, Messrs. [Henri] Lefebvre, [Martin] Pawley, and [Alain] Touraine, I see people primarily preoccupied with the conditions of enslavement that still are at hand in society, where technology is a dominating force rather than a liberating force: technology as a reinforcement of capitalist domination and elitist rule. Interestingly enough, as you cross the line between the first two speakers and the second two (again, I exaggerate slightly), as you cross the line, the interest in concrete educational possibilities declines, as, what to me is, a higher social realism emerges. I do not hesitate as chairman to put my own salmon on the floor, as the Irish say, in this respect. That is, I do think that there is a lack of social analysis and great creative inventiveness in the first two speakers, and a prominent and often very convincing social analysis of our educational predicament in the second three speakers, or second three paper contributors, but an evident disinterest, at least so far, in what the content of an education should be under conditions of capitalist, hypertrophied technological rationality.

There are different ways of handling this. I do not mean to give a full summary, but let me simply point to a few features of the responses, which the speakers made and will presumably amplify with respect to the social situation they perceive. M. Lefebvre sees the United States as a kind of overdeveloped country, par excellence, in which the sorcerer's apprentice is the capitalist producer, and the architect and planner tends to be reduced to his assistant, his amanuensis, the apprentice of the sorcerer's apprentice, you might say. And, space for him is a mirror, in a sort of Aristotelian way, space is a mirror in which the disjuncture, the disarticulation, the irrationality of our society is reflected. Consequently, his call is for a criticism based on a potential rationality, which is absent in the society, and on the principle *si dubitas circumspique*: if you really take the hard look at the environment around you, you will find what's the matter with the whole society. So that, the architectural design student ought to be essentially a social critic, whether he builds buildings or not, whether he makes contributions to the ongoing design process or not, is not so firmly articulated in his paper, and perhaps he will have a word to say to us on that question.

Mr. Pawley, for his part, sees the chaotic corporate society as sacrificing hecatombs of trained students, by defining them, first, as form givers to the society and, then, depriving them of the career opportunities in which form can indeed be given to the society, reducing them to salaried workers in firms public or private, where their imaginative enterprise is crushed out, if I could loosely paraphrase.

Mr. Touraine begins to focus again on rulers and victims, but the stress in his paper is strongly on the present university, the degree to which it inhibits progress in the area of design and to which it might be a contributor to this design; and he carries us, in that sense, into the heart of the educational question that is involved here and that began to be really broken open this morning, in this morning's session, and to which this one in the end, I hope, will be devoted.

Mr. [Sheldon S.] Wolin did not contribute a paper on time, and has thus earned the privilege of, so to speak, becoming, in some degree, a transformer of what he has listened to, in terms of the previous discussion, to introduce some of those considerations into the articulation of this afternoon's confrontation between social analysis, or social theory, and educational potentiality. I would like to ask him to lead off with perhaps ten minutes of discussion that will set the frame, and then we hope that we will have a very free back and forth here within the framework of these two coordinates—social analysis and theory, educational possibility and opportunity—in which our members will duly tear each other apart for a while. After that, as has previously been the case, we will, of course, open the topic for the participants of the other panels and the public assembly. Professor Wolin, would you like to lead off?

SHELDON S. WOLIN: After listening to Professor Schorske's resume, I'm glad I did not present my paper on time, not because I feared it would be distorted, but because I feared it would have been presented with an epitaph. Therefore, I'm grateful for having been delinquent. I'll try to do three things in the few minutes that are allotted to me: first, I'll try to characterize what I think have been some of the major assumptions (all of which I'll reject) in much of the discussion that's taken place over the last two days; second, I'll try to show where some of those assumptions lead; third, I'll try to suggest alternative ways of thinking and alternative possibilities of action. These will center on what I shall loosely call "political education," and mean it in a very broad sense. The context of my remarks is a context, which, if I had time to elaborate, I would call the context of technological society. What I mean by technological society, very briefly, is the constellation, the complex composed of science, technology, and modern corporate structures; and these are, from my point of view, basically structures of power, basically structures of domination. Now, within that context, and within the context, too, of these meetings, I'm reminded that about a century and a half ago Saint-Simon sent out an appeal to the propertied classes of Europe asking them to contribute subscriptions to what he called a "Council of Newton" in which the intellectuals, the poets, the mathematicians, the physicists would all come together, live off the bounties supplied by the propertied classes of Europe and proceed to think in the best interests of humanity. I feel there has been something in this Saint-Simonean strain in the discussions up till now, but they show, I think, just as Saint-Simon's projects and proposals showed, that utopias need not be the fantasies or the projections of the oppressed. Utopias can also be reflections of the anxieties of those who sup at the table of the existing system and who, by virtue of their anxieties and fears, proceed to project utopias, which really lack the distinguishing element of utopias, namely novelty.

For, the premise of much of the thinking which I detected, at least in the last day or so, was thinking which really basically believed that the existing order has at best committed, or its policy makers or decision makers have committed, certain "mistakes," and that basically a reordering means nothing more than replacing irrational or obtuse decision makers by those who are more enlightened. There has been, in my view of things, very little of an assumption that the existing order of things may, in fact, be deranged, that it may be deranged in terms of rewards, in terms of distributive justice, in terms of the distribution of power, in terms of the distribution of justice, as well. Hence, they seek, and, hence, I think there has been a good attempt to seek, in terms of our preceding discussions, a form of utopia, which is basically a redemption of the present.

For example, one kind of illustration has been that there has been relatively little discussion and relatively little critique of why existing society has become what it has become—why we are where we are. There has, instead, been an assumption that where we are constitutes a departure point from which we can curb the excesses of that system and then proceed to happier days. There has been very little grappling, I think, with some of the issues that a group such as this has to grapple with. There has been no mention, for example, of racism; there has been no mention, really, of the triviality of much that passes for work in contemporary society; there has been no discussion of colonialism, of war, of arms races, and things of that sort. Most of these are probably, again, viewed as, at best, irrational decision making or, at worst, perverted priorities, but not derangement.

Accompanying this has been, I think, a kind of co-optation of fashionable language that used to be language of revolt—language that talked in terms of alienation, freedom, and things of that sort. Now, that language, I find, has been assimilated to the construct called "systems theory," so that, in effect, that language which used to be language of revolt is now language of justification. Freedom becomes an input, or, as it was said this morning, we try to "design values." Now the whole formulation, I think, of design and systems theory rests upon certain assumptions which, again, if time permitted, really ought to be trotted out because they are not neutral notions; they are notions which do not merely imply choices, as all conceptualization does imply choices. They also imply forms of language and forms of sensibility, which I think rest upon a very important set of values, most of which I would closely identify with existing technological structures, so that all of the kinds of discussions which have occurred, and the utilization of systems theory and design, are really, in many respects, euphemisms for forms of control and forms of direction, which, again, have not been fully or candidly faced.

I would also suggest, too, that there has been a good deal of dogmatism, in terms of preceding discussions, dogmatism that is shown, perhaps, mostly in terms of what questions have not seemed to be questions. That is to say, for example, there has been a kind of dogma, which establishes two dichotomies. One, those who accept the blind advance of technology and those who reject the blind advance of technology, as though the world were composed of two choices, namely Wernher von Braun, on the one hand, and some hippies, on the other. This, I don't think, is a fair formulation of what the via media might be: that there are all kinds of problems that go way beyond technological assessment and the evaluation of alternative technologies. It would seem to me that a fair inspection of technology really ought to ask the fundamental question: whether the form of technology which we know is or is not, simply, a particular product of a particular kind of economic system and social arrangement.

There has been, too, a kind of dogma of what the past signifies. The past basically signifies either something that has been escaped from, or which happens to house a few treasured artifacts that can be retrieved or rescued from that past and suitably praised. The past, much more, as a context of significance, the past as memory, the past as embodiments of what humanity has meant in terms of self-understandings: this, I think, has been largely neglected.

Similarly, I think there's been a dogma about the nature, so to speak, of contemporary knowledge. I have found very little discussion, except perhaps by Mr. [Anatol] Rapoport, suggesting that much of social-science knowledge—all of which I think, much of which, has been assumed in terms particularly of systems theory—may not be anything but trivial.

Finally, I think there has been a kind of dogmatic assumption that human inventions, which bring new forms of human power, are fundamentally neutral, and that what they basically require is, again, that good and rational people happen to, or should be the ones who decide how those new technologies and new forms of power are utilized. Now, I don't think it's accidental that systems theory has been—insofar as there has been—the sort of favored example of a kind of social theory about how design ought to proceed, about how architects ought to view their communities, about how a potential Universitas should relate itself to society, because I think, in a very real way, systems theory is the intellectual correlate of technological society. Systems, like much of technological society, don't have histories, they are basically constructs, whether they be cybernetic constructs or even, in a certain sense, more mechanical kinds of constructs. Machines and systems, as I suggest, do not have theories: they only have interconnected parts, and, as a result, like technological society itself, which, as a precondition of its advance, have had to slough off the past in terms of habits, memories, sensibilities, and so on. Systems theory, too, makes short shrift of memory. Memory becomes retrieval of information, retrieval of stored information, which, again, I think is significant. So that systems theory, I think, in a certain sense, is an aptly chosen word because the kind of imagery it conjures up to my mind is the imagery of an object floating in space: it is, indeed, like technological society itself.

Now, because it does not—systems theory and much of the thinking surrounding it—because it does not have a genuine historical dimension, either in terms of a critique or in terms of an understanding of how it got where it is, it views no kinds of inherited claims regarding oppression, injustice, and accumulated wrong. These simply are not dimensions in terms of which it thinks. Instead, it conceals these kinds of problems, basically, in terms of talk about infrastructure and superstructure again as rather disembodied kinds of forms.

But where does this leave us? It leaves us, I think, with the kind of basic question that Professor Schorske raised at the outset toward which we are to address ourselves: the problem of the university and its relationship to the society, the society that I have dubbed "technological society" for purposes of this afternoon's discussion. Now, if we think about technological society and we think about the university's relationship to it, there's one fact that seems to me quite interesting. When we look around us in the world, we see what I would describe as mind-created structures. Whether they be deliberate, formal, organizations, whether they be universities, whether they be bureaucratic structures, whether they be cities that are planned, or what have you, we live in a kind of mind-dominated universe; I would even go so far to say we live in a theory-saturated universe.

In relationship to this kind of world the university has become, itself, a kind of embodiment of mind, which caters to this sort of mind-created world. The university has become, in many ways, not merely a caterer to that kind of world, but a codifier of that kind of world—a codifier in which values such as cumulative knowledge become important, in which values of innovation become important, but values such as criticism and genuine deviance become disvalued, become threats to the kind of steady growth of innovative and cumulative knowledge, which assumes we continue to push farther the same frontiers, push them back, that we have, so to speak, seen from the past.

In that regard, therefore, those who are, so to speak, in the context of our discussion, interested in the relationship of students in terms of that university, find themselves either falling into the language of apprenticeship or falling into a kind of vestigial Marxism, which suggests that because the workers no longer represent an object of sentimentality, the students can perform that kind of function. But, I would suggest that even those who seem to be quite sympathetic to student aspirations and student oppressions in the last decade or so, must also inspect their own kind of formulation of the place of students, and ask whether students themselves have not been objectified into manipulable objects suitable to the kinds of dreams and visions of academic people.

Well, if we ask where does this leave us and where do we go, and, if time permitted, I would try to say that the most apt analogy for our kind of age, is an analogy that would take us back to the Reformation. I don't mean to say that in any kind of antiquarian sense, but simply in the sense that the Reformation shows us the importance of a very significant kind of human activity, a kind of human activity in which a church that was the most significant human structure of its time, was de-structured; in which men and women learned the experience of what it meant to de-structure, of what it meant to destroy, of what it meant to question at various kinds of levels, and proceed to evolve and establish a wide range of associational ties, and associational bonds, and associational communities.

Now, what I would emphasize here is this importance of de-structuring as a form of experience in which students and teachers can be involved; and I would, just to close this point out, I would like to draw attention to what I think was a very apt remark of yesterday, namely, the importance of trying to assess the possibilities that exist in the world now that would enable us to move toward experiences of de-structuring I detect in the kind of interests which students are displaying today, not only in the area of environmental problems, not only in the area of law, not only in the area of medicine, not only in the area of social welfare, not only in the area of education, but also, of course, preeminently, in many respects, in the area of design and architecture. There is, I think, a very important blend that is being practically worked out in many areas, a blend of action, a blend of knowledge, a blend of skill, a blend of expertise, but a blend, above all, that takes individuals not only to communities but into communities. And, there is a very important lesson there which relates to the Universitas, namely, the lesson, perhaps, that the best way to form a university is not, perhaps, to centralize it and to specify its identity in terms of space and of time but, rather, to think of it much more pluralistically, as a kind of invisible church, if you will, of believers whose main ties are those of spirit and outlook, rather than physical plant and physical location.

Now, just one final point, and I'll make it very quickly. The final point, I think accompanying this is a very important suggestion about what a new form of politics may well have to take in this kind of world we live in. I think that the politics of growth, about which there has been so much alarm and dismay in recent years, points perhaps to a new form of politics which not only involves de-structuring but, I think, also involves a politics of nurture, as I would call it: a politics that is less concerned with exploiting environments and human materials, and human relationships, and power relationships, and much more, perhaps, sensitized to the fact not only that the world is small and there's very little in it in the way of resources, but also that, in fact, the true politics may be one in which a care for things that live, human and non-human, may be, in the last analysis, the kind of bond that ties us together. Thank you.

SCHORSKE: Ms. Keller would like to say a few words.

KELLER: I'll start out with my optimism. I'm already dizzied by the beginning of this session: I have to sort out all these big ideas in my own mind, and so let me become very simple.

I work with designers a great deal of my time, and I work in planned communities, and I'm trying simply to do a very difficult thing with a group of architects and anthropologists, namely, how do you evaluate what is going on in a community today, what are the forces—technological, and power, and political, and moral—that are acting on this particular group of people at this time. We don't even have concepts to think about this coherently; that's what I'm about to do, and my paper was not optimistic or pessimistic, I was trying simply to say that we are all aware, and in this room particularly, that there is a tremendous change underway toward something. We're not agreed as to where. Some say it's going completely to the end point, or to death, to destruction, the apocalypse. And, others say, no, it's coming to a new beginning, to a new birth, and I suppose I would count myself among the latter, at least at symposia such as these. I don't know what I would do here if I took the first point of view.

All right, given that as background, let me indicate some of the things that struck me as important to discuss in this kind of meeting. I took seriously Mr. Ambasz and company's request that we think about a new converging point: they call it Universitas. Maybe it's a bad idea, Emilio, that we gave an old term a new accent; maybe one should have invented a wholly new phrase because too many people have talked about universities. I didn't interpret it that way. I was asked to think about what such a new creation, a new creature, a new animal would have to concern itself with and maybe worry about, and that's what I tried to do.

Second point: I take seriously the fact that we're not here, in this particular room, as politicians and labor leaders, and so on; we are here dealing with ideas, and I like to deal with ideas very much. I want to have an exchange of views, not only statements of positions and not very grandiose formulas about the state of the world, and I think you can disagree with me, but if I make myself clear enough at least there is then a basis of some kind of exchange. Simply put, the idea of this new creature would have to take into account, the way other institutions are not capable of doing, a totally, what I consider a radically new world view. And I'm willing to bet that before new institutions can come into being, and before new people can be created, world views have to change via some processes from the old world, to be sure. I don't know how to get away from the old world; we're living in it, we're born in it. But some new possibilities are here at stake, and what are some of these?

I think that a new technology is underway, with some domination—and every system means domination on some level, really—so it will have some power elements that are nasty and unbearable but it will also have some liberating forces. I think it has the chance to give us opportunities for diversity, for greater wealth than we've had before. So I consider some new technology—automation, electronic revolution, the communications revolution—as some of the key levers of this emerging world. Along with this—I would never just stick to one dimension such as technology—there are new resources that we have to make use of. When I talk about "we," I mean an ascendant image of the world; not everybody in the world became industrial, some countries did and they served as models for others. So, this new electronic society will stress speed, it will stress non-territoriality; it cuts absolutely through the heart of our conventional institutions of work and the family. I don't want to get too detailed on this, but I'll be glad to discuss a few of these things if they come up naturally. It cuts through our notion of permanence, it's a society in which an emphasis—and I'm only talking now about priorities and emphases—will be placed on provisionalism, impermanence, and mobility, to name just three of the major forces of the time. And the mobility is not just territorial: the mobility is spiritual; also contact mobility. If I can literally contact electronically people millions of miles away, that's a contact we have great difficulty dealing with today, because we are so stuck on territoriality.

Now, in the paper, I also stress the idea of community, because I think we lack a viable notion about that necessary element of social life. The older communities are in decay, new ideas are still wanting to be created, and I think we can't talk about Universitas without talking about the context in which it will be placed, and, therefore, I will stress the larger milieu rather than the smaller institution, which is how I interpreted your mandate, Emilio.

Now, it seems to me that in your [Working] Paper, which you say was ambiguous and abstract and general, and I'm sure everybody could find their level, as it were, I still think you were confused or caught up between this problem of territoriality versus non-territoriality; it came up repeatedly. On one end, you wanted open-ended, very fluid, very alive kinds of learning situations and practice situations, and on the other, you talk about an institution that looks just a little like some amended universities that I'd change.

Now, perhaps we will have to combine these two because we're creatures of the emerging world and of the older world. And so my image (and I will end with this as my introductory remarks) of this new possibility for convergence of ideas is the image, first of all, my favorite image, of a circus, second, of a ship, and third, of a hotel, perhaps like the Plaza, which you think is imitation Europe, or perhaps any other favorite hotel. Now what do these have in common? They have a momentary fixed location point, but they're always in motion, and they have the experience of moving through a changing scene, and that is what I think we should emphasize as one of the first elements. That's all I have to say at the moment.

SCHORSKE: The floor is open.

MARTIN PAWLEY: My paper dealt quite simply with a suggestion that we could analyze the nature of the university at present, from which I don't believe the Universitas Project, as I understand it, can ever be wholly divorced: that we can analyze the university at present far more accurately and more alarmingly if we assume that it has a military model rather than an ecclesiastical one. That was the substance of my paper; my conclusion in the paper was, more or less, that I used the examples of World War I and World War II, and, principally, the example of the French army. The mutiny in the French army in 1917 and the collapse of the French army in 1940 I took as parallels for the probable performance of our university system when it comes to confront the crisis so eloquently summarized by Mr. Goodman this morning.

Simply, I believe, on the basis of that analysis, that the capacity of our university system to defend technological society against that crisis which he outlined, is zero, absolutely zero: it will perform as well as the French army in 1940. I believe that this crisis has analogs and, of course, proceeds from a situation in society which can best be described by the development and the cancerous growth of privatization, of retreat from the public realm, and from a total disbelief in the administration, the capabilities, and the potentials of elites.

What, then, can the Universitas Project possibly carry out? I was much illuminated yesterday by the parallels with the Bauhaus. I'd like to just briefly summarize my conclusions on those because I think that the parallel is a realistic one, and, in many ways, if the prognosis for the Universitas was as hopeful as the prognosis for the Bauhaus, we might be more cheerful than we are. As Professor Schorske indicated, I fear belatedly, it was the liberals who knocked the financial props from under the Bauhaus by means of the dissolution of the Soviet republics formed in Thyringia and Bavaria. This was done by [Gustav] Stresemann and by the Social Democrats. From then on, the administration of the Bauhaus, under [Walter] Gropius and [Marcel] Breuer and others, decided upon political neutrality, which led to the exclusion of communist students first, and later artists, and so forth, and eventually to the non-politicism of [Ludwig] Mies van der Rohe and the collapse under the Nazis. This was the origin, this whole process was the origin of the socialist architecture, which, particularly in the field of housing, survived to be constructed in a capitalist society—with results that we are now beginning to understand, and which in my view explained the massive rejection of the principles of modern design by the mass populations of Western society.

Now, a complicity with the broader scale of social forces, as Mr. [Jivan] Tabibian suggested, was the only success of the Bauhaus; it was an influence rather than an institutional success, but a formal influence deprived of its context and, thus in its product rendered absurd. Political neutrality, as I believe we now clearly see, leads to bureaucracy and, thus, by default and by our linguistic environment, to totalitarianism and, hence, the current identification of modern design with bureaucratic totalitarianism.

The differences between the Bauhaus and Universitas in this regard are profound and profoundly depressing. First, the Universitas Project propagates no revolutionary design image; it talks about deriving one. Second, it has not even a revolutionary resource to be kicked away; it begins where the Bauhaus finally ended up, with an appeal to organizations like the Ford Foundation, reactionary elites, existing sources of finance. Third—and this point proceeds from the other two—lacking a radical design base, a radical political base, and a radical resource base, it seems to me to lack also an identity. Perhaps its organization and mode of operation could provide this, but these have not been revealed or, indeed, discussed except in the paper contributed by [Hans Magnus] Enzensberger, who is not here for reasons that I believe most of you know, and that paper no one yet has referred to.

Now, this basic identification between the Universitas Project and the conventional or existing university, I think, is undeniable; the name implies it, the connection has been made time and again in the last two days. The summary of its impotence and its fate in that connection, I believe, was best made by Professor Rapoport yesterday; he said if the Universitas produces, or if Universitas graduates a product which is saleable and which is bought by the elites, then it is committed to the goals, the systems of administration, and the general values of those elites. If it does not, then where the hell is it going to get its money? This is absolutely elementary, and, in my view, absolutely true, and I think it eloquently dismisses the idea of the university as a suitable venue for a project which is to reinvigorate and present totally new perspectives to the concept of urban design.

So, what then can be a possible answer? There's only one that occurs to me, and I put this forward as a suggestion that is not developed in any way: that is, that if we accept the logic of social reaction against the incompetence of the elites, as expressed in student revolt, we see that it progresses backward in terms of age, presumably down toward zero. It starts with dissident intellectuals of middle age, it progresses to postgraduates, it progresses to undergraduates, and now, particularly in the French example, which is, of course, a paradigm because of the events of 1968. In the French example, after 1968 it has progressed back further to the *lycée*, that is, to secondary education.

Thus, I propose that if the Universitas Project has a revolutionary aim, and I mean a revolutionary aim in the context of the inevitable tendencies toward the disasters outlined by Mr. Goodman, if it has a revolutionary aim then it must, again, I quote Mr. Tabibian, it must encourage deviant behavior, it must reward that behavior. The conventional university structure does, indeed, reward deviant behavior but it does so by a method that is only admirable in its symmetry, that is, as you progress through the university system you must first undergo an apprenticeship of conformity; you later, assumedly, if you are brilliant, clever, ingenious, or lucky, you reach a position where the more deviant the proposal you make, it receives a higher award, your advancement in the academic profession is assured. And, in that process, of course, because of the time factor involved, you have, of course, grown used to having wine with your meals, having a car to drive, and a house in the suburbs, and a number of acquisitions, possessions, and orientations, which are, of course, indivisible from those of the elite which you profess to attack. Thus, under the conventional university structure, deviant behavior is rewarded, but, at the same time, it is rendered impotent by complicity.

Now, the *only* way in which that situation can be avoided, in my view, is that this process should be directly reversed. That is, that deviant behavior should be encouraged at the earliest level and not at the latest. And I don't mean by the "earliest level" the first year of undergraduate life, I mean before university status is reached at all—I mean in terms of primary schools, and in terms of secondary schools. This has an advantage, which goes beyond the ones that I've mentioned. On the scale effect, the pyramidal structure of education in our society is such that millions receive primary education, thousands receive university education, hundreds receive postgraduate educations, and a few achieve the status of being, in my view, emasculated intellectuals who can say what the hell they like and it doesn't have any effect.

If we could introduce a revolutionary design concept, or, more accurately, a revolutionary design critique of our society at a primary or secondary school level, we would at one stroke achieve a wider application of these ideas—simply numerically, more people would be involved—and, second, we would achieve that these ideas could be expressed at a level which is necessarily prior to that at which possessions are acquired, complicity is evolved, and a general commitment to the status of elite is reached.

I suspect that this begs the question, if indeed anyone bothers to ask it, as to what could be taught at such a level, and I do have an answer for it—or a proposal. But I will leave that for now, and if it arises later that's fine. Otherwise, I think that summarizes the position taken by my paper and the position that I have been forced to, as a result of the last two days, come to.

SCHORSKE: May I ask a question in this connection, which is, in terms of the way in which higher education has become, or has been made complicit in the purposes of the ruling groups in the existing society, as your analysis suggests, what is your ground, what is the point of entry politically, which will exempt the much more common socialization mechanism of the elementary and secondary school from similar pressures?

I'm puzzled at the somewhat utopian cast of your proposal, given the form of the analysis that prevails in your diagnosis of higher education and its discontents and ills.

PAWLEY: It proceeds entirely from a pragmatic observation, and that is that most educational innovations in our society over the last hundred years have found their way into primary and secondary education. To my knowledge, no significant innovations have found their way into university education. As I suggested in my paper, it is our addiction to terms such as professor, faculty, and a number of others, that prevent us from seeing the university for what it is, that is, an institution which, in my view, is a defeated army; it cannot do the job we ask it to do, or which our elites ask it to do. It cannot do either. If there is a political standpoint, it must proceed from the assumption of a standpoint of, I was going to say political innocence, but I would say political non-contamination perhaps, which can literally only be found as one regresses in age and experience, and commitment and corruption, if you like. Thus, it is necessary at the earliest possible stage, and as one advances in age and commitment, corruption, and so forth, it becomes less and less possible. That's my view.

SCHORSKE: Mr. Meier

RICHARD L. MEIER: Actually, within our own design schools it's possible to do what you ask, and it works, it fits into the elementary school education. It started out actually from the Berkeley disturbances, where they allowed the students to create a good share of their own curriculum, in which case, they created their own courses for alternative futures, discovered that the futures were rather empty, and then decided to go in for action. One of the actions that turned out to be very productive was to go into the school system and to start asking the kids themselves how to redesign their environments. Now the Berkeley school system happens to be fifty percent Black and fifty percent White. And the White live on the hills, and the Black live on the flatlands. And those streams, even though they're going through the same structures, were kept very, very separate, and the administration knew no means of mixing these two subcultures until the architect came along and then suggested, you know, we can do things to this environment, but, of course, first we have to think about it. And so he got some butcher paper, and he got it on the table and said, "Now what do you want to do?" And, whenever they got consensus, they pasted it on the wall. But they discovered that this was not enough. They had to have a tape recorder, and they had to construct a dance, and every time there was consensus, there had to be a ballet and a dance and some music that would fit whatever was the consensus; so then there was the epitome of action, fitted together with the design, and they could do the dance, play the music, or they could look at the wall. And it was really the combination of these three that made it so attractive that the Whites from the hills asked to come in to this urban laboratory. And the school administrators were overwhelmed, "This was exactly what we wanted to create for years, but we didn't know how to do it." But the man was drafted: the irreplaceable man.

KELLER: Could I ask a question also? Is it possible to break into these speeches? Mr. Pawley, I don't understand how you can sit there and say that there has been no significant innovation in the university in the last two hundred years. I don't understand that. If it's just for political rhetoric, then I'll accept it, but you can't mean that. And how, in the same breath, can you say that the high schools will make these innovations. Now what do you mean by significant innovations?

PAWLEY: Quite simply, I mean innovations, which seemed to me to bear any relation to the brief, pungent analysis of the crisis that confronts us and which is allegedly implicit in the Universitas Project, which was made by Mr. Goodman this morning. In relation to that I see no innovation, no.

KELLER: But that crisis has hardly begun to be formulated, and two hundred years ago they could hardly address themselves to this crisis, so crisis is relative to the times. Do you throw out—I'm just asking, really—I mean, would you throw out all medical and scientific innovations, just to take these two examples?

PAWLEY: No, you're shifting the grounds. I said that there had not been educational innovations, I didn't say two hundred years, I said one hundred, although I admit the figure could be fifty or sixty or seventy or whatever. But, what I meant was relevant to the crisis to which I believe the Universitas Project intended to address itself.

KELLER: Okay. I'll let it go.

HENRI LEFEBVRE [in translation]: Ladies and gentlemen, I apologize once again for having to speak French, but it seems to be the only language in which I can express myself correctly. Yesterday, I was very happy and I congratulated myself for finding myself amidst university friends who were studying such interesting things as values, and also studying the values of such sciences as semiotics, economics, sociology, etc. Today I'm also very, very happy, and I congratulate myself even more because I'm witnessing an historical event, I should say a biblical event, in the midst of the Tower of Babel. I would like to add, however, that I think, and I'm sure I'm not the only one to think that the Tower of Babel also saw the event of linguists.

In view of the difficulties inherent in trying to open a dialogue, under the circumstances, I doubt that I have succeeded in doing what I had set out to do in my mind, in other words, to compare Marxism, European Marxism, as I think I represent it. And I hasten to say that it is a Marxism free of all political dogmatism, and democracy as it is understood in this country. I would also like to say something rather realistic, in which terms we could have set the problem: If there were to be a check for two million dollars placed on this table, what would we do with it?

I seem to feel in this company a kind of terror that seems to inhibit whatever dialogue we were willing to enter into. And it weighs heavily on our conscience, it is well known in Europe, it is a kind of terrorism that prevents one from speaking, it is very diffuse and indefinable; it is not political, it is not due to capitalistic trappings, it is not due to authority, it is not even due to the weight of traditional ideas. I don't know how one can translate such a good French word as *terrorisme* into English but this is what seems to be what is inhibiting us.

I shall give an example of something that happened to me in France recently: I was addressing a group of young architects and I was telling those young architects that, circumstances being what they are, they were all working for a profit, and there is a certain value added to work which is profit and which seems to be inherent in their work, and they thought I was obscene because I was referring to something shameful just as some parts of the body better remain there because they are shameful; well some things had better remain unsaid because they are shameful, also.

Things being as they are, it would actually be my wish to fold that little paper back into my pocket and wait and see whether anybody comes up with an interesting answer to the question of what do you usefully do with two million dollars. However, there is such a thing as rules of the game, and this being so, I shall recite my little lesson. I shall say, at first, that there are a number of scenarios for the future, which one can possibly envisage in view of the circumstances of the moment. If we look at them all, very few of them seem to be favorable to the project we have at heart, to the Universitas Project that we are considering. Some of them, however, would be more favorable. For instance, in the future there could indeed be that very deep transformation that some people seem to think is possible. In France, for instance, we could solve the important problem of immigrant workers: we have three and a half million immigrant workers in France and if we could solve that problem, they could suddenly change the future. The same thing could be said about the question of Black people in the United States. So we should try to introduce a discontinuity in history, at the same time, maintaining a continuity of knowledge, so that whatever we know now may be of some use in, let's say, one generation or in the year 2000.

There are, of course, very unfavorable scenarios that come to mind. There is an example, of course, of the very survival of man as a species; it can be considered that man could be largely eliminated either through a third world war, or through pollution, or any such destructive happening. But, in order to keep on working, we have, to some measure, to retain at least a slightly favorable idea of the future. And so we go back to the Bauhaus, which has been referred to by my friend Jean Baudrillard and by Meyer Schapiro yesterday. What did the Bauhaus introduce that was entirely new at the time? It was, to my mind, the production of space, of course, around the year 1920, although all societies before had produced space, the idea of space creation emerged and became clear. Objects, as such, were no longer created that were finding their place in space, but the power, the technology or whatever that was necessary to create space itself as a new concept and as a new product emerged, and that was a new idea that was introduced then.

And, therefore, so again, this new idea emerged around 1920, that there could be such a thing as a global production, as a production of space as a whole, and as a concept, but it happened also that this production happened in a capitalistic world and so space as it was created was sold, and it could only be sold by bits and pieces, and so space became fragmented, and the production of space became antagonistic with production as a capitalist phenomenon.

I think that this notion of the production of space is extremely important, and I shall keep on dwelling on it and give two examples to illustrate my position. This morning, Chris Alexander gave a very interesting exposé, and also some years ago he published an article, and I'm sorry if I don't quote it in English in the right way, in French it was entitled "The City Is Not a Tree." In France, at roughly the same time, we had arrived at roughly the same conclusion by entirely different means. We had set out to find out the form of space which was produced by bureaucratic society, and we had come to the conclusion that a bureaucratic society produces space in the shape of a tree, because only in space so shaped can all the controls be exercised from one given central point that commands all the other branches.

The second example, and I'll refer to what my friend Mr. Castells has said, is the example of the historical center of the City of Paris, which is a very good, lively, and ongoing example of class struggle. In the beginning of the nineteenth century, when the French bourgeoisie seized power, it set out to destroy the center of Paris, and more recently, in what can only be termed "state monopolistic capitalism," the French central market, Les Halles, was also very seriously threatened—they're not entirely destroyed because we still have some faint remnants of democracy in Paris, in France. But our beloved one that died about a year ago, General de Gaulle, wanted to have Paris central market torn down and, very symbolically, replaced by the stock exchange—I mean the Ministry of Finance.

(I'm sorry about the Ministry of Finance: I've just written a monument to capitalism.) So anyway, in France the stock exchange is not important enough to be placed anywhere, let alone in the historical center of the city. So, as I've stressed the importance of the production of space, and I insist that space is a social product: space is not a blank product, space is not a neutral space on which to write something, space is a social product. I have to state it again. And this is one concept that I think could very usefully be part of the curriculum of that university, Universitas that we are discussing. It could study the production of space in history, for, ever since animalistic societies, pre-historic societies, or archaic societies up to the present world, it has taken many faces and it has used the tools of the moment. So, space, as we produce it now could come to terms and could also put to use the revolutionary transformations of our thinking, of our modes of living, of acting, and of the tools that are disposed of. This is one of the things that could very usefully be studied by a new institution.

SCHORSKE: May I ask whether there is anybody on the panel or on the floor, perhaps Mr. Castells or Mr. Christopher Alexander, whether they would like to comment on the issue of spatial organization as reflective of the society they exist in, or whether this problem of criticism which is raised by M. Lefebvre is a problem which has reality for them.

I would also like to ask that you make your remarks brief. I don't want to exercise terror, but, on the other hand, monopolization of time, and we have such little time left, would be unfortunate. Mr. Goodman.

PERCIVAL GOODMAN: I'd just like to say this, that space, I think, is a social production, and to give an example of that. Louis Sullivan, the American architect, objected very strongly to the notion that there should be Corinthian columns on a bank building, because he felt that Corinthian columns were, in fact, not functional. Now, what Louis Sullivan did not understand was the function of the Corinthian column on the bank building. The function of the Corinthian column on the bank building was, in my mind, twofold: one was that it impressed the depositor, and the second was analogous, and this was pointed out by Samuel Butler in a new utopian novel called *Erewhon* [1872], where he called the temples "musical banks," and people went to the bank for this false coin which, in fact, was given out by the churches. So, what we must look at is not the superficial notion that the architect had that he was designing a pseudo-Renaissance building, or a pseudoclassical building. The banks knew what they were about, and certainly know what they're about in terms of just what Arthur Drexler said this morning, quoting Gordon Bunshaft. When I look at the Chase Manhattan building, what I am impressed by is not the functionalism of modern architecture, what I am impressed by is the impersonal might of the Chase Manhattan Bank which is given by that gigantic scale and that impersonal quality of the detail.

SCHORSKE: As a footnote to what you just said, I remember the public-relations release at the time when the Chase Manhattan Bank was opened, which lauded in the building its "soaring angularity." That was the epithet attached to it.

ARTHUR DREXLER: I would like to address a question to Professor Lefebvre about a statement of his that puzzled me very much. If I understood him correctly, he described the Bauhaus, as I believe he did in his paper, as having invented space. There must be some level that he means this on that would be intelligible to me. Taking it on a familiar, professional level having to do with the history of architecture, the statement involves many contradictions, not simply in terms of the entire history of architecture, as one has, I think, with some reason, supposed that space as an architectural invention is something that occurs under the Roman empire and is successively reinvented from epoch to epoch. In modern times, the Bauhaus, I would have said, so far from having invented space, or even a particular space appropriate or peculiar to our own time, so far from having done that, I would have supposed that the Bauhaus had invented a new thing that preempted a familiar space. It is the disappointment at discovering that this new thing, after the thing itself has become familiar and widespread, has in no way changed the space; it is disenchantment with this, the disappointment of this discovery, that has put the Bauhaus into a certain disrepute. I would add, incidentally, that the Bauhaus in the United States did not enjoy the admiration which, I think, is still held in Europe. That's a question.

SCHORSKE: I'd like to ask Mr. Castells, but first I think the question was addressed to M. Lefebvre. And then I will recognize you Mr. Castells, and Ms. Arendt.

HANNAH ARENDT: I just want to say one word about the Bauhaus.

SCHORSKE: Okay, fine.

ARENDT: Because it's so important, I feel.

SCHORSKE: M. Lefebvre.

LEFEBVRE [in translation]: In reply to your question, I did not mean to say that the Bauhaus had invented space; I meant to say that the Bauhaus had discovered that in the modern capitalistic society there was such a thing as a production of space—that space itself became a product. This very notion has not actually been made entirely explicit, it hasn't fully formulated itself, it is implicitly contained in some of the things that we do, think, or say, but the concept, as such, is still emerging. A building is no longer a single monument that defines the space around it by the radiation or whatever it emits. It is the sum of the buildings that are conceived in relation to the space that they create by their interaction. In the past, as I have said, architects were concerned with the building of monuments, or of buildings, but now they seem to be more concerned with the interaction of their various creations. But, again, as I have said, it is not yet entirely explicit even today, although there is some work being done, for instance, with great uncertainty in the United States by somebody like [Robert] Venturi. It is not, to my mind, a concept we've entirely defined and come to terms with.

SCHORSKE: Requests to speak are from Mr. [Manuel] Castells, Mr. Pawley, and Mr. [Gyorgy] Kepes. Mr. Castells.

MANUEL CASTELLS: Well, just a comment. I agree completely, of course, with M. Lefebvre's statement that space is a social production, of course it is a social production, but that is the point of departure of any sociological analysis. And, we have to go through that evidence, and we have to ask: Which kind of socially good action, which is the center of that social process of production, which are the different processes of production, and which are the contradictions in each of these processes? I mean, we have to go through a social theory of space. I mean, it is the same nonsense if the historians have to do a theory of time: there is no theory of time; there is history. Now, in my opinion, some of the papers presented here were speaking at that level, and were trying to discuss some specific aspects of that social theory. And I think that's the essential point to stress. The statement by Suzanne Keller, before, pointed out the most important thing, in my opinion. Our work, our job is to do that, is to think about that kind of social problem, because, anyway, in another sense, we have no superior right over another people to speak about communities, to speak about urban spaces in the world, and so on. If you want to transform space politically there are a lot of places to do that. But if you are here it's because you have a capacity to think about such problems, and that capacity could be the tool for the real transformation of that kind of life.

PAWLEY: Perhaps it's a little rude, but I think that Professor Lefebvre's suggestion, the implication that we wouldn't know what to do with two million dollars needs answering. It was, of course, a rhetorical question; he did not want nor, indeed, leave space for an answer.

If I had two million dollars, I would not give it to any institution, which was producing graduates for Mr. Logue, who, I quote, wants, "a better product than the one we have now." I wouldn't give it to any institution connected with Christopher Alexander, whose sure grasp of our social and economic realities was expressed in the statement he made this morning: "A housewife who wants to build a house can come into our office." I wouldn't give it to any institution connected with Suzanne Keller, who will presumably use it for the development of telefaxes, videophones, and all kinds of other crap. What I would do with the two million dollars—and I will make it very plain—is that I would fund an institution or organization whose people would be either primary school children or secondary school children, and who would be given absolutely free breadth to develop secondary or tertiary or alternative uses for consumer products such as Coke tins, packaging, and things like that. Our only possibility to survive, in my view, the crisis, as Mr. Goodman expressed, consists in a *détournement*, a French word with which M. Lefebvre is very familiar, a *détournement* of nature, of a consumer society which it is now beyond our capacity to either end or substantively change. That is what I would do with the money.

GYORGY KEPES: Actually, I just want to make two points. It seems to me that the emphasis was on the wrong issue. I had a rather close firsthand contact with the Bauhaus because I worked with Gropius. I was in Berlin at the critical moment of the disintegration of the Bauhaus, and I also just could not help following and reading the history of the Bauhaus.

To say that the Bauhaus was a design school, I think, is in itself a mistake. The second, to make statements that the Bauhaus had a space concept I think is a completely illogical concept. If one wants to speak about certain types of space notion—what some people refer to as the Bauhaus notion—then one has to trace it to [Theo] van Doesburg, [Cornelis] van Eesteren, [Aleksandr] Rodchenko, [Vladimir] Tatlin, or whoever else—the Vesnin Brothers in Russia. And it was a stream which came from an accumulated force of insights, technology, political, social, and if you tried to project the Bauhaus existence and tried to interpret this kind of projection into sociological conclusion, by making it as it would be a Bauhaus notion, known in a certain moment of history, I think, shows a complete misunderstanding of the issues. And that's what I felt. It goes through many levels of this discussion that we are philosophizing without knowing the facts, and I hope I'm not being insulting, but I have to say so.

But the fact is that there is a certain situation that has a tremendous complexity. And we pick out a few probability data and we try to make from a few samples a faithful conclusion, which gives a completely wrong basis for further discussion. I think what happened, and maybe it's worthwhile just to think about it, is that the Bauhaus as an idea, had a continuity, for instance, [Henry] van de Velde, who suggested a great deal of very essential ideas, but like everything in life, it's a reaction against something. And sometimes what we react against is more important than how we reacted. The real pioneers—and it sounds maybe very, very dangerous to say such things—William Morris and [John] Ruskin had a greater understanding of the issues we are speaking about than anything that happened after. When William Morris said that the only birthright of labor is *freudenleben*, he put his finger on the most essential building element of our life: and it is not the spatial units, it is the human material, which makes life. And if we don't go back to this essential insight, I think we could create very beautiful esoteric structures, with a beautiful outside that will collapse like many things that have no real foundation.

EMILIO AMBASZ: I want to assure whoever doubts it that Mr. Pawley's is a really very subtle analysis. It doesn't mean that diapers would teach diapers. The idea he's proposing has a very good, sound historical foundation. In 1948, the Ministry for Education in Argentina was in charge of introducing the national doctrine into schools. They decided that the universities had already a certain position that wouldn't permit them to do it, high schools neither. But elementary schools were the place where the nationalist position of imperialism could be introduced in the easiest manner. They then proceeded in style with the university project of indocrination. The fact that they have succeeded is that I have written the Universitas Project.

KELLER: I just wonder how you expect children to solve the problems that we can't solve, I don't mean we in this room, I just don't understand how.

OCTAVIO PAZ: A new revolutionary class: the problem I think is very sad, because we are talking about critical university or universities, or Universitas, and that is very important, but the university cannot be the real revolutionary class. We are looking for the revolutionary class. The revolutionary class was the working class, and it seems that it's no more this; that is the real problem. Now, we are going to make such substitutions, for instance, children? I

love children; in medieval days they did a lot of things, but they are not revolutionaries. That is very clear.

Now, what can we do? Again, the production of space: of course, space
is social, art is social, but it is not only social. There are some parts of art that
cannot be—when you talk about banks and buildings, they are beautiful, they
are horrible, they are power, they are money, but they have something that is
not historical, exactly historical; they are not only social. Architecture as art
cannot be reduced only to social terms. There is something which transcends
that. And what is that? We could call it dreams. History produces dreams.
When a society produces dreams, we can see the dreams. When society produces waste only, as capitalist society, and bureaucratic society, it produces only
waste, not dreams. That is the big problem; our society, the capitalist society,
and also the Eastern society, with the mask of socialism, are producing only
waste. What can we do? This culture is not only social; it's social but in a contradictory sense, in a deep Marxist sense, culture is a contradictory product of
economic structures. We can do a small thing. We can have criticism. The
Universitas can be a good model if we can criticize all societies and all powers.

ALAIN TOURAINE: I would like to come back to the university problem but
start with a comment on the discussion that has been going on among Ms.
Keller, Mr. Pawley, and M. Lefebvre. I think our chairman was right when
he was opposing, at the beginning, optimistic and pessimistic views.
Nevertheless, I'm more impressed by the common elements and the common orientation among the three speakers, because I think the three of them
could be labeled as nihilists. Some of them are optimistic nihilists, others are
pessimistic nihilists, but they are all of them nihilists, and, by way of consequence, defend an extremely elitist concept of the university.

Ms. Keller says that the world is changing, all the way along it can be
defined just by its change, so there can be no content in education, in the university, and we just need some people able to cope with a constant change.
Mr. Pawley says the university is like an outmoded, disbanded, and demoral-
ized army, and so we cannot do anything with it, and anyway, Octavio Paz is
certainly right to say that if revolution comes from somewhere it's not from
the university, as such, and M. Lefebvre gives a good conclusion saying that
there is such a discontinuity, that we should wait a long while, up to the
year 2000.

Meanwhile, what will happen? Elites, small elites, revolutionary or conformist, will take care of education problems. The rest of the population will
be left aside. It's a movement back to oriental monarchism or, to a certain
extent, in the Western world, to Oxbridge, to the French *Grandes Ecoles,* or to
the best American liberal arts colleges. It's the kind of elites which are
defined by their independence, and where this kind of dandy revolutionism
can be closely linked with the formation of a new ruling class.

I think that is very far from the real problems of universities, in general, and Universitas, more specifically, because it's not possible to be entirely optimistic or pessimistic or to use clearer terms. Any kind of university system has to be, at the same time, central and positive in terms of implementation of some cultural orientation, of some model of knowledge, and, at the same time, it is caught in a social situation, and more concretely, in power relations. So, the problem is to understand how it is possible for a university to define itself, at the same time, positively in relationship with the creation of knowledge, and, at the same time, critically, in terms of its position in a system of social class and social power.

On the first point I'll be very, very short, but I think it's a point which should have been studied more carefully. The Universitas Project is important and valid, I think, in its main intention, because, after all, it tries to define a certain concept of knowledge, which is clearly in the evolution of our system of knowledge—which passed from the study of notions to the study of concepts to the study of principles to the study of systems. And, we passed from a formal knowledge to, more and more, not concrete but more operational knowledge, passing from a study of a theological order to a study of exchanges, to law and mechanics and commerce and then to the planning of industrial resources and now to this inclusion of human and natural problems into the concept of design.

And, here, I think, we should remind ourselves, at least, that it's useless to speak about university and education and research if we don't accept the very simple idea that the first and most fundamental task of a university is to develop a fundamental model of knowledge. Now the main problem is, the university is not just the creation of knowledge. It is an institution, it uses resources, it prepares people for tasks and jobs and so on, and so it is involved in the social structure, it is part of the social structure. And, furthermore, I think it is necessary to eliminate a kind of easy solution. From time to time, I have the impression that some people here believe that the solution is very simple, that, after all, we're entering a new age, a post-Promethean age, where we can get rid of all problems and constraints of accumulation, and our main task is to have a cybernetic view of society and to maintain fundamental equilibrium, to avoid pollution, overpopulation, and so on. And so, in some sense, either it is no more accumulation, there are no more social classes, no more power, and the entire world can be like a local community, and so there is no problem.

I think that even if these problems are very important, they can be extremely misleading, and it's a kind of utopian way, which is absolutely contradictory to our present society. Our society is not interested in equilibrium, fundamentally, but in development, progress, change, call it as you like it. An American anthropologist once said that the only affluent society he knew was the Kwakiutl. They were so rich they could destroy part of the riches for a potlatch; our society is certainly not ready to do so, and we have a rate of invest-ment that is high, so that we live in a society that consumes the smallest part of its product that we knew in history. So, we cannot avoid the problem of the position of the universities or educational systems in a class relation.

What I want to say, very briefly, is that we can oppose two types of uni-versities, according to the place they have in the social system. Both can develop the same cultural orientation, have the same role in the production of knowledge, but have different and opposite meanings in terms of their social role. Or, to put it in slightly more abstract terms, every university has two main roles: one could be called theory or, if you like, production of knowledge, and the other one is ideology and elements of organization of the social order.

Now what I want to say, in very general terms, and rapidly, is this: that one type of university is a unified, organized, integrated, and planning type of university, and this is a model of university which is most directly linked with the ruling classes. And, actually, if we consider the history of the aca-demic system, especially in this country, the main fact is a progressive inte-gration of an academic system. It is an old idea, which has been expressed by David Riesman, by Bernard Berenson, by many people, and which I think is quite true. The fact that the academic system, let's say, in the United States today has three main functions: the first one, which is a system of production of knowledge which binds very closely the academic system, or, let's say, the head of the snakelike procession, to use Riesman's expression, with the polit-ical power, and the economic power; second, a role of integration, hierar-chization, and exclusion; and third, a role of education, I mean of reproduction of the social order. Every time a university system speaks about education, it's a reactionary system. To refer again to the history of this coun-try, it was between the two world wars that the theme of education and, more specifically, of general education, was developed—at Columbia first, at Harvard during the presidency of [Abbott Lawrence] Lowell, and finally at Harvard which produced in 1945 the Red Book, probably one of the most reactionary documents ever issued by the American academic system. And they were, all of them, speaking about education.

Now, education, maybe we could say design, to a certain extent, in the present vocabulary, means to give the main role to the integrative function of society, and the professors, the academic people, the name of their profes-sionalism, actually manage the system within a general frame of reference which is congenial with the interests of the ruling class. So, what I would indicate very briefly is that if we want to have a university that is at the same time creative culturally, which is an instrument of theory, of creation of knowledge, and which has a socially critical function, we could devise a cer-tain number of elements of organization. I just want to mention three or four principles.

First of all, I think it is necessary to separate production of knowledge and management of institutions. In this country the liberal ideas of academic freedom, such as it was used in 1915 with the creation of the American University Professors' Association, has been progressively transformed into an element of junction between a professional role and a management role. So, I would say that a critical university is, first of all, a university where the theoretical function of academicians is separated from the management of institutions. And that's a very important point.

Second, I would say that the demand and supply of knowledge should be completely separated. In the same sense, scientists should be organizing institutes; and the type of education that students receive should not be determined by the needs and orientation and interests of scientists. In the same sense, students should have a completely independent organization and should be able to make demands on the academic system and so, after that, we should have some kind of transaction between the two elements.

Let me say, at the same time, that we should have a relatively complete separation between three circles in academic organization. First of all, the central nucleus, which is production of knowledge. Second (and these ideas are not too far from some ideas which have been expressed at MIT recently), a second circle is, let's say, applied knowledge, or training of professionals, where the control should not be entirely in the hands of academicians, but partly in the hands of scientists, partly in the hands of professionals. And, third, the social use of knowledge, which should be completely open to the [members] of the university, to watch that all social demands can express themselves and not just demands coming from the power elite.

My fourth and last point was that it seems to me essential that the aim of education should be to transform [the elite role of] the student. I think Europe is lagging far behind the United States, and the United States is lagging far behind the Soviet Union, for example, in that the continuous permanent education should become something completely central, and the student as a specific social category should disappear. [*Editor's note: At this point a gap of undetermined length appears in the tape and transcript.*]

So, my conclusion would be that the real position of the university is not to be a center of opposition, is not to be a center of integration, but the university should be the place where the positive element, which is the creation of knowledge, and the critical element, which is the struggle against organization and power centers, should be connected. This, I think, should be the main problem for any kind of university, to be creative culturally, and critical socially at the same time.

MEIER: I guess I have to follow directly from Alain Touraine. I didn't realize I had so much in common with him, and that we have now turned the corner. I think that design, the challenge for the future, the part that makes it most fun (I can't be a nihilist, because it's so dull), the part that's most fun is synthesizing, taking the components, partly of new knowledge, partly of old knowledge, and putting it together into new things, new directions, new institutions, etc. At the same time, when this document came I realized that it really had a major impact upon other institutions so that I decided I really shouldn't be a critic myself but simply transmit the document to advanced students in my own institution and discover what they thought about what was being proposed here.

One of the first things that came out very strongly is that, obviously, we're arrogant. Why should a group be choosing the values and goals in advance for the people who are going to participate in an institution and make it work? To a very small extent, this may be needed in order to provide it with some kind of a constitution or framework. But, almost everything we've discussed has to be redone again by the people who will make such an institution work.

The next thing they pointed out was that the document appeared to be pre-technological rather than post. It had not taken into account the technology that already exists that is affecting design, in concept as well as in action. For instance, almost everybody has been talking about statics when it's the dynamics of film and that sort of thing that are going to be far more important; imagery is going to be on film in the future, and people will live a thousand lives in one lifetime because of the potentials of moving from print to film. This is one big new space that has to be looked at. So the technology of fitting together the imagery of the past with that of the future had not really been taken into account by this kind of an audience, nor could it, very well.

So then, this really posed the question: What is the challenge for a new institution? In fact, the students said, What is it they're proposing that we can't do now? We can do it now. All the things that they're proposing are going on right now. Then we can give all sorts of examples. It's just a matter of initiative on the part of either the students or the faculty or the two together.

Well, there is one thing that has to be done, and it probably has to be done here; it can't be done at Berkeley or Paris or London or anywhere else, it has to be done right here. And this takes a view of the future for which I'm really indebted to Erich Jantsch, because last spring he brought to Berkeley the world planners, either in philosophy or as much action as is possible today. And from this we could begin to see what the content of the books that are now being written will probably be and pose some of the problems that will be the problems of this decade that will last at least for a generation. But, so far, the books are not written. And those problems were really created by, on the one hand, the telecommunications advances that enabled the whole world to be unified; and the connections exist right here in Manhattan with the whole world—very high volume capabilities. The other one is that an invention, actually between the Russians and Swiss bankers, of all things, of moving Eurodollars across national boundaries, and the two together had then brought about the construction of these large edifices called multinational corporations.

But this is only the beginning. And the next stage has already happened, only nobody's yet writing about it, and that is: the high technology of the United Sates has been cosmopolitanized. And, if one goes to the engineering schools one finds that the technological will has already gone out of America, that our engineering schools have had to recruit for their most advanced courses from all over the world, that almost half of the new faculty that is being added to American technological schools got their first degree overseas, generally in China or in India or in Iran or in Greece, or in places like that. So here is a structure that already exists, is expanding more rapidly than any national state; the headquarters, we're in the shadow of them right now. And the new people that they're going to recruit are already trained or being trained in American technological institutes with the high technology. And they have no ethics. There's no community, as such, and there's no feeling for style, and there are series of tasks that have to be done, and, in fact, they have to be done right here in the shadows of the skyscrapers. And, it has to be done both with an organization and with a spin-off organization, it has to be done behind the scenes, and it has to be done in a revolutionary fashion. An institution has no single purpose such as we've been talking about here. The Universitas that I had been imagining, actually referred to the meaning of the term, that there was going to be a multivalued approach that was still going to start from knowledge the way Alain Touraine had suggested, and then move there to action on every different front, rather than, in some cases, critics, who put up the signs and say you cannot go beyond here, it is inhumane, and in other cases it is synthetic, in the sense that it creates new things in the new spaces that are opened up.

Now as far as I can see, the New Town approach would have to be a colony, of whatever would be done in this particular location, otherwise it's only a little parochial effort. If we fail, or if such an activity does not occur, if the humanizing and the provision of ethics, or the multinational corporation does not occur, I actually join the pessimists. In other words, I see Malthusian catastrophes; I see political catastrophes, human tragedies of an order much larger than the last war, and even nuclear ones. And that these are the risks that we take if we don't find some kind of an institution that brings the new forces that already are in being, technological, organizational, etc., and puts them under control. I'd better stop.

SCHORSKE: Are there other comments?

KELLER: Could I link two people, Mr. Touraine and Mr. Meier, together for a moment? I'd love to know, Alain, first of all, whether or not you take seriously these technological and these multinational institutional forces that are arising, whether these trends and tendencies, you would take seriously; whether you think they're important, or whether you still hark back to another kind of rhetoric, substantial rhetoric to be sure, but still where economics in the old-fashioned sense, in my view, is everything, and everything can be reduced to money, or whatever. I would just love to hear your views, I'm not challenging, I'm just curious.

Touraine: Just one sentence. I take it quite seriously, and I'm seriously against it. And that's a large part of the problem, because if we refer precisely to the period of the old type of economic organization, after all, the university did not play at that time a very important role. After all, the Industrial Revolution in England or in Scotland was made by people who were not university educated, and the bourgeoisie in the nineteenth century, the American tycoons, did not care too much about university, at least during their active time. But now, precisely the type of economic and social organization we have, be it in the West or in the Soviet Union, it is much more socially integrated. It is not just a system of production, but it is a system of production, information, consumption, communication, and that is why the university cannot be neutral, cannot be just put aside today. And the forces that act toward an integration of the academic life into the interest of planners just on the top of their skyscrapers is much more dangerous. These forces are much more dangerous than before. That is why I think the university must be, in that sense, disintegrating and critical. And, at the same time, I reacted when I read the [Working] Paper to the idea of Manhattan as the capital of the world. I don't think it's the capital of the Chinese. If I feel myself as being a little bit Latin American, and fortunately it is the capital city of Latin America, but I don't consider the brain drain, and the exploitation of Latin America, as an element of a nice worldwide integration. And, in that sense, I think the university should be militant today. What I oppose is a view which would define the role of the university just on that ground, because this opposition is just nothing if it doesn't rely on something positive, or to use Lefebvre's vocabulary, if the opposition to the social relation of production is not supported by a positive role in the development on the forces of production, on the development of knowledge.

Anatol Rapoport: I would like to address Mr. Meier. He pointed out the crucial aspect of whether or not these power centers are imbued with some kind of an ethos which is acceptable. Can he cite an historical analog whereby centers where great powers concentrated, where empires being built, and so forth, somehow were imbued with that kind of an ethos? In other words, is there any reason on the basis of historical experience to suppose that such might occur?

MEIER: Well, for planners, yes. In Britain you'll find just that thing happening after the imperialism of the nineteenth century.

RAPOPORT: After imperialism?

MEIER: That's right. It is superimposed on the imperialism.

RAPOPORT: In other words, after the disintegration of imperialists?

MEIER: No, no. Simultaneous with it.

SCHORSKE: May I intervene in this discussion? I do think the British example is right, but I would pick a different time. I think the philosophic radicals were the people, in the early nineteenth century, who began a certain ethic inside the colonial administration of England which ultimately became internally linked with other anti-imperialist forces so that the emendatory or ameliorative thrust of the bureaucracy itself, when it proved illusionistic, also had certain technical know-how and understanding that made possible an anti-imperialist momentum inside the British system itself. I think it has happened elsewhere, too. Mr. Paz.

PAZ: Another example: in Spanish imperialism, of course, there were some of the priors of the Church who, in the name of Christianity, denounced the atrocities of the Spaniards in the New World. Well, that is the same thing, the constructive thing; the constructive persons in this country are the destructive persons, the persons who are able to side with the horrors of the American imperialism in Latin America and everywhere.

RAPOPORT: But is this relevant to the question that I have raised? We have, of course, ethical repugnance, we have, for example, people who top the American hierarchy who are sincerely horrified by the genocidal actions in Vietnam, and so on. But does that make a difference? Does that mean that such adventures will not be undertaken? Does that mean that the arms race will somehow be curbed on the basis of such ethical considerations? Does that mean that the dangers we face will be genuinely reduced simply because people somehow become aware of ethical implications of power?

MEIER: I have actually had to think through a good share of this kind of future and I can say that the main counterforce against the tragedies that have been imposed upon us by nationalism are likely to be cross-cut, not necessarily modified in strength initially, by a new kind of loyalty. And this is why I say there's a new raw material for large-scale worldwide organization, where they create communities of their own, nonlocal communities.

RAPOPORT: They're cartels?

MEIER: No, no. These are communities of people who love each other, communicate with each other daily, and they manage world operations, they're powerful in that sense, that they make decisions. And you have many different communities that are coming into force, including the non-corporate ones, following right behind, which are called the international organizations—in fact, the "BINGOS," the business-oriented, and the "INGOS," the international non-governmental organizations. And both of them are growing at roughly the same rates.

RAPOPORT: I seriously asked that question. You say that they do have power, I question that; I'd like to be informed on that. What sort of power do they have, and how do they use it?

LEFEBVRE [in translation]: It might be a bit late, but I want to introduce an ideal methodology. I think that we should establish a distinction between what is relevant to our discussion and what is not relevant. I do not think that we can preoccupy ourselves with such things as class struggle, or student struggle, or oppression. I don't mean that it is not interesting, that we are not concerned very directly with those things, or by those things, but I don't think they're relevant to what is bringing us here together.

SCHORSKE: May I speak to this point very briefly? It does seem to me that we have had, in the discussion here, a real problem which is relevant, and that has to do with the issue of political entry, how do we make a political entry? It was raised this morning by Mr. Logue in one way, by Mr. Castells in another. We've had a variety of ways in which this issue was posed and I think to that degree it is necessary to get into where there is a real integration between intentions of designers who can come with humane intentions and technological skills to a society which can only, in certain respects, use their services. To the degree that social systems, and the way in which one orients oneself to social systems, are fundamental to the carrying out of tasks that I think are easier to establish among us at a technical level, I think the questions do retain a certain validity and relevance.

There was a question over here, an intervention.

KENNETH FRAMPTON: Well, it is an intervention. It's become a rather long intervention. I feel that one of the points that seems to have been constantly articulated during the discussion is the question of whether or not, though no one specifically put it in these terms, design can be a revolutionary agent in society. And I feel that design, by definition, cannot be revolutionary but must be revisionist or ameliorative. And, therefore, in a certain sense, a

Marxist-Leninist school of architecture or school of design is a contradiction in terms and can only concern itself not with design but, as the speakers made the point yesterday, with destruction. And I think, that, for me, relates to the issue of technological reversibility because I think there is a romanticism abroad which takes various forms, and I even feel that Christopher Alexander's propositions are an example of that romanticism, which unconsciously perhaps has in mind some pre-industrial community structure as Ruskin had in mind, and as Morris had in mind, that men would make their own products and employ the act of doing so, and in which communities would be able to determine their own environments.

Unfortunately, I think that state of affairs is contingent upon a mode of production which is organic, the community being bonded together by having identical, more or less very little division of labor, and almost problematically engaged in the same activities. A little bit like the romanticism of the 1950s when architects sought to re-create the community set of, say, Mediterranean fishing villages, in a neocapitalist society. So that the issue of technological reversibility, I think, brings up an issue for a university of design, which, I think, perhaps gives some hint as the main focus to which a university of design should address itself. And, I'm somewhat disappointed with the fact that the interdisciplinary aspect of a university of design has not been emphasized enough, for my taste, this whole discussion. And I think this question of focus turns upon the whole issue of the GNP as an abstraction, which can never be satisfied, and upon the issue of an ideology of waste set against, on the other hand, the fact that one cannot make anything without waste, and so I feel that a university of design is really, by definition, a university of confrontation which must bring itself into conflict with the optimization of production which the abstraction of an ever-escalating GNP presupposes.

While, at the same time, it is in the predicament that it cannot reverse all the technical systems which are already stacked up. And, it hypothetically sits in this predicament, when it has to appeal to some source of a political mandate, and that's what I find the most depressing thing about the whole project because it seems to me that those who are in power in society are interested solely in the optimization of the GNP, and they will not permit any university of design of any significance to come into existence which concerns itself with the confrontation of these issues of ideology and waste.

CASTELLS: Yes, I think we have a problem. They are kind of sympathetic propositions, to me, propositions that are rejecting any possibility of integrating some kind of business of the university, if I can put it in that way. But, the trouble with this kind of position is, why are you here? I mean, if you think really that nothing can be done at the level of cultural politics except by an institution, it is nonsense to be here. You have to be in the world, on the task.

So, if we are here, it is because there is some kind of possibility to combine political action at different levels and in different situations. I mean, it's a very old problem in politics. The problem is that the terms of the opposition between anarchism which is completely outside the system, and utopia and democracy, which have tried to combine the legal and illegal action in the sense of a different logic inside that society, keep changing. So, the only point is why we can't have that perspective. I think we can do better, but this political issue we have not discussed completely.

And just a few words to take up some conversation with Professor Schorske: Which kinds of disruptive institution do you use for the term I talked about this morning? We have, for instance, the possibly at a very low level, to support the movements of urban populations by having this movement, by having people to organize, to demand movement, to counsel us—sociologists, cultural leaders. That's a task, a very low-level task, that has been done everywhere in the world now. But I think that an institution couldn't exist only for that task; that professionals can do this, but not an institution. If we think about some kind of historical example, I think the best activity of that kind of institution could be the possibility of some reflection of the political problems in a particular sector of sociological contradictions. I mean, when you are really in the movement, it is practically impossible to stop the movement and think about it. But if you had some kind of intellectual confrontation, not in the immediate moment of the fight, to start with, but quite closely tied to that movement, not in the time, not in the space, but in the activity, so you have, at the same time, the kind of creative and critical institution we were talking about.

I have in mind an example, the faculty of Vincennes. As you know, there was an experimental university built up after 1968 by the French government and sponsored by the Ministry of National Education. But, in this faculty you have, at the same time, several departments that are working very closely on technocracy, I mean, were training people for the technocracy. But you have, too, some departments and some possibilities to do theoretical work. You have a lot of politics, too, but the important thing now is political problems that are arising from the social practice being discussed in organized seminars, and producing theoretical tools to understand and to change that situation.

I don't know, of course, that kind of institution is much more directly tied to the political problems of a university of design, but if we had the idea that there is a political culture and there are some political problems, urban problems, the difference would not be a very important obstacle. The only problem in that respect, in my opinion, is that Vincennes was built because of the May 1968 movement. Well we don't have to be dogmatic, I don't think that the history has to be the same all the time. I wouldn't say May movement, but I would say some kind of Quixotic movement [should be] supporting your attempt. That's the question.

EDWARD J. LOGUE: I have the feeling that I think M. Lefebvre was expressing, that the meeting is attempting to build a very large and solid theoretical base for a rather slender and fragile practical problem. The chairman yesterday afternoon began with an elegant series of polarities to which I would add only the polarity between the designer and everyone else. I can't speak as a designer but at least as someone who three or four years ago confronted the problem that you face, which was how to build a design school from nothing, this was at the poor, beleaguered State University of New York at Buffalo. We adopted exactly the same solution that you have, which was to invite all of the most dissatisfied and intelligent people we know to come and visit us and tell us what was bothering them. And the message was very plain, which one of them expressed by saying the present generation of architects is not competent to train the next generation of architects. We opted for a systems analysis solution, which I'm not sure was the correct one, it was just going out of fashion the way semiology is now. We caught up two years later with semiology, and the dilemma as we understood it was that designers, most of them, most of the present generation, are trained by one variant or another of the Beaux-Arts atelier method: they spend sixty to eighty percent of their time in the design studio, at the drawing board subjecting their work to the criticism of their peers or their teacher-critics. And this produces something in them and in the profession, which is known as the ability to design, or to manipulate forms and materials in three dimensions in a functional and satisfying way, although in practice it turns out to affect only perhaps twenty-five percent of them who will ever go on actually to practice this craft and perhaps only five percent of them or less who will practice it very well.

They have lost the sense of control over the environment, they can no longer draw to their profession the other strengths—sociological, legal, political, whatever—they feel they need to make significant decisions. And while Gropius has argued eloquently for what he called total architecture and for a design-team approach to this, it comes only haltingly. The problem, I would say, is how to recapture that fine arrogance that the Beaux-Arts tradition had in which it assumed to be able to control the environment completely, from the landscaping to the paperwork.

The question, another way of putting it, would be how to train Ed Logues, and if you don't like Ed Logue, how to train an Ed Logue that you would like. And, to this, I feel, we are bringing a host of questions which don't fundamentally answer that particular question, where there are in existence, as I think Dick Meier has been trying to suggest, there are in existence analogs as to how it can be done. I think of the visual design studio in Rochester, which is run on an extraordinary combination of professional standards and total freedom. In the beginning, the students simply arrived and the director said, All right, what do you want to do? And, after two weeks of chaos, they came to him and said, We want a course in basic design problems.

Another is, I think, I hope a partway contradiction to what Mr. Pawley was saying, is the organization I'm associated with, the New York State Council on the Arts, which, believe it or not, does succeed in being revolutionary and conservative at the same time within the limits of the kind of corruption and co-option to which I would confess. We do manage to support institutions like this one and yet also the Street Theater, the Earth People's Park, the radical workers, and their ladies auxiliaries.

I think that at meetings like this it's always disappointing that there are so few people here who are willing to defend American technology, and I think Dick Meier produced the proper answer: it's one that was suggested some years earlier by David Riesman in connection with the Peace Corps, and Dick Meier was saying that the international concerns in this country find it necessary to take all of the people who believe in the American system and send them overseas. This is because having them around here is very embarrassing, they just get in the way, and the Peace Corps has served somewhat the same purpose.

I say this as a confessed co-opted and corrupted person, and one who would argue within the limits of the examples that I was giving and that Dick Meier was giving, that it is possible in a restricted, admittedly, and flawed way, to make some kind of beginnings of education on a group and participatory basis and of structured and functioning organizations that can work in this unhappy society of ours.

SCHORSKE: Ladies and gentlemen, I'm afraid that with that illuminating confessional we will have to close off the discussion. Mr. Tabibian is to summarize the yield of the four sessions for us in a bare thirty minutes, or to at least send us off with a closing and encouraging word, as I understand it. Is this correct? We open the floor to Mr. Tabibian.

JIVAN TABIBIAN: I had to take some rather copious notes in the last two days, and they're sort of my security blanket to know that they're available if I want to be specific. I'm sure, at first, we're sort of curious about what lies behind the presumption that one can sort of summarize the meeting. There are a couple of things that lie behind the presumption: by the very fact that you think it is a difficult task, the expectations to be fulfilled are very low, so, therefore, the possibility of failure is not that great. The second thing is that, in some ways, not romanticizing the notion of challenge, failure itself doesn't mean much to me personally. Challenges are cultural constructs, and I am either immune to it or have been decontaminated by observing how certain societies have worked themselves up to meet certain challenges, such as this present one. And finally, being the last speaker, there is almost no possibility for counter-argument, and, furthermore, it also gives me a legitimate way, even if in a subtle way, to smuggle in some of my own personal thoughts, and

I will tell you how I will do it. I will try to smuggle it, first, through the framework I will use to integrate what has been said—that is the subtle part—and at the very end I give myself the right to say a couple of sentences which are more explicitly ideological.

Finally, I must, so to speak, be grateful, I can't thank them, that this afternoon both Professor Schorske and Professor Wolin spoke, because, in some ways, they directed me further in a sort of framework and organization that was emerging. Therefore, I remain very grateful to the insights that were provided in their presentations. If I were to be left to my own devices, I would have, in some ways, concluded the session with the presentation of Professor Wolin. In terms of the organization and designs of social interactions, which are meant to maximize the flow of ideas, and the explored new ideas, I must say, that the design of this particular enterprise this afternoon, or the whole two days, could have been improved if we had so organized ourselves that the afternoon's discussion would not have been able to avoid referring to the questions raised by Professor Wolin. I thought that the moment he finished, the entire discussion would go in that direction; we did manage, successfully and miraculously, to evade that kind of almost obvious invitation.

There is no way to summarize; I'm not going to restate. I'm trying to organize the elements that have been presented in the following way. It's a model that I'm proposing to fit into the various thoughts that were presented. Though we did raise the question of life, I'm going to dispense with the question, and I say that, ultimately, in a non-controversial way, we might agree that the basic motivation behind all this is not survival, so much, but maybe, an agreement, without defining what it consists of, an agreement that we have the objective to improve the quality of life of human beings. So, I will use as a point of departure the quality of life as an implicit principle that sort of guides our thinking. And I will further, and artificially and simplistically, propose that we are talking about various aspects of the quality of life, or rather many elements of the quality of life, and these are in fact the physical, the physiological, the biological, namely, those that are related to the comfort of existing, of living; those that are related to the interpersonal, in terms of the quality of relationships that individuals indulge in; the social and ethical combined, namely both the quality and the effect and the perception and the meaning and the norms associated with being a social animal, namely, living with others, with roles and meanings and, ultimately, with values. So these are the aspects of the quality of life that are both, so to speak, at the origin of our motivations, and the coordinates within which we pursue what one might call an improvement: not necessarily a progress in an identifiable sense, but an improvement which is made in the experiential sense.

Therefore, the Universitas Project begins from the question: What can we do in order to, in a systematic, organized, deliberate, and particularly intentional way, improve the quality of life? And what emerged in the last two days: that there were, in fact, two fundamental approaches, two fundamental world views, so to speak, two orientations to the question of how to go about changing the quality of life: *change*, as a neutral term, and assuming that that change for everybody pursuing it implies a change in a desirable direction. This change, though it is a neutral term, for some people in the last two days, means, in fact, improving that which is, while for others it has meant drastically altering what it is. Therefore, the question of more and better of the same versus different is an essential question. This is, in some ways, related to the question whether what we are observing is a degeneration of something that is inherently positive, what Professor Wolin was talking about, and therefore possibly can be redeemed, versus something that is inherently wrong and therefore needs to be replaced by a genuinely new system.

Now, I organized my thoughts sort of spatially on a piece of paper, and language, linearly, cannot do justice to the interrelations that are spatial, but on the one hand, therefore, we have the group of people who want to improve, and those who drastically want to alter. Then the question arises, both of those face the question: How and by what means? Because there is as much argument about how to improve as there is argument about how to drastically change. And here the further separation occurs in terms of changes that are—or improvements, namely continuity versus discontinuity—to be taking place through institutions or structures or roles, the whole family which I will later elaborate, on the one hand, or versus through values. The discussion of the first session indicated that there is a recognition of a realm of values that might ultimately generate changes experientially, while discussions at other times indicated that the changes occur in institutions and then later translate themselves into values. As all such, by the way, attempts of organization, this is a simplification, and I ask for your indulgence.

Now, the two modes, the two motivations—improvement versus drastic change—and value as an institution, dictate all methodology, and first let me characterize the difference in those methodologies. Those who are oriented toward improving, and who ultimately philosophically believe in the possibility of redemption, they are people who speak of problem solution, they are people who speak about professionalism, and they are people whose philosophical orientation is empirical, pragmatic, and realistic. While, on the other hand, people who are asking for a drastic change, their orientation accommodates, in fact tolerates, and at times necessitates, a form of thought which is speculative, which is postulative, and is not embarrassed or impatient with philosophical or metaphysical questions. So, I mean, this is the orientation in thought; and intellectual posture derives out of a fundamental relationship to the intrinsic validity and legitimacy of the system, whether it is to be saved or whether it is to be dumped.

Therefore, one system of thought is basically oriented toward the maintenance of the system, by adaptation, while the other one is oriented toward the disruption and the destruction of the system by replacement. One is reparation; the other is replacement. There is a difference between the reparative motivation and the disruptive and replacing motivation.

As a footnote and a digression, let me go around and say something else, and say that if you are in the reparative systems maintenance orientation, the integration that you notice between societies and cultures, you can think of it as an internationalism of a healthy type, a *pax Americana* in the technological sense, but if you are of the other type, the same integration is better labeled as *imperialism*. The very labeling of the process indicates your attitude toward the legitimacy and the validity of the system that you are either saving or trying to change.

But, from outside, suppose we were to say, What are the constraints and the limitations that face either orientation? Let me first take some of the limitations that face the, so to speak, disruptive, subversive, transgressive mode. Its limitations are this: it cannot, or it has not in our discussions, dealt with the question of scale, in the sense that it romanticizes the success of solutions that can or have occurred on a small scale. The second question is that it faces the question of power, both power internally and externally, namely, the distribution of decision-making authority within small groups, but particularly the relationship of that small group to the larger society at large. For instance, if the Universitas is such a disruptive institutional undertaking it is difficult to specify at this point what will be the nature of its politicization internally, as well as what will be the nature of its politicization vis-à-vis other institutions. But the disruptive mode cannot anticipate and define a priori, in an explicit and specific way, the nature of political relationships. This is almost inherent to the proposition of drastic replacement of those systems.

Finally, there is, so to speak, an insensitivity to variations in this mode. While it starts from the necessity of pluralism, it cannot integrate pluralistic values in a coherent system and, therefore, must believe that if things are left, so to speak, to their own open-ended devices, that how many is inherently possible, and that the result and outcome of revolution will not necessarily be more disruptive than the results of the system that it has destroyed. This is a certain kind of optimism, that is, an optimism related to the harmony that can replace an old order by a new order. Now, this may not necessarily be so, but I have not heard that our discussions were able to answer these questions in any other way but for me to come to these conclusions. I think if dealt with, these questions might be answered, but at the level to which they were developed, the proposals to replace the existing systems did not adequately deal with these questions.

Now the constraints, or the limitations or, rather, the inadequacies of the reformist approach are of a certain type. First of all, they cannot demonstrate that the further massive injection of existing methodology contains, so to speak, the seed of its own salvation. The interesting proposal about the fact that maybe more and better variations of what we already have as technocrats would solve it, whether it's the combination of Berkeley, Harvard, and Yale, or whatever, in some ways, forgets that our existing decision-making elites are very heavily staffed already by those people. Namely, the people who are, in fact, making those decisions represent that mode of thought. The concrete political, social, and environmental problems that we experience have not taken place in their absence, or in their ignorance, or independently of them; namely they are intrinsically related to the decisions of those whose ideology and technology is the one that advocates further reform. Therefore, it cannot guarantee, in some ways, that more of the same is necessarily going to produce different than the same.

The second question is that the need to save the system has to cope with the question of . . . (By the way, the bar closes at 5:30. Depending whether I want to say what I want to say or not, I should either advocate prohibition or alcoholism. Okay. All right.) . . . the question of the other sort of contradiction it faces, or difficulty it faces is that the need to save a system as a system faces the question of having to resolve the optimization of individual and humanistic ethics with the ethical systems. It has not so far demonstrated that the existing way of thinking has solved the technical intellectual problem of, so to speak, reconciling and harmonizing individual ethic and system ethic.

Another problem is that this kind of orientation is only reactive in nature. I don't want to use the word *reactionary*, but reactive in nature, namely, problem solution requires an identification of an existing problem; therefore, its overall orientation is to respond to existing difficulties rather than anticipate difficulties. It's the lack of anticipation that, therefore, creates a gap between the experience of inadequacy and the technology of responding to that inadequacy. Therefore, at best a society that is oriented to that kind of reformism will always imply a group of people who are caught in that gap and who are always waiting for their turn to have their lots improved or bettered. So this society must agree, this orientation must recognize, that it makes peace permanently with the notion of a group of people who are waiting for their turn to benefit from the evolving resources and technologies with which their problems can be solved, because the solutions can never anticipate, so to speak, the problems in this frame of reference.

Another thing is that the very realism leads both to the recognition of jurisdictional and political fragmentation, and adopts toward that jurisdictional and political fragmentation a passive or retreatist attitude, and, on the one hand, advocates a systemic integration, and, on the other hand, it begins from the recognition that that system is decisionally and jurisdictionally fragmented. While we want a systems orientation that is highly integrative, we are invited to recognize and admit and live with the phenomenon of the jurisdictional fragmentation that exists, say, in New York State or in any large metropolitan area in the nation at large.

And, finally, the question of technical solutions: while I agree with the urgency of problems that Mr. Goodman has suggested, the question is that to define our problems as technical invites further technical solutions. We cannot, in fact, deny the fact that in the last fifty or sixty years technology was applied without sensitivity to problems. In fact, most of the technologies from which we suffer were technologies developed as problem solutions, they were developed as solutions to problems, and therefore the reformist orientation must understand that its incapacity may be mostly due to its inability to anticipate nth-degree side-effects and anticipate them in such a way that they do not only respond to present problems, but they are able to respond to the very problems that they themselves have to and will create. And even if those problems are not considered problems in the consciousness of the present, recognizing a change in the dynamic nature, they may in fact be considered problems in the future. Many of the issues that we consider today as problems, if described, but not experienced, to people a hundred years ago, they would not have considered them problems and therefore not included then in their evolving technologies their own answers and their own solutions.

Now, at this point, I want to make a further distinction. Within those orientations, those who are reformist, and that's why I really don't see that much difference between the orientation of Mr. Alexander and the orientation of Mr. Logue, in this reformist orientation I would suggest that there is a distinction, however, between a participative versus an elitist attitude. The elitist attitude is of two types. One is an elitism where a monolithic elite, either enlightened or otherwise, is in charge of, as philosopher king or a king without being a philosopher, is in charge of dictating or establishing proper rules of the game, and paternalistically or otherwise saving themselves and others from ultimate destruction, or leading them to it, and, pluralistically speaking, where elites are accepted as realities and that therefore the problem of social design is one of reconciling those elites, or creating a consensus of elites, and, in a pluralistic way, resolving the conflicts of those elites, where democracy becomes, in fact, that of concurrent majorities, in the sense of traditional American democratic theory.

Now the participative one itself is not a very simple one. There are two kinds of participative notions, one where, if given the chance, individuals are able to harmoniously express themselves and somehow their individual decisions will all resolve, sort of through an invisible hand, into a meaningful compromise and synthesis, and those people who believe in participation but who do not believe in the invisible hand, and believe that that participation must be structurally induced. So these opinions were also expressed here, where some people believed that while participation is good it ought to be left to the devices and somehow impulses and intuitive motivations of people, while others thought that the designer has a role to even structure the modes in which that participation is to occur.

Now, participation elitism is a question that really occurs and is meaningful in the context of systems maintenance. When we move to system destruction or the replacement of systems, this time the dichotomy is not between participation and elitism. This time the dichotomy is elsewhere. In this case, it's the question of the breakdown of the system and its replacement occurring intentionally versus it occurring, what I would put in quotation marks, "naturally" or "accidentally." If it is to occur intentionally, some people propose that intentional disruption of systems is due to occur by the deliberate manipulation of symbols and signs while others here suggest that they ought to occur by the deliberate manipulation or design of social structures. Now, in some instances, both of those are based on either a romanticism or an optimism that we do, in fact, have the ability, either by manipulating symbols or by manipulating structures, to induce historical discontinuities. However, on the other hand, the people who believe that these discontinuities are to occur naturally, particularly from a historicist point of view, again have sort of varying sub-attitudes. One is that of thinking of this accidentally, in which case the only valid position is of passivity, with a certain aesthetic anarchism that underlines it: and let's stop and see what happens, and whatever happens, simply because it's not what we have now, it's going to be good in itself, and let's sort of delight in the cataclysmic revolutionary situation, versus those who do not accept that passive attitude and believe that those discontinuities, structural or otherwise, can be induced or accelerated or given a push in the right direction. These are the ones that are, in the true sense, the deliberate, organized revolutionaries.

Now there is a difference between a revolutionism that eventually leads to a bureaucratization of totalitarianism, versus the others, who believe in the inevitability of accidental discontinuity, who are basically aesthetically oriented anarchists.

Now, at this point (there are only two, three minutes left; you're tired), I would like to introduce the very critical notion that Professor Wolin suggested, the notion of de-structuring. I thought, in some ways, I could understand that notion because the problem of interstitial spaces that I was proposing was meant in the direction of structures that are sort of decomposing themselves, not literally falling apart but in the reshuffle acquiring new meaning. Now this de-structuring applies to this, so to speak, broad and simplistic taxonomy in the following way: those who want to replace the system are basically either working for or hoping for a de-structuring. While those who are working for improvement, the term they would rather use is probably a "re-structuring." Now, the question of the Reformation is only to be raised in my mind with the following critical issue. The Reformation was succeeded—the de-structuring of the Church was succeeded—with new structures with which we are seeming to take issue, we have certain reservations if not very serious objections to the new structures that succeeded the de-structuring of the Church. What is the assurance we have that the de-structuring that is going to follow or somehow accompany the technological society, to what extent the de-structuring of the technological society includes anymore the promise of new structures that are in some ways more humane and humanistic. We can posit and specify, hopefully, what they ought to be. As Professor Wolin suggested, it might be the politics of nurture. If we were to conceive of a new order, rather than the Church or the technocratic society, of a new type of society whose quality and normative characteristics are in the area of nurturing, in fact then the de-structuring would not have been in vain. But to simply advocate and work for that de-structuring without knowing what the direction of what follows is, is at best a dangerous statement, and therefore poses all anew all the previous statements that I already made.

Now, incidentally, there is no need to believe that the improvement versus replacement has to be, in terms of actual historical events, mutually exclusive. Instead of thinking toward a synthesis, as I think our overall Western orientation toward the desirability of synthesis goes, instead of thinking of them as sort of in a synthesis in which we salvage some of the past and work toward the totally new, I propose that what may, in fact, be happening at times is a simultaneity of the two at least on the level of separate consciousnesses, as well as separate actions in different groups and different societies.

As a conclusion, let us talk about the problem of Universitas and how it relates to this. The question of the Universitas fits into this bubble in the following way: both are genuine questions about what it means, and really the questions about what it can do relate to the framework in the same way. The question is: Is the function of the Universitas to indulge in an analysis of society, to determine both cognitively and normatively whether one or the other mode should be the prevailing one? Namely, the function of the Universitas may at best be one of determining whether we ought to repair the system or replace the system.

And, if one went beyond this theoretical, analytic, social-theoretic analytic phase, the second presumed function of the Universitas about which there was some discussion, is if we decided which to do, whether it is to prescribe means and methods with which to do it. Therefore, the discussion and the argument of the role of the Universitas fits in terms of these four quadrants: whether to change or to improve—drastically change or improve—and whether particularly to assume a role of social criticism or whether to also generate tools of social prescription.

Now, in talking about these various roles, one notices inherently a separation between those who are impatient and those who, in some ways, are patient. But the patience and impatience are not purely here psychological categories, as they are epistemological categories. In the sense that there are those who are oriented toward immediacy, and observable short-range results, and those who, though they think that we are in a critical period, because of that very critical nature of the situation, believe that for once we should take the time and go through a speculative and postulative phase, before we come to immediate, and short-term solutions.

This dichotomy, in some ways, and the particular critical nature of the situation in which we are, reminds me of the kinds of discussions that went on during the French *résistance*. During the *résistance* the very necessity of action brought up the question: Can we at a period of such stress and disaster indulge in philosophical discussions about the nature of man, the nature of freedom and responsibility, about pluralism, about participation, about free will? Do we really have the time to take time and think about ourselves and meaning and humanity and survival? Or do we, under the pressure of action, the necessity of action, sort of indulge in action and let action generate its own logic and its own ideology? I think that, in some ways, the same kind of dilemma we face, the more critical a situation is, the more there is a very understandable pressure to respond to it in a sort of immediate, mindless way, immediate and practical way, and rationalize that impatience by this tremendous threat, this specter of immediate destruction and of doomsday. "We have no time" means, in fact, that our thoughts should be oriented toward solving immediate problems. On the other hand, we say because we do not have time that the mistakes can be costly, and if the mistakes can be costly there is a necessity, even at the risk of missing the boat, to cogitate about whether that's the right boat to take.

Now, these two situations are very critical in my mind, and really run through exactly, particularly this afternoon's sessions. I am less impressed by distinctions of optimists/pessimists, as impressed by those who believe that actions are, in ultimate ways, their own salvations. While others who believe that action without a prior philosophical and speculative commitment and exercise create situations that are ultimately and really irreversible. The irreversibility of acts should be our first and foremost inducement and invitation toward, so to speak, a more careful and patient consideration of all ideational systems. I can continue, but that's enough.

POSTSCRIPTS

EDITOR'S NOTE: The participants
in the Universitas symposium were
asked to submit written statements
on their impressions and opinions
as to the course of the two-day
event. Eleven brief responses were
received and are published in this
section. Several of these texts
have been translated recently
by Marguerite Shore.

Brief Thoughts About the Symposium
By Jean Baudrillard

It is clear that this type of colloquium remains too subservient to the constraints of the university's respectability. Certain practices (see the proposals of Christopher Alexander) come up with an exposition that is merely abstract and reductive; certain theoretical hypotheses should be more thoroughly explored—given the dissemination of viewpoints and the need to distribute meaning according to intellectual labels. The organization of the symposium itself (set work sessions, limited hours, concentric public areas, groupings by affinity) contributed to this "neutralization." While this flexible and free formula is, in fact, a compromise, what does it indicate about the enterprise in general? In this instance, there was nothing to judge. But, it clearly reflected *a certain state* of the Project: to acknowledge a phase of uncertainty and compromise, not regarding its goals—at this stage, this sort of project doesn't need to have a defined "goal"—but, rather, regarding the conditions for its emergence and possibilities.

It seemed to me that the participants, too focused on a limited exchange of viewpoints, did not achieve *a grasp of the collective responsibility* regarding the Project, which might have led to a more radical posing of the question, What does this sort of initiative make possible? Also: What are the opposing forces? Now, the purpose—and it doesn't matter which new institution we take the responsibility to create—should be to change the relationship of forces or to overturn them. The absence of this crucial interrogation seems more serious to me than that of the "Blacks," noted by one of the participants.

Thus, what does this initiative impose, what does it stimulate? Is it the *theoretical* demand for a global critical analysis of this society, the parallel demand for a transmutation of values? Is it a certain number of antagonistic, marginal, "alternative," latent, or insurrectional social *practices*, which all reveal the need for a life change? Is it simply the trustees' *economic* redistribution of a definite significant budget?

I don't believe that anyone (even the most favorably positioned) knows this with certainty; all the goals exist together. But we need to be aware that, for the university, each one corresponds to a very different institutional (or counter-institutional) model.

The first hypothesis corresponds to a model of theoretical and intellectual experimentation, a global super-laboratory of knowledge, a brilliant and transcendent institution that, for knowledge, will be a bit like the World Trade Center will be for trade in future decades. More or less long-term, an institution focused on the storage and redistribution of *knowledge* (or innovation, or creative imagination) will have to deal with institutions of *power* and will have to turn toward compromise and coexistence with them.

The second hypothesis leads to a model of social experimentation, to a social counter-institution, which would develop, if on a limited scale, a model of social relationship, and relationship with the resolutely *deconstructive knowledge of the dominant model.* Few things have been attempted thus far in this sense: raising the contradiction between university (in the broadest sense of the term) and life, giving *the very invention of knowledge,* and not its results (always more or less aligned with power), the dimension of a new collective relationship. Can this model be institutionalized? In any case, the experience can be passionate and decisive.

The third hypothesis leads, radically, to the opposite: to a model of a super-modernist brain trust, a subsidiary of the technocratic system, which would "generously" maintain it. In this prestigious neo-institution, an "elite without power" (intelligentsia) and the structures of power would exchange their guilty consciences. One would seek the illusion of participating in power and changing the course of the world; the other would draw from it alternative expressions to *maintain* the course of the world.

In any case, it is clear that the Project will have to play it tight if it is to avoid becoming merely an expression of the "post-technological" revival of a dominant technology that plans its own future crises; and, at this point, it will try to select the systems of political and social innovation that will be most useful in terms of its future crises. Henceforth, we can trust technocracy to take control, *programmatically,* of the "liberation" of the new productive forces—knowledge, information, etc.—in a word, all the accumulation of multiple and interrelated knowledge (no longer specialized) that might be the object of a university of the future. A manipulation of this genre could come under the most revolutionary auspices. The system, even in its most "generous" form, only contemplates its reproduction and the institutionalization of all the new forces that arise, to better control them (as it did for the working class through parties and unions).

That's the entire problem: will the Universitas, planned for the year 2000, be the place where the theoretical, practical, and scientific imaginations are institutionalized and, dangerous in their wild state, become a domesticated force in the service of what the system seeks above all: foresight and control? Or, will it be a vibrant fragment of a counter-institution?

After May 1968, these problems arose in France for new universities, but they still have not been able to be truly implemented; between a rather weak, scarcely inventive, traditionalist technocracy and an obstacle in the form of extreme leftist, also almost traditionalist, politics, questions, conflicts, and solutions have not been able to be dealt with radically. It seems to me that what makes the experience passionate in the United States is the radicalism of the situation—on the condition, once again, of becoming aware of the opposing forces.

(Translated by Marguerite Shore)

After the Symposium: Tower of Babel, Screen, or Establishment of a Real-Life Situation?

By Manuel Castells

The first reaction of those who lived through the stimulating experience of this symposium is a certain embarrassment over the extreme confusion in which it unfolded. Despite efforts at organization, a systematic format, and occasionally even bureaucratic procedures in the sessions, everything seemed vague and lacking in goals, with an exchange of views difficult to accomplish. This makes very clear that the problem was not one of failure, but of an objectively determined social situation. Confusion was only defined in relation to clarity; yet an analysis of the symposium as a social act should take as its starting point a definition of the implicit and explicit goals, of the discrepancies between them, as well as the gap between the symposium and the different levels of achievement and potential for each of its goals. But, rather than return to that jungle, let's take the easier road of establishing a few reference points for the different explicit levels of the Project within which the symposium took place.

1. With regard to the goal of *legitimization* (intellectual, academic-scientific, political) of the Universitas Project, we can state that the goals were not only met, in large part, but, furthermore, that it was necessary to have a certain level of confusion in order for legitimization to maintain its double character of explicitness and differentiation. Or, to put it more clearly, mutual understanding wasn't necessary for so many serious people with opposing views to make simultaneous declarations of exactly the same depth. The point here is not to denounce a certain manipulation of the participants, who were not dupes but, on the contrary, to indicate this astonishing fact: Why did everyone (particularly when the people involved were so different and contradictory) play the game? Despite the definite pleasure of spending time in New York, something else has become clear: the idea that a confused need for a new type of intellectual apparatus, whatever it may be, has become one of the central problems of intellectual workers of our era. And the myth of the flexibility of North American institutions awakens a distant hope in this sense.

2. With regard to the literally *theoretical* goal of the symposium, on the other hand, undefined goals and intellectual spontaneity made matters worse, in the sense that little new was said in relation to the content of the texts. Indeed, it was almost impossible to hold a discussion, with presentations and speakers at very different levels, and following a logic that did not correspond with their aims. Thus, if there were real contributions, notably on two fronts, the university and the symbolic analysis of the urban, as well as isolated contributions (the excellent paper by Anatol Rapoport comes to mind), there was a failure to establish a field where powerful ideas might be

expressed and transformed beyond the perspectives outlined in advance. This is normal, but it is also unfortunate, because the gray matter and level of involvement of those present should have allowed us to create much more in terms of intellectual output, had we set out to do so.

3. As far as the *institutional* goal, the creation of a Universitas "critique" of the urban environment, there were many discrepancies. Thus, forming an assessment of this is much more complicated. Indeed, there were two kinds of well-reasoned responses (leaving aside several comical interventions, which are part of the folklore and "entertainment" that always has to play a role at this kind of gathering), and both are based on strong arguments: those that lean toward a technocratic approach to problems of the environment (for them, the university and institutions already provide a work environment that needs simply to be adjusted, made more systematic, provided with different means); and those that place every critical institution in the realm of utopia and, therefore, either denounce the contradictions between the Project's goal and its institutional and financial support, or demand the establishment of a phalanstery of philosophers outside social practice.

These two viewpoints seem as logical as they are external to the explicit purpose of the Universitas, unless the symposium was the utopian counterpart of a truly technocratic project.

Yet, if we make a serious assessment of the Project, the whole problem for those few, rare individuals who tried to foresee the possibilities of a *cultural policy*, with the necessary compromises as well as requisite assurances, was to stake out positions in the complete absence of precise information regarding the circumstances surrounding the Project. Therefore, by definition, a political (in the broadest sense of the term) stance, the goal of which is to accomplish and reorient the project, cannot begin from an idea, but requires a situation. This would rule out any real engagement on unknown territory.

So, it seems to me that these are the real issues of Universitas: rejecting technocracy and tempted by utopia, it follows a secret policy, which cannot be judged by these results. In this sense, the symposium could not be of help to the Universitas. Utopia and dreams, but never arms, can only be the warrior's repose. Too often, arms are controlled by dealers.

(*Translated by Marguerite Shore*)

Post-Crypt to the Symposium
By Gillo Dorfles

Over the course of the symposium, numerous considerations emerged, which deserve more careful analysis and which could be an important point of departure for a subsequent definition and establishment of a Universitas like the one hypothesized, beginning with Emilio Ambasz's introductory Paper.

Here, it is only possible for me to set forth some of the reasons for major discrepancies that, according to me, were brought out during the discussions. Among these, I would like to stress the following. Many presentations hinted, repeatedly, at the growing importance in today's world of the principle of people's increasingly accentuated mobility, instability, and temporariness and, therefore, their relationship with the city and their surroundings. (I remember, for example, Suzanne Keller's phrase: "Impermanence will become a fact of life. We ought not proceed on the assumption that we will always need a fixed territorial organization in which a fixed population will reside permanently.")

This is one of the points that I feel is most dangerous, in that it addresses the future organization of the education we should anticipate in a university of design.

The moment has arrived when we need to realize that many of the situations and movements that until recently were considered progressive or avant-garde should now be considered outdated and even obsolete. These include the excessive technological mirage, the rejection of craftsmanship, and the conviction that, in the future, too, mobility and instability must be fundamental to the existence of our relationships, indeed, even more than they are today.

Instead, I am of the opinion that, in the near future, many of these situations that seem up-to-date today or in harmony with the times will end up being counterproductive and will be doomed to complete abandonment and reversal. In other words, it is somewhat likely that, as before, man will be destined to reflect bitterly on his current condition of instability, insecurity, and disconnection from his habitat and his surroundings; and he will be led to seek a situation that is very different from the current reality or from the one that now promises to be shared by most of the highly industrialized nations and also seems destined to spread to others.

Naturally this does *not* mean: reestablishing preexisting family and individual values (namely, rebuilding the nuclear family on patriarchal principles, returning to the concept of family and single-family dwellings broadly applied at the end of the last century). Rather, it is likely that the institution of the family—as so many sociologists have predicted—is destined to break apart even more thoroughly; and it is equally likely that the single-family dwelling—until recently dominant in certain countries (England, Sweden, the United States, etc.)—will be replaced increasingly by larger human group-ings, condominiums, and multifamily dwellings. But, it is also likely that we will witness, in a way that is unimaginable today, a marked return to the coun-tryside, to certain traditional and agricultural activities, completely different from nineteenth-century and pre-industrial activities, yet no less important.

Certain observations (such as, for example, the one made by Christopher Alexander, regarding the ongoing experiment in Sweden for new forms of human settlements) would seem, indeed, to acknowledge what I am saying. These observations would demonstrate another important phenomenon to which I have long alluded in some of my writings: a return to the sponta-neous "free" activity of the individual, including in the area of design. This activity might lead to a restoration of individual creative and design possibil-ities and could allow an escape from the danger, on the one hand, of "other-directedness" (which has already been analyzed so intelligently, beginning with the renowned writings of David Riesman), and, on the other hand, of what I have called, in my 1968 book *Artificio e Natura* (artifice and nature), *banausic* work (from the ancient Greek term for menial work, *banausia*). What I mean is an escape from that type of work, so frequent today, where both laborer and expert have no awareness of the true purposes of the work for which they are responsible or to which they are subjected.

And so, the only way to achieve a type of habitat that is not totally "other-directed," but which in itself has a structurally autonomous principle, guided by the individual or by a community of individuals, is to offer the pos-sibility (obviously within an overall macro-territorial plan) of the formation of self-guided urban or territorial centers.

A singular example, and one that also is rather well-known and studied, was the *cidade livre* (free town) that arose alongside Brasilia, through the autonomous proliferation of laborers who were working on the construction sites of that partly absurd, hetero-imposed city. Well, as we know, the *cidade livre* seemed much more vital, at least initially, than the hyper-advanced city designed by Lucio Costa.

Naturally, these considerations are not meant to suggest a condition of continuous architectural and social anarchy; they are only intended as an affirmation of the need for a truly modern and progressive school of design to leave room for new ideas (and not those that are *falsely new* but, in effect, already depleted).

One final observation seems appropriate (also to respond to some points brought up during the debate to which it was impossible to reply). Regarding my thesis about the importance of the "affective memorization" of one's sur-roundings and, generally, of one's residential environment, perhaps I did not sufficiently specify how this is intimately connected with the *architectural and ecological semantization* to which I alluded. Well, it seems obvious to me that, without the presence of some established recognizability—the ability to decodify linguistic elements that address and that can address the various structures of an environment, natural as well as artificial—we will increasingly lack the presupposition that is indispensable if a "memorization" is to take place. Today's citizen often lacks sufficiently explicit points of support to help him build a network of associated images that leads to the establishment of a specific "environmental memory." This is what must be remedied in the study of environmental design, and, generally speaking, in architectural and urban design, as it will be able to be studied and taught in a future Universitas.

(*Translated by Marguerite Shore*)

Postscript
By Stuart Hampshire

The symposium on the Universitas Project showed, at least, that no established habits of political planning or of sociological analysis or of aesthetic theory have the support of any of the assembled group of intellectuals from different countries. Certainly, French Marxist revisionism, as represented, amounted to no clear program for changing society or its methods of education. In fact, I was left with the impression that, of all forms of conservative thinking and of academicism, the variant of Marxism that omits the role of the revolutionary proletariat is the most conservative in its effects on social thought. The French speakers at the conference left me with the impression that they were deeply attached to the traditions of the French intelligentsia and to the institutions, customs, and privileges that support the intelligentsia, and that they were proud of its traditional wit, articulateness, and detachment from common concerns. It seemed clear to me that a Universitas designed by them would support speculative philosophy, the rhetoric of radicalism, and the lecturing habits of university professors; but no general doctrine of the causes of violence, poverty, and technological misery emerged, and no program to remedy them.

I think it was surprising, but also fortunate, that the example of the Bauhaus did not occur in the forefront of the discussion from the beginning: fortunate because quite different historical lessons can be drawn from the eclectic, internally diverse, and historically changing institution; and also because the terms of the conference, avowedly utopian, made [William] Morris and [John] Ruskin far more relevant thinkers than [Walter] Gropius, [Vasily] Kandinsky, or [László] Moholy-Nagy. In fact, the Project really required, and requires, a reexamination of the modern movement, which goes back to [Adolf] Loos and beyond. The problem is a widespread resistance—conscious and unconscious—to the conditions of life that advanced technology had imposed, and soon will impose. This all-embracing resistance is so radical that only so-called utopian thinking can answer the questions that it raises. We ought to be talking about the ideas that concerned Morris, only with much more knowledge and much more experience.

The definite conclusions left in my mind at the end of the discussion, were, one, that really radical thought about planning social priorities and social costs is to be expected in America, the home of unapologetic capitalism, rather than in the Common Market countries. This is so for a variety of reasons: first, because the failure of the cities in the United States is so complete as to demand systematic solutions quickly from even the most conservative politicians and businessmen; second, because American universities have developed within their faculties many architectural and design schools which are genuinely experimental, even if also eclectic and sometimes politically discrete and detached: the necessary studies on the necessary scale can be undertaken in America, and probably nowhere else; and third, for the more obvious reason that the United States has, in historical terms, only the most recent and fragile customs of living together, not the entrenched customs of European societies, and, therefore, the possibility of a break with the past is taken seriously and leads to more than an intellectual game.

My second conclusion is that a meeting on planning, and any conference on broad issues of social policy, requires the presence of some natural scientists, even if their effect is only to criticize and restrain. A room full of philosophers, poets, historians, administrators, without a scientist who is not a social scientist, does not represent the intellectual and imaginative resources that we have. Also, Universitas will need natural scientists from several disciplines. Their view into the future is more worth attention than the view from any other discipline. Not only that, but the cast of mind of natural scientists is a necessary corrective to speculative intelligence.

Last, one could be alarmed (I was) by the assumption made at the conference, and particularly by American and French speakers, that all important questions about human beings, which are not questions about their physical state, are social questions. Octavio Paz very politely dissented from this assumption, and this intervention of his was, for me, the most memorable speech of the conference.

There is always the danger that if one meets to discuss the future of planning, one may hope to plan the future: "the future," here, including the future of art and consequently culture. The liberal belief, to which I subscribe, is that one plans settings, not what is done within the setting that permits and favors the important activities. "Society" is just the name of arrangements, and not of what the arrangements are for.

Symposium Afterthoughts
By Erich Jantsch

Before the symposium, many things about the Universitas Project excited me—most of all that it had been taken under the wing of The Museum of Modern Art, one of my great loves in this city for twenty years, a place of taste, imagination, measure, and quality. I experience quality as an almost physical joy, a joy of life which grasps mind and body, and is spiritual as well as erotic and sensuous—be it watching the New York City Ballet (before its degradation commenced), reading the *Neue Zürcher Zeitung*, going to the theater in London, looking at Toronto's new City Hall or at the John Deere Building in Moline, Illinois, eating at Lasserre's in Paris, or going through The Museum of Modern Art in New York. I naïvely anticipated gaining a similar experience from the symposium, really sensing the genius loci at work. In this anticipation, I felt stimulated to write a paper, which became much broader and much more readable than the planning theories which currently brought me into some of the conventional reward schemes.

Not only did I feel at the symposium that my excitement was not shared by more than a very few participants, I was also appalled by the lack of vision, not only of what was to be created, but even of current reality: these never-ending arrogant, even imperialistic, claims by jealous disciplinary thought; the petty views of science in the light of logical positivism or French structuralism; the helpless evocations of some long-gone Bauhaus tradition; the inability to break through conventional patterns currently established by schools of architecture or environmental design; the blindness with respect to the changing cultural environment; and the insistence on the physical aspects of design.

The grandiose idea of a place for education for "the design and management of the man-made milieu" was pulled down by the specialists into the same trap in which they comfortably sit themselves. Significantly, it was the women (who can never become so brilliantly stupid in science as men can and, therefore never so narrowly trapped), who wanted to help it out—Hannah Arendt, Suzanne Keller, and, in the audience, Denise Scott Brown. For some moments, it seemed as if the challenge of the design of a human culture—not just its physical manifestations—would move the discussion into focus, before it was lost again. With it, any questioning of the role of education, any sense for cultural and social dynamics, and any sense of design became lost. What the symposium discussed mainly was bureaucracy, how to turn out "products" (by which term were meant people!) to serve the status quo, how to please "the decision makers," some of whom seemed to be present and to take alternating benign and threatening attitudes toward the idea of a new place for education having an impact in areas of current power play.

In the context of many discussions I had soon after the symposium with my friends from academia on the East Coast as well as the West Coast, the symposium became part of the beginning of a nightmarish development, which seems to have started in the United States. By this I mean the systematic stamping out of interdisciplinary approaches everywhere, fragile and insignificant as they may appear, in their early phases of development. Student unrest has made the American establishment extremely sensitive to anything that might qualify as "subversive." Interdisciplinarity, which, of course, is subversive to any firmly established power, has been found out. The consequences can no longer be overlooked: the Center for the Study of Science in Human Affairs at Columbia University and the Harvard Program on Technology and Society, both prematurely terminated (Columbia University even openly announcing its turning away from any "problem-oriented" thinking); the Program of Policy Studies in Science and Technology at George Washington University being starved out by government agencies, which reorganize under new names but do not want any innovating approaches; congress instructing the government repeatedly to cease funding of "multidisciplinary" work; RAND Corporation, RAC, and other systems analysis groups threatened with dissolution; the Planning–Programming–Budgeting System, which forced long-range thinking and the assessment and evaluation of systemic impacts of programs, slowly deteriorating since the inception of the Nixon Administration, and now effectively dropping out from government planning procedures; a breakdown of planning and design in favor of the short range, the linear, and sequential approaches to problem solving; the technological modes of thought and action in dealing with social and cultural systems; and the revival of the economic ends-means approach of the 1930s, of incrementalism and "muddling through."

In the light of all this, the ugliest episode of the symposium does not surprise me any more: I am speaking of the "take-over bid" pronounced by the head of the Urban Development Corporation of the State of New York, who was also the most ardent advocate for "schooling down" (as Ivan Illich would say) students in the old way to make them "good products." Half lure, half undisguised threat, this offer to accommodate the Universitas Project in one of his agency's development projects and to trim it to his ideas of a "training" place met with a sigh of relief from some of the participants and sponsors of the symposium. The track on which the Universitas Project seemed set at the end of the symposium is only too familiar. It is the same track on which the original idea of a European systems university got rerouted (by civil servants and industrial federations) to become the International Institute for the Management of Technology in Milan (IIMT), a place for short "efficiency training" of people from industry and government. The original question (Here is an idea—how can it become funded and implemented?) becomes reversed (There are available funds—what idea might suit the strings attached to them?).

I find the "political wisdom" of taking the way of least resistance disgusting, cowardly beyond any necessity, sterile, and despicable. I want to attach myself to, or contribute to, or exercise leadership in this area; the principle of leadership is inseparably linked to the challenge of design—of the design of human systems, in particular. I was excited about the prospects of such leadership, of participating in it. Now, after the symposium, I feel disappointed. It will take a stronger kind of leadership to pull the Universitas Project back from the lulls of an easy life, and to make it meaningful in terms of dynamic human culture and society. I feel this is still possible.

Postscript
By Suzanne Keller

The conference on Universitas was yet another, albeit most enjoyable, example of the difficulties of communication among different disciplines, nationalities, and personalities. Some of these difficulties may have stemmed from vague instructions (too much freedom, no less than too little, can be a problem) or from professional rigidities, but most had to do with the nature of public dialogues in general.

I, for one, thought it regrettable that the meetings took place before a passive audience of critical observers. This, in itself, inhibits an easy exchange of views, a genuine groping for a common language, and the all-important liberty of making a fool of oneself, explicitly at least, during the discussion. Yet, all these are somehow necessary if the monologues of strangers are to move toward intellectual togetherness. In the presence of an audience, there is a tendency to play the United Nations game, that is, to rise to the imaginary defense of one's discipline, country, or ego.

As for substantive content, I felt the group to be divided on a number of fundamental issues, reflecting diverse intellectual and temperamental inclinations. One division occurred along the optimism-pessimism dimension, which, incidentally, I find fairly standard in groups dealing with futurism. Another concerned the different perspectives people wished to emphasize: general ideas—no matter how abstract or tentative—or real undertakings in a context of political or economic constraints. I myself thought that this conference was far from any implementation stage—that it needed first to sort out ideas and impressions, suggest possible lines of development, and work toward formulating significant parameters. I thought the concern for political feasibility somewhat premature. In line with this, I also had the impression that a number of people were convinced that the constraints were greater than the options, and that really novel ideas were bound to be rejected by the members of one or another establishment. On the contrary,

I believe that in view of the various crises facing us, our ideas are indispensable and will get a hearing if we are persistent enough. In my own experience, I find decision makers often resorting to this or that timeworn formula because they know of no better one. To improve this situation we need good ideas as much as favorable political and economic conditions. Thus, I considered our first responsibility at this meeting to be the development of some new ideas and proposals irrespective of their immediate applicability or popularity.

Another characteristic theme concerned an anti-technological bias, which has been with us a long time. Once again, I thought this dated and unproductive. I agree that one must work toward a humane technology, one controlled by human beings in the service of human needs and goals, but this is not going to come about by exiling technology or turning our backs on the new civilization already in our midst: first, because this is patently impossible and, second, because I do not see any way out of the morass and misery of our world except by finding better ways of creating, distributing, and sharing the necessities of life—which is impossible without technology. If there is another way, I wish someone would tell me.

Finally, I found too little futurism for my taste and too little willingness to let one's imagination run wild. I realize that this meets with skepticism (benign or irate) in some quarters, but I think it both desirable and necessary. I think that a set of goals, a sense of direction, and some visions of tomorrow need to be articulated in this era of change and crisis. Without a vision, it was said long ago, perhaps at a similar historical juncture, the people perish. And one of the first requirements for Universitas is a vision or, rather, many visions, of its possible future.

Report on the Discussions of January 8–9, 1972, at The Museum of Modern Art
By Henri Lefebvre

The following reflections serve as a supplement, for the time being, to the discussions that took place at the Museum.

1. In the course of these discussions, questions concerning the future university and the experimental city were fully touched upon. Why? Wouldn't one reason for critical examination be the very character of the symposium itself? We had planned to have "panels," that is to say, a debate among specialists. The presence of an audience, in a very pleasant location, transformed these encounters into a series of presentations. Of course, the major inconvenience of a "panel" was avoided: discussions among specialists tend toward complicity and the milieu becomes self-enclosed. The Delphe method, preconceived and presented as rigorous, does not avoid the dangers of this com-

plicity. In any case, the opening up of the "panel" (which no longer was anything resembling a panel) to an audience of more or less enlightened amateurs introduced a different problem. Each person expressed his thesis; there was no clash of opinions, and no conclusion was reached.

2. Meanwhile, a conclusion was vital at the end of these discussions. The majority of the participants had envisioned listening to or applying an existing science: political science or law, economics, semiology, etc. It seems that each of them thought their "discipline," their "specialty" should in turn dominate the new university and determine the exploration of urban space, and govern any eventual experimental city. The discussion, however, revealed the failure of these extrapolations. In the end, the appraisal is an acknowledgment of failure. For example, semiology collided with economic considerations, and, conversely, the economic calculations and sensible prognostications of economic realists appeared laughable when confronted by the demands of theoreticians for meaningful space.

The hypothesis of a new science (or of several new sciences) concerning a new "object," a transformed institution, was not developed.

3. As far as I'm concerned, I appreciate that new realities—which are literally *unlimited* when compared with those that determined the concepts, categories, and ways of thinking and measuring—demand new sciences, or at least radically changed sciences.

Here is a significant example: there are many books and articles of a serious nature concerning *urban economics*. Specialized economists have studied the effects of urban phenomena on centers of production, the diversity of particular "services" for companies and industrial production. They have studied, albeit incompletely, the costs of production in the industrial sectors involved in construction, equipment, etc. They have gone so far as to analyze the networks that are formed by connections between companies and businesses, etc.

Here and there, in the publications and projects, one can catch a glimpse of the beginning of an outline of a new science, one that I will call *the political economy of space.*

Here is how one can define it, in my opinion. Its definition takes off from the (critical) Marxist concept of classic political economy. The study, such as it appears in the framework of industrial production, is, for Karl Marx and for Marxist criticism, a study of *scarcity*. It rests on the momentary or long-term *scarcity* of goods. It is *political* in that it allows for a distribution of *poverty* in such a way that this distribution is carried out under the cloak of justice and knowledge. *"Summum jus, summa infuria."*

So, what is the situation today? Goods that were scarce in the past, beginning with bread and agricultural products, have lost that important "uniqueness": scarcity. They have become abundant and even overabundant (whether in a latent or declared state of overproduction) in the big industrialized "developed" countries and, therefore, on a world scale, while shortages persist in the so-called underdeveloped countries. This explains the persistent relevance of political economy. The "discipline," as such, is in a state of crisis in the powerful countries. It has disintegrated as a science—replaced by empiricism and pragmatism, market studies, marketing, publicity, etc. While previously scarce goods are now abundant (and unequally distributed, to be sure), previously abundant goods have become scarce, and unequally distributed. In other words, they become "commodities"; they become scarce. It's necessary to continually increase *production*. I was among the first to call attention to and emphasize the importance of this significant phenomenon of new scarce commodities. Important, but *superficial,* phenomena (pollution, deterioration of the environment), hide these serious and profound changes. Space is already one of these new scarce commodities. Soon, air, light, water—in short, the *elements*—will be added to the list.

The elements and their spatial surroundings therefore take on *value* (use value and exchange value). They enter the system of exchange—that is, production, allocation, distribution—in other words, the political economy, but it is no longer the classical political economy concerned with "products" in the normal sense of the term, as objects. As it happens, the lack of space bears no resemblance to what we used to call scarcity. At least in part, space is not well maintained, if not an outright provocation. It has a "spontaneous" side, for the processes that give rise to it are poorly understood, and even more poorly controlled. But do we want to control it? It is more profitable to maintain a scarcity of space around certain points and "privileged" sectors.

To be more precise, space itself is open on all sides. The technical innovations allow one to "build" on the surface of the seas, on the ocean floors, in the mountains, in the deserts, even in interplanetary space. The lack of space is only recognized in particularly defined "places." What we are talking about, therefore, is a *contradiction*, which carries new characteristics within itself. It is no longer only a contradiction in the relationships of production. It is a *contradiction of space*. The contradictions and conflicts *within space* (with all their strategic implications) have not disappeared—far from it. *Contradictions of space* surround them, and bring them to a higher degree of acuity.

Through an even deeper and more bizarre contradiction, as space simultaneously becomes known, recognized, explored, and elaborated on an enormous scale, as an entity it is fragmented and pulverized through retail sales.

Under these conditions, we already know that "real estate" and "construction" have ceased to be secondary mechanisms or annexes of industrial and finance capitalism, but have passed to the top level (once again, unequally, to use again the well-known expression that referred to the great law of unequal development).

The exchangeability of any given place for another demands that it be comparable to other places of the same, or an analogous, space. The exchange value drives down the monetary value, and each commodity appears in the chain of supply and demand in relation to the "cost of production," or the socially necessary labor time. Other elements (notably speculation) intervene to distort the workings of the law of value, of supply and demand, of intrinsic value, of price, etc.

An indispensable ability to compare has been achieved through production of cells for human habitation that are practically interchangeable (and ultimately are), differing only in surface area and volume, and subordinated, therefore, to a severe quantification that extends to their surroundings (the spaces in-between, routes through the area, etc.). Natural characteristics, sites and so forth, disappear in this homogenization.

Will the use value disappear in this homogenization of fragments of commercialized space? Will space be reduced to a sign of prestige and superimposed social "standing," to internal differences within the system, to value produced through sale, with and after the disappearance of its natural characteristics?

No. The buyer will continue to buy the use value, which influences the exchange value. He will not buy only a (more or less) habitable volume, convertible and interchangeable with other volumes. He purchases *distance* which links the domicile to other places, to centers (centers of commerce, leisure, culture, work, decision-making bodies) and which renders that particular volume more or less desirable. But it isn't exactly that desirability that plays a role: yes, it is a distance, a *space,* but it allows an economy of time. We buy use of time.

"Classic" exchange value and use value can therefore be found, but in the context of a complex relationship, which no longer coincides with the "classic" analysis of the great economists, above all, Marx. The two poles of value are situated in space. The reference to social labor (the necessary means), otherwise known as the cost of production, persists, but less emphatically. The competitive element is no longer a factor in setting prices strictly in accordance with value (at the "true price"). What one pays, reaping a benefit or incurring a loss, partially escapes monetary quantification and can, in effect, take on significance with regard to the semantic and psychosociological order. Space becomes *insignificant* with regard to old symbols and symbolism, and, at the same time, becomes *super-significant* with regard to new semiological aspects. In the final analysis, use value defines itself in hierarchical terms: practical advantages, symbols of prestige, capacity for power (relationship to power). New contradictions arise (between center and periphery, between those who rise to power and those who escape it, etc.). Everything is in the controllable and controlled framework of a partially artificial lack of space.

The political economy of space is, indeed, an area of economics with political implications, even more precisely, a strategy or strategies. This political economy of space is in its infancy, not clearly distinguished from urban economics, which once again represents only one particular example of classic economics and traditional political economy. But the political economy of space is destined to develop rapidly. Will we be able to intervene in this process? Will operational concepts be provided? Definitely. This doubles the importance of the most pressing questions: "Who? For Whom? For What? Why? How?" Or, to put the question another way, it is the question of power.

It goes without saying that this political economy of space, inasmuch as it is a social practice in the global framework of the existing society, does not cancel out the production of consumer goods (durable and nondurable). It tends to displace the essential questions, but does not go so far as to abolish them. The problem of management of means of production remains integral, although partially displaced in the direction of organization and management of space.

It also goes without saying that on the theoretical level, the political economy of space implies criticism of the reality it exposes. The critical analysis of production of things in space stresses contradictions, as Marx did in *Das Kapital*. In other words, the critique is internal and arises from scientific knowledge, and has nothing in common with moralizing or philanthropic criticism.

The economic reality tends to break down and divide itself into sectors. General models fail. The economy divides itself as follows: an economy of agricultural products, an economy of industrial products, a political economy of space, etc.

Finally, this analysis is only one piece of a global study of *the production of space*. This analysis is radically different from the proliferating studies of space that offer nothing but descriptions. These fragmentary studies, parceled out and divided up, could be put to use, just as the political economy of space could make use of urban economics and regional geography. But it is necessary to go beyond the limits of these partial studies. The production of space tends to dominate social praxis without achieving its purpose, given current social relationships of production. It presupposes, even under these conditions, the use of technically developed productive forces—initiatives by a group or class—and individual interventions by real people, within the institutional framework, for the purpose of achieving practical goals. Meanwhile, these serve as conveyers of ideologies and representations, particularly representations of space.

In my opinion, this is the significance that emerges from the totality of our recent discussions. These extensions of research do not rule out other investigations, for example, on the subject of celebrations. Are there urban celebrations? Where? How? Are trade shows celebrations? Is recreation integrated into what already exists? What should we think about political celebrations? Violent celebrations? What is the connection among transgression, creativity, and celebration?

(*Translated by Marguerite Shore*)

Postlogue
By Richard L. Meier

The foregoing scenario, which depicts what could happen to a Universitas conceived for Manhattan, in the locale of The Museum of Modern Art, is even more incomplete than the representation of its living predecessor. It was left open because competing concepts need to be used in the founding of an effective institution. They provide a tension that keeps intellects and perceptive faculties alert. The offspring, the student generation, is crossbred; it is vigorous, responsive, enterprising, and impressive. Unless the hybrid is sterile, the third generation most often reverts to an undistinguished mean. There is, however, a fair chance that a hardy new strain—a more effective adaptation to a complex challenging environment—will be established. Although it guides one's thinking, this biological analog must fail, because genetic combinations are arranged through only two sexes: by its very definition Universitas might have three equivalents, perhaps more. What new ideas put forward at our meeting might be joined to what I was able to lay out to produce a still greater range of developmental potentials?

The morning session of the first day argued about value, changed in such a way that the audience, which was both younger and older than the disputants (an interesting case of the excluded middle), could not relate the differences to any known choices that must be made in the course of building an institution. The discussion was not made more comprehensible by the French contributors, who felt that values ceased to exist as a cultural force after the May 1968 student rebellion; discussions of values, they said, had become irrelevant, and it appeared that only Americans were interested in perpetuating the exchange of thoughts on the subject.

The afternoon session on aspects of the theory of signs should have been more relevant because it provided a potential theoretical base for a Universitas dedicated to design. However, the symposiasts presented ideas cultured by unproductive propositions. They seemed to favor an institution dedicated to nihilistic revolution, which, admittedly, implied its own early death. The audience became restive; it could even have been called hostile. Very few of them were tuned to the nuances of debate between various schools of semiologists and semioticians, or the new undogmatic Marxists. (I had been sensitized the previous year by several doctoral candidates who had arrived via Paris and who had lost contact with the edginess of the audience of which I was then a part.) Denise Scott Brown, from the back of the room at the end of the day, focused the unrest in a series of questions that should have been posed to the discussants, if this exchange of views was to be constructive.

A group of us scheduled for the program the next day met at dinner that night to consider this contretemps in intellectual exchange. A failure at this stage might mean the indefinite postponement of a highly worthwhile development. It was obvious that we were faced with a crisis in belief. Western aesthetics were again falling apart; the leaders of the priesthood were in a mood of black despair. Yet, the discourse thus far had only back-tracked. The old taboos for the elite were respected, and the style of violating the taboos of the popular culture was maintained.

It was necessary for someone to challenge the naïve faith in New Towns: Suzanne Keller accepted the task. Beyond that, some kind of blasphemy was needed to open the system. My paper had started in that direction. Indeed, some members of the Museum staff had regarded it as satire—a tongue-in-cheek presentation—because many of its propositions were unthinkable as proper strategies. I pointed out privately to one staff member that for a well-indoctrinated, middle-of-the-road intellectual such as himself, a proposal for working with world business is shocking and, therefore, must be set aside as non-serious. Our group agreed that my remarks to the symposium should go beyond the paper and introduce some blasphemy to raise controversy about real issues that could be argued in the months to come. What follows is drawn from my notes. Not quite all of it was said because the clock allowed too few minutes.

The state of the world poses a challenge to the Universitas that was ignored by the planners of the symposium and the speakers (except perhaps by Rexford Tugwell). It arises from the rapid postwar growth in world trade, transnational movements of people, and new channels for the transmission of information. Old institutions no longer work adequately, as indicated by the monetary crisis we are still experiencing, which was precipitated by the amplified flows of Eurodollars and related securities. We must look forward to many other institutional crises in the future, not only in the exchange of goods and services.

Why tolerate them? Why not throttle the growth of the multinational corporations that now dominate world trade? They provide us with a new hope for peace, along with increasing prosperity. A world dominated only by nations acting in self-interest is highly vulnerable to war, but when strong economic interests cut across international boundaries—increasingly, even the Iron Curtain—the risks of deadly conflict, including nuclear wars, are lessened.

I am indebted to Erich Jantsch, who brought world planners to Berkeley in the spring of 1971 and gave us a chance to discuss prospects for the future of the world. These men came from the "BINGOS" (business-oriented international non-governmental organizations) and the "INGOS" (international non-governmental organizations), as Johann Galtung has differentiated them. There were also philosophers and social scientists. We were able to discuss with them the forces that lead, almost inexorably, to integration and a consequent reduction in the significance of national boundaries.

Some things have happened that will produce strong effects in the next two decades, even though they are not evident today. One of these is the huge expansion in telecommunications capability that is mentioned in the paper itself. Another starts from the observation that simultaneous with the speedup in aerospace technology and the headlines it produced, the youth of America lost interest in technology. Engineering schools experienced an increasingly rapid decline in enrollment, so the colleges filled their places with persons who received their first higher education (from) overseas. The more theoretical and advanced departments of technology in America have often had a majority of such students, of whom Chinese, Indian, Iranian, Korean, and Arab have been the most common. Thus America has cosmopolitanized an asset that had been uniquely developed in its laboratories; but it has very few jobs for such graduates. The multinational corporations are the natural employers of these technologists, many of whom cannot go home again. Their backgrounds allow them to become the internationally mobile cadre of technologists from whom the future managers and executives will be selected. Some of them will come back to Manhattan to direct the empires of the "BINGOS," and others to work for the United Nations and the international professional groups.

The problem is that their disjointed education has created many personal difficulties. This class of technologists has neither ethics nor style. Their early work will be isolated from critics, so there is little likelihood that a body of ethical principles or a set of aesthetic standards will evolve. They require self-controls of various kinds built up through further education and experience, along with a flock of consultants to raise the level of sophistication.

Where is there a better site for such education and experience than here in the shadow of Rockefeller Center? I propose an institution dedicated to the task of teaching, criticizing, and helping private, public, and professional world organizations. The need is obvious, but the will is not apparent.

If the effort is not started now it will need to be created later, somewhere in the same vicinity. If it is delayed for as much as a decade, we must anticipate increased likelihood of catastrophes such as the world has not experienced before. They could be breakdowns in the political order due to failures in bargaining. Equally likely is a Malthusian disaster far greater in scope than the Irish Potato Famine, which is the last one of these recorded. The possibility of an exchange of nuclear weapons would also be enhanced by insufficient effort addressed to the sharing of values about the environment, designed and natural, across national and cultural boundaries.

We need an institution that creates an international idiom both for conscience and design.

The Universitas Symposium in Retrospect
By Anatol Rapoport

Although the symposium was not characterized by dramatic clashes of irreconcilable views, I felt the presence of a wide gap between participants whose attention was engaged primarily by the directly manipulable environment (buildings, streets, organization of space) and those whose concerns lay elsewhere. This is not to say that there was a lack of realization that the material and the nonmaterial environments are intimately related. On the contrary, this point was made, emphasized, and repeated many times. The gap had to do with the nature of the shaping that can be imposed on each of the two aspects of the environment and, hence, the nature of the institutions that initiate, support, or permit such shaping.

An architect is concerned with the "organization of space." The nature of this field of design is such that it must be carried out in accordance with the specifications of the designer. Streets, buildings, and managed landscapes are faithful replicas of their representations in pictures or models. The consumer of architectural design knows what he is getting or buying.

The concerns of the philosopher, the social critic, or the poet are characteristically with the nonmaterial symbolic environment of man. While the nonmaterial environment ("the quality of life") obviously depends to a considerable extent on how the material environment is shaped, the problems of "designing" the former are by no means as clear as those of shaping the latter. Indeed, the question of whether deliberate "designing" of social, political, and educational systems is at all meaningful, let alone whether it is desirable, by no means elicits unequivocal answers except from people committed to extreme technocratic or anti-technocratic positions.

Attempts at deliberately designing man's nonmaterial environments have certainly been made. Some of the modern states have come into being as a consequence of conscious acts, motivated by preconceived notions about the nature of man-in-history or man-in-society and, hence, about the sort of nonmaterial environment that best fits him. Invariably, such "designed" societies have developed along lines altogether different from those envisaged by their designers (the "founding fathers"). Moreover, the degree and the nature of the discrepancy are by no means objectively ascertainable, as it is in the case of comparing realized physical objects with their blueprints.

In short, while as a consequence of progressive growth of technology and of the increase in size of social units under central control, the idea of designing and realizing certain aspects of the physical environment is flourishing; the counterpart of this idea—that of designing a livable nonmaterial environment—has either injected elements of an Orwellian nightmare into the images of the future or has remained the focal point of sterile controversies. The reason is not far to seek. Institutions (largely, determinants of the nonmaterial environment), to the extent that they are deliberately designed, are designed either by wielders of political power or by those who seriously challenge that power in the political arena—or else by utopians. In the first instance, means of implementing the designs are available, but the process of implementation directs the realization of the designs toward serving the interests of the power elites, however these interests may be rationalized in terms of laudable social goals. In the second instance (when the challengers are reformist or revolutionary political coalitions with well-formulated programs), the design of a reformed or radically reconstructed social order serves more as a rallying point for recruiting adherents than as a concrete plan of action. In the third instance, the utopias remain dream visions. A prominent and inescapable impression from historical experience is that the original aims of a designed social order become perverted or degraded to the extent that means of implementation become available. I had hoped that the session on semiotics would be devoted to this theme (the relations between the activating potential of symbols constituting an ideology and what turn out to be the concrete referents of those symbols). However, this theme was not brought out at that session.

To my way of thinking, the symposium was dominated (or perhaps ought to have been dominated) by the following dilemma. Design means foresight. Something is designed to serve some need coupled with knowledge of how the thing designed will serve the need. The realization of the purpose of design is effective only if the need can be stated sufficiently explicitly. For, only then can we clearly discern whether the realized design has fulfilled the purpose or not. Such is the case when a piece of technology is designed. The design of a vehicle to take some men to the moon and back has been an unqualified success in terms of the specific purpose for which the vehicle was designed. For, the men actually went to the moon and came back. The design of a nuclear bomb was another instance of success, because the bomb can demonstrably do what it has been designed to do. The latter example illustrates dramatically that "success" can be claimed only if the criteria of success are strictly confined to the effective realization of a very specific purpose, that is, if one foregoes asking sometimes quite obvious questions that immediately suggest themselves, questions of how the realized purpose fits into a larger scheme or how the needs of some people that have been satisfied relate to the needs of other people or even to other needs of the same people or to future needs. Technocrats eschew such questions. Since the symposium was certainly not dominated by technocrats, questions of this sort were fully aired. It cannot be denied, however, that such questions are, in a way, at cross purposes with questions related to design proper; because the designer *must* work for a purpose and must, at least for the duration of his work, fix his attention on purposes that are assumed to be "good" and that "stay put." For this reason, some questions raised at the symposium must have been disturbing to some of the participants. I would have liked to see a more explicit confrontation on that issue.

Success is addictive and not only in the primitive ego-feeding sense. Success in large-scale enterprises is achieved by inculcating the participants with a sense of collective solidarity and by developing virtuosity by intricate coordination of efforts. These experiences are gratifying to probably most people, and this is an important reason why people derive satisfactions from participating in organized activities. If the specific goals of an organization are achieved, the satisfactions are intensified. Consequently, there is a resistance against questioning the "ultimate purposes" served by the successes; or else a tendency develops to rationalize the goals of the organization in terms of wider goals, presumably served by it. A well functioning, i.e., victorious war machine, with its well-defined goals that are easily rationalizable ideologically, is a prime example of an institution that nurtures addiction.

In the case of a war machine, the schism between its supporters and its enemies is rather clear-cut. The enemies reject the goals served by the machine and with them its very raison d'être. In the case of an educational institution, such as a university of design, ambiguities arise that must be faced. An educational institution is characteristically described as "serving the needs of society." Most of us live in societies where consensus on the "needs of society" is practically impossible to achieve, because critics of existing social systems keep raising the thorny question of *whose* needs are identified with the "needs of society." They will not accept "the needs of society" as a meaningful concept, at least in the present "advanced" societies. Consequently, any discussion centered about the design of educational institutions, especially educational institutions that are themselves concerned with problems of design, necessarily take directions only tangential to the problems of design. Such discussions cannot be expected to be concentrated on questions of equal interest to all participants. The symposium on the Universitas was no exception.

I would have liked to hear more explorations, in depth, of the central theme of higher education in Western societies. For this central problem is relevant to the design of any educational institution, and especially one like the Universitas. Those who continue to "believe in" institutionalized higher education recognize its three avowed purposes: to enrich the inner life of the educated, to perpetuate a cultural heritage, and to "produce" people with socially useful skills. Those who have given up the hope of harmonizing these three purposes or who have rejected outright one or more or them, declare all institutionalized education to be useless or even harmful. I count myself among those who cannot see how, in most so-called "advanced" societies, the freedom-nurturing purpose and the "social usefulness" purpose of higher education can be reconciled. Yet, I cannot bring myself to disavow loyalty to institutionalized higher education in the same way that I have disavowed conventional "patriotic" loyalty to the nation state. Is my reluctance to "write off" the university simply a rationalization of my "class interest" as reflected in the comfortable position I occupy in the academic world? Or can the idea of a university as a community serving worthy human purposes (as distinguished from "the needs of society") still be implemented, in particular, in an institution such as the Universitas purports to be? If so, who will be motivated to study in such an institution? (There is no problem with the motivation to teach: professors are paid.) After having studied at the Universitas, what will people do later? Will they be offered or will they accept jobs as architects, industrial designers, city planners, or managers in presently existing institutions and firms? If so, will the purpose of the Universitas become simply that of serving existing institutions "better" (in terms of the traditional purposes of those institutions)? A plea for that sort of training institution was made by at least one participant. Or, will the graduates who enter the working world expect to change the purposes of existing institutions? Or, perhaps undermine or subvert at least some of them? If the latter, how will the Universitas be financed, and where will its graduates get jobs?

Such are the questions that brought me to the symposium. They remain unanswered. I must confess that I did not expect to have them answered. I came away with the impression that the symposium served an important purpose of providing a forum where questions of this sort could be aired. They are not new, being persistently raised all the time in circles concerned with higher education. But they are well worth iterating.

The Creative and Critical University
By Alain Touraine

1. Universities speak readily of the need to adapt to changes in society. They have to, due to the increased demand for higher education, as well as the development of new and highly specialized fields of work. Less frequently, they reform themselves or modify their functioning, their system of decision-making, their relationship to authority, their pedagogy, or their qualifications.

It is even rarer for them to confront the central issue of their social purpose. This question is essential today. Furthermore, it is necessary to go even beyond a critical analysis of the social utilization of knowledge, to reflect on the very nature of knowledge, the creation and dissemination of which is the university's mission.

The Universitas Project is important precisely because it proposes a new vision of knowledge.

We propose a general interpretation: knowledge moves from the definition of principles to the analysis of systems, to the degree that societies gain a greater capacity to act on themselves and have a growing need to know the conditions of their activity. In a society where capacity for self-transformation is weak, knowledge is the recognition of the organization of the world and of the essence and working of the human spirit. Formal knowledge, classified into trivium and quadrivium, seeks to impose order on the world of phenomena and to free logic from ideas.

The development of market capitalism and the State as organizer and protector of trade is linked to the development of a new system of knowledge, organized around principles of balance and the functioning of mechanical or juridical bodies. With the large-scale development of capitalist industrialization and, thus, the increased ascendancy of man over nature, knowledge of movement of natural systems became the primary goal. Evolution and historicism were the most general principles of this knowledge.

Today, economic development is linked more than ever to the capacity to manage systems. But, at the same time—and here is the most interesting new development for defining the university—society's action on itself is no longer limited to the manipulation of "nature." The separation between the natural and social sciences—a classic notion of nineteenth-century German thinkers—is increasingly eradicated, both in social practice, because large organizations serve as communications systems between both protagonists and integrated technical bodies, and in theory, where ideas circulate among biology, linguistics, and economics.

All highly industrialized societies, engaged in decisive efforts for economic transformation, act directly upon human relations, attitudes, and needs. The separation between public and private life, work and non-work, disappears. The economic and political decision-making centers extend their domination, beyond the facts of production, to those of communication and consumption. Social sciences are formed in response to this new situation. The university can no longer define itself by knowledge of the order, or even the movement, of things; its intellectual task is to analyze the conditions and forms of the functioning and transformation of systems of human activity.

Such is the general implication of the theme of the environment, beyond style and strictly pragmatic goals.

The university is, thus, no longer separated from its object of study, as was the thinker, reflecting on the nature of the world. Its knowledge activity is part of the system of actions it is studying. Critical reflections on the conditions and social use of knowledge have also become inseparable from the university's progress.

2. The problem lies at the heart of university work, but it is so agonizing that almost everyone seeks to escape it, going in opposite directions.

For some, the problem that I've just posed is nothing but the expression of old habits. Our society defines itself by change, not by principles. It fully recognizes capitalism's huge innovations, which multiply trade, open markets, knock down borders and regulations, and replace ascribed positions with achievement, and personal relations with strategies, interests, and negotiations.

It's all about giving free reign to technical progress, to economic calculations, and the mobility of people, goods, and information.

Within the realm of the university itself, what's essential is to open access to knowledge, to stimulate innovation, to erase obsolete and constraining barriers, which separate the traditional domains of research and teaching.

This large theme of modernization merits the same criticisms here as those that were addressed by developmental sociologists. The most fundamental criticism is that reality does not correspond to this optimistic image. Instability, inequality, and contradictions do not disappear in a supposedly all-inclusive market society. Cities rot, the gap between rich and poor on a world scale is growing or holding fast, opening the university to the masses does not mean its democratization. New conflicts, new social movements appear, and the illusions of those who believed they had seen the end of ideologies in the 1950s are carried away by the massive renewal of utopias, ideologies, and challenges to them.

What is directly called into question in the university is the relationship between science and power; the vanity of a "professionalism" that doesn't want to see that the orientation of research is linked ever more closely to the needs of power.

These evident observations lead other observers and players to entirely reject the link (considered diabolical) between knowledge and the Promethean labor of accumulation and development, which imposes the dependence of knowledge on power.

The themes of stability and participation are counterposed to those of growth and achievement. The university must be a place for community and expression, just as knowledge must research the conditions of man's integration into nature, and the ecosystem's requirements for survival.

This is a democratic, Charles Fourier–like image in an extreme form, which takes up the populist themes already evident in America at the end of the nineteenth century, and which has always nurtured an antiauthoritarian tradition in pedagogy.

This position has a certain critical value: it contributed to the shake-up of the established order and its reassuring discourse, and spurred debate.

But it also merits criticism, in turn. If we want a true university for the masses, in the first place we have to liberate what we call "the people" from the domination under which they suffer. Otherwise, putting the university in the service of the people means turning it over to notables, or transforming it into a ghetto that will suffer under the full weight of alienation.

And, if the university serves the purpose of popular power, its concerns are no longer expression and stability, but rather the mobilization, development, and reinforcement of power's capacity for action.

Populist utopias seem to me to be a mix of defense of the privileges of those who are the richest segment of ruling societies, and uncontrolled moral crisis subordinated to the demands of profit and power.

3. In our type of society, the university can be neither "modernist" nor "pseudo-populist." It can only be antiestablishment, which, in the first

instance, means that it must denounce the confusion between knowledge and the social utilization of knowledge. It shouldn't address stability, pollution, or urban crisis, but, rather, the struggle against capitalism, autocracy, and technocracy. It must uncover the social problems masked by so-called "natural" situations: the financial speculation that lies hidden in the city, the profit in work, the class privilege in education.

And, it is only in basing itself upon knowledge, and conceiving of knowledge as the explanation of how society acts on itself and its environment, that this social critique can lead in a positive direction. Otherwise, it will get lost in a lyrical illusion that poses no serious threat to the system of power, and will be easily co-opted by a consumer society that knows how to interpret demands for expression and power in ways that reinforce the dominance of the ruling class. The university cannot exist outside power, on the margins of society, while the development of knowledge plays a central role in the functioning and evolution of highly industrialized or post-industrial societies.

The university cannot be completely immersed in society, as it is also a force for production in society, but this very role, like all scholars, is close to the power on which its resources depend, and which has the means to influence it.

The more the university accepts a self-image of its own neutrality and its exclusive "professionalism," the more easily it subordinates itself to the dominant interests and ideologies. Therefore, the university must be critical and antiestablishment, above all, in search of social reality beyond self-satisfied discourse and the seeming neutrality of technical education.

Student pressure and initiative on the part of all academics to reveal social and cultural demands that have no independent or reliable means of expression should help prevent the university from becoming an instrument for reproducing the social order and, quite the contrary, turn it into a locus of analysis and consciousness of the conditions and orientation of how societies function and how they change.

This operation presumes certain changes in the way that universities function. I have indicated a few of these changes in my paper, and I would like to briefly highlight a few others.

— A university is not isolated; it is part of a university system and, more broadly, part of an educational system. These systems are organized into a hierarchy that replicates the social hierarchy. Thus, it is necessary to very consciously carry out antihierarchical measures, which can only proceed by attempting a horizontal differentiation between institutions. The theme advanced by the Germans from the *Gesamthochschule* should be an essential goal of all university reform.

— A university must systematically favor culturally deprived students, both young and adult, not only to achieve a better equality of opportunity but to struggle against the university's own discourse, which mixes up scientific content ideology with the dominant culture.

— Finally, the university must be militant. I certainly do not demand that the university identify itself with a particular social or political force, but it must fearlessly play an analytical and critical role, above all, with regard to itself. In this period of large organizations, it is no longer possible for a critical awareness of society to be expressed only by independent and isolated intellectuals. A university must be capable of committing itself to denounce lies, to expose what is hidden, to show what choices were made in what appear to be events resulting from natural developments or pure technology. This presumes internal debates, and, often, there will not be sufficient agreement to take a collective position. But enlarging its realm of intervention should at least be the intention of a university. That such a commitment entails risks is certain. But the moment that a university's major concern is to avoid taking risks, to secure its future, to be accepted, it has already made a choice—that of conforming to the established order. I do not think that the involvement of certain American universities in the struggle against the war in Vietnam meant that they abandoned scientific research. It was not the most mediocre teachers who played a leading role in offering a political critique of decisions, information, and institutions—far from it.

The role of the university today is too important to allow it to turn back, to shut itself off within its ivy-covered walls.

(*Translated by Marguerite Shore*)

Afterthoughts Concerning the Education of Designers
By Rexford Guy Tugwell

Reflection on the dialogue in January (1972) concerning the shape and purpose of an educational institution centering on design has reinforced the feeling that too little attention is being paid to environmental constriction from man-made causes.

This shows itself particularly in buildings and their surroundings, but extends inevitably to whole cities and towns. It is, of course, necessary to accept natural conditions and to work with and within them. Geography and climate are the most obvious of these. The proximity of rivers and harbors, surrounding mountains and plains, the character of soils and immediate resources— these are geographic. Temperature and humidity ranges, rainfall, probability of inversions, fogs and the like—these are climatic. Both have to be accepted.

New York has an underpinning of hard rock; Chicago has a fresh-water lake; Los Angeles is located in a basin; Washington is in a humid, watery area. Every urban situation, in fact, is different, and if recognized for what it is, may be taken advantage of by designers in order to produce something unique.

Certain man-imposed limitations tend to prevent this. As long as land is privately exploited, there will be designing calculated to suit the demands of those who insist on uses of the highest density. This tends to prevent the proximity of work and living places since commercial uses are more profitable when squeezed together. This, in turn, creates problems of transportation from bedroom to business localities, an enormous expense that falls on the public. It prevents the development of spacious amenities and creates the congestion so familiar in all large American cities.

Designers themselves cannot escape from these constrictions, which are imposed by the economic environment. They may, however, join in pleading for the freedom necessary to civilized management; and, in any case, they ought not to be blind to such constrictions on their work. Occasionally they are able, as in satellite towns or in new cities, to demonstrate the effect of free space; but the problems of the great urban concentrations continue to grow worse, and solutions are not to be found in designing alone, however imaginative.

It does not seem unreasonable for an educational institution to consider the relationship of design to the economic environment and, while doing what can be done under difficult conditions, identify the source of the difficulties and, as well, the alternatives.

The other strong impression from the discussions has to do with the confusion of design with planning. It is impossible to plan without some control of the resources to be made available. Designers must operate within this condition; but they do not have responsibility for making the condition. That this relationship is little understood is shown in a number of ways, but, as well as any, in refusal to consider the conditioning of time.

The passage of time is the one inevitable fact to be dealt with. It has measured units; but what may happen within these units is something to be discovered only by the most sophisticated forecasting techniques, and then only within imprecise margins of error. Yet one characteristic is known. There will be innovations. There will be altered demands (in education, medicine, transport, communications, for instance).

The effect of these realities on the arts of design ought to be cautionary. A building for almost any purpose more than twenty-five-years old (say) will be obsolete. Immense permanent investments in hospitals, transport facilities, and so on, can become an incubus if too great a commitment is made. This makes a problem for designers they are reluctant to recognize. They have a propensity for permanence, for making a mark; but this is a futile hope. Things change, some, of course, more rapidly than others, but all do change. The best a designer can do is to merge his work usefully in the ongoing creation of future institutions.

It is suggested that these considerations deserve to be put before beginning designers as they pursue their education. They should be part of any educational program.

Biographies of the Participants

CHRISTOPHER ALEXANDER (1936-)
Architect, educator, and design methodology theoretician; Universitas symposium panelist

Christopher Alexander was born in Vienna, Austria, in 1936, and raised in Oxford and Chichester, England. He attended Cambridge University, where he received a BA in architecture and an MA in mathematics. He earned a PhD in architecture at Harvard University with a thesis later published as *Notes on the Synthesis of Form* (Harvard, 1964), for which he was awarded the first Gold Medal for Research by the American Institute of Architects in 1970. Alexander was appointed Professor of Architecture at the University of California at Berkeley in 1963. In 1967, he became a founder and Director of the Center for Environmental Structure, Berkeley. He was later a Professor in the Graduate School and, as of 1999, has been Professor Emeritus of Architecture at Berkeley.

Alexander is the creator of Pattern Language, an approach to architectural thinking based on the idea that one set of universal laws determines the structure of a city, a building, or a room. Originally intended to enable every citizen to design and construct his or her own home, Pattern Language resulted in a liberation from architectural dogma; its abstraction of the process by which organic and inorganic forms evolve presented a coherent alternative to the use of imposed grids and zones in environmental and urban design. Alexander's ideas have perhaps had a greater impact on computer science than on architecture; theoretical structures that he defined are now recognized as general frameworks in computer programming and software development. Alexander has designed and built numerous buildings, lectured widely, and is the author of many books and papers. Among his key publications are: "A City Is Not a Tree," *Architectural Forum* 122, nos. 1 and 2 (April and May 1965): 59–61, 58–62; Alexander et al., *A Pattern Language: Towns, Buildings, Construction* (New York: Oxford, 1977); *The Timeless Way of Building* (New York: Oxford, 1979); Alexander et al., *A New Theory of Urban Design* (New York: Oxford, 1985); and *The Nature of Order* (New York: Oxford, 2002).

EMILIO AMBASZ (1943-)
Architect, industrial and graphic designer, inventor, and museum curator; director of the Universitas Project

Emilio Ambasz was born in Resistencia, Chaco, Argentina, in 1943. He left Argentina in 1966 to study at Princeton University, where he completed the undergraduate program in one year and earned an MFA in architecture the following year. He was a visiting professor at the Hochschule für Gestaltung in Ulm in 1967, and a co-founder of the Institute for Architecture and Urban Studies in New York under the auspices of The Museum of Modern Art, also in 1967. In 1967–69 he was Philippe Freneau Professor of Architecture at Princeton, and in 1970 he became Curator of Design at The Museum of Modern Art. At the Museum, Ambasz organized numerous influential exhibitions and wrote their accompanying catalogues, notably *Italy: The New Domestic Landscape* (1972), *The Architecture of Luis Barragan* (1976), and *The Taxi Project: Realistic Solutions for Today* (1976).

In 1976 Ambasz established Emilio Ambasz & Associates, an architectural and industrial design practice in New York and in Bologna, Italy. His pioneering architectural work established him as a leader in the field of "green," or sustainable, architecture, with such award-winning projects as the Fukuoka Across Building and the Mycal Cultural and Sports Center in Japan, the Glory Museum in Taiwan, the Conservatory at the San Antonio Botanical Center in Texas, Monuments Towers Office Building in the United States, the Venice-Mestre Hospital and the Nuova Concordia hotel and residential complex in Italy, and the Museo de Arte Moderno de Buenos Aires in Argentina. Ambasz has invented and patented numerous industrial and mechanical designs, including the world's first automatic ergonomic office seating system, Vertebra, for Open Ark in 1977, and track lighting systems for German and Italian manufacturers (Logetec, Osiris, etc.). He was Chief Engineer and Design Consultant for the Cummins Engine Company in Columbus, Ohio, from 1978 until recently. Among his many furniture designs are the Visor stacking chair for Knoll, the Brief office chair for Poltrona Frau, the Qualis office chair for Tecno-Europe, and the portable desktop for IBM. Ambasz's extensive and innovative body of work has been accorded many honors and awards over several decades of practice in which he has "sought to reinterpret the poetic aspects of modernism and the relationship between architecture and the landscape."

Ambasz's work has been the subject of numerous exhibitions internationally, and his publications include many books by him and about him and his oeuvre. Notable among these are: Mario Bellini et al., *Emilio Ambasz: The Poetics of the Pragmatic—Architecture, Exhibits, Industrial and Graphic Design* (New York: Rizzoli, 1989); Peter Buchanan et al., *Emilio Ambasz, Inventions: The Reality of the Ideal* (New York: 1992); *Emilio Ambasz: Natural Architecture, Artificial Design*. Intro. Terence Riley (Milan: Electa, 2002); Michael Sorkin et al., *Analyzing Ambasz* (New York: Monacelli, 2004); Fulvio Irace, *Emilio Ambasz: A Technological Arcadia* (Milan: Skira, 2004); and *Emilio Ambasz: Casa de Retiro Espiritual*. Intro. Peter Buchanan (Milan: Skira, 2005).

HANNAH ARENDT (1906–1975)
Historian, political theorist, philosopher, author; Universitas symposium panelist

Hannah Arendt was born in 1906 in Hannover, Germany, and was raised in Königsberg and Berlin. In 1922, she began her studies in classics and theology at the University of Berlin, but by the following year had entered Marburg University where she studied philosophy with the phenomenologist Martin Heidegger, later moving to Heidelberg to study with the psychiatrist and existentialist philosopher Karl Jaspers. Involved in Zionist politics from 1926, and fearing Nazi persecution, Arendt fled to Paris with her first husband, the Jewish philosopher Gunther Stern, in 1933. There she met Heinrich Blücher, a German political refugee, whom she married in 1940. Following detention in separate camps as enemy aliens, Arendt and Blücher reunited and fled to the United States the next year. In America, Arendt worked as a writer and editor, and later as a professor at many universities, among them the University of California at Berkeley, the University of Chicago, and, from 1967, at the New School for Social Research in New York. Arendt died, in 1975, world-renowned as one of the most original, challenging, and influential political thinkers of the twentieth century.

Arendt's wide-ranging philosophical inquiries produced no systematic body of thought but covered diverse topics such as totalitarianism, revolution, freedom, thought and judgment, the history of political thought, and the ordinary character of human and political experience. Her first book, *The Origins of Totalitarianism* (New York: Harcourt, 1951), touched on many themes that recurred in her subsequent work: the possibility of a humane and democratic public life, and the examination of historical, social, and economic forces that threaten such life. Her next book, *The Human Condition* (Chicago: 1958), undertook a thorough historical-philosophical inquiry into the origins of democracy in the ancient world and its practice in the modern political era. In 1961 she traveled to Jerusalem to cover the trial of Nazi Adolf Eichmann for *The New Yorker*, which produced the work for which she is best known, *Eichmann in Jerusalem: A Report on the Banality of Evil* (London: Faber, 1963). Rather than view Eichmann as a purely malevolent agent, Arendt found that he operated his massive program of genocide unthinkingly, as an ordinary innocuous individual who followed orders efficiently and without any concern for their human dimension or ultimate effect. Thus, she rendered her controversial conclusion that the extermination of the Jews had resulted from the absence of sound judgment, through banal activity, much like any other bureaucratic operation.

Notable among Arendt's other publications are: *On Revolution* (London: Faber, 1963); *Men in Dark Times* (New York: Harcourt, 1968); *On Violence* (New York: Harcourt, 1970); *The Jew as Pariah: Jewish Identity and Politics in the Modern Age* (New York: Grove, 1978); and *The Life of the Mind*, 2 vols. (San Diego: Harcourt Brace Jovanovich, 1978).

JEAN BAUDRILLARD (1929–)

Sociologist, cultural critic, and postmodern theorist; Universitas essayist and symposium panelist

Jean Baudrillard was born in 1929 in Reims, France. He studied German at the Sorbonne University in Paris, became a German professor in a lycée, and worked as a translator and critic while continuing his studies in philosophy and sociology. In 1966, he completed his PhD thesis, "The System of Objects," under Professor Henri Lefebvre, and in 1972 joined the sociology faculty as an assistant professor at the University of Paris at Nanterre. Since 2001, Baudrillard has been a professor of philosophy of culture and media criticism at the European Graduate School in Saas-Fee, Switzerland.

World-renowned for his investigations into hyperreality, especially as it relates to America, Baudrillard's philosophy centers on the twin concepts of *hyperreality* and *simulation*. These terms refer to the virtual or unreal nature of contemporary culture in an age of mass communication and mass consumption. As a philosopher of consumer society, Baudrillard was heavily influenced by Karl Marx's discussion of commodity fetishism, which he rearticulated through developments in linguistic structuralism.

Among Baudrillard's many books are: *The System of Objects*. Trans. James Benedict (London and New York: Verso, 1968); *The Consumer Society: Myths and Structures (Theory Culture and Society)*. Trans. George Ritzer (London: Sage, 1997 [1970]); *Simulacra and Simulation: The Body, in Theory*. Trans. Sheila Faria Glaser (Ann Arbor: Michigan, 1994 [1981]); Baudrillard and Mark Poster, eds., *Jean Baudrillard: Selected Writings*. Trans. Jacques Mourrain (Stanford: 1988); and *Symbolic Exchange and Death:*

Theory, Culture & Society. Trans. Iain Hamilton Grant (London: Sage, 1993).

MANUEL CASTELLS (1942-)
Sociologist, city and regional planning educator, and author; Universitas essayist and symposium panelist

Manuel Castells was born in Hellín, Spain, in 1942, and lived in Valencia and Barcelona. He studied law and economics at the University of Barcelona in 1958–62, where, as a student activist against the Franco regime, he was forced to emigrate. On a political refugee scholarship, he graduated in public law and political economy from the Sorbonne University in Paris in 1964, and went on to obtain a PhD in sociology from the University of Paris in 1967. He also holds doctorates from the Sorbonne and the University of Madrid. His distinguished academic career includes the teaching of the methodology of social research and research in urban sociology at the University of Paris, first at Nanterre, and in 1970 at the Ecole des Hautes Etudes et Sciences Sociales, Paris. He has also taught in Madrid and Barcelona, and served as visiting professor and lecturer at numerous universities throughout the world. In 1979 Castells was appointed Professor of Sociology and City and Regional Planning at the University of California at Berkeley. In 1994–98 he served as Chair of Berkeley's Center for Western European Studies, and, in addition to many other honors, in 1998 received the Robert and Helen Lynd Award from the American Sociological Association for his lifelong contribution to the field of community and urban sociology. In 2003, he became Professor Emeritus at Berkeley.

As one of the intellectual founders of the New Urban Sociology, Castells has conducted extensive cross-cultural studies of social transformation, including focusing on urban social movements and community organizations, economic and social transformations associated with the information revolution, and, most recently, the social and economic implications of the Internet. He has engaged in research on several continents, and served as an advisor to UNESCO and many other international organizations and governments. His current work aims at understanding the new society that is emerging out of the technological revolution and the global economy.

Among his influential publications are: *La Question Urbaine* (Paris: Francois Maspero, 1972); *The Economic Crisis and American Society* (Princeton: 1980); *The City and the Grassroots: A Cross-Cultural Theory of Urban Social Movements* (Berkeley: 1983); *Informational City: Information Technology, Economic Restructuring, and the Urban-Regional Process* (Oxford and Cambridge, Mass.: Blackwell, 1989); John Hull Mollenkopf and Castells, eds., *The Dual City: Restructuring New York* (New York: Russell Sage, 1991); *The Information Age* (Oxford and Cambridge, Mass.: Blackwell, 2000–03): Vol. 1, *The Rise of Network Society* (1996), Vol. 2, *The Power of Identity* (1997), Vol. 3, *End of the Millennium* (1998); and *The Internet Galaxy: Reflections on the Internet, Business, and Society* (New York: Oxford, 2001).

GILLO DORFLES (1910-)
Painter, teacher of aesthetics, and writer on art and design; Universitas essayist and symposium panelist

Gillo Dorfles was born in Trieste in 1910. He became a painter and author of numerous essays on aesthetics. He lectured widely in Europe and the

United States and was Professor of Aesthetics at the University of Trieste. In 1948 he founded the Concrete Art Movement (Movimento Arte Concreta; MAC) together with fellow artists Gianni Monnet, Atanasio Soldati, and Bruno Munari. Dorfles was the pivotal theoretician of the group, exhibited widely, and wrote many catalogue introductions for his fellow painters. In 1949 and 1950, he had one-man exhibitions at the Libreria Salto in Milan; he participated in numerous Concrete Art group shows, notably in 1951 at the Galleria Bompiani in Milan, a traveling exhibition to Chile and Argentina in 1952, and the large *Esperimenti di Sintesi delle arti* exhibition in 1955 at the Galleria del Fiore in Milan. Dorfles taught aesthetics at the University of Milan and has written many books on contemporary art and industrial design.

Among his numerous publications are: *Kitsch: The World of Bad Taste* (New York: Universe, 1969); *Architetture ambigue: Dal neobarocco al postmoderno (Immagine e consumo)* (Bari: Dedalo, 1984); *Liberatore: Sculture, 1970–1990* (Milan: Electa, 1993); *La moda della moda (I Turbamenti dell'arte)* (Genoa: Costa & Nolan, 1984); A. Rocca and G. Dorfles, *Atlas of the Milan Triennale* (Milan: Charta, 2000); and *Introdução ao Desenho Industrial* (São Paulo: Edgard Blücher, 2002).

ARTHUR DREXLER (1925–1987)

Exhibition designer, museum curator, lecturer, author, and director of the Department of Architecture and Design, The Museum of Modern Art; Universitas panelist, chairman of the third session

Arthur Drexler was born in New York in 1925. He attended the High School of Music and Art, studied architecture at The Cooper Union for the Advancement of Science and Art in 1941, and served in the United States Army Corps of Engineers in 1943–45. After the war, he worked as an architectural draftsman in New York, a designer for George Nelson Associates in 1947–48, and an architectural editor for *Interiors Magazine* in 1948–50. In 1951, he was hired as Curator of Architecture at The Museum of Modern Art; in 1956 he became the Director of its Department of Architecture and Design, a position he maintained until his death in 1987.

From 1951 to 1986, Drexler's Museum exhibitions were "encyclopedic" in range, including textiles and automobiles, historic preservation and the work of the great modern architects; and the shows themselves were often benchmarks in the history of twentieth-century design. He directed and sponsored many groundbreaking exhibitions and was responsible for the catalogues that accompanied them. During his tenure, the Museum's collections of design objects, graphic arts, and architectural drawings and models underwent their greatest period of growth. He acquired the first automobile for the collection as well as the 1945 Bell-47D1 Helicopter, among countless other historically important and beautiful objects. His exhibitions of architecture and urban planning were often vehicles for his profound concerns for quality, education, and social justice. Drexler was a founder and Trustee of the Institute for Architecture and Urban Studies in New York, a consultant to the jury for the Pritzker Architecture Prize, a member of the Society of Architectural Historians and the Society for the Arts, Religion, and Contemporary Culture, and the recipient of the Medal for Architectural History of the American Institute of Architects. He lectured widely at various universities and was a leading arbiter of architectural merit for three decades.

Among his many books are: Henry-Russell Hitchcock and Drexler, eds., *Built in USA: Postwar Architecture* (New York: MoMA, 1952); *The Architecture of Japan* (New York: MoMA, 1955); *Introduction to 20th Century Design from the Collection of The Museum of Modern Art* (New York: MoMA, 1959); *Ludwig Mies van der Rohe* (New York: Braziller, 1960); *The Drawings of Frank Lloyd Wright* (New York: MoMA and Horizon, 1962); *Charles Eames: Furniture from the Design Collection of The Museum of Modern Art* (New York: MoMA, 1973); Drexler, ed., *Architecture of the Ecole des Beaux Arts* (New York: MoMA, 1977); *Transformations in Modern Architecture* (New York: MoMA, 1979); and Drexler, ed., *The Mies van der Rohe Archive of The Museum of Modern Art* (New York: Garland, 1986).

RONALD DWORKIN (1931–)

Political philosopher, lawyer, and legal educator; Universitas essayist and symposium panelist

Ronald Dworkin was born in Worcester, Mass., in 1931. He received BA degrees from both Harvard College and Oxford University, and an LLB degree from Harvard Law School as well as one from Yale Law School. He was admitted to the New York bar in 1959, and was a professor of law at Yale from 1962 to 1969, when he was appointed Professor of Jurisprudence at Oxford and Fellow of University College. He holds a joint appointment at Oxford and New York University, where he has been a professor in the School of Law and the Philosophy Department since 1975. Professor Dworkin has lectured widely at schools such as Stanford University, Western Reserve University, Northwestern University, Cornell University, and Witersrand University in South Africa,

among others. He is a Fellow of the British Academy and a member of the American Academy of Arts and Sciences. He is the author of many seminal articles and books on important legal and philosophical topics, among them *Philosophical Issues in Senile Dementia* (1987) and *A Bill of Rights for Britain* (1990).

His representative publications include: *Taking Rights Seriously* (Cambridge, Mass.: Harvard, 1977); *A Matter of Principle* (Cambridge, Mass.: Harvard, 1985); *Law's Empire* (Cambridge, Mass.: Harvard, 1986); *Life's Dominion: An Argument About Abortion, Euthanasia, and Individual Freedom* (New York: Knopf, 1993); *Freedom's Law: The Moral Reading of the American Constitution* (Cambridge, Mass.: Harvard, 1996); and *Sovereign Virtue: The Theory and Practice of Equality* (Cambridge, Mass.: Harvard, 2000).

UMBERTO ECO (1932–)

Novelist, scholar, literary theorist, semiotics educator, and philosopher; Universitas essayist and symposium panelist

Umberto Eco was born in 1932 in Alessandria, Piedmont, Italy. He entered the University of Turin to study law, but changed his course of study to medieval philosophy and literature, ultimately earning a doctorate in philosophy in 1954 with a thesis on St. Thomas Aquinas. He then entered the field of journalism as Editor for Cultural Programs at the state-owned television network RAI. His thesis was published in 1956, and a second book on medieval aesthetics was published in 1959, which established him as a leading medievalist. He lectured on aesthetics and architecture at the universities of Turin and Milan between 1956 and 1965. From 1959 to 1975, Eco worked as a senior nonfiction editor at

Casa Editrice Bompiani in Milan, and became a columnist and writer for a diverse range of journals, developing his ideas on the open text and semiotics. In 1962 Eco published *The Open Work*; in 1966 he was appointed Professor of Visual Communications in Florence, and in 1969 Professor of Semiotics at the Milan Polytechnic. By 1968, Eco had published his seminal book in the field of semiotics, *La struttura assente* (the absent structure), later revised and retitled *A Theory of Semiotics* in 1976. In 1971 he became the first professor of semiotics at Europe's oldest university, the University of Bologna, and went on to earn many academic accolades. He also taught and lectured on semiotics at many universities in the United States and in Europe.

By the close of the decade, however, Eco's career took a radical change in direction with a novel set in the Middle Ages, *The Name of the Rose* (New York: Harcourt, 1983 [Milan: Bompiani, 1980]). This work, intended as a mystery that could be read as an open text—enigmatic, complex, and open to several layers of interpretation—met with huge critical and commercial success, and suddenly thrust its author into an international spotlight outside the world of academia. It has sold over nine million copies, won countless prizes, and was made into a film in 1986. The second of his three novels, *Foucault's Pendulum* (New York: Harcourt, 1989 [Milan: Bompiani, 1988]), proved to be another immediate success, and firmly established Eco as an important novelist worldwide. Eco's work is said to illustrate "the postmodernist literary theory concept of hypertextuality, or the interconnectedness of all literary works and their interpretation." He has defined the novel as a machine for generating interpretations.

Among his many other books are: *Semiotics and the Philosophy of Language* (Bloomington: Indiana, 1984); *The Aesthetics of the Cosmos: The Middle Ages of James Joyce*. Trans. Ellen Esrock (Cambridge, Mass.: Harvard, 1989); *Six Walks in the Fictional Woods* (Cambridge, Mass.: Harvard, 1994); *The Island of the Day Before* (London: Decker, 1995); and Eco, ed., *The History of Beauty*. Trans Alastair McEwan (New York: Rizzoli, 2004).

Hans Magnus Enzensberger (1929–)
Poet, essayist, editor, and translator; Universitas essayist

Hans Magnus Enzensberger, was born in Kaufbeuren, Bavaria, Germany, in 1929, and is considered to be Germany's most important living poet. He was educated at the University of Erlangen, the University of Hamburg, and at the Sorbonne University in Paris (1952–53). He received a PhD from the University of Freiburg in 1955. Widely celebrated for his poetry, he is also acclaimed for his work as an essayist, journalist, dramatist, editor, translator, and publisher. Enzensberger published his first book of poems, *Defense of the Wolves*, in 1957, and a second, *To Speak German*, in 1960 (both Frankfurt: Suhrkamp). Together, these volumes made him famous as his country's "angry young man." In 1965 he founded *Kursbuch*, a periodical that provided a forum for literary and political discussion. Also between 1965 and 1975, he was part of Group 47, an association of writers that had gathered to reassess and revitalize German literature since the Nazi period of World War II with a new cosmopolitan German culture. Known as an important political voice in postwar Germany, he undertook a thorough critique of the political system and the mass media, and urged intellectuals to participate in the political reorganization of Germany, especially during the 1968 international student movement. In 1968 he resigned a fellowship at Wesleyan University in protest against United States foreign policy and moved to Cuba. His books of that period, *The Havana Inquiry* (1970) and the novel *The Short Summer of Anarchy: Life and Death of Durruti* (1972), deal with political, social, and cultural subjects in the contemporary world. He examines various types of conformity, criticizes the Left's ineptitude in addressing society's problems, and searches for a new political direction.

Among Enzensberger's many books are: *Mausoleum: Thirty-seven Ballads from the History of Progress* (New York: Urizen, 1976); *The Sinking of the Titanic: A Poem* (Boston: Houghton, 1980); *Europe, Europe: Forays into a Continent*. Trans. Martin Chalmers (New York: Pantheon, 1989); *Civil Wars: From L.A. to Bosnia* (New York: New Press, 1995); *The Number Devil: A Mathematical Adventure*. Trans. Michael Henry Heim (New York: Holt, 1998); *Zig Zag: The Politics of Culture and Vice Versa* (New York: New Press, 1998); *Lost in Time* (New York: Holt, 2000); and *Elixirs of Science* (2002).

KENNETH FRAMPTON (1930-)
Architect, architectural historian, educator, and author; Universitas symposium speaker

Kenneth Frampton was born in London, England, in 1930. He attended the Architectural Association School of Architecture in London from 1950 to 1956; ARIBA 1957. After two years in the British Army and a year in Israel, he joined the London architectural firm of Douglas Stephen and Partners, where he became an Associate. In 1965 Frampton left for the United States, and taught at Princeton University until 1968; in 1972 he joined the architecture faculty at Columbia University in New York, and became involved as well with the Institute for Architecture and Urban Studies in New York. Since 1974 he has been the Ware Professor of Architecture in the Graduate School of Architecture and Planning at Columbia University, and from 1993 to the present, Director of Columbia's PhD Program in Architecture (History and Theory).

An influential and widely respected historian, theorist, critic, lecturer, and writer, Frampton has taught and lectured at numerous schools of architecture in the United States and internationally, and participated in many conferences and seminars. He has received countless fellowships, honorary degrees, and awards, and served on many architectural juries throughout the world. He has consulted to various schools, publishers, private companies, and municipalities, and his professional associations include the Royal Institute of British Architects, the Berlage Institute, Amsterdam, the Architectural League, New York, the American Academy of arts and Sciences, the American Institute of Architects, and the Aga Khan Award for Architecture. His architectural projects include housing in England, Israel, and New York.

Frampton has published numerous essays in books and journals, and is the author of some of the most notable architectural books of his time, among them, *Modern Architecture: A Critical History* (London: Thames & Hudson, 1980; rev. enl. ed. 1985); *Modern Architecture and the Critical Present* (London: Academy; New York: St. Martin's, 1983); Frampton and Mark Vellay, *Pierre Chareau* (Paris: Editions du Regard;

New York: Rizzoli, 1985); *American Masterworks: The Twentieth-Century House* (New York: Rizzoli, 1995); *Studies in Tectonic Culture: The Poetics of Construction in Nineteenth and Twentieth Century Architecture* (Cambridge, Mass.: MIT, 1995); *Labour, Work, and Architecture* (London: Phaidon, 2000); *Alvaro Siza* (New York: Phaidon, 2000); *Le Corbusier* (London: Thames & Hudson, 2000); Frampton, gen. ed., *World Architecture: A Critical Mosaic 1900–2000.* 10 vols. (Beijing: China Building Press, 2000); *Tadao Ando* (New York: Monacelli, 2003); *Steven Holl* (New York: W. W. Norton, 2005); and *Ten Shades of Green: Architecture and the Natural World* (New York: W. W. Norton, 2005).

PERCIVAL GOODMAN (1904–1989)

Architect, planner, teacher, utopian social critic, painter, and designer; Universitas symposium speaker

Percival Goodman was born in New York City in 1904. He studied at the Ecole des Beaux-Arts in Paris in the mid-1920s, and began his career as a designer in New York in 1928, creating art deco interiors at the better department stores (Saks & Co., I Magnin), hotels, and wealthy private clients. His later work, in a career that ultimately spanned sixty years, was marked by a strong commitment to architecture using social ideals in design. Along with residential and business buildings, in the 1950s he became one of the most prolific synagogue architects in the United States. His religious buildings were the first to combine modern architecture with contemporary abstract art for which he commissioned works from contemporary American modernists.

Goodman taught architecture at Columbia University from 1946 to 1971,

deeply influencing many of his students with his keen social conscience and a utopian conviction of the power of modern architecture as a vehicle for social change. In 2001 a retrospective exhibition of his architectural work, paintings, and book illustrations was held at the Miriam and Ira D. Wallach Gallery of Columbia University; the catalogue, Kimberly J. Elman and Angela Giral, eds., *Percival Goodman: Architect, Planner, Teacher, Painter* (New York: Princeton Architectural Press, 2002), considers the architect's work within the modernist movement and offers a personal and critical assessment of his achievement as a socially conscious practitioner.

Goodman is the author of the planning textbook (with his brother Paul Goodman) *Communitas: Means of Livelihood and Ways of Life* (New York: Columbia University Press, 1947; Vintage Books, 1960; second. ed. Columbia University Press, 1990), which is still in use today; *The Decay of American Cities–Alternative Habitation for Man: A Plan for Planning* (1966); and *The Double E* (Garden City, N.Y.: Doubleday Anchor, 1977).

STUART HAMPSHIRE (1914–2004)

Philosopher, educator, and author; Universitas symposium panelist, chairman of the first session

Stuart Hampshire was born in Healing, Lincolnshire, England, in 1914. He received a degree in philosophy at Balliol College, Oxford University, in 1936, and was a fellow and lecturer in philosophy at All Souls College, Oxford, in 1936–40. During World War II, he served in the British Army and Foreign Office. After the war, he taught at University College in London (1947–50), and at New College, Oxford (1950–55).

In 1963, he was appointed Professor of Philosophy at Princeton University, where he eventually became chair of the department. In 1970, he became Warden of Waltham College, Oxford, returned to Princeton University (1984–90), and also taught at Stanford University in California. He was made a Knight of the British Empire in 1979, and was a Fellow of the British Academy and a member of the American Academy of Arts and Sciences.

Hampshire was one of the anti-rationalist Oxford thinkers, among such figures as Isaiah Berlin and Bernard Williams, who gave a new direction to moral and political thought in the post-war era. Inspired by his study of Baruch Spinoza, he centered much of his thinking and writing on the factors that influence knowledge and the origins of free will. Departing from standard philosophical methodology tied to science and logic, he believed that aesthetics, ethics, and political philosophy are parts of a single inquiry: the philosophy of mind. He developed ideas on the human condition linking human freedom to an understanding of one's own disposition, genetic heritage, and childhood experiences. He argued that self-knowledge depends on social interaction, and held that any theory of ethics must take into account the fact that although human nature is historically and genetically conditioned, it is also revisable because of the possibility of self-conscious intentional action. In his extensive examination of such subjects as human motivation, epistemology, metaphysics, ethics, and aesthetics, his approach reflected his particular interests in psychoanalysis, literary theory, and art criticism. Hampshire died in Oxford in 2004.

Among his many published works are: *Spinoza* (Harmondsworth: Penguin, 1951), *The Age of Reason: The Seventeenth*

Century Philosophers (Boston: Houghton, 1956); *Thought and Action* (London: Chatto, 1959); *Freedom of the Individual* (New York: Harper, 1965); *Freedom of Mind and Other Essays* (Princeton: 1971); *Two Theories of Morality* (Oxford: 1977); *Morality and Conflict* (Oxford: Blackwell, 1983); *Innocence and Experience* (Cambridge, Mass.: Harvard, 1989); and *Justice Is Conflict* (Princeton: 1999).

ERICH JANTSCH (1929–1980)
Astronomer, physicist, engineer, educator, and author; Universitas essayist and symposium panelist

Erich Jantsch was born in Vienna, Austria, in 1929. He received a PhD from the University of Vienna in 1951, and did postdoctoral study at Indiana University, Bloomington, in 1951–52. He worked as an astronomer in Vienna until 1957, and as an engineer and physicist in Switzerland until 1962. He served as a consultant to the European Organization of Economic Cooperation and Development (OECD) in Paris between 1962 and 1968, and concentrated on the fields of urban and regional planning, public health, and the conservation of natural resources in the United States at the University of California at Berkeley, the Institute of International Studies, and many other institutions around the world. The main thrust of all his work is in understanding how open systems, scientific as well as human, work and in bringing together science and the humanities in a unified view. His writings are mainly in the areas of planning theory and cultural and institutional change. He has served as a visiting professor and lecturer to many institutions, among them MIT, Technical University in Hannover, Germany, Portland State University, and the University of

California at Berkeley; he has also consulted to numerous governments and businesses, and made an attempt to synthesize all known self-organizing processes, from the big bang to the evolution of society, into a comprehensive worldview. Jantsch died in 1980.

He is the author of: *Technological Forecasting in Perspective* (Paris: OECD, 1967); Jantsch, ed., *Perspectives of Planning* (Paris: OECD, 1969); *Technological Planning and Social Futures* (New York: Wiley, 1972); *Design for Evolution: Self-Organization and Planning in the Life of Human Systems*. Ed. Laszlo Ervin (New York: Braziller, 1975); Jantsch and Conrad H. Waddington, eds., *Evolution and Consciousness: Human Systems in Transition* (New York: Addison-Wesley, 1976); *The Self-Organizing Universe: Scientific and Human Implications of the Emerging Paradigm of Evolution* (New York: Pergamon, 1980); and Jantsch, ed., *The Evolutionary Vision: Toward a Unifying Paradigm of Physical, Biological, and Sociocultural Evolution* (Western Press and the Association for the Advancement of Science, 1981).

SUZANNE KELLER (1930–)
Sociologist, educator, and author; Universitas essayist and symposium panelist

Suzanne Keller was born in Vienna, Austria, in 1930, and came to the United States in 1939. She became a naturalized citizen in 1944, and graduated from Hunter College, in New York City, in 1948; she received her MA and PhD degrees in sociology from Columbia University in 1950 and 1953. After conducting postdoctoral research at Princeton and the MIT Center for International Studies, she taught at Brandeis and Vassar colleges, and then spent 1963–65 in Greece as a Fulbright lecturer, and 1965–67 at the Athens Center of Ekistics. In 1968 she became Professor of Sociology at Princeton University, and was the first woman in the history of Princeton to receive tenure. In 1991 she was inducted into the Hunter Hall of Fame upon receiving an honorary degree; in 1993 the Suzanne Keller Award was established at Princeton to honor outstanding achievement in the sociology honors program. She is presently Professor Emeritus of Sociology at Princeton.

Her recent book, *Community: Pursuing the Dream, Living the Reality* (Princeton: 2003), is based on a thirty-year study of a single community, Twin Rivers, in New Jersey, from its creation as a planned development to the present. It has broader and deeper aims than most sociological studies, going beyond mere description and endeavoring to develop common principles of life that could be applicable to other human communities in the cyberspace age. Her study uniquely combines her extensive in-depth findings of three decades of monitoring, interviewing residents, collecting records, and first-hand observation with timeless questions of how a group of strangers can create an identity of place, shared goals and institutions, a spirit of reciprocity, and deal with issues of individuality versus the common good. She also addresses how design can enhance or deter community spirit.

Keller's many books include: *Beyond the Ruling Class* (New York: Random, 1963); *The Urban Neighborhood: Strategic Elites in Modern Society* (New York: Random, 1968); Keller and Donald Light, Jr., *Sociology* (New York: Random, 1975); Keller, ed., *Building for Women* (Lexington, Mass.: Lexington Books, 1981); Keller, ed., *Marriage and Family Today* (New York: Random, 1983); and Keller et al., *Understanding Sociology* (New York: McGraw-Hill, 1995).

GYORGY KEPES (1906-2001)

Painter, sculptor, exhibition and graphic designer, architect, photographer, filmmaker, educator, writer, and editor; Universitas essayist and symposium panelist

Gyorgy Kepes was born in Selyp, Hungary, in 1906. After graduating from the Royal Academy of Fine Arts in Budapest in 1926, he joined the Berlin studio of the Hungarian artist László Moholy-Nagy, a teacher at the Bauhaus who experimented with diverse materials. He left Berlin for London in 1936, but the next year followed Moholy-Nagy to Chicago and taught in the New Bauhaus / Chicago Institute of Design until 1943, and at North Texas State Teachers College and Brooklyn College. In 1945 he moved with his wife Juliet to Cambridge, Mass., and began teaching at MIT as Professor of Visual Design. His work there with students led him to propose a Center for Advanced Visual Studies at MIT, dedicated to exploring the connections between science and art. It was officially founded in 1967, with Kepes as its director, a position he retained until his retirement in 1974. He was also a visiting professor and lecturer at many schools around the world.

As an abstract painter, Kepes exhibited widely (Katherine Kuh Gallery, Chicago; Art Institute of Chicago; Royal Academy, Copenhagen; San Francisco Museum of Art; and Museum of Fine Arts, Rome, to name only a few); he developed works that ranged from book design to light and kinetic sculpture, and included exhibitions and large environmental works. Much of this work was interdisciplinary and often collaborative, and expressed his deep sense of serving human values through design. These, as well as his photographic and film projects, were the key elements in his lifelong mission to understand the nature of vision and reveal a common ground where science and art could communicate. His executed works and projects were always related closely to his roles as educator, writer, and editor. As editor of the Vision + Value Series, published in New York by George Braziller, Kepes prepared many volumes of essays by leading members of the scientific, scholarly, and artistic professions centered on understanding visual formulations of various contemporary cultural themes, with interdisciplinary communication the consistent goal. He was a member of the National Institute of Arts and Letters, a fellow of the American Academy of Arts and Sciences, and the recipient of many honorary awards. Kepes died in Cambridge in 2001.

Among his many influential books are: *Language of Vision* (Chicago: Theobold, 1944); *The New Landscape in Art and Science* (Chicago: Theobold, 1956); Kepes, ed., *The Nature and Art of Motion* (New York: Braziller, 1965); Kepes, ed., *The Education of Vision* (New York: Braziller, 1965); Kepes, ed., *Structure and Art in Science* (New York: Braziller, 1965); *The Man-Made Object* (New York: Braziller, 1966); Kepes, ed., *Arts of Environment* (New York: Braziller, 1972); and *Gyorgy Kepes: The MIT Years, 1945–1977)* (Cambridge, Mass.: MIT, 1978).

ARNOLD KRAMISH (1923-)

Physicist, historian, and author; Universitas essayist and symposium panelist

Arnold Kramish was born in Denver, Colorado, in 1923. He received a BS degree at the University of Denver in 1944, and an MA degree from Harvard University in 1947; in 1947–48 he did graduate work at Stanford University in California. As a young man, Kramish had worked on the Manhattan Project, and came to know some of the leading figures in the Allied war effort. He served as a consultant to the United States Atomic Energy Commission in 1947–51, and worked at the Rand Corporation in Santa Monica and Washington, D.C. He served at the American Embassy in Paris as United States Science Liaison Attaché to UNESCO and to the Organization for Economic Cooperation and Development (OECD) in 1970–76. He was a consultant to such organizations as the International Bank for Reconstruction and Development, the National Science Foundation, the Twentieth Century Fund, the Presidential Task Force on Disarmament, and headed the Institute for the Future and the Institute for Strategic Studies. Kramish was also technical director of a White House Study for a Strategic Defense Initiative in 1981–84, and an advisor to the undersecretary of defense for policy in 1984–91. In 1994 he was a Senior Fellow of the Global Access Institute.

Among his books are: *Atomic Energy in the Soviet Union* (Stanford: 1959); *The Peaceful Atom in Foreign Policy* (New York: Harper and the Council on Foreign Relations, 1963); *The Atlantic Technological Imbalance: An American Perspective* (New York: Pergamon, 1968); *The Future of Non-Nuclear Nations* (Leske, 1970); and *The Griffin: The Greatest Untold Espionage Story of World War II* (Boston: Houghton, 1986).

Henri Lefebvre (1901–1991)

Sociologist, philosopher, educator, and writer; Universitas essayist and symposium panelist

Henri Lefebvre was born in 1901 in the south of France. He attended school on the west coast of France at Brieuc and in Paris. He was the most prolific French Marxist and existentialist philosopher of his time, influencing the development of philosophy, sociology, geography, political science, and literary criticism. He expanded Karl Marx's theory of economic exploitation into a general theory of alienation in everyday life, arguing that modern capitalist society encouraged abstraction and fragmentation of community. During World War II, his manuscripts were burned by the Vichy regime, and he was persecuted for his Leftist writings by postwar authorities. He obtained a position at the university in Strasbourg in the 1950s, and by 1963 he had published his doctoral thesis as *La Valée de Campan*, for which he was lauded as a founder of the study of rural society. He returned to Paris as a professor at the new suburban university at Nanterre, where he was an influential figure in the 1968 student occupation of the Sorbonne University and the Left Bank. At Nanterre he developed his critiques of the alienation of modern urban life and investigated the cultural construction of stereotypical notions of cities, nature, and regions. He questioned the modern movement toward specialization and developed one of the first theories of what came to be known as globalization. Lefebvre was one of the original thinkers who pioneered the field of understanding human behavior in the context of everyday modern life. He died in Navarrenx in 1991.

Lefebvre was the author of numerous books; among them are: *L'Existentialisme* (Paris: Editions du Sagittaire, 1946); *Sociology of Marx.* Trans. N. Guterman (New York: Pantheon, 1968 [1966]); *The Production of Space.* Trans. N. Donaldson-Smith (Oxford: Blackwell, 1991 [1974]); and

Writings on Cities. Trans. and eds. E. Kofman and E. Lebas (Oxford: Blackwell, 1996). See also Rob Shields, *Lefebvre: Love and Struggle: Spatial Dialectics* (London: Routledge, 1999).

EDWARD J. LOGUE (1921-2000)
Urban planner and lawyer; Universitas essayist and symposium panelist

Edward J. Logue was born in Philadelphia in 1921. He received a BA degree at Yale University in 1942, and graduated from the Yale Law School in 1947 after serving in the Army Air Force in World War II. He worked briefly as a lawyer in Philadelphia, and then moved to New Haven, where he became legal secretary to Chester Bowles, Governor of Connecticut. He was Chief of Staff to Ambassador Bowles in India in the early 1950s, and then returned to New Haven as Development Administrator under Mayor Richard C. Lee. In 1960, he accepted a position as head of the Boston Redevelopment Authority under Mayor John F. Collins, with unusually wide powers, and changed the face of modern Boston: he was responsible for the Government Center, Prudential Center, and the much imitated Faneuil Hall/Quincy Market Restoration that revitalized downtown Boston. In 1967, after running unsuccessfully for Mayor of Boston, he studied at the John F. Kennedy School of Government for a year, and was invited to New York in 1968 by Governor Nelson A. Rockefeller to head the newly created New York Urban Development Corporation (UDC). There, in seven years, he was responsible for thirty-three thousand low and moderate income housing units statewide and the creation of three New Towns: Radisson near Syracuse, Amherst near Buffalo, and the transformation of

New York's Welfare Island into Roosevelt Island. Logue was an honorary member of the AIA, a member of the American Institute of City Planning, the American Planning Association, and many other organizations. He received countless awards and citations of excellence in urban affairs, and was a leading advocate of the responsibility of public policy to build affordable housing. He is known as a preeminent force in the field of urban innovation. He died in Martha's Vineyard in 2000.

Logue is the author of many articles, speeches, papers, and reports, all in the Yale Library. See also: Thomas H. O'Connor, *Building a New Boston: Politics and Urban Renewal, 1950–1970* (Boston: Northeastern, 1993).

RICHARD L. MEIER (1920-)
Chemist, planner, behavioral scientist, and futurist; Universitas essayist and symposium panelist

Richard L. Meier was born in Kendallville, Indiana, in 1920. He attended Northern Illinois State Teachers College in 1936–39, and received a BS degree from the University of Illinois in 1940. He received a PhD at the University of California, Los Angeles, in 1944, and did postdoctoral work on a Fulbright scholarship at the University of Manchester, England, in 1949–50. After working as a research chemist, he became an assistant professor at the University of Chicago (1950–56), a research social scientist at the Mental Health Research Institute, University of Michigan, Ann Arbor (1957), and a professor of resources planning at the University of Michigan (1965–67). In 1967, he became Professor of Environmental Design at the University of California at Berkeley, where he was named Professor Emeritus in 1990. He served as a visiting lecturer at Harvard University and at the Center of Ekistics, Athens, in the early 1960s, and has consulted on social and resource planning with several corporations and schools, such as MIT and Harvard. He is a member of the American Chemical Society, the American Sociological Association, the American Geological Society, the Society for International Development, the Federation of American Scientists, the Society for General Systems Research, and the Marine Technology Society.

Among Meier's many books are: *Science and Economic Development: New Patterns of Living* (Cambridge, Mass.: MIT, 1956); *Modern Science and the Human Fertility Problem* (New York: Wiley, 1959); *A Communications Theory of Urban Growth* (Cambridge, Mass.: MIT, 1962); *Developmental Planning* (New York: McGraw-Hill, 1965); *Planning for an Urban World* (Cambridge, Mass.: MIT, 1974); and *Urban Futures Observed in the Asian Third World* (New York: Pergamon).

Hasan Ozbekhan (1921–)

Planner, economist, systems analyst, and educator; Universitas symposium panelist

Hasan Ozbekhan was born in Istanbul, Turkey, in 1921. He received a BS degree from the University of London in 1943, where he also did graduate work until 1945, when he immigrated to Canada. He later became an American citizen. He was associated with Massey-Harris, Ltd., in Toronto, until 1951; was Executive Vice President of the U. S. Brenner Corp., in New York, in 1951–55; and Consultant, Special Management Research and Program Development, General Electric Corp., in Ossining, New York, in 1956–63. Between 1964 and 1969, he was Director of Corporate Planning of the System Development

Corp., Santa Monica; in 1969–71, he was General Manager of International Development and Director of Planning for Worldwide Information Systems, Los Angeles. In 1971, Ozbekhan entered academia with an appointment as Professor of Statistics and Operations Research by the Wharton School of Economics of the University of Pennsylvania. He was subsequently Chairman of the Graduate Group in Social Systems Sciences and Professor of Management at Wharton, and is currently Professor Emeritus of Management at Wharton. As a consultant, he did science policy design for the Turkish government, and a large study for the French government analyzing the nature of present events, which constitutes the basis of the present policy for the future of Paris.

During the early 1970s, he was considered one of the most prominent planning theoreticians of his time. He is widely known as a co-founder of the Club of Rome, a semi-secret, international, nongovernmental, nonpolitical organization comprising a network of scientist, humanists, economists, and business leaders whose purpose was to study the nature of human events in a rapidly changing world and propose ways to ameliorate the "predicament of mankind." Prior to his joining Wharton, Ozbekhan was a principal author of its original proposal to apply system dynamics computer modeling technology to understanding the dynamics of social systems in large corporations and cities in order aid to high-level decision makers around the world. Among the subjects addressed in the proposal were international development, hunger, birth control, investment, and environmental programs. He was also a formative influence in creating the Institute for the 21st Century.

Among his publications are: *The Isle of Princes* (New York: Simon & Schuster, 1957); *Technology and Man's Future* (Rand, 1966); "The Triumph of Technology: Can Implies Ought," in Stanford Anderson, *Planning for Diversity and Choice* (Cambridge, Mass.: MIT, 1968): 210; "Planning and Human Action," in P. Weiss, ed., *Hierarchically Organized Systems in Theory and Practice* (1971): 123, 183–192.

MARTIN PAWLEY (1938–)
Architect, architectural critic, and writer; Universitas essayist and symposium panelist

Martin Pawley was born in 1938 in London. He studied architecture at the Oxford School of Architecture, the Ecole Nationale Supérieure des Beaux Arts in Paris (1958–59), and at the Architectural Association School of Architecture in London in 1968. He practiced architecture for a number of years and taught at the Architectural Association, and in the United States at Cornell University, Rensselaer Polytechnic Institute, Florida A & M University, and UCLA. He has worked as an architectural consultant to governments and other organizations, such as the government of the Republic of Chile (1972–73), the United Nations (1975–77), the state government of Florida (1977–79), and the City of Los Angeles Planning Department (1979–80). He served as architecture critic for *The Guardian* newspaper from 1984 to 1991, and the *Observer* from 1992 to 1995, during which time he was consulting editor of *World Architecture* magazine. He has worked in television, lectured, and participated in many architectural conferences, such as "Resourcing the Future," and "Building Audacity." He continues to write a weekly column in the London *Architects' Journal.*

Pawley's writing has appeared on a regular basis in numerous periodicals; among his many books are: *Architecture versus Housing* (New York: Praeger, 1971); *Frank Lloyd Wright: Public Buildings* (New York: Simon & Schuster, 1971); *Building for Tomorrow: Putting Waste to Work* (San Francisco: Sierra Club, 1982); *Theory and Design in the Second Machine Age* (Cambridge, Mass.: Blackwell, 1990); *Buckminster Fuller: A Critical Biography* (New York: Taplinger, 1990); *Future Systems: The Story of Tomorrow* (London: Phaidon, 1997); *Norman Foster: A Global Architecture* (New York: Universe, 1999); and *Twentieth-Century Architecture: A Reader's Guide* (Boston: Architectural Press, 2000).

OCTAVIO PAZ (1914–1998)
Poet, essayist, playwright, translator, editor, educator, and diplomat; Universitas writer (a poem) and symposium panelist

Octavio Paz was born near Mexico City in 1914. He attended the National Autonomous University of Mexico in 1932–37 and published his first book of poetry, *Luna Silvestre*, in 1933, and a second book in 1936. In 1937, at the height of the Spanish Civil War, he traveled to Valencia, Spain, to participate in the Second International Congress of Anti-Fascist Writers, and joined a brigade fighting the army of the fascist dictator Francisco Franco. Upon his return to Mexico the next year with the aim of popularizing the Spanish Republican cause, he became a founder of the journal *Taller* (Workshop), which signaled the emergence of a new literary sensibility in a new generation of writers in his country. He received a Guggenheim Fellowship in 1943 to study modernist poetry in the United States (Berkeley and New York City), and in 1945 joined the Mexican Foreign Service; he was sent to the United States and then to France, where he wrote his fundamental study of Mexican identity, *The Labyrinth of Solitude,* in 1950 (New York: Grove, 1961), and where he participated in various activities organized by the surrealists under André Breton. In 1962, he was appointed ambassador to India. His work as a diplomat for over two decades allowed him ample time to write many "phosphorescent, political, passionate, complicated, moral, and hauntingly lonely" volumes of poetry and prose. In 1968, he resigned his diplomatic post in protest against his government's bloody suppression of student demonstrations in Tlateloco during the Olympics in Mexico. He then taught at the University of Texas at Austin and the University of Pittsburgh in 1968–70, at Cambridge University in 1970–71, and held the Charles Eliot Norton Chair of Poetry at Harvard University in 1971–72.

He ultimately returned to Mexico where he worked as an editor and publisher, founding two important magazines dedicated to the arts and politics: *Plural* and *Vuelta.* He received many honors and awards, and lectured and taught in various schools throughout the world. Among many other prizes, he was awarded the Miguel de Cervantes Prize, the most important in the Spanish-speaking world, the prestigious Neustadt International Prize for Literature in 1982, and in 1990 received the Nobel Prize for Literature. Paz died in Mexico in 1998.

Notable among his many books are: *Marcel Duchamp, Or The Castle of Purity.* Trans. Donald Gardner (London: Cap Goliard, and New York: Grossman, 1970); *The Other Mexico: Critique of the Pyramid.* Trans. Lysander Kemp (New York: Grove, 1972); *The Monkey Grammarian.* Trans. Helen Lane (New York: Seaver, 1981); *Poema 1935–1975* (Barcelona: Seix Barral, 1981); *The Collected Poems of Octavio Paz, 1957–1987.* Ed. and trans. Eliot Weinberger (New York: New Directions, 1987); *Convergences: Essays on Art and Literature.* Trans. Helen Lane (San Diego: Harcourt Brace Jovanovich, 1987); and *Sunstone.* Trans. Eliot Weinberger (New York: New Directions, 1991).

ANATOL RAPOPORT (1911–)

Mathematician, musician, biologist, pioneer in systems sciences; game theorist, semanticist, peace studies educator; Universitas essayist and symposium panelist

Anatol Rapoport was born in Lozavaya, Russia, in 1911. He came to the United States in 1922 and became a naturalized citizen in 1928. He studied music in Chicago and in Vienna, and performed as a concert pianist. He then attended the University of Chicago as an undergraduate and graduate student, receiving a PhD in 1941, and served in the United States Army Air Force in 1942–46, achieving the rank of captain. He taught mathematics at Illinois Institute of Technology in 1946–47, mathematics and biology at the University of Chicago in 1947–54, and was professor of mathematics at the University of Michigan and Professor at the Mental Health Research Institute at the University of Toronto, in 1955–68 and 1969–70. In 1970, he became Professor of Psychology and Mathematics, and in 1984 Professor of Peace Studies, at the University of Toronto, from which he retired as Professor Emeritus. He is a member of various professional organizations, including the Mathematical Association of America, the Biometric

Society, the International Society for General Semantics, the Society for General Systems Research, the American Academy of Arts and Sciences, the Canadian Peace Research and Education Association, and Science for Peace.

Rapoport is a leading figure in the systems sciences and in peace research. He spearheaded many scientific innovations, including the application of mathematical methods to biology and the social sciences. He is one of the rare thinkers of his time in combining philosophy and science, and in his originality and rigor in unifying ethical concerns and aesthetic appeal with the sciences and systemic thinking. His early concentration in mathematical biophysics led him to the study of parasitism and symbiosis, and then into the context of human systems in terms of conflict and cooperation, which occupied him throughout the remainder of his professional career. His lifelong inquiry into human social values was accompanied by his utilization of mathematical and system-based methods as well as his urgent ecological concerns, views on aggression, theories of conflict resolution, and profound belief that science and the information revolution, by following enlightened goals rather than appetites of acquisition and power, could lead to peace and a higher quality of life for humanity. He has published widely in scientific and humanistic journals, has lectured and consulted extensively, and is the recipient of high honors internationally.

Among his many books are: *Science and the Goals of Man* (New York: Harper, 1950); *Fights, Games, and Debates* (Ann Arbor: Michigan, 1960); *Strategy and Conscience* (New York: Harper, 1964); *Two-Person Game Theory* (Ann Arbor: Michigan, 1966); *Conflict in Man-Made Environment* (Harmondsworth and Baltimore: Penguin, 1974); *General Sys-*

tem Theory (New York: Abacus, 1986); *The Origins of Violence: Approaches to the Study of Conflict* (New York: Paragon, 1989); *Peace, An Idea Whose Time Has Come* (Ann Arbor: Michigan, 1993), and *Skating on Thin Ice* (Toronto: RDR Books, 2002).

MEYER SCHAPIRO (1904-1996)
Artist, art historian, educator, critic, and philosopher of aesthetics; Universitas symposium panelist

Meyer Schapiro was born in Siauliai, Lithuania, in 1904, came to the United States three years later, and became a naturalized citizen in 1914. He graduated from Boys High School, New York, in 1920, at sixteen, and entered Columbia College on both Pulitzer and Regents scholarships. After graduating three years later, he embarked on a course of graduate work in art history at Columbia. His doctoral dissertation, accepted in 1929, on the Romanesque sculptures of the cloister and portal of Moissac, a French abbey built in 1100, treated such historical works for the first time as art rather than as documents leading to the Gothic style. He brought into his argument medieval church history, theology, social history, folklore, and illuminated manuscripts. A part of his work was published in *The Art Bulletin* in 1931, and his exceptional work was immediately recognized. Schapiro had accepted a teaching position at Columbia in 1928, and his long distinguished teaching career was primarily spent there, although he lectured at many other schools during the ensuing decades.

Along with the arrival of European modernism, the postwar period saw the development of a New York School of Painting, Abstract Expressionism, for which Schapiro became a primary interpreter, validating the movement in intellectual, historical, and moral terms in his popular lectures. On the basis of his brilliant, insightful lecture style, Schapiro was considered one of the most original and inspiring teachers of his time, "like having Plato in the living room," according to one artist, but his published output was small until the 1970s, when the publisher George Braziller began a multi-volume series of his essays and lectures. In 1966–67 Schapiro was Charles Eliot Norton Lecturer at Harvard University, in 1968 Slade Professor of Art at Oxford University, and in 1974 visiting lecturer at the College de France in Paris. In 1973 he became Professor Emeritus at Columbia, which awarded him the Alexander Hamilton Award for distinguished service and accomplishment in 1975. He was elected a member of the National Institute of Arts and Letters in 1976, among many other honors. Schapiro died in New York in 1996.

Among his published works are: *Vincent van Gogh* (New York: Abrams, 1950); *Cézanne* (New York: Abrams, 1952); *Words and Pictures* (Mouton, 1973); *Selected Papers: Romanesque Art.* Vol. 1 (New York: Braziller, 1977), *Modern Art: 19th and 20th Centuries.* Vol. 2 (New York: Braziller, 1978), *Late Antique, Early Christian, and Medieval Art.* Vol. 3 (New York: Braziller, 1979); *Romanesque Sculpture of Moissac* (New York: Braziller, 1985); *Theory and Philosophy of Art: Style, Artist, and Society* (New York: Braziller, 1994); *Mondrian: On the Humanity of Abstract Painting* (New York: Braziller, 1995); *Words, Scripts, and Pictures: Semiotics of Visual Language* (New York: Braziller, 1996); and *Impressionism: Reflections and Perception* (New York: Braziller, 1997).

CARL SCHORSKE (1915–)

Historian, educator, and author; Universitas panelist, chairman of the fourth session

Carl Schorske was born in New York in 1915. He attended Columbia University, where he received a BA degree in history in 1936; he earned MA and PhD degrees at Harvard University in 1937 and 1950. He was Professor of History at Wesleyan University, Middletown, Conn., in 1946–60, taught at the University of California at Berkeley in 1960–69, and at Princeton University in 1969–80. He became Professor Emeritus at Princeton in 1980. In 1981, he received the Pulitzer Prize for general nonfiction and a McArthur Foundation Fellowship, and is the recipient of many other awards and honorary degrees. He is a member of the Royal Academy of Fine Arts of the Netherlands, the American Academy of Arts and Sciences, the Austrian Academy of Sciences, the American Historical Association, the Institute for Architecture and Urban Studies, and the Institute of Humanities. He has lectured widely and consulted to the United States Office of Strategic Services and the Council on Foreign Relations. Known for his erudite work on the cultural and political history of Vienna, Schorske has also analyzed the nature of historical inquiry in the modern period, and the relationship "between history and the supposedly rootless modernism."

Among Schorske's books are: Schorske and Hoyt Price, *The Problem of Germany* (New York: 1947); *German Social Democracy, 1905–1917: The Development of the Great Schism* (Cambridge, Mass.: Harvard, 1955); Schorske and Elizabeth Schorske, eds., *Explorations in Crisis* (Cambridge, Mass.: Harvard, 1969); *Fin-de-Siècle Vienna: Politics and Culture* (New York: Knopf, 1980); *Gustav Mahler: Formation and Transformation*

(New York: Leo Baeck, 1991); and *Thinking with History: Explorations in the Passage to Modernism* (Princeton: 1998).

DENISE SCOTT BROWN (1931–)

Architect, planner, and urban designer, theorist, writer, and educator; Universitas symposium speaker

Denise Scott Brown was born in Nkana, Zambia, in 1931, and raised in a suburb of Johannesburg, South Africa. She attended the University of Witwatersrand in Johannesburg (1948–52) and the Architectural Association School of Architecture in London (1955). After traveling and working in Italy and England, she came to the United States with her first husband, the late Robert Scott Brown. She studied at the University of Pennsylvania where she received a master of city planning degree in 1960 and a master of architecture degree in 1965. While teaching at the university she met the American architect Robert Venturi, whom she married in 1967; that year she also joined her husband's Philadelphia architectural firm, now known as Venturi, Scott Brown & Associates, where she is principal-in-charge of many projects in urban planning, urban design, and campus planning, and also participates in a broad range of the firm's architectural projects. Scott Brown has taught urban planning at various prominent universities and is noted for her innovative interdisciplinary studio courses for architects, social scientists, and urban designers as well as a focus on the built environment, empirical methods, and the use of media studies as resources. She has also served numerous schools as a board member, advisor, jurist, and consultant as well as a lecturer and teacher.

Her recent projects include campus planning for Brown University and Tsinghua University in Beijing. At the University of Kentucky, she directed precinct planning in parallel with the design of a new Biomedical/Biological Sciences Research Building. She led master planning and design of a new hospital for Lehigh Valley Hospital–Muhlenberg, and directed the University of Michigan Campus master plan and plans for several of its sub-campuses, culminating in the design of the University's Life Sciences Institute, Undergraduate Science Building, and Palmer Commons complex. She has also directed campus plans for the University of Pennsylvania, Williams College, and the Radcliffe Institute of Advanced Studies at Harvard University. Among many other projects, Scott Brown has written and advised on urban planning issues related to the development of the World Trade Center site in New York and Philadelphia's Penn's Landing as well as a plan for the Bouregreg Valley in Morocco.

Her bibliography includes many articles in journals and books; she is also author (with Robert Venturi) of the following books: (also with Steven Izenour) *Learning from Las Vegas* (Cambridge, Mass.: MIT Press, 1972, rev. ed. 1977); *A View from the Campodiglio: Selected Essays, 1953–1984* (New York: Harper & Row, 1984); and *Architecture as Signs and Systems for a Mannerist Time* (Cambridge, Mass.: Belknap Press, 2004).

THOMAS A. SEBEOK (1920–2001)

Linguist, anthropologist, semiotics educator, and author; Universitas panelist, chairman of the second session

Thomas A. Sebeok was born in Budapest, Hungary, in 1920. He left Hungary in 1936 to study at Magdalene College at Cambridge University, but immigrated to the United States the following year and became a citizen in 1944. He earned a bachelor's degree from the University of Chicago in 1941, and MA and PhD degrees from Princeton University in 1943 and 1945. While at Princeton, he commuted to Columbia University to study linguistics with professor Roman Jakobson, who directed his doctoral dissertation. He went to the University of Indiana, Bloomington, in 1943, to assist in running the largest Army Specialized Training Program in foreign languages in the country, which he eventually directed. Assigned to teach courses in the English department, he went on to create Indiana's renowned Department of Uralic and Altaic Studies. He was offered the directorship of the Research Center for Anthropology, Folklore, and Linguistics at Indiana, and also had several fellowships at Stanford University to work in biology. By 1956, as Indiana's Distinguished Professor of Linguistics, he had created the Research Center for Language and Semiotic Studies, and established programs in semiotics, holding one of two chairs in the world in the discipline at the time, the other being held by Umberto Eco. In 1991 Indiana awarded Sebeok the title of Distinguished Professor Emeritus of Anthropology, of Linguistics, of Semiotics, and of Central Eurasian Studies. He died in 2001.

As a linguist studying Finno-Ugric languages, he traveled to Central and Eastern Europe, including Lapland, the former Soviet Union, Mongolia, Mexico, and the United States. His studies in grammar and phonology were complemented by his interest in anthropology, folklore, and literary studies in folksongs, charms, poems, and games. He carried out some of the first computer analyses of verbal texts, and by 1960 was known as a scholar who overcame academic boundaries between disciplines. He expanded the definition of semiotics in the mid-1960s by turning to the study of nonverbal and animal communication (biosemiotics). He published and lectured widely, was award countless honors internationally, and edited many scholarly journals, notably among them *Semiotica*, the journal of the International Association of Semiotic Studies.

Among his best-known books are: Sebeok et al., eds., *Approaches to Semiotics: Cultural Anthropology, Education, Linguistics, Psychiatry, Psychology* (The Hague: Mouton, 1964); Sebeok, ed., *Portraits of Linguists: A Biographical Sourcebook for the History of Western Linguistics, 1746–1963* (Bloomington: Indiana, 1966); *Animal Communication: Techniques of Study and Results of Research* (Bloomington: Indiana, 1968); *Perspectives in Zoosemiotics* (The Hague, Mouton, 1972); *Contributions to the Doctrine of Signs* (Lanham, Md.: University Press of America, 1976); *I Think I Am a Verb: More Contributions to the Doctrine of Signs* (New York: Plenum, 1986); *Semiotics in the United States* (Bloomington: Indiana, 1991); and *Signs: An Introduction to Semiotics* (Toronto: 1994).

Jivan Tabibian (1937-)

Political theorist, urban planner and designer, management consultant, educator, and diplomat; Universitas essayist and symposium panelist, summarized proceedings

Jivan Tabibian was born in Beirut, Lebanon, in 1937, to Armenian parents, and was educated in French schools, at the American University of Beirut (1957–59), and at Princeton University (1959–62). He later became a United States citizen. During an academic career of some thirty-five years, he taught various subjects at a number of American universities, beginning with political theory and international politics at Wake Forest University in North Carolina (1963–64) and at the University of California, Los Angeles, where he was also on the faculties of the Graduate School of Business, the Neuropsychiatry Institute, and the School of Urban Design (1963–75). He was also on the faculty of the School of Urban and Regional Planning at the University of Southern California (1968–91), and Dean of the Design Program at the California Institute of the Arts, Burbank (1969–73). From 1968 until recently, he was associated with the International Design Conference in Aspen, Colorado, serving on its Board of Directors and eventually as an advisor to the Board. In 1973, he and noted designer Milton Glaser co-chaired the IDCA program. Tabibian has served on numerous other boards, both private and public, corporate and institutional, such as the Sundance Institute for Film and Television in Sundance, Utah, for which, as an urban and regional planner, he created the facility's master plan in 1982–85. In 1982, he was a founding faculty member of the School of Management and Strategic Studies at the Western Behavioral Sciences Institute in La Jolla, California, participating in its programs until 1992 and remaining a Fellow of the International Leadership Fellowship.

Parallel to his academic career, Tabibian has had an extensive consultancy practice in the areas of policy, planning, corporate management, film, marketing, and regional development (1967–94), with assignments in the United States, Mexico, Latin America, Japan, the Middle East, and Europe. In 1984–89, he was the managing director of DGEI, a trading company, in Paris. Since 1998, Tabibian has been the Ambassador of the Republic of Armenia in Vienna, initially for bilateral rela-

tions as well with Austria, Hungary, Slovakia, and the Czech Republic. Presently he is exclusively ambassador to international organizations—the United Nations and the OSCE in Vienna. "The promise of democracy" remains the focus of his intellectual attention.

Among his publications are "The Alienated Professional," in Reyner Banham, ed., *The Aspen Papers: Twenty Years of Design Theory from The International Design Conference in Aspen* (New York: Praeger, 1974); "Demystifying the Movie Business," in *The Off-Hollywood Film Guide* (New York: Random House, 1996); "The Twilight of Humanism," *The New Business of Design* (1996); and a series of articles on post–Soviet Armenia politics and society in *AIM* (1992–99).

ALAIN TOURAINE (1925–)
Sociologist, educator, activist; Universitas essayist and symposium panelist

Alain Touraine was born in 1925 in Hermanville, France. He was educated at the Ecole Normale Supérieure in Paris, where he graduated in history in 1950 and received his doctorate in literature in 1965. In 1952 he was a Rockefeller Fellow and studied sociology at Harvard, Columbia, and Chicago universities. In 1956 he founded the Research Center for the Sociology of Labor at the University of Chile, and in 1958 founded the Industrial Sociology Workshop of Paris (which became the Center for the Study of Social Movements in 1970). He also served as a researcher at the French National Research Council between 1953 and 1958. In 1960 he became senior researcher at the Ecole Pratique des Hautes Etudes (now the Ecole des Hautes Etudes et Sciences Sociales). Touraine taught at the Department of Literature of the University of Paris at

Nanterre from 1966 to 1969. In 1981 he founded the Center for Sociological Analysis and Intervention, from which he retired in 1993. He is an officer of the Légion d'Honneur and of the Ordre National du Mérite.

The principal body of Touraine's work consists of a focus on an area of his field that he used as a title for his 1965 book: *The Sociology of Action*. In its initial phase, mainly based on field studies in Latin America, his research initiatives were devoted to the sociology of labor and workers' consciousness. A second period was concerned with social movements, beginning with his studies of the events of the student demonstrations in May 1968, and then focusing on military coups in Latin America and the Solidarity movement in Poland. In the 1970s, he was known as the foremost authority on social movements around the world. He subsequently turned to social problems associated with urban development. In what may be designated his third period, ongoing today, Touraine is primarily concerned with the subject as the fundamental agent of social change. He is widely known as the originator of the phrase "post-industrial society."

Among his books are: *The Post-Industrial Society: Tomorrow's Social History*. Trans. Mayhew (New York: Random, 1971 [1969]); *The Self-Production Society*. Trans. Derek Coltman (Chicago: 1977 [1973]); *The Voice and the Eye: An Analysis of Social Movements*. Trans. Alan Duff (New York: Cambridge, 1981); Touraine et al., *Workers Movement*. Trans. Ian Patterson (New York: Cambridge, 1987); *The Return of the Actor*. Trans. Myrna Godzich (Minnesota, 1988); *Critique of Modernity* Trans. David Macey (Cambridge, Mass.: Blackwell, 1995); and *Beyond Neoliberalism*. Trans. David Macey (Cambridge: Polity, 2001).

REXFORD GUY TUGWELL (1891–1979)

Economist, governor, political advisor, and educator; Universitas essayist and symposium panelist

Rexford Guy Tugwell was born in Sinclairsville, New York, in 1891. He studied at the University of Pennsylvania's Wharton School of Finance and Commerce, where upon graduation (BS 1915 and MA 1916) he was recruited to the Wharton teaching staff. In 1917, he moved to the University of Washington, which he followed by periods at the American University in Paris and Columbia University, where he eventually became Professor of Economics. His scholarly writings stimulated debate on such issues as the role of planning in government and constitutional reform. In 1932 Franklin D. Roosevelt enlisted him as an adviser during his presidential campaign. After he was elected, the president appointed Tugwell Assistant Secretary to the Agriculture Department; in 1934 he was promoted to Under Secretary. He was one of the original members of Roosevelt's brain trust, and a major force behind the New Deal economic package, contributing many innovative concepts in the battle against economic depression. Although he was a strong supporter of economic planning, Tugwell was conservative in his views about federal relief programs. He helped to plan the Agricultural Adjustment Act and directed the Resettlement Administration, a new agency created out of an amalgamation of several programs, which was designed to cut down on rural poverty.

In 1937, he resigned from the Roosevelt administration and became vice president of the American Molasses Company. However, the following year he returned to public service as chairman of the New York Planning Commission under Mayor Fiorello La Guardia. There, he broke new ground with a city budget that broadened minority opportunities in jobs and civil service. In 1942 he became governor of Puerto Rico, where he improved the civil service, established auditing procedures, and helped diversify the Puerto Rican economy. He then returned to teaching political science at the University of Chicago (1946–57) and became a senior fellow at the Center for the Study of Democratic Institutions at Santa Barbara, California (1957–66). He died in Santa Barbara in 1979.

Among Tugwell's numerous books are: *Mr. Hoover's Economic Policy* (John Day, 1932); *The Battle for Democracy* (New York: Columbia, 1935); *The Stricken Land: The Story of Puerto Rico* (Greenwoods, 1947); *The Democratic Roosevelt: A Biography of Franklin D. Roosevelt* (Garden City, N.Y.: Doubleday, 1957); *The Light of Other Days* (Garden City, N.Y.: Doubleday, 1962); and *The Brains Trust* (New York: Viking, 1968): *Roosevelt's Revolution: The First Year, a Personal Perspective* (New York: Macmillan, 1977); and *The Diary of Rexford G. Tugwell: The New Deal, 1932–1935*. Ed. Michael Vincent Namorato (New York: Greenwood, 1992).

SHELDON S. WOLIN (1922–)

Political scientist, social critic, author, and educator; Universitas essayist and symposium panelist

Sheldon S. Wolin was born in 1922 in Chicago. He attended Oberlin College (BA 1946) and Harvard University (MA 1947 and PhD 1950). He taught political science at Northwestern University in 1950, at Oberlin in 1950–54, at the University of California at Berkeley in 1954–71, and at Princeton University beginning in 1961. He is presently Professor Emeritus of Politics at Princeton. He has lectured at various universities, has been a Harvard University Fellow, a Sheldon Fellow, Fulbright Fellow, Magdalen College, Oxford, and a Rockefeller Fellow, and is a member of the American Political Science Association. His 1960 book *Politics and Vision: Continuity and Innovation in Western Political Thought* (Boston: Little, Brown) has influenced generations of political science students. In a collection of eleven essays published in 1989, *The Presence of the Past: Essays on the State and the Constitution* (Baltimore: Johns Hopkins), Wolin provides a detailed critique of the American state, from ideas of democracy promulgated by Alexis de Tocqueville to American political culture of the 1980s. In arguing that the ideas behind the United States Constitution and democracy, with their mechanisms for holding political power accountable, have been eroded by the privatization of public functions, he writes that the resulting immunization of power against public scrutiny far exceeds " the power capacity envisioned in the Constitution." Other "elegantly written" essays provide intellectual analysis of a variety of texts in political theory, illuminating "old texts with new questions."

Wolin has published widely in journals and reviews; among his other books are: Wolin and Seymour Martin Lipset, eds., *The Berkeley Student Revolt: Facts and Interpretations* (Garden City, N.Y.: Anchor, 1965); Wolin and John H. Schaar, *The Berkeley Rebellion and Beyond: Essays on Politics and Education in the Technological Society* (New York Review, 1970); *Hobbes and the Epic Tradition of Political Theory* (Los Angeles: Clark Memorial Library, 1970); and *Tocqueville Between Two Worlds: The Making of a Political and Theoretical Life* (Princeton: 2001).

The Univercity: A Fable

To culminate his long tenure in a fitting manner, the Governor of the Northeastern Region conceived of creating a new city. Intent on minimizing the political and financial struggles, which in the past had invariably deformed the destiny of other cities, he proposed that the new city be designed and managed by the University of the Northeastern Region.

This University had been established more than a century ago, to contribute solutions to the problems of an evolving rural society. Having fulfilled its task with a modicum of accomplishment, the University was, nevertheless, becoming increasingly aware that the main areas of intellectual speculation and artistic imagery had been shifting from an anxious observation of the natural milieu to an anguished inquiry into the nature and praxis of the man-made environment. The Governor's intentions suited the University's need for intellectual expansion, and the proposed task was accepted.

The new city was to be the University's laboratory for urban and institutional innovations—preventive health care, personal and mass transportation systems, different forms of neighborhood government and communal living, new working and leisure pattern—these were just a few of the ideas the University intended to test there.

The Grant Act that once had sponsored the creation of the original University was unearthed. By carefully stretching some of its original meaning, the Regional Legislature granted the University large extensions of public land. The University's financial arm—the Bank of Univercity, as the city was to become known—issued bonds on this land to finance construction. To avoid land speculation, Univercity and its surrounding countryside were to remain the property of the Northeastern University. Land for industrial use could only be leased, while, to further experimentation in social groupings, housing leases would be signed not by a family, but by each of its members as individuals.

Another branch of the University, its Urban Planning and Development Institute, was put in charge of designing the city, supervising its construction, and managing the new city's infrastructural services. It was also to supervise some of its superstructural aspects, especially those pertaining to educational, cultural and leisure activities.

The new city's physical plan was to be based on the concept of open-ended systems. It was to provide an urban system capable of interacting with its surrounding context, and of receiving new or removing old sub-systems without unduly affecting the rest of the city's processes. The technicians of the interdisciplinary design team hoped that the city resulting from such a dynamic model would foster the maximum of social communication.

A varied and representative cross section of the Region's population willingly settled there, once Univercity's concepts and goals became known. In a few years, the population became stabilized at 100,000 inhabitants and, in a relatively short time, it became the much talked-about showcase its founders had hoped for. Naturally, in its first stages, Univercity underwent the normal adjustment problems, but on the whole it prospered as had been projected

As time passed by, however, an indefinable yet perceptible shift in Univercity's goals and behaviors began to take place. No one has yet been able to establish exactly in what manner and why, but it is suspected that some of the experiments on which Univercity was based got out of control, generating totally unexpected secondary and tertiary consequences.

It would seem that the beginnings of the change were subtle and, in turn, gentle. It is assumed that it all began when, in opposite corners of the city, altars to Revolution and Redemption were built. Although no one actually believed in gods, playing off the divinities against the others was perhaps a useful device for gaining terrain for their own human goals.

Later, the citizens established a cemetery in the center of the city. The Future was buried there several times, only to be exhumed periodically by a few who felt they could not go on without its forwarding image. In another part of the city, members of a much different group devoted themselves to exorcising the guilt of history by making collective gestures endowed with the power to obliterate individual memories, they believed. These seem to have been the same who decided their newborn babies should be considered 120 years old. It is surmised that they did so not so much hoping that the ever-present knowledge of the end would prevent their engaging in harsh longings or the pursuit of vain glory, but, rather, wanting their children to grow up with the awareness that any wager against mortality was an insane challenge.

As generations changed, uncertainty, which in olden times used to dress itself up as language, gave way to purposeful silence. Music and mathematics became Univercity's form of mystical experience and epistemological transaction. Words, forgotten and aimless, roamed the city, gradually returning to the chaos to which they had once belonged.

On festive occasions, the days blended into the nights as the inhabitants gathered to promenade their feelings and dance their passions. The rest of the time they remained in the quietude of their places, making objects or turning thoughts. With these creations, they hoped to reconcile their desire with their own fears. It was felt that the power of these creations depended on their meaning not becoming known until they had become form, and the most powerful constructs were assumed to be those which remained closed up in their recondite condition until ready to reveal themselves. Stones and water—and all examples of real and imagined creation— were revered as inner forms that had not yet revealed their signs.

Those without a gift for numbers and deaf to sound dedicated themselves to architecture. At one end of town, they delineated a parcel of land in the almond shape of an eye, digging until water level was reached. With the earth that had been removed, they built a square platform at the opposite end of town. On it, they drew an orthogonal grid, building at every crossing square towers ten steps wide and one hundred steps high. *The first tower was made of sandstone and the last of ice, but all seemed to be of the same material, so subtle was the series and so large the number.*

At this point, however, even conjecture must stop, for none can claim to know how or why Univercity disappeared. It might have been possible to surmise some of the changes that took place in Univercity by observing transformations that also occurred around that time in some of the neighboring cities that survived the disappearance of Univercity; but this task would have been hindered by the fact that almost all records of the history of Univercity itself have literally vanished

Numberless hypotheses are brought up about the end of Univercity. There are those who maintain that the Regional Government at first tolerated the unexpected turns Univercity had been taking, rationalizing it as a useful experiment which they could well afford, as long as it remained circumscribed. But later, as its influence began to pervade the ways of perceiving and acting upon reality of the people of other cities in the Region, the Government decided that it was imperative to bring Univercity to a fast and thorough end.

The speculative variations on the possible reasoning behind such a decision are immeasurable. While some maintain that it came about because Univercity taught a subversive alternative to the prevailing conditions, others believe that it was becoming increasingly evident to the people of the region that Univercity could only remain the exemplary model as long as they were willing to continue toiling to maintain an ideal they themselves could never hope to become.

Whenever a few of us risk gathering in secret to evoke its unbearable absence, we quietly tell each other that Univercity is still somewhere in the Region, transparent and alien by its own will. For us, Univercity is still here, waiting for none, but willing to be turned once more into a fable by the passing shadow of those who may unite for a perfect instant to bring its image to light.

Emilio Ambasz, 1972

[This text was written by Emilio Ambasz at the close of the symposium that forms the subject of this volume. It has been published previously in *Emilio Ambasz: The Poetics of the Pragmatic* (New York: Rizzoli, 1991).]

Index

Trustees of The Museum of Modern Art